D0330944

Quest for the Presidency
1992

Quest
for the
Presidency

1992

by PETER GOLDMAN

THOMAS M. DeFRANK

MARK MILLER

ANDREW MURR

TOM MATHEWS

with

Patrick Rogers · Melanie Cooper

TEXAS A&M UNIVERSITY PRESS

COLLEGE STATION

To the craft of reporting
and to the men and women who,
in an age of attitude,
still practice it

Copyright © 1994 by Newsweek Inc.
Manufactured in the United States of America
All rights reserved
First edition

The paper used in this book meets the minimum requirements of the
American National Standard for Permanence of Paper
for Printed Library Materials, Z39.48-1984.
Binding materials have been chosen for durability.

Library of Congress Cataloging-in-Publication Data

Quest for the presidency 1992 / by Peter Goldman . . . [et al.]. —
1st ed.
         p.   cm.
    Includes index.
    ISBN 0–89096-644-3 (alk. paper)
    1. Presidents—United States—Election—1992. 2. United
States—Politics and government—1989–1993. I. Goldman, Peter
Louis, 1933–   .
E884.Q36   1994
324.973'0928—dc20   94–5403
                                                              CIP

The first man put at the helm will be a good one.
Nobody knows what sort may come afterward.
                    —Benjamin Franklin, at the
                    Constitutional Convention,
                    Philadelphia, 1787

Contents

Preface

This book is the eyewitness story of a momentous American election—one in which power shifted between parties, ideologies, and generations, and the established political order was shaken by the strongest third-force challenge in eighty years. It is a work of narrative journalism, undertaken initially for *Newsweek;* a far shorter version appeared as a special issue of the magazine, published a day and a half after the last polls closed on November 3, 1992. But those of us involved in producing it understood even then that, in the course of a year and a half in the field, we had gathered a unique record of a rare moment in our political life—a season in which, as one of our sources told us, something *happened.*

This book is that record, published whole for the first time. It was reported from a privileged inside position. Members of our special election team operated separately from the reporters, writers, and editors responsible for *Newsweek*'s weekly coverage of the campaign. Our understanding with the various candidates, their staffs, and their consultants was that our findings would be held in strict confidence until after the votes had been counted. Had we come into any information explosive enough to change the outcome of the election, we would have proposed to our editors that we shut down the project and publish it. We found nothing so shattering as that, nor did we expect to. Our intent rather was to write what our late proprietor Philip Graham once referred to as a first rough draft of history—an intimate look at the men and women who enter upon our quadrennial quest for the presidency and at the bumpy road they travel toward that prize.

Our passkey into their lives, their thoughts, their hopes, their fears, and their strategies was our promise of confidentiality and our history of having kept that promise in two past works in this series. They in turn offered us a degree of access they could not grant to the daily and weekly press and have rarely allowed to authors of past books in this genre. The most generous of all with time and entree, fortuitously, were Bill and Hillary Rodham Clinton and their aides and advisers.

The principals in all the contending campaigns were helpful to us, but we are especially grateful to the Clintons and the Clintonians for daring to be so open, even in their moments of highest stress and deepest gloom. We believe that our you-are-there portrait of their campaign, based largely on the reporting of Mark Miller, will help our readers understand the mind, the heart, and the operating style of the man who became our forty-second president.

It is perhaps important to say what this book is *not*, given what may seem to some readers an odd coupling between a team of journalists and a publisher of scholarly works. Our connection with the Texas A&M University Press has been the source of great pride and pleasure for us, a partnership grounded in our shared belief that political journalism can be serious enough to merit the attention of serious minds. But this *is* a work of journalism, not of scholarship, or of political theory, or of public policy. Readers will search it in vain for a detailed analysis of the various "plans" offered by the candidates or for a moral commentary on the state of our society and its institutions and processes of self-government. This is, rather, a book about what has come to be called practical politics—the inside story of how presidents are made, and broken, in the late twentieth century.

It is wholly a work of original reporting. It includes a substantial appendix of primary materials in the form of previously unpublished campaign documents, but otherwise has none of the appurtenances normally associated with books published by university presses; there are no footnotes, no source notes, no bibliography. If the book bears any family resemblance at all to any academic discipline, it is nearer to military history than to political science. It is the on-the-ground chronicle of a democratic war of succession—of battles won and lost, of strategies that worked or went awry, of princes and their generals glimpsed in victory and defeat.

The book is the product of what newsmagazines call *group* journalism—a form common to them but rare enough elsewhere to require a word of explanation. It is journalism from the ground up, rooted in aggressive, full-court reporting by a team of correspondents; the work of the writer is to weave their discoveries and their insights into a coherent whole and to set it in the context of its time. The anchor of our reporting team was Thomas M. DeFrank, on detached assignment from his duties as *Newsweek*'s deputy Washington bureau chief and senior White House correspondent. He brought the experience and the connections of twenty award-winning years of president watching and of our two previous *Quests* to his coverage of President Bush's campaign for reelection. Miller, who has been a *Newsweek* writer and reporter in Washington, New York, and, currently, Los Angeles, lived inside the Clinton campaign and provided the material for our up-close account of the governor's rocky journey to the White House. Andrew Murr, a *Newsweek* correspondent also based in Los Angeles, covered the campaigns of Ross Perot and Clinton's strongest Democratic rivals: Bob Kerrey, Paul Tsongas, and Jerry Brown.

The three lead correspondents went into the field in the late summer of 1991, at a point when Tsongas was the only announced candidate, and continued their reporting well past Election Day—a postmortem sweep that added greatly to our data base and to our understanding of the events of 1992. The team was joined early in the campaign year by Patrick Rogers, a correspondent based in New York, who charted the rise and fall of Pat Buchanan's challenge to a sitting president of his own party. Tom Mathews, a coauthor of the 1988 entry in the *Quest for the Presidency* series, wrote major portions of the magazine version of the story. His understanding of politics and his elegances of language have helped shape the book. Melanie Cooper was our senior researcher, though she could more accurately be thought of as vice president in charge of everything. She was responsible not just for the literal accuracy of the work, to which she brought her always sharp eye and keen insights, but for its soul as well. To these labors, we added a wide further range of assignments, from running logistics to choosing pictures to writing captions to acting as our principal liaison with the publisher; she discharged all of these duties willingly and well.

The pictures in these pages are the work of an extraordinary group of photojournalists. Four of them—Jacques Chenet, Larry Downing, John Ficara, and Wally McNamee—covered the campaign as *Newsweek* staff photographers of great creativity and skill. A fifth, Ira Wyman, an artist at his trade working on assignment for the magazine, was granted unusual inside access to the Clinton campaign and has been most generous in sharing his photos with us.

Our further debts are numerous. *Newsweek*'s managing editor, Kenneth Auchincloss, a man of wisdom, tact, and great kindness, supervised the magazine version from day one to publication and has been a source of aid and comfort in its expansion to book form. Our editor-in-chief and president, Richard M. Smith, and our editor, Maynard Parker, made the necessarily large investment in the success of this project; we are grateful to them. Stryker McGuire, then chief of correspondents, helped assemble our reporting team. He and his successor, Ann McDaniel, kept it going through the problems and privations of lives lived almost wholly on the road.

Among our comrades in arms involved in *Newsweek*'s week-to-week coverage of the campaign, Eleanor Clift and Ginny Carroll were particularly helpful to us. But we profited as well from our connection with one of America's great news organizations; the work of Jonathan Alter, Howard Fineman, Joe Klein, Ann McDaniel (again), Tom Morganthau, Evan Thomas, Bill Turque and others made up an important second stream of reporting and commentary, supplementing our own efforts. Nancy Stadtman, the magazine's chief national-affairs researcher, provided an indispensable who's who in the various campaigns and a day-by-day chronology of key events in the election year. Abigail Kuflik and Danzy Senna joined our research team in the later stages of the magazine version and worked with great skill and sangfroid in the closing rush to publication.

We are indebted as well to our friend and colleague Ted Slate and to the staff of the fine library he built at *Newsweek*. Mata Stevenson and Ron Wilson, principally among them, led a never-ending chase for vagrant facts and figures and unfailingly found them. Guy Cooper, Joe Romano, and Dubravka Bondulic of the magazine's photo department conducted the search for many of the pictures that appear in these pages, and Richard Pena of the photo lab produced the prints. Rollene Saal, as *Newsweek*'s literary agent, helped greatly in our hunt for the right publisher.

That search led us finally and happily to Texas A&M University, soon to be the site of George Bush's presidential library. The connection came about in important part through the good offices of Dr. George C. Edwards III, the director of A&M's Center for Presidential Studies. We are grateful to him; to N. Camille North, who was senior sponsoring editor for this work; and especially to the excellent Mary Lenn Dixon, managing editor of the Press, who edited our manuscript with great grace and care.

Most of all, we are indebted to the men and women who *lived* the quest for the presidency in 1992 and who helped us in various ways in *our* quest. Not all are prominently featured in the manuscript, but each has been of great help to us, in ways they will recognize, and we would like to extend our thanks to all of them here—to Roger Ailes, Darcy Anderson, Collier Andress, Phil Angelides, Lud Ashley, Tommy Attaway, Loretta Avent, Fred Barnes, Bettina Barnett, Bob Barnett, Bob Barrett, Jacques Barzaghi, Heather Beckel, David Beckwith, Paul Begala, Sandy Berger, Eric Berman, Charles Black, Diane Blair, Linda Bloodworth-Thomason, Rich Bond, Bob Boorstin, Michael Bourbeau, Brent Bozell, Jerry Brown, Bay Buchanan, Pat Buchanan, Shelley Buchanan, Eric Bucy, Regan Burke, Bob Burkett.

And to President George Bush, George W. Bush, Patrick Caddell, Lisa Caputo, Andrew Card, Paul Carey, Dave Carney, Andrew Carpendale, Bill Carrick, James Carville, Alex Castellanos, Dick Cheney, James Cicconi, Penny Circle, Torie Clarke, President Bill Clinton, Hillary Rodham Clinton, Steve (Scoop) Cohen, John Connally, Peggy Connolly, Bob Corn, Tony Corrado, Joe Costello, April Cotton, Virginia Cox, Kelly Craighead, Amanda Crumley, Mitch Daniels, Richard Darman, Tad Devine, John DiStasio, David Doak, Jacqueline Domaignue, Mike Donilon, Tom Donilon, Chuck Douglas, Ken Duberstein, Patricia Duff, Jeff Eller.

And to Jeff Ely, Rahm Emanuel, Mort Engelberg, Tricia Enright, Paul Erickson, Alex Evans, Jodie Evans, Karen Ewing, Tony Fabrizio, Will Feltus, Liz Fine, Richard Fisher, John Fitzpatrick, Marlin Fitzwater, Jeff Forbes, President Gerald Ford, Michael Ford, Sally Ford, Gary Foster, Jim Francis, Jody Franklin, Steve Fridrich, Ron Fried, Andrew Friendly, Karen Frost, Craig Fuller, Chris Gallagher, Jr., Bill Galston, Paige Gardner, Jack Gargan, Mark Gearan, Alixe Glen, Mary Ellen Glynn, Leslie Goodman, Matt Gorman, Bob Grady, Phil Gramm, Stan Greenberg, Frank Greer, Hugh Gregg, Judd Gregg, Tom Griscom, Mandy Grunwald, Stacey Hadash, Mark Halperin, Larry Harrington, Tubby Harrison, John Hart, Nancy Hernreich, Harrison Hickman, Cathie Hill, Eleanor Hill, Sharon Holman, John Jay Hooker.

And to Bill Hoppner, Peter Hutchins, Harold Ickes, Gwen Ifill, Steve Jarding, Ed Jesser, Paul Johnson, Hamilton Jordan, Dennis Kanin, Will Kanteres, Mickey Kantor, Tommy Kaplan, Maura Keefe, P. X. Kelley, Bob Kerrey, Andrew Klein, David Kotok, Bill Kristol, Lionel Kunst, David Kusnet, Peter Ladd, Celinda Lake, Jim Lake, Bob Larkin, Judy Laterza, Avis Lavelle, David Leavy, Charlie Leonard, Ann Lewis, Beverly Lindsey, Bruce Lindsey, Nackey Loeb, Tom Luce, Mary Lukens, Frank Luntz, Jim Lyons, Dennis McClain, John McConnell, Mike McCurry, Kate McDonald, Don McDonough, Nancy McFadden, Scott Mackenzie.

And to Jack Maguire, Fred Malek, Gary Maloney, Capricia Marshall, Murphy Martin, Paul Maslin, Mary Matalin, David Mathews, Sylvia Mathews, Garry Mauro, Michael Medavoy, Mort Meyerson, Mark Middleton, Scott Miller, Richard Mintz, Betty Mitchell, Robert Mosbacher, Greg Mueller, Clay Mulford, Mike Murphy, Dee Dee Myers, Adam Nagourney, Paul Nagy, President Richard M. Nixon, Paula Nowakowski, Billy Nungesser, Mark Nykanen, Jim Oberwetter, Kevin O'Keefe, H. D. Palmer, Max Parker, Andy Pavin, Anna Perez, Michael Petrelis, Howard Phillips, Martha Phipps, Jim Pinkerton,

Roman Popadiuk, Clyde Prestowitz, Jim Pribyl, Jonathan Prince, Steve Provost, Meeghan Prunty, Martin Puris, Vicki Radd, Tim Raftis, Justin Raimondo, Tom Rath, Bruce Reed, Mame Reiley, John Reilly, Sig Rogich.

And to Ed Rollins, Simon Rosenberg, Mark Rosenker, Joe Rothstein, Andy Russo, Sal Russo, Allan Ryskind, Chris Sautter, Heidi Schulman, Mitchell Schwartz, Brent Scowcroft, John Sears, Eli Segal, Ricki Seidman, Dave Seldin, John Shakow, Michael Shea, Brooke Shearer, Derrick Shearer, Laurie Shields, Bill Shore, Bob Shrum, Sam Skinner, Rodney Slater, Craig Smith, Judy Smith, Curt Smith, Matt Smith, Wendy Smith, Nancy Soderberg, Adam Sohn, Stephanie Solein, Patti Solis, Stu Spencer, Gene Sperling, Jim Squires, Fred Steeper, George Stephanopoulos, Greg Stevens, Roger Stone, Richard Strauss, Robert Strauss, Stephanie Street, Orson Swindle, Mike Synar.

And to Joe Tarver, Sheila Tate, Pete Teeley, Robert M. Teeter, David Tell, Ginny Terzano, Susan Thomases, Harry Thomason, Chris Tremblay, Joe Trippi, Niki Tsongas, Paul Tsongas, Jeffrey Tuchman, Paul Tully, Owen Ullmann, Vaughn Ververs, Richard Viguerie, Ileana Wachtel, Shari Waldie, Mike Waldman, Ann Walley, Redman Walsh, Sean Walsh, David Watkins, Betsy Weinschel, Ian Weinschel, Dianna Wentz, John White, Michael Whouley, David Wilhelm, Degee Wilhelm, Clayton Wilhite, Carter Wilkie, Pete Williams, Richard Winger, Tom Winter, Fred Woods, Robert Zoellick—and others.

A personal note: One of my obligations as the writer on the team was not just to set down the events of the year but to try to understand the context in which they occurred. I was greatly assisted in this by a series of conversations with men and women who belong to that loose grouping called the political community but who appear only briefly, if at all, as players in the narrative. They come from all points of the political compass, bringing with them lively, informed, and provocative minds. They have been generous with their time and their thoughts, and I owe my particular thanks to ten of them—to Doug Bailey, Linda DiVall, Al From, Geoffrey Garin, Ed Goeas, David Keene, Celinda Lake, David Petts, Kevin Phillips, and Richard Wirthlin.

Joe Trippi and Michael Ford, two friends who will figure prominently in my next book, have waited patiently for me to get on with this one. In the interim, they, too, have enriched my understanding not just of the campaigns they served but of the theory and practice of politics in our time.

There is Tony Fuller, my dear friend and coauthor of the first of these *Quest* books, among other works. He and I talked politics relentlessly through the campaign year and beyond, and my own views have been influenced by his sharp perceptions and his fine ironies.

And there is always Helen Dudar, the writer, critic, and first reader, without whose wisdom and love nothing would be possible.

PETER GOLDMAN

New York City
June, 1994

I

A Quiet National Crisis

I don't think ANY *government person makes you feel confident.*
—A woman voter
in a Clinton focus group,
summer, 1992

I.

The Autumn of a President

For much of a year, George Bush had drifted on the tides, like a Sunday sailor oblivious to the thunderheads piling high on the far horizon. The country was sliding into what a leading student of our politics called a quiet national crisis—a loss of faith not merely in the president or the Washington culture he embodied but in that durable vision of progress called the American Dream.

The current of unhappiness ran deeper than the normal ebb and flow of partisan feeling in an election year; it challenged the very order of our politics and the inflated expectations it had encouraged in us after decades of over-promising and underachievement. The engines of economic growth, superheated in the '80s, had stopped turning. The institutions of self-government seemed too corroded by money, vanity, and cynicism to do anything about it. The optimism once regarded as a national birthright had given way to fear of the future and anger at the politicians who had mortgaged it for short-term gain for themselves and their patrons. In another time and another society, an elder of Bush's own party said, the mood could accurately have been called prerevolutionary. And yet the president seemed first blind to and then baffled by the danger, even as it threatened to engulf his presidency.

His polltaker, Fred Steeper, had been among the first of the president's men to see it, and then only faintly, as an odd anomaly in his polling. The numbers didn't add up, Steeper thought, poring over his printouts one chill October afternoon in 1991 like a medical detective first confronting the symptoms of a troubling new disease. On the one hand, his client seemed the picture of political health, with a glowing 70 percent approval rating in the afterlight of Operation Desert Storm in Kuwait and Iraq. On the other, a virus of pessimism—a queasy feeling that the country was seriously off on the wrong track—was spreading across Bush's America and had by then infected half the population.

Steeper was an understated man, his imagination tethered firmly to earth by his data. They told him that the odds still greatly favored Bush's reelection. But the dissonance between the president's ratings and the popular mood wasn't right, wasn't *normal*. Steeper found himself haunted by the ghost of an earlier and far grander wartime leader who had been cast aside by his people once the guns fell silent. "I'm worried about the Churchill parallel," he confessed to a visitor to his high-tech offices in the Detroit suburbs. What would happen if the president's trend line going down crossed the arc of America's discontent going up? Could Bush, like Winston Churchill, wind up on the discard pile of electoral politics?

The more closely Steeper looked into the similarities, the more they tormented him, and in mid-December he set forth his concerns in a short memo to his friend Robert Teeter, who would be managing the president's campaign. Steeper had argued in earlier communiqués that Bush could not simply rest on his successes in foreign policy—that he needed to engage with the ills of the economy and go to war with the Democratic Congress to show that he really understood what was going on. Nothing much had happened, and Steeper's pre-Christmas memo used the Churchill analogy to underscore the need to get moving. Sir Winston and the Conservatives, he reminded Teeter, had been turned out of office less than two months after the victorious end of the war against Hitler. Bush, too, had had his triumphs, but, as Steeper dourly noted, "the country [had also fallen] into a recession. Leaders are not necessarily reelected for their foreign policy and wartime successes, even when monumental."

The Churchill Parallel became part of the working vocabulary at the White House that winter, as both the numbers and Bush's inattention to them worsened. His people had been after him for months to get on with the business of seeking a second term. "It's just a two-month sprint," he would say, waving them off; the real campaign wouldn't begin till Labor Day, 1992, and there was no point getting excited before then. So dreamy was his disengagement that, at mid-year, one of his own children had felt it necessary to call him and ask point-blank whether he really meant to stand for reelection.

"I haven't made up my mind," he had replied, closing off further inquiry. It was as though saying yes, even in the family, would begin the worst year of the rest of his life.

The Man from Nowhere

Bush would run, of course, and by the conventional markers he relied on in all things, he saw no reason why he should not win. The polls a year out looked good, at least to him; they were his daily affirmation that people still liked him and still took patriotic pride in his triumph of arms in the Gulf. Sure, the doom criers said the economy was in a bad way. But Bush and his closed circle of advisers didn't believe it, and even if it were so, no one yet appeared to be blaming him.

Neither did the opposition then seem especially formidable. The Democrats most feared by Bush's war counselors had run for cover when his favorable rating in the polls hit 91 percent after the war; the early betting favorite was Bill Clinton, and when his name was mentioned among the president's men, the dismissive one-word answer was usually, "Women." There were no third-force candidacies to trouble their slumber. Ross Perot, the crotchety computer-systems tycoon, was presumed to be happily occupied piling up his third or maybe his fourth billion dollars, and Pat Buchanan's right-wing polemics were still the stuff of op-ed commentary and talk TV.

There was, moreover, the comforting private assessment of Bush's friend and strategist Bob Teeter in late September, 1991, that his defeat was—how to put it?—highly unlikely. Teeter was an ineffably cautious man, and he hastened to add that the election was going to be closer than most people thought. But he liked the president's core strengths—the fondness America seemed to feel for him personally and, with his successes at war and diplomacy, a new respect for his leadership as well. He was not seen as larger than life, as Ronald Reagan had been in his prime. But he had something at least equally precious: people thought he was *real*, and they had come to believe that he knew how to be president. Given their warm regard, Teeter thought, it would take worse than a worst-case train of events to unseat Bush; it would take what he called a doomsday scenario.

What was missing from his reading and from the president's was the subtext of jeopardy—the unquiet spreading like a dark stain beneath the bright surface of Bush's popularity. His own people, making the case for him, did not pretend that he was really of Churchillian size. One of his middle managers described him over lunch with a friend one day as having been an "adequate" president; nobler adjectives seemed somehow inappropriate even to his publicists, at least in their off-duty hours. But the temper of the times seemed to beg for something more than mere adequacy—for a strength and clarity of purpose that seemed quite beyond Bush's reach. He was instead the president as majordomo; a succession of patrons from Richard Nixon to Ronald Reagan had found uses for his breeding, his excellent manners, and his obliging nature and then had left him to manage the estate just as the bills were coming due.

His political coloration had always been borrowed from his patrons and his party constituency, no matter how much further right their views were from his own. His résumé, commonly called gilt-edged, was in fact gilt by association with other men and their ideas about the public good; there was no real Bush agenda beyond muddling through. His domestic policies were a hash, reflecting his own inattention to them, and the New World Order he proposed to build in the post–Cold War era had a certain shapelessness to it, like a house constructed by do-it-yourselfers in the dark. It seemed to consist, for the most part, of scrambling to manage crises once they had occurred—crises too often fomented by onetime "friends" who owed their power to American money and arms.

Bush thus remained rather an indistinct figure, for all his years on public view. He was not really *from* anywhere—not Connecticut, where he grew up, or Texas, where he kept a voting address, or Maine, where he and his family were summer people. He was instead a man of Washington and was, like many such men, rootless in place, time, and ideology. The capital in his lifetime had become a walled city, in spirit if not literal fact, and the president had taken on the pallor of the governing party seated permanently within its gates.

He had himself been born to a gentleman ideal of public service as the obligation of his class—a debt of stewardship that had led him from one job to the next till he finally reached the White House. He had no larger credo and was by turns mystified and annoyed when people demanded to know what more he stood for. No one had had to ask Ronald Reagan that, as David Keene, a conservative Republican strategist who had served both men, observed in the winter of Bush's decline. Reagan had run for president because he wanted to *do* something, and being president had offered him a way to do it. But there was nothing Bush truly hungered to do. He had run, in Keene's view, to be president—to sit in the Oval Office and, in his reflexive way, to serve.

He was at his happiest and best at foreign affairs; it was, as he often remarked, the one arena where you could make things happen without ordinarily having to go beg Congress for permission. Bush would claim, with pardonable hyperbole, that he had overseen changes of almost biblical proportion in the world as it had existed for nearly half a century. The Berlin Wall had come down. The satellite peoples of Eastern Europe had freed themselves from bondage. The Soviet Union had literally disappeared from the map, along with the threat of a global nuclear war. Communism was dead in all but a last few outposts around the world, and so was anticommunism as an organizing principle in the politics and policies of the West. For a brief time before a New World Disorder spilled over the stage, it was possible for serious scholars to debate whether history itself had ended.

Bush for the most part had been a bystander at these events, reacting to them rather than shaping them. It was in fact Reagan who, at reckless cost to America, had finally spent the Evil Empire into bankruptcy. But its disintegration had happened on his successor's watch, not his. It was Bush who got to preside over the last rites for Soviet communism and to negotiate an end to the forty-year balance of nuclear terror. And it was Bush who inherited and fitfully used the resulting new opportunities open to America as the last real superpower on the planet. He and James A. Baker III, the friend Bush had installed as secretary of state, even got the Arabs and the Israelis into the same room talking. One of the crueler ironies history held in store for the two was that they would witness the first tangible fruits of their diplomacy not as actors but as guests in somebody else's Rose Garden.

"It's Vague Out There"

The president's own apotheosis as world leader rested heavily on his success at mobilizing a global alliance against Saddam Hussein's aggressions in 1990. The "war" was a lopsided one, though the first estimates of the Iraqi body count were grossly inflated; its battle scenes, so far as the media were permitted to show them, consisted of smart bombs flying down chimneys and Saddam's "combat-hardened" soldiers flinging down their arms. The troops he had committed to the Mother of All Battles had proved to be the Fanny Hill of All Armies, gifted most notoriously at surrender.

There would be questions afterwards about whether Bush's earlier coziness with Saddam had invited the Iraqi invasion of Kuwait in the first place and whether he had ended the war too soon, leaving a man he had called worse than Hitler still in power. But the quibbles were lost at the time in the flutter of a million yellow ribbons. It was a famous victory, and Bush had, for a season, become a national hero. His reelection seemed all but assured. His chief of staff suggested that the members of Congress might just as well go home for the next two years; the president wouldn't be needing them anymore.

The champagne corks, as it turned out, had popped too soon; the halo effect of the war had dimmed with the worsening of the economy. A very few analysts marked it at the time, indeed, as the beginning of the end for Bush—a desert mirage that had blinded him and his courtiers to the reality of his situation. One of these was Richard

Nixon, who, in the descending winter of his life, remained a shrewd handicapper of politics. "Bush will be defeated when he comes up for reelection," he told a young confidant in the spring of 1991. His friend, agape, reminded him that the president's approval rating at that moment was close to 90 percent; the conventional wisdom was that he would win his second term almost by acclaim. "Popularity from foreign-policy accomplishments is fleeting," Nixon replied. "If the economy is bad in the fall, he will be defeated—and the economy *will* be bad."

The former president's prediction was on the money. The ground war had been a marvelous hundred-hour diversion from a recession that was then already eight months old and was still in train. But the flags were laid by for another day; the parades gave way in the public consciousness to the unemployment lines and foreclosure sales that had been there all along. Bush practically alone seemed not to notice, and the impression spread among his countrymen that his mind was elsewhere, not on them or their travail.

Little in his demeanor suggested otherwise. He had been elected without a mandate and had governed without a program; he had neither the interest in designing one nor the heart to go begging Congress to enact it. During his long ascent to the presidency, he had confided to friends that his days as CIA director had been by far the most exciting of the many chapters in his public life. The world was Bush's playhouse, and the Agency had been his window into its secrets. Mention domestic policy, one pal said, and the president's eyes would glaze over; his people learned not to schedule meetings on the subject later than, say, 2:30 or 3:00, when there were always excuses for him to play hooky.

His distaste came across, for an ominously growing number of Americans, as a lack of conviction about the things that mattered most to them. The two most memorable lines he had spoken in his rise to power had been his charge in 1980 that Reagan was preaching voodoo economics and his dare to Congress in 1988 to read his lips—he would brook no new taxes. Both principles had been abandoned when they became inconvenient, and no new articles of faith had sprung up in their place. "I still can't tell you what he stands for," a senior campaign aide lamented, "and I've worked for him for ten years."

The people in his service despaired of his suddenly growing a Vision Thing, a term he himself had given to the language some years before, or even producing a more prosaic to-do list for a second term. He had neither the flair nor the patience for high concept; George was a good and a smart man, a close friend from his long-ago days in Congress once said, but he appeared never to have thought about any public matter for longer than two minutes. He ran his presidency on a piece-work model, addressing problems serially as they were thrust upon him. Where Reagan had favored broad strokes, Bush painted by the numbers; inspiration tended to fail him when he was placed before a blank canvas and asked to do the big picture.

His want of poetry had finally caught up with him, after a lucky lifetime in politics. He was coming to seem a provisional figure, a man who offered an aura of experience, judgment, and competence when what America most wanted of him was hope. To many and finally a majority of the governed, his passivity came to seem a form of retreat; it was as if he sat in a room shuttered against the harsh concerns of the workaday world. In the summer of 1991, a nonaligned Democratic polltaker asked swing voters in a series of focus groups in the Middle West if Bush reminded them of anyone in children's stories or nursery rhymes. The most frequent answers were Rip Van Winkle and Little Boy Blue—two folk characters who, when they ought to have been up and about their business, were asleep instead.

By autumn, the nation's view of its president was hardening into a judgment that he either didn't get it or didn't give a damn. Danger signs flared like lightning against a night sky, none more ominously than in a by-election that November for a U.S. Senate seat in Pennsylvania. The overwhelming favorite was Bush's friend and onetime attorney general, Richard Thornburgh, a popular former governor; he went into the race with a 44-point lead in the polls over Harris Wofford, a worthy but obscure chair-warmer then occupying the office by appointment. Thornburgh's worst mistake, among many, was advertising his connections with Bush and his ease in the corridors of power in Washington. In a season for outsiders, he became the inside man and lost to Wofford by a landslide.

Bush seemed mainly bemused by the outcome; it was as though he had seen a pair of oncoming headlights in his lane on a highway but had not yet guessed their meaning. He found it hard to grasp the spreading disaffection of his compatriots, mistaking their desperation for ingratitude; he wondered aloud, at one point in his slide, where the *honor* was for his service to his country and his triumphs in the world. As his support wilted, his bewilderment grew. By the spring of 1992, he would scan what had become an alien political landscape and complain, "It's vague out there."

His people shrugged. They had long since reconciled themselves to his limited imagination and his shallow depth of field. Maybe he would get lucky again; maybe the Democrats would oblige him, as they had in 1988, by nominating somebody eminently beatable—somebody, for one example, like Governor Clinton. What you couldn't do was *fix* Bush, one of his young middle managers said on the eve of his last campaign. It was too late for that. By Election Day, his last as a candidate for public office, he would be sixty-eight years old.

2.

The Age of Anxiety

R onald Reagan did have a Vision Thing, a picture of a glorious
   American future drawn from a mythic American past. He called
it the Shining City on a Hill, and it had been his life's work as a public
man—a tapestry of fact, fiction, rumor, hope, and dream stitched into
one heroic whole. It served him well for most of his two terms not
because of its resemblance to reality, which was slight, but because he
himself seemed to believe so passionately in it. It was only when he had
walked away, leaving the keys to the city in the hopelessly prosy hands
of his successor, that it came to be seen more nearly as it was: the
Gipper's last movie set, all gleaming facades propped up by temporary
carpentry and borrowed cash.

What his reign had postponed was the gathering crisis of American
politics, a leveling wave of cynicism that put Reagan's own place in
history at risk along with his heir's future in office. The golden age he
once seemed to promise had turned out to be merely gilded; it was, as
the Republican political analyst Kevin Phillips argued, a go-go period
uncomfortably like those of the 1880s and the 1920s—a time of pyra-
miding wealth bought, or borrowed, at great economic and political
cost to the many. Its biggest beneficiaries were the top 1 percent of the
population, who had raked in 60 percent of the new money. Its price
was an explosion of debt at every level, from credit cards to junk bonds
to treasury paper to bad bank loans—and a real economy crawling
along at its slowest rate of growth since the Great Depression.

Most ordinary Americans had in fact stood still or slipped back
during their eight-year tenancy in the Shining City, and with the turn
into the '90s, the discovery that prosperity hadn't meant prosperity for
everybody gave rise to an acrid new politics of blame. The new morning
in America was as hot with rebuke as judgment day, with Reagan
standing alongside his protégé in the dock. The Gipper's fall from his
great eminence happened with surprising force and velocity. Three
years after his departure from Washington, he was history, and not as
one of its heroes. He had shrunk in stature to Jimmy Carter's size and

was more widely blamed than Carter for having brought on America's economic miseries.

What he had left his successor was an unplayable hand: the beginnings of a prolonged slowdown that felt like a recession even in those interludes when it didn't fit the technical definition. Reagan had "won" the Cold War at terrible cost to the victors—a stretched-thin economy living on the cuff and overinvested in the manpower and machinery of war. It was as if that strategy aptly called MAD (mutual assured destruction) had seeped from military doctrine into economic thought; a greatly escalated arms race had finally beggared the late Soviet Union, but it had helped bring the United States to the edge of insolvency as well.

The process had been going on for nearly half a century, but Reagan had accelerated it, raiding the treasury like a tapped-out householder borrowing to stay a day ahead of the bills. He had sold first himself and then America on the belief that you could cut taxes, grow the military, and balance the budget all at the same time. You couldn't; when Bush called it voodoo economics, he got it essentially right. Taxes actually rose for most people in the Reagan years. Deficits spun wildly out of control. The demands of the Cold War diverted money, energy, and thought from the most basic civil needs: roads, bridges, schools, safe streets, accessible health care, even reviving the economy when, inevitably, the party ended and the hangover set in.

Reagan's bequest to Bush was in some measure a garrison state—a nation burdened by military commitments it could no longer rationalize, let alone afford, and a defense establishment on which it was heavily dependent for exports and jobs. The distortions had been masked by the Vegas economics of the '80s, a time when high rollers made large fortunes doing deals, not making things, and when the Dow-Jones Industrial Average was widely mistaken for a measure of our general well-being. The economy had already begun stagnating when Bush moved into the Oval Office, and during his second year there, it had slipped into recession. Unemployment rose to nine-year highs, and bankruptcy supplanted mergers-and-acquisitions as the hot new specialty in corporate law.

Reagan, with his arts of illusion, had endured a much sharper downturn in the early '80s and had recovered in plenty of time to win reelection by a forty-nine-state landslide. But Bush found himself prey to a new strain of recession that seemed immune to the workings of the business cycle and resistant to the old remedies. Even when the normal measures said it was getting better, the economy kept devouring jobs and draining consumer confidence. The president was a patently mortal man, subject to the laws of gravity, and hard times brought him crashing to earth. The single constant in an otherwise volatile political season was the progressive collapse of his support. The Gulf war, once thought his guaranteed ticket to a second term, would come to be seen as having been only a false remission—a pause in a long downward slide toward oblivion.

In The Götterdämmerung Vector

Bush had the further bad luck to be seeking reelection at a time of deepening estrangement of the governed from their government. The divide was not a new one. Its ancestry, as the young Democratic polltaker David Petts noted, was at least as old as the Whiskey Rebellion of 1794; by 1992, it had been widening for twenty years. It had been glimpsed in the third-force candidacies of men as disparate as George Wallace in 1968 and John Anderson in 1980. It had boiled over in the tax revolt of the late 1970s. It had sent outsiders like Carter and Reagan to Washington, with implicit mandates to clean house.

For a time in the early years of his presidency, Reagan seemed to be healing the breach, less by his actual achievements than by the sheer force of his person. It was one of the great ironies of his reign that, having run against the federal government, he restored a measure of faith in it; the polls recorded a growing majority of people who believed that it could actually be made to work for them.

The breakpoint came in the autumn of 1986, in the view of analysts in both parties, with the disclosure of the Iran-Contra affair—the three-cushion play in which Washington had tried to ransom some American hostages by selling guns to the Ayatollah Khomeini and then had diverted part of the proceeds to the anticommunist rebels in Nicaragua. The mazy detail of the scandal counted less, politically, than Reagan's insistence that he hadn't known what was going on and hadn't been alert or curious enough to ask. His plea that he had been out to lunch the whole time would have been damning enough if anybody had believed it. Not many did. In the prevailing public view, the Gipper had lied to the people, and having placed their trust in him, they took it personally. He had become just another politician after all, and with his reduction from icon to ordinary man, a Republican analyst said, his presidency effectively ended after six years.

Reagan never recovered, and neither did his heir, whose plea that he hadn't been "in the loop" privy to the Iran-Contra intrigue was suspect almost as soon as he uttered it. The first six years of the Reagan-Bush era had been an optimistic time, a reassertion, on the most mixed evidence, of America's claim to the special favor of God and to a manifest destiny in the world. In the last six, the glow had faded and died; pessimism had become the norm in our national psyche and cynicism the dominant mode of our politics. In the election that seated Bush as president, half of adult America stayed home, an abstention rate unmatched in America since the Jazz Age and unheard of anywhere else in the democratic world. Nonvoters, as the dropout Democratic pollster Patrick Caddell would observe, had become our unacknowledged majority party—a coalition, he called it, of the discontented, the disillusioned, and the disfranchised.

By 1992, they could no longer be ignored; the alienation of the people from the institutions of politics and government, and from that faceless giant known collectively as The Media, had risen to a frightening flood tide. It was, David Petts thought, as if a contract had been broken between Washington and the rest of the country. Bush, in Petts's polling and focus groups, had come to stand for foreign policy, period, and Congress was the house of bounced checks. There was, he thought, a huge disconnect between them and the quotidian worries of middle-class life in America; the governing class saw its subjects dimly, if at all, through the smoked glass of limousine windows and the impersonal measure of polls.

The view from the far side of the glass, peering in, was not flattering to the new American oligarchy. By spring, Linda DiVall, a Republican pollster with a heavily congressional client list, would do a survey advancing as a proposition that the entire political system was broken— that it was run by insiders who didn't listen to working people and couldn't solve their problems. In the world's oldest constitutional democracy, three voters in four agreed. DiVall was a matter-of-fact woman, not given to visions of politics in what one radical journalist called the Götterdämmerung Vector. But she wondered if she would have got a much different result polling in Moscow just before the people rose against their Soviet rulers.

For the disaffected, each day's news seemed to bring fresh grounds for unbelief in politics and government. The sputtering economy was itself a daily indictment, of Congress as well as the president; each blamed the other, but their helplessness ran together in the public mind and translated into nonfeasance in office. The national debt had quadrupled in the Reagan-Bush years, to $4 trillion and counting. Savings and loans were collapsing. Banks were wobbling under backlogs of bad debt. Corporate giants were paying for their fevers of acquisition in the '80s at exorbitant interest rates. Real estate values crumbled, and not just for the builders of empty urban office towers;

the real victims were ordinary householders whose net worth was roughly identical to the resale value of their homes.

There was a price for the revels of the Reagan years, and it fell most heavily on working America. Corporations shored up their profits and retired their debts by "downsizing" or "rightsizing" their payrolls, which sounded nicer than letting people go, and by "reengineering" the way they ran their businesses, which meant that the laid-off employees were unlikely ever to be invited back. The very nature of work in America was changing, away from permanent jobs with high wages and generous benefits. A sizable fraction of working people lived in a Kleenex economy: nearly a fourth of the labor force in the early '90s consisted of temps and part-timers, who were cheaper to maintain and easier to dispose of when they were no longer needed.

The consequence was a brutal squeeze not just on the poor but on the middle class as well. Housing foreclosures were up. The homeless became part of the American townscape, in small cities as well as large. New college graduates had trouble finding work. Laid-off professionals drove taxis and caddied at country clubs. Personal bankruptcies reached record highs. So did dependency on the dole in its various forms, with some of the newly dispossessed among the clients. One American in ten was on food stamps, one in eight living in poverty; one family in four had been directly touched by unemployment. For those who had jobs, household incomes were stuck roughly where they had been in the early '70s—and they stayed at those levels only because longer hours and working wives had become the norms of middle-American life.

Morale fell along with the economic numbers. The feeling that America was on the wrong track—a standard polling measure of the public mood—had been a majority view for most of six years and was fast approaching a national consensus. The Bush years had become a new age of anxiety, unconnected to the old standards of measurement. Unemployment had been worse during the Reagan recession—the worst, indeed, since the 1930s. But it had come and gone like a summer fever. The ills of the '90s had the feel of a chronic condition, a wasting disease of the sinew and spirit. In the American psyche, as the young Republican pollster Ed Goeas observed, this recession wasn't just about jobs—it was about fear of the future.

The sense of danger hung like smoke on the air, and with it, the suspicion that no one was in charge—no one with the strength, courage, and vision to keep the country from sliding deeper into decline. Tokyo eclipsed Moscow in the American nightmare; in Fred Steeper's focus groups for the Bush campaign, people worried obsessively about the Japanese and spoke of the happy ending of the Cold War only if you reminded them of it. Pessimism supplanted hope in the American Dream; great majorities felt that their own standards of living were deteriorating and believed, against the grain of history and myth, that their children would do even worse.

There were multiplying parallels to the boom-and-bust cycle of the Roaring Twenties, as Kevin Phillips was among the first to remark in print. They ranged from what he called "the triumph of Upper America"—the rich in both periods got enormously richer—to the stubborn insistence of the president that nothing was really wrong. In fact, something was. A reputable academic institute proposed that America had already entered "a contained depression"; the term may or may not have precisely fit the economy, but it surely described America's deepening self-doubt.

In the circumstances, it was not hard to sustain the spreading public impression that Washington was fiddling while the nation burned. There were reasons for its inaction, first among them the mountain of IOU's signed jointly by Republican presidents and Democratic Congresses in the '80s. Their check-kiting had bought six years of plenty, or its appearance. But Washington had drained its own resources in the process; it was hard to speak imaginatively about public policy when the government was running nearly $300 billion a year in the red.

Neither was it thought possible for politicians who valued their lives and careers to speak about raising taxes. The taboo was a relatively new one, a further legacy of the Reagan-Bush years. In a not very long ago time, as David Petts remarked, Americans grudgingly accepted taxes as their half of a transaction with government—the dues one paid in the expectation of services and benefits in return. But that understanding had faded with the '70s and collapsed in the '80s; the new view, championed most effectively by Reagan, was that government couldn't be trusted to do anything much with money except move it from middle-class families to "welfare queens." Much would be said in the 1992 campaign about the gridlock in Washington—the result, in most analyses, of divided party control of the White House and Capitol Hill. In fact, the two parties had made the mess together. The real paralytic agent was terror; it was hard to vote to raise taxes or spend money on the general good without thinking ahead to the negative ads one could surely anticipate in one's next campaign.

One resource the Federal City did have was a gift for inappropriate metaphor—a way of turning a want of bread into a plenitude of circuses. The House of Representatives was discovered to have built the friendliest bank in America, the one place left where the management smiled on the habit of the members of writing rubber checks to cover their own deficit spending. The sins of venality on the Hill are many and various, but the blizzard of overdrafts was easily comprehended by every citizen with a checkbook; before the year was out, some of the miscreants would pay for them with their political lives. The all-white, all-male Senate judiciary committee similarly distinguished itself with its televised hearings on a charge of sexual harassment brought against Clarence Thomas, a black Supreme Court nominee of modest stature at the bar, by his sometime staffer Anita Hill. The inquiry embittered him, pilloried her, and made it hard to remember when or why the Senate had dubbed itself the world's greatest deliberative body; the spectacle revealed nothing so vividly as the character of the men who conducted it by their own old-boy rules.

The sideshows only reinforced the growing popular supposition that the government was at once corrupt and irrelevant—that its sole concerns were maintaining itself in power and servicing its monied client groups. The real-world concerns of the early '90s had to do with jobs, schools, medical care, mortgage payments, college bills, and crime. Even a lengthening life span had become, for many Americans, a mixed blessing; children worried about nursing-home bills for their aging parents, and breadwinners laid off at age fifty faced the suddenly terrifying question of how they would survive for twenty-five or thirty more years.

Politics, in the view of growing numbers of Americans, had little to do with any of that; the principal interest of its practitioners seemed instead to be their own survival and betterment at public and private expense. Their cynicism, even their criminality, was widely assumed. A hit movie of the day proposed quite seriously that John F. Kennedy had been the victim of a coup d'état involving practically every agency of government short of the Bureau of Mines. Paranoia suffused our real-world politics as well; a national poll brought in a two-thirds majority verdict that a sizable number of the people running the country were crooked—a level of suspicion unmatched even at the height of the Watergate scandals.

Voting No as the Best Revenge

The quest for the presidency in 1992 thus began as a kind of Kabuki drama played to an audience grown weary of its stylized makeup and its ritualized forms. Politics had become a game for professionals, men and women for whom America was not so much a country or an idea as an assemblage of movable "coalitions," "constituencies," and "target groups." They had grown technically expert at their work in the century and a half since winning elections had first emerged as a business rather than a civic duty. But two neglected nonpartisan focus-group studies in the early '90s suggested that they had lost touch with a larger reality. What the inquiries independently discovered was an incipient collapse of faith in American democracy—a breakdown so serious and so far advanced as to call into question the very legitimacy of the government, the Congress, and the electoral process.

One of the inquiries, a ten-city tour of the American psyche commissioned by the Kettering Foundation in 1990 and 1991, found levels of revulsion so high that people no longer felt they lived in a democracy at all. The nation, in their view, had fallen captive to a clique of politicians, PACs, lobbyists, and mass media responsive only to special interests and to themselves. Elections had become charades, all empty rhetoric, slung mud, and profligate spending; the citizens and their concerns had been crowded almost entirely out of the picture.

Doug Bailey, one of a bipartisan team who did a separate study for the Centel Corporation, shared the view that the mood bore a distant resemblance to the revolutionary tides sweeping the former Soviet empire; the saving difference was America's long experience with and faith, however battered, in the possibility of change by orderly process. Bailey, a pioneer political consultant, had himself largely abandoned the business after nearly a quarter-century serving moderate Republican clients; he had got discouraged by the rise of a class of men and women for whom public office was not a calling but a living, to be sustained by the slavish reading of polls and the tireless pursuit of campaign contributions.

What people longed for, Bailey believed, was leadership. What they were getting, as he and the Democratic pollster Peter Hart wrote in a summary of the Centel study, was a system "rigged by the incumbents for the incumbents, and for the vested interests that fund their campaigns." The voters, in such a setting, were an inconvenience—a beast to be propitiated at two-, four-, or six-year intervals and then forgotten till the next election. An analyst who worked on the Centel project watched Hart outline its findings to a group of members of Congress and was struck by a sense that at least half of them actively *hated* the people they had been sent to Washington to serve.

The voters appeared to have caught on, and their mood was dangerous to all professional politicians, of whatever party or persuasion. On the day he left for Moscow as Bush's ambassador, Robert Strauss, the Democratic power lawyer who had witnessed much history and brokered some of it in his seventy-two years, ventured to a friend that the faith of the people in their country was the lowest he had ever seen it. They loved America, he said, but they no longer believed that it could deliver for them, and so had accepted as a fact of life that they were going to be screwed. In such a climate, voting no could be the best revenge; it became quickly evident that 1992 would be a time when incumbents fell and insurgencies bloomed, challenging a two-party architecture that had been more or less securely in place since the extinction of the Whigs before the Civil War.

The burden fell most heavily on George Bush. He was victim in part to our habit of asking too much of the men who have held or sought our highest office. A presidential election has come to resemble a pilgrimage of the lame and halt to a holy place in the range of hopes, prayers, and expectations it excites. Nobody mortal could satisfy them all, and Bush—unlike a Roosevelt, say, or a Reagan—did not have the art to pretend that he could. Hope, which dies hard in America, would seek other vessels. Bill Clinton, the man who would emerge as the leading Democratic challenger, was a bright and talented politician, but his most compelling claim was that he was new.

Bush was not. After twenty-odd years in Washington and twelve in or around the White House, he was, or seemed, the system made flesh—the leader of a power elite operating at a great remove from workaday America and its discontents. His incumbency and his handsome Washington portfolio were no longer the negotiable instruments they once had been. He entered his last campaign in trouble not, or not simply, because of his lack of great achievement or of soaring ideas. He was in peril because, in a season of blame, he was there.

3.

The Winds of Rebellion

A presidential election is the grand pageant of American democracy—
a spectacle in which the events on stage are invested by actors
and audience alike with larger-than-life meaning. Parties are pre-
maturely buried and as suddenly disinterred; mighty coalitions are
pronounced dead, and realignments confidently proclaimed; old ideologies are consigned to history, and new ones divined in the exit polls
before the victor is seated; a back-bench senator named Kennedy or a
B-movie actor named Reagan is raised overnight to national icon,
only to be returned with time and reexamination to the ranks of
fallible men.

And yet, watching the events of 1992 unfold, it was more than
ordinarily hard to escape a sense that an order of things was cracking—that, whatever the denouement, the accustomed patterns of
politics would not soon be the same again. The simultaneous crises of
faith in the economy and faith in the government had loosed powerful and unpredictable winds of rebellion across the landscape, and
the party that had monopolized the presidency for most of the past
quarter-century was not alone in their destructive path. The two-
party system itself was under siege: it was the year of the outsider, a
time of mutiny within each of the major parties and of passion, finally
disappointed, for a billionaire salvationist who represented no party
at all.

As the avant-garde of a new politics, Pat Buchanan, Jerry Brown,
and Ross Perot were an implausible lot, each badly and in the end
fatally flawed. But each in his way argued with surprising effect
that there was no two-party system anymore—that America had
fallen into the hands of a single incumbent party obsessed only with
power, not principle, and sustained by money and chicane. And each
in his way offered something that the regular parties no longer
seemed able to provide: a sense of empowerment for people who felt
abandoned by what had become, in their eyes, a professional governing caste.

The Primal Scream

The common offering of the outsiders was politics as primal scream—the accusation, delivered at high pitch, that the American Dream had been betrayed by one set of elites or another for personal and political gain. The identity of the villains varied according to the ideology of the candidates and their tribes. But the insurgencies of 1992 had shared roots in what the late historian Richard Hofstadter called the paranoid style in American politics—the suspicion that the Dream was being subverted from within by money and faction—and this time their vision had support both in demonstrable fact and in serious intellectual argument.

Their manifesto, if one could be singled out, was a slender volume called *Promises to Keep,* by the sometime Kennedy-Johnson thinker-in-residence Richard Goodwin. The book had its most powerful influence on Governor Brown, who borrowed from it liberally, but the ideas and passions it advanced had far wider resonance in the chilled-out politics of 1992. Goodwin's brief was that American democracy had been corrupted by "a profane combination of private interests with public authority"—an alliance bottomed on the ever-increasing cost of getting elected and the consequent willingness of office seekers to sell their souls on the open market.

The interests of the people, in Goodwin's critique, had become secondary to the appetites of politicians and of the "money power" that bankrolled their campaigns. The two major parties had become nothing more than twin conduits for personal ambition; in a country that spent upwards of $3 billion on elections, as America had in 1988, the public agenda was ipso facto in the hands of the people who picked up the bills. The idea of the commonweal was a quaint antique. "Corruption, anxiety for office, and mediocrity rule the land," Goodwin wrote. The worst nightmare of the Founding Fathers, the triumph of faction over the general good, was coming true, and it would take nothing less than "a popular revolution" to stop it.

As it happened, a sizable fraction of the people were ahead of the prophecy; by the time Goodwin published, they were already attaching themselves to various champions, not all of them as respectable as the insurgents who offered themselves for president. At its outer extreme, the search for a voice for the disfranchised had led to the likes of David Duke, a cleverly retouched ex-Klansman and neo-Nazi who had run successively for senator and governor in Louisiana and had done alarmingly well. His appeal was widely presumed to be racist, his success one more event in a pattern of reemergent bigotry in the land. But in a postmortem study of Duke's U.S. Senate race, the state-of-the-art Democratic polltaker Geoffrey Garin found a wider thread than race uniting his supporters. The people most likely to vote for Duke were the people who felt least well represented in the government as it was.

The rebels of 1992 found newer and more powerful ways of connecting with them and their grievances; Duke would make a half-hearted run in the presidential primaries, but a new age of political technology was dawning, and he was lost in it. What Brown and Perot discovered, each in his way, was the use of modern electronics to converse with the voters instead of merely talking at them in nine-second sound bites and thirty-second ads. Each turned call-in talk shows and toll-free 800 phone numbers into instruments of popular democracy—Brown, the beggarly revolutionary, to finance his campaign with donations of $100 or less; Perot, the billionaire populist, to float the mere idea of a third-force candidacy on *Larry King Live* and raise an instant army of volunteers.

Together, they changed the face of presidential campaigning, making even the most artful video politics of our recent past look practically paleolithic by comparison. Their plunge into interactive electronics would prove rapidly catching; by summer, Clinton would have an 800 number, too, and he and Bush would be popping in on chatmeisters from Katie Couric at daybreak to Arsenio Hall at midnight like rival martial artists plugging their latest action movies.

But the challenge to the old order ran far deeper than the addition of new tricks to the trade of political communication. The real revelation of the year of the insurgents was the vulnerability of the two-party system to outsiders with the will, the resources, and the command of new-age techniques to tap into the mood of rebellion rising against the government. What Perot showed, in his season in the sun, was that you could simply ignore the forms and rituals of party politics entirely and offer yourself directly to the people—the candidate as the embodiment of their unfiltered will. And what Brown demonstrated within his party was that you didn't have to be a billionaire to take on the system credibly. Burdened though he was by his flaky reputation and his rusted political skills, he simply announced his manifesto and his phone number, and a river of money flowed in, the small checks adding up to large round numbers.

State of Siege

There would be those, indeed, who saw in the events of 1992 the beginning of the end of two-party politics—or at least of the unchallenged dominance of the two aging parties that had governed the nation for nearly a century and a half. America had got so used to the existing arrangement that it had almost come to seem part of the constitutional order. Binary politics was deeply embedded in our state law as well as our national history, and challenging it was a daunting enterprise. Its longevity owed in important part to its genius at coopting rebel movements, soaking up their ideas, their energies, and their passions before they got out of hand; the last successful third-force candidate for president had been Abraham Lincoln of the infant Republican Party in 1860.

But as Republican strategist Ed Rollins remarked in the fall of 1991, long before he had thrown in with Perot, the old system was showing symptoms of morbidity. The realignment of power to the Republicans once thought to have arrived with Ronald Reagan had turned instead into a *de*-alignment, the falling away of voters from both established parties. Neither, in Rollins's reckoning, could any longer bank on more than, say, 30 percent of the vote. Between them lay a no-man's land inhabited by 40 percent of the country, independents who were at best indifferent to and at worst repelled by the old brand names.

The flight from party politics owed partly to its recent record—arguably the longest run of underachieving presidencies in a century or more—and partly to its perceived remove from everyday reality. The 1988 campaign was widely judged to have been the emptiest in our recent past; at a time of rising danger to the economy and momentous change in the world, the two men seeking our highest office debated which one hated criminals more and which more ardently revered the flag. Handlers as a class were widely blamed for the reduction of presidential politics to a game of Trivial Pursuit. But the candidates bore a full share of responsibility as well; neither George Bush nor Michael Dukakis offered a real reason for his election.

Their candidacies in turn had been windows into the sad state of our party politics. The major parties had grown old badly—had fallen victim, in Kevin Phillips's dour assessment, to a slow and probably terminal illness equivalent to Alzheimer's disease. Their national headquarters in Washington had become the investment banks of our politics, devoted mainly to raising large sums of money from people with vested interests in the business of government and redistributing it to those candidates they considered worthy. Worthiness usually meant electability; the biggest checks accordingly were written to incumbents, underwriting their permanence in office—and, too often, their great distance from their constituents.

The system made eminently good business sense when incumbency was still an unmixed blessing—when, for example, 98 percent of the members of Congress seeking reelection regularly won. But in 1990, their average margins of victory sank disquietingly low, and by 1992, their edge would dissipate even further. Twenty House members would be defeated in their own party primaries, the biggest purge of its kind since World War II. Dozens more chose early retirement and large one-time severance packages rather than breast the tide. Term limits for members of Congress, a novelty in Colorado only a year before, became a national cause. Women challengers found themselves suddenly in vogue; in the boys' club of our politics, no one quite so graphically represented change.

It was fashionable among academics and journalists in the early 1990s to identify the Democrats as the party in deeper danger. With the turn of the decade, a whole shelf of books proclaimed them moribund, a party soon to be in the company of the Whigs as candidates for historical dioramas at the Smithsonian Institution. Their misfortunes, it was argued, could no longer be blamed on an unlucky run of candidates from George McGovern to Michael Dukakis or on the supposedly greater guile of the Republicans at winning elections. The ills of the Democrats, it was proposed, lay closer to their institutional soul; they were so deep in decline as to be dependent on hard times to return them to the White House.

They had, so the argument ran, turned their backs on the values and needs of the great American middle class; instead, they had too closely embraced the outcasts of our society, from yippies to feminists to gays and, most especially, to blacks. They were in bondage to their client groups, the faded remnants of what once had been the New Deal coalition. They were addicted to the welfare state and to the taxes and bureaucracies necessary to sustain it. They had become, most damagingly of all, the Levelers of our time—a party committed to the massive transfer of the nation's wealth and opportunity not just from the rich but from working America to the undeserving poor.

Neither had the Democrats functioned effectively as an opposition party, carrying the attack to Bush from their own bastion of power on Capitol Hill. As in past boom times, they were, as Kevin Phillips noted, the prisoners of their own complicity in the policies that had brought the economy low. But they were captive to their institutional folkways as well. In 1991, two brash young Democratic consultants, David Petts and Michael Donilon, then partners in a polling firm, argued in memos and meetings for a more consciously provocative approach—creating and passing a Democratic legislative agenda and challenging the president to veto it if he dared. They got nowhere; the inertial forces working against confrontation and for compromise were too great.

The books proclaiming the party moribund were not inaccurate as to its recent past—its long passage in the desert since the murder of John Kennedy and the forced exile of Lyndon Johnson. It could indeed be fairly argued that the Democratic majority in presidential politics and the liberal ideals that had nourished it had died with FDR; since then, liberalism had gradually become a dirty word and the Democrats a minority party. But something was missing from the picture: the possibility that the party had a future and that it might be different from its past. By the time the obituaries reached print, the Democrats were already in the process of rediscovering the middle class, and the presidential field in 1992 reflected their reawakened concern. Jesse Jackson, who had run as the tribune of the poor and disfranchised in 1984 and 1988, chose not to do so this time; the party and its ultimate nominee would thus be spared the embarrassment of having to barter with him and his constituents at the expense of the white tax-paying classes. The single old-time liberal fundamentalist seeking the party's nomination was Senator Tom Harkin of Iowa, and he would be among the first driven from the field.

The survivors were mostly men of the postmodern center. They still believed in government activism, but activist no longer meant big, and the have-nots were no longer to be the sole or even the main clients. The programs most in favor with the New Democrats, as they styled themselves, were broad-based benefits designed principally for the well-being of the middle class and only incidentally for the poor. Welfare had been supplanted on their agenda by welfare reform, and civil rights for minorities by expanding opportunity for all. Their touchstone issues had to do with lowering taxes, creating jobs, and—most of all—making college and medical care accessible and affordable for Middle America. The poor, while not forgotten, would have to await their deliverance by a generally rising tide.

The heart transplant was by no means complete. The body of the party was still powerfully influenced by its organized constituency groups, and with the rise of Bill Clinton, symptoms of rejection set in. At least one senior party official watched his ascent at a fearful distance and sought to retard it by planting stories in the media that he was unelectable in November. The counterargument from Clinton's advocates was that the old Democratic politics hadn't produced many winners either. The mythic old New Deal coalition had not been fully functional since the New Deal, when first the depression and then the war bound its hopelessly mismatched constituent groups together. In the half-century since the death of Franklin Roosevelt, there had been just four Democratic presidents, and only Lyndon Johnson among them had, under extraordinary circumstances, run up a clean majority of the vote.

Clinton embodied the more moderate politics of the Democratic Leadership Council (DLC), a centrist group he had chaired for a year and had used as both a springboard and a brain bank for his ambitions. Its ideas on reinventing the welfare state were hotly debated within the party, but its arithmetic was hard to argue with. The Democrats in their heyday had helped to create a large and prosperous middle class and then had walked away from it, ceding its symbols, its values, and its votes to the Republicans. What was left of the party's natural base had withered to what looked like a permanent minority in presidential elections. By 1988, the old Democratic hard core of white liberals and blacks had shrunk, in DLC executive director Al From's reading of the exit polls, to 29 percent of the vote.

Yet there were those who believed that the Republicans were an even more endangered species—a spent force after too many years in power and too little of enduring worth to show for it. Much had been written about their supposed "electoral lock" on the presidency; they virtually owned vast expanses of political real estate in the South and West, while the Democrats had practically nothing dependably bankable beyond the District of Columbia.

But there are no permanent majorities in a democracy as large and various as America; even our longest-lived ruling coalitions, from Andrew Jackson's to FDR's, have been alliances of convenience that lasted for roughly a generation and then came undone. The gods had favored George Bush and his party in 1988 with a weak opponent and an economy that still looked good on paper. His easy victory inspired a whole new round of commentaries about the death of the Democrats. On paper, and there were reams of it, the idea was tempting. In fact, the inevitable fault lines were already appearing in the New Republican Majority first drawn together by Richard Nixon a quarter-century earlier, and by 1992 they were opening wide. What distinguished Nixon's coalition from its predecessors was that the man who built it had lived to watch its unraveling. The occasion of sorrow was said to have been mitigated for Nixon and his Main Street tribe by their contempt for the High Street president in office at its decline.

There were still bright young men with bright young ideas in Bush's service, post-Reagan conservative ideas about using government in nonbureaucratic ways to address social concerns. Their views bore a certain family resemblance to those of DLC's resident thinkers, so close that members of the two groups sometimes thought of themselves as parties to the same conversation. But access to power was limited for the reformers in Bush's Washington, and their nearly boyish faith in their agenda was often mocked by their elders in the White House. They had run into that late period in the life cycle of governing parties when the central idea is not what more you can do for your country but how you can stay in power. The great burst of intellectual energy that had suffused and rationalized the early Reagan years had played out. The Republicans actually in charge had entered upon what one of the young bloods called their Decadent Period—a time when pragmatism had become the ruling ideology and the party of change was in danger of becoming a propaganda machine for the status quo.

What was missing was a fighting faith of the sort that had bound the Reagan majority together and allowed people to think of his early years in office as a revolution. History had conspired against the coalition that had won five out of the past six presidential elections, by margins that averaged out to landslide dimensions. Like the Democrats before them, the Republicans were prey to their successes as well as their failures. The disintegration of the Evil Empire had left Reagan's legions without a common adversary; anticommunism had lost much of its relevance in a world with no communists left who mattered greatly to America's security. The new enemy was economic decline, and with the advent of lean times, the old Republican agenda came to seem less important than the issues of day-to-day survival.

The party majority had survived earlier recessions during its long run in power from Nixon to Bush. But in Kevin Phillips's view, it was victim to deeper, longer-term cyclical forces—an undertow much like those which had dragged the Republicans down along with the economy in the Gilded Age and the Roaring Twenties. Phillips had been one of the architects of that majority in the Nixon years; he had envisioned a new Republican victory coalition anchored in the Sun Belt, a term he coined, and bound together by the economic interests and the social values of Middle America. The majority had subsequently passed into the hands of other tribes with other agendas, but they had managed to sustain it in power so long as the cash registers kept ringing, the Reds remained a menace, and Reagan could still brush away care with a smile.

By 1992, as Phillips argued in his eerily prophetic book *The Politics of Rich and Poor,* it had come near the end of its run. The coalition had drifted far from its beginnings in what he called the cloth-coat Republicanism of the Nixon years; in his view, the new-money fortune hunting of the Reagan era and the old-money conservatism at Bush's court had brought the Grand Old Party back round to its bad old image as the champion of the rich. To be so perceived was not helpful, politically, in hard times. Phillips doubted that the party majority he had helped design could long survive the end of the boom it had promoted; it had become George Bush's lot in our political history to be helpless witness to its unraveling.

It remained as risky as ever, on the eve of battle, to underestimate Bush in a political fight. It was true that his successes in public life had been mainly by appointment or ordination—that, on his own, he had lost nearly as many elections as he had won. What made him dangerous was his nearly acrophobic fear of falling from great heights; it was when he looked down that he showed himself willing to do almost anything to win.

But he seemed oddly diminished, in spirit as well as size, as he prepared himself fitfully for his last campaign. An air of defeatism stole over his troops with his steady decline in the polls and appeared at times to infect him as well. Rumors swirled about his seeming state of entropy. There were published speculations that he was not well; that he planned to stand down voluntarily, at his own wish or Barbara's command; even that, in his ongoing war with English syntax, he was showing suggestive signs of a brain disorder called aphasia.

The stories did not stand up to scrutiny; the only reality they reflected was the president's weakened political situation, refracted through the distorting glass of the media. And yet there was a palpable air of finality about Bush's last stand—a fin de siècle feeling that, whether he won or lost, an old era in American politics was ending and a new one was struggling to be born.

II

The Challenger

The only thing more unpredictable than an election is just being born. Is life itself. You get in an election, it's like you're kicking down a fucking door, and you got no idea what's behind it.

—James Carville, strategist
to the Clinton campaign,
January 1992

4.

The Man Who Would Be President

The painters were redoing the governor's mansion in Little Rock, and Bill and Hillary Clinton were sleeping fitfully in the guest house out back. It was the summer of 1991, the season of George Bush's nearly total dominion over our politics. So daunting were his poll numbers that, out of the entire Democratic Party, only a half-forgotten ex-senator named Paul Tsongas had so far been brazen enough to challenge him. But the Clintons were a couple with large and shared ambitions, a common hunger powerful enough to make them reckless of the odds that had scared everybody else into hiding. The mere scent of opportunity, however remote, had been enough to trouble the young governor's rest that night, and as day broke over Arkansas, he sat straight up in bed.

The sudden movement wakened Hillary. She could guess what was on her husband's mind; they had been talking about it off and on for weeks.

"We have to do this, don't we," she said. She meant run for president, and it was a statement, not a question.

"We don't have to do anything we don't want to do," he replied.

"But if we don't," she said, "what will our excuse be?"

It could get ugly, he said. Dirty.

They both knew what he meant. The whispers about him and other women had plagued him for much of his career in politics and had seriously strained their life together. He had considered declaring once before, in 1987, and had gone so far as to invite friends down to Little Rock for the ceremonies. But at the last moment, he had stood down. His announced reason was that his daughter, Chelsea, then seven-going-on-eight, was too young for the rigors of a national campaign. In fact, as intimates knew, the concerns that he and Hillary shared were more specific than that. What they really feared was that questions would be raised about his rumored sexual adventuring and would damage them all—their daughter, their marriage, themselves.

The problem hadn't gone away. But Chelsea was four years older now and had been well tutored by her parents on what to expect from politics, including the likelihood that people would say bad things about her daddy. And this time, Hillary, too, felt ready for whatever came; it was said around the statehouse, indeed, that she was the tough one in the Clinton family—tougher, certainly, than Bill. There were things the two of them believed in, the public passions that had survived the worst passages of their private life. America needed to hear them, Hillary thought, and there was no better forum than a presidential campaign.

She knew it wouldn't be easy. She had read the polls and watched one after another of their more famous Democratic contemporaries dither or duck for cover—Mario Cuomo, Dick Gephardt, Bill Bradley, Jay Rockefeller, Lloyd Bentsen, Al Gore, Jesse Jackson. Maybe Bush *was* invulnerable, as everybody then said; maybe no Democrat could win. To Hillary, it didn't matter. She looked on the 1992 campaign as a kind of practice run anyway, a chance for both of them to travel the country, talk about their issues, and make themselves known. If nobody cared, fine—they could go home and wait till next time. At least they would have tried.

You've *got* to run, she said, with a finality suggesting that the case, for her, was closed. And so it was: in the months to come, Clinton would date the beginning of his quest for the presidency to that moment and to Hillary's words.

The Natural

It could as easily be said of William Jefferson Clinton that he had been running for president all his sentient life. He was a frankly ambitious man in the one trade in America in which, as he himself remarked, ambition was thought to be unseemly; nobody ever criticized Michael Jordan for all the hundreds of practice jump shots he must have put up as a kid, Clinton mused, but if you lusted in your heart for high political office, as he did, you weren't supposed to show it. He was old enough, in his middle forties, to remember a time when politics was still considered an honorable and even a noble profession, and it remained a calling for him long after it had fallen into public disrepute. He saw no reason why he shouldn't want to succeed at it; if you were serious about wanting to change people's lives, he often said, there was no better way.

Politics was a source of affirmation as well for a man who appeared to need it—whose own sense of himself seemed to depend in some measure on his ability to make other people like him. He was good at the game, perhaps the best of any serious presidential contender of his party since John F. Kennedy; one of his thirtysomething managers called him, a bit wistfully, the candidate of a lifetime. He carried himself with that special ease born of the conviction that he could talk anybody into anything. His self-possession, a senior aide said, bordered at times on arrogance—a belief, shared with Hillary, that the two of them were the smartest people on the planet. And yet there was the hint of something vulnerable about him; at middle age, Clinton was still the schoolboy charmer who listened attentively, spoke well, did his lessons, aced his tests—and, when he did get into mischief, eased his way out with a half-apology and a soft little curl of a smile.

His interest in issues was real and his grasp of them formidable. The half-flattering, half-dismissive term "policy wonk" would become a staple and then a cliché of the journalism about him. The label was in fact better suited to a Jimmy Carter, say, or a Michael Dukakis—men who addressed the complexities of government with the air of having crammed all night for a final exam. Clinton attacked them with feeling, sometimes too much of it, as when he smothered one-part problems with five-point programs; at times, he could be the man with too many plans. His defense, when his managers complained, was the example of George Bush in 1988. Bush, he said, had run on a two-plank platform: read my lips and the other guy's a bum. It had got him elected, but the old Vince Lombardi dictum was wrong—winning *wasn't* everything. If you didn't have an agenda to govern by, something you wanted to accomplish, there was no point running at all.

Clinton was further blessed with a gift for making instant connections with people. He could dominate a whole room with his raw physical presence—he was a wide-bodied six-feet-two—or win voters singly with a word, a touch, a grin, and a steady, attentive gaze. It seemed not to matter that, as one of his most loyal troopers put it, his attentions were a mile wide and an inch deep. For those few moments he rationed to you, friend or stranger, he made you feel as if you were the most important person in his world.

Critics measuring him for the presidency would say of him that he was perhaps *too* ingratiating, too eager to please whoever was in front of him at whatever cost. The more serious among them wondered whether or not he was tough enough for the job—strong enough, that is, to say no at the risk of being disliked. The more contemptuous called him Slick Willie for his tendency to rearrange fact and shade meanings to accommodate his own needs and the desires of his audience of the moment. The nickname had first been hung on him by a notoriously hostile editor down home, but it would recurringly haunt him in 1992 because, to a sizable fraction of the electorate at key points in time, it seemed so neatly to fit him.

Clinton himself hated hearing the name, but he acknowledged the inner need that made people think there was something to it. His father, William Blythe, a construction-equipment salesman, had died in a highway accident before Clinton was born; he had been raised for much of his boyhood by an alcoholic stepfather who regularly took a strap to him, his mother, and his half-brother, Roger. He had put at least a temporary a stop to the whippings by threatening to fight back, but like many children of abusive parents, he felt a deeper, more desperate impulse to try to be the peacemaker—to contrive, by being a pleasing boy, to head off trouble and hold the family together. He was a young man and his stepfather was dying of cancer when they finally reconciled, closing the circle. But the meliorist in Clinton, as he himself understood, had never really been laid to rest.

Neither had his thirst for achievement, on the fastest track he could find to the highest level he could imagine. His boyhood had not been so Dickensian as it was sometimes made to sound by the profile writers of the media and the propagandists in his own campaign. It was true that his mother had had to park him with his grandparents for several years in a backwater Arkansas town called Hope after his father died, and that his stepfather had exorcised his own demons by abusing his family. But Clinton had never felt unwanted or unloved, not, anyway, in retrospect. He would speak of his growing-up years instead as having been an *intermittent*, not a constant, hell—a state he thought roughly synonymous with being alive.

The residue, for him, was not bitterness or self-doubt but a passion for achievement—a drive not so much to flee his beginnings as to transcend them. There was something almost desperate about his hunger, an urgency that played out as a chronic lifelong workaholism; it was not until he was in his forties that he looked back and realized that he had lost a part of his childhood on his the way up the ladder. But where others of his generation, equally driven, sought the measure of their worth in money, he felt drawn to public office—to the chance to write his signature on the world. His inspiration was John F. Kennedy, whom he had met fleetingly in his teens as a member of the Arkansas delegation to Boys Nation. The surviving pictures of their handshake captured the firelight of longing in Clinton's ducked head and upturned eyes.

His path took him to Georgetown, Oxford, and Yale Law, a dance step ahead of the draft and the war in Vietnam. Then he went home to Hot Springs, Arkansas, with his book-learning, his dreams, and, in short order, his Yale sweetheart, Hillary Rodham, a lawyer and law professor of modern views and precocious reputation. As true children of the '60s, they sat up nights during their courtship talking about the art of changing public policy, and when they married, it seemed part love match and part political alliance. People who knew them well guessed that their common causes helped bind their union together when the tales of Bill's wandering eye threatened to pull it apart.

Hillary kept her family name and pursued her own career, with one of the state's major law firms. But her husband's rise in politics was a joint effort beginning even before they were married. He declared for Congress when he was barely old enough, at twenty-seven, to serve. He lost, narrowly, to an entrenched Republican incumbent whom everyone else thought untouchable; that a mop-topped young liberal who had first tasted politics in the McGovern campaign should have come within four points of winning was enough to establish him as a comer. In two years' time, he was elected attorney general. In four, at age thirty-two, he moved into the governor's mansion for what would be the first of five terms.

It was very nearly his last, in large part because he acted as though it might be. He was victim to the hubris of the young, and to a certain contingent sense of life as well—the legacy of the late father he had seen only in family photos. The likeness to himself haunted him and seemed deeper than their striking physical resemblance. He had grown up, he would say, feeling that he, like his dad, would never have enough time. The governor's term was only two years then, and Clinton tried to cram too much into it; when the legislature choked on his do-everything agenda, he treated its members as if *they* were Boys Nation and he the reigning grownup in the house. He was, moreover, as careless of costs as he was of feelings. As he discovered at reelection time, he had made himself an easy target with his overreaching.

He knew he was in trouble the day an old man approached him in Fort Smith and told him bluntly, "I wouldn't vote for you if you were the last man on earth."

Clinton asked why not.

Because, the old-timer said, Clinton had raised the fee for auto-license tags to help pay for his programs.

Clinton gestured toward the Oklahoma state line, a short distance away. Over there, he said, licenses cost three times as much as they did in Arkansas, even with the increase.

"Son, you just don't understand," the old man said. "That's why I live on this side of the border."

Clinton lost that time, to a Republican businessman who caught him flat-footed with a savage attack campaign. The lessons were chastening. Advocates of the Slick Willie school of Clintonology said that defeat made him a trimmer, willing to compromise his principles in the interest of a deal or maybe just approval. Clinton himself preferred to say that losing had matured him, politically and emotionally. It taught him to see politics as a marathon, not a sprint; you had to husband your energies for the few issues that mattered most to you and not try to do everything at once.

In the months thereafter, he climbed in his car and began what amounted to a journey of rediscovery, of himself, his party, and his state. That he would attempt a comeback was never in doubt. The question was how, and Clinton sought the answers in reading—a forty-book syllabus in political economics—and in travels among the voters who had only just rejected him. The books taught him how ill-prepared America was to compete in a changing world economy and how government could be part of the solution. The voters told him just what they thought of him and the activist Democratic tradition he embodied. He was too young. He was too brash. He didn't listen. He had moved too fast on too many fronts. He was trying to govern a state when he couldn't even run his own household; why else would a *real* man let his wife run around using her maiden name?

He had set out on his pilgrimage not knowing if he had a future. His successor was busy undoing much of what he had done, and the talk around the courthouses was that Arkansas was on the verge of becoming a Republican state. But Clinton had another of his wayside epiphanies during his travels, and he called Hillary excitedly from a little country store on the road one night to tell her about it.

"You know," he said, "I think I can run again, and I think I can win."

"Why?" she asked.

"Because I just had this incredible conversation with this old boy," he bubbled. "He just looked at me and said, 'Bill, me and my wife and my boys and their wives, we all voted against you. We *leveled* you.' I asked, 'Why'd you do that?' He said, 'I had to. You raised my car tag.' I said, 'Would you vote for me ever again?' And he said, 'Sure—you're the least likely to ever do that to me again.'"

Clinton's case for a second chance rested on an apology for having botched his first—"I made a young man's mistake"—and a promise to focus on a stripped-down agenda of things that really mattered to a poor, rural state like Arkansas: a modern manufacturing economy and an upgraded school system. He shucked some of his liberal baggage— his over-the-ears haircut and his opposition to the death penalty were only the most conspicuous casualties of his remaking—and Hillary became Mrs. Clinton instead of Ms. Rodham on public occasions. Her surrender to Arkansas's sensibilities on the matter was her idea, not his. She had concluded that her symbolic declaration of independence was getting in the way of the issues she and Bill *really* wanted to talk about.

He won in a landslide that time, and the next, and the next, by margins approaching two to one. His governing room, even with his more modest program, was limited by the poverty of his state. There was no Arkansas Miracle, only an inchmeal crawl toward the late twentieth century. The price of progress, as Clinton himself would admit, was sometimes a certain flexibility about protecting the environment when it got in the way of creating jobs. But his ideas and his skills at getting them executed ripened with time. His fellow governors, in 1991, voted him the best in the business, and Senator Sam Nunn of Georgia, meaning it good-humoredly, referred to him as having been a rising star in the party in three different decades.

The irony was that, even as he came to national prominence, his star was in decline in Arkansas. He had had his little dalliance with running for president in 1987 and had wound up instead placing Michael Dukakis's name in nomination at the convention, at mind-numbing length. It was a bad introduction to America for a man who aspired to the White House; he appeared to have achieved his fifteen minutes of celebrity as the butt of jokes in late-show comic monologues.

His reception back home was worse—a nearly palpable feeling of ennui with the middle-aging boy wonder after his ten years in office. He wondered for a time in the spring of 1990 whether he shouldn't voluntarily retire. He was in line for the chairmanship of the Democratic Leadership Council, the clubhouse for upwardly mobile southern moderates like himself; the forum that went with the job would be a way for him to keep his higher ambitions alive without going through a bruising fight for reelection. Not even Hillary was sure he would seek another term until the day he announced, and even then, he was worried enough to put in a Mayday call to a media consultant, Frank Greer, in Washington.

"I really need your help," Clinton said. "I think I'm in terrible trouble. I'm at 46 percent, and I'm dropping like a rock. All they're thinking is, 'Ten years and taxes. Why do we need to reelect *this* guy?' You want me to run for higher office? Well, if you don't get your ass down here right now, I'm never going to be able to run for dog catcher."

Greer answered the SOS, though with an agenda larger than winning a provincial election; he had recognized Clinton early on as a potentially hot property and had been agitating him for two or three years to run for president. The two, in some ways, made a natural pair. Both were sons of the South, born a month apart, and both had got into politics as young men inspired by the example of John F. Kennedy; Greer was a fifteen-year-old page in the United States Senate the day JFK was shot. While Clinton sought public office, Greer migrated into the business of helping other people achieve it; he had started his firm in 1980 and had built it into one of the capital's richest and winningest ad factories. But something was missing from the picture, as Greer came to realize. All those years, in all those races, he had been looking for Mister Goodbar—a candidate who, like the lost prince of Camelot, believed in government, knew where he wanted to take it, and could use television effectively to bring the people along with him.

He was sure he had found his man in Clinton, and while his firm was overextended that season, he felt he couldn't say no; in their long-running series of conversations, he himself had urged Clinton to seek reelection as a stepping-stone to larger things. So Greer flew in with Stan Greenberg, a smallish, tweedy Yale professor who had gone into the polling business; they had worked together on some seminal studies of why traditional blue-collar Democrats had defected to Ronald Reagan in the industrial suburbs of the North and how they could be won back. A quick scan of the terrain in Arkansas that spring was enough to persuade the two consultants that Clinton had good reason to worry. He had kept his core promises to improve the state's infrastructure and upgrade its schools, but he had had to raise taxes to do it, and people were saying that he had been in office too long. He hadn't figured out a message, a rationale for his reelection beyond his record.

With his art and his handlers' artifice, Clinton cobbled up a plan for the future and managed somehow to reposition himself as the agent of change. In the end, he won going away. But victory had had its price— the almost offhand promise, in a debate, that he would put his well-known national ambitions on hold and serve out his full four-year term. He meant it at the time, or so his people believed, and in the earliest days of his renewed lease on the governor's mansion, he appeared to be acting on it. He plunged into the 1991 state legislative session in a sixty-three-day fury of activity and made it his most productive ever, signing most of his agenda into law. But in the bone-weary aftermath, he and Hillary began to wonder and talk about whether there was anything more they could accomplish in Arkansas—

whether, indeed, they shouldn't be raising their sights to higher office and larger goals.

The first tickles of restlessness were at war with Clinton's political instincts—his sense, widely shared in both parties, that Desert Storm had all but guaranteed Bush's reelection. Greer thought otherwise, but his relentless nagging kept bumping into his friend's native caution.

"The economy is going to hell in a handbasket," Greer said, almost begging. "Middle-class incomes are going down. We're going to be able to make the economic argument that built the Democratic Party. We can do it again."

"Frank," Clinton interrupted, "tell me once in history where the winner of a successful war, in *this* country, has ever been defeated."

Greer couldn't think of anybody.

"And Frank," Clinton said, "I never served in Vietnam." His explanation of why he hadn't rather oversimplified the story, though it had worked well enough for him in Arkansas politics. He had played by the rules, he said, and had finally lucked out of the draft with a high lottery number. His concern, though, was whether people would think he could serve as commander-in-chief, never having worn his country's uniform.

"Bill, I never served in Vietnam either," Greer said. As long as Clinton hadn't dodged the draft or gone to Canada, he would be okay.

Clinton's sales resistance by then had lowered considerably, and his pledge to stay put in Little Rock came more and more to seem a self-imposed prison sentence. It wasn't so much that the alignment of the planets favored him; on the contrary, Bush did look unbeatable in any but the most imaginative reading of the polls. It was rather the openness of the field on the Democratic side and the axiomatic truth that ambition, in politics, abhors a vacuum. If Al Gore in particular had shown signs of interest, Clinton would have stood aside; the senator had made something of a name for himself nationally in a first turn around the track in 1988, and while the effort had gone badly, he maintained a kind of pride of place among the younger southern mentionables for the presidency. But Gore, like everybody else, was holding back, and Senator Chuck Robb of Virginia, once thought their chief rival for territorial rights to the New South, was disappearing into a fog bank of personal and public scandal.

The turning point, on Frank Greer's calendar, was the day in May when Clinton did a speech at the DLC's annual convention in Cleveland. His text amounted to a manifesto for a postmodern Democratic politics, beyond the stale old contention between liberal and conservative. The choice that counted was between yesterday and tomorrow, he argued, and the party's future lay in getting on the right side of the equation. His star turn was brilliantly received, and Clinton took it on the road that spring and summer, pumped up by the excitement it seemed to stir. It was, Greer thought, as if he had cleared a first hurdle in his mind—as if the possibility of running for president had at least become thinkable.

But his pledge not to was a higher hurdle, and relays of friends and consultants who met with him came away doubting that he could get over it. Just before the Fourth of July, two of them tracked Greer to his vacation cabin on Orcas Island off the coast of Washington and told him their worries. "We think you're losing your candidate for president," they said. Bill was hung up on The Promise. He was at the point of deciding not to run.

Greer rang off and called Clinton. The governor indeed had been stewing, partly about his commitment to stay put, partly about the impact on his family if he did choose to run. He still had reservations about whether Chelsea was old enough, and he worried as well about whether it would be fair to Hillary. She had been serving as chairman of the Children's Defense Fund, with a chance to reach a national audience on issues she cared greatly about. "She's always put her career on hold for me," he said. Shouldn't he wait four years and give her a chance?

Greer took a pass on the Chelsea question; that, he said, was something the Clintons would have to work out as a family. But he argued that a presidential campaign would be a better stage for Hillary as advocate than any private-sector organization could provide. And the promise to stay out his term as governor? Don't make a decision, Greer urged Clinton, without talking to the people of Arkansas and finding out what *they* think; after twelve years of Reagan and Bush, they might not be as unforgiving as he thought.

Clinton began his journey of exploration on Independence Day, with a jammed schedule of events. That night, he called Greer back in a fever of excitement. Everywhere he went, he said, there had been people with signs and buttons, urging him to run. Greer smiled; he had helped seed the crowd with claqueurs for Clinton.

In the weeks that followed, Clinton got back in his car and cruised the state, seeking leave from the voters to run for president. His itinerary was kept secret, to throw the press pack off the scent; his entourage consisted of a single aide, Mike Gauldin, until Hillary joined up for a final swing in August. Their sense of the response, backed up by polling, was that Arkansas would release him from his commitment. It was a short step from there to their conclusion, in the small hours of morning, that he *had* to run—and before the summer was out, a shadow Clinton-for-president campaign was in motion.

Bill's List

There was, as the Clintons both knew, a far larger threat to his hopes than a broken campaign promise. It was the gossip—pervasive, knowing, and detailed—about his supposed infidelities. It was as dangerous and as unpredictable as a bomb with a time-delay fuse. Clinton might tiptoe around it for a while, but it was primed to go off—and as the fall of Gary Hart four years earlier bore witness, the stories could be his ruin if they came out on anything but his own terms.

The tales had been out there for years, sometimes with names attached, sometimes not. No one had substantiated them, though at least one regional newspaper had tried; its reporters had tailed Clinton several times to see if he wound up at night's end with a woman-not-his-wife. The surveillance had come up empty each time. But the rumors had persisted and had very nearly become a matter of public record when, in the midst of Clinton's reelection campaign in 1990, a sometime state employee named Larry Nichols filed a lawsuit naming five women he claimed had been Clinton's girlfriends—among them a television anchor, a newspaper reporter, a statehouse staffer, a former Miss America, and a bottle-blonde saloon singer named Gennifer Flowers.

Clinton had escaped that time, narrowly. The parentage of the suit was suspect; Nichols had been sacked by the governor for having misused state phones for his own purposes and had been a bit too transparent thereafter about his desire for revenge. The court records were kept under seal, and when Nichols called a news conference to air his charges, most of the Arkansas press ignored him—all, indeed, except a single radio deejay who broadcast the story. One editor who cross-examined Nichols for an hour concluded that he didn't *know* anything; he appeared instead to have been plucking rumors out of the air and proclaiming them to be fact. The editor spiked the story.

The Clintons themselves appeared to have worked through their problems somewhere within what they called the zone of privacy they insisted on for themselves and their daughter. That zone was one they guarded jealously as long as they could. It was known that they had met cute, as old-time Hollywood scenarists used to say, in the Yale law library during their student years. She was down from the Chicago suburbs and Wellesley, the child of a Goldwater Republican household; he was back from his Rhodes and on the rebound from a broken relationship; both were political, and both ferocious overachievers. He had been eyeing her from a distance, trying to work up the nerve to speak to her. She had noticed, and, that day in the library, had clapped her book down on the table and marched on him.

"Listen," she had said, "if you're going to keep staring at me and I'm going to keep staring back, we should at least know each other's names. Mine's Hillary Rodham. What's yours?"

He couldn't remember.

It took a bit more time, but they started dating and fell in love; when she left the beginnings of a career in Washington to join him in Arkansas, she thought of it as a surrender not to his will but to her own heart. They were less like personalities than complementary ones, come together on the common grounds of marriage and politics. She was a quick, sharp, centered woman who had had great successes as a lawyer for various private and public interests. Her mind was more disciplined than her husband's; she was a focused, linear thinker where he was spontaneous and creative, even sloppy. Each needed the other. Clinton's life would have been chaos without someone like Hillary, a friend said, and hers would have been lonely if she had married someone in her own image; people would be too intimidated to come to her house for dinner.

As it was, they capitalized on their differences, working out their own division of labor like partners in an alliance. She was less politician than advocate; to people who didn't know her, she seemed the sum of her causes. He was the more relentlessly public person, the permanent campaigner, with a quick grin and a warm word for everyone. Some of the women in their circle, seeing his extravagance with his feelings, worried for Hillary. There was a promiscuity about Clinton quite apart from the question of whether he was or wasn't the secret swinger he was so widely rumored to be. Friends wondered privately how much emotion he had left over for his wife, having squandered so much on strangers in the normal course of his days.

The marriage, so far as the Clintons were willing to expose it to view, had not been as idyllic as its beginnings. There were, as Hillary carefully put it, the *rumor*-type problems about Bill and women; there were as well the inevitable collisions between two strong-willed people who tended to work too hard, care too much, and explode too loudly and quickly, especially when they were tired. They seemed, as they professed to be, comfortable together. Still, it was plain between the lines of their serial accounts of their union that they had at least talked about the possibility of divorce.

They had chosen instead to stay together, holding to the contemporary view that marriage and parenting were not shelters from the storm but labors to be "worked at." Neither of them was a quitter, Clinton said, and, anyway, they found life somehow richer and more meaningful with one another, which struck him as a fair definition of love. To people around them, their relationship seemed something less than a picture-book romance and yet more than just an "arrangement" between two driven people with only their ambition in common. There was a tenderness between them, tinctured, on his side, with an air of having only recently rediscovered his wife after years of taking her for granted.

But there was something businesslike, too, as if the two of them were colleagues in a grand public enterprise. She had been a major player in his governorship, notably when she managed the design and marketing of a program of educational reform, and as his presidential candidacy took shape, no adviser was as influential or as feared. She was Hillary *Rodham* Clinton, or HRC, in campaign communications, and sometimes "H-Bomb" behind her back. She was a stubborn and aggressive woman, and while she did not flaunt her power within the campaign, neither did she trouble to hide her feelings when things displeased her. The two of them seemed consumed by a common flame. What they each lamented, separately contemplating their lives, was that they hadn't left themselves time enough for fun.

They did not go into the campaign blind to the dangers of scandal. Yes, the local press had given them a bye, but the rules of play in national politics had changed since John Kennedy's secret dalliances. A boundary had been crossed the day, in 1987, when a reporter from a reputable newspaper asked Gary Hart straight out at a press conference if he had ever committed adultery. The genie was out of the bottle; after that, no area of behavior was off-limits, no line of questioning too prurient, no plane of sanctimony too high for the character police of the mass media.

Clinton's own first impulse was to stonewall—to declare up front that he wouldn't answer what he called "have-you-ever" questions about what he then still imagined to be his private life. But as Hillary argued early and aggressively in his pre-announcement strategy meetings, that wouldn't do anymore; it seemed only to excite further speculation. "We've got to put a stop to this," she told Greer and Greenberg one day at the governor's mansion. By "this," she meant the gossip problem; it was, she said, more serious than they seemed to think.

At her urging, they decided to do some sort of preemptive strike at a breakfast meeting with reporters in Washington in mid-September, a date Clinton had already accepted as his formal introduction to the national press. It was Hillary as well who shaped the response he would give if, as seemed likely, somebody asked him if he had ever cheated on her. He would be frank, up to a point. He would concede that their marriage had had its difficulties, but he would add that they remained a family, bound to one another as man and wife and as Chelsea Clinton's parents. The details of their problems were nobody's business but their own. What mattered was that they were still together and planned to stay that way.

Clinton's start-up management team thought the line might just work; there was no Other Woman in the picture, not then, and both press and public seemed to be nursing a bit of a hangover after the pursuit and kill of Senator Hart. In fact, many of Clinton's people presumed that he *had* had extramarital affairs and hoped that none had been too recent. His team was no more immune to the buzz about him than anyone else—or to the suspicion that, where there was so much smoke, there had to be fire.

What they could not bring themselves to do was raise the subject with him point-blank; even when they gathered in Washington on the eve of the breakfast, it was Clinton himself who finally broke the embarrassed silence. "All of you are nice not to bring it up," he said, "but I know all of you are concerned." He and Hillary would deal with the matter as forthrightly as they felt they could, he said. The discussion drifted on to something else; no one had the stomach to press him any harder, or even to rehearse him in his lines. It was plain that night and the next that their candor would stay strictly within the bounds Hillary had laid out. They would declare their problems healed and their marriage whole, and draw the line against further questioning there.

So it played at the breakfast, to the great relief of Clinton's handlers. Most of the questions were about public policy, a drug as addictive to Clinton as heroin to a junkie; one of his own top hands called him Propeller Head, and over the eggs, bacon, sausage, biscuits, and grits that morning, he was in full twirl, outlining his vision of a new Democratic politics and his commitment to tax relief for the middle class. It took a while for his inquisitors to get around to more personal matters, and when they did, his fidelity to his script was pitch-perfect. "Hillary and I have been together almost twenty years," he said. "We're committed to our marriage and its obligations, to our child, and to each other. We intend to be together thirty or forty years, whether I run for president or not, and I think that ought to be enough."

The answer seemed to work; the next questioner changed the subject, and the pursuit seemed less heated for a time thereafter. In fact, it was only less visible. Several major news organizations were already nosing around Little Rock, pursuing women whose names were alleged to be listed in Bill's Black Book. The very day he declared his candidacy in early October, a reporter stood at the edge of the press pack, recounting a conversation he had lately had with a prominent Democratic campaign consultant.

"What's going to get him?" the reporter had asked. "His dick or his record?"

"Both," the consultant had confidently replied.

For a time, the campaign tried with some success to parry the A-question, demanding that the reporters raising it explain its relevance to the issue of whether or not Clinton was qualified to be president. But the effort was like trying to push toothpaste back into a tube. The suspicions were too widespread, and the people raising them weren't just nosy reporters—they were the party activists whose faith Clinton would need if he was to thread his way to the nomination.

He ran into their doubts one November day at the airport in Tampa, at a closed meeting with two dozen or so uncommitted delegates to the Florida state party convention. The questions ranged widely over the usual public concerns until, well into the session, a woman came at him head-on.

"What about the rumors?" she asked. "There is ugly stuff. Stories of womanizing. What are we to believe? What surprises will there be?"

Clinton began with what had become his own rote reply—that the rumors were fictions made up by the Republican opposition in his last gubernatorial campaign. But as he talked on, his growing anger with the press rose in him and finally flared, out in the open, like a fire in dry grass. "This is more than Gary Hart or any of those guys had to face," he complained. Hart had got caught in a current affair. Clinton had not; he felt he was being measured unfairly by a new standard, one that acknowledged no statute of limitations on sins of the past.

The trademark smile and the nibbled lower lip were gone; Clinton's agitation was visible. "They do all this damage to me," he said. "They throw all this garbage at me, they nose around, but they don't have the guts to say they didn't find anything. To be a candidate today, it's almost like you have to have never married, or been divorced, or never made a mistake. Or *lie* real good. We've spent twenty years trying to make people's lives better, and this is the kind of crap that gets thrown around."

He sensed that he was on dangerous ground—that his handlers would raise hell with him later—but he was still hot, and he kept going. "I'm sick and tired of all this," he said. "You want me to tell you I've had a mistake-free life, a boring life in which I didn't learn anything. I ain't going to do that." He would promise, obliquely, that his pants would stay zipped from then on—that he would do nothing in the campaign to embarrass or betray his supporters. But he wasn't going to button up about the press. One publication, he said, had gone so far as to run through a list of his personal phone calls for the past year, phoning everyone on it and asking why he had called.

"How would you like that?" he asked his inquisitor.

"Well," she answered, "*I'm* not running for president."

The questioning segued to other, less delicate subjects. But there was a vein of self-pity in Clinton, as in most politicians under stress, and when the woman told him afterward that she had only wanted to give him a chance to speak to the subject, he flared again.

"J. Edgar Hoover didn't do much more to people than what's been done to me," he said.

He moved on. But the question, in all its variations, lingered, and so did the multiplying inquiries into his past. One major newspaper questioned a woman staffer of Clinton's so aggressively on the subject that she burst into tears. Another journal was said to have approached one of his alleged past girlfriends with a proposition bordering on blackmail: either tell your story anonymously or look for your name and picture on page one. The supermarket tabloids were offering checks in large round numbers for kiss-and-tell stories—and so, as soon became evident, were the skin magazines.

Clinton was, precariously, the front-runner in the Democratic field when the sound of premonitory thunder first rumbled in the pages of *Penthouse* that autumn. He occupied less than a column in a longish sexual memoir by an Arkansas rock groupie named Connie Hamzy; the rest had to do with her adventures fellating as many as two dozen singers, musicians, and roadies, by her own count, in a single night. Even she conceded that her supposed encounter with Clinton had never got past the groping stage. One of his people, she wrote, had approached her at poolside at a Little Rock hotel one summer day in 1984 and said the governor would like to meet her. She had agreed, so she said, but after a bit of fondling and a scramble through the hotel corridors, they couldn't find a suitably private trysting place and so finally gave up.

Clinton's own version, spun out over dinner at a favorite Mexican restaurant, La Fogata, in San Antonio one evening, was radically different. He had been at the hotel for a meeting, he said, and was in the company of an aide and several other people when Hamzy approached *him*. In her account, his side of the dialogue consisted of come-on lines and moans. In his, *she* was the provocateuse:

"Come inside this stairwell," she had said.

"Naw," he had replied.

"Well, here's what you're missing," she had said, flipping down her bikini top to show off her breasts.

The temptation, Clinton said, had been resistible; he had walked away, and that, in his recollection, was that.

His reaction to the *Penthouse* story was almost preternaturally relaxed, given how tender he had become on the subject; it was, rather, Hillary who wanted to go to war. It had fallen to Bruce Lindsey, an old family friend and adviser, to brief her on the details and on Hamzy's sometimes lurid language about her audience with the governor.

Hillary smiled thinly. "Bill does not want to overreact to this," she said. But as the day went on, her temperature rose, and with it, her insistence on a strong response. The woman had to be shown up for what she was.

In the end, cooler heads prevailed. Clinton's command fell into a crisis-management mode that would serve it well in stormier weather yet to come. His young spokesman, George Stephanopoulos, churned out a short, curt denial—"It never happened"—and his managers rounded up statements from three eye-witnesses who were prepared to back him up; their names were made available to reporters who raised the subject. The missiles otherwise stayed in their silos. The measured response was enough to smother the story in the mainstream media, most of which ignored it entirely or gave it only glancing notice. The subject of Bill's List was enveloped once again in a public silence, broken only by the sound of a time fuse ticking.

5.

Waiting for Godot

To one veteran Democratic strategist, the field of candidates assembling for the primaries in the fall of 1991 looked like the missing-man formation flown over Air Force funerals: there was a hole against the sky where a lost hero ought to have been. On paper, the six contenders might have been an admirable panel for a debate on the future of their party after a quarter-century wandering in the desert. They embodied every important shading of Democratic belief from conservative to moderate to liberal to neo-nihilist—the view, championed by former governor Jerry Brown of California, that the salvation of the party of Jefferson, Jackson, and Franklin Roosevelt lay in blowing it up and starting all over again.

And yet, in the days before Bill Clinton emerged as a dominant force, they seemed to be men of the most ordinary clay; each, indeed, had been drawn into the race in part by the conviction that the others looked so eminently beatable. The party's marquee-name politicians had fled to their bunkers at the sight of Bush's postwar poll ratings, never imagining that he could slide so far so fast. Of those who actually did take the field, only Brown was well-known, and for all the wrong reasons. He had reigned over the nation-state of California with some success for eight years and had twice before run for president, each time stirring a flutter of excitement. But he was most famous for his idiosyncrasies, a quirkiness of style and mind that had got him inseparably stuck with the nickname Governor Moonbeam.

The others had almost no public profiles at all—not, in any case, on a national stage. Bob Kerrey of Nebraska was a first-term senator with his own ethereal modes of life and thought; Governor Moonbeam, meet Cosmic Bob. Senator Tom Harkin of Iowa was an antique, a '30s-style farmer-labor populist confined to the back benches by his retro politics and his thumb-in-your-eye attitude. Paul Tsongas had been a senator, too, until a siege of cancer had forced him home to get well and make money; he was remembered, if at all, as a thoughtful but somewhat mousy man, Elmer Fudd with a public-policy agenda, and he had been out of politics entirely for seven years. L. Douglas Wilder of Virginia had had his moment of celebrity on the day, in 1989, when he became the first black man ever elected governor anywhere; in the two years since, he had largely faded from notice beyond the boundaries of his own state.

And Bill Clinton? To the tastemakers of Washington, he looked at first glance like yet another in a flawed line of Jimmy Carter clones—a wrong-way carpetbagger running as the son of a moderate New South. The idea of a southern candidate was tempting as geopolitics, given the urgent need of his party to break the Republican lock on America below the Mason-Dixon line. But in the view from the capital, the South had been sending forth all the wrong sons. Carter had been too wet, Al Gore too wooden, Jesse Jackson too hot and too black; the others had been as forgettable as the names and likenesses on old baseball trading cards. And now came Clinton, preceded by his reputation as a man with a motor mouth and a slippery zipper. That loose grouping of operatives and journalists known within the Beltway as the political community knew little else about him, and with his late entry into the race, he had had no time to fill in the blanks in their understanding.

Together, the six declared candidates labored under the judgment that they were the Democratic B-team—the end-of-the-bench substitutes who get to play only when the game is presumed to be hopelessly lost. They were victim in some measure to the first law of contemporary politics, which holds that availability breeds contempt; it was as though wanting the presidency badly enough to seek it was itself a mark of defective character. But it was likewise true that none of the contenders was a man of great stature or glittering credentials, and most were carrying personal baggage of one sort or another. All that distinguished them, so the Beltway sages said, was their gall; they alone in their party were damned fool enough to hit the gaming tables after the *real* players had concluded that the dice were loaded and had walked away.

They were quickly dubbed the Six-Pack, as if their diverse candidacies came in a half-dozen small and interchangeable containers. The lunchtime regulars at Democratic haunts like The Palm and Duke Zeibert's in Washington inspected them critically, looking for a potential winner among them, and concluded that none of them would do. As with each new field of Democrats for a generation, it was their lot to be measured against a myth: the lost glories of Camelot and the remembered glitter of its ruling family. Revisionist history had treated John F. Kennedy badly. His party's nostalgists had not, and neither had popular sentiment; the class of '92 accordingly found themselves running against his ghost.

The contest was an impossible one, but the dream of a hero kept recurring with each new failure at the polls, and the particular pallor of the cast gathering in the fall of 1991 brought it back in vividly heightened colors. The early days of the campaign were political theater played, so far as the critics down front were concerned, by a company of understudies. The script was a variation on *Waiting for Godot*, who, as in the original, was nowhere in evidence; actors and audience alike kept stealing glances at the wings, as if waiting for the real star to make his entrance and steal the show.

The Golden Boy

There had to be a favorite, of course; a media-age campaign without a front-runner is like a Grand Prix rally without a Porsche, and the handicappers' choice that fall was Bob Kerrey. His entry into the race, on the last day of September, had been a show of the sort handlers dream of, so well-wrought that even the clear, cool autumn skies appeared to have been prearranged. The senator stood before the Nebraska state capitol, drawing on its solidity and strength, with a crowd of five thousand of his homefolk at his feet. No camera angle had been neglected, no touch of local color overlooked. A choir from Boys Town sang patriotic airs. A rural high-school band played "Born to Run," once Gary Hart's campaign theme. Even Kerrey's ex-wife had been induced to show up; it was the first of his political events she had ever attended.

The buzzwords had been as carefully attended to as the visuals. It was no longer fashionable, as it had been in Reagan's time, to pretend that prosperity could be bought on the cuff; the idea of sacrifice was in vogue, and Kerrey, like most of his rivals, presented himself as its advocate. He spoke of a need for "renewal in America," a commitment to "build for greatness" again after a time of drift in government, cynicism in politics, and greed in public and private life. But the real resonance of his speech lay in its direct appeal to the baby-boom generation, with whom Kerrey felt one in spirit if not quite in age. He had borrowed more than just a Bruce Springsteen song from the Hart campaigns; he had plugged into their tribal music as well, the demand of fortysomething Americans for power after the twelve-year gerontocracy of Reagan and Bush. "I want to lead America's fearless, restless voyage of generational progress," Kerrey said. The media had their sound bite, and the campaign its signature line.

Kerrey was not the first politician to be mesmerized by the sheer number of the boomers, as if the fact that they had all grown up watching "Leave It to Beaver" and listening to the Beatles made them a potentially cohesive political force. Hart had tried to marshal their energies, twice, and had failed. But Kerrey, in the winter-book wisdom, was everything Hart had wanted to be and wasn't—the candidate who could finally lead a new generation to power. He was still young enough, at forty-eight, to speak the boomers' language; brave enough to have earned a Congressional Medal of Honor in Vietnam and then to have stood up against the war back home; attractive enough to have won the movie star Debra Winger as his part-time live-in lover; liberal enough to appeal to the activists who often dominate Democratic primaries—and yet bright and curious enough to move past the stale old vocabularies of party and ideology.

Neither was he afflicted with false modesty; Kerrey had never been a no-not-me kind of guy. He had succeeded at everything he had set his hand to, in the restaurant and health-club business as well as in his midlife career change to politics. It was no longer surprising to him to be mentioned as a possible candidate for president; the chat had begun when he was not yet forty and barely through his rookie year as governor of Nebraska, and it had trailed him to Washington with his election to the Senate in 1988. There would be fits and starts on his way into the race three years later, but awe of the job or of the competition was not among the deterrents.

He was, indeed, a long step ahead of his more nervous advisers in his confidence. Maybe it was too soon, several of them said during a conference call while Kerrey was still sorting his options. Maybe his portfolio was a little light, after a single term as governor and less than three years as a senator from a smallish state.

"Bob," one worrier said, "why don't you wait until 1996?"

"Oh, hell," Kerrey's pollster, Harrison Hickman, said, breaking in from the Washington end of the line. "If he can't beat *this* field with raw talent, he's not going to beat the next group with four more years of preparation."

Kerrey was inclined to agree. From his angle of vision, a confidant said, Bill Clinton was a marginal guy—a backwater southern conservative who would nibble at the edges of the big problems and never really make things happen. Tom Harkin? What could *he* do? Nobody *liked* him. Doug Wilder? Jerry Brown? They looked pretty much like ciphers. And poor Paul Tsongas? Kerrey, like practically everybody else in the early going, praised him for his personal and political courage, but compliments for Tsongas were like tips for valet parking; they didn't cost much, and you knew the guy wasn't going very far.

Next to the lot of them, Kerrey felt ten feet tall. He believed, that is, in his own clippings—the stories anointing him the golden boy in a field of has-beens and wannabes. His people would come to wish that the notices had been less glowing and that they had had more time to get the senator's act together, combing the bugs out before it hit Broadway. The cost of his late start and his big-bang entry had been to raise high expectations of him—"unbelievably high," Jim Pribyl, an old friend who had managed Kerrey's run for governor in 1982, lamented afterward. "It was practically the Second Coming of Jesus."

The first coming of Kerrey as a presidential candidate was something less than his admirers had had in mind. He had always proceeded more by impulse than by plan in his short political career, waiting for a seam to open and then rushing headlong into it. "My life has not gone in a straight line," he told his Senate chief of staff, Billy Shore, a survivor of the Hart campaigns, and his processes of thought were no more orderly. His mind, and his speech, seemed to work by free association and were not always easy to follow. The more literal members of the press and the political community had tried to over the years and, failing, had saddled him with his nickname Cosmic Bob.

He was more accurately the existential hero as candidate, a man who lived in the moment and found it useless to calculate three weeks, let alone three years, down the road. He appeared to have left his faith in linear thinking on the battlefield in Vietnam, along with a piece of his leg. His experience there had taught him with brutal clarity that the unexpected—the absurd—was a part of the human condition. He had somehow emerged whole out of a long, bitter recuperation from his wounds, but he could not be induced to live his life according to some rigorous design. He seemed to prefer the whispering of his own inner voice—a sense of I'm-OK well-being that was at once a source of his appeal and an impediment to his hopes.

His people had thus been obliged to start without him. With his arrival in Washington, several of them had lunched one noonday at Primi Piatti, a trendy Italian restaurant a few blocks from the White House, and had begun what amounted to a two-year conversation about running him for president. It had been rotisserie-league politics, a fantasy game built around a make-believe candidate. Over time, the dream had faded into what Harrison Hickman called The Nightmare Scenario. Bob, Hickman warned the others, would keep them waiting till, say, Labor Day, 1991, and only then scan the horizon. If he sensed an opportunity, he'd go; if he didn't, he wouldn't.

And so it played. Kerrey idled through the spring and summer, occasionally signaling to his people that he was *thinking* about running. But he did none of the usual cloud-seeding with strategists, policy experts, or prospective donors—nothing to advance his candidacy beyond the daydreaming stage. Memos flew among his consiglieri, among them one from a former Nebraska congressman, John Cavanaugh, setting out all the detail work that had to be done if Kerrey was serious. Hickman looked through it, his discouragement growing page by page. It struck him that the document should have been titled, "I Was Going to Run for President But I Forgot."

It was close to Labor Day, just as Hickman had guessed, before Kerrey finally made his decision. It jelled for him the day in late August when he sat in front of his TV set back home in Lincoln, watching the unfolding story of the old-guard Soviet coup attempt against Mikhail Gorbachev. What set him off was George Bush's apparent willingness, in the first hours, to bargain with the plotters. Kerrey, outraged, picked up the phone and rang his man Billy Shore back in Washington.

"Billy, I'm going to get into this thing," he said, and he didn't mean later; he had to be dissuaded from announcing that day.

As it was, his people had less than six weeks from then to liftoff, and the enterprise would never quite recover from the haste of its beginnings; it would be fairly said that Kerrey's candidacy had peaked the day he announced. An organization was pasted together—a melange of friends, staffers, and strategists drafted from Kerrey's own circle and from Billy Shore's black book of old Gary Hart campaigners. One of the Hart people, Sue Casey, was installed as manager. The ensemble *looked* like a campaign—a safety net of sorts, Hickman thought, under an untested candidate. But its weave was seriously flawed: nobody except a couple of part-time outside advisers had any command-level experience in presidential politics.

Neither were they going to get much help from Kerrey, as he made plain early on; he seemed to place more faith in destiny than in hard work. "I don't know anything about how campaigns run," he told his media man, Joe Rothstein, "and I don't intend to learn."

"You don't have any choice," Rothstein said, more prophetically than he could have known at the time. "You're about to get a big education."

Saint Paul

The man who had beaten Kerrey and everybody else into the field was perhaps the unlikeliest candidate in the recent history of our politics: a cancer patient in remission who said he was running as "the obligation of my survival." Paul Tsongas had been a first-term senator of postmodern views and budding ambition when, in 1983, he was informed that he had non-Hodgkins lymphoma, a cancer of the lymph nodes. The disease was then thought invariably fatal, and he was given eight years at the outside to live, if he was lucky. He had chosen at first to ignore the death sentence and had gone back to the career curve he had designed for himself: seeking reelection to the Senate that year and running for president in 1988. But his condition had worsened to a point where he had had to give up his dreams and force himself through a course of radical experimental therapy nearly as devastating as his illness.

He had come through it cancer-free, so far as his doctors could tell, and except for a minor recurrence in 1987, he had had no further problems. His deliverance had been more nearly probation than reprieve. There had been no real way to recalculate his life expectancy, so he had dropped out of politics, gone home to Lowell, Massachusetts, and begun a vastly better-paying second career as a lawyer, a lobbyist, and a member of various corporate boards—his way of guaranteeing a future for his wife, Niki, and their three daughters if he should die young.

But as his health and vigor returned, so did his dormant case of presidential fever, burning hotter than ever. Tsongas began thinking of illness as a metaphor, cancer as an analog for a sick economy. Cured of one, did he have a duty to treat the other? It came to him that the answer was yes, and that he couldn't wait until 1996. The Old Paul Tsongas, he thought, would have done that—would have reckoned the odds against his beating Bush and waited for a better day. The New Tsongas was animated instead by what he could only describe as *purpose*—a mission to deliver his party and his country from what he saw as their inexorable decline.

In the winter of 1990–91, with the drums of war beating loudly in the Persian Gulf, he visited his doctor and friend, Tak Takvorian, for one of his semiannual checkups. While Takvorian poked and probed, Tsongas ran his own battery of tests. He was working on a manifesto setting forth his ideas about a public-private partnership to revive the economy; would he be up to doing a book tour to promote it? Could he campaign for some other candidate for president? Or run a symbolic one-state candidacy of his own—a commuter candidacy between Lowell and New Hampshire, just across the border? Or what about big casino: a full-blown national campaign?

Takvorian finished his examination. The tests were negative for cancer, as they had been for three years. Tsongas was in good shape; he swam competitively, he worked out, he watched his weight, he was vigorous in body and mind.

You're fine, Takvorian told him. You can do anything you want.

Tsongas tried out his dream on Niki first. She liked it; her own law firm was dissolving, but they felt secure enough financially to afford his adventure. Then they gathered the girls, Ashley and Katina, both teenagers, and Molly, who was nine. The grave look on their parents' faces scared them. Was Daddy sick again?

"It's something worse," he told them. "I want to run for president."

There was nothing imposing about Tsongas, not by the cruel standards of politics in the television age. He was a bright, knowledgeable man with a dangerously sharp wit, trained often on himself; it was a saving grace for a man who had been nicknamed Saint Paul for his piousness long before he set out to save America. But as he cheerily admitted, he was not the most charismatic guy ever to come down the pike into national politics. He wore rumpled suits in unpresidential shades of gray and had a nearly matching indoor pallor; the combination made him look tired even when he wasn't and stirred recurring rumors about his health. His speeches, until he submitted late and grudgingly to coaching, were all coughs, mumbles, lisped words, popped eyes, dancing eyebrows, and sentences that didn't quite end, instead trailing off into silence.

On television, he was an anachronism, unpretty, uncoiffed, and uninflected. He looked small and uncomfortable on-screen and sounded reedy; his commercials used hired announcers in preference to his own thin voice. In person, he was sometimes preachy and usually teachy, with frequent resort to audiovisual aids. Once, his people tried to ban chart paper and blackboards at his events, fearing that they made him look schoolmarmish. Tsongas was unfazed; at his first stop under the embargo, he snatched up a campaign placard, flipped it over, and was soon happily decorating its white backside with one of his doomsday graphs tracking the American economy downhill.

Tsongas could fairly counter that his want of standard "candidate skills," as the tradesmen of politics called them, hadn't stopped him in the past; he had never lost an election. But his problems were more than skin-deep. He was burdened by what one of his strategists, a tough-talking South Boston pro named Ed Jesser, referred to as two big fucking albatrosses around his neck. One was his history of cancer; there were people out there, Jesser guessed, who wouldn't even let him run the local 7-Eleven for fear he might die any minute. The other was his fellow technoliberal Greek from Massachusetts, Michael Dukakis.

Jesser could just hear people all over America moaning, "Oh, God, not another gutless dweeb who isn't going to get pissed off if an entire motorcycle gang drives through his living room and rapes his wife."

Tsongas had, moreover, embarked on his "journey of purpose" in the spring of Bush's near canonization—a time when the president's popularity had soared to an astral plane normally traveled only by employees of NASA. It even rained on Tsongas's announcement speech, as if the gods were sending him a sign. He was unintimidated; the president, he reckoned accurately, had been on a downward trajectory before the war and was unlikely to stay aloft forever. Tsongas had felt more daunted by the possibility that Bob Kerrey or Bill Bradley might run; he regarded them both as formidable candidates with ideas not unlike his own. He had called both of them, prepared to step aside if either had told him, "I'm in." But Bradley had said he wasn't running, and Kerrey, ambiguous as usual, hadn't said he was.

The other people then being mentioned did not scare Tsongas or excite his admiration; it was him or nobody, in his view, and he had taken to the streets like a Jehovah's Witness canvassing for souls. Through the spring and summer, he was a lonely and, some thought, risible figure, hawking his eighty-two–page pamphlet—*A Call to Economic Arms,* he called it—and preaching his neo-Calvinist theology of work, sacrifice, and self-reliance as the means to a better future.

The message, as time would tell, was not without its allure to a public grown weary of unpaid bills and unkept promises. The problem, it would be said, was the messenger—a man who presented himself as the voice of truth and yet had trouble getting anyone to listen.

The Museum Piece

In the year of the New Democrat, Tom Harkin was the living embodiment of what everybody else was running against—a leather-lunged heartland populist summoning America back to a future modeled after Harry Truman's Fair Deal. The senator alone in the field offered himself as a traditional liberal—the equivalent, in our recent politics, of announcing that one has a social disease. Through the summer and early autumn, he roamed the landscape calling for an "American perestroika," largely at the expense of the rich, and joyously laying the wood to the man he liked to call George Herbert Hoover Bush. His pleasure seemed undisturbed by those critics who suggested that somebody might want to check Madame Tussaud's and see if one of her waxworks was missing. He had the Democratic left all to himself, and if he owed this stroke of fortune to the fact that nobody else wanted it, it didn't matter; he had his own field in which to stand and wait, like everybody else, to be struck by lightning. His claim to serious attention rested on the belief that it would take just such an act of God for any Democrat to turn Bush out of office. What Harkin offered the starved party faithful was, if not victory, at least a satisfying fight. He wasn't one of these *modern* Democrats, he said, who thought they had to act like Republicans to get back in business. Naw, that was wrong; one Republican party was more than enough. He was an old-time, in-your-face, jobs-and-opportunity Democrat, a fighter who, by his own admission, didn't mind sticking his finger in your eye to win an argument, a vote, or an election.

It was almost a matter of pride with him that, after ten years as a congressman and seven as a senator, he was known around Washington as a mean son of a bitch. He was by choice a loner, almost a recluse by the standards of so indefatigably social a city, and when he did find himself in company, he said what he thought without regard for the usual niceties. He had learned during a tour as a navy fighter pilot that once you got in that cockpit, you were alone. *Your* ass was on the line, and you'd better be aggressive, in his view, because if you weren't, you died.

His early noodlings about running were the occasion of some puzzlement back home in Iowa; one of the state's leading Democrats tumbled out of his chair laughing upon being informed that poor old Tom was considering the race and called it the dumbest goddam idea he had ever heard. But Harkin was an angry and a driven man, a coal miner's son who had neither forgotten nor forgiven his mean beginnings. Like Richard Nixon, say, or Bob Dole on the other side, he was an Alger hero with an attitude—a store of grievance that suffused his politics and fired his special resentment of the son of privilege who occupied the White House. When he finally declared his candidacy in mid-September on a borrowed farm southwest of Des Moines, his tone was combative almost from the moment he began to speak. "I'm here to tell you that George Herbert Walker Bush has got feet of clay," he said, "and I intend to take a hammer to them."

For a time, his rivals were obliged to take notice of the crowd noise at his rallies and the steady growth of his treasury; by the end of the year, he had raised $2.2 million, second only to Clinton. A lot of the checks had been written by trade-union political action committees, which only reinforced the impression that Harkin was a man of Washington and a servant to the old Democratic clientele. But that was where

Harkin's base had always been; he wore his union label out on his sleeve, and labor in turn had always generously reciprocated his affection.

Its gifts in the fall of 1991 included not just money but what would prove to be Harkin's best single day of the campaign—an occasion made sweeter by the fact that it came principally at Clinton's expense. The AFL-CIO put on the first major confrontation of the Democratic hopefuls at its annual convention in Detroit, a venue as homey for the senator as his own front parlor. He found the delegates hungry for red meat, and he dished it up in bounteous portions; when *he* was president, he said, he would be the scourge of "every double-breasting, scab-hiring, union-busting employer in America." The speech brought down the house; had Mario Cuomo's name not still been in play at the time, the barons of what remained of Big Labor might have embraced Harkin on the spot.

Clinton, by contrast, all but disappeared into the drapery, the victim of contradictory advice from his coaches and of his own tendency to go recessive in multicandidate events. He had planned, with the encouragement of his centrist chums from the Democratic Leadership Council, to challenge the unions under their own roof—to scold them for featherbedding and remind them, as he did all his audiences, that the flip side of opportunity was responsibility. But Wilhelm and Greer pushed for a less provocative approach. Clinton, they said, would be playing to a suspicious crowd. The best he could hope to do was keep them uncommitted, and the way to do it was to make himself as agreeable and as credible as he could.

"Remember, it's the way you say it that's more important than the specifics," Greer told him during a prep session. The best message he could deliver was just to go out and "look presidential."

Clinton looked merely bland instead, his message of change reduced to a pudding as sweet and lumpy as tapioca. His people knew he had done badly, although, as custom required, they put on their happy faces when he came back to his holding room afterward.

"Did you think it was okay?" Clinton asked.

"Bill, you hit a home run," Greer said. "They expected you to come in with horns. Our strategy was to get through this—to reassure them and not make any enemies. You did better than that."

The overnight press notices were nowhere near so charitable, and when he read them next morning, Clinton was furious, with himself and his team. "I screwed up," he said. But his capacity for blaming himself was never limitless, and, as often happened, he turned on his handlers. They had briefed him badly, he groused; they had sold him an "accommodationist" game plan, when, he went on, "this is not an accommodationist campaign. If we're always playing defense, we just become like everyone else." His people were thinking tactically, not strategically, and it was compromising his entire candidacy.

"It's just not happening," he grumbled. "There's no big picture."

In the event, it would matter little that Clinton had lost the day, and even less that Harkin had won it. The senator's fortunes had always been yoked in a curious way to Bush's; his brawling style had a certain partisan appeal so long as the race looked hopeless, but as the president's support eroded through the autumn, the Democrats began shopping elsewhere for somebody with a live chance to win. Harkin's money, once the envy of the field, was disappearing as if into a black hole. His ads, and the well-recommended team that produced them, had disappointed him. His politics of grievance appeared to have bumped its limits even on the ravaged economic ground of New Hampshire; his poll ratings there were stuck in single digits, well below that arbitrary class of men known to the savants of politics as The First Tier.

His campaign was failing, and in desperation, he sought a consulting opinion from an outsider, a veteran Democratic operative with no candidate of his own to counsel. They met one night at Harkin's house, out of sight of his own management team; only the senator and his wife were there. It was mid-January. The first primaries were barely a month away. Harkin was despondent.

It's a mess, he said. I'm dead in the water. What should I do?

His visitor's advice was blunt: get a message.

By then, it was too late. Harkin had already planted himself on the wrong side of all the equations by which Clinton, Tsongas, and the others hoped to frame the race: he was old against new, insider against outsider, the believer in big government against the believers in reinventing government. Nobody would notice or care when he won Iowa, since he lived there. The tastemakers of politics and the press had treated him from the beginning like an artifact more suited to a museum of American history than to the Oval Office. He was Mister Wrong, in their dismissive judgment, and the search for Mister Right went on without him.

The Invisible Man

For two nights in November, the senior hands in L. Douglas Wilder's unlikely run for president sat in focus-group facilities in New Hampshire and stared through panes of one-way glass into the face of racial prejudice in America. The campaign polltaker, David Petts, had designed a blind test pitting Wilder against the rest of the field. There were no pictures, not at first. The groups—four of them over the two evenings—would be introduced to each of the candidates through his biography, his record, and his promises and then would be asked to judge them sight unseen.

The Doug Wilder story, in the telling, proved irresistible—the saga of a self-made man who had fought his way up from poor beginnings; had won a Bronze Star for valor on Pork Chop Hill in Korea; had made a great success at law and then at politics back home in Virginia; and finally, as governor, had somehow closed a $2 billion shortfall in the state budget without raising taxes or crippling vital public services. For the focus groups, it was a case of love at first listen. When Petts polled them, Wilder was the early favorite in all four sessions.

And then they saw him, in a television ad made for his breakthrough campaign for governor in 1989. Out of a flutter of flags and a cloud of pieties, Wilder's face appeared; it was nearer beige than black, but his color was out in the open, and the effect was devastating to his hopes. With the ad still on-screen, the groups would begin whispering among themselves, then muttering out loud.

"He's *black!*" a woman gasped in one session.

"I was hoping you weren't going to tell me that," another said. "I was really starting to like him."

"*I* might vote for him," a man said, "but my neighbors never will."

At one of the sessions, in Nashua, Petts stepped out of the room during a break, leaving the group alone for a few moments while he conferred with his colleagues behind the looking glass.

"You know what we need?" one man said, unaware that the room mike and a hidden video camera were still running. "We need somebody like David Duke to put these people in their place."

"That's right," a second man agreed.

A couple of others nodded. Nobody objected—not one person.

We're in fucking New Hampshire, Wilder's media man, Joe Trippi, was thinking, and fucking David Duke just rolled through a Democratic focus group. We're *dead,* Trippi thought. We're absolutely fucking dead.

Petts went back into the room, this time to try out various pieces of Wilder's message against what his rivals were selling. He asked the group to rate each man's offerings on a scale of one to ten. Clinton and Kerrey were putting up fives and sixes for their ideas—not bad, not great. But Wilder's pledges to attack the deficit without raising taxes and to put America's needs first on his agenda, ahead of foreign entanglements, rang up tens around the table.

"That's what we need to hear!" a man exclaimed, listening to the litany.

There was a buzz of agreement, until the chat got back to the man who had started it.

"But you know what?" he said. "I've lived in New Hampshire my entire life, and no black man's gonna get elected here. You can't do it. He's *black.*"

Wilder's support melted away, all of it, and it became plain as the sessions unfolded that nothing he said or did could win it back. Some of the focus groupies held his color against him. Others said they didn't, but they were prisoner to what Petts would later call a secondary racism; they simply assumed that a black candidate couldn't win, and they weren't interested in casting any symbolic votes—they were looking for a winner. Either way, they were closed to argument. The guy was black. Forget it. No way. Case closed.

The irony was that Wilder had never intended to run an explicitly black campaign—to present himself as a cooler, better credentialed version of Jesse Jackson. He had had his own black period coming up in the legislature, as a young man with an Afro and an attitude. But he had succeeded at the state level as a classic southern moderate, distinguishable from his fellow Democratic governors in the region mainly by his slightly darker skin tone. He didn't much like Reverend Jackson and, one adviser said, had no interest in claiming his abandoned place in the primary debates as this year's token black-guy-off-to-the-side. Wilder's dream in presidential politics was one with his strategy: to take the next step beyond what Jackson had achieved and run as what he was—a tested career public servant who happened, incidentally, to be black.

Neither was he out to win a plaque in the African-American hall of fame for his contributions to The Race. Whatever sense of black history informed his candidacy had been brought there by the mostly white team of advisers, staffers, and consultants who, starting in the spring of 1991, had egged him into it. The governor's own motives were rather less abstract. One of the white boys asked Wilder's longtime friend and guru Paul Goldman what made him run—whether it wasn't some feeling of obligation to the black past that kept him knocking on doors marked WHITE ONLY. "He doesn't care about history," Goldman, then the state party chairman, answered with a laugh. Wilder, like most politicians, was in the game to win, hold, and exercise public office. History was a luxury for his white recruits; they saw at least a chance of getting a black man on a major-party ticket for the first time ever, and they wanted to be a part of it—even if, as one of them conceded, it meant trying to make Wilder into somebody he wasn't.

It was understood by them—and, friends said, by Wilder himself—that he was in fact running for the vice-presidential nomination this time around. The plan was a reprise of the long game he had played in Virginia, where he had first put in four years as lieutenant governor and let white people get used to seeing a black man in high state office. They did; when he went on to run for governor, he got 42 percent of the white vote and won. His interlude as number two had, so his people believed, been indispensable to his becoming number one, and it would be again if he were ever to reach the presidency. The un-spoken objective of his campaign, one of his innermost circle said privately, was to *force* his way onto the ticket in 1992 and so position himself for a real run at the top later on.

That it would take force, in this aide's view, was a given; the party was fixated on winning back the white voters who had defected to Reagan and Bush and was, as usual, taking the blacks for granted. But Wilder was not without cards in a game otherwise rigged against him. If he could turn out a large and solid black vote, the more warlike of his scenarists imagined, he could do to Bill Clinton what Jesse Jackson had done to Al Gore in 1988; he could break Clinton's lock on the South, damage him in the big cities, and—with a little help from Paul Tsongas, say, or Bob Kerrey—stop him short of a first-ballot nomina-tion. The winner in that script would *have* to treat with Wilder. "We'll hold the party hostage," one aide said; it was the only leverage they had.

The plot had its temptations for Wilder. There was a vindictive streak in him, a trait deepened by a lifetime of slights, large and small, visited on him by white men of power. Its target, in the settling winter of 1991–92, was Bill Clinton; Wilder didn't like or trust him, and when he felt unfairly blindsided by his rival governor in an early de-bate, the race became a grudge match for him.

"Bill Clinton made a big mistake," he told his seconds afterward.

They thought Wilder was talking about getting revenge in the next debate.

"No, I don't mean that," Wilder said. "I mean Bill Clinton will never be president."

The problem was that, to make good the threat, he would have had to run precisely the kind of race he was so determined to avoid: a campaign trading consciously on the color of his skin. Trippi, the media man, urged just such a course on him, churning out draft after draft of a speech presenting Wilder as the grandson of slaves and a child of the ghetto in a time when its boundaries were still enforced by

Jim Crow laws. It was a hard sell; Wilder had got to be governor running as a fiscal conservative whose color was incidental to his beliefs, and he wanted to offer himself for president the same way. His resistance put Trippi in the uncomfortable role of having to play the house cynic, telling a proud black achiever that no one would listen to him—that he had to run on his race and not his record.

"Why?" Wilder asked drily at one meeting. "This is America."

"You want to watch these focus groups?" Trippi replied.

Wilder didn't have to. He had been briefed on them by then and had reacted impassively; at sixty, he was quite beyond surprise at being told what people of color may or may not aspire to in white America. But much of the heart had gone out of his campaign with the discovery of its limits. His popularity had collapsed at home, in part precisely because he had gone off adventuring in presidential politics halfway through his term as governor. His people had an increasingly hard time dragging him away from his bleeding budget to go canvass New Hampshire or bone up on national policy. There *was* no Wilder campaign, one aide said in a moment's private despair. Its organization was malformed, its strategy incoherent, its candidate disengaged; Wilder had put his name and his future in Virginia politics at hazard for what looked increasingly like a fool's errand.

There were many reasons why his candidacy came, as it did, to an early and unhappy ending. Wilder was not, for one thing, a figure of great size or expansive vision; he belonged to that breed identified by Richard Nixon as politicians of prose, more at home with the mechanics of power than with its larger possibilities. He had not prepared himself well for the run, and in his face-to-face encounters with his rivals, he was often embarrassed. His pinch-penny approach to government placed him well to the right of the hard-core Democratic activists who tend to vote in primaries—the furthest right of anybody in the field. He was betrayed by his sometimes spiteful temperament; his candidacy was upstaged by a long-running public quarrel with Senator Chuck Robb, a page-one slanging match that had the look of a political suicide pact.

But Wilder was caught as well on the horns of the American Dilemma—the still unresolved tension between our public ideals and our private prejudices. He found himself, as a result, in a lose-lose situation: he was ignored if he talked about the issues and was scolded for "playing the race card" if he mentioned his blackness at all. His prospect for success on his qualities as a man or on his record as governor, after half a term in office, would have been slight if he had been white. As a black man, beyond his potential as a spoiler, he had no chance at all. As two nights of focus groups in New Hampshire made plain, he was the Invisible Man come to presidential politics; his color was all people saw, and when he left the field in January, a month before the primaries began, it was as if he had never been there.

The Prince of Tides

One night in December, 1990, Edmund G. (Jerry) Brown, Jr., sat with a little group of consultants in a chain Mexican restaurant in Alexandria, Virginia, and talked about his future in politics—if he still had one. Brown was in a funk. He had been the wunderkind of the '70s, twice governor of California and twice a candidate for president. But his rocket ride had flamed out in the '80s; he had left the spectators laughing—at him—and after a long sabbatical, he had had to take on the chairmanship of the state Democratic Party just to get back into the game.

His main duty on the job had been grubbing for money, and two years at it had given him the look of a banker, which was essentially what he had become. At fifty-two, the middle-aging whiz kid had gray sideburns, a gold Rolex, and a wardrobe of expensive Italian suits that didn't quite hide a swelling paunch. He hated his work, and he was looking for a way out, one step ahead of a dump-Jerry cabal even then forming against him. He wanted to make a comeback, he told his companions across a field of denuded burrito platters and empty diet cola bottles. He was thinking of running for senator in 1992 and seeing what happened.

"Do you want to be senator?" one of the consultants, Joe Trippi, asked. "Or do you want to be president of the United States?"

"Well, I want to be president," Brown said. He was thinking of the Senate mostly as a launching pad.

Trippi, then still nonaligned for 1992, was intrigued enough to have joined the taco klatch; he had fond memories of Brown going back to his own student days in San Jose in the '70s and still thought he had what it took to be president in spite of all his baggage. The guy was just going at it the wrong way. The two colleagues at table who had set up the meeting, Bob Corn and Jeff Ely, had tipped him in advance on Brown's Senate-first strategy. Trippi, forewarned, had rehearsed his response—a kind of Socratic lesson in the folly of seeking the presidency as a Washington incumbent of any kind.

Look at Nixon in 1968, he told Brown. "What office did he hold?"

"None," Brown said.

"Right," Trippi said. "Now, 1976, who gets elected president?"

"Carter."

"Right. What office did he hold?"

"None."

"1980, who gets elected president?"

"Ronald Reagan."

"Right. What office?"

"None."

"Can you recall how many U.S. senators have ever become president of the United States?"

"No," Brown said. "How many?"

"Well, I don't know," Trippi confessed, "but I think since I've been alive, one. John Kennedy."

The catechism was still in progress when another consultant, Mike Ford, came in late from his home office in the Maryland exurbs. He and Trippi had been through many wars together, dating to the Teddy Kennedy insurgency of 1980. They thought of each other not merely as friends but as brothers, two incendiary spirits who believed that their party needed something more than wrinkle cream to stay alive and vital; it would take radical surgery, a transplant of heart and soul.

"We were talking about whether I should run for the Senate or for president," Brown said as Ford eased his large ex-jock's body into a chair.

"Well, what do you want to do?" Ford asked.

"I want to be president some day."

"Okay, in 1968, who was elected president?" Ford began.

Brown looked from Ford to Trippi, suspecting, not unreasonably, that he had been set up. Still, a faint but distinct aura had begun to glow around the head and shoulders of Governor Moonbeam, and when he headed home for California the next afternoon, it was still there.

It took him an uncommonly long time to process the idea through the random-access channels of his mind. In the past, he had always seemed to operate more on whim than on prolonged ratiocination; he had made his name as the prince of tides of our politics, an intellectual surfer grabbing a wave, riding it for a while, then scanning the horizon for something newer, bigger, and better. It had been a dazzling trip while it lasted. The young Jerry had been New Age even by the advanced standards of La-La Land, and it won him a kind of national celebrity; he was that odd-duck boy governor out there who ate bean sprouts and tofu, slept on a mattress on the floor, kept company with Linda Ronstadt, spoke in koans about how less is better here on Spaceship Earth—and yet somehow had made California work. His earlier presidential adventures had struck sparks while they lasted; it was his timing that had undone him, not the gigawatt electricity he seemed to radiate.

And then it had all gone away. The novelty had worn off, and the applause for Brown's intellectual wire-walking had given way to ridicule at his moonbeamishness. He ran for the Senate in 1982, lost badly, and walked away from politics altogether for six years. He had used part of the interlude working on a still-unpublished memoir, part of it sampling new life experiences like a hungry diner working a smorgasbord table. He had lived in a Mexican village, studied Zen at a monastery in Japan, and worked for a short time as a volunteer in Mother Teresa's House of the Dying in Calcutta.

What his wanderings appeared to have kindled in him was not so much a vision as an itch—a nostalgia for his old life so powerful that he begged his way back through the only entryway available. The sign on the door said party chairman. The desk inside offered him a front-row look at what politics had become while he had been away. The view was not a pretty one; the residue of Brown's two years on the job consisted of nausea at the degree to which money had come to dominate the process and resentment at being blamed for not having raised enough of it to buy the 1990 state elections for his party.

The experience, as he would describe it to his people, had been a radicalizing one—an education in the real corruption of our politics. He had taken the job hoping, so he told friends, to lead a rejuvenation of the party at the grassroots. What he had become instead was a croupier, raking in chips from every Democratic interest group and every monied liberal at the table and shoveling them back out to Democratic candidates and apparatchiks. Brown *had* been good at it, but it was hard for him to escape the feeling that what he was bankrolling was the decay of democracy; as the price of winning public office went up, the number of people who actually voted kept going down. "I suddenly saw it's the money," he told his followers. "It's the money that prevents anything from being done."

He was left with a mission but not a pulpit or a plan. Continuing as chairman was not among his options, even if he had wanted to stay on; his enemies in the party, numerous and well placed, were already planning his ouster when, in the budding spring of 1991, he spoiled their fun by resigning. But for months thereafter, he dithered between running for the Senate, as he first planned, or for president, which looked infinitely riskier to his already battered name and reputation.

"The only thing is, I could be really embarrassed," he told Trippi in one of their early talks. His enemies in politics and the press would dredge up all the old Moonbeam stories and make a public laughing-stock of him.

"Yeah," Trippi said, "but fantasize for one second about what would happen if you won Iowa. 'Cause if you did *that*, that would erase everything."

Brown was unpersuaded. He vacillated deep into the summer, and when he finally resolved one day in July to go for broke, it seemed as much a prophetic as a political decision; it was as though he had journeyed back in time to quattrocento Florence during his travels and had come back as Savonarola to cleanse the American polity of sin. His message, simply put, was that the money changers had taken over the temple of our democracy, buying influence for themselves and their clients. His means for driving them out would be making them irrelevant. He gathered some of his advisers one night at his house, a converted firehouse in San Francisco, for a dinner of leftover sushi with brown rice and a glimpse at the puritanical new discipline he proposed to bring to politics. Whether he ran for senator or president, he said, he wouldn't accept contributions of more than $100.

The news was received with some horror by the few professionals in his entourage. The legal limit was $1,000, and even that was short money for a contemporary media campaign.

"Why don't you do it for $250?" one of his guests, a young pollster, pleaded.

"No," Brown said. If you really meant to make a statement, the max had to be something people could conceivably afford; it was the only way to turn the fat cats out of the process and let America back in.

His sense of mission was reinforced by his fellow exile Pat Caddell, the broody pollster who had left Washington in disgust four years earlier and moved west to Los Angeles to seek his fortune in other lines of work. Caddell had spent his last years in politics raising alarms about the growing alienation of the voters from the process and looking for a candidate who would give flesh to his apocalyptic views. The search had led him to Gary Hart, the failed phenom of 1984, and later to his friend Joseph Biden, a nonstarter in 1987. He had all but given up hope when Brown began his meditations on 1992. The spell came over Caddell again, and he appeared at the doorsill to Brown's psyche, a bearded, bear-sized apparition with a four-year-old book of revelation under his arm.

The 156-page document was called *In Search of Mr. Smith*—the hero of a long, fictional prologue about a senator who comes out of nowhere and takes the Iowa caucuses by storm. Its thesis was that American politics and government were ruled by an "elite reality" having little to do with the everyday lives and discontents of the people. Its protagonist was a young man in his forties bearing "a dual-engined message of populism and new generation leadership" and speaking directly to the voters by satellite and cable instead of in thirty-second ads. Predictably, given its authorship, the recipe worked. "This campaign," Caddell's Senator Smith declared in his hour of triumph on caucus night, "was staked on a fundamental belief that the majority of Americans are not apathetic—just ignored—and that if given a true voice they would rise as a mighty river surging through the political life of our country. . . . The issue is empowerment, and the way to empower people—is to *empower* people. This election is not about electing 'me' but 'us.'"

Brown, who inhaled ideas as insatiably as a druggie freebasing co-caine, incorporated Caddell's into his own and began forming a radical critique of what the system had become in the third century of the American republic. Its nub was that the country had fallen into the hands of a permanent oligarchy of incumbent officeholders and the monied interests that financed their elections; the losers were the people, and the ideal of popular sovereignty. As a vision, it was all midnight and no sunrise beyond the vague promise of "real change"; there would be times when this critique made Brown seem, in his humorless way, to be running for national scold. But it was powerful enough to conquer his ambivalence about what to do in 1992. "Running for president, somebody is *listening,*" said Jacques Barzaghi, a French cineast who had been Brown's alter ego for years. "Even if you are number six or number seven. Or number one hundred—who cares?"

The manner of Brown's entry was an accurate preview of the way his campaign would run: three months passed between his decision and his actual declaration, and even then, it took two days and two insomniac nights at the last possible moment to cobble his speech together. Caddell had kicked in a draft. So had Mike Ford, a tough veteran pol who felt equally at home in the world of ideas. Brown was working on his own version; his crib sheet, in turn, was a manuscript copy of *Promises to Keep,* Richard Goodwin's pessimistic new book on the debasement of American politics.

The dueling authors closeted themselves in a hotel suite in Phila-delphia. The candidate sat in the living room, wearing only a pair of loose boxers and dark knee-high socks, and punched away at a laptop computer. Caddell and Ford worked on their versions in the bedroom. Barzaghi floated among them, a spectral figure with a shaven head and a tattooed body swathed in black leather and denim; the competition of writerly egos tickled his Gallic irony.

There was, for example, the bicker over the word "empowerment." Brown considered the term and the idea it embodied—returning power to the people—to be the very heart of his campaign. But he tended to overwork it, and at one point, Ford tried to slip in "magic" as a substitute.

Brown caught him. "Why are we using 'magic' rather than 'empowerment?'" he demanded.

"Well, governor," Ford said, "we've used the word 'empowerment' fifty thousand times, is why. Let's say 'magic.'"

"I don't like 'magic,'" Brown said. "What do you think we've got to use 'magic' for?"

"'Cause you're Goofy, is why," Ford teased. "It's like Disney World. You know—the Magic Kingdom?"

Brown didn't get it; he had not recently visited American mass culture in the course of his intellectual wanderings. But the speech finally came together, and against the appropriately revolutionary backdrop of Independence Hall, he declared his intent not merely to run for president but to tear down the whole cracking architecture of American politics from within. "This candidacy is not simply about me," he said; it was about "you, and you, and you"—an entire citizenry disfranchised by "the collapse of our two-party system" and the rise of a single incumbent party in its place.

He was as lonely as a street-corner preacher, standing in front of the cradle of our liberty and offering to lead what amounted to a second American revolution against a new ruling class. Its launch was raggedly advanced and ill-attended; only a small knot of reporters and noonday passersby witnessed it live, and the larger political world gave it only passing notice. The apostle of a new order was still Governor Moonbeam in his early notices, just as he had feared, and his words were drowned out by the sound of the old order laughing.

The Cuomo Overhang

With Brown's late entry, the field was complete. But the autocrats of the luncheon tables in Washington found it hard to credit that that was all there was—that the Democracy was bound for the Super Bowl with a lineup of scrubs. The anxiety of the Federal City gave way to dread as Clinton began his inexorable rise toward the top of the pack. Was the party on the same old ruinous course, awarding the nomination to yet another obscure and vulnerable loser? Could no one be found to save the Democrats from themselves?

Many nominees for the part were proposed over the coffee cups and

Perrier bottles—men whose attraction seemed to increase in direct proportion to their unavailability. But the name most frequently mentioned was that of Governor Mario Cuomo of New York, a star in the fantasy lives of Democrats dating to his eloquent keynote speech at the party convention in 1984. It was hard for the declared candidates even to be noticed, let alone be taken seriously, until Cuomo spoke. The wait was a long one; the sorting-out process was held largely in suspended animation while the governor sat at his great remove in Elsinore-on-the-Hudson, brooding over his duties and his possibilities like a medieval scholastic pondering the Five Ways of Saint Thomas Aquinas.

Cuomo had gone through a similar public agony in 1988, seeming to enjoy the unsettling effect on the party, the press, and the real candidates. The tease had led nowhere then, and with its rerun in 1991, the senior leaders of Cuomo's party found it, as one said, more than a little tiresome. Some had come to doubt that he would *ever* leave the security of his own duchy in New York for the thinner air of national politics. But this time, there were signs that the winks and the flashes of ankle might be real. A shipment of slick Cuomo brochures materialized in New Hampshire during the fall, and friends of the governor were working the phones, urging prominent Democrats to hang loose until he had decided what to do.

His ruminations made planning difficult for the declared candidates; they were all laboring under what Bill Clinton's people called the Cuomo Overhang, waiting for Mario to make up his labyrinthine mind. When Clinton's fledgling team gathered in Little Rock early in November to talk strategy, it was, one participant thought, like having two parallel conversations in the same room at the same time. Some game plans factored Cuomo into the race, others counted him out; the conferees had to keep interrupting one another to find out which set of assumptions was on the table at any given time.

With Cuomo in, they all knew, they would have a much steeper path to climb. There would be an instant stature gap between him and everyone else in the field; he would have the name, the team, and the money, plus that extra allure that went with having played hard to get for so long. There was some talk, indeed, of ceding New Hampshire to Cuomo and making a stand instead in the South, where Clinton would have the home-field advantage. But Hillary put her foot down and ultimately prevailed. If Cuomo got in, she thought, Bill should run as the Un-Cuomo—just draw a line in the dirt and say, "These are my values, those are his." Cuomo's were old. Bill's were new. It would be the dialectic they had always wanted: a generational struggle for the hearts and minds of the party.

Cuomo did not oblige them with a clear signal as to his intentions. On the one hand, he kept repeating his incantation that he had no plans to run and no plans to make plans. On the other, he seemed drawn to the prospect of making the Democratic case against the excesses of the Reagan-Bush years. On scanty evidence, the assumption spread that he *must* be running, and when he kept putting off a final decision, insisting that he first had to get his own state's chaotic finances in order, the boys who lunch said that that was just Mario being Mario; he was stringing out the suspense as long as he could.

He couldn't string it out forever; for all practical purposes, time would be up for him on December 20, the filing deadline for the primary in New Hampshire. The mind of Mario Cuomo was thicketed with irony, and he had long looked at the quadrennial war there as a droll spectacle—a bunch of presumptively sane and competent men scrambling around a small state in pursuit of a meaningless Wednesday morning headline. It was dumb, but if he didn't get in the game there, he could find himself chasing a homeboy named Clinton around the South, which could be even dumber.

There were accordingly winks and nods around Washington when, on the twentieth, Cuomo's people laid on preparations for his last-minute plunge into the race. Planes had been chartered for the sprint from Albany to Concord, and a microphone had been ordered up for Cuomo's use when he got there. The long wait was over, or so everybody thought. Godot was making his entrance at last.

Bill Clinton was due in Nashville that day to see a doctor about his chronically disappearing voice. His plane had just touched down when his deputy manager, George Stephanopoulos, called from Little Rock to go over the draft of a statement welcoming Cuomo to the war. But as he was being patched through to Clinton, Stephanopoulos was interrupted by urgent calls from one and then another friend at party headquarters. It looked, they said, as if Cuomo might be having second thoughts.

"Governor, don't get off the plane," Stephanopoulos told Clinton.

He glanced at his TV set. It was tuned to CNN, the constant companion to modern political operatives, and there, sure enough, was Cuomo, explaining why he wouldn't be a candidate after all. He had *wanted* to run this time, he said, really and truly, but his first obligation was to his state, and he couldn't just go off to New Hampshire with his budget bleeding red ink all over the capitol floor.

Stephanopoulos did an improvised simulcast, repeating Cuomo's words into his cellular phone. At the other end, Clinton listened in sober silence. Then he dictated a new statement wishing Cuomo well and remarking that, as a fellow governor, he understood.

Another staffer, Richard Mintz, called Hillary at the governor's mansion with the news.

"He's not running?" she exclaimed.

"No, Hillary, he's not," Mintz said.

"Oh, my God," she said. She could feel the landscape of her life changing, possibly forever. The campaign wasn't a rehearsal anymore, or a traveling seminar on the issues. Now it was real, and Bill was the front-runner. It was more than a little scary.

6.

The Look of a Winner

Luck is a precious element in politics, worth more than a seven-point program or an eighteen-carat smile, and in the autumn of his ascent, Bill Clinton seemed to be garlanded with four-leaf clovers. Mario Cuomo had kindly got out of his way, along with the rest of the Democratic first team. So had Jesse Jackson, a torment to the party and its white-bread nominees for nearly a decade. Clinton's remaining competition looked a great deal less than formidable. The media, for a season, seemed smitten with him; the smell of success is aphrodisiac, and just so long as Clinton looked like a winner, young, bright, exciting, and amply monied, his notices were as warm as first love.

But fortune had blessed him rather too much too soon. Clinton was like a talented rookie who had not yet seen his first big-league curve ball; all he had shown so far—all he had had time to show—were the easy heroics of the batting cage. In the standard-issue commentaries of the op-editorialists, the late start of the campaign was declared a mercy for the country after the tiresome two- and three-year marathon runs of our recent past. In fact, the shortened season damaged most of the candidates and would nearly destroy Clinton, propelling him to the head of the class before he himself was ready or anyone else knew who he was.

His indefinition, indeed, would prove to be his greatest single vulnerability; it meant, as things worked out, that America would first get to know him through the least flattering moments of his past. The myth of Bill Clinton was that he had been plotting his climb to the presidency forever. The truth was that his real preparation for the race had been mostly intellectual, his long soak in the literature of economics and public policy, and in the early going, his speeches showed it; they were like cold oatmeal, good for you, perhaps, but leaden and lumpy going down. He hadn't bothered introducing himself before he started talking, which gave his new ideas a disembodied sound. The merit badges he won for being Mister Substance gave way with time and repetition to the complaint that he was a walking syllabus of solutions to all of America's problems, some of which people didn't even know they had.

What Bill Clinton wouldn't talk about was Bill Clinton. The campaign had calculated that, as George Stephanopoulos put it, being specific about problems and solutions would be the first test of character in the chill political climate of 1992, and Clinton had gone about it with a vengeance. His team tried valiantly to squeeze the disparate bits and pieces of his message into a series of three long speeches at Georgetown University in the fall and winter, outlining his plans for the economy and the world and his vision of a "New Covenant" of shared responsibility between the people and their government. In the world according to Bill, the young would repay their student loans with public service; people on welfare would ultimately have to graduate to work; the rich, who had profited from the laissez-faire policies of the '80s, would pay more taxes while the squeezed middle class and the working poor paid less.

The speeches were handsomely wrought; apart from Paul Tsongas's pamphlet, they were the closest any candidate had then come to proposing a coherent design for the American future. But they attracted only routine attention from the press, accompanied by the private complaint that Clinton had run on a bit long and provided a bit too many details. The grumbling was not without foundation; even at his best, Clinton at a lectern tended in the early going to be long of wind and low on soul. At his worst, one of his consultants fretted, he risked becoming Dukakis with a drawl—a technocrat so bloodless as to seem no more than the sum of his programs.

The problem, Stephanopoulos thought, was marrying what Clinton *thought* to what he *felt;* if they could only take care of that—if they could get more of *him* into his public appearances—he would win. The question was how to go about it. The attempt to humanize Clinton kept bumping into the wall of his reticence about revealing his feelings or dwelling on the boyhood traumata that had helped form him. "I don't know what to do about all this psychobabble," he complained one day, exasperated at the latest efforts of the press to explain him. He understood its importance—better, he reckoned, than Bush did—but that didn't mean he had to like it.

The best response, his people kept insisting, was to explain himself—to define who he was and where he came from before his enemies painted his portrait their way. But in the first months of his campaign, he couldn't bring himself to lower his guard. So far as the press and the voters were concerned, Clinton consisted of his agenda and his deceptively open-looking face. He wasn't going to go around parading his emotions, he said, or handwringing about his abusive stepfather. He hadn't been brought up that way; his mother had taught him never to put his troubles off on anyone else, and he wouldn't. His style instead was that of a salesman: grin, lock eyes, and keep talking about the product. He was by his own choice an entirely public man, an assemblage of pixels on a screen with no third dimension. The price was to be connected by free association with other such men; a disturbing fraction of voters, exposed to his smile, his southern accent, and his relentless sincerity, were reminded of Jimmy Swaggart, say, or Jim Bakker—the soiled divines of televangelism.

There were pages from his past, and Hillary's, that they hadn't even opened to their own team; the scary thing, one of his young aides lamented long before the mud started flying, was that his people didn't know him themselves. They hadn't asked him about his sex life or his family finances, and they weren't aware of his gimme-shelter adventures avoiding the draft—not, at least, in any detail. They were reduced like everybody else to combing the public record for what it revealed of his weaknesses; their dossier for the defense was accordingly light on his personal life and heavy on the shortfalls in his ten-year run as governor of a small, poor southern state.

Neither had they figured out how to use Hillary effectively to help warm up his persona. They talked among themselves about scheduling more joint appearances as a token that the robo-wonk was after all a flesh-and-blood family man. But Hillary wouldn't trivialize herself or her marriage, she said, by serving as a prop at his events in the saucer-eyed Nancy Reagan manner, and she was even more adamant about not allowing Chelsea to be dragged into the campaign. Her insistence on these matters bought more space for herself and for her daughter. The cost was a certain hardening of her own image. By spring, a sizable number of voters would see her as the yuppie wife from hell, all career and no home life; the impression was widespread that she and Bill were childless.

The trouble was that the campaign didn't know what else to do with her, except to turn her loose with her own schedule of events— usually in secondary media markets—and have her do variations on Clinton's stock road speech. She was better at it than he was in some ways, though she lacked his ease and élan in crowded rooms; her version of his talk was shorter and more to the point, and she was far quicker than he at absorbing the sometimes daily changes in message required in a '90s-model campaign. It became seductively easy for the two of them to brag on their "unprecedented partnership," as Clinton once called it, and to do jokes about how voters could buy one and get one free. Only with time would they realize that what they were describing sounded too much like a his-and-hers co-presidency, whereupon they began toning it down.

The more immediate problem, in the start-up months, was incorporating Ms. Clinton into any larger strategic design. She complained sometimes about how Bill was flying around with his big entourage while she was out there all by herself, scurrying through airports and dashing to speeches with little or no guidance as to what she was supposed to say. He was the candidate, of course, but she brought her own expertise in policy and politics to the table, and she didn't like being treated as an afterthought. She felt left out of the loop, and it would be months before she was assigned a chief of staff whose most important duty was keeping her in it—seeing, for example, that she was on the routing list for every important communication in the campaign.

The problem was just one of the growing pains of an enterprise starting too late with too few experienced people and too little internal coherence. Even by the standards of 1991, Clinton had been slow to the gate, the next-to-last man to declare. His base of operations then was a downtown storefront in Little Rock, with a few phone lines, a single fax, and no cable-TV hookup. To one early recruit, Richard Mintz, it looked more like the headquarters of a city-council campaign than the nerve center of a presidential candidacy.

Clinton's start-up staff was not much more imposing. He had brought along a couple of aides from the statehouse and a couple of longtime chums, Bruce and Bev Lindsey, the first in a human wave of FOB's (for Friends of Bill) and FOH's (for Friends of Hillary) who would attach themselves formally or informally to the campaign. But the early recruits were frequently young and green, and to the extent that the Clintons let anyone share authority, the design of the campaign fell into the hands of outside consultants—a core group of Beltway professionals of the sort Clinton was nominally running against.

Reputations can be made in politics by the quality of one's hired hands, and Clinton's were, on paper, an impressive lot. His ad man, Frank Greer, and his pollster, Stan Greenberg, had blue-chip reputations in Washington. So did his fund-raiser, Robert Farmer, a lusty, flashy publishing millionaire whose talent at coaxing money out of other people's pockets had effectively bought the 1988 nomination for Michael Dukakis. His success then had established him as a master of the new reality of primary politics: victory goes to the campaign that starts fund-raising early, sells its product well, and finds its way to the most important benefactors—those who can write checks for the maximum permissible $1,000 on their own bank accounts and bring in large numbers of similarly well-fixed friends as well. The mere presence of Farmer's name on the roster sent a particularly powerful signal to the political community; it was Clinton's warranty that he would be well provided for financially and was therefore to be considered a serious man.

The campaign would score the coup of the season, moreover, the day it signed an itinerant gunslinger named James Carville and his partner, Paul Begala, as its strategists-in-chief. Carville, at forty-eight, was a late-blooming grandmaster at the chessboard of politics, a failed lawyer out of Louisiana who had traveled a lot of bad road in his second career. He was forty-two years old when he won his first race, an old guy, relatively speaking, in a young person's game. He had been flat broke when he got a tentative assignment from Gary Hart to go organize the South in 1983. The day he left Washington, trudging toward Union Station in a cold April rain, he had forty-seven dollars in his jeans and everything else he owned in a garment bag. He was lugging it along Massachusetts Avenue when the shoulder strap broke. The bag hit the wet pavement. So did Carville; he sat down on the sidewalk and cried.

The job with Hart fell through. But Carville's fortunes had greatly improved since then, and so had his skills, honed fine in a run of winning senatorial and gubernatorial races. The defeat of Bush's man Dick Thornburgh in the 1991 Senate by-election in Pennsylvania was only the latest, but its degree of difficulty and its fortuitous timing had made him and Begala the hottest properties in town. The two of them shopped the presidential field, leaning toward Bob Kerrey at first but settling finally on the more natural fit with Clinton. In the sitzkrieg of autumn, with no real contests on the calendar to write about, the media interpreted their signing as a major event. CLINTON WINS CARVILLE PRIMARY, said the headline in the *Washington Post*.

What Clinton had in fact got was a person who cared about little in life except winning elections and who had learned that the way to win them was by a monomaniacal focus on message. Carville was a man of considerable guile but no pretensions. He gave himself none of the airs of his richer, higher-toned contemporaries, with their house accounts at fine downtown restaurants and their sleek suites in Georgetown or the tonier Virginia suburbs. He was a tightly wound man, tall and wire-thin, with a sharply angled face, a frightening smile, and wide-set, dangerous eyes. His working gear was a T-shirt or sweatshirt and a tattered pair of hip-hugger jeans, with ironed-in creases and a see-through view of his boxer shorts. His office was in his Spartan basement-level apartment on Capitol Hill, where he slept nights on a threadbare couch opposite his own desk and Begala's. They had never troubled to hang out a shingle; all that identified them as the season's hottest consulting firm was a bumper sticker plastered on the front door, a memento of one of their old campaigns.

Carville traded on his southernness and his mad-dog reputation, just as the late Lee Atwater had; to look, talk, and occasionally behave like a bit player in *Deliverance* could be exceptionally good for business. Rivals nicknamed him Jaws, and his own unlikely girlfriend, Mary Matalin, whose day job was deputy manager of the Bush campaign, called him Serpent Head when she was mad at him. Carville preferred his own nom de guerre, the Ragin' Cajun, which accurately described the warrior spirit and the pop-to discipline he brought to the campaign. Begala was the gentler of the two partners and the more theoretical, with interests in policy as well as politics. Carville had little taste for abstraction and none at all for public service; he was instead a mercenary who lived from war to war.

The campaign he joined was not nearly the efficient machine it might have seemed from its high-powered, high-priced consulting team or from its early press cuttings. The Clintons had found a talented young manager in David Wilhelm, but his only battle stars for running anything had been won in Chicago mayoral races. His inexperience at national politics seemed to suit Clinton fine, since it guaranteed real control to Hillary and himself. Deep into autumn, the candidate was serving de facto as his own manager, scheduler, and political director, and the resulting organizational problems only got worse as the campaign grew in size. No one was really in charge. The Clintons, by chance or design, had seen to that.

Partly as a result, Carville, who *needed* control to work his spells, found his early months a misery of protracted meetings, conference calls, and overelaborated prep sessions for big events. His patience with crowded rooms and extended discussion was notoriously short; with time, his colleagues learned to set out desk toys at his place at table so he would have something to play with when he got bored. He was a high-maintenance personality as well, an officer who required the unshared attention of his client and the adoration of his troops. The diffusion of power and the competition for Clinton's ear sent him into a sulk that would last intermittently into spring and would finally end only when a palace coup put him clearly in charge.

But the period of the Cuomo Overhang had its benefits for Clinton. While the press and the pols were watching obsessively for a puff of white smoke from the statehouse in Albany, he had time to seek his own stride as a candidate, to run some early trial heats against his known rivals—and, most critically of all, to get his fund-raising machinery in order. The keystone of his strategy from the start had been to bank enough in contributions and federal matching funds to last him through the March primary in Illinois. If he was doing well by then, the smart money would flow to him as if by force of gravity. If he was doing badly, it wouldn't matter if he was broke; he would be back in Little Rock anyway, watching the rest of the race from the bleachers.

The problem, in the first weeks, was that there was barely enough in the till to keep the doors open at headquarters. Bob Farmer, the wizard fund-raiser, had turned out to be little more than a name on a letterhead for Clinton. Farmer had warned the governor up front that he had taken a new job in Boston and so could be no more than a part-timer in the campaign. But even with that caveat, his contributions had been minimal, to Clinton's annoyance, and the local talent in Little Rock were only too clearly in over their heads. In the entire month of November, there were no fund-raising events at all, and the campaign was in serious jeopardy of bleeding to death.

The man who rescued it was a brash young Chicago pal of Wilhelm's named Rahm Emanuel, who would come to be known around headquarters as Rahmbo for his profane speech and his assaultive style. He moved in as finance director in what traditionally had been the drought season in political fund-raising even in good times, the month between Thanksgiving and Christmas. In 1991, the Democrats were finding it drier than ever; their traditional angels were feeling pinched by the recession and discouraged by what then still seemed the improbability of beating Bush. Emanuel, undaunted, set a $2.2 million target for the period and flogged his people relentlessly to meet it. November, with its blank calendar, gave way to a December dense-packed with twenty-seven fund-raisers in twenty days. By the turn of the year, in spite of their late start, Emanuel's team had reached their goal and run up the campaign's overall receipts to $3.3 million—by far the largest single stack at the table.

Clinton's strategy did not come together so quickly or so tidily. He and his generals didn't have to worry about the Iowa caucuses; Tom Harkin's favorite-son candidacy had taken the state effectively off the table for everybody else. But the importance of the season-opening primary in New Hampshire was puffed up, as a result, from hype to hyperinflation. For Clinton, the need to compete there was a detour on the road south, where he and the voters at least spoke a common language. Still, he was obliged to follow the rest of the herd into the state, with no very clear idea of what to do when he arrived or how to proceed if he did well.

His handlers guessed early on that he would not—that they were probably going to have to explain away a second- or even a third-place finish. The state was presumed to be a natural for Paul Tsongas, since he lived just across the Massachusetts line and had been day-tripping into New Hampshire for months. The consensus of the wise men was that a Tsongas victory there wouldn't matter; nobody took him seriously enough to care. But Clinton did. The guy was dangerous, the governor told his people, because he *believed* he could win; a man so persuaded wasn't going to be running any soft-edged vanity campaign. The further problem was that Tsongas's messages of responsibility and investment in the future sounded so like his own. "Every vote he gets," Clinton said after one early encounter, "is a vote I lose."

But Tsongas was not the candidate he feared most over the longer road past New Hampshire. The sages of politics, scanning the field, were as impressionable as tourists at a souk; they were easily drawn to flash, glitter, and artful spieling, and in the days before Clinton's levitation, the seductions of the marketplace led them to Bob Kerrey. The senator, it was confidently said, would bring a dash of glamor and excitement to a race otherwise peopled by a wonk, a flake, a black, an antique, and a survivor of the Big C. He was likened, in the more extravagant advance commentaries, to the young Jack Kennedy come to lead the return to Camelot.

With time, it would become apparent that it was the *idea* of Bob Kerrey that people had fallen in love with; the real article, while bright and charming, was only too plainly unready for the big time. But his glittery image preceded him into battle, like sunlight flashing on burnished armor, and Clinton watched Kerrey's approach with wary eyes. The two had gone head-to-head for the first time at an event on Chicago's North Pier in October, and the crowd had been overwhelmingly with Clinton. "I kicked his butt," he told his handlers afterward, with some pride but surprisingly little pleasure. Kerrey, he said, was a tough, competitive son of a bitch. It might not have been such a great idea to show him up so early—not with a whole winter's payback time before the primaries.

"An Inch Away from Moonbeam"

Clinton needn't have worried. It was back-to-school time for Bob Kerrey, just as his handlers had warned him, and he had a lot to learn. The first lesson was that in the big-chill politics of the '90s, it would take more than raw charisma to get somebody to the White House. There had always been something indistinct about Kerrey, a certain blurriness of thought and focus. His pollster, Harrison Hickman, spoke of him privately as the political equivalent of an inkblot test: ask twenty voters what they saw in him and you'd get twenty different answers. The quality had sometimes served him well in the past, but as he wandered through his first weeks as a presidential candidate, it became a nearly disabling weakness. He hadn't even worked up a serviceable everyday speech, let alone anything so focused as a message; he trampled applause lines and slid around points like a slalom racer trying to avoid them. If vagueness had counted, Cosmic Bob might have won on points. "He's an inch away from Moonbeam," John Reilly, a smart, earthy Washington lawyer serving as a senior adviser to the campaign, warned early on. His team tried to fix him, with advice and sometimes scripts. It didn't take. Kerrey, a proudly unmanageable man, resisted prompting. The trouble was that, without it, he seemed not to know quite what he wanted to say.

What he *didn't* want to talk about was Vietnam or the medal of honor he had brought home from his tour there as a Navy SEAL. His handlers nagged him to use his war stories; only one voter in twenty had any idea who he was, and his heroics were a powerful way of introducing him to America. "You need to talk more about yourself," his New Hampshire director, Paul Johnson, wrote him in a memo in November. Kerrey was a new guy on the block, and the first thing people wanted to know about him, Johnson said, was whether they would like having him as a neighbor.

Kerrey didn't bite; he didn't even want the warm-up speakers at his rallies talking about his wound or his medal. Sometimes he would tiptoe up to the brink, speaking affectingly of how much he owed a country that had healed and educated him at government expense "when I came back." But even on these occasions, he wouldn't say back from where. "Jesus, Bob," his senior political adviser, Larry Harrington, told him one day, "some people might think you came back from the *moon* or something."

The pounding from his managers was relentless, and Kerrey finally gave in to them. But, as with many of his sudden enthusiasms, he overdid it. On his best days, he made moving connections between his story and his issues; his recovery from his wounds became a paradigm of how government could help others less fortunate, as it had helped him. At his worst, the story seemed to be all there was to his candidacy; the new complaint in the media and elsewhere was that he had become little more than a walking biography—a man with not much to talk about except himself.

The bio problem was only a symptom of a larger indiscipline in the campaign, the consequence of the weakness at the top and of Kerrey's own indifference to the rules of play. His senior hands, Sue Casey among them, were members of what came to be known as the Let-Bob-Be-Bob school, which meant allowing him to find his own way at his own pace and banking on his personal allure to get him through the rough patches. But Bob being Bob sometimes radiated a kind of unseriousness—the casual air of a bright college boy figuring he could ace his finals without cracking a book. While Clinton burned enough midnight oil to capsize a supertanker, Kerrey idly watched *The Fabulous Baker Boys* on a VCR, starting in his hotel room one night and finishing in a van en route to his first speech the next morning.

What he seemed not to get, or care about, was how much hard labor it took to master the relentless, message-driven politics of a contemporary campaign, and there was no one at his side to keep him at it. His regular traveling companion, Billy Shore, seemed to be humoring him instead; there were distressed reports from the road of their laughing when nothing was funny and clowning in open view of the press and the public. "It's unbelievable," a field operative told headquarters. "It's two guys out here giggling."

When he did get serious, Kerrey too often seemed lost; some of his people began to wonder if there was something seriously wrong with him. His standing as the white knight in the lists was slipping quickly away from him, and when their paths crossed again at a meeting of state party chairpeople in Chicago a month after their first encounter, Clinton was no longer shy about denting Sir Bob's armor.

The setting was in fact a perfect showplace for Clinton, a test against the entire field of candidates, and he was at the very top of his game. There were none of the leaden programmatic passages that weighed down even his best speeches; he made his points instead with horror stories about real people who had lost their jobs or their health-care benefits while their supposed servants in the government bickered over who was to blame. "Washington, D.C., has become a city of irresponsibility," he said, and he did not exempt the Democrats from the indictment. The sad truth, he said, was that most voters "don't care much about politicians of *either* party. . . . The American people have lost faith in the political process, and they have ample reason."

The speech put Clinton out front in the first competition that counted: the chase after that magic incantation known in the trade-craft of politics as a Message. In the consensus view, Kerrey's was blurry, Tsongas's dour, Brown's shrill, Harkin's out of date, Wilder's practically nonexistent. Clinton's was suddenly crystal clear, at least in outline; his talk was the beginning of his presentation of himself as a new kind of Democrat, leading his party beyond its old ideas and old role as the servant of its client groups. In the Q&A period afterward, a woman in the audience asked him if he was really a Democrat or just a Republican in clever disguise. Clinton didn't know at the time that his own man Frank Greer had planted the question, but he was no less ready for it. He was indeed a Democrat by instinct, heritage, and conviction, he said, and by genetic code as well; so devout had his grandfather been in the faith that he believed he would be going to Franklin Delano Roosevelt when he died.

Clinton got a standing ovation. Kerrey bombed; his young managers had considered skipping the cattle show entirely, on the theory that, as one put it, the party regulars were a bunch of idiots anyway and were beneath the senator's attention. They finally decided to send him, but as things worked out, he could as profitably have stayed home. His flight in was diverted to Milwaukee and fogged in on the tarmac there for seven hours. While he sat earthbound, he got out a laptop computer and started reworking his speech. With each new draft, it got murkier and murkier, until it was as impenetrable as the weather.

It hardly mattered. When Kerrey finally arrived in the hall, he mumbled his text into a dysfunctional mike and then left town, neglecting the mix-and-mingle time required of candidates seeking favor at such events. It was Clinton instead who, in the nearly universal view, won both the beauty contest onstage and the Mr. Congeniality competition in the hospitality suites. When the two men cleared town, they left behind a litter of torn-up scratch sheets rating Kerrey the front-runner. For the first time, the party establishment had to take Clinton seriously. He had begun his warp-speed climb to the top—and Kerrey his lazy downward spiral back to earth.

His descent was well advanced when John Reilly, a veteran Democratic warrior with combat ribbons dating to the Robert Kennedy insurgency of 1968, showed up at a message meeting in Washington in early December and did what he called a human-helicopter critique of the operation. Reilly had held back for a time, recalling how an earlier generation of gray eminences had volunteered their advice to the Mondale campaign in 1984; they had been known around headquarters as the Fuckheads and were humored only because of the damage they could do you in the press and the political community if you ignored them. Reilly, at sixty-three, didn't want to be like them. But his advice, unlike theirs, had been invited, and he was old-fashioned enough to care deeply about the causes he took up.

He had watched with growing dismay as the campaign drifted under the split leadership of its manager, Sue Casey, who had been a ranker in the Hart campaigns, and its chairman, Bill Hoppner, a businessman and sometime Kerrey chief of staff with no national political experience at all. No one, so far as Reilly could tell, was in charge. The epiphany, for him, had been the day not long before when he had arrived at a meeting and found an empty chair at the head of the table. "Who the Christ is running this thing?" he wondered, and when no answers became apparent, he figured the time had come to speak his mind.

The disarray, he said at the December meeting, had got to the point where Kerrey was in danger of being written out of the race. The media tended to see a campaign as a mirror of the candidate, and the mess at his headquarters on K Street reflected badly on the senator—maybe terminally so. The pundits were getting ready to declare that the whole thing was imploding, and unless his team found a way to keep that perception from hardening—a way "to freeze the linebackers," Reilly said—the stories would start popping. "If Kerrey called a press conference tomorrow," he guessed, "half the press would think he was getting out of the race."

The core problem, in his withering view, was leadership. "Decisions don't get made," he complained. "Things just happen." They had already spent $220,000 on media and had only a few weak ads to show for it. They had no polling in New Hampshire, nothing to build a strategy on. A straw vote in Florida and a network debate on NBC-TV were coming up, and nobody was thinking about them. They didn't have enough committed, seven-day-a-week people with serious national experience. They weren't growing enough to get serious or, at least as important, to *look* serious to the media.

At a point in Reilly's harangue, someone tried to cut him off, suggesting that the meeting wasn't a suitable forum for his complaints.

"It's the only forum I have," Reilly shot back, plunging ahead with his case.

He avoided going after Casey or Hoppner directly, not wanting to show them up in front of the help. But when he spoke of the need for a command team "layered" with new people, his meaning was unmistakable. "This is a national campaign," he said. "It's Yankee Stadium. It's The Show. If a candidate has a second-class campaign, he can't be anything but a second-class candidate."

Hoppner did not disagree with the assessment; all he really wanted was to go home to Nebraska and occupy that stately distance from the trenches normally reserved to campaign chairmen. Casey, the incumbent CEO, fought back. "You're exaggerating the problems," she told Reilly. The things he had complained about were all being taken care of.

But much of the middle-rank staff around the table had sat through Reilly's helicopter tour of their world in silent agreement. The first rumblings of a coup were indeed already audible in the corridors on K Street, and within the fortnight, it had been carried out. With a final nod from Kerrey, command responsibility passed from Casey to a new "campaign director," Tad Devine, a blooded veteran operative who had been helping out part-time and whose price for taking over was complete control.

The plotters hoped improbably that Casey wouldn't take her demotion too hard and would stay on, minimizing the mess. She didn't oblige them. Two days before Christmas, she quit the campaign and went home to Denver, leaving it to the new crowd to apply CPR to Kerrey's nearly lifeless candidacy. The front-runner had stumbled back to the starting line and would have to begin all over again.

A Shadow Play in Orlando

One day in mid-December, a taut, wiry young man clothed in an Armani suit and a South Boston manner checked into the Buena Vista Hotel in Orlando and assembled a troop of volunteers for a look around. His name was Michael Whouley, and he had been sent to Florida to wire the state Democratic convention for Bill Clinton. The main event was to be one of those games politicians play—a nonbinding straw poll of interest mainly to the bettors, tipsters, and touts waiting for the real action to begin. But it would be the only match before the primaries with somebody actually keeping score, and it was a safe guess that the media would be swarming all over it, ready to embrace the victor as the front-runner du jour. Clinton wanted to win it, badly. Whouley's job was to make sure he did.

He was starting late on an uphill journey. The campaign had only lately hired a skilled national-party functionary, Jeff Eller, to run its Florida operations, and by the time Eller posted Whouley to Orlando, the convention was just five days off. Kerrey's people on the ground had been making noises for weeks about playing to win, no matter how wobbly their home office in Washington might look. Harkin was working the state hard, with most of the labor delegates already on his side and a professional phone bank prospecting for more. A few diehards were trying to get something going for Cuomo—enough, with luck, to tempt him into the race.

Clinton's prospects, two weeks out, had looked less than promising. His people hoped to get him 1,000 of the 2,200 delegates, enough for a convincing victory in a multicandidate field. But they had no more than fifty or so votes in hand, and while their tracking and mailing operations had got up and running since then, the Clintons would be arriving in Orlando not much farther than halfway to their goal.

The battle thus would have to be won at the convention, and Whouley attacked the problem as meticulously as General Norman Schwarzkopf plotting the liberation of Kuwait. He set up a command post in room 643 at the Buena Vista, then headed downstairs and led his scouting party on a yard-by-yard reconnaissance tour of the lobby, the corridors, the conference spaces, and the ballroom where the delegates would gather. A photographer shot pictures along the way. They would be blown up and mounted on the walls in Whouley's war room; all he would have to do was glance around him to figure out where to move the Clintons, say, or post a bunch of placard wavers, or order up a spontaneous demonstration.

But his real coup came when he scanned the farther reaches of the ballroom and saw an opening high above the floor, a window overlooking the entire hall. Whouley was staring up at it, wondering what was on the other side, when an aide leaned out and called down to him in triumph. It was the audiovisual control booth, a room fitted out with sophisticated sound equipment—and, by happy chance, the hotel's stock of walkie-talkies. Whouley struck a deal to rent nineteen of them for $1,500, with the unspoken understanding that the control booth itself would be thrown in. The room was thus annexed to the Clinton campaign before any of his rivals knew it was there. Out of it, Whouley's crew would run two separate radio networks—one for the advance team steering the Clintons around the hotel, the other for the floor leaders in the hall.

The electronic edge, combined with some old-fashioned convention politicking, produced exactly the effect Clinton's stage managers wanted: the *appearance* of a big, vibrant, and probably unstoppable campaign. Nearly every delegate who signed up for Clinton was commissioned as a whip and given a hat and T-shirt appropriate to the rank. At points in the proceedings, whips would find themselves whipping other whips, but it worked. Claques of supporters greeted the Clintons wherever Whouley sent them; most of them were teenagers bussed in from Arkansas, but that worked, too. Goodies flowed as if from a cornucopia—stickers, fans, penlights, and, at a Saturday night delegate dinner, 2,000 Chinese fortune cookies containing the message BILL CLINTON'S GOING TO BE IN YOUR FUTURE.

Whouley's boys couldn't buy a happy ending, though they spent around $50,000 trying; the candidate had to perform, too, and when his team gathered in a small meeting room at the hotel to prep him for his speech to the convention, he looked off his game. He had wakened with a cold and a headache, and his mood was grumpy as his coaches swirled around him, pummeling him with talking points. When Greer finally got him to rehearse, his voice was hoarse and raspy, his manner tired.

"Put some emotion into it," Greer said. "So far, it sounds like a great policy speech."

"I'll lay plenty of emotion in," Clinton answered curtly. "I'm sorry, I can't give you any emotion now. I've only got enough emotion in this voice for one speech."

Hillary popped in with her own scouting report on the buzz in the hotel corridors. They already knew about the whispers, emanating from Harkin's camp, that Clinton was antilabor. In fact, Hillary said, it was worse than that.

"It's the whispering on jobs," she said. "It's not labor—it's *jobs.*"

The news touched an exposed nerve with Clinton. He had worked hard to bring jobs to Arkansas, he said heatedly, and people there knew it. Look at the steelworkers' union: they were supporting him down home, even as their national leadership was trying to force them to support Harkin, and he wanted to say just that in his speech.

Greer interrupted. "Force" was too strong a word, he said. They needed something softer.

Clinton exploded. "Let's get tough!" he said. "It's a mistake to suck up to them. And don't pander, damn it! I'm going to pound the *crap* out of them on it. I think we ought to *kick* them."

"Throw the gauntlet down," Hillary echoed.

There was an awkward silence in the room.

"This is great for me," Clinton said finally, sounding a little contrite. "You guys get me pissed off. It's group therapy."

If so, it didn't help his performance much. His speech, the first on the card that Saturday morning, was flat, and so was the audience response. Harkin scored far higher on the applause meter with his Bush-bashing, and Kerrey was at his emotive best talking about how government could do for others what it had done for him in his own desperate hours. "There are lives at stake, *lives* at stake in this campaign," he said, with a passion verging on anger. The crowd fell dead silent—a stillness more powerful than applause.

But Clinton had the rest of the day to recover any ground he had lost, and he did. He and Hillary dashed separately from caucus to caucus, occasionally passing one another on the escalators and trading messages in their own verbal shorthand. They were brilliantly received practically everywhere. The black caucus gave Clinton a standing ovation. The women's caucus, made wary by rumors that he was soft on the abortion question, wound up mostly in his corner.

By the end of the day, he had the straw poll locked up, with nearly seven hundred sure votes in hand; all that was left for Whouley and his crew on Sunday morning was to move two computers into their skybox overlooking the hall and tot up the final score. They watched the numbers popping on-screen. A lot of delegates had got an early start home, but of those who stayed to vote, Clinton got 54 percent, to Harkin's 31 and Kerrey's meager 10.

Whouley smiled the smile of the director on opening night of a hit musical, soaking up the applause from a seat in the back of the house. The events unfolding before him were meaningless in real terms, as insubstantial as shadows on a wall. But in the politics of our time, reality was in the eye of a professional class of beholders, and victory belonged to those masters of illusion who framed reality for them. The news out of Orlando was that Clinton had won, and if the resulting headlines had no negotiable value, it didn't matter. What mattered was that he *looked* like a winner in a game where appearances are everything; the show in Orlando confirmed his arrival at the head of the pack.

7.

The Scent of a Woman

Dee Dee Myers was at her desk at headquarters in Little Rock one Thursday in mid-January, fielding a call from a reporter, when the first small chunk of sky fell on Bill Clinton. An assistant had just brought over a note, and Myers, the governor's pert young press secretary, scanned it as unhappily as if it said the biopsy had come up positive.

"Uh oh," she said, reading aloud to herself. "'*Star* magazine links BC with five women.' I'd better kill this."

It was the moment Clinton's people had dreaded from the beginning: the whispers about Clinton's supposed sexual athletics had escalated from vague rumor to cold print, with names, times, and places attached. The *Star* exposé, when they saw it, was not itself the stuff of their bad dreams; it was a rehash of the old Larry Nichols case, the lawsuit brought by a state employee who claimed to have been fired because he knew too much about the governor's womanizing. His accusations and his list of Bill's girls had melted under scrutiny when he first filed the suit, and their revival in a lurid supermarket scandal sheet did little to heighten their credibility. For forty-eight hours, Myers thought she actually *could* kill the story, or at least contain it. She hit the phones, and so did Stephanopoulos, on the road with the candidate. In a day's frantic pleading for sanity, they managed to talk the major networks and the mainstream pencil press into spiking the allegations.

But another media food chain was forming around them, one they hadn't anticipated and were powerless to stop. The story squirted from the bottom-feeding *Star* onto Fox Television's evening newscasts that night and from there to the raunchier big-city tabloid dailies the next day. Their interest in turn attracted the attention of the respectable media, and their loud headlines—WILD BILL, shrieked the *New York Post*—made useful visuals for even the more sober-sided TV newscasts; they could hardly be blamed for showing how badly the penny press was behaving. The story of the story had *become* the story, a way for more fastidious editors and producers to publish all the juicy details without dirtying their own hands. It had a certain legitimating effect as well on further inquiries into Clinton's past. In short order, serious reporters who had once occupied themselves setting down his views on public policy were asking about his sex life instead.

The first of them were waiting for Clinton when his small campaign plane touched down in Boston for a fund-raiser that day. Stephanopoulos held him back while the three reporters aboard got off, then told him that the *Star* was about to publish some sort of sex story. The campaign hadn't seen it yet and didn't know exactly what was in it. Neither did the reporters waiting in ambush on the tarmac, or at the fund-raiser, or at Clinton's next port of call in New Hampshire later in the day. But that didn't stop them from raising questions or Clinton from denying all. When a local anchorperson in Manchester asked if he had ever committed adultery, his eyes widened. "If I had," he said, "I wouldn't tell *you*."

As the frenzy built, Clinton's first impulse was to walk through it and even to joke about it; maybe all those reporters who had been so enamored of him till then, he said, were having an attack of "buyer's remorse." At a rally in Bedford, New Hampshire, two nights later, he did a hoarse but spirited run through his stump speech, then opened the floor to questions. A woman got up and said she had one for Hillary, who was in the house. Wasn't a candidate's fidelity to his wife a relevant issue for voters to ask about?

Hillary never flinched. If she had one fear in the campaign, intimates knew, it was that Bill might let *both* of them down. Her confidence in herself was another matter. She and her husband had known from the first, she said, that they would be hit with accusations—the kind that appear in tabloids next to the stories about people born with cow's heads. "From my perspective," she said, "our marriage is a strong marriage. We love each other, we support each other, and we have had a lot of strong and important experiences together that have meant a lot to us." Sure, "issues" had come up between them, as they did in any marriage. But they were nobody else's business; there had to be some "realm of protection" from public gaze. "Is anything about our marriage as important to the people of New Hampshire as whether or not they will have a chance to keep their own families together—"

The rest of her answer was lost in an explosion of cheers. In the back of the hall, James Carville whooped and clapped his hands; Hillary, he thought, had just knocked the ball out of the park. Afterward, she and Bill retreated to their room. An aide who dropped in on them found them giggling like two kids on a date. They sent out for Greek food, watched in-room movies on television, and waited for the next day, hoping it would be better.

It wasn't. Clinton skated through his schedule easily enough, but on a televised debate on Station WMUR in Manchester that night, the moderator, Cokie Roberts of ABC News, asked each of the candidates to speak to his most talked-about vulnerability. When she got to Clinton, he was composing his answer to the widely heard charge that he wasn't tough enough to stand up to the traditional Democratic interest groups. Instead, Roberts asked him about the rumors of his philandering. He managed to ad-lib a vigorous-sounding response, denouncing the gossip and blaming the Republicans for spreading it. The answer pleased his handlers, who believed as a matter of tradecraft that the best defense is a good offense. The question upset them. In seventy-two hours, the Bimbo Issue had oozed from the pages of a rag like the *Star*, as Clinton called it, into the respectable press and now into the formal discourse of presidential politics.

In public, Clinton put on his game face, which consisted, usually, of a nibbled underlip and a smile. "I want to be president because I think I can do the best job," he mused aloud that night at the Manchester airport, killing time till takeoff for New York. "But if it doesn't work out, I'm way ahead in life. Whatever happens, I'm going to be okay. Hillary and I have talked through this whole thing exhaustively. I knew they would try to do this; it's flattering that they think I'm gonna win, I guess. They don't think they can beat me on the issues." If the press was overplaying the whole thing, so be it; he couldn't control that. "Whatever the rules are," he said, "I'll play the hand I'm dealt."

Still, beneath his public calm, there was about him the air of a man silently cursing the fall of the cards. The *Star* story had been relatively easy to deal with, given its seedy origins; he had only to attack his attackers to blow it away. But he knew he and Hillary hadn't snuffed the issue—hell no, he said. It was a fair bet that there would be more sex stories, and Clinton resisted any suggestion that he try to preempt them by addressing the issue head-on, saying straight out whether he had or hadn't cheated on his wife. He found it hard to give simple, direct answers to questions that touched on his private life—so hard that his own people were still flying blind through the haze of his past.

In fact, he had ample ground to believe, or fear, that more bedroom slippers would soon be dropping. The campaign had sound intelligence that *those people*—Clinton's blanket term for the scandal sheets, the tabloid TV shows, and the Republicans—were down home offering women money to say he had bedded them. They were working Nichols's list, and other women as well. One of the latter, a single mother in Arkansas, had called Clinton's office in tears to report just such an offer. "You're trying to raise your kids," a stranger had told her. "We can make it a lot easier on you."

But the quarry the *Star* seemed to be stalking most avidly was Gennifer Flowers, an underwhelmingly talented lounge singer who, with Clinton's help, had got herself a day job on the Arkansas state payroll. She had been mentioned in Nichols's lawsuit, and while she had denied all at the time, the boys from the tabloids were chasing her with an offer she finally couldn't refuse. In January, a woman had called the campaign to report that two men with British accents had approached her, looking for Flowers. They said they worked for the *Star.* She gave them Flowers's number, then phoned in the alarm. Not long thereafter, Flowers herself had rung up Clinton. She had said, as he would recount it afterward, that she had been offered fifty grand and a job in Los Angeles—the whole nine yards—to say they had had an affair. "She said, 'I asked them if it had to be true,'" Clinton remembered, "and they said, 'Hell, no. Don't you know the press? They'll run *anything.*'"

She seemed safely on board. But a week after the first *Star* story appeared, the campaign was tipped by friends in the press that a second was about to pop—a kiss-and-tell tale with corroborating evidence. The word reached Clinton in Washington, where he had done yet another cattle show before a national mayors' conference. It was nearly midnight when he and Bruce Lindsey got to a bank of pay phones outside the meeting room and began a frantic canvass to see what the *Star* had this time. They learned little beyond a single, ominous fact: Gennifer Flowers had vanished and nobody knew where she was.

That night, Clinton told Hillary that a new and potentially more damaging story was about to land on them. The next morning, the campaign principals hit the phones in their various bunkers for their daily eight o'clock conference call. Their mood was self-congratulatory. A new public poll confirmed what their own surveys were showing, that Clinton was holding onto the lead in New Hampshire; the sex story had done minimal damage. The money, too, was looking good. The total raised to date would pass $4 million that day, Rahm Emanuel reported, and that didn't include federal matching funds. By primary day, he said, "we'll put $6 million in their hands."

But the bad news soon eclipsed the good. At eleven o'clock, a fuzzy photocopy of the *Star's* next edition rolled out of the fax at headquarters in Little Rock. MY 12-YEAR AFFAIR WITH BILL CLINTON, the headline shouted, PLUS THE SECRET LOVE TAPES THAT PROVE IT! Inside, the mystery of Flowers's disappearance was solved: she had been at the *Star*'s offices in the New York suburbs for several days talking, for a price that had ballooned to six figures. What she had said was scorching—that over the long course of their liaison, Clinton had been fond of jogging over to her place for bouts of energetic lovemaking; that he had once begged her to have sex with him in the men's room at the governor's mansion while his wife was around but not looking; that he had talked about leaving Hillary for her but had decided not to, because a divorce would hurt his political career. Flowers had, moreover, taken to taping their phone conversations— "to protect myself," she said—and had apparently caught the governor in a number of indiscretions. The most damaging, in the *Star*'s recounting, had the sound of a cover-up being born. "If they ever hit you with it," Clinton was alleged to have told her, "just say no and go on. . . . If everybody is on record denying it . . . no problem."

Dee Dee Myers handed a copy of the spread to David Wilhelm, the campaign manager. They began reading.

"This is devastating," Myers said finally, breaking the glum silence. The story was bad enough. The tapes made it worse. They didn't directly confirm Flowers's account, but her conversations with Clinton had obviously been pretty chummy, and they had an authentic feel. One quoted him on the advantage to Bob Kerrey of being single: "Nobody cares who he's screwing." To the staff, that sounded just like Clinton talking.

Wilhelm reached for the phone and rang New Hampshire headquarters. Clinton and his traveling party weren't there; they had abruptly pulled off the road and holed up in a twelfth-floor hotel room in Manchester, trying to figure out what to do. Wilhelm got Mitchell Schwartz, the state campaign director, instead. Schwartz sounded as if he had been run over by a truck.

Next, Wilhelm phoned Frank Greer.

"Our smoking bimbo has emerged," he said. "It's Gennifer Flowers."

Alarm spread at headquarters. Phones rang constantly. Wilhelm found himself juggling two and three conversations at once. The national party chairman, Ron Brown, checked in from Washington, fearful that they had another Gary Hart fiasco on their hands; he wanted to know how Clinton was going to handle it. Wilhelm tried to sound reassuring, without notable succcess. Staffers crowded into his office, looking for comfort. Some of them had served with Hart and were in deep déjà-vu; the final days with Gary, one of them was thinking, were just like this. "As long as Clinton is telling the truth, we'll be okay," Myers said, trying to stay calm. "It's just going to take us a week to dig out." But her wishful thinking bumped into the secret suspicion, widely shared in the campaign, that some of the rumors about the governor were true and that the Flowers story might just be one of them. Without knowing the answer, the command group moved into its crisis mode, contacting its scattered advisers around the country. Frank Greer called back, this time with Stan Greenberg, the polltaker, on the line.

"What's Bill's reaction?" Greer asked.

The governor acknowledged that he had talked to Flowers, Wilhelm said, but denied that they had had an affair.

The tapes bothered Greenberg. "Why was he talking to her?" he asked sharply.

She had been calling *him*, Wilhelm said. She was distraught about the allegations involving her, so Clinton maintained, and he had only been trying to calm her down.

"Those things sound very damaging to me," Greenberg said.

Greer didn't think so—not if they were put in the proper context.

Greenberg cut him off. The tale of the tapes, he said, was very troubling.

A young press aide, Steve Cohen, popped in. Ted Koppel had offered to put Clinton on his late-evening show *Nightline* that night to answer the charges. The command group liked the idea at first, but weren't sure what Clinton should say or whether to send Hillary on with him.

"I'm not sure it's worth escalating to that point," Greer said.

"Who are we kidding, guys?" Myers said. "This is full-scale nuclear war."

It was a war waged in the first hours without its commander in chief and some of its general staff; they were still effectively incommunicado. Headquarters had faxed the story to their hotel, and at a point during the morning, Clinton called Hillary from an airport pay phone in Manchester to brief her on the allegations. Then he and his party set out in the sleet and snow to do an event in Claremont, a three-hour drive away. For most of the ride, he buried himself in a copy of *Lincoln on Leadership*, saying little. He seemed, as sometimes happened, to have withdrawn inside himself.

While he tuned out, his handlers found themselves in a daylong debate as to whether the *Nightline* booking was such a good idea after all. For most of that time, Wilhelm led the charge for Clinton's going on and doing a "sinners repent" appearance on the show—something more direct than his past allusions to having had unnamed "problems" in his marriage. "*Do* it is my strong recommendation," he told the road party. The story could be ruinous if they tried to tough it out.

But Carville, on tour with the candidate, had been against the *Nightline* date from the start. For one thing, he said, Clinton wasn't ready, physically or psychologically, to go rushing into any high-pressure, high-stakes TV interview when they didn't even know how the story was going to play in the legitimate media. There was, moreover, the awkward issue of exactly what it was he could say. He had already denied having slept with any of the five women in the first *Star* article, including Flowers; he could hardly backtrack now, tapes or no tapes. When he had first briefed Hillary by phone on the new story, she had told him, "Let's just go for it. Tell them the truth and get this off our backs." The problem was that his own team hadn't had the brass to ask him what the truth was—not till Carville finally put the question to him.

The *Star* was wrong, Clinton insisted. He told Carville that he hadn't had intercourse with Flowers, using the common vernacular verb. The reply, on close inspection, did not exhaust all the varieties of sexual activity available to them. Was Clinton really denying all, or was he ducking once again behind a narrow legalism? His staff would never know; they could only go forward on his word that Flowers's story, as told, was "not true."

They finally decided against the *Nightline* date, pleading bad weather in New Hampshire as an excuse. In fact, Clinton was too tired and harried to go on, and Hillary, weary of all the dithering, had decided on her own to stay in Atlanta. As their surrogate, Little Rock offered up Greer's newly recruited partner Mandy Grunwald, a tough, smart, profane woman described by one acquaintance as Lee Atwater in a Chanel suit. She lived up to her notices that night, turning the attack back on Koppel for dignifying trash-for-cash journalism with serious attention. Even he got defensive, and the question of what Clinton might actually have done to, for, or with Gennifer Flowers somehow got lost in the noise.

Both Clintons were well pleased with Grunwald's performance. But she had only bought them a day or two at most, and Clinton's people knew it. The Flowers story was starting up the now-established chain from the supermarkets to the networks, and the British scandal sheets were said to be offering up to $500,000 for more Bill-and-me confessions. At least, Clinton joked, trying to cheer his people, he was driving up the cost of sleaze. At worst, it went without saying, he could be dragged under by it; the press and the party insiders were already composing Clinton's political obituary. "If we don't turn this into a positive," Carville's partner, Paul Begala, warned that night, "we're going down."

They were still rehearsing lines and sorting invitations from the talk shows when Don Hewitt, the producer of *60 Minutes*, offered the Clintons a truncated prime-time edition right after the pro-football Super Bowl. Clinton had doubts about the offer and spent what one senior hand called a goosey day in Little Rock thinking about it; neither he nor Hillary was disposed to go beyond what they had already said on the subject. But Carville, this time, argued vehemently for accepting the invitation. "Do we really not think that, by October, the entire American public will have heard of this?" he said in one conference call, sweeping reservations aside. The problem wouldn't go away. It was best to confront it now.

If Clinton needed evidence, he found it waiting for him at the Little Rock airport at daybreak the morning he returned to the road. As he got out of his car, a woman TV reporter poked a mike in his face and told him—incorrectly, as it turned out—that the next week's *Star* would allege that he and Flowers had done cocaine together. Would he care to comment?

Clinton paused for a moment, looking as if he had just taken a punch to the solar plexus. When he spoke, his tone was soft and deliberate. "I have never used cocaine in my life," he said. "*Ever.*"

A few minutes later, settling into his seat on the charter plane, he muttered, "Boy, I *hope* she said that, because anyone who knows me knows that is totally untrue."

"But you're dealing with people who don't know you," Bruce Lindsey, his seatmate on the morning's flight to Washington and Boston, told him.

"That's okay," Clinton said. "They'll come after her on this. It will come out all right."

He fell into a moody silence, trying to focus on the speeches he was to give that morning. He couldn't. The scandal had broken his concentration and his stride. For all he knew then, his life in politics could be ending.

"If this is it, I'm not through," he told Lindsey after a time. "But we've got to find out if that's it."

More packs of reporters were waiting for him on the ground in Washington and Boston, with sex much on their minds. Clinton flogged himself from one media mob scene to another, wearing his calm like a mask. His speeches were drowned out by the din; as Gary Hart before him had discovered, it was hard to talk public policy in a hurricane.

What was plain was that the story wouldn't go away, and Carville used the moment to attack Clinton's last hesitancy about going on *60 Minutes*. At Logan Airport, they picked up a copy of the *Boston Globe*. There was a leaked story from an unnamed senior aide to the effect that Clinton would indeed appear on the show and would confront the infidelity question head on. Clinton glanced at the headline, plainly irritated. "That's the danger of going on *60 Minutes*," he said, "because the legitimate press will use it." It would be a kind of hunting license, a justification for raking up all the other rumors about him.

But the media frenzy was already out of control, and if Clinton didn't take his case strongly to the people, Carville told him, it was over. "Governor," he said, "there were fifty reporters in Washington. Most of them were not there because you were going on *60 Minutes*."

"I can't keep responding to a new story each week," Clinton said.

Carville and Stephanopoulos agreed; all the more reason, they said, to try to quash this one now.

"But how can I get to that point?" Clinton asked.

Do *60 Minutes*, Carville said, and then shut up. Tell the press, "I'm not responding, I'm not responding," until they tire of the pursuit.

Carville had finally won his point. But when he wakened in his ninth-floor room at the Ritz Carlton at six o'clock that Sunday morning, he felt overcome by embarrassment for the Clintons, having to discuss their marriage on national television. He started to weep and couldn't stop for a half-hour. The other senior hands drifted into his room for a prep session, and then Hillary, beating her husband by a half-hour. While they waited, the group peppered her with questions. She talked about how important her family was to her, and soon, *everybody* was weeping, herself included; she was very worried, she said, that she would cry on TV.

Then Clinton came in, looking composed and ready. Neither he nor Hillary wanted the usual coaching; he simply outlined what they were prepared to say, and that was that. None of his people raised the question of whether he would or should explicitly confess having committed adultery. They did some skittering around the subject, but no one wanted to touch it.

Finally, they all descended to the third-floor room where the interview was to be taped, and the Clintons took their places, sitting together next to a fire. The heat quickly intensified. "Who is Gennifer Flowers?" the interviewer, Steve Kroft, began. "You know her."

"Oh, yes," Clinton replied.

"How do you know her?" Kroft pressed. "How would you describe your relationship?"

"Very limited," Clinton said. He and Hillary went through their repertoire of prepared lines about loving one another, caring deeply about their daughter, and sticking by their marriage through the bad times as well as the good. Kneeling off-camera, Don Hewitt twice begged Clinton to confess to adultery. Twice, Clinton declined; it was enough, in his view and Hillary's, to say that there had been "problems" between them and to assume that, in the context, everybody would know what they were talking about. At the close, Kroft asked Clinton why he wanted to be president. His answer was powerful and emotional, a homily on his calling to change people's lives. Once again, in the control room, Carville was weeping.

Aboard the Gulfstream jet on the flight back to Little Rock, the mood was ebullient to the point of giddiness. There was an undercurrent of suspense about how the show would play, but Clinton and his traveling companions were pleased with his performance, and Hewitt had assured them that it had been great television. "The last time I did something this important was the Kennedy-Nixon debate," he had said, "and I like to think we helped create a president. I'd like to think we'll do it again."

On the ground, Clinton had asked Carville if he played hearts, his own favorite card game.

"Better than you'll ever hope to," Carville had replied with a sly grin, and once the flight got airborne, they sat down to a game.

Carville's mood, already playful, was further brightened by an occasional splash of bourbon from a bottle he had smuggled aboard. At one point, he threw down a low card and tried to claim a trick without anybody noticing. Clinton, who missed nothing, caught him. Carville shrugged and grinned again.

"I just like to be in charge," he said.

They dealt another hand, and then another. As always, Clinton played to win, relying on that all-or-nothing strategy known in the game as shooting the moon. If it worked, you scored big-time. If it didn't, you lost badly.

"We may go down," Carville guessed after a while, "but at least this thing is behind us."

Clinton agreed, sort of; they hadn't seen the show yet. "This thing could go down like a turd in a punch bowl," he said.

The jet touched down a few minutes before air time. Carville and Stephanopoulos headed reflexively for headquarters. The high of the plane ride was giving way to anxiety again.

"Our lives are in the hands of a bunch of editors," Carville said.

"James, we've done all we can," Stephanopoulos replied.

Their worst fears were realized, at least in Clinton's eyes. He had taken his limousine home to the mansion to be with Hillary and Chelsea and had watched the show in rising fury. Their deal with CBS, as he understood it, was that they would be on for fifteen to eighteen minutes, and that the interview would touch on other aspects of the campaign, not just the scandal. But the version forty million Americans saw was only eleven minutes long, and it was all personal. The parts he had thought strongest had been left on the cutting-room floor. That closing answer on why he was running, for example—even the TV crewmen were gasping, it was so impassioned, he said, but it had never got on the air.

Clinton went to bed that night so angry he could barely sleep, and when his people came by for him early the next morning, he was still steaming. "It was a screw job," he said, en route to Jackson, Mississippi, in his small campaign jet. "They lied about how long it was going to be. They lied about what was going to be discussed. They lied about what the ending would be. It couldn't have been worse if they had drawn black X's through our faces."

Carville felt his hopes for a turnaround melting away. "There are going to be a hundred cameras in Jackson," he said glumly, and it was going to get worse, not better; Gennifer Flowers would be holding her own televised press conference, live from New York, on CNN that afternoon.

Her show at the Waldorf-Astoria was extraordinary even by the standards of the tabloid era in political journalism. The woman scorned, posed before a blowup of her *Star* cover, wore a crimson ensemble and a pouty, heavy-lidded gaze. The press gallery, one of the largest of the season, bombarded her with such questions of moment as whether Clinton had used a condom during their sporting moments together. Clinton heard parts of the event over a car radio en route from Mississippi to Louisiana for a speech at the state capitol. Hillary, campaigning in South Dakota, tracked him there, and he slipped into a legislator's office to take her call. She was furious at CNN's live coverage of the event, and she wanted to fight back.

Carville was disposed to agree, once he had seen the evening newscasts. Two of them, CBS and ABC, led with Flowers and played segments of her tapes without verifying them; there was reasonable ground to suspect that they had been doctored. The story was turning into "the crack cocaine of journalism," Carville thought; everybody in the press wanted to get off on it, and the campaign as a serious enterprise addressing serious issues was getting lost in the smoke.

That evening, while Clinton did a fund-raiser at the home of one of the Longs of Louisiana, Carville slipped into a bedroom looking for a phone. He plunked down on the bed, a solitary figure amid the opulence, and rang Mandy Grunwald in Washington.

"I think we're going to have to go to war," he said. "The problem with going to the mat on this is it's five days our message gets killed. But I think we're going to have to go all out."

A counteroffensive was mobilized, with Carville out front leading the charge, and the campaign seemed briefly to be stabilizing. One public survey, in the *Boston Globe,* showed Clinton leading Paul Tsongas by sixteen points. Another, on ABC, suggested strongly that America was Gennifered out; huge majorities thought the media had said enough about the Flowers affair and should quit poking around in the private lives of the candidates anyway.

Clinton was jubilant when he heard the numbers at an air terminal in New Orleans; he high-fived Dee Dee Myers and pumped his fist in the air. But when Hillary came on the line from South Dakota during a four-city conference call, she took him down a peg, scolding him for his taped conversations with Gennifer. It wasn't the borderline intimacy of the calls that troubled her, not in the thick of the campaign. It was instead her husband's carelessness; she instructed him half-teasingly that he would have to kick his habit of eating, watching TV, working a crossword puzzle, and talking on the phone all at the same time.

Clinton's problems were in fact much deeper than his telephone manner. His opening to the nomination depended on his showing in New Hampshire; if he didn't run at least a strong second there, his strategists thought, it would be an invitation to somebody else—a Cuomo, say, or a Dick Gephardt, or a Lloyd Bentsen—to jump into the race to save the Democracy from another Black November. He had started late there and for a time had seemed mired in fourth place.

But as his numbers began to move up, his strategy team had caucused in Little Rock between Christmas and New Year's and had decided to escalate from a token run at New Hampshire to an all-out war to win. Soon after the turn of the year, they put up a deliberately minimalist Frank Greer ad, with Clinton talking earnestly into the camera for sixty seconds about how he had a comprehensive plan for the economy. Its objective was to "put government back on the side of the forgotten middle class." He had invited voters to read it themselves, and the campaign had circulated copies to every library in the state. The mere fact that you could find it in so institutional a setting was itself a kind of validation; if it was in the library, it must be real.

The ad would prove one of the most powerful of the season. It had helped propel Clinton into first place within a week, and his lead had been solidifying nicely till Gennifer came along. Before she talked, Clinton's state coordinator, Mitchell Schwartz, had been privately predicting victory by fifteen points or better. Afterward, Stan Greenberg's polling for the campaign showed Clinton ahead by only five. There were, moreover, disturbing undercurrents in the focus groups Greenberg doted on—questions about Clinton's strength, honesty, and family values.

"You realize if this hadn't happened," Greenberg told Clinton when he delivered the numbers, "we would have won by a landslide."

He still thought then that they *would* win, and the overall vital signs seemed to support his guarded optimism. Money and endorsements still flowed to the governor wherever he went. His campaign treasury gave him a safety net that none of his rivals could match, and his ground operations in the key states, while never quite as strong as their notices, were still the envy of the field. He had bought himself some breathing room in a private sitdown with Ron Brown in Washington, reassuring him that the worst was over; there would be no more embarrassments to him or the party.

But there was a nearly surreal dissonance between the apparent prosperity of the campaign and the siege mentality setting in among Clinton's inner circle. What most of America knew about him was that he might or might not have slept with Gennifer Flowers, a question he had not directly answered on *60 Minutes*. If he couldn't somehow make himself heard on the issues that had got him where he was, he and his high ambitions could come crashing back to earth.

The WYSIWYG Factor

For Democrats in the election business, it was panic time, a season aflame with memories of Gary Hart and reawakened fantasies of a young Lochinvar riding out of the West—or an old Lochinvar from the East, North, or South, for all anybody cared—to come to the aid of the party. A couple of days after the Flowers story broke, two well-seasoned young consultants, Joe Trippi and Paul Maslin, sat nursing beers after work at a planning retreat for a Senate candidate in Oregon and stared into what looked like a looming disaster for the whole Democratic ticket—one that could drag down their state and congressional clients in the fall. Maslin, a pollster without a horse in the presidential derby, ventured at first that Clinton could probably survive the scandal and win the nomination, for whatever it would be worth.

Trippi, an ad man, had got hold of copies of the Bill-and-Gennifer editions of the New York daily tabloids. He shoved them across the barroom table.

Maslin hadn't seen them. He scanned their loud headlines. His face reddened under his usual clinical mask. He got up and excused himself to go look for a phone.

"We've got to get Gephardt into the race," he said.

All of a sudden, the hunting season was on, and the cadre of office-holders, consultants, lobbyists, fund-raisers, and headquarters appa-ratchiki who make up the permanent Democratic Party were looking furiously for a hero. It was a measure of their desperation that the numbers they most frequently rang belonged to men of Washington—Hill people like Dick Gephardt, Lloyd Bentsen, Bill Bradley, and Sam Nunn. The petitioners knew that the weather was not favorable to insiders; Maslin himself had only just spoken eloquently at the retreat about how the feelings of ordinary Americans about their government had moved past anger to an even more corrosive despair. But the hour was late and the hunger strong in the party for a tested major-leaguer—somebody bright, clean, experienced, and uncontroversial who under-stood the rules of play.

Suddenly, the background music in the Democratic quarters of Washington was the susurrous whisper of Rolodex cards and the Chic-let click of Touch-Tone phones—the sounds of a party seeking deliv-erance from its sixth defeat in its last seven tries at the presidency. Hope sprang in odd places, like wildflowers poking through the rubble on a demolition site. A draft-Cuomo headquarters opened in a second-floor walk-up in Concord, New Hampshire, trying to rekindle a dead fire; the governor did not actively encourage the effort, but he seemed, as usual, to enjoy the attention. In the Senate, relays of petitioners found their way to Bentsen, a man much admired in the capital for his courtly bearing, his worldly wisdom, and his scene-stealing turn as Michael Dukakis's running mate in 1988. Even the fact that he was then pushing seventy-one had a certain attraction; his age certified that he was a grown-up with hormones presumably under control.

But it was Dick Gephardt who excited the most vivid rescue fanta-sies, particularly among his colleagues in the lower house and their retinue of aides, consultants, and lobbyists. It mattered little that his last try for the nomination, in 1988, had run out of gas and money in the early going, or that he was probably best remembered as that guy with no eyebrows among the seven Wonder Bread candidates contend-ing for the prize. The Federal City had long since rationalized his failure; it was widely accepted, more on faith than on evidence, that you rarely won on your first try anyway and that losing was therefore good for you.

Gephardt had redeemed himself, at least within the Beltway, in his new role as majority leader. He seemed to understand better than Tom Foley, the speaker, or George Mitchell, the Senate Democratic leader, that the function of an opposition party on issues of principle is not to accommodate but to oppose. His friends in Congress, the core of his 1988 campaign, seemed ready to support him again. One said excitedly that there were fifty more like himself, prepared to mount a draft movement at the merest nod from Gephardt.

The thought had in fact occurred to Gephardt during the summer of 1991. He had seemed, on his election as leader two years earlier, to have renounced any plan to run for the presidency soon again. But people who knew him well sensed the onset of what one called a mini-midlife crisis—a feeling that he had spent twenty years in politics working his way up to a job that seemed suddenly to be suffocating him. He had been hit hard emotionally, friends said, by the successive resignations of two friends and colleagues in the leadership, Tony Coelho of California and Bill Gray of Pennsylvania. Each had got entangled in official investigations. Each had tired of the guff and had walked away, giving up once bright futures on the Hill to return to the private sector; Coelho was making money on Wall Street, and Gray was storing up good works as head of the United Negro College Fund.

Gephardt seemed to colleagues to envy them their liberation and to feel marooned where he was in a life he didn't like. He had tasted the headier wine of presidential politics; then he had been cast back to Congress, a second banana again, waiting for Speaker Foley to retire or die. Hating one's job wasn't exactly a great rationale for a presidential candidacy, a friend said; if it were, 200 million Americans would probably be chasing one another around New Hampshire with position papers and bumper strips. Still, Gephardt was tempted; in July, he sent a staffer on a covert mission to Iowa to scout the terrain.

But by the time a new wave of suitors arrived at his doorsill in January, he appeared to have got over his brown study—or at least whatever illusion he had had that there was a chance for him to succeed. It would be widely published during the winter that he had ordered up staff studies of how he could jump in late and steal the nomination. In fact, what he asked for was an analysis of why it *couldn't* be done: too many filing deadlines had elapsed and too few delegates were left to be won. The coauthor of the white paper, Bill Carrick, who had managed Gephardt in '88, called it the This-Is-Impossible memo, which was precisely his understanding of his commission. Gephardt wasn't running; he just wanted something authoritative he could show around to the suitors who thought they were his friends.

There would be further supplications down the road, to Gephardt and others; long after the issue was settled, the fantasists of the Democracy were still spinning daydreams of an "open convention" that would save them all from what seemed certain doom if Clinton—or any of the other active candidates—should win the nomination. In fact, the this-is-impossible memo had it right. A generation of reforms, intended to democratize the process, had rigged it instead in favor of the candidate who started early and raised the most money. A latecomer declaring in January, 1992, would have had a hard time finding primaries to run in before early May; by then, more than half the delegates would have been bespoke, a commanding majority of them for Clinton.

The word in computerese for the party's situation was WYSIWYG: what you see is what you get. There was no hero waiting in the green room to go on and no script with what the frightened elders of the party would have considered a happy ending. The candidates already on-screen were what there was, and if Clinton didn't collapse under the weight of his problems, one of the others was somehow going to have to beat him.

Only Connect

It had become depressingly plain by then that Bob Kerrey was not what the power brokers of the Democracy had imagined him to be—not, anyway, in his maiden voyage in presidential politics. He seemed to some of his own people to be at sea on troubled waters; one of his senior strategists was telling colleagues privately during the days of the Cuomo Overhang that Kerrey wasn't ready—that if Mario did get in, maybe Bob should get out. His campaign wasn't ready either. His new management team was only just settling in, with less than two months left before the primaries began, and was discovering just how bad things were.

At age thirty-six, Tad Devine, the new boss, had been around the track before with Carter, Mondale, and Dukakis and had managed Lloyd Bentsen's vice-presidential campaign in 1988. But nothing had prepared him for what he saw when he moved into headquarters on K Street between the holidays to take over as Kerrey's campaign director. There were only a couple of television sets with lousy reception and no satellite dish to bring in CNN and C-SPAN; trying to run a

'90s-model campaign without all-day TV, Devine thought, would be like driving a car with his eyes closed. The office help picked up the phones sporadically during what most people think of as business hours and then went home, leaving a single answering machine to receive incoming calls. Devine ordered the machine unplugged, the tape destroyed, and the phones staffed nights and weekends. "We are closed when the campaign is done," he said.

He tried to set an example himself, in the manner of a stepfather who has just acquired a dysfunctional family. He showed up for work at seven in the morning, surprising the young volunteers clipping the day's papers; they didn't usually see the grown-ups on their early-bird watch. "I'm here," Devine told them, "and I'm not leaving. This is a campaign." He instituted a daily shape-up meeting of the mid-to-senior staff at 8:30 A.M. and often ran planning sessions on Sunday, underscoring his wish that the operation go on a seven-day week.

Devine was unhappy with the ad strategy in place, and he moved swiftly to replace his inherited media man, Joe Rothstein, with a pricey new pair of consultants, David Doak and Robert Shrum. Kerrey resisted at first, but Devine was making it a him-or-me proposition; if the senator sided with his old pal, he would have to find a new manager—his third—on the very eve of the primary season.

"Look," Devine told Kerrey late one night, forcing the issue, "those kids in New Hampshire are working hard. They're doing the job. They need some air cover."

"Where'd you learn *that?*" Kerrey asked.

"Not from the same place you did," Devine said. "But I know you get it."

In the end, he prevailed, and Doak and Shrum got the account. Within a week, their first ad went up, a stark little monodrama on trade; it showed Kerrey posed in front of a hockey net, promising to "play a little defense" against the Japanese for a change. It seemed for a time to touch a nerve—the fear, visible in polls and focus groups, that America was not merely in a recession but in a scarier long-term economic decline and that Japan was rising to primacy. Its timing, moreover, could not have been luckier. The Friday night it went up, the network newscasts were showing footage of Bush throwing up at table at a state dinner in Tokyo, the low point in what was already a bad trip. In a single weekend, Kerrey's share of the vote moved up from single digits to 16 percent, good enough for third place and a claim to membership alongside Clinton and Tsongas in that mythic club known as The First Tier.

The problem was that he had no money for a sustained ad offensive or anything else important to a new-style campaign. Devine had been told when he signed on that they would go into the new year with $850,000 in the till, which sounded pretty good to him. But the campaign's books, when he peeked into them, were as indecipherable as hieroglyphics had been before the Rosetta stone. Devine sent for help in the person of Tony Corrado, a master of campaign finance who had abandoned the trenches to write and teach at Colby College in Maine.

"Come down for the weekend and tell me what we've got," Devine begged.

What they had, as Corrado quickly confirmed, was a mess—a book-keeping system so primitive that hundreds of thousands of dollars had been spent with no adequate accounting and for no discernible purpose. The nearest thing he could find to a budget memo allotted $1.7 million for January and February. The number was as real as Tinker Bell. The money wasn't there.

"Tad, you've got $250,000 at best," Corrado reported.

Devine's heart sank. He regarded New Hampshire as a media state, no matter how many times you read in the papers that it was a kind of Jurassic Park for old-fashioned, front-parlor politics; the whole thing came down to getting 40,000 people to vote for you, and the most efficient way to turn them out, in Devine's view, was television advertising. Fudging just a bit, he had told Doak and Shrum they had a million in the bank to play with. Now he had to call Shrum with the bad news.

"Shrum," he began, "you remember that million dollars I said we had?"

Shrum did, vividly.

"I thought I was lying to you by $200,000," Devine said. "Turns out I was lying by about $800,000."

"What are we going to do?" Shrum asked.

Devine knew what *he* was going to do for starters; he coaxed Corrado aboard full-time and put him to work cleaning up the mess. The picture improved, but the campaign had started too late and had made too little visible progress to persuade the money boys that Kerrey was any longer a good bet. By mid-January, Corrado submitted a *real* budget memo reckoning that, with all their patting and pruning, they would still come up $1.1 million short for the first two months of the new year. His tone on paper was clinically flat. His two-word summary to Devine was less guarded: "You're fucked."

It took some financial legerdemain and the power of prayer to keep Kerrey in business. Somehow, his team made it happen; Corrado juggled the bills, and the campaign somehow got a second ad up, this one with Kerrey on location in a hospital emergency room talking about national health insurance. The vagaries of lighting gave his face a ghastly greenish hue, and the senator, who was having a hard enough time getting comfortable with his new media wizards, hated the spot; he said it made him look like "Doctor Death." But health care was the hot issue of the season, and on the advice of his team, Kerrey ran with it, to a point where he sometimes seemed to be waging a one-note campaign.

The health issue had been compromised for him anyway by the disclosure early on that his own restaurant chain back in Nebraska provided coverage for only a smallish fraction of its workers. The campaign couldn't think of a good answer and so never offered one, relying instead on the vain hope that the complaint would go away. It didn't; at a focus group a month after the story hit print, people were still buzzing about it.

"He's the first guy to come up with health care," a man said.

"Yeah, but he doesn't give it to his workers," a middle-aged woman replied. She was for Clinton.

"Nine hundred employees, he doesn't give them health care," a man said.

The Flowers story had broken by then, but the pro-Clinton woman dismissed it as mud-slinging. "Clinton's not going around saying don't cheat on your wife," she said. "In my mind, it's not an issue. The Kerrey thing is."

Devine sat watching in dismay. *Kerrey's* got a character problem, he was thinking. His best single issue had become a negative for him, another cheap promise by another lying politician.

Nothing else seemed to be working for him either. Devine, with some trepidation, had arranged what the trade calls a come-to-Jesus meeting with Kerrey—a session of straight talk about unpleasant facts. They met in a hotel room around the corner from campaign headquarters so they could be alone. Devine had brought along a couple of discouraging new polls. "You're more than twenty points behind," he told the senator bluntly; the mini-surge had stalled out, and Kerrey was sliding backward into the second tier. Money, already scarce, would get scarcer. "If we pursue this aggressively, we will be a million dollars in debt," Devine said, and even then, success was far from guaranteed. The only hope he saw was to go negative against Clinton and try to drive down his numbers. They would have to pray that any votes they knocked loose would move to Kerrey, not somebody else.

To Devine's relief, Kerrey was prepared to go for it. He seemed serious about changing America, to a point where going after Clinton was not merely a matter of tactics. The Republicans would tear him up in the fall, Kerrey told Devine, and it would be a dereliction of their duty as Democrats not to make the case against his nomination. "Lives are at stake," Kerrey said. It was one of his own standard lines, but he seemed to Devine to believe it.

The attack strategy never got in motion; with the Flowers scandal breaking over Clinton, it seemed prudent to let his past destroy him without the senator's help. But Clinton didn't cooperate; on the contrary, his numbers kept rising, and Kerrey wasn't moving at all. A reporter spied Tad Devine rushing out of a campaign event one day and asked him what Kerrey had to do in New Hampshire. "*Connect,*" Devine answered, barely breaking stride. The press picked up the word, much to Devine's dismay and even more to Kerrey's; to him, as he complained in his van one day, "connecting" sounded less like politics than electrical engineering.

But it seemed to capture the distance between him and the voters—a distance he seemed unable to narrow even as he got better at the game. He was stuck back among the also-rans, and as he struggled for traction, the elders of his party, who had once invested great hope in him, began to look elsewhere for a savior. Clinton, in their eyes, was irreparably damaged goods. Tsongas was a nonstarter, a man afloat mainly because everybody else was sinking. Harkin was going nowhere. Brown was a bad joke. Wilder was gone, the first dropout, before the fight had fairly begun. And Kerrey? The mysterious alchemy of politics—or, more accurately, political perception—had taken the sometime golden boy and transmuted him into a loser.

Treading Water

While Kerrey started his slow descent beneath the waves, Paul Tsongas appeared to be barely treading water. The script he had worked out with his longtime friend and manager, Dennis Kanin, was not unlike Clinton's except for its leading man. The race, they believed, would cook down sooner or later to a replay of Mondale versus Hart in 1984, a matchup between an old and a new Democrat, and Tsongas hoped to use his early start to establish himself as Mister New.

The problem was getting the touts along the paddock rail to take him seriously. Back when he had been the only guy out there, his antistyle and his chutzpah had had a kind of curiosity value for the media; there were some not unflattering stories about his courage in speaking out against the old liberal theology of his party and in taking on George Bush when other men of larger reputation were cowering under their desks. But the novelty soon wore off, and with it, whatever faint glow he had managed to generate. The short attention of journalism wandered on to speculations about who else would enter the race and when. The resulting dope stories sometimes neglected even to mention Tsongas's name.

The whiteout in turn made it hard for him to attract money or operatives with combat ribbons in national politics; nobody wanted to work for or waste money on somebody who looked like a sure loser. Tsongas trekked on anyway with a confidence that had always been there and that seemed to intimates to have been reinforced by his having beaten the Big C. His previous campaigns, dating to his maiden run for city council in Lowell in 1969, had *always* been treated as jokes at the beginning, and he had won them all. His magic in his new incarnation was his conviction that he embodied a cause so large that, as his man Jesser guessed, he didn't give a fuck if he lost—not so long as he was heard.

In fact, he did want to win, and believed that he could, without quite knowing how. In the dog days of summer, his press secretary, Peggy Connolly, told him point-blank that she thought they were in some kind of black hole; nobody cared that he was running.

"We're going backwards," she said.

"This doesn't feel bad," he answered. There had been darker days in his Senate race, days when he'd thought seriously about folding his hand and walking away. "This feels *right*," he added. "I don't feel the same despair."

There wasn't much to support his calm, beyond the home-court advantage accruing to a candidate who lived within an hour's drive of a majority of the voters in New Hampshire and who understood the depth of their economic distress. As the field solidified in early autumn, a private poll there showed him out front, five points ahead of Kerrey and eighteen ahead of Clinton. His people faxed it around to the national press. The response was a stifled ho-hum. He was *supposed* to be winning New Hampshire; if he couldn't win there, his own people conceded, it would be fair to ask where he could.

Neither did it seem to count for much that he scored well in some of the early debates, waving his austere economic plan as a symbol of his independence and accusing his main rivals, Clinton and Kerrey, of taking *their* cues from ad men and pollsters. The new rap against him in the party and the press was that he was "unelectable," which mattered more, in the nature of things, than his claim to be new, different, thoughtful, and unencumbered by old ideologies or special-interest

IOUs. He and Niki had spent more days in the state than any of the others, doing coffees, town meetings, and Rotary dinners. Nobody noticed; at times, it *was* as if nobody cared.

His people knew by then that they would have to attack his vulnerabilities straight on. He couldn't really escape the Greek-from-Massachusetts problem, since that was what he was; all he could do was display his humanity and his sense of humor, hoping people would see for themselves that the only things he had in common with Dukakis were their MA postal code and their Attic bloodlines. But he himself had figured out a way to get at the question of his health—to show the world that, in Jesser's earthy words, he didn't look like a guy who was going to fucking die real soon. His inspiration came from his own regular workout routine: while his rivals were running for the presidency, he would swim for it.

Tsongas was a dedicated lap swimmer and an occasional competitor in meets for men over fifty, a club he had only recently joined. For some time, he had allowed news photographers and camera crews to shoot him doing his lengths in the pool; the pictures were his way of telling voters to forget about the waxy skin and the baggy eyes—he really was all right. The photo ops seemed to work on a retail basis, and Tsongas, in his running conversations with Kanin through the summer and fall, had proposed upping the ante—building his first TV spot around footage of him in the swim.

The costuming alone was a rarity in the history of political advertising: the candidate clad only in a pair of Speedo racing trunks a scant inch or so more modest than a bikini. The setting, in a lap pool, was similarly daring, given that the presidency was mostly a desk job. Even so loyal a soldier as Ed Jesser thought the ad was a dumb idea at first blush, and when he and Tubby Harrison, the campaign pollster, were summoned to a studio in Boston to look at the footage, he went prepared not to like it.

It wasn't until the tape rolled that he changed his mind. Tsongas's ad man, Michael Shea, had studied swim meets on television as part of his homework for the assignment and had noticed the visual power of the butterfly, the most taxing stroke of all. It wasn't Tsongas's favorite, but he could do it competently, and at Shea's suggestion, he did. The effect on Jesser and Harrison was electric. Tsongas was swimming directly at them, rising, sinking, rising again by sheer force of muscle and will. He looked so *powerful,* Jesser thought, headed right in your face like he was gonna swim through a fucking brick wall.

With the others kibitzing, Shea and his fellow media man, Fred Woods, picked the best five seconds, sprinkled in some old still photos and some language about "guts" and "swimming against the current," and got out the first ad of the primary season. It went up before Thanksgiving, against the tradition in politics that it was a mistake to start advertising too early. Kanin and his colleagues relied on a contrary premise: if you got your ad up first, you would have the tube all to yourself.

The strategy seemed to work for a time; a newspaper poll in early December showed Tsongas leading Bob Kerrey, then his closest active competitor, by twelve points in the horse race and by nearly twenty in favorable ratings. But the surge barely lasted out the holiday season. With Bush entering his long slide, the party at large, and the activists likeliest to vote in New Hampshire, were looking for somebody who could win, and little about Tsongas fit the standard criteria. Not even Clinton's struggles with the womanizing question seemed to help. Tsongas had to answer the equally deadly charge that he was a loser, and having a plan wasn't enough; in the early weeks of winter, his clippings were mainly about other people passing him in the polls.

The new front-runner was Clinton, and Tsongas's team saw the particular danger in his rise. They were two similarly inclined men auditioning for what Kanin had envisioned as the Gary Hart role in the unfolding melodrama—the outsider with new, postliberal ideas about reviving the economy and the psyche of America. They had hit it off when they first met in Washington during the summer, before Clinton was officially a candidate, and their mutual respect appeared to survive the early rounds of competition between them.

"Paul really seems to like Bill," Clinton's man Frank Greer told Kanin when the two campaigns crossed paths in Los Angeles in September.

"Yeah, he does," Kanin agreed.

Bill seemed to like Paul, too. "Why don't we get it over with now?" Greer ribbed Kanin when they met again later in New Hampshire. "Let's get them together as a ticket."

At the time, it was just a joke, but it quit being funny with the realization that each man was a threat to the other's chances. Tsongas did respect some parts of Clinton's platform—means testing for social security, a tougher line on welfare and domestic spending, measures to upgrade education. But he gagged on Clinton's proposal for a modest tax cut for the middle class as a gesture of fairness after the rich-get-richer policies of the Reagan-Bush years.

Tsongas guessed where Clinton was coming from; he had seen the same polls and attended the same party meetings about how the Democrats had to win back the middle class if they were ever to renew their lease on the White House. But you couldn't make polls or interest-group politics a basis for action. Kerrey had been doing that with his Japan-bashing and his one-note hammering on health care, Tsongas believed, and now came Clinton with his gimmicky little tax cut—ninety-seven cents a day for the average family. It seemed to Tsongas irresponsible to try to buy votes out of the federal treasury with the deficit already out of control, and he and his people decided to make an issue of it—an issue not merely of policy but of character and morality as well.

It was the only way in which Tsongas could be persuaded to join the gathering assault on Clinton's person. The Flowers affair ought to have destroyed the governor, if recent history was any guide, but he appeared to be limping through it and even, for a time, to be expanding his lead in the New Hampshire polls. Kanin and Jesser, in their frustration, wanted to use it. Tsongas refused. Character, in his view, could be adequately revealed in a candidate's programs and promises; you didn't have to get personal to show up a man of glib speech and weak will for what he was. His blunt instrument of choice instead was a tough ad on the Clinton tax cut. It opened with an up-from-under shot of ninety-seven cents tumbling onto a glass tabletop, looking, by design, like very small change. The voice-over amounted to an attack on Slick Willie without once having to mention Clinton's name. "Some candidates" were trading in cheap gimmicks and bigger deficits for political gain, the ad said, but not Paul Tsongas: "Paul Tsongas offers straight answers. . . . Paul Tsongas won't shortchange our future."

The spot was delayed by a long, internal soul-search as to whether or not it was wise to flout the usual rules by making so hard a case against a tax cut; it was one thing for Tsongas to talk about it in speeches and front parlors, where he could explain his opposition, and another to reduce his case to the simplicities of a thirty-second ad. The holdup proved fortuitous for Tsongas. The ad went on the air in early February, just as a second shoe was dropping on the Clinton campaign, and this time it wasn't a bedroom slipper. It was an army brogan—a style of shoe that Clinton had contrived never to have to wear.

The Fortunes of War

The wonder was that the Clinton campaign never saw it coming—not, at least, with the destructive force it carried. As a matter of prudence, their opposition-research shop had collected its own dossier on how Clinton had escaped the draft and the war in Vietnam in his college years, in case one of their rivals tried to make an issue of it. But they considered it a minor matter, in part because Clinton himself seemed so little concerned about it; the whole thing had been hashed over in his Arkansas campaigns, he said, and he had survived. When George Stephanopoulos worried aloud about its damage potential at a staff meeting late in December, the Clintons shushed him and changed the subject. No one, Hillary said, was going to get Bill to stop talking about how much he had opposed the war.

What none of them reckoned on was how the issue would grow and take fire under the burning lens to which the media had lately subjected the "character" of candidates for president. In broad outline, what it mainly proved was that Clinton was a man of his generation, or of that part of it sufficiently blessed by luck, flight, privilege, or student deferments to have avoided being called up and shipped to Vietnam. The roll of the fortunates was a long one, including such personages as the president's son George W. Bush; his vice president, Dan Quayle; and his secretary of defense, Dick Cheney. All had been of age to serve in the war. None had fought in it. But Clinton's escape had involved some occasionally fancy footwork, and so would his serial attempts to explain it. As he had in the matter of Gennifer, he sounded like a man trying to smooth-talk his way out of a scrape. It scarcely mattered whether his stories washed or not; he was entering the season of Slick Willie, and it would almost be his ruin.

He was campaigning in Manchester a bare twelve days before the New Hampshire primary when Jeffrey Birnbaum of the *Wall Street Journal* broke what would be the first in a flood of stories on how he had stayed out of uniform. The accounts would be various, the evidence confusing. The nub of the matter was that Clinton had been halfway through his two-year Rhodes program at Oxford when his local draft board started breathing heavily down his neck. He told the board that he would be going on to law school at the University of Arkansas when he finished his studies abroad and had arranged to join the ROTC program there, a legitimate alternative to active military duty. He got his fresh deferment and headed back to England in time for the new academic year. By his own account, he had barely got there when he had an attack of conscience about riding out the war as a student while people he had grown up with were dying. He had voluntarily put himself back in the draft, he said, and had expected to be called; he was spared only when a lottery system was instituted two months later, and he lucked out with a high number.

But the *Journal* produced two witnesses who gave the story a less innocent cast. One was the aged Republican secretary to his draft board, who claimed that Clinton had been given special treatment.

The other was the then head of the ROTC program, who said that Clinton's commitment to sign up had simply been a way to avoid the draft and that he had reneged on his promise. Neither had made such assertions in the past, a fact duly noted by Clinton in his encounters with the press that day. His answers seemed at first to satisfy the pack, and the campaign went ahead with plans to let the Clintons go home to Little Rock for a last weekend's rest before the homestretch. Only James Carville opposed the furlough, and not even he had the heart to make a fight of it. Clinton had been feeling fluish all winter, his nose red and runny, his voice reduced to a wheezy croak. It was hard to argue that he didn't need the downtime.

His team imagined at the time that the whole storm would blow over in a day. Their confidence was reinforced when Stan Greenberg, the polltaker, convened two more of the focus groups on which he and the campaign relied almost to the point of religious belief. The sessions started with a videotape of Clinton taking softball questions on the draft from a TV interviewer and knocking one after another out of the park. Greenberg and Frank Greer sat in a dark, cramped observation booth, watching anxiously through a one-way mirror. Around them, untouched Chinese carryout dinners congealed on their plates.

The first group, all women, ended the suspense. They seemed well satisfied with Clinton's defense. "It just seems like he's under attack a lot," one said. "A lot of people didn't serve in Vietnam. So what?" No one objected; on the contrary, when the moderator ran a Clinton TV ad, another of the women said, "He gives me hope. For some reason, he made me proud to be an American."

Greenberg and Greer were jubilant. "Reporters are in another world," Greer said. "They're trying to drive this thing. They're trying to *make* the news."

In a final straw vote, seven of the ten women chose Clinton, to two for Tsongas and one for Jerry Brown. Greer reached for a phone to call Little Rock with the good news.

"You know what our response should be?" Greenberg said. "Bemused. 'We're the front-runner. You've got to expect it.'"

The second group, all men, filed into the room. They worried Greenberg; they might be harder on Clinton over the draft issue than the women had been. His fears were unfounded. There weren't as many Clinton voters among the men, but they, too, seemed to buy his explanation. "I consider this stuff to be irrelevant," one said, "and I'm sick of the media feeding us this stuff when we really want to hear about the issues."

Greer jumped out of his seat and hugged Greenberg. Happiness, in their trade, was a warm focus group, and Greer got back on the phone to David Wilhelm in Little Rock to share the glow.

The news was welcome but not very nourishing; Wilhelm, normally good-humored and gregarious, was wondering why he had ever got into politics in the first place. There were days when he felt as if what he was running was not a campaign but a counterintelligence service, chasing rumors about women and now the draft. As a kid coming up in Chicago, he had imagined that politics was a way to do some good in the world. But now, having got to the top of the trade and checked out the view, he was like a young priest fighting doubt. For people in D.C., he brooded over dinner at the Capital Hotel one night that weekend, politics wasn't about issues or message, as he had once imagined. It was a *business*, concerned only with whose stock was up and whose down. Clinton's was down, and the party insiders were nervous, *plenty* nervous; those who had got on the bandwagon because they thought he was electable were getting off.

Wilhelm was not alone in his gloom. A couple of public polls had gone sour in New Hampshire, showing Tsongas back in the lead. Greenberg didn't believe them, but his own poll was still in the field, and the campaign was filled with dread as to what his numbers might show. At a strategy meeting that Saturday afternoon, there was some distracted talk about whether to increase the advertising buy in New Hampshire or save the money till later. "This week is life or death," Carville said, scanning the room through slitted eyes. "If we have to spend an extra $200,000 to take a chance, let's take a chance."

Afterward, everybody adjourned to a favorite hangout, a steakhouse named Doe's, and then to a staffer's home for a surprise birthday party for Stephanopoulos. The celebration more nearly resembled a wake. Bruce Lindsey, a charter FOB, speculated privately about whether they shouldn't just end the campaign—whether it was worth the pain to carry on.

Someone asked Lindsey when that might happen.

"When Hillary says it's too much," the FOB replied.

Hillary, as it happened, was far from surrender; she was in a warlike mood, lacerating anybody, including her husband, who seemed to her less than militant about fighting back. Clinton himself was in a state nearer denial, as if he didn't understand what was happening to him. The two of them met with the campaign command on Sunday night at the governor's mansion, in a conference room furnished to look more like a study. Hillary wore a green sweatsuit and house slippers. Clinton was in jeans, running shoes, and a light blue Yale sweatshirt. His voice was still raw, his manner agitated. But it wasn't the opposition or the press he blamed for his difficulties, let alone himself. It was instead the stunned group of advisers in the room, and he scolded them at blistering length for their sins.

The one he had uppermost in mind was his proposal for some modest tax relief for the middle class. He had never wanted it in the first place, he said heatedly, but they had talked him into it, and now Tsongas was slapping him around for it, accusing him of pandering for political gain. Clinton seemed not to get that the real problem was the wider assault on his character—that it had knocked him off his message for days on end and had cast the shadow of doubt on *all* his campaign promises. "That damn middle-class tax cut has cost me my credibility on economic issues," he railed. He was fixated on a symptom, not the cause.

He was still going when Carville slipped off to call Greenberg. The new poll they so feared had just come in from the field in New Hampshire, and Greenberg, at home in Connecticut for the weekend, had jotted the returns on the back of an envelope. They were bad. The draft charges were hurting. Clinton had dropped 9 points in five days. Tsongas had surged ahead by 11, at 32-21.

"We're in free fall," Greenberg told Carville.

Carville mumbled something noncommittal into the phone and rang off. He kept a poker face. He was standing near Clinton and didn't want him to read the bad news in his expression.

Once again, the campaign found itself in turmoil. Carville was openly lamenting that they had done those focus groups on the draft issue at all, let alone that they had taken their upbeat tone seriously. They had let the story hang out there all weekend with the candidate chilling in Little Rock and the campaign in its slow-response mode. Now, their numbers were in the toilet, and what support they still had was going wobbly. Ron Brown was back on the line from Washington, worried anew about Clinton's viability. "There's been some slippage," Wilhelm told him, without saying how much. "You can't take the shots he has and *not* slip. The issue is whether we can show he will fight back. I'd say we have forty-eight hours to project that."

Fighting back became the order of the day. The question was how, and no one was quite sure. While Clinton was doing a speech at a high school in New Hampshire, his expanded road party sat in a conference room off the principal's office debating media strategy for the last week before the primary. Four new spots had been made over the weekend. Three promoted Clinton's economic ideas, and some of his people thought they still made the strongest case for him. But Carville, among others, argued heatedly for the fourth ad—an in-your-face assault on the tabloids and the Republicans for trying to destroy Clinton. "We're *collapsing!*" he shouted over the phone to one of the soft-liners. "They don't believe us right now. This crap has taken its toll on us. We ain't gonna put up some fucking *plan* spot to do what we have to do. We gonna run *third* if we don't do something about it."

But they didn't have a strategy in place, and a huge pack of reporters was waiting in the cold for Clinton outside the school entrance. He was going to have to face them, and he would have to make it good. In the conference room, his troops rehearsed lines for him, knowing that what he said would be less important than how he said it.

"This is your show," Stephanopoulos told Carville, deferring to the senior strategist in the group.

Carville was pacing the room, psyching himself up first. His hands were jammed into his pockets. His eyes were as narrow and threatening as gunports in a fortress wall. He was muttering furiously to himself.

"We're in extremis," he said. "It's time to get the fibrillators out."

"Spoken like a good Catholic," Begala said, smiling. He had been around James long enough to recognize his warm-up drill.

"I just can't stand a quitter," Carville muttered. "I just can't stand a damn quitter."

"You've got to wind him up," Begala said.

Clinton walked into the room. Carville started winding. "Go out and kick some ass," he said finally. Clinton did.

But a new land mine lay just down the road, and the campaign already knew it. ABC News had got hold of a copy of a letter Clinton had written twenty-three years earlier to the army colonel who had accepted him for the ROTC. The letter explained in the most anguished terms why he wouldn't be keeping the commitment. Taken as a whole, it was a document of its time, a young man's cri de coeur against the war. Its worst vice was the occasional purple of its prose; otherwise, it could be read to confirm Clinton's story that he had, however briefly, exposed himself to the draft. After an advance look, Carville professed to find it "exculpatory," a word he had earlier applied with more hope than confidence to the Gennifer tapes. "The letter is our friend," he said, making a mantra of it. "The letter is our friend."

But with the Flowers affair, the media environment had changed around them, from the honeymoon attention that had accompanied Clinton's rise, to a destructive new mode anticipating his fall. A curious synergy had taken form between the sex and the draft stories, each reinforcing doubts raised by the other about Clinton's basic integrity. The exegetes of the press had judged his responses about his sex life to have been uncandid and were already looking for more of the same in his account of how he had managed to miss the war. They were accordingly less inclined to see the letter whole, as Carville had hoped, than to deconstruct it, and they would find much in it to reward a selective reading. Two morsels in particular stood out in the soup of Clinton's emotive language: he had thanked his ROTC patron for "saving me from the draft" and conceded that he could not otherwise have avoided it without spoiling his "political viability." The phrases, ripped from context, could be taken as a plea of guilty not merely to draft-dodging but to incipient Slick Willitude as well. Clinton, in this reading, was a man so consumed with ambition that, even at age twenty-three, he had been willing to say or do anything to stay out of the war and still preserve a future in politics for himself.

The sudden change of weather caught him off guard, and while his public smile remained pasted on, his private reaction was a sulfurous mix of anger at the media and pity for himself. The night before the story of the letter broke, he sat brooding in the darkness in the back of his van, en route from Boston to Manchester with a couple of his roadies. What passed for dinner was a sandwich and a Diet Coke, and he attacked them without visible pleasure. His mind was on the letter, and on the word of ABC's Ted Koppel—mistaken, as it turned out— that the network had got it from a source in the Pentagon. Clinton felt himself doubly victimized, by Republican dirty tricksters and by a cynical press motivated mostly by "commerce and naked power."

"I mean, no one has ever been through what I've been through in this thing," he told his traveling companions. "*No* one. Nobody's ever had this kind of personal investigation done on them, running for president, by the legitimate media." By their own ordination, the press had become the arbiters of character in American politics, and, Clinton complained, their standards had become "a moving target." He had said up front that his marriage had not been perfect, and had thought that that ought to be enough—"unless," he added, "I did something like Gary Hart did." His hedged response had satisfied the people, or so he seemed to believe. "At least," he said, "they think I'm entitled to be treated like Hart was instead of being murdered, you know, in this sort of relentless, foaming-at-the-mouth stuff that the tabloids are doing."

What he hadn't reckoned on was that the rules had changed since Hart was seen with a nubile young blonde at his place in Washington and photographed with her during a cruise aboard a pleasure boat aptly named the *Monkey Business*. It was no longer required that you get caught in the act in a current affair; under 1992 rules, Clinton said, the press would take the word of a woman who had denied in the past having had a liaison with him and who now had been paid a six-figure bounty by the *Star* for changing her story. It was *crazy*, Clinton said. It was sick. "I mean, I'm just telling you," he continued, tearing off a bite of his sandwich, "I think that it is almost blood lust. I think it is an insatiable desire on the part of the press to build up and tear down. And they think that is their job—and not only that, their divine right."

And now they were going after the draft story with the same fervid heat they had brought to the bimbo hunt. Clinton guessed, indeed, that the new quest was part frustration at the defeat of the old. "They felt guilty," he said, sitting deep in the night shadows, "because I'd already told them all they needed to know. And they whored around anyway and spent hundreds of thousands of dollars, the legitimate press, looking into me, and they didn't find a damn thing that they could run with." But it struck him as partly arrogance as well: "You're dealing with a group of people that basically believes that, for whatever reason, they ought to have the right to determine the outcome of this election. And they can justify anything, *anything,* under the guise of the First Amendment. And there ain't no way to win with it."

He would have thought, for example, that at least one paper would have applied the same investigative energy to the question of whether the draft letter had in fact been leaked by the Pentagon for partisan advantage. But no: they had seized instead on its language and were combing it for meanings like scholars pondering the Dead Sea scrolls. The whole draft business, Clinton said, "has been gone over several times. I've been totally exonerated. But they know they could get big hits if they could somehow get somebody to change their story. So therefore, that's far more important to them than whether hungry people get fed. That's why they let the bad guys win all the time. *They* don't care—it just confirms their cynicism and enables the game to go on."

He didn't mean to suggest, he said, that his past wasn't an issue. "People are entitled to know that I was hard against the war and didn't want to go," he explained. "Those are the facts. What I don't think is appropriate is for them to come out here twenty-three years after the fact and think that they can, like Sherlock Holmes, somehow fathom every little subtlety of what every little word meant and uncover some great hidden truth." The business about his "political viability," for example—all he had meant at the time was that he wanted and intended to work for change inside the system. "I mean, how the hell did I know I'd be here? How the hell did I know whether I'd ever be able to get elected to anything or not?"

His sadness, as he framed it in his backseat soliloquy, was mainly for the American people. "They want this election to be about *them*," he said. But his concern for the republic was suffused with a sense of his own victimhood; he felt singled out for martyrdom by the established "ins" of both parties and their allies in the press because he stood for *real* change, not just rearranging the deck chairs on the Titanic. Like most men who seek the office, he genuinely believed that he was better than anybody else running, and he had no doubt that he would have been the easy winner "except for this"—the gauntlet of scandal he had been obliged to run.

He had been damaged, he knew that; the sheer cumulative weight of what had been dumped on him had made people wonder what was or wasn't true and whether he was any longer electable. He professed not to care that the Washington power elite, including some of the leadership of his own party, was writing him off as terminal and shopping for another hero. "They're irrelevant," he said. "I just have to win." What troubled him more, he said, was his conviction that winning should be *about* something—something important. His voice, in the night shadows, was wistful. "I just think that it's a sad thing that what you have done and the things you've tried to do are so diminished in a deal like this," he said. "That the things that really will matter once you get in office play so little a role."

Still, the letter had to be dealt with, and the campaign played what it thought was its strongest hand: release the text and attack the administration for having leaked it. The line was more than mere tactics. Clinton's people believed what they had been told, that the letter had come from the Pentagon, and their outrage was real, not manufactured. They felt victimized, and their passion carried them off into an alternate reality, a paranoid world of dirty tricks plotted and executed at the highest levels of government. Carville backgrounded the press at the Days Hotel the next morning, barely containing his anger. Then he joined the traveling command in a second-floor room. Clinton, coat off and tie loosened, paced the floor with a Styrofoam cup of coffee. Begala sat at a table, banging out a statement on a laptop computer. The others peppered Clinton with advice.

"George Bush said he would do anything to win," Carville started, trying out a line in a voice taut with anger, "and the Pentagon got the message."

"It's not about you or the election," Greer said. "It is about the country. It has to be in the context of fighting for the future."

Clinton listened, mostly in silence. He was, relative to the others, a dove; his anger at his situation had not got the better of his political instincts. "Be very careful," he warned. "This is a test of character, and if you're going out there trying to make this more than it is, that will say something about your character. My sense is, if I play offense, we will be going too far." Neither was he moved by Carville's view that the letter was necessarily his friend. It could be misread to make him look like an ambitious schemer. "To say this letter is a home run," he said, "is overstating it."

In the event, it looked more like a strikeout. When the campaign distributed the text to a hangarful of reporters that morning, it was like handing out copies of *Lady Chatterley's Lover* to a crowd of schoolboys; they tore through it, looking for the good parts. Clinton was tattooed with questions about his integrity, his patriotism, his fitness to be commander in chief—and, just as he had guessed, his apparent precocious ambition.

The gambit had backfired. When Clinton's men got back to their war room at the hotel, the overnights from Greenberg's tracking poll were waiting for them. They were bad. The free fall had got steeper; even before the flap over the letter, Tsongas's lead had widened from eleven points to twenty, and the internals showed a troubling vein of doubt about Clinton's honesty. The letter could only make it worse; when Begala skimmed the first Associated Press account, leading with Clinton's thank-you to the ROTC man for saving him from the draft, he knew it was a goddam disaster.

Clinton, moreover, was about to lose his trump card: the word from Koppel that the letter had been leaked by the Pentagon. He was scheduled to go on *Nightline* that night, and Stephanopoulos broke from a strategy meeting to call the show's producer. They spoke for a few moments. Then Stephanopoulos hung up, looking stricken.

"We're fucked," he said. "Koppel didn't know what he was talking about." The *Nightline* people had rechecked who gave them the letter, and while Koppel would speak only to Clinton about the matter, it was plain that the source hadn't been the Pentagon after all.

Begala, who had been working on talking points for Clinton, slumped over his laptop. "This isn't happening," he said. "I'm going to wake up from this and find out it's this cold medicine I'm taking."

"This is a big problem," Stephanopoulos said. Clinton himself had gone way out on a limb that morning, and so had Carville on background, accusing the administration of playing dirty tricks. Their surrogates were hitting the same note. One of them, Congressman Dave McCurdy, was in Washington at that moment demanding an investigation. It was too late to call him off. The *Nightline* appearance was bare hours away, and they had to rewrite the script.

"I think we're in pretty big trouble," Stephanopoulos said. He was the house pessimist, a guy who went dark, as he put it, if the weather turned bad. But this time, everybody else agreed.

"We can't back off the show," Begala said. "It's still in our best interest to try to communicate directly with the American people."

Stan Greenberg thought Clinton should "make this a story about America"—about a whole generation torn asunder by the war. "Because if we get into the give and take on this letter, we're going to lose," he said. "The only way we win this thing is generationally."

"We don't want to get into plumbing-the-depths-of-his-psyche questions," Begala said, agreeing.

Stephanopoulos snorted. "This is what they're asking," he said. "I've been through it for the last three days."

"If he asks us a question and we look like we're not answering it, that feeds exactly into this notion of 'Slick Willie,'" Carville said. He had been lying on the couch, his body a thin, horizontal line barely denting the upholstery. "Go back to the letter," he said. "The letter is your friend."

He picked up a photocopy and started reading, his metallic accent reflavoring Clinton's words. Stephanopoulos jumped in, playing Koppel, skeptical and probing.

Greenberg got the picture. Clinton couldn't duck specific questions about the letter, "but," he said, "we have to figure out how to get to the larger question of generations and history. And we've got to get to the question of how this affects him being commander in chief, because if we don't get to that question, we're dead. That's where the voters are walking all over us."

They tried out responses, wishing all the while that they had had more time to prepare. Their own desultory research into Clinton's draft history hadn't turned up the letter, and if Clinton remembered having written it, he hadn't told them. As a result, they had been blindsided, and now Koppel was waffling away the best defense they had managed to throw together.

Somebody flicked on the TV set in the room to see how the local newscasts were treating the story. "New problem stirred by old letter," a promo on one station said. They switched channels. Another teaser came on: "Bill Clinton faces new allegations about his draft record."

Carville got up from the couch and fished a beer out of a sinkful of ice. "If all else fails, try a Samuel Adams," he said. With no bottle opener near at hand, he jammed the cap between the door and the frame and pried it loose, spraying beer on the floor.

"Shit," Stephanopoulos said softly. "We're going to come in fifth."

The newscasts, local and network, turned out to be less damaging than they had feared; one station, running a beat behind the day's developments, reported Clinton's charge that the Republicans were behind the leak. "Well, damn!" Carville exclaimed, too pleased to care that the story wasn't true.

Afterward, the core group returned to their war-gaming for *Nightline,* prepping themselves to prep Clinton. The main concern, for most of them, was that Clinton not get drawn into a microanalysis of what the letter meant; if that happened, Mickey Kantor, the campaign chairman, said, "we're going down a slippery slope."

"Don't scare him about the letter," Carville warned. A scared candidate would look tentative on TV.

"I'm not scared of the letter," Kantor said. "I just don't want Clinton spending thirty minutes on it."

Clinton himself seemed distinctly unscared when he and Hillary came in from the night's last rally; his manner was calm and his mind's eye seemed to have turned inward, as if he were a method actor getting into character for a play. He listened to some of the concerns in the room, among them the potentially deadly question of whether he could be an effective commander in chief. His response was a long, impassioned speech on his fitness for the role and his feelings about the war in Vietnam. When he finished, his handlers fell silent for a moment, then stood, applauded loudly, and pantomimed leaving the room. He would do just fine.

He wondered if he should bring a copy of the letter with him. Some of his handlers thought he should. Hillary cut them off. "Why bring a copy with you?" she said. Doing the show would be like appearing on a witness stand; you *never* brought potentially damaging evidence with you. "Say, 'Ted, I don't have a copy,'" she told her husband.

"What does the letter show?" Grunwald said, steering the talk back to its content.

"It shows that I was telling the truth," Clinton said.

"But why did you write the letter?" Stephanopoulos asked, playing Koppel again.

Because he thought he owed the ROTC chief a direct explanation of why he was dropping out, Clinton said.

"Keep with the bigger picture you started with," Hillary prompted;

his speech to the people in the room was more powerful than any further explication of the text.

Clinton was still upset at finding himself trapped in a time warp, a middle-aged public man held accountable for the private agonizing of a college-age boy. "One of the problems with this whole thing is that everyone is looking at this as a forty-five-year-old man who is running for president," he complained. It hadn't been easy for him to do what he had done back then. "One of the few tangible memories I have of my father is a picture of him in uniform," he said. "I grew up believing in the honor of the military. It *killed* me to turn against the war."

Begala thought they could work with that; Clinton could talk about how his boyhood memories of his dad and the experience—the *searing* experience—of opposing the war had shaped the man running for president.

"When I ask young men and women to serve," Grunwald said, playing with a line, "it will be in a war supported by the American people."

"I like that, Mandy," Hillary said.

"If I ask young men and women to give up their lives, it won't be for a war that the American people don't support," Clinton echoed.

There were more lines, more talking points, till Hillary finally called a halt. "Don't overthink this, Bill," she said. "Don't overtalk this. Talk from your gut."

As they broke up, Begala volunteered one last offering, another line of Grunwald's: "You know, Ted, the only times you've invited me on your show it was to talk about a woman I never slept with and a draft I never dodged."

The "never" was a step further than Clinton had yet gone in his statements about Flowers, but he and Hillary both loved the line, and it became his lead card on the air that night.

The show went well enough, thanks in part to Koppel's unwonted delicacy. He read the whole letter aloud, and the cross-examination that followed was teatime mild. But Clinton never quite recaptured the passion that had briefly lit the room during his prep session.

"*Nightline* was good," Mandy Grunwald remarked to Hillary a couple of days later, "but compared to what happened before—"

She didn't need to finish the thought; Hillary understood. Her husband had showed more life and passion in prep sessions than he had on the air.

"What gets him revved up?" Grunwald asked.

"He's *always* tightened up in front of TV cameras," Hillary said. "It's like he thinks, 'This is . . . *television!*'"

The irony was that the medium would save him. The Koppel interview was the first round in a closing media blitz—a high-risk sprint through five live-TV appearances in five days. The best, for his talents and his cause, were two paid half-hours in which he took questions directly from voters—a format that would come to be known within the campaign as "Ask Bill" and would be frequently revived whenever he got in trouble. The questions mostly supported his contention that real people cared about real problems, not whom he had bedded or how he had got out of the war.

Clinton seemed to borrow fire from them. His speeches, going into the homestretch in New Hampshire, were his strongest of the campaign; it was as if he felt his life in politics slipping away and was waging one last, desperate fight to save it. His standing in the polls, public and private, seemed to stabilize. Tsongas's seemed to be going soft. He had all but dropped out of sight, cutting back his schedule to one public event a day. There were fresh speculations about his health, till he invited the cameras back to poolside to shoot him swimming again. To Clinton's men, it looked more as if what ailed Tsongas was front-runneritis—a disease marked by tics, twitches, and night sweats about doing something dumb and blowing a big lead.

"Forget about Tsongas," Greenberg said, scanning his latest poll the Friday morning before the primary. "They're pulling off of him."

"You just pray one thing," Carville joked grimly. "That Tsongas goes out there in a Speedo at least once a day."

Their comfort was premature—the ease of men who knew that their candidate needed no more than a strong second-place finish and who clung to the belief that he might still win. In fact, Tsongas was more durable and Clinton more damaged than they knew. The calm in the campaign was the peace of the roller-coaster car at the top of its arc, just before its plunge straight down.

8.

The Comeback Kid

It had been the winter of talking trash, a season in which the candidates trekked from arena to arena insulting one another like a lost troupe from the World Wrestling Federation. Their debates were the undercard of the primary process; they were of little real consequence except as make-work for handlers and divertissements for the sportsmen and scribes waiting at ringside for the main event. But CNN chanced to have scheduled its installment in the seemingly endless maxiseries for the Sunday before the New Hampshire primary, and Bill Clinton approached it as edgily as if his comeback from the boneyard of politics depended on how well he did.

His mood was cranky as he set out from Manchester to Nashua in a red campaign minivan the Saturday before the big show. His handlers piled in with him; the half-hour ride was the only time they could wedge into the schedule to begin his warm-ups. The buzz among them as they got started was about why Paul Tsongas had dropped mostly out of sight for the past several days. In fact, he was holed up nursing a painfully infected eye. But mysteries in politics are usually food for paranoid thought, and Clinton was not immune. He guessed aloud that Tsongas was spending a hundred hours prepping for the debate. The fantasy gnawed at him and became fresh ground for complaint about his own handlers, whom he often tended to blame when things went wrong. "I've basically been both under- and overprepared," he groused, looking back at them from the passenger seat. That was why he hadn't done as well as he should have on the debate tour. He had been too passive. He hadn't felt well armed.

Hillary, sitting just behind him, thought he might be getting too *much* advice from his cornermen, not too little. Whenever he felt his circuits getting overloaded, she said, he needed to tune them out. "The important thing, Bill," she told him, "is for you to say what you're comfortable with."

His handlers didn't disagree in principle; the problem was that what Clinton was most comfortable with was the minutiae of public policy—

the more of it, the better. He tended to get bogged down in detail when what he really needed to do was soar.

"Keep your focus on the big prize, the big picture," Mandy Grunwald, a rising star in his eyes and Hillary's, told him. "Let *them* bicker about details."

"What's the objective in this debate?" Clinton asked.

"The objective is to make it about something *big*," James Carville said. He had smuggled an open bottle of Sam Adams out of the hotel and was holding it between his knees, sustenance for the ride. "We're not just having another election. What we do here really matters in what kind of country we are going to have. Every time you can take it to be the big choices, the better it is for you."

"And make them look small," Grunwald said.

"Yeah," Carville said. "It's okay to argue and to be as aggressive as possible, but make it big, governor. You can't look at Paul Tsongas and see his face on the side of Mount Rushmore. Where you do best is when you talk about what kind of country we need, where you want to take the nation. Paul Tsongas has no idea of the world outside New Hampshire. You've got to hit the big ideas." He took a swig of beer. "I know it's risky, but shit, we're in a risky position. The bigger we are, the harder they're going to fall."

What Clinton didn't need was any further exegesis of the draft letter. Carville's idea, if the letter came up at all, was to use it as a pivot—address it briefly and broadly, then turn away to the here-and-now struggle with America's economic competitors overseas.

"We're in a war *now*, don't make no mistake about it," Carville said.

"I like that," Hillary agreed.

"Every time you can hit that, hit it," Carville said. "It's *you*, man. There's no one better at that than you."

It was Hillary who, near the end of the ride, finally broke their awkward silence about what only lately had been Topic A: the issue of her husband's alleged philandering. The hired hands still felt queasy discussing the subject in his or her presence in any terms more specific than "character." They needn't have worried; her tone, when she raised it, was clinical—the attitude not of a woman scorned but of an adviser addressing a matter of practical politics. She was expecting aggressive, even hostile questioning from the two CNN newscasters on the panel. One of them, Bernard Shaw, was the man who had kayoed Dukakis in a 1988 debate by asking how he would react to the rape and murder of his wife. The other, Ken Bode, seemed to Hillary to be "obsessed" with the question of how Gennifer Flowers had got a state job with Clinton's help.

"You've got to be ready for The Question," she said. "If you can't keep your promise to your wife, how can we trust you to keep your promises to us?"

Clinton sat in opaque silence, betraying neither worry nor pain. His passivity was his normal mode in strategy discussions; he usually loved to talk, but when *he* was the subject, he became a listener, filtering the noise for what he thought he could use. He didn't say how he would handle the sex question, or even try out a line, as he sometimes did, and nobody pressed him further.

He seemed more engaged when Grunwald tactfully changed the subject to Tsongas. Saint Paul had begun to grate on Clinton and his team, in direct proportion to his rise in the polls. They spoke of him less often as courageous; their private word for him instead was "sanctimonious," often with the epithet "son of a bitch" attached. What irritated them most was Tsongas's regular declaration that he was not Santa Claus, implying that Clinton was. Clinton had to be ready for that one, Grunwald said. Tsongas was sure to use it in the debate.

"*My* strategy with Paul," Hillary ventured, "is to say, 'You know, Paul, you've got the story half right. We *do* have to level with people. But we also have got to understand the pain they're in.'"

"They don't want a lollipop, they want a leader," Grunwald said, composing out loud.

"They don't want a handout, they want a hand *up*," Clinton said.

"What you do," Hillary advised, "is praise Tsongas as a big contributor to the big picture, but say he's just not getting it."

Carville spun a favorite old campaign yarn about his legendary Louisiana homeboy, Earl Long, who had once found himself in a race against a man who was both a Baptist deacon and a Ford dealer. "I'd buy my car from him, that's how honest he is," Long had said, "but if you need to buy *two* cars, you'll have to go somewhere else. He's not big enough to handle it."

Clinton laughed.

"That's what you gotta do with Paul Tsongas," Carville told him. "He's a good guy. Got a lot of character. 'You tried hard—you're just not there.' This race is about big things. You've got to make it about *two* Fords, not one Ford. The presidency is about a *fleet* of Fords."

They were pulling into Nashua. Someone remarked on the big turnout of Clinton supporters.

"Yeah," Hillary said, with a grim smile. "People also come to see the freak show at the circus."

Her own instincts were, as always, combative, and when she and her husband drove from a rally to a more formal prep session back in

Manchester on Sunday morning, she tried in her own way to get him pumped. She had really liked it, she told him, when he said at the rally that an economic plan like Tsongas's was just a piece of paper—that it needed energy and vision behind it to make it real.

"That is the difference between you and Paul Tsongas," she said. "That's it in a nutshell, and that has *got* to come out in the debate tonight."

His advisers were waiting for them in an improvised war room at the Days Hotel. The core group sat around a table. The lesser players hovered behind them. Their sense of urgency was palpable—a belief, hardened into conviction, that Clinton's survival might well hang on his performance. Carville had been stalking the room all morning like a caged tiger, eyes narrowed, murmuring one of his private litanies to himself. His job was to slap the candidate into shape, get him into a gladiatorial mood, and when Clinton arrived, Carville was ready.

"We *want* this debate," he told Clinton. "We *need* it. Because of what's happened to us, people are going to be looking at you." Carville was partial to the aphorism, attributed to Frederick the Great and Napoleon among others, that God is on the side of the big battalions. It was important, he said yet again, that Clinton go big—that he be the biggest guy out there with the biggest ideas and show that he had heart to fight for them. "Get itching for the first question," Carville said. "Forget this slow beginning—*jump* on that son of a bitch like a snake on shit. Right from the start. No sense sitting back thinking, 'Gee, this is a big debate.' You got to be the horse in the stall pawing for that first question."

What if it was the A-question? The consultants were less shy this time; they had convinced themselves that one of the CNN people would ask Clinton something about his fidelity to his wife.

"Be prepared on all the questions to challenge any that are beyond the pale," Paul Begala said.

Clinton slid easily into character, the outraged husband slapping back at an imaginary interrogator. "On our worst day," he began, "my wife deserves better than that, and you ought to be ashamed of yourself."

"Don't lose that," Frank Greer said. Clinton didn't, though it would be weeks before he would actually get to use it in combat.

There was worried talk at another point about what Ken Bode might do. In their imaginings, they had demonized him as the panelist most likely to come at Clinton on Flowers, the draft, or both.

"I think I ought to kick his brain hard," Clinton said.

"Kick him *hard*," Hillary seconded. She always liked to see him fighting mad.

"If you're going to get angry," Grunwald said, "and I *love* getting angry on this stuff, say, 'I can't believe you are asking this when, outside this studio, there are people losing their homes. The people of New Hampshire have moved on. Why can't you?'"

"And not deal with the *facts?*" Clinton asked. His own habit under attack was to do the verbal equivalent of a legal brief, trying to smother the allegation of the day in petit-point detail. The idea of ducking behind the big picture seemed to make him uncomfortable.

"Do you feel like kicking his ass?" Carville asked, sensing Clinton's unease. "*Do* you?"

"Yes," Clinton said.

"Then *kick* it," Carville told him.

They were disposed to kick Tsongas's, too; at the very least, they had to keep him from widening his lead in the polls and pushing Clinton back to the second tier. One way was to hang the guy with his own words, carelessly uttered, to a young man who had lost his job and wondered what Tsongas might do as president to help repair his broken self-esteem. Tsongas's response had been realistic in fact but wintry in expression. I'll provide the jobs, he had told the young man; you worry about you.

"Can we get a copy of that?" Clinton exclaimed. "*Please* get me a copy of that."

"You want to pounce on him," Grunwald said.

"It's not that he's *bad,*" Begala said. "It's just, he only gets half of it."

Clinton fell into an extended variation on a main theme of his stump speech—a homily on the need for a candidate for president to have some rationale larger than simply wanting the office.

"*Preach* to them," he said when he was finished.

"Yes," Grunwald said. "Exactly. Preach to them."

They guessed he would have to talk about his electability as well, given all the mud that had stuck to him. They were themselves shell-shocked under the daily barrage of punditry declaring Clinton dead, with supporting quotes from anonymous party leaders in Washington.

"This election is about whether we will change," Clinton said, framing one possible answer.

"You have to take on the people who are saying this," Greer seconded.

"I don't mind Washington giving up on me," Clinton said, trying that approach. It was in fact a badge of honor, given all the other things the ins had got wrong.

Hillary liked that version, but the session was running long, and, knowing her husband's tolerances, she pushed his coaches to wind it down. Mostly for fun, they tried out a few of what Carville called bullshit questions—the sort of trivia tease that could find its way into a debate. Someone asked Clinton his favorite movie.

"It's *9½ Weeks,*" he joked. The film told the dark, steamy tale of a woman living in bondage to a man and liking it.

"A sense of humor is important," Greer said. "One of the problems in focus groups is that they think you're too perfect."

Perfect? Clinton laughed. "I'm a fat, slightly hard-of-hearing, middle-aged man."

Carville did a last pep talk, his own heat rising as he went along. "If something feels right and feels bold, dammit, *do* it," he said. "Draw a line in the dust, and if they come across it, get angry. Your ass is on the line tonight, and you need to show people you're willing to fight for yourself and for them. Don't give them any technical explanations."

The impact on Clinton was unclear, but Carville had worked himself into a fine frenzy. "No one has faced this kind of campaign before," he said. "*No one* has. This is your opportunity. The other thing is that this country really *is* about to go down the crapper."

There were giggles in the room. Hillary, who loved Carville's passions, stifled a laugh.

"I'm serious," Carville said. "It's something worth fighting for."

As it turned out, the best single bit of advice had come from George Stephanopoulos—a contrarian aside to the effect that Clinton might not be attacked at all and so needed to be prepared with a strategic Plan B in case there wasn't any flak to catch. The suggestion had got lost in the crosstalk. The consultants had done what they are paid to do, to anticipate the worst and to ready their clients for it. Clinton was accordingly well armored against artillery rounds that never flew—not, anyway, at him. The fire was directed mostly at Tsongas for challenging his party's time-worn creed.

On most scorecards, the "winner" of the evening, if there was one, was Bob Kerrey. The losers were Clinton's handlers; they traded embarrassed jokes about how wrong they had been about what to expect. Clinton had comported himself well, but there had been no fireworks, and there would be no bounce in the polls, nothing to narrow what was then a seven-point Tsongas lead in Stan Greenberg's polling. If anything, Clinton appeared to be sliding; early returns from a *Boston Globe* poll on Monday placed him fourteen points behind.

The news hit like a hard right to the midsection. Several of the command group dragged themselves downstairs to the hotel dining room that evening for a dinner of tough steaks and bad wine. They had to speak softly—a couple of reporters were at the next table—but, among themselves, they did not try to conceal their misery.

"There was just too much to overcome," David Wilhelm said. He had just flown in from Little Rock; he had stayed at his battle station there, trying to hold things together while the rest of the command team hit the trenches in New Hampshire. He looked shell-shocked. He was shaking his head as if the votes were in and the campaign over.

A waiter brought a portable phone to their table. In close succession, Greenberg took two calls. The first was an update on the *Globe* poll, and Greenberg started jotting the numbers on a brown paper place mat. They didn't look that great, but they weren't quite as bad as the first sweep, either. The late returns had closed the margin from fourteen points to eleven. At least Clinton was moving in the right direction.

His people were still trying to be happy at the news when the second call came in, this one from Greenberg's assistant, Joe Goode, in Washington. Goode had a report on their own polling. Greenberg listened, his face impassive. Occasionally he grunted an acknowledgment; otherwise, he said nothing till the two reporters behind him had finished dinner and cleared out. Then he wrote a new set of numbers on the placemat:

Tsongas	34
Clinton	18
Kerrey	14
Harkin	11
Brown	6

Clinton was sinking; he had lost six points in three days. Kerrey, revived by the debate, was breathing down his neck. A pall fell over the half-dozen or so handlers around the table. They were looking into a very deep hole. If the numbers held up, Clinton could be dead. "Kerrey's going to pass us," Mandy Grunwald said bleakly.

Greenberg reluctantly agreed.

"We have to plan for the worst," Grunwald warned. She pushed some plates aside and started writing scenarios on *her* place mat. None of them was very happy. "Kerrey comes in second," she said. "That kills talk of a new candidate. He goes on to South Dakota and wins, and then to the South. Money comes in. It kills Paul Tsongas and Bill Clinton. Kerrey becomes unstoppable." She contemplated that for a moment, then began writing again. "Or," she said, "Clinton comes in a weak second. What matters is the spread. Twenty percent or above and he survives. Below twenty and Clinton is probably dead." In either case, the money would stop; all Clinton could do then would be to empty his bank account, head for Georgia, and fight for survival nearer his own turf.

The dinner had turned into a death watch. A staff meeting was scheduled for 10:30 that night, but how could they reveal the new numbers without destroying morale?

"*Lie,*" Wilhelm told Greenberg. "You have to lie. This will cause a panic."

Greenberg said no; he agreed only to limit his briefing to the *Globe* poll and keep his own numbers to himself.

"Too many questions," Wilhelm muttered to himself. "Just too many questions."

The group headed back upstairs, still trying to figure out how to break the news to the candidate. Their first order of business was to call off the staff meeting; they were afraid their faces would betray what they were thinking—that Clinton was doomed. Instead, they regrouped in Carville and Begala's room on the second floor. Stephanopoulos lay on one bed. Carville sprawled on the other, stripped to his T-shirt and undershorts. Grunwald and Begala sat beside him. Room service materialized with two beers and a glass of wine. Nobody touched them. The TV was on, and CNN was reporting on its own closing poll. Its findings were closer to the *Globe*'s than to Greenberg's doomsday readout. The network had Clinton trailing by thirteen, at 35-22.

They were watching the time, knowing Clinton would be back soon from a last frantic day's campaigning. He devoured poll numbers and would want Greenberg's latest as soon as he walked in the door. Carville didn't think they should tell him how bad it was. The others felt they should. "Clinton has to be told," Greenberg insisted, and Grunwald silently agreed. *He* has to be prepared, she thought, and *we* have to be prepared.

"We have to tell him the truth," Begala said, but it didn't have to be *all* gloom and doom; maybe the two public surveys, the *Globe*'s and CNN's, would cushion the blow for him.

Stephanopoulos was sliding into one of his dark moods. Like the others, he had thought that Clinton had bottomed out in the final days and had started moving up again. As is common with candidates and campaigns in trouble, they had been seduced by the turnout and the noise at his rallies, forgetting that the crowds hadn't just materialized; they had been "built," as the term of art had it, by professional advance men.

"So what we did all week was prevent a meltdown," Stephanopoulos said miserably. "Let's face it—our crowds were fake."

"We just energized our supporters," Wilhelm said.

What haunted them all was the sense that they might be looking at the end of the campaign—that Clinton might even have to quit on primary day if he ran a bad third.

Stephanopoulos wasn't *that* gloomy. "He'd never not fight," he said.

Carville dressed and headed out to see Clinton. Begala, Greenberg, and Grunwald padded along after him, worried that James might be *too* blunt. The numbers could break Clinton's spirit if they weren't carefully presented.

They found the candidate in Mickey Kantor's room, slumped in a straight chair with his head propped on one hand. Hillary had fled for cover in their own suite, not wanting to hear any more bad news. Clinton was gray with fatigue. He looked profoundly sad.

Greenberg outlined the three polls, saving his own for last. He hoped his was wrong, he said.

Clinton didn't think so. He lacerated himself yet again for having bought into the middle-class tax cut and for not having responded quickly or strongly enough to the draft business.

"I'm dropping like a turd in a well," he said. "We're going to get *killed.*"

"We don't know that," Grunwald said. The other two polls looked better than Stan's, and, she said as sunnily as she could, "Majority rules."

Clinton seemed to want reassurance, and Grunwald tried to provide it, marshaling every reason she could think of for believing that the situation wasn't really so bad. Clinton would finish second, she said. Kerrey would fall short; the media would write him out of the race and proclaim Tsongas and Clinton the finalists—a pairing that should favor Clinton. And anyway, Grunwald went on, by now desperate for silver linings, the Democratic primary wouldn't even be the story of the day; most of the attention would be on how badly Pat Buchanan embarrassed George Bush on the Republican side.

Clinton looked at her. She was a woman of striking effect, nearly six feet tall, with a pale, angular face set off by inky black hair. She did not trade in sentiment; she had made her way into rooms once occupied solely by men and had commanded their attention with a mind as tough and speech as profane as theirs. Clinton seemed to want to believe her and to take some faint cheer in her words—that desperate mix of wish and hope more often found in hospital waiting rooms.

"Listen to me," Kantor interjected. "Hear me out. You're the best candidate in the field. You're a young man. You're forty-five."

The campaign chairman's words, meant to be comforting, were not. He was telling Clinton in effect not to despair—there would be another chance for him in another election year.

Clinton listened stonily. He would say afterward that while the numbers had depressed him, he hadn't really believed them; they didn't match the response he had felt out among the people. But for his troops in the room that night, his wan look gave him away. In his own mind, Mandy Grunwald thought, he knows it's all over—his candidacy, his career, his dreams of being president. Her sadness mirrored his, though she tried to hide it. He looked to her like a man who couldn't quite believe that this was where it would all end: in a room at a Days Hotel in Manchester, New Hampshire, before the first primary of his first national campaign.

What the Tarot Cards Said

Polling results are the tarot deck of politics, and while Clinton sat in his rooms gazing at what he was sure was The Coffin, his rivals were scanning their cards for portents of what the primary held in store for them. Tsongas was looking not merely for victory, which seemed all but assured; he wanted affirmation for what had, in the last days of the battle of New Hampshire, become not merely a candidacy but a crusade. What Kerrey sought in *his* cards was something rather more modest. The onetime golden boy was hoping for some sign that he was still alive.

For days, even weeks on end, the senator appeared to have hit stall speed. His share of the vote stayed frozen between 9 and 11 percent, and the issue was no longer whether he would win—it was whether he could squeeze past Tom Harkin into third place. He joked about his static market share in his speeches, telling of how he had dozed off in his room one night and wakened to a voice on TV intoning, "Nine-nine, ten, nine-nine, nine-eight, nine-nine." He imagined, he said, that he was tuned to the Winter Olympics and was hearing how the judges had scored the latest gold medalist. He wasn't; the numbers, in his story, were his own day-by-day returns in the tracking polls.

His handler-in-chief, Tad Devine, had warned him two weeks out to forget about winning New Hampshire. "We've just gotta get out of here," he told Kerrey—a goal that might have been a de facto slogan for his campaign. The painful irony was that the enterprise seemed outwardly to be prospering under its new management; the mechanics were more efficient, Kerrey's speeches were getting better, and with Clinton's slide, some money had finally started to flow in from panicky

Democratic bettors in search of a fresher horse to play. There had been enough in the till to pay for a credible ad campaign by a media firm of blue-chip price and reputation. But none of the masterworks issuing from the atelier of David Doak and Bob Shrum seemed to be moving voters. People *liked* Kerrey, if his handsome 60 percent favorable ratings were to be believed; he just wasn't closing the sale.

"I think you're the best candidate," a voter he met at a health club one night told him, "but I can't vote for you."

"Why?" Kerrey asked.

"The press says you're not connecting," the man said, "and you're behind in the polls."

The polls, in Shrum's view, had by then become part of the problem; there were just too many public and private head counters out there tracking the tiniest overnight blips and hiccups of public opinion. To Shrum, it was as if the dynamics of the primary had fallen prey to a political variant on the Heisenberg uncertainty principle—the theory in physics that observing a phenomenon changes it. The poll rankings, published daily, had become a self-fulfilling prophecy; Kerrey was stuck in third place because he was stuck in third place, and nothing he said or did seemed to help.

Not even national health insurance, the centerpiece of his campaign, was working for him. He had rattled some of Clinton's people with it earlier in the year, simply by claiming that he had a health-care plan and Clinton didn't. David Wilhelm, Clinton's manager, had thought at the time that they needed to get something together fast, and when Stan Greenberg phoned Little Rock headquarters from Washington one day in January, Wilhelm enlisted him in the effort. "Kerrey is all over us," he told Greenberg. "Why give him this? Let's just kill it. Let's have a plan. Then he can't say anything."

The flutter then had lasted until James Carville and Paul Begala plugged into the discussion on a conference line from their semi-subterranean office on Capitol Hill. They had helped design Harris Wofford's stunning upset in the Pennsylvania Senate election two months earlier, with health care as their cutting issue. But its power, in their eyes, had been in the idea, not the details. People saw health coverage as a problem and wanted something done about it.

Carville's voice on the line was accordingly a splash of cold water on the idea of trying to produce an instant plan. "Well," he said in an irritated drawl, "if you really want to give Kerrey an opening, go out and try to put one together in a day or two."

"But tactically, why give him this opening?" Wilhelm asked.

"We don't want them to turn our economic debate into a health-care debate," Stephanopoulos said.

"We won't put it out in the next twenty-four hours," Wilhelm promised.

Carville's voice came back on the speaker. "Bob Kerrey has no economic plan," he said. "Bill Clinton does. Bob Kerrey has no foreign policy. Bill Clinton does. For Bob Kerrey to say Bill Clinton doesn't have a plan is like Mickey Rooney calling Wilt Chamberlain short."

Wilhelm retreated a step. The plan could wait awhile; what they needed was something to tell the media in the meantime.

"I'm going to call these guys and say Bob Kerrey's full of shit," Dee Dee Myers, the press secretary, kidded.

Wilhelm laughed and shook his head. "This was a great meeting," he said, "to arrive down to that."

The flurry had blown over; with the passing weeks, even Kerrey began losing faith in the issue and had to be talked into staying on it. He did, to little effect; it gave his campaign a one-note sound, and when that note didn't resonate, he had little left to fall back on. Toward the end, his team put up an ad called "November," touting him as the Democrat most likely to beat Bush in the fall. The new spot was a concession that the attempt to sell Kerrey for what he was had failed. Instead, the ad defined him by what he was not: he wasn't "regional" like Tsongas or "old" like Harkin, and, the script said pointedly, "no one can question his patriotism."

But the claim that he was therefore the one electable man in the field was mocked by the polls, including his own. The ad did produce a bounce of nearly three points for Kerrey in its first twenty-four hours on the air. "The word for the day is 'surge'," said one of the senator's publicists, Mike McCurry, who saw to it that the press was briefed on the finding. The bad news was that the bump only got Kerrey to 10.4 percent, ahead of Harkin, to be sure, but still far back of the leaders. The blip, and the celebration, barely lasted out the twenty-four-hour news cycle; the word for the next day once again was survival.

To be so stalemated was a new and hard experience for Kerrey, who had never lost in his short career and had till lately regarded his competition in the primaries as pushovers. They weren't, and his rivalry with them was hardening into dislike. Tsongas, for example—it was tiresome hearing every day how he was the last honest man in American politics.

"He's sanctimonious," Kerrey remarked to an aide, Will Kanteres, on the campaign plane. "What is it about Greeks from Massachusetts? Are they *all* sanctimonious?"

Kanteres, a Greek from New Hampshire, said no—only the Greeks from Republican families.

"'I'll tell you the truth,'" Kerrey said, mimicking Tsongas. "What do you say to respond—'I *won't* tell you the truth?'" He paused as if to consider the idea, an ironic smile playing over his lips. "No, *that* won't work," he said.

Nothing else did, either. Tsongas kept floating above reproach, and Clinton seemed to be sliding around it. Kerrey himself was affronted by the manner in which Clinton had escaped the draft and the war, and by his shifting explanations of how he had managed it. But his attempts to turn the scandal to his own advantage were compromised when his chief pollster, Harrison Hickman, faxed an anonymous memo on Clinton's draft record to the *Boston Globe* in an attempt to keep the story alive. The mere fact of its anonymity gave it the odor of skullduggery, and when the *Globe* traced it to Hickman's fax line, alarms went off in the campaign.

Hickman called Devine in New Hampshire, knowing that, since Watergate, the mere appearance of doing dirty tricks had become a capital crime. "You're going to have to fire me," he said.

At first, Kerrey was inclined to agree. But in the van en route to his next event, Devine and McCurry talked him out of it, on the ground that it would only make a bad story bigger. Hickman was permitted to stay on, minus a layer or two of skin; Kerrey flayed him privately in barracks language and pilloried him in public as "Harrison Hitman."

In fact, the frustration Hickman had responded to was one shared by Kerrey and most of his troops—a sense that the press was giving Clinton too easy a ride on the draft issue. In their view, the boys on the bus had grown up to be middle-aging baby boomers, many of whom had avoided the war on college deferments and so looked on Clinton as one of their own. On Valentine's day, Kerrey's man Billy Shore had dashed off some unloving doggerel about them:

> Roses are red,
> Violets are blue,
> Clinton dodged the draft
> And so did most of you.

Jokes didn't help, and neither did anything else. As the primary drew near, Kerrey was still spinning his wheels, unable to get traction. Devine's official line, in conversation with reporters, was that the senator needed only to finish in the top tier. Somebody asked him what that meant. "It's sort of like pornography," he replied. "You know it when you see it."

But in his private ruminations, Devine was reduced to prayer for a closing rush strong enough to produce what he called The Big But. His model was Michael Dukakis, who had run behind Dick Gephardt and Paul Simon in the 1988 Iowa caucuses and had lived to tell the tale. Dukakis had claimed that he "won the bronze," prettying up the fact that he had actually lost, and the network analysts had bought it; the commentaries had started out, "Governor Dukakis finished third, *but.*" In Devine's reveries, Kerrey didn't need to overtake Tsongas and Clinton, not just yet. A strong close and a bronze medal would be good enough in New Hampshire; he would then be the alternative to the front-runners when they inevitably fell. Never mind that Kerrey wasn't moving at all, let alone finishing with a kick. "We're one 'but' away from the nomination," Devine told himself, seeming to believe it.

Paul Tsongas harbored larger dreams. The obligation of his survival, as he had called it, was no longer simply a felt duty to run for president; it appeared to have become a calling to purge the entire political process of its mendacities, large and small, about what really needed to be done to set America right. The moral strain that had got him the nickname Saint Paul took on an almost belligerent edge as it moved front and center in his campaign rhetoric; at times he seemed less candidate than apostle, with The Book—his economic plan—as his writ and righteousness as his sword and shield. "My job is to turn the economy around," he said one day at an event in Concord, making it sound like God's will. "There are some Democrats who will find this very hard to take. So be it," he intoned. "So be it."

It is a not uncommon affliction of office seekers in the heat of battle to come to see themselves, sincerely, as the children of a higher destiny and their rivals as enemies of all that is right and good. But the virus was particularly easy to catch when one's chief competitor was a man as soiled in combat as Clinton. One of the daily torments of life in the Tsongas campaign was the television imagery of the bionic governor smiling his way through the storm of rebuke when, by the normal rules, his bones should have been bleaching by the roadside. The fact that he was alive, well, and running a presentable second in the polls seemed to act as a goad to Tsongas. As primary day drew near, he strayed more and more from his winning message of sacrifice and investment into a fog of pieties about his own lonely commitment to speak hard truths.

The change in pitch, and the slowdown in his scheduling to one event a day, caused some distress to the more warlike of his handlers. Not even his self-deprecating humor was enough to leaven the mix, not, anyway, for his pollster, Tubby Harrison. Clinton had got up off his back and started to run again, Harrison mused, while Paul had *disappeared*. Instead of campaigning visibly and hard, he had become a philosopher and a comic—a guy out there talking about the meaning of life with a few jokes sprinkled in to keep the crowd awake.

In the process, Harrison thought, his message had got smaller; it was fine to run around saying you weren't Santa Claus, but at a point you had to say who you *were*. Paul was waving The Book around too much, and when he did talk policy, he said things like "I'm pro-business" instead of "I'm pro-jobs" or "I'm pro-growth." It was catching up with him. He was still ahead, but he wasn't *moving* anymore. Harrison's last guess before the primary was that Tsongas would win by eight points when it could have been twenty or better—enough to have knocked Clinton out of the race.

"He's not doing what he's supposed to be doing," Harrison complained to the campaign director, Dennis Kanin. "He's coasting."

If so, it was a dangerous mode for so vulnerable a candidate. The days had long since passed when his competitors had tossed flatteries at him like pocket change; with his surge to the top, he became their target rather than their mascot, and their pleasure in zinging him was heightened by their irritation at his sometimes holier-than-thou tone. Their response was a form of excommunication: Tsongas, they said, was a Republican sitting in the wrong pew.

His honeymoon with the press was wearing thin, too, as his man Ed Jesser had warned him it would. With Clinton's fall and Tsongas's rise, his candidacy had gone from invisible to the center of a mob scene. Its new prosperity was measurable by the number of TV crews shadowing him and was certified on what Jesser called the Fourteen-Camera Day, all fourteen of them trained on the onetime consensus loser who suddenly seemed alight with a winner's glow.

"Is Tsongas dyeing his hair?" a member of the pack asked Peggy Connolly, the press secretary.

Connolly asked what prompted the question.

"He looks younger," the reporter said.

It wasn't dye, Connolly said. It was called confidence, and Tsongas had it.

But there would be a delayed price for all the attention, Jesser had told Tsongas at the time. "We're going to read more crap than you'll ever believe about what your favorite food is, how good Niki is, all of the kids," he said. "They're going to latch onto five local pols in

Lowell who are colorful, and they are going to tell everyone about you. And you're going to be Mr. Wonderful. Nobody will lay a glove on you. That'll last for five days. And once they've done that, they'll kick the shit out of you. You are going to become a scumball lobbyist who wasn't in the war. You probably knew the war was coming— that's why you joined the Peace Corps. That other wave will come."

The upside in being discovered so late was that there wouldn't be time before the primary for the wave to gather destructive force. There were stories out there to be done under the invasive new rules, about Tsongas's lobbying activities and his corporate connections to nuclear power. Being back in the pack had afforded him a kind of protective cover; he hadn't mattered enough for media people to descend on Lowell, Jesser said, and scour up locals prepared to say what an asshole he was. But there was a more insidious downside, one from which the campaign would never quite recover. During its months in the shadows, the enterprise had been surviving day to day, with planning, hiring, and fund-raising all stunted. When it finally emerged into daylight, it didn't have the means to capitalize on its sudden success.

Neither was Tsongas wholly prepared to cope with the attacks when they came. He had been running a low-energy campaign toward the end, and when Clinton came roaring back after the draft story, crowding the pages of his daybook from edge to edge with events, the contrast could hardly have been sharper. Tsongas's own people spoke worriedly among themselves of the "stamina gap" that had opened between the two men. There were rumors about his health, fanned by operatives for the other candidates in saloon conversations with reporters, and he could no longer kill them by swimming a few laps in the pool. *His* daybook looked like a wallflower's dance card; the kindest interpretation anyone put on its sparsely inked-in pages was that Tsongas must be sitting on his lead.

The more common speculations were darker than that. Tsongas had long since blocked out the Wednesday before the primary as a day off, partly on the advice of such old stagers as Fritz Mondale, Gary Hart, and Michael Dukakis; if you wanted to keep your sanity, they all had told him, it was important to pull off the road and catch your breath when you could. Tsongas's plan was to spend his day enjoying his family and beginning preparations for the CNN debate. But when Peggy Connolly cruised the bar at the Wayfarer Hotel in Manchester at midnight the night before, she was waylaid by reporter after reporter asking her if something was *wrong* with Tsongas.

By then, something was, though nothing nearly so dire as the rumormongers were suggesting. Two weeks out, Tsongas had visited a mill, and a flying wood chip had hit him in one eye. Conjunctivitis set in and spread quickly to the other eye, turning both into swollen pink blobs. The preliminary debate-prep session was moved from Boston to a room at the Sheraton in Lowell, closer to home, to make it easier on him. Even then, he wasn't up to it. He was in pain so sharp that he couldn't concentrate; his coaches watched him sitting with his head tilted back, opening and closing his eyes, and called off the session. Kanin's stomach knotted. He couldn't tell Tsongas his fears—what could the poor guy do?—but he could feel the whole race slipping away.

The first thing they had to do was get him back out for a couple of days dense-packed with New Hampshire events; a swim for the cameras in Concord was one of them, as a token that he wasn't in a cancer ward somewhere. Kanin sent an aide to an optometrist's for an assortment of glasses in various styles. Their purpose was wholly cosmetic, to hide Tsongas's crimsoned eyes. He looked terrible without them, but they made him self-conscious, and he sometimes left them off.

They were still a problem when he showed up at Saint Anselm College in Manchester for the CNN debate. His prepping had gone well after the false start; he and Kanin had worked particularly hard on answering the charge that he was soft on nuclear power, a touchy issue in the state. But his eyes were still red and bleary, and in the time before he went on, he tried on pair after pair of glasses from Kanin's stockpile. His people watched on monitors till he found a look he liked—or, rather, preferred to having no cover at all. Then they sent him out into combat for the last time before the primary.

They almost wished they hadn't. They had correctly guessed that Harkin would attack him straight off about nuclear power. What they hadn't anticipated was that everybody else would join the assault; it was one Christian against four ravenous lions, and they ate Tsongas alive. He never found his stride, never created one of those "moments" that make the highlight film on the newscasts. In his holding room, Kanin sat in gloomy silence amid a knot of staffers watching on a monitor, shouting lines that Tsongas should have said but didn't. Even his two younger daughters caught the bad vibrations. They were upset that everybody was picking on their father and, Peggy Connolly thought, a little frightened that all the grownups in the room were yelling at the TV.

Tsongas knew he had done badly. "All I could think about was the glasses," he told Kanin afterward. His family and staff tried to buck him up, and when Jack Germond, a columnist doing instant analysis on CNN, astonished them all by declaring Tsongas the winner, a cheer went up in the room. Kanin didn't believe it. He had almost seen the points peeling away from Tsongas's lead. His only solace was that not many people had been watching the event live; the press, as it turned out, was too absorbed with the horse race to pay the debate much attention, and Tsongas's poor showing accordingly got lost in the noise.

So, to Senator Kerrey's misfortune, was his "victory" on the consensus score sheets. If anybody cared, it didn't show up in the campaign's polling that Sunday evening; the senator was still mired in deep third place, and when his vote-tracking specialist, Jack Maguire, set up shop for a last sweep on Monday night, there was no reason to expect anything much better. As his canvassers began their calls, Maguire sat alone in his office in Concord, Massachusetts, just south of the New Hampshire state line, and made score marks on a yellow legal pad. The common presumption in the campaign was that they would reveal the dimensions of Kerrey's defeat.

What Maguire saw in his scratchings amazed him; for a giddy hour and a half, it was possible to believe in miracles. Tsongas was *destroying* Clinton. He had been stalled at 35 percent of the vote for several nights, but Maguire was logging in three ticks next to his name to every one for Clinton. Tsongas was at 40 percent and climbing, maybe as high as 50. Clinton's trend line was static. Kerrey's was inching up; a strong finish for him, coupled with a bad shellacking for Clinton, would put him right back in the chase.

As it happened, Maguire had tapped into the same wave that had so frightened Clinton's handlers. The difference was that he was still polling when, at midevening, it began to recede as suddenly as it had formed. The old configuration of the race was reasserting itself. Clinton was coming on strong. There were three scratches next to his name now to every four for Tsongas; he was still in second, but if he kept moving, Maguire thought, he could get to 30 percent, and Kerrey would be back in the soup.

The numbers were only half crunched when Tad Devine called in from the road for a reading. The turn in the tide wasn't yet definite; the overall totals still looked bad for Clinton and good for Kerrey, and Devine dashed back to headquarters to share the news. As he burst in the door, he saw Bob Shrum and Mike McCurry at the top of the stairway to the second floor.

"I got the numbers," he said.

He headed up the stairs. Shrum and McCurry hurried down. They met in the middle and, standing in the half-light, contemplated a suddenly brightening future.

"Definite third," Devine said excitedly. "Possible second—maybe."

Tsongas was at 35. Clinton had fallen back to 16. Kerrey had 12 or 13 percent—14 if you counted those undecided voters who were leaning his way. He was ahead of Harkin and right on Clinton's tail. The movement over the past three days was all in the right direction. They might just get that Big But after all.

Kerrey's men went to bed that primary eve dreaming of still more; the tarot deck of politics had once again woven its hypnotic spell. The overall polling totals they had been looking at didn't show the abrupt shift in the tides in Clinton's favor during the evening; the numbers instead were a mirage, a dreamscape of possibilities they hadn't dared imagine and didn't really have. In their reveries, Kerrey was getting airborne at last. His ads were finally working. He had the momentum. Even the elements seemed to favor him; the forecast for morning was snow, and their man on the ground, Paul Johnson, had put together what they felt sure was the best get-out-the-vote operation in the state.

"If you can get us to 15 percent, we'll be okay," Bob Burkett, Kerrey's finance chairman, told Johnson.

"If we get to 20," Bob Shrum said, "we'll win the nomination."

Declaring Victory

It didn't snow for Kerrey, but there wasn't much else for George Stephanopoulos to feel good about as primary morning broke over New Hampshire. Stephanopoulos wasn't even sure he could get himself out of bed. He was a short, dark, thick-maned young man of thirty-one, a Greek Orthodox prelate's son with the face of an altar boy and the intensity of a true believer for his secular causes. It wasn't languor that made him want to sleep in; as deputy communications director for Michael Dukakis in 1988, he had been nicknamed Twins for doing the work of two people, and his normal day in his new posting began at six in the morning.

He had been Clinton's first outside hire for the campaign—the Rhodes scholarship in his résumé helped—and had since become his alter ego, a mirror reflecting and magnifying the candidate's own moods. If Clinton was cut, Stephanopoulos bled; if Clinton felt blue, Stephanopoulos went black. It was going to be a black-and-blue Tuesday, he sensed, and he lay under the covers longer than he usually let himself do. "I just can't *do* this," he was thinking. By nightfall, the whole doom-haunted effort would be over.

He finally dragged himself out of bed and downstairs to the makeshift command center in room 206 at the Days. Even in good times, an election day is a torment for handlers, a march of long, empty hours spent waiting for small scraps of news. The times didn't look good for Clinton, and the only thing left to fill the day was to plan his orderly southward retreat. Stephanopoulos and Bob Boorstin from the PR shop sat down to help Paul Begala with a briefing memo for the candidate on what lay ahead. They were hard at work when Stan Greenberg bustled importantly into the room with the first returns on the day's exit polling.

Begala looked up from his word processor. "What's the bad news?" he asked, expecting nothing else.

"No, it's pretty good," Greenberg said. Clinton was behind Tsongas, but he was drawing more than 20 percent of the vote—the magic number he needed, in their calculations, to be perceived as real. The rest of the pack was far behind.

Stephanopoulos sighed heavily, almost theatrically. "As long as we have distance between us and Kerrey," he said, "that's all I care. We can beat Paul Tsongas."

The memo in progress suddenly got easier to write, and its authors began recasting it to reflect the emerging new reality. Kerrey was dying if not dead; Clinton's task, starting that night, would be to treat him as if he no longer existed and frame the race beyond New Hampshire as a two-man affair, a stark choice between himself and Tsongas. Words flew from Begala's fingertips onto the screen: "It's Moses vs. The Mechanic. The Visionary vs. The Technocrat. . . . You challenge; he chastises. You promise hope and opportunity; he promises pain and limited horizons. You view the presidency as the vital center of the nation, and this election as a struggle for the very soul of the nation; he sees the president as secretary of commerce."

Carville left the poets to their labors. He wasn't much for memos; it was part of his brief to bear the news to the candidate, good or bad, and he had gone into one of his private isometric warm-ups for the task. He paced the room, muttering about various forms of torture and flogging himself lightly with a length of rope he had picked up somewhere. Occasionally, as a punctuation mark, he paused and twisted it into a hangman's noose.

Begala glanced up at him and shrugged. "James is the only Shiite Catholic I know," he said, returning to the memo.

Suitably pumped, Carville ducked out to find Clinton. After a time, he reappeared in the room.

"He feels pretty good," Carville reported. "I said this is early stuff and it changes a lot."

"Yeah, but did he *hear* you?" Begala asked. You didn't want to get his hopes up too high; the fall would be steeper if the picture changed.

"It doesn't matter if he heard," Stephanopoulos said. "Let him have a couple of good hours."

More returns drifted in, better, if anything, than the first batch. It was Tsongas 35 percent, Clinton 25, Kerrey and Harkin 11 each. Carville snatched the readout from Greenberg's hands. "Where's my candidate?" he said, disappearing out the door again.

Mandy Grunwald came in and sat down at the word processor, working on lines for Clinton to use that night. She and Begala came up with the magic words that would turn a silver-medal finish into pure gold: "Thank you, New Hampshire, for making me the Comeback Kid," she wrote.

"That will get him on the network news," Begala said. In the new politics, getting on the news was the next best thing to winning.

While the others clung together for support, the Clintons stayed mostly alone in their suite, the candidate resting his weary body and his cracked voice. He had wakened at peace with himself, he would say later, and by the time he headed out to the Merimac Inn at five o'clock for a two-hour round of satellite-TV interviews, he was in exuberant spirits. It was as if he were *winning*, not just staying alive, and his glow helped shape the media perception of what was really happening. Bob Farmer, his campaign treasurer, came by between interviews to congratulate him.

"If those exit polls hold up," Clinton said, "we're smokin', son."

Still, he kept wanting reaffirmation that his situation was as good as it looked, and Stephanopoulos stepped out periodically with his cellular phone to get fresh numbers for him.

"It's almost like I'm just waiting for something bad," Clinton said. "Next one, I'll probably drop to 12 percent."

"I'm calculating how many hours there are left to vote and how far you *could* drop," Stephanopoulos confessed. The important thing was for Clinton not to dip below 20 percent, and that wasn't happening— not so far.

"I'll tell you what," Clinton said, fighting euphoria, "I'll feel like Lazarus if these polls hold up."

But his pleasure was not unalloyed. One of the polls, by the *Los Angeles Times*, showed him doing best on such personal qualities as caring, experience, and leadership.

"What more can you ask for?" Stephanopoulos said.

"*Message*," Clinton said quickly. "They killed us on message."

The modern campaign is a reductionist exercise, and that alchemical formula called message is its heart and soul, as central to politics as scripture to the church. The requirement was neither mysterious nor unreasonable on its face; it meant simply that a candidate ought to be able to make a clear and compelling case for his or her election, in as few words as possible, and stick with it day after day no matter what else happened. To be "on message," in the argot of the new politics, was the highest virtue. To stray or be knocked "off message" was thought to be a potentially mortal sin.

The quest for a negotiable message was harder than it looked; it had defeated such certifiably bright men as Walter Mondale, who had got the wrong one, and Michael Dukakis, who had seemed to have none at all, and Clinton was unhappy with the way it had been going in his embattled campaign. His theme of opportunity and responsibility— the New Covenant he had preached on at eloquent length in the fall— had never quite got cooked down to a digestible size and shape. His early lead had been built instead on the perception that he was the Democrat most likely to succeed in November, and the electability vote, he told Stephanopoulos, had always been a weak reed to rely on. It was a "pile-on" vote, he said, and once the storm of scandal broke over him, it was lost.

His message thereafter had been drowned out by the noise of the battlefield. Simply by weathering the assault, he had established himself as a tough and even leaderly man, a fighter who wouldn't buckle under pressure. But in the din about his sex life and his escape from the war, it was hard for people to tell what he was supposed to be fighting *for.*

The subject was a festering sore spot with Clinton, a suspicion congealing into angry certainty that his side had let him down; he was even then building toward one of his recurring blowups. But the night felt too good for recrimination. The status-quo boys in Washington had all but buried him, and he had proven them wrong. When the marathon interview session finally broke up, he made for the freight elevator, the secure back way up to his suite. As he stood waiting for it to come, he raised his fists and banged the doors in triumph, celebrating his own survival.

His team had gathered in his bedroom to talk about what he should say at his celebration that night and, more important, when he should say it. In the politics of appearances, the victory often goes to the candidate who claims it most convincingly, whether or not he has the most votes. Mickey Kantor led the charge for an early appearance, before Tsongas went on, and Hillary, decisively, seconded the motion.

"You don't think I should congratulate Tsongas on his apparent victory?" Clinton asked.

"No!" Hillary said. "*We're* the ones declaring victory. What's so great about getting 32 percent of the vote in the state next door to your own? The whole idea is for us to set the agenda and force Tsongas to respond to *us.*" Clinton didn't have to slam him; he just had to say that the next day was the beginning of the rest of the race and that, as the one candidate with a truly national campaign, he was ready for it. "Paul Tsongas couldn't name ten people for him in South Dakota or California or anywhere else," Hillary said.

Clinton followed the script, to brilliant effect; he used his handlers' line about his being the Comeback Kid with such conviction that everybody believed him. It wasn't enough to erase the fact that Tsongas had beaten him, 33 to 25 percent, in the final accounting. But with his early appearance and his exuberant manner, he had won the game within the game; on sheer salesmanship, his fourth of the vote became the stuff of a comeback in the overnight commentary and so robbed Tsongas's victory of much of its glow.

Tsongas seemed to sense as much. He and his team had chosen to delay his appearance, waiting for the real returns to catch up with their early prophecy that he would win by eleven points or better. It didn't happen; Clinton upstaged him, and when Tsongas finally presented himself to his followers at Razzberries, a restaurant near the Manchester airport, he was in what for a winner was an oddly ungracious humor. He spoke yet again of what he *wasn't* for—the particulars resembled the Clinton and Kerrey platforms—and of the pain he would be asking people to bear if he were to be elected. "We're going to climb that mountain," he said grimly. "We're going to *sweat.*" There was no larger, more generous vision in his speech, no shining city on a hill beckoning voters across the chilly plain of his politics. "I'm not running to be Santa Claus," he said one more time. "I'm running to be president of the United States, and there's a difference."

Tsongas at least had something to celebrate. Bob Kerrey did not; he had barely crept in third, with 11 percent of the vote, a point ahead of the luckless Harkin, and the Big But he had been chasing went to the Comeback Kid instead. There would be no charge of momentum for Kerrey, no fresh flow of cash to keep his candidacy going. His finance committee met that evening and concluded that, if he did expect to go on, he would have to spend a lot more of his time on the phone begging contributions. For Kerrey, who hated having to ask strangers for money, the prospect was as appetizing as a plate of broccoli to George Bush. He was losing his heart for the whole venture anyway; in the senator's rooms at the Wayfarer that night, Tad Devine had to talk him out of quitting the race then and there.

It was Clinton alone who went to bed happy. He had reestablished himself as a live contender and had sent a powerful message to what, in his pleasure, he dismissed as the Beltway crowd—the elites of the party and the press in Washington. He was alive and well. *Their* boys were not; the two senators in the race had fared badly, a write-in campaign for Mario Cuomo had fizzled, and the white-knight fantasies that had titillated the Democrats all winter would get harder to sustain with each passing day and each missed filing deadline. The lords and ladies of Washington, like it or not, would have to learn to live with Clinton, and the process was already starting. Why else would Speaker Tom Foley have called him, congratulating him on his showing and offering to work with him in some—ah—discreet way?

But Clinton's euphoria was gone by morning, the victim of the hard realities of his situation. All he had bought in New Hampshire was extended life, not victory, and the price in money, energy, and coherence had been high. Practically his whole command team had parachuted into the state just to get him through the primary with his skin still on. Everything else had been put on hold. The two biggest days of the early season were bare weeks away—first Junior Tuesday on March 3, with Colorado, Maryland, and Georgia largest among the prizes; then Super Tuesday on March 10, with its heavily southern array of eleven primaries and caucuses in a single day. It was crunch time, and so far as Clinton could see, they weren't ready. No new ads had been cut, no polling decisions taken, no strategies set in place, no defenses prepared for the next wave of attacks by the opposition and the press.

They weren't even sure where to go. Clinton's generals had decided early on that they couldn't let him get typed as a regional candidate, as Al Gore had been to lethal effect in 1988. He needed to win something outside the South before Super Tuesday to show that he had national appeal, and in the days before the draft controversy broke, it had looked as if he could do just that; he had been leading in the polls almost everywhere. The ground had changed since. The plan had not; as Bruce Lindsey would put it later, they had quit thinking, and bad targeting was one of the consequences. Within the week, Clinton would be suckered into contesting the Maine party caucuses and the South Dakota primary, two low-stakes games he had almost no hope of winning.

The campaign was back in crisis, verging on panic. Behind his public smile, the Comeback Kid was seething. On the flight south to Georgia the morning after the primary, David Wilhelm and Bruce Lindsey tried to brief him on the plan, such as it was, for South Dakota. Clinton stopped them; in his exhaustion, he was still fighting the last war.

"I think we should take on some of this 'I'm not Santa Claus' crap," he said. Tsongas was vulnerable, or should have been. The trouble, Clinton complained, was that nobody with any political sense had really put the guy's vaunted program under a microscope. Clinton's own top hands had been too busy piloting him through New Hampshire even to have read Tsongas's book.

What hurt more was that Clinton's own plan, his claim to serious regard as a candidate, had got swallowed up in the clamor about *him*. He knew he had got through New Hampshire by sheer force of will and personality; they had taken to calling him Robocandidate there for his refusal to lie down and die. After all these weeks and months, that was all anybody knew about him—that he could take a hit. At the end, he had tried to turn that perception back to what he stood for; the hits he had taken, he had said in speeches and interviews, were *nothing* compared to the hits the American people had taken under Reagan and Bush. It hadn't worked. "Even in the last week," he told Wilhelm, "my message was totally blocked out by all this stuff. When I went on the air and reinvented myself, they had totally forgotten the plan."

The parallax view of his candidacy was plainly wounding to a man whose sense of himself was so bound up with his ideas about public policy. *He* had become the subject, he told his aides, when the campaign ought to have been about a larger cause. In his agitation, he berated himself for not having demanded a new spot in the last week advertising his economic platform and his proposal for a national-service program for young people as a way to work off student loans. Instead, he had signed off on ads full of "pretty pictures and music"— typically political stuff in a year when being seen as a typical politician could be fatal. All New Hampshire proved, in Clinton's mind, was that people hadn't wanted to let his candidacy die young. What he hadn't done, he said, was give them sufficient reason to elect him president.

"We Don't Have A Clue"

What Clinton had to do first was dispose of Tsongas—go after the guy harder than he had so far been willing to do and from an angle further to the populist left than he had ever intended. He had hung back from the attack, even when his warm feeling for Tsongas had begun giving way to annoyance. But if the race was really down to the two of them, attack became a matter of strategic necessity, and Clinton was no longer hesitant about it. It was, for one thing, a way to define his own candidacy by contrasting himself with Tsongas. And it had the sweet taste of revenge—a chance to vent his rising anger with a man who had ridiculed him as a panderer.

The process began at his very first stop, in Atlanta, where Governor Zell Miller, a Carville and Begala client, spared the candidate having to bloody his own hands. "Bill Clinton is too gracious to say this," Miller told a crowd at the CNN Center, "but it's time to tell the truth. The truth is that Paul Tsongas will lead the party we love right down that well-worn path of defeat." When he laid down the cudgel, Clinton picked it up and in a matter of days was swinging it with visible relish and bloody effect. He attacked Tsongas as no more than "an economic mechanic" selling more of the trickle-down economics of the '80s. "I am tired of what is cold-blooded being passed off as courageous," he said one day in Denver; *his* program would put *people,* not corporations, first.

But off-camera, he was irate at the ragged state of his campaign coming out of New Hampshire and its seeming inability either to shape or to stick to a coherent message. Nothing seemed to be going right. On one particularly wretched day, Bob Kerrey came flying into Atlanta from his essentially empty victory in South Dakota and immediately lit into Clinton in vivid terms as unelectable—a loser who, come autumn, was "going to get opened up like a soft peanut" on the evidence of his own past. The line, from the pen of Bob Shrum, made a devastating sound bite. Clinton's contribution to the newscasts that night was equally irresistible and hardly more flattering. He had been in a studio doing a round of TV interviews when word reached him, incorrectly, that Jesse Jackson would be supporting Tom Harkin in the South. The result was the portrait of the candidate as an angry young man, throwing an unpresidential tantrum over what turned out to be an open mike. "It's a dirty, double-crossing, back-stabbing thing to do," he exploded. "For him to do this to me . . . is an act of absolute dishonor."

This time, the public glimpsed a Clinton familiar to his inner circle but rarely seen outside it: a man of short and explosive temper under stress. Once again, his message got lost in the sound and fury; once again, his field commanders were sunk in despond. Carville had headed south out of New Hampshire before the returns were in to run the campaign in Georgia. They would be okay there, Carville thought, and not just because of bubba pride; they had the formidable help of Zell Miller and his statewide connections. The trouble was that they were still so vulnerable everywhere else. The only thing Clinton had going for him at that moment, Carville believed, was the weakness of the field. Clinton should have been blowing them away. He wasn't; their deficiencies were the only reason he was still alive.

Clinton himself had been fraying visibly under the strain, and when he spoke one-on-one with Stephanopoulos in his suite in a downtown Denver hotel at the end of February, his aggravation showed. He was sitting on one of the twin beds in a small, dowdy room, looking angry. Nothing was working, he said. For the first time in all his years in politics, he didn't know what to do.

Stephanopoulos didn't know, either. His own spirits had sunk to a point where he was thinking of leaving politics; it had become a daily struggle for him just to get up and go to work. But he knew he had to mask his own feelings. There was a debate that night to prep for, and he couldn't let Clinton sink into self-pity.

"Governor, I know you're frustrated," he said, but they needed to get down to the business at hand. It was going to be a long campaign. The message would get out, and the forum that evening was a place to start. You have things to say, Stephanopoulos told Clinton. You'll have a good debate.

"I *always* have a good debate," Clinton said, sounding petulant, "but it doesn't matter."

Stephanopoulos tried to be cheering. Kerrey, he said, was tapped out, living on borrowed money and time. Tsongas would get some mileage out of Junior Tuesday, but that was okay; it would be a two-way race then, and Clinton could win it.

Clinton nodded and went back to work on some radio spots. But when he met with the prep team in his sitting room later, he started up again, this time about the ads. His media man, Frank Greer, was known in the trade for his strongly emotional spots, beating the Republicans at their own symbolic game. The problem had come because his operatic style collided with his client's own wounded sense of who he was and what his campaign was supposed to be about. "The message we've been sending is totally wrong," Clinton said. The ads weren't specific enough; they were all flags and rallies and soaring background music, and while he remained personally loyal to Greer, he hated the product. "It undermines everything I've stood for," he said. "It's not working. Nothing's moving any numbers."

His people were trying to get him back on track, but he kept rolling. He was running as the candidate of change, the one man who would challenge the status quo, he said; it was the very heart of his campaign, of who he was, and it was being obliterated. "We've failed to capture that," he railed. "We've just failed. And it's really discouraging. It was the ultimate wound out of New Hampshire. I see it now—coming out of New Hampshire, we should have said here is a guy who was down and he's back because of issues."

The handlers reminded him gently of why they were there: to practice for a debate. In an environmentalist state, they were expecting
him to be attacked on his environmental record, and they tried out
ways to respond. The bottom line was that Clinton wasn't Tsongas, or
Kerrey, or Bush—three men complicit in the failures of the past.

"The strength of this campaign has been its message of change,"
Begala said.

It was the wrong thing to say; it touched a sore spot, like cold water
on a bad tooth, and Clinton was off again. The message of change had
been subverted by the strategy they had used to save him in New
Hampshire, which was essentially to forget about it. "I think we have
to face the fact that we're no longer the candidate of change," he said,
"and nothing we've been doing has changed that."

"And we've got an opportunity to change that today," Begala reminded him.

Clinton ignored him. "We've been miserably unprepared for the
last two weeks," he said. "We haven't had a strategy, and we have to
face that. We've been running national mailings and national ads that
aren't worth anything and are not related to issues." The words were
spilling out now. "We have to analyze everything we've done wrong,"
he said. "We don't have a *clue.*"

He got up to get ready for a fund-raiser; its timing, before the
debate, was a further irritant to him, but it was too late to reschedule
it. Stephanopoulos followed him into the bedroom and, while Clinton
changed, asked if he wanted to reconvene the prep session when he got
back.

"All I know is I don't want another debate prep I don't have any
confidence in," he snapped.

In the sitting room, his coaches did a quick damage assessment.

"We've got to keep him off of everything that's wrong with this
campaign," Lindsey said.

True, Greenberg said, but Clinton was on to something important:
they *hadn't* talked seriously about what their strategy should be. "It's
crazy to go on like this. There's no clear sense we know where we're
going, and you know why? We *don't.*"

"We can't do that today," Lindsey said.

They weren't going to do much more prepping, either; Clinton came
back from his fund-raiser still smoldering, and Begala cut their planned
second sitting short. "The only idea I want to convey is this," he said.
"You are the candidate of change. All it is, is: they're old and we're
new. And that will define you and give people reason to vote for you."

In his dressing room at the Denver convention center that night,

Clinton withdrew from all of them, turning inside himself. His people took that to be a good rather than a bad sign; it usually meant he was on and would perform well. He sat at a makeup table with his wire-rim reading glasses on, making notes from a couple of clippings on the differences between his plan and Tsongas's. Stephanopoulos sat on the counter. The others stood. Mostly they left him alone, speaking only when he asked a question.

"You need to be more of a happy warrior," Greer said at one point.

Clinton didn't respond. The room was silent except for the soft scribbling of his pen on a packet of three-by-five index cards. At one point, he turned to Begala and asked for some funny lines.

Begala offered one that had served Clinton well in speeches: "I've had so much garbage dumped on me, I'm practically a human landfill."

"I don't know why you want to remind people of that baggage," Greer said.

"Because it's *out* there," Stephanopoulos answered.

"It's *absolutely* out there, and that's why we're not doing better," Clinton said.

It was time to go on, and Clinton headed for the set. Greer trailed along behind him. The others hung back in a holding room to watch the show on a single small TV set.

"I think he's ready," Stephanopoulos said, more than a bit wishfully. "I think he feels good."

So it seemed, at first; Clinton was in stride, hitting all the right buttons about change and drawing the agreed-on line between his people-first economics and Tsongas's pro-business plan. "He *is* the smartest boy in the class," Begala exulted at one point, and when the group reviewed their scorecards at mid-debate, they had their boy and Jerry Brown ahead on points. Tsongas, by contrast, seemed off his feed. It was gang-up time on Saint Paul again, mostly on nuclear energy, and his responses under fire got small and pouty. Kerrey was flailing, and Brown didn't matter. The night belonged to Clinton.

"Man, this is exactly what we wanted," Begala said. "He's on substance, he's on change, and he's pushing them."

"He's on," Stephanopoulos said. "He's confident. He's *back.*"

But momentum, in televised debates, can be as fickle as a hot streak at a gaming table; it can be wiped out in one bad play, and Clinton, in his frazzled state, was an easy mark. There were just twenty minutes to go when he joined the assault on Tsongas, charging that he would build "hundreds" of new nuclear power plants around the country.

Tsongas looked stricken. "That is a lie," he said. "That is a lie. That is a lie."

"No one can argue with you, Paul," Clinton said. "You're always perfect."

"I'm not perfect," Tsongas shot back, without missing a beat, "but I'm honest."

For Tsongas, it was a bad moment, damaging to his image as a man above the petty squabbling of politics. For Clinton, it was worse, an arrow to the heart, and the silence in his holding room was the sound of despair.

"It was so *unnecessary,*" Lindsey said.

"It was going so well," Stephanopoulos said, burying his head in his hands. "Paul Tsongas just won this debate."

The show ended, and Clinton joined his team.

"I just got so sick of that 'I'm no Santa Claus,'" he said, his mood still smoky. "'I'm the only one this, I'm the only one that.'"

His people found it hard pretending to be happy. The debate was the campaign in microcosm, a struggle in which Clinton's beliefs about governance kept getting engulfed by questions about his character. This time, worse yet, he had wounded himself; in a game ruled by sound bites, most of America would see nothing of the debate except Clinton inviting rebuke and Tsongas delivering it, right between the eyes. It was the mistake of a candidate wandering off course into a preserve of his own, a private zone of rancor at the world and pity for himself. His people were in danger of losing him to his furies, and unless they could get him back, it would be difficult for him or them to get his candidacy on track and moving again.

9.

"Goin' Home"

The campaign jet was southward bound from Baltimore to Macon, Georgia, deep in the heart of what ought to have been Clinton Country, but the candidate was still in a state of acute distemper with everyone—the opposition, the press, his own team, himself. It was the day before Junior Tuesday, and his morning, always his worst time, had been spoiled by a fresh round of polling. Tsongas was beating him in Maryland, Colorado, and Minnesota. Even Georgia, the state he had been counting on as his firebreak, was in some danger; the *Atlanta Constitution* had just come out for Tsongas, upsetting Clinton greatly, and Governor Zell Miller, his most important ally in the state, had warned James Carville, "We're not bleeding—we're *hemorrhaging.*"

The Clinton road show had taken on the air of a death march, and the gloom had infected its star. "Goin' home!" Clinton had crooned happily to himself, breaking camp in New Hampshire only two weeks before. Now he *was* home, or headed there, and as his jet streaked across Dixie, he was telling his combat-numbed troops, "This battle may be over."

He had started the day at a Metrorail subway in Maryland, smile in place, shaking hands in the early March chill and gamely telling reporters to forget the polls—"this thing is going in the right direction." Out of their earshot, his mood was foul and his sense of direction the opposite of what he had claimed. He was still growling at his strategists and, most particularly, his ads. "They have not captured the essence of my economic message," he railed at his traveling party. "They've lost Minnesota. They've lost Maryland." He wanted new ads, fast, this time with him on camera framing his race with Tsongas as a choice between yesterday and tomorrow; more trickle-down Reaganomics or a new commitment to invest in the future.

His aides had taken the beating in glum silence, hoping that, as usually happened, the storm would blow over. It didn't; almost as soon as Clinton had buckled into his seat for the flight south, the stage smile fell away, and he erupted again. His voice, raw with overuse, was a furious whisper. His fist pounded the armrest in time with each hoarse word. In the seats nearest him, Paul Begala and George Stephanopoulos sat looking blank and saying nothing. It was useless to argue with Clinton when he was in one of his moods; it was best just to shut up and let him ventilate.

At the top of his list that morning was, yet again, the middle-class tax cut; it had become a canker on his spirit, both cause and symptom, he thought, of all that had gone wrong in his campaign. His complaint had a strong odor of denial about it, given his own complicity in the plan and his refusal to concede that the underlying problem was not his program but himself. He was, as his people understood, a man haunted by the ghosts of his past; the media had wakened them in New Hampshire, and he had responded with what looked like verbal sleight of hand. His campaign there had been like a failing carnival, all spiel and no show. His campaign promises, including the tax cut, had either been eclipsed by the controversy or had been seen through a prism of mistrust in everything he said.

But it was no good telling him any of that; the tax cut had become an obsession for him, and in his revisionist history of where it came from, he had all but exempted himself from blame. All he had really wanted was a tax credit for children, he complained, "but I got talked out of it by too-cautious advisers who said not everyone has kids." They had sold him on the tax cut instead, and it had come to be seen as the cornerstone of his whole economic program. He was getting cuffed around for it, not just in debates but on the editorial pages; his adoring old notices as a man with a sophisticated plan had given way to a new wave writing him off as a politician with a simplistic view of the economy and a tacky gimmick purporting to fix it. It had been a mistake and worse; it had "destroyed the integrity, the vitality of everything I stood for and worked for for the past ten years."

"We have let *Tsongas* become the candidate of the future," he rasped, thumping the armrest, "and that's why we are losing. 'If you're not for progress, you're yesterday's politician. If you're for dividing the pie, you're yesterday's politician.' Don't kid yourselves— we let him do it. We helped him by our stubborn insistence on running this middle-class tax cut and our stubborn refusal to run the new ideas of my campaign."

It wasn't so much the cost that hurt him as the injury to his pride. Tsongas was winning what Eugene McCarthy once described as the A students—the upmarket, college-schooled, issue-oriented people who led and sometimes shaped public opinion. "I am (*thump!*) very (*thump!*) angry," Clinton said. "I've worked my butt off, I've raised all this

money so *I* could be the candidate of new ideas." He wasn't; it was
Tsongas instead who had become the darling of the editorial writers,
and Clinton's own team had let *that* happen, too, without a peep of
protest. "We need to beat them up," he said. "This is *war.* This is
conflict. My staff isn't playing offense."

The way to begin, in his view, was with his advertising. There had
been a debate in Maryland the night before, the third in two days, and
he had dominated it by distinguishing himself from Tsongas. "We have
never had an ad that captures my economic message like I did last
night," he complained. "*Never.*" They had a million dollars in wasted
ads out there; they, and the campaign, had to change, and not, he said,
to the stale old class-war rhetoric they had been drifting into. "You've
got to be *for* something," he insisted. He wanted ads that opened with
something positive about him and his program, and then explained
how his ideas were newer and better than Tsongas's. He had a plan,
but its integrity, and his, had been eviscerated by the middle-class tax
cut. He wanted a new approach, and, he growled, "I don't care *how* it
polls."

Some of his own people had come to think that he and they cared
rather too much about polling; they had done far more surveys and
focus groups than any of his rivals, and Clinton had signed off on all of
it. They blamed his anger in part on his fatigue; his tantrums usually
happened when he was tired. But it flowed as well, one staffer believed,
from his wanting to have things both ways—to devour polls and still
pretend they did not influence him. His campaign had in fact become
poll-driven, this aide said; for two months, they had been doing everything because of a poll and then had been surprised when their dependency showed. There was no risk anymore, so there was no edge to the
campaign. They had lost it by trying to play it safe.

Still, Clinton's generals saw a silver lining in the storm cloud of his
rage. "Where his frustration with the middle-class tax cut is very
valuable," one of them told another, "is in breaking him of this tyranny of poll data. What he doesn't admit is that he is overly reliant on
polls. He'll go on a two-day jaunt about left-handed blonde women
who no longer support him."

"That's Bill Clinton, campaign manager," the second staffer replied.

"No," his colleague said. "That's just Bill Clinton."

Their first move to appease him was to clear his schedule the next
afternoon so they could shoot some new commercials. But what
should they say? What *could* they say? The questions about Clinton's
character were like a great cloud blotting out everything else in his
campaign; it was hard for him to be heard if people didn't believe him.

His strategists convened by conference call to talk about the problem. Their spirits were low; most of the road party didn't see a way for Clinton to get through Junior Tuesday whole. Neither was there a clear answer to the basic dilemma before them: should they go at the trust problem frontally, owning up that Clinton had one? Or could they find some formulation of his message so big, so compelling, that people would lay aside their reservations and give him the benefit of the doubt?

Carville, as usual, spoke up for the big idea. "We got to get one thing and get to the core of this election," he said from Atlanta, his voice a throaty growl on the speaker phone.

Frank Greer argued that the character question had to be dealt with first; otherwise, it wouldn't matter *what* Clinton said on the issues. "We've got to do something to regain trust," he insisted.

Stan Greenberg agreed. Carville didn't. "My belief in a campaign," he argued, "is take one thing and drive it home as hard as you can."

"It's all about accountability," Begala replied. "Values."

"Let's decide on one thing," Carville said impatiently. The clock was running, and the campaign seemed adrift, with no clear focus. "If it's values," he said, "do values. If it's accountability, do accountability."

"Do one thing and drive it home," Begala agreed.

"If we want to do accountability," Carville said, "tie it into the '80s. Paul Tsongas versus the future. All I keep coming back to is, let's find one thing, let's do it, and let's start Wednesday morning and say, 'This election is about—'"

"You've seen how upset the governor is," Begala reminded the others. "He does not want his message reduced to populist economics. He will not go with a straight populist dichotomy of Wall Street versus Main Street. He wants to go beyond the politics of the past."

"He can't stand the idea that Paul Tsongas is getting credit for new ideas," Stephanopoulos said.

"It just tears him up that Tsongas is thought to have a more sophisticated economic plan," Begala added.

"And that Clinton's a rube with a middle-class tax cut," Stephanopoulos said.

Greenberg, the numbers man, thought Clinton should quit worrying so much about it. The high-end vote was only a quarter of the electorate. "Our core audience is non-college women who don't trust us on values," he argued. "He's got to relate to them in some way on values."

"Stan, I understand what you're saying," Stephanopoulos said, "but those are not the voters he's focusing on."

"Then he damn well loses this election," Greenberg said sharply.

They were talking about advertising approaches when Carville cut in again, reminding the others that there was only a week left till Super Tuesday. "We got just one spot," he said. "I'm just telling y'all that we've got to draw a distinction with Paul Tsongas."

They tried out some approaches. None quite clicked.

"We can't do fifteen messages," Mickey Kantor said finally. "We'll be lucky if we get two ideas across. We're doing better with our contrast with Tsongas, but we all know the problem we're having: people don't trust Bill Clinton."

"I agree with that," Greenberg added, "and I think if we don't address that, we won't win."

Someone interrupted with the latest poll numbers. They weren't good. In Colorado, Tsongas was leading, and Jerry Brown was coming on strong, challenging Clinton for second place. In Florida, a must Super Tuesday prize for both men, Clinton and Tsongas were dead even; the only comforting news was that, in the year of the outsider, most people saw Tsongas as a creature of the system—a former senator with corporate strings attached.

"Now, that's the contrast," Greenberg said.

"Are you saying that's what we communicated in Georgia?" Carville asked. He was nearly shouting. "I'm *drunk* if the voters picked up on that. This race has not been about the contrast between Paul Tsongas and Bill Clinton. It's been about Gennifer Flowers and the draft. If it is so critical, then let's make this about trust."

The ad couldn't *just* be about trust, Greenberg objected. Couldn't they do the contrast on economics in a way that made people *like* Clinton a little more?

"I believe so," Greer said.

"I believe *not,*" Begala shot back—not, anyway, in the week remaining before Super Tuesday.

"If this race is on trust, we will get our clocks cleaned," Kantor worried. "Let's do responsibility first, then tackle trust for Super Tuesday."

"Respect first, trust and love later," Grunwald said.

"The question is, are they more comfortable with Bill Clinton at the end," Greenberg went on. "If they're not, I don't give a damn *how* good the contrast is."

"What basically we have," Stephanopoulos said, "is that Bill Clinton's plan is new and tough, and that's the contrast." If that meant ducking the character question for now, so be it. "Our central problem is they don't trust us. But you're not going to get people to trust you in a week."

Not many people in Clinton's campaign really believed he *had* another week; they straggled to work on Junior Tuesday thinking that the show was about to close on the road. They had all but written off Maryland, and they were going to lose Colorado as well. Their offsetting "victory" in Georgia would be so underwhelming in scale and so heavily discounted in advance that no one would care. Bruce Lindsey, the candidate's friend and adviser, wished he could pack it all in and go home. Stephanopoulos was barely going through the motions. In Little Rock, Rahm Emanuel, the fund-raiser, and Richard Mintz, who had lately become Hillary's manager, went out for a recklessly long and vinous lunch. The jokes were of the gallows genre; the serious topic was what they would do now that the campaign was over.

In Atlanta, Clinton headed for a church, where Greer had a camera crew waiting to shoot the new commercials. He submitted to the required makeup artistry, then joined his roadies in a Sunday-school classroom and took a seat in an undersized chair for a briefing on what they had come up with.

"We're not going to accomplish, between now and Super Tuesday, all of our goals," Carville said. His tone and his hyperkinetic manner were uncommonly subdued. "I'll be honest with you," he added. "If today goes like I think it will, we're going to be in the fight of our political lives. We're not going to be able to erase every personal doubt or get our message all the way there." All they could do by Super Tuesday, he told Clinton, was sharpen the choice between him and Tsongas to a single point of difference, and they had to do it fast and well.

"We can't fix everything with one ad," Carville said.

"We can't fix it overnight," Clinton replied, "but we can fix it."

He was trying to buck everybody up, including himself. It was hard. He said he had talked with Hillary the night before about the unhappy pass they had come to and had found her in "emotional free fall." The others fell deathly still; his voice was the only sound in the room.

Then he got up to do the shoot. His people hadn't had the heart to tell him that talking straight into the camera was his worst look on television. He was *too* good at it, too smooth; it called Slick Willie to mind. His best side came out when he spoke extempore with real people, and Greer had assembled a group in an adjoining room as props for the ads. Clinton would talk to them about what had gone wrong in the '80s and what he proposed to do to set things right.

While he was out, Carville, Begala, and Stephanopoulos hung back in the classroom to talk.

"We have got six days, that's all," Carville said. They had an unhappy candidate on their hands, and they were *still* looking for the defining difference between him and Tsongas.

"How do we keep it from getting so damn petty?" Stephanopoulos wondered. "Look at what's happened in the last five days. He's gone further and further into the toilet because he can't contain his frustration." All their advice would be useless if Clinton himself didn't focus on what he wanted to say; in fact, he ought to ignore his consultants and work through his message on his own. They would be driving to the airport that day, and, Stephanopoulos said, "I'm going to tell him to write down ten sentences."

Carville wanted a fax copy of whatever the exercise produced.

"You got to tell him to do that," Stephanopoulos said. "It's the only way to break the tyranny of the consultants."

"Well, you better be sitting up there in that car with him," Carville answered.

They brooded some more, still groping for words.

"Strategy is not a priority in this campaign," Carville said suddenly. "In fact, we have *bad* strategy. This campaign works too hard and thinks too little."

"But how do we change that?" Begala asked.

By defining the race as a real choice, Carville answered; maybe by making it a battle for the soul of the Democratic Party. "I want to have a real focus," he said.

The soul-of-the-party business troubled Stephanopoulos; it could cast Clinton as the Old Democrat running against a man who was *really* challenging the settled liberal orthodoxies.

"That's Clinton's worst fear," Begala said. "That he'll get sucked into some Tom Harkin–style prairie populism. Into being something he's not."

"The only way we can survive this is if we convince people that Paul Tsongas is not a Democrat," Stephanopoulos said. "This is still a Democratic primary."

Survival, in their depressive mode, looked like the best they could hope for that day. Their life-or-death state, out of the seven up for grabs, was Georgia. Its friendly party leadership had scheduled the primary early for Clinton's advantage, as a kind of appetizer for his expected feast on Super Tuesday the following week. In the game of expectations, Clinton not only had to win it, he had to win it big; he couldn't come out of Georgia looking like a bleeder. He had everything going for him there, from the governor down to the county courthouses. But Carville, as Clinton's man on the ground in Atlanta, was worried. There had been too much damage, too many days in which they had let themselves get knocked off their message. Carville thought Tsongas might top 30 percent of the vote, a deep embarrassment for Clinton and a bad portent for the next rounds.

"We've been blocked," Carville said.

"It's true," Stephanopoulos replied. "We have not had a good story in two weeks. No one knows anything about us except we've got problems."

"We need a hit person who goes out and hits Tsongas all the time," Carville said. "If Paul Tsongas wins the Florida primary—"

"—he wins the nomination," Stephanopoulos finished.

They were staring wanly into the future. There didn't seem to be much of it left.

Carville found a piece of chalk, stood at a blackboard, and scratched out, "Narrow Focus!!!" People first versus business first—that was the contrast if Clinton would buy it. "It's not perfect," Carville said, "but it's all we can do. We got five days."

And the people's trust—could Clinton ever get it back?

"It's going to be tough," Carville said, "but the only way we can ever regain it is to be in the race after today."

There was a break in the shoot, and Clinton came back into the classroom. It had been going well, he told them; he had used his '80s versus '90s message, and for the first time, he had felt as if he had been communicating what his candidacy was really all about.

But as he stepped outside to go on filming, this time with a multiracial group of children in the church schoolyard, he seemed visibly rattled. His "comeback" in New Hampshire had not been as cleansing as he had hoped; he hadn't yet won anything anywhere, he was in for a long night that night, and his prospects for Super Tuesday, a week away, looked dicey. He was running, in effect, against himself, or that caricature of himself born in the tabloids and embellished daily in the mainstream media.

"We can't go a day without a story on it," Stephanopoulos said dolefully. He was sitting on a pylon in the schoolyard, just out of camera range, watching Greer arrange the players for the next scene. "It's deadly," he went on. "It's slow poison. People can talk for days about not having a strategy, or having no clear message, which is true. But the real truth is, he has had a ton of mud dropped on him and no one can see him. Read the papers. It's all you see."

The No-Win Scenario

Ten days before Junior Tuesday, Tad Devine had wandered into the office of his sidekick, Tony Corrado, seeking shelter from the telephones. Their guy Bob Kerrey was off in South Dakota trying to save his candidacy; his expected victory there was pretty much a gimme, since he came from just across the state line, but he had to have a quick win somewhere just to stop the bleeding. The far harder question was where to send him next in the briar patch of southern and western primaries coming up, and Devine wanted somewhere quiet to think and talk about it.

"Let's get out of here," he said. "We need inspiration. We have to figure out how we're going to win this nomination."

Corrado glanced up from his paperwork. Devine was carrying some notes and a cellular phone. Corrado scooped up his own stuff—a wad of index cards and delegate counts—and followed his pal down to the street.

"We're going to kick this guy's ass," Devine said, meaning Clinton's. "We just have to figure out how to do it."

They flagged a cab and headed for what was perhaps the most secure safe house in Washington for two political operatives plotting strategy: the National Gallery of Art. Their search for the muse led them past the Leonardos, the Raphaels, the Monets. Corrado lingered over a series of Walker Evans's disturbing photos of the casualties of the Great Depression. Devine hung back, his cell phone pressed to his ear, returning his backed-up calls in a low murmur. The usual lunchtime parade of art lovers glared at him as they strolled by.

Finally, the two men retired to the museum cafeteria and set up shop at a table, spreading their notes and cards in front of them. The puzzle was how to navigate Kerrey safely through alien territory over the next several weeks to Michigan, where he might have at least a fighting chance. It was going to be tough. Among the prize states, Tsongas had staked out Maryland, and Clinton looked solid in Georgia, South Carolina, and the cluster of southern states voting on Super Tuesday. There wasn't much left for Kerrey, and even if there had been, he was nearly broke.

"Okay, how do we light up the board?" Devine asked. They couldn't win the next rounds; the imperative instead was to survive them, and he saw only one way. "We have to change the game," he told Corrado.

His idea was essentially to finesse a schedule that was stacked against Kerrey anyway. Devine called his plan "delegate accrual," though it rather resembled General Giap's strategy for Vietnam: you fought for patches of ground back in the boonies and let the big targets wait until the time was ripe. They would play hard in only one state, Colorado or Georgia, on Junior Tuesday and then shop the map of Super Tuesday states for the friendlier congressional districts; the objective would be to pick off delegates in retail rather than wholesale numbers. If Kerrey and Tsongas each got enough, they could at least keep Clinton from running away with the day and the nomination.

A light bulb went off over Corrado's head. The plan reminded him of an old episode on *Star Trek,* one in which Captain Kirk had beaten a computer war game called the No-Win Scenario. He had done it the only way possible: he had reprogrammed the computer and made a no-win game winnable.

In the quiet of the cafeteria, the two handlers started shuffling papers, looking for a way for Captain Kerrey to do the same. They began with a search for congressional districts in which he might get 15 percent of the vote, the threshold level you had to beat to win your proportional share of the delegates. They scoured their lists for likely targets. They punched numbers into a pocket calculator. They scribbled furiously on note cards. In the end, they reckoned that there was a chance—just a chance—that Clinton would come out of Super Tuesday with no more than 650 delegates of the 2,145 he would need for the nomination. His edge would be big but not yet insuperable. Kerrey would have lived to fight another day, on friendlier ground.

Devine laid out the plan to the rest of the command group the next day, then headed west to Colorado to explain it to Kerrey. They connected on the campaign plane between Boulder and Denver, sitting side by side in the forward cabin with Kerrey's road crew around them. Devine was excited. His face was flushed. His forelock tumbled down his brow. He was sweating, and his glasses slid down his ski-jump nose. There was some good news that day—Kerrey was leading in the exit polls out of South Dakota—but he needed to know that it was the *last* good news he would be hearing for a while.

"You gotta stay in the boat," Devine told him. "You gotta keep your head down. It's gonna be a tough couple of weeks. You gotta stay focused. You gotta stay focused on the long-term strategy."

He outlined it, pulling no punches. They would be floating over the next two weeks with no money to speak of, but that was okay, Devine said, so long as they kept accruing delegates. The short-term objective was just to stay in the hunt till the South was behind them; if they could keep Clinton in sight, they would have a shot at overtaking him as the campaign moved north and west. It was a long-haul strategy, Devine admitted, but that was okay, too. He showed Kerrey his legal pad full of numbers, demonstrating, like a proof in math, that it could be done.

"Does your wife know about this?" Kerrey asked him, smiling. Devine was always moping about the time he had to spend away from his family back in Providence. The question was a joke between two men who had only lately got comfortable with one another; it told Devine that Kerrey was aboard.

The plan was never more than self-delusion, a dream of the sort that flourishes in bunkers when the generals cannot bear to admit defeat. Kerrey soldiered through it, broke but game. He spent a couple of days in Georgia, lobbing bombs at Clinton as a man of character so flawed as to render him unelectable in November. Then he headed west back to Colorado, the state Devine had finally settled on as their prime target for Junior Tuesday. Kerrey's last available dollars went into a flash media buy there over the weekend before the primary, an ad attacking Clinton *and* Tsongas on their environmental records.

It was all spun wheels. On primary day, Kerrey was in Arizona, the next station on his long journey nowhere. Devine followed him there. The exit polls during the day were ugly. The real numbers, when Devine caught up with them the next morning, were worse. He had slept badly; to save a few dollars, he had shared a room with the campaign baggage handler, and people had been phoning all night with questions about luggage and logistics. Still groggy, Devine rolled out of bed and flicked on the TV news. Clinton's victory in Georgia was the big story. Kerrey hadn't won anything anywhere, or qualified for any delegates. In Colorado, his ad slamming the two front-runners appeared only to have driven votes to Jerry Brown; the onetime golden boy had finished out of the money. The plan hadn't worked. The No-Win Scenario had devoured another victim.

Devine switched off the set, pulled on his clothes, and headed out into the corridor, knowing it was over. Billy Shore, the senator's body man, found him there.

"He wants to get out," Shore said.

They headed for Kerrey's suite. The senator was sitting on a couch, surrounded by his team. They weren't so much planning for the future as wondering whether there was one. Tony Corrado had worked up a financial plan for the next two weeks. Usually, he presented a choice among "high," "medium," and "low" budgets. This time, the only options were "low" and "skeletal," and even the latter came to $1 million. There was no prospect of raising it; the money boys, along with everybody else, had finally written Kerrey off as a loser.

Should he keep going anyway? He had already polled the room when

Devine arrived. The response was plain in their long faces. Kerrey turned to Devine. Tad was the house optimist; maybe he had an angle. "What do you think?" Kerrey asked him.

"You're toast," Devine said.

They scrubbed a fund-raising trip to Florida that day and flew back to Washington instead. Kerrey met with his staff, choking up a bit as he spoke to them, and later with the Senate colleagues who had backed him. Their advice was to get out, gracefully and soon.

The next morning, before a gallery of aides, volunteers, and reporters on Capitol Hill, the fallen favorite announced his withdrawal from the race. His irony was in full flight, and his words were eloquent, a summons to fundamental change in America—"not timid change, not change at the margins, but radical change, to restore a sense of purpose and mission to our experiment in self-government." The message had finally come together, when it was too late. In the audience, a few of his people cried. It would be said among some of them later that Kerrey's farewell had been his best speech of the campaign.

Honey, I Shrunk the Message

The day, had anybody noticed, was Paul Tsongas's; he had won three of the seven states at stake on Junior Tuesday, more than any of his rivals, and had done presentably well everywhere else. But the night, when the arbiters of prime time render their judgments in such matters, belonged to Bill Clinton. He was in downtown Miami at 6:30, wrapping up some local TV interviews, when Stephanopoulos came in with the latest exit polling. Tsongas's expected victory in Maryland wasn't exactly a blowout, and he was in danger of losing Colorado to—of all people—Jerry Brown. And Georgia? Clinton smiled and punched a hole in the air. He was thrashing Tsongas, by better than two to one. Georgia had saved his political life.

His victory there was a sweet one, made sweeter by the fact that he and his people had spent the past several weeks reading death notices for his candidacy. Some of the pols they had counted on had started to *bleed,* as Carville put it, back when it looked as if Clinton might get burned in the first southern primary. Senator Sam Nunn, nominally an ally, had done virtually nothing to defend him on his draft record, and much of the old Jimmy Carter crowd had been flirting with Tsongas. They would be serving crow for supper that night on some of the finest tables in Georgia, and Carville, for one, planned to enjoy the spectacle. "George," he told Stephanopoulos, "I'm gonna go up to the City Club, have a couple of martinis and a steak, and make a list of everyone who tried to fuck us in the last week."

Georgia had restored Clinton's credibility as well, or so he believed. He thanked the South for that, he told Dee Dee Myers. It wasn't called the Bible Belt for nothing; people there were more religious and therefore, Clinton felt, more forgiving. They could look at him, know his sins, and still believe in his redemption—and, believing that, they had listened to him. For all the time he and his handlers had spent agonizing over it, his retooled message—people-first economics—had finally clicked. What his victory proved was that he could exploit the open ground to Tsongas's left and still run as a new-model Responsibility Democrat.

It didn't even seem to matter to the instant analysts that he had been *expected* to carry Georgia or that it was the only state he had won. "NBC was great," Stephanopoulos told him happily after a fast scan of the evening newscasts, "and Rather led with 'Clinton comes alive in Georgia.' And the interesting thing: the exit polls asked why people didn't vote for Paul Tsongas. They said he was for big business."

Again, a smile broke luxuriantly over Clinton's face. He still felt sickish, as he had all winter; his voice was a croak, and he was ashy with fatigue. "I just want to go to bed," he said. "I don't know that I can function. I feel *baaad.*" But he and his campaign were back in business, and before he turned in, he called Governor Miller, whose name and connections had helped put him there. "Zell, you really laid down for me," he said. "If you'd *tried,* ol' boy, you might have done me some good." They both laughed; then Clinton got serious again. "You stood up for me and gave me credibility," he said, "and the people could *hear.* I can turn this around. I'm real happy. This is going to be stunning. No one expected this. This will send them a message."

If so, it was bitterly received by Paul Tsongas. He was under the impression that *he* was the one who ought to have been celebrating that night; he felt so good about his showing, indeed, that he decided to sleep in the next day instead of doing the morning shows, thus wasting a chance to share his message and his victory glow with the voters in the crucial states just ahead. The one important debit entry on his balance sheet for Junior Tuesday had been Colorado. Brown *had* won it, and Clinton had slipped in second by a bare percentage point. Tsongas, once the heavy favorite there, had run an embarrassing third; a thirty-point lead in the early polls had melted away to less than zero.

But he had won Maryland, Utah, and Washington state and had finished second in the other three states on the calendar. No one could write off his candidacy as a hothouse New England flower anymore;

his win, place, and show finishes had all come far from home. He hadn't even done all *that* badly in Georgia. The final score there was Clinton 57 percent to Tsongas 24; still, for a northern interloper to go from zero to a fourth of the vote on enemy territory in two weeks was no mean achievement. "They said that I was a regional candidate," Tsongas exulted at his victory party that night. "They're right: North, South, East, and West."

He proclaimed himself The Breakthrough Kid, cribbing from Clinton's bag of tricks. It didn't work for him, and another twig was added to the growing fire of his anger at his rival; it had reached that heat at which Tsongas even envied him his slickness. Clinton's people seemed able to lower expectations and then beat them, where Tsongas, as he himself remarked with sour irony, had trouble creating any expectations at all. "They are the most accomplished spinmeisters," he complained one day on the road in Georgia. "Whoever came up with that 'Comeback Kid' line did a great job. I'm in the minor leagues in comparison."

Tsongas's campaign by then was taking on the air of a grudge match; he didn't like Clinton anymore, and his animus only deepened as his rival tried to rehabilitate himself by bashing him. Tsongas had come out of New Hampshire the putative front-runner, and he believed, on the basis of incomplete returns, that he had won the Maine caucuses soon thereafter. It would be several weeks before the victory was awarded, narrowly, to Jerry Brown instead. Even then, Tsongas had the best numbers on the scoreboard. But to his growing annoyance, Clinton seemed to be winning the perceptions game with arts more commonly associated with club fights and bondage films: the ability to absorb punishment and seem to enjoy it. What Tsongas's victories bought him was attention when what he really needed was credibility. He was still seen less as a live contender than as a curiosity, a quixotic figure out there speaking truth to power. It all seemed admirable as long as it lasted; still, the presumption from the first had been that the Empire one day would strike back.

Even that pale glow was dimming, moreover, as Tsongas's message got smaller and more defensive. In New Hampshire, he had had time to be expansive, to talk about sacrifice today as an investment in a greater tomorrow. In the headlong fly-around politics of the South and West, all that survived was the sacrifice. As Bob Kerrey twitted in one debate, the un-Santa was beginning to sound more like the Grinch who stole Christmas. For the middle class, there would be no tax relief in a Tsongas presidency. For old folks, there would be cuts in social security. For farmers, truckers, commuters, and Sunday drivers alike, there would be a nickel-a-year rise in the tax on a gallon of gasoline. Tsongas's honesty, once inspiriting, had begun to sound merely suicidal. It was as if he were building a college with shiny new labs, dorms, and classrooms, Tubby Harrison told Dennis Kanin one day, and then refusing to let anybody in.

His candidacy was suffering as well from advanced Gary Hart Syndrome, the growing pains of a small campaign coming too suddenly into its maturity. He had bet the farm on New Hampshire and put everything else on hold; in states where Clinton had phone banks, Tsongas had answering machines. His little troupe had graduated from a minivan to a charter Boeing 737 in a single day, just to accommodate the mob of reporters who had lately discovered him. The problem was that Tsongas's team wasn't ready for the upgrade, strategically or financially, and as they boarded their new jet, they had only the rudest semblance of a flight plan to tell them where to go.

While Tsongas was still hot, his man Dennis Kanin had been working the phones nearly full time, trying to coax in more cash and more A-team political operatives with past national experience. Some money came in—enough, anyway, to keep the enterprise afloat for a while. The pols were another story. Kanin desperately needed backup help running day-to-day operations. He was not himself a natural executive, and on those days when he had to be on the road with Tsongas, nothing at all got decided. He had hoped that success would bring in fresh recruits, and the campaign had doubled its headquarters space in downtown Boston in anticipation of their imminent arrival. But most of the new chairs were occupied perforce by rookies or short-timers. The best of the veterans were either bespoke by other candidates or were too skeptical of Tsongas's chances. "Wait and see," they would tell Kanin, or, "It'll take a few weeks to work things out."

In truth, the campaign was playing catch-up ball when it was too late to catch up; they were reduced to prayer for the Last Clinton Story—the final scandal big, fat, and juicy enough to wipe that little smile off his face and send him home. There was, realistically, no other hope; just as Hart had in 1984, Tsongas had outrun his resources, in the till or on the ground. In the recent history of our politics, party nominations have all but invariably gone to the candidate who has raised the biggest war chest and the strongest army before the fighting started. Clinton answered that description in 1992, and while his bank account was not limitless, there was enough in it to position him for the early kill contemplated in his strategy.

He was further blessed, as Tsongas was cursed, by the calendar and particularly by that Dixified contrivance called Super Tuesday. A smattering of northern and western states would be at stake that day, but if

Tsongas won Massachusetts, say, or Rhode Island, nobody would care; chalk up two more predictable wins for the homeboy from Lowell. The day amounted instead to a southern regional primary, designed by its sponsors as a sort of mantrap for well-heeled Yankee liberals of the sort who had lately been winning the party nomination and losing in the fall. It hadn't worked so far; Fritz Mondale in 1984 and Michael Dukakis in 1988 had fared badly in the South on Super Tuesday and had still escaped alive. This time, it was finally a homeboy who had the money and the soldiery, and Jesse Jackson wasn't around to drain off black votes, as he had to Al Gore's sorrow in 1988. There would be nobody to spoil Super Tuesday for Bill Clinton—nobody, that is, except himself.

Kanin had always known that Super Tuesday was potentially death for Tsongas. He had thought briefly of skipping its major battlegrounds entirely and sending Tsongas on to the next rounds in Illinois and Michigan, where he would at least be on a level playing field. But there were too many delegates to be won in the South and too much face to be lost by fleeing. The plan the Tsongas command finally settled on instead was a bit like playing roulette in Las Vegas, a game requiring a certain recklessness of the odds favoring the house. They put most of their chips on Florida, where their polling ten days out showed Tsongas fourteen points ahead, and made side bets in the pricey media markets of Texas and Tennessee.

It would all prove squandered money and time. Tsongas was paying the price of front-runnerhood with few of the fringe benefits; everyone else was piling on him, and Clinton in particular appeared to be building his whole candidacy on Tsongas's destruction. At first, the attacks were not much more than irritants, as when Zell Miller roughed him up in Atlanta or when a couple of Clinton aides, on separate occasions, referred to Tsongas in print as a son of a bitch. With each episode, Tsongas complained personally to Clinton; the governor pleaded not guilty, and that appeared to be that. But the rigors of the road and the frustrations of the race were beginning to tell, and as they did, Tsongas's mood darkened. He began to suspect Clinton and his allies of suggesting that he was not merely a fake Democrat but somehow un-American as well.

The spark that lit the fuse had been a page-one *Atlanta Journal* story quoting yet another Clinton surrogate, Lieutenant Governor Pierre Howard of Georgia, as saying, "Tsongas is not Greek for Bubba." It was only a variant on a joke Howard had used in his own campaign to explain *his* locally suspect first name; Pierre, he had told the boys in the courthouse squares, was French for Bubba. But Tsongas didn't know that, and he was hypersensitive to any suspected slight on his ancestry, sometimes even the mention that he was Greek. When his man Ed Jesser got hold of the *Journal,* he folded it carefully to keep Tsongas from seeing the story.

The secret kept only till Tsongas arrived at his suite at the Omni Hotel and was given a courtesy copy of his own. When Jesser and another aide, Andy Pavin, came by to deliver him to a Jefferson-Jackson Day dinner that evening, he came out of his bedroom clutching it. His face was an angry mask.

Jesser glanced at his watch. Three thousand Georgia Democrats were waiting in a hall across the street, and he and Pavin had twenty minutes to get Tsongas there. The question was whether they should. Tsongas had disappeared inside himself, a sure sign of his rage. His shoulders were hunched forward. He was pacing the floor in a tight little circle, eyes darting around the room in search of someone to yell at. When he glanced at the paper, he saw only blood.

"Ed, what are we going to do?" he asked Jesser finally. Jesser knew it wasn't really a question. The guy was going to go to the dinner and tear some new assholes.

"They're saying my mother and father are scum," Tsongas said. "They're saying my children are scum."

It was time, and they started across the street. Niki Tsongas was calm. Her husband was still spluttering. At his side, Dennis Kanin was trying to hose him down; it wouldn't help Tsongas's cause to take on the entire Georgia party, but as they walked into the cavernous hall, it sounded as if he might do exactly that.

In desperation, Jesser looked around for someone he knew and found his way to Jimmy Carter's son Chip. The bubba line, Chip explained, was a joke, a political pun intended for Georgia Democratic insiders, and there was no percentage in raising a ruckus about it. "It's a shot for Clinton, and it'll work," he said, "but Paul shouldn't do that here."

Jesser dashed off to catch Tsongas. By then, some other locals had got to him and told him the same story. His fires were banked. His speech was all Democratic bonhomie; the only edged line in it was a mild gag at Zell Miller's expense, and it got a big laugh.

But Tsongas's sense of grievance remained, an open wound inflamed by the daily pounding he was taking, and he soon found fresh ground for offense. For days on end, Clinton had been painting him as Reagan Redux, promoting trickle-down tax breaks for millionaires and corporations and nothing for the middle class. That was bad enough for so proud a man. What put it over the top was Clinton's declaration, at a press conference in Dallas, that the nation could no longer sacrifice fairness to growth. "It won't work," he said. "It's not America."

The quote lost something in the translation from Clinton's hoarse drawl; a fair number of newspeople in attendance thought, and reported, that he had said Tsongas's ideas weren't *American*. The Associated Press wrote its account that way, and within hours, newspapers and radio stations around the country were running with it.

Tsongas was on a day trip to Arizona when the story ran. He didn't respond immediately, but on the long flight back to Florida, his outrage came to a high boil. He charged down into a thicket of microphones and cameras waiting on the tarmac and announced that henceforth he was going to call Clinton "Pander Bear"—an appropriate name, he chided, for a man who would say or do anything to get votes. "The use of the term 'not American'—that was *code*," he said. "I resent it. . . . It was code to say, 'He's different. He's ethnic.' Let me say to Bill Clinton, there are a lot of people in this country who come from ethnic stock. We are Americans."

The press, habituated to looking for angles in everything, decided that his outburst was just politics, probably aimed at Hispanic voters in Florida; why else would Tsongas have waited thirty hours and two thousand air miles to complain? The Clinton command thought it more likely that Saint Paul had taken leave of his senses. They had been waiting in some suspense for him to mount an effective response to their attacks on him. He hadn't. Instead, he had fallen into precisely the trap they had set for him. He had got so mad at Clinton, and so resentful of his success, that he kept forgetting to say why he would be a better president. Not even his ads promoted what he actually stood for; his message was that he *had* a message, and Clinton didn't.

His pain was intensified by a feeling of abandonment by his own party. The brass at national Democratic headquarters seemed to him to be taking sides with Clinton in the policy debate between the two men, putting up generic TV commercials advertising tax relief for the middle class as "a better way." In fact, it was Clinton's way, though the spot named no names; the party *was* throwing in with him.

It was irritating, Tsongas grumbled one day, flying across Florida; the Democratic establishment had *always* been against him, and now they were crawling into bed with Clinton, putting up someone they knew to be vulnerable in the fall. They just didn't give a damn, he guessed aloud. They didn't even care if they lost the election—they just didn't want to have to change the party. His challenge to the middle-class tax cut had hit them right at their core. The sad thing was that their core consisted wholly of polling data; the party Tsongas had identified with all his life had come to that.

His sense of estrangement was shared by his disciples. One of them, Ed Jesser, was assigned to represent the campaign at a party-sponsored gathering of money men in Florida a few days later, and he hitched a ride in from Texas on a small jet chartered by the Democratic National Committee. He sipped a Budweiser and tolerated the surroundings happily enough, till one of his fellow passengers, Ron Brown, the party chairman, leaned in to twit him a little. Brown had been early to sense the inevitability of Bill Clinton, warts and all, and had begun the process of outreach to him in various public and private ways. His interest, grounded in the unhappy recent history of the party, lay in having a nominee in place as early and bloodlessly as possible and getting on with the campaign that really mattered against George Bush. But to Tsongas's men, Brown's stance looked like favoritism, and Jesser couldn't resist the chance to let him know it.

"So, Ed," Brown asked him, smiling sweetly across the divide, "if Paul gets elected, what do you get out of it?"

Jesser popped the tab on a second can of Bud and drained a long draft.

"The chairmanship of the party," he said, smiling sweetly back.

Jesser's speech to the fat cats the next day was short—less than a minute, by his internal clock—and it pointed to a practical moral: "Paul Tsongas will kick the living shit out of George Bush in a general election, and he's the only one who will." The big givers were unmoved, and their checkbooks stayed mostly in their pockets and purses. The money game had long since been lost to Clinton, in the fall of 1991, and Tsongas's candidacy was dying slowly of malnutrition—not just a want of resources but a contraction of its own spirit as well. The candidate had worked himself into a siege mentality, and as his rancor grew, his message got even smaller. There were days when what he seemed to stand for, in his speeches and his ads, was his anger.

The sad part was that he understood precisely what was happening to him. A requiem air had stolen over him in the last days before Super Tuesday, a sense that a prize he had almost had in his hands was slipping away from him. Texas was gone by then—his own polling showed that—and Florida, his do-or-die battleground, was going; that fourteen-point lead had melted down to a seven-point deficit in three days. There was some small cheer for him in the news that seven Florida newspapers had come out for him. But as he flew back into the state from Nashville on the Sunday before the voting, spent and sad, he did not try to hide his bitterness or his gloom. Yes, he said, the endorsements were gratifying; they told him that he had changed some people's minds, and if he did end up losing, as he had begun to sense would happen, he would have a scrapbook to show for it. At least there would be that.

He understood the artistry of how Clinton and his handlers had undone him. It was smart politics, he mused; the constant attacks had knocked him off his message. But he felt he had had no choice except to answer in kind. People all over the country, all over the world, were forming their first impressions of him, watching him closely to see what would happen when he took a hit. If they concluded that he wouldn't hit back, his presidency would be a nightmare. It had been his duty as well to speak out, or so he felt in his anger; he had by then lost whatever respect he had once felt for Clinton and wanted to let everybody else know just what kind of person he was. He wished, indeed, that the race had come down to him and Bob Kerrey instead of Clinton. If he lost to Kerrey, he said, he wouldn't feel so bad.

He sat in silence for a few moments, staring straight ahead at the bulkhead of his forward cabin. A lunch of barbecued chicken lay half-eaten before him. "I gotta trim my sails," he said finally. Whatever happened, he had no complaints; he felt he had served a purpose just by having tried. If it all ended that day, he said, he could walk away from the plane and his entourage, climb into his Jeep and drive home to Lowell. His tone suggested that he might look back in anger, but never in sorrow or regret.

"We're Back"

Bill Clinton and his coaches sat around a wrought-iron table on a hotel balcony in downtown Dallas five days before Super Tuesday, basking in the brilliant late-afternoon sunshine and the glow of renewed life. They had gathered to prep the candidate for the latest debate, on ABC-TV that evening, but for the first time in weeks, they felt they had the luxury of talking issues and tactics, not the appropriate defense for the latest scandal. Bob Kerrey had dropped out that morning. Tom Harkin was barely clinging to life. Jerry Brown was coming off his surprising victory in Colorado with nowhere visible to go. The last man left in their path, so far as the men on the balcony could see, was Paul Tsongas, and he seemed to have lost his way in the South; he kept going to the wrong places and saying the wrong things, as if he had lost the will or the ability to fight off Clinton's attacks.

The character issue hadn't gone away, of course; the press was seeing to that with its ongoing prowl over the back roads of Clinton's life. He had been hit again with the subject only that morning, at a sitdown with the editors of the *Dallas Morning News*, and had flared at their suggestion that there might be more to come—"things," as one of them put it, "like photographs on 'The Monkey Business.'" Clinton had barely been able to control his anger. "I wonder who else could have stood up to what I've been through," he said. He had told the world that he wasn't perfect, but the media hadn't been willing to settle for that; they had set off instead on a "hysterical search" for fresh dirt and, by so doing, had brought their own character into question. "You do have the right to know, do I believe in my family and its obligations, the commandments preached at my church?" he told the editors, his agitation visible. "Yes, yes, and yes. If I become president, will I lie, cheat, and steal? No."

But the tale-telling seemed at least to have receded from the front pages, and as he sat out in the early spring sunlight, surrounded by his team, Clinton's mood was as mellow as it had been since his brief turn as the front-runner in New Hampshire. "Do you realize," he asked, "the last day we had like this was when the *Manchester Union Leader* showed me seven points ahead?"

"We're back on track," Paul Begala said.

"Yeah, we're back," Clinton answered, though he still wasn't quite comfortable with how they had got there. "I just don't want to win this from the left," he said.

"Your mind is in a left-right position," Carville told him.

"No, my mind isn't—the *press* is," Clinton replied. They were beginning to treat the new neopopulist strain in his rhetoric as a paint job—a purely tactical move to isolate Tsongas on the right.

"Listen," Carville said. "The right position is, 'The '80s are over. Let's get on to what we need to do in the '90s.' The left-right thing is so *old.*"

"It's not left-right," Begala said. "It's right-wrong."

But what if Tsongas went on the attack on ABC that evening? Clinton had to watch how he responded; they didn't need a repeat of his crack in the Denver debate about Paul being perfect.

"It's not that he's *bad,*" Stephanopoulos said, striking a cautionary note. "He's just *wrong.*"

"It's real important not to be petty," Frank Greer added. "We have still got a serious trust problem." The trick, he said, was to look presidential—to seem "passionate, sincere, and under control."

"I understand," Clinton said. "I'll be all right." He didn't like being picked at, and there was a trace of irritation in his voice.

But trust *was* a problem, Stan Greenberg went on, and getting petty with Tsongas would only feed into it.

Clinton cut off the discussion there. He was the candidate, and he had his own sense of what people wanted to hear from him. "They want to know that I didn't dodge the draft," he said. "They may or may not want to know if the Gennifer Flowers story is true. What they do want to know is that, if it is true, it's not true *now*. I know what I'm talking about. That's really what they want to hear."

When they finally adjourned to the TV studio, Clinton had to wait out some last-minute haggling about the format for the debate, and his people used the time to try to relax him. Hillary grabbed his shoulders and shook him from side to side. "Just have fun," she told him. *She* wouldn't; the debates were still an agony for her, too painful to watch, but she managed a smile for him.

"I'm loose," Clinton said. "I may get up and lead them in a rap song."

He headed for the set. Hillary left to be by herself, as usual, with the TV off. The others crowded into a holding room and watched the show on a monitor in mixed awe and unbelief. Clinton was in form, his sheer presence dominating the stage as if he were the host and ABC's butter-smooth anchor, Peter Jennings, just a supernumerary. Tsongas, by contrast, looked and sounded comatose; he couldn't seem to find the answers to Clinton's jabbing attacks on his economic plan.

"This is going too well," Carville fretted, forty-five minutes in.

"It sure is," Stephanopoulos said. "Something is going to happen."

Nothing did; Tsongas was just sitting there, letting Clinton tattoo him. It must have been his disappointment at getting kicked in the gut on Junior Tuesday, Carville guessed, because Tsongas sure as hell couldn't have been surprised by Clinton's strategy of attack. "We didn't telegraph it, we *telephoned* it," Carville said, his glee showing. "We *faxed* it. We *satellited* it. We wrapped it in a diaper, put it on a stork, and *flew* it to him."

He glanced at the monitor. He had worried that Tsongas would come back with *something* after the last commercial break, but he didn't. Carville smiled a wolfish smile. "This guy's having a hard time holding altitude," he said.

He was having a harder time finding a beachhead anywhere in the South. His big media buys in Texas and Tennessee mystified the Clinton command; in their reading, he had never had a chance in either state. Florida had made better sense, at least on paper. It was the least purely southern of all the states of the Old Confederacy; with its admixture of locals with refugees from the Snow Belt and the islands, it could barely be said to be *a* state at all. The owlish Greek from Massachusetts was not quite so extraterrestrial there. Several early polls, public and private, showed him running dead even with Clinton. His own had placed him briefly ahead.

But the state had become a honey trap for him, a place as seductive and finally illusory as its theme parks and its Art Deco beachfronts. The polls that had so beguiled Tsongas had frozen the race, in the public mind, as an evenly matched fight. It wasn't, and both sides knew it; with less than a week to go, Tsongas had fallen seven points behind in his own soundings and sixteen behind in Clinton's. The trouble was that the media were stuck with their dated numbers and were still talking up the possibility of an upset, creating expectations that Tsongas could not possibly meet. The night of the ABC debate, Begala told Clinton that several eminences of the national press were predicting flatly that Tsongas would win.

"Good," Clinton said, smiling. "Let 'em think that. Tell 'em it's a terrible struggle."

It more nearly resembled a rout in the making. The only thing even about it was the size of the media buys for the two camps. The Clinton campaign had a vast edge in organization on the ground—the job of wiring Florida had only begun with their triumph at the state Democratic convention in December—and a superior feel for the local folkways as well. Clinton had spent the day after Junior Tuesday working the teeming condo colonies in South Florida, which had helped deliver the state to Dukakis in 1988. His people had fitted him out with a yarmulke and some applause lines about how he was more fierce than Tsongas in his devotion to the defense of Israel and social security. "You ain't seen nothing yet," Stephanopoulos kidded, watching from an approving distance. "Florida is Pander City, and we're going to do it."

For most of the week leading up to Super Tuesday, indeed, the campaign seemed to be purring along in overdrive. Clinton had his prime rival on the ropes and most of the others heading for the exits. Kerrey dropped out that Thursday, and Tom Harkin soon followed. He had hung in for one last roll of the dice in South Carolina on Saturday and had run a dismal third. On Sunday he called Clinton in Tyler, Texas, to say that was it; he was dropping out of the race. The friction level between the two men had been high, but Harkin was a good loser and Clinton a gracious winner; he loved the sport of politics too much to gloat.

"You've been a hell of a guy, the way you've carried on in the last two weeks," he told Harkin. "I think you did your best last week, and you never got credit for it."

"The great news is, we had a good night campaigning in Ohio," Harkin said. "The bad news is, when you're out of bucks, you're out of gas." It was over for him; he was going home, but whenever Clinton was ready, he wanted to talk about what he could do to help.

Clinton thanked him and rang off. He seemed to marvel at how Harkin was handling defeat; there had been no bitterness or self-pity, traits to which he himself was not immune. "What a classy guy," he said.

But he himself had flown back into bumpy weather that weekend, and this time Hillary was with him. For some time, they had known that Jeff Gerth, the *New York Times*'s premier investigative reporter, was poking around into their finances and particularly a land-development deal they had got into during Clinton's long-ago tour as Arkansas attorney general. The enterprise had been of a piece with the small-world phenomenon among successful Arkansans, the clubby networking of a few hundred leaders in business, government, and the bar for fun and profit. In 1978, the Clintons had hooked up with a longtime chum, James B. McDougal, and his wife in a fifty-fifty partnership they called Whitewater Development. They had bought 230 acres of land in the Ozark Mountains, divided it into forty-two lots, and waited for the customers to queue up for vacation homes.

The buyers had never come; Whitewater, in the Clintons' account, had turned out to be more nearly a white elephant, and while the company had survived over the years on life support, the partners had gone their separate ways. Bill became governor; Hillary had her law practice in one of the state's preeminent firms; McDougal, after a brief turn as a statehouse aide in the first Clinton administration, would preside over the rise and then the ignominious fall of a large savings and loan. For the principals, inured to the Arkansas Way, the venture was nothing more sinister than a chummy business deal gone bad. The Clintons, who were well-off but not rich, insisted that they had been burned on their piece of the action; an accounting firm hired in the effort to contain the story would place their losses at nearly seventy thousand dollars.

But the *Times* saw darker shadings in the picture, intimations of sweetheart deals and conflicts of interest, and when Gerth pressed for answers, the Clintons' storied damage-control operation broke down. The job of assembling a dossier for the defense on money and draft questions had been preempted from the campaign by a group of lawyer friends of the Clintons, among them Hillary's bright but spiky pal

Susan Thomases. The task force had taken rooms in a downtown Little Rock hotel and, with an air of great secrecy, had begun combing the available records for problems and fashioning appropriately lawyerly answers. The *Times*'s inquiry into the Whitewater affair had been one of the first on their screen, and Thomases, along with a lawyer for the campaign, met with Gerth in New York during the run-up to Super Tuesday.

Their real agenda had been to get the story killed, or at least delayed; the campaign didn't need another mess with Super Tuesday only days away. But the device they had used was less than felicitous. The problem, Thomases had told Gerth, was that many of the relevant documents couldn't be located; nobody knew where they were. Gerth had seemed to her to be a reasonable man, and she had come back to Little Rock sure that she had bought some time for the truth squad to work up a fuller response. She hadn't. The words "missing documents" are as intoxicating to investigative journalists as Chivas Regal to a barfly. The mere fact that documents *were* missing, and that the campaign had turned the matter over to lawyers, had made the whole affair smell even riper, and the *Times,* after some sharp internal debate, decided to hurry the story into print.

An early copy rolled out of the fax at Clinton headquarters at dusk that Saturday evening, three days before the megaprimary. CLINTONS JOINED S&L OPERATOR IN AN OZARK REAL ESTATE VENTURE, the headline read, neglecting to mention that McDougal had not been in the S&L business at the time. The account that followed had a slapped-together look—some subeditors at the *Times* had thought it unready for publication—and was considerably harder to follow than Clinton's alleged adventures with his draft board, say, or with his favorite Little Rock lounge singer. But there it was on page one of the publication that, more than any other, sets the daily agenda for the national print and broadcast media. The campaign command could almost hear the dominoes falling; within twenty-four hours, everybody would be chasing the story, demanding to know whether the Clintons had at the very least been heedless of appearances—and, oh, by the way, where *were* those missing documents?

A sizable stash of them, as it turned out, were easily retrievable at the Rose Law Firm, where Hillary was a partner; three young aides hurried there that Saturday night and reappeared within two hours, each carrying a carton stuffed with papers and forms. The work of going through them was stalled for two hours more while the lawyers, claiming privilege, haggled with the campaign staff over who should do it. The dispute was resolved less by reason than by terror; as one participant would put it, they thought they might be looking at the third strike—Flowers, the draft, and now this. A mixed group of ten lawyers and laypersons closeted themselves in a room at headquarters and rooted through the files till nearly dawn.

The *real* quick-response team took over Sunday morning, with Stephanopoulos and Begala directing operations out of Clinton's suite at the Warwick Hotel in Houston. "I was at risk," Clinton told them, blocking out what he wanted to say. "I did lose money. No special treatment. It ought to be clearly defined and specific." Some others in the campaign, Hillary among them, believed that the *Times* was out to stop Clinton and that they ought to say so in their response. Begala and Stephanopoulos argued against it, and as draft statements and backup documents came in by fax from Little Rock, they toned down the smokier language; it just might invite a new round of damaging stories. "I don't want to be in Gerth's face," Stephanopoulos said. "I just want it to go away."

They set out later for Austin, the next stop in a fly-around tour of Texas. Clinton's own demeanor seemed untroubled; not even his worst enemies in Arkansas had seriously charged that he had used his position to enrich himself. His concern, and the campaign's, was for Hillary, who for the first time had become a target of the scandal chasers. The *Times* story reported that her firm had done legal work for McDougal's troubled S&L and that she herself had successfully put forward two "novel proposals" to help him with the state securities commissioner.

When his plane touched down, Clinton called her—"to make sure her head's okay," he said—and then went off to do an event. Begala and Stephanopoulos lingered at the terminal; a press conference was to be held there, Clinton's first since the Whitewater story appeared, and they needed to get his statement patted into finished form. The simpler and cleaner they made it, they believed, the better it would play. The unspoken concern in the campaign at all such moments was that Clinton would overexplain himself, leaving a whole double hand-ful of new loose threads to be pulled and plucked. What he most needed this time, one senior hand said, was to keep his mouth shut.

"You have one concern," Stephanopoulos told him. "You did not get involved with an S&L owner. At the time of the investment, he was just an old friend."

"We don't want to pick a fight with the *Times*," Begala said. "About as strong as we should go is, 'They didn't quite get the facts straight.'"

"What should I say about Hillary?" Clinton asked.

"You should stick to the big stuff," Stephanopoulos said. The point, he continued, was that Hillary had always scrupulously avoided getting into conflict-of-interest situations. Her partners inevitably did handle matters involving the state—Rose was one of only a few major firms in Arkansas—but she didn't take that kind of work herself or share in the profits from it.

"You got to defend Hillary big-time," Begala urged.

"What they need to know," Stephanopoulos said, "is that you were financially at risk in this deal."

"Remember," Bruce Lindsey added, "less is more."

"Less, less, less," Stephanopoulos said.

The press conference went well for Clinton, or well enough to squeeze much of the juice out of the story. He got across the central points that Whitewater had been a deal between two old friends, not a governor and an S&L prince, and that it had been "a big money loser" for him. A thick packet of the no-longer-missing documents seemed to back him up; the all-night search party had done its job. On the way out, a local radio reporter chased Clinton to his plane and asked if the flap had done his candidacy serious damage.

"Of course not," he said, his eyes pained. "I mean, look at the facts."

In the ensuing days, the press would do just that and would find them mainly confusing. The life span of scandals in politics usually is in inverse proportion to their complexity, and the Whitewater tale, with its squirmy numbers and its missing connectives, was hard to follow— or to follow up. "God willing, it goes away in a day," Begala reassured Clinton as they were leaving Austin, and for the most part, it did; the story would stay dormant till long after it mattered to Clinton's chances of winning. But it fed the appearance of taint about his candidacy—the sense that he was bumping along from scandal to scandal and would sooner or later run into the one that would do him in. The search for the Big One had progressed from an itch to a passion, even an obsession, for some sectors of the press. Clinton's candidacy was hanging by a thread, one leading news executive lectured a reporter who seemed to him slow to the chase. It was implicit in the scolding that their publication should be the one to sever it.

The Whitewater story seemed, moreover, to have made Hillary fair game for the hunters—the subject of inquiry into her conduct in her dual role as power lawyer and governor's wife. The experience was a scarring one for her; her anger with the media for its treatment of her husband had been building up since January, and now, with her own ethics in question, it had got intensely personal. In public, she smiled and spoke dismissively of the whole affair. "Oh, there's no scandal," she said when it came up in one tarmac interview in Florida. "That's just a totally inaccurate story." Among friends, she was less restrained in her fury; when one asked her about the Whitewater story and its front-page display, she replied tartly that she had given up reading the *Times*.

To her, the whole episode was one more example of what she saw as the superficiality of modern political reporting, and its cynicism as well—the presumption of wrongdoing by anyone in public life. The campaign had afforded her an up-close look at the news business and the guys who run it, and, she said privately, she had found it most depressing. It was a *game*, a commercial enterprise for them; politics had become a blood sport, and the historic role of the media in the process had somehow got lost. "This piece is a classic example," she said, bouncing around the secondary media markets of Florida in a small prop plane the day after it broke. "They wanted to get Bill Clinton. I think the story was printed to have an effect on the election."

That she should be the instrument was a source of particular pain to her. She had become her husband's first protector as well as his closest adviser in the campaign; when his schedulers packed his days so densely that he didn't have time to sleep or think, she did not hesitate to intervene. But now her conduct was being used—unfairly, she thought—against him. "What's really terrible," she said, "is finding out that things your father told you are true. He used to tell me, 'Hillary, don't ever forget two things about the establishment: it hates change, and it will always protect its prerogatives.'"

The experience, and the cloud it left over the campaign, seemed to take some of the pleasure out of Super Tuesday for both Clintons. The returns gave them more than ample ground for popping the champagne corks. Clinton overwhelmed Tsongas across the southern and border states, and in Hawaii as well; Florida fell by eighteen percentage points, Texas by forty-six, Tennessee by forty-eight, Mississippi by sixty-five. He carried eight states in all and swept up 450 more delegates in a single day, pushing his overall count to above 700; he was a third of the way home, with no one left to beat him except himself.

Tsongas, by contrast, had to settle for so-what victories in Massachusetts, Rhode Island, and Delaware. His consolation prize had been a poll the day before showing that he had done slightly better than Clinton in separate trial heats against George Bush. "Let the record show," he had said with wistful irony, "that there was at least one day when I could be elected president." There wouldn't be many more such days, not after Super Tuesday; it was plain that his short but extraordinary run on the stage of national politics was nearing its end.

The presumption that Clinton was the nominee was visible in the swollen train of reporters, retainers, and hangers-on who crowded around him. "Who *are* all these people?" Hillary asked, wandering into the mob scene. Get used to it, a reporter told her; the skeptics had become converts overnight, and the retinue was only going to grow.

And yet there was something joyless in Clinton's mood as he sat for the obligatory round of interviews with the network anchors that night. He had waited like a fighter in his corner, jaw muscles working, while his trainers gave him some last pointers.

"Forget about process," Stephanopoulos pleaded; people wanted to know what he would do, not how he had won.

"*Change*, Bill," Greer said. "People want *change*."

Their advice seemed wasted; all the anchors wanted to talk about was how damaged he was by his personal problems and how he could possibly overcome people's doubts about him. Clinton handled the inquiries smoothly, turning the questions away from his dossier to his message. He did forget about process and talk about change, whenever his interrogators let him. People had put aside their doubts, he said, because he was fighting for something much bigger than himself.

But his frustration with the questions was evident, and when he routed himself out of bed to do the early shows the next day, his pettish early-morning mood was worse than usual. He had just had the biggest day you could ask for, and the papers were still questioning his viability, still asking whether the scandals were over. He sat with darkened brow while a crew from *Good Morning America* was setting up in a hotel room for the day's first interview. He seemed so downcast in his moment of triumph that, with the lights about to flare on, his man Frank Greer felt obliged to offer him one last bit of advice. "Look *happy*," he told Clinton, who tried.

IO.

The Downside of Charisma

In a kinder, gentler world, nobody would have had to remind Bill Clinton to smile. He had come rocking and rolling into the industrial north, the battleground where, according to his original plan, he was supposed to lock up the nomination. The alignment of the planets looked favorable, at least to the naked eye. Stan Greenberg's first polling report gave Clinton "manageable" six- and seven-point leads in the twin primaries in Michigan and Illinois the following week, and that was just for starters; his margins in both states would widen quickly into double digits as the dimension of his victories on Super Tuesday sank in.

And who was left to stop him? His last remaining rivals were Paul Tsongas, who was already being written out of the race, and Jerry Brown, who had never been seriously counted in it; the Clinton team was only just beginning to appreciate the danger posed by a man who had a microphone and a cause and didn't give a damn what he said. There was no one else, in the field or behind the tree line. The dread at national Democratic headquarters over Clinton's march toward the nomination was giving way to a kind of cheerless resignation to it; the party and its nervous candidates would have to live with him at the head of the ticket, like it or not.

And yet the Little Rock command group was in an oddly edgy state as they decamped to Chicago and set up their northern command post in a suite at the Palmer House Hilton. On the one hand, Greenberg's confidential report on his Illinois polling showed "the seeds of a much more positive image" for Clinton, a tingle of newness and excitement about him that reminded people of John Kennedy. On the other, two voters in three harbored serious questions about his authenticity—whether he wasn't quite literally too good to be believed. "Slick and smooth is the downside of charisma," Greenberg wrote, putting the best face he could on his findings. "It is troubling, to be sure, but it can be turned into a positive."

Not all his colleagues were quite so sanguine; it was plain that

Clinton's success at jawing his way out of one mess after another had exacted a larger cost in credibility. His people were coming to understand that the final battle would not be Clinton against Tsongas, or Brown, or any of the phantom candidates said to be awaiting his collapse. It would be Clinton versus Clinton, Trust-Me Bill against Slick Willie, with his dreams of the presidency riding on which side of him won.

The prospect worried James Carville. He approached a campaign as if it were a poker game, trying constantly to divine what the other players were thinking behind their game faces. He knew what *his* play would be if he were across the table, advising Tsongas instead of Clinton. He would have Tsongas go right at the Slick Willie business: "Tell me what you want to hear, and I'll tell you what Bill Clinton will say." He also knew how he would have Clinton inoculate himself against such an attack. The first imperative, as usual with Carville, would be to go big; Clinton always did better when he focused on the forest rather than the trees. But he had to get bold as well, and the question among his generals was whether it was in him to risk giving offense to anyone.

The concern was not a new one; the suspicion was widely held among Clinton's staff that he really did want to be all things to all people. The impulse, in their view, was partly a game with him—a continuing challenge to his confidence that he could talk anybody into anything. But some of his handlers thought they detected in him a deeper hunger for approval, almost as if a simple majority wasn't enough for him; he seemed to want to win by acclamation. That wasn't going to happen, of course, and if he kept on trying to please everybody, he would only reinforce the suspicion that he *was* Slick Willie—one more fast-talking, self-seeking politician trying to get ahead with easy flatteries and empty promises. It was a problem, Carville thought, and they would be crazy to deny it. The guy had to show he was for real. He had to risk something somewhere to be president.

But Carville, always moody, was beginning a descent into one of his glooms—a period of frustration with the candidate and the campaign. He was used to being the man in charge, the driving force at the center of things. In this campaign he wasn't—not, anyway, to the degree he seemed to need. There were too many people at the table, too many voices contending for Clinton's ear, and Carville's metallic drawl grew more peevish when it was heard at all. He was pulling back into himself, disengaging, by his own later admission, from much of what remained of the primary season. Denied the wheel, he became a distant and not infrequently grouchy backseat driver.

The dark cloud was settling over him when, a week before primary day in Illinois and Michigan, Greenberg came in from a briefing session with Clinton. His mission had been to keep the candidate on message, casting himself as a man of the people and Tsongas as a paler, mumblier clone of Ronald Reagan. The contrast was working fine in their advertising. One particularly wicked new spot, written by Grunwald, skipped through the pages of Tsongas's *Call to Economic Arms,* lingering over some of its more provocative passages: "Page 22—he proposes a capital-gains tax cut for the rich. . . . Page 21—cuts in cost-of-living increases for older Americans. . . ." At the end, the monograph flipped shut, face down on a table, while a sonorous voice asked, "Isn't it time we closed the book on the '80s?"

The ad had first gone up in time for Super Tuesday and had drawn blood. "They finally read the book," Tsongas's pollster, Tubby Harrison, mourned at the time. The plan had become a weapon against its author, and when Stan Greenberg tried out the ad on focus groups in Illinois, its effect was deadly.

But its offscreen star was still having trouble getting into character as a neopopulist. Clinton hated the criticism he was taking for it in the press and the spillage it was causing him in the polls, particularly among upscale, college-educated voters. They were the jury of his peers, one of his counselors said; he wanted them to like him, and it hurt his vanity to have them desert him for Tsongas. He was just as intellectual as Paul, he complained privately. He had thought at least as hard about the problems of the country and had come up with a lot of good solutions. But his strategists kept wanting him to flank Tsongas on the left instead of meeting him head-on in a contest of their essentially centrist ideas. Clinton was uncomfortable in the role—*very* uncomfortable, one handler said—and Greenberg had had to do a bit of a hard sell to keep him at it.

"I told him, 'First, don't reinvent the message,'" he reported to Carville. "'We want this economic contrast with Tsongas.' I came back to that three times."

Carville liked the strategy; what worried him was the way Greenberg, like most pollsters, dressed up his advice in data. "I'm just telling you, the more you give him, the more screwed up he becomes," he said. "It's ethnic voters this, suburban voters that."

"The issue he's focused on is how he's running among Catholics," Greenberg said. There were a lot of them in Illinois and Michigan, and it worried Clinton that he wasn't bringing them around.

"What can we do about Catholics in a week?" Carville growled. "Nothing."

Greenberg agreed; the main thing, short-term, was to keep Clinton on what looked like a winning track. "I spent the end of the meeting with him entirely focused on him delivering the economic message," he said. "I grabbed him in the hall afterward, and I don't think he is off the reservation."

"We for people, he for companies," Carville said, slipping inexplicably into a B-movie Native American accent. "He for '80s, we for '90s. See Tonto."

"But the longer we put this off . . ." Greenberg started. He meant dealing with Clinton's credibility gap, not just among Catholics but among educated women as well; they had never quite forgiven him Gennifer Flowers or accepted his denials that anything naughtier than a few phone calls had happened between him and her. Yes, he was winning the primaries, but the deep currents of distrust could come back to haunt him in November if he didn't find a way to allay them.

"You're right, in the long term," Carville interrupted. "But we got one week. We need one thought. We don't need *nuances*—we need a *message.*"

Clinton needed to show some spine as well, and he made a good beginning with a pair of speeches in the Detroit area, one to a white gathering in the industrial suburbs, the other to a black crowd in an inner-city church. The strategic design was to reunite the old Bobby Kennedy coalition, but not by truckling to its divided constituencies; his speeches instead challenged the whites to lay aside their racial prejudices for the common good and, in more muted tones, urged the blacks to break the cycle of welfare dependency in the ghettos. Both speeches were bravura performances, Clinton at his emotive best, but he was especially pleased with the response of the whites in a Reagan Democratic enclave to his appeal to come home to their party. The talk plainly touched a chord, and as he walked back to his holding room, he pumped his fist in triumph. "God, that was great!" he said.

So were his polls; a fresh batch from the two primary states showed his leads widening and his positive ratings on a sharp upcurve. The zap-Tsongas strategy was clearly working, and as Clinton sat down with his handlers in their Chicago war room to prep for a debate, their advice was to stay with it. The only trick, in their view, was not to get personal with Saint Paul—just stick to the major economic differences between them.

"The more finger-pointing we do," Carville said, "the less well we do. The bigger you go, the better. Our favorables haven't been this high since pre–Gennifer Flowers."

"We're dealing with thirty-point leads in both states," Greenberg said. "Our positives are in the sixties and our negatives are dropping. We want to do nothing that makes us look political or petty. We want it to be big. I think people have concluded that we're the only big candidate."

"You got to be big," Carville echoed.

"Don't let him get to you," Greenberg warned. Tsongas already *had* got to Clinton with a new TV commercial, proclaiming himself the honest man in the race. "He's no Bill Clinton, that's for sure," the voice-over said. "He's the exact opposite. Paul Tsongas. He's not afraid of the truth." The ad stung; Clinton privately called it "hateful," and his people didn't know how he might react if Tsongas tried to go live with the attack that night. It wouldn't do for a man so damaged to protest his sincerity too much. "Don't get into the honesty debate," Greenberg warned. "Don't do it. It doesn't serve you."

There was the further possibility that Tsongas would come out crowing about having been endorsed that day by the *Chicago Tribune*. Clinton hated it when that happened; he had been losing the battle of the editorial pages to Tsongas, and while he kept winning primaries anyway, he took each fresh rejection badly.

"That really shows you what a pathetic, elitist culture we live in," he grumped.

"Oh, this is the paper that endorsed Ronald Reagan and George Bush," Carville said, on-message as usual. "They want the '80s to continue."

"Jeez," Clinton exclaimed, "that's all I need to know. Oooooh, that's so good!"

But what if Tsongas opened other fronts—Clinton's record in Arkansas, say, or his economic plan?

"You are thirty points ahead," David Axelrod, a Chicago media consultant, told Clinton. "Let him attack you, but don't stoop to his level."

David Wilhelm was Axelrod's pal, but this time, he disagreed. "Do not sit on a lead," he said. If Saint Paul got pious, Clinton could ask him why, on the eve of the Texas primary, he had suddenly amended *his* plan to include tax breaks for natural-gas producers—an important interest group in the state.

"Don't get prissy," George Stephanopoulos objected.

"That's not prissy," Wilhelm said.

"You don't want a debate on pandering," Stephanopoulos argued. "Why do you want to do *that?*"

"Because he *does* pander," Clinton answered. He had long since tired of Tsongas throwing the charge at him.

They tried out more questions, more answers, till Clinton finally signaled an end to the session. "Stan," he said, turning to Greenberg, "what's our major objective tonight?"

"If we come off presidential and big, and they come off small and petty, we win," Greenberg answered. "Deliver the economic message, that's the key. Don't be afraid to be tough."

Clinton's performance, in the event, was on-message but off-pitch, in the manner of a man under instruction not to make a mistake. It didn't matter; his competitors weren't exactly lighting up the screen either. Tsongas was still smarting at how his strategy of attack had backfired against him on Super Tuesday, tarnishing his image as a new kind of politician. In the aftermath, he had decided to leave the trash-talk largely to his television ads—a new one went on the air that night—and to use his live appearances mostly to promote his message of economic renewal. The New New Democrat was accordingly subdued; the few mortar rounds he lobbed at Clinton during the debate landed without visible effect.

Brown did no better, for all his wild-man reputation. As his ringwise senior adviser Mike Ford noted in a pre-debate strategy memo, nearly half the voters in a new ABC News poll doubted that Clinton was honest enough to be president. "This guy has a credibility problem," Ford wrote. "Pound it." The advice somehow got lost on what Ford privately alluded to as the Mondo Bizarro landscape of the Brown campaign—an enterprise in which order was nonexistent and dissonance was the norm. If Brown had read the memo, it didn't show that night; he could as usefully have stayed home.

The battle for the Midwest was settling into a comfort zone by then for Clinton and his men, a feeling of confidence fed by their widening leads in the polls in both states. Tsongas, to be sure, moved up a bit in Illinois over the weekend, but Brown, riding a wave of trade-union support, was slipping past him into second place in Michigan. The two men were canceling one another out, fighting for the leavings of what promised to be another banquet for Clinton.

He could no longer seriously hope to cinch the nomination outright that Tuesday, as he and his strategists had once imagined possible. Still, he wouldn't have to wait very much longer; he had the word of party chairman Ron Brown on that. Brown had slipped into Detroit during the week for a secret meeting with Clinton; discretion dictated that their dates *had* to be secret so long as other contenders were still technically alive. But that would all end, Brown said, if Clinton could only keep himself and his winning streak going through the April primary in New York. Pull that off, the chairman told him, and it really *would* be all over; the party and its almost-candidate could then bring their flirtation out of the closet and start working together on how to beat George Bush in the fall.

Teatime for Hillary

It wouldn't be quite that easy. The Sunday before the primaries, a new cloud had drifted up over the horizon line, shadowing what till then had seemed a sunny and limitless view. The problem this time had to do with Hillary and her independent life in the law. The *Washington Post* had published a story in that morning's editions reporting that her firm had done significant work for the Arkansas government during her husband's years in the statehouse. The report appeared on its face to be no deadlier than a common cold; nothing in it contradicted Ms. Clinton's declaration that she had refused her share of the profits from that side of the firm's business. Still, life was always suspenseful in the Clinton campaign—a continuing education in how little its managers knew about the private affairs of their client and his wife.

Neither they nor America had experienced anybody quite like Hillary Rodham Clinton before—not, certainly, in a presidential campaign. She didn't fit the old stereotype of the political wife, the helpmate whose public duty it was to hang adoringly on her husband's words and, if he got elected president, to go find something unarguably good to do as her "project." But she didn't quite suit the new model, either. Other candidates' wives of her generation had pursued their own successful careers outside politics and yet, in election years, had honored the old forms. They still ornamented stages when and where their husbands' handlers thought it necessary, sometimes bringing the children along to complete the effect. If they had anything to say about the strategies or the substance of the campaign, they most often said it privately, as pillow talk.

Hillary was different. She was not just wife, mother, lawyer, public advocate, and principal breadwinner in the Clinton family; she was openly and unabashedly a partner in her husband's success. Intellectually, she was his peer; in politics and government, his last-word adviser; on the trail or in the legislature, his star salesperson, excepting only himself. She had been a free spirit at least since the day when, at age twelve, she announced to her stoutly Republican family that she was going to marry a Democrat when she grew up. "Hillary!" her great-aunt Adelaide had answered, aghast, "you must not say that— not even in jest!" She *had* married a Democrat, and her concessions to his career had mostly been matters of appearance—her agreement to use his name, for example, and to preside at state occasions at the governor's mansion when her own schedule permitted. In things that counted to her, she maintained her separate identity, both as a lawyer and on the sometimes bumpy ground of her marriage.

People accustomed to the older archetypes—the matronly Barbara Bush, say, or the imperial Nancy Reagan—weren't quite sure how to take the New Woman on the block. Was she the wife as victim, waiting up nights for a philandering husband to come home? Or the yuppie American princess with a headband, a power suit, a career curve, and a feminist attitude? Or the *real* boss of the House of Clinton, the puppeteer who would run her husband's presidency? Or was she, as a new round of stories would suggest between the lines, the ultimate inside player—a lawyer capitalizing on her connection with her husband the governor? Any or all of the above seemed possible, given how little anybody outside her own network of friends and admirers actually knew about her. The signals were scrambled, and Hillary didn't always make it easy to sort them out.

It was as if she couldn't. She belonged to a generation of professional women who had had to fight their way up alone in a man's world—a world in which it could be mistaken for a sign of weakness to reveal oneself or one's feelings. She lived instead inside her cool veneer, at least in her public life. Women in focus groups, particularly women less educated than she, felt threatened by her. "We don't need another Nancy Reagan," several said. Campaign staffers stewed over her resistance to letting them root around in her professional affairs. She stood on her attorney-client privilege. They saw a higher good in electing Clinton president, which meant protecting him against the large and small surprises that kept jolting his candidacy. "Our research on ourselves is not near, not *near* as good as it should be," Carville worried aloud one day.

The *Washington Post* story was one more distraction they didn't need, falling as it did on the day of the second debate in three nights for the Illinois-Michigan television market. It was much on their minds when Clinton joined them in their war room in Chicago for a coaching session; you didn't have to be a rocket scientist to guess that *somebody* would raise the Hillary question on the air that night.

"I think Tsongas is going to come at you mean and hard," Hillary herself warned.

"Hit *him* hard," Paul Begala said, smacking his fist into an open palm. "I can't believe someone who lobbied for Michael Milken and Drexel Burnham would lecture you about your wife."

"That's good, that's really good," Hillary agreed.

"That's if he crosses the line," Begala said.

"Let me tell you," Carville added, "if he attacks Hillary, I would jump. You have the license to just *jump* on him."

"If you hear the word 'Hillary,' don't let him finish," Stephanopoulos said.

"That's an open door," David Wilhelm said.

"Don't be Michael Dukakis," Mickey Kantor added. Dukakis hadn't struck back under attack—hadn't even managed a show of emotion when he was asked how he would react to the rape and murder of his wife.

After a time, Hillary got up to leave for her next event of the day. "I'm going to the debate alone?" Clinton asked her in mock terror. She looked back at him and smiled. They both knew how hard it was for her to watch him in a debate or Chelsea in a ballet. She was so tough in so many ways, Clinton would remark later, but not on debate nights. She would come to the studio with him when she could, and hold his hand when he got there, and then just walk away before the shooting started.

"I'll try not to screw it up," he promised her.

"Defend my honor," Hillary said. They both laughed.

A troop of aides accompanied him instead and sat in his holding room with him while he was layered with makeup. "I know this is the eighth event of the day, and I know you're tired," Carville told him as he headed out to the set. "But things are going our way. Be happy."

Clinton took his place onstage. "We're one hour away from winning Illinois," Wilhelm said, wishing it were already over.

Tsongas was sharp in the first couple of rounds, the sharpest of the three. Still, Clinton seemed loose and relaxed, and he didn't say anything dumb; all he needed to do, his handlers thought, was survive.

"Well, ten minutes almost gone," Stephanopoulos said, looking up at a clock.

"Eat it up," Carville urged Clinton's image on a monitor. "Keep it in play."

More time went by, more harmless questions and answers. No one had asked about Hillary. Maybe no one would.

"So what are our talking points?" Wilhelm asked, thinking ahead to the postgame schmooze with the press.

"No blood drawn," Carville said. "Nothing tonight changes the dynamic of the race."

They were one spin behind the events onstage. Bill Bonds, a Detroit TV newsman on the panel of inquisitors, asked the candidates one by one if Clinton would be electable in the fall, given his "recent problems." Tsongas was up first. In their holding room, Clinton's handlers held their breath.

"The most important thing is not winning," Tsongas began, "but winning with a mandate to govern."

"He punted!" Stephanopoulos crowed.

"He doesn't have the courage to go after us," Begala said.

Jerry Brown did, though "courage" was not exactly the word his own more sober strategists might have chosen. Brown had called Mike Ford that afternoon to ask whether he had any new thoughts about the debate. So slack ws the campaign's press operation that Brown hadn't even seen the *Post* story, and Ford thought better of telling him about it. Anything that looked like an attack on Hillary would just give Clinton a chance to play the outraged husband. "No, just stick to your message," Ford advised.

But the term "Brown strategist," applied to Ford or anyone else in his free-form campaign, was something of an oxymoron; the candidate shopped widely for ideas and acted on whatever fancy seized him. One of the people he called that day was consumer advocate Ralph Nader, who read him the Hillary story. Brown lit up, and when the question of Clinton's electability came around to him, he decided on the spot to throw the bomb.

"Yeah," he said, "I think he's got a *big* electability problem."

Bonds asked what it was.

"It was right on the front page of the *Washington Post* today," Brown answered. "He is funneling money to his wife's law firm for state business." The *Post* hadn't actually said that, but Brown was undeterred. "That's number one," he went on. "Number two, his wife's law firm is representing clients before the state of Arkansas agencies— his appointees. And one of the keys is the poultry industry, which his wife's law firm represents." The industry was polluting Arkansas rivers, Brown said, scaling new heights of indignation, "so it's not only corruption, it's an environmental disaster."

"It doesn't sound like you could run as his vice president," Bonds commented drily.

"No, it doesn't," Brown replied.

Opportunity had just knocked, and Clinton seized it, right on cue. "Let me tell you something, Jerry," he said, reddening perceptibly. "I don't care what you say about me . . . but you ought to be ashamed of yourself for jumping on my wife. You're not worth being on the same platform with my wife."

Brown, looking stricken, repeated the charge.

"Jerry comes in with his family wealth and his $1,500 suits and makes a lying accusation about my wife," Clinton said.

"It was in the *Washington Post*," Brown countered. "Are you saying *they're* lying?"

"I'm saying I never funneled any money to my wife's law firm," Clinton answered. "*Never.*"

The show ended, and Clinton stalked back to his holding room, still hot. His sense of the politics of the moment had not deserted him; he figured that his words hadn't mattered so much as the pictures of him sticking up for his wife under a slanderous attack. But his anger with Brown was unfeigned. "He'll say *anything*," he fumed, eyes flashing. "*Anything.*"

"You did fine," Carville told him.

"It's so personal," Clinton said. "I don't mind Tsongas hitting me on my record or on distortions I've made, but . . ." He paused, shaking his head. In fact, he *did* mind Tsongas hitting him, and he had to concede that the guy had landed a few good shots that night.

"It wasn't new," Carville said. "It was rehash. You defended your wife. We had a good debate."

Tsongas had a better one on most score sheets, at least for the first fifty-five minutes. In his holding room, Ed Jesser watched Clinton's set-to with Brown at the close with great satisfaction; they were two guys down in the gutter tearing at each other while Paul watched coolly from the sidelines. Tsongas came in smiling, for a change; his usual expression after a debate was a blank stare, but this time he was as ebullient as his troops. Their mood was reinforced by a fresh poll showing him within ten points of Clinton in Illinois— eight among likely voters—and that was *before* the debate. They had just won the last TV event that mattered. They felt reborn, back in the race.

They dreamed sweet dreams that night. On Monday morning, Tsongas's manager, Dennis Kanin, wakened in a sunny mood and called his wife, Carol, to share it.

"What did you think of the debate?" he asked.

"I'm depressed," she said.

Kanin was surprised. "Why?" he asked.

"People like a guy who stands up for his wife," she said.

Kanin spent that afternoon in the hotel room of his colleague Tim Kraft, working on strategy for the states down the road. The television was tuned to CNN. Every fifteen minutes, or so it felt to Kanin, images of Brown baiting Clinton and Clinton scolding Brown filled the screen. You wouldn't have known there was anybody else in the race. Paul Tsongas had disappeared.

Kanin glanced at Kraft. His unhappiness showed.

"It's been like this all day," Kraft told him.

The day indeed was Clinton's. But victories in media politics are measured out in news cycles, the intervals between morning, evening, and late-night news programs, and his time was nearly up; after a run of less than twenty-four hours, his victim wife was about to become the yuppie princess again. The unlikely setting for her latest metamorphosis was the Busy Bee restaurant in Chicago, and its catalytic agent was her own husband. The two of them had popped in to work the breakfast crowd, a bit of faux folksiness intended mainly for the cameras. The photo-op went fine. It was when Clinton spied a knot of reporters roped into a corner up front that the trouble began; he made for them and opened himself to what he knew would be hostile questioning.

The aides in his company winced. Clinton had rarely been able to resist such encounters; by his own admission, he loved sparring with the boys and girls on the bus, confident as he was that he could outthink and outwit any reporter alive. "You keep playing this game of 'gotcha,'" James Carville had scolded after one such encounter; Clinton was daring the press to try to catch him out in a fib or a gaffe, and, Carville warned, "it only takes once."

"Yeah," Clinton had replied, "but they didn't get me *that* time, did they?"

They didn't get *him* at the Busy Bee, either; he weathered a flurry of questions about his wife, her firm, and its dealings with the state. The trouble began when a network reporter, Andrea Mitchell, asked him if they could speak to Hillary.

"Sure, ask her anything you want," he said expansively.

A look of surprise crossed Hillary's face; till then, she had stood silently behind him, nursing a Styrofoam cup of coffee and letting him do the talking. But her faith in her own gift for argument was a match for her husband's in his, and she stepped forward, blinking into the glare.

It was a mistake. A local TV reporter began what amounted to a cross-examination on the proprieties of life as a governor's wife, demanding finally whether it was suitable for her even to be connected with a firm doing business with the state. She flared. "I suppose I could have stayed home and baked cookies, and had teas," she said. "But what I decided to do was to fulfill my profession, which I entered before my husband was in public life."

The instant flap was one of the sillier of the season. As Clinton explained, cleaning up behind her, she wasn't against tea, cookies, or homemaking in general; she had been talking only about her ceremonial role as first lady of Arkansas and doyenne of the governor's mansion, not her family life with her husband and her daughter. But in the reductionist world of sound-bite politics, the context didn't matter. It sounded as if Hillary had come out against home, hearth, and motherhood, and Clinton's handlers didn't have to wait for the six o'clock news to know that they had another mess on their hands.

Paul Begala eased up to Hillary in the crush and suggested that she might want to do some damage control—maybe talk later about the difficult choices women faced trying to reconcile their careers with their household obligations. "I'm going to say what I feel," she replied, sounding defensive. "That's all there is to it." She did try over the next few minutes to amend the record, but her protestations that she had never meant to disparage homemakers got lost in the noise. Explanations were futile in a world in which the principals in a campaign for president got an average of nine seconds of air time in which to say what was on their minds.

The ensuing media storm did nothing to quiet the jangle of nerves in the Clinton war room; in the private chat among the handlers that day, the feeling was implicit that they had yet another New Hillary on their hands—the candidate's wife as loose cannon on a rolling deck. Her stumble at the Busy Bee, while unfortunate, was forgivable; those things happened in campaigns. The talk in the room was less charitable about the reluctance of the Clintons to be open about themselves with their own managers. "This Hillary stuff is coming," one senior hand said the day the *Post* story broke, "and we've got to get ahead of the curve."

Instead, they remained hopelessly far behind it. A lawyer and an accounting firm had been put in charge of the record-vetting process, shut away from the campaign command. The Clintons were treating a political issue like a legal matter, and, in the view of their handlers, were making it worse as a result.

A fresh bit of fuel for their unhappiness had turned up quite by accident at Little Rock headquarters only that day, in the form of a memo Hillary had written to her partners in 1986. In Clinton's reelection campaign that year, there had been some flak about her having accepted a share of the earnings for work the firm had done for a company handling bond issues for the state. She hadn't technically violated her rule against profiting from public funds; a private company was paying the bills, not the Arkansas treasury. Still, she said in the memo, she planned to return the money she had received in the past for the bond business—it totaled $10,000 or so—and she wouldn't be accepting her cut in the future.

The memo could have been exculpatory, in Carville's favorite word for found documents; it could have been spun to show just how far Hillary had been willing to go to be above reproach in her financial affairs. The problem was that neither she nor anyone else had told the campaign it existed. They had had to find it themselves, and with investigative reporters swarming all over Little Rock, they had to assume as a matter of prudence that other copies might fall into less friendly hands. The distinction between the two kinds of money wasn't clear to the handlers, not at first. The potential damage was. Out in public, Hillary was saying she had "never, ever" taken money from state business—and here, in her own words, was the suggestion that maybe once upon a time she had accepted just a teensy bit.

"We stand a chance of losing the presidency because of our research on ourselves," Carville said when news of the find reached the war room.

"It sucks," Hillary's chief aide, Richard Mintz, agreed.

"It worse than sucks," Carville said. "Sucks can be put in a positive light. This is a disaster."

Wilhelm's wife, Degee, came in with a note for him to call Jeff Eller at the campaign press office in Little Rock. Eller was the one who had found the memo. The note said "urgent," and Wilhelm hurried out to a phone. "This is the story tonight," he fretted.

While they waited for him, the others complained among themselves about the little land mines that kept going off in their path—the stories they should have known about but didn't.

"Let's not beat ourselves up over this," Mickey Kantor said, looking for a silver lining. "This is not Bill Clinton sleeping with another woman. It's an issue we have to deal with."

Should they do a preemptive strike—maybe put out a statement explaining Hillary's arrangement with her firm their way? Stan Greenberg thought so. So did Kantor. But Mandy Grunwald worried that Hillary herself was becoming an issue; like her husband, she was being introduced to America the wrong way, not as herself but as her hard-edged caricature in the press. The questions about her were bigger than the particulars of her law practice "and," Grunwald said, "she walked right into it with the 'cookie' line."

"You can talk about this for fourteen hours," Kantor told them, "but she is not going to back off from who she is."

"Well, she will have to be part of the conversation," Greenberg said, "but we have to have a serious discussion of who Hillary Clinton is as the wife of a Democratic presidential candidate."

Wilhelm came back in from his call to Little Rock. The press indeed was all over the story of the Clintons as a provincial power couple, widening its net to include Hillary as well as Bill. The *New York Times* alone had four investigative reporters in town. "They're going after this," Eller had warned Wilhelm; the campaign needed to do something to blunt it.

But what? The group talked inconclusively for a half-hour about doing a statement, never quite reaching a decision; the only useful outcome was an agreement to have a delegation sit down with the Clintons the next day and talk to them about the perils of their secretiveness. "I've had blind dates with women I've known more about than I know about Clinton," Carville said at one point, his disgust writ large on his face. He was not alone in his anger. "The *arrogance,*" one senior hand spluttered after the meeting broke up. No other word seemed appropriate; they were in the thick of a presidential campaign, and the Clintons seemed to think they could just finesse their way through it, like a couple of smart-alecky college kids cruising through exam week on their facility with words.

"I Am Now the Message"

They didn't know it yet, but Paul Tsongas and his troops had just experienced their last happy days of the campaign. Tsongas had arrived in the Midwest burdened by low hopes, bad numbers, and a suit of tarnished armor. Michigan was already gone when he got there—so far gone that Jerry Brown was challenging him for second place—and Illinois hadn't looked much better. Clinton had wired the state organizationally and, after Super Tuesday, was surging in the polls. Within his first twenty-four hours on the ground, Tsongas had slipped from nine to twenty-one points behind.

And then he and his little entourage wandered into one of those white-light dreamscapes that open before dying campaigns—an almost magical sense of well-being nourished by crowd noise, press attention, and low-budget, small-sample polling. After a shaky start—a lecture on tax policy to a roomful of students at a vocational high school—he had got his speeches back on his economic message. Clinton's credibility gap was widening, thanks in part to a fresh round of Tsongas attack ads; nearly half the state didn't believe Clinton spoke the truth, and when he marched in the Saint Patrick's Day parade in

Chicago on Sunday, some people along the sidewalk laughed at him as he went by.

Suddenly, the whole Tsongas campaign seemed to be on a contact high. It was like being in a different state from the one they had touched down in a few days earlier, Dennis Kanin thought. If so, it might appropriately have been renamed the State of Euphoria, a place where all days were sunny and even bad omens looked good. A public poll in Sunday morning's *Chicago Tribune* put Tsongas thirty points behind, which, in the new mind-set, was excellent news. In Tubby Harrison's private tracking, the gap was down to ten points and closing daily. "We got a real shot here," Tubby was telling the road company from his offices in Boston. At the very least, Tsongas should run a decent second, enough to beat the expectations game and keep him alive. At the outside, he might actually astonish everybody and win.

Only on primary day did they wake up to the discovery that it had all been a mirage. The splash of cold water was a first round of network exit polling, leaked to both campaigns during the day by friends in the media. Michigan was a disaster, just as Tsongas and his team had expected; he was running a weak third, behind both Clinton and Brown. Illinois, in its way, was worse. His surge, if it ever existed, had gone into reverse after the last debate. It *was* as if Tsongas had disappeared. Clinton was leading by more than thirty points.

The Tsongas entourage was en route to O'Hare airport for their flight to Connecticut, the next stop on the long primary trail, when the polling caught up with them. That's ridiculous, Kanin told himself; it couldn't be *that* bad. But when they got to O'Hare, he found his Illinois coordinator, Kitty Kurtz, looking grim.

"I heard a crazy number," she said, "but I discount it totally."

They compared data. Hers were almost exactly the same as his. Clinton was leading, 52-19. Tsongas was only a few points ahead of Brown, who hadn't even contested the state.

The news was received with a great deal more cheer in Clinton's war room. "Goodbye, Saint Paul!" Begala whooped.

"If these numbers hold up, we've got to pile on," Carville said. "Make Tsongas go limping out of the race. Make him answer questions about nothing else."

"So when he goes into Connecticut, he's not going to have a chance to get his message out," Begala said. "This is going to be Gennifer Flowers for him."

Clinton descended to the Palmer House lobby to do his victory speech before a huge American flag, one more symbol repossessed from the Republicans. Then he headed through a storm of confetti and cheers to a holding room to prep for the usual post-primary interviews. The real returns were coming in on television. The margin looked much smaller than it had in the exit polls. Clinton's smile disappeared. Had they pumped their own expectations too high? Was Tsongas going to make it close after all?

Stan Greenberg tried to reassure him. He had gone over the poll numbers carefully, he said, and was sure they would hold up. "Have I ever been wrong?" he asked Clinton playfully.

"Once," Clinton said. He meant the night before New Hampshire, when Greenberg's polling had shown the campaign on the brink of collapse.

The two men looked at one another. The tension broke. Clinton started to laugh. The numbers on-screen fattened nicely thereafter; in the end, Clinton won both states by identical two-to-one landslides, over Tsongas in Illinois and Brown in Michigan. The nomination was in reach, if not yet in hand.

Tsongas, too, knew what the returns meant. He himself had framed the primary in Illinois as his first major showdown with Clinton in neutral territory, and he would be punished in the perceptions game for having lost it so badly. He conferred with his braintrusters on the flight to Connecticut. There wasn't much to say, and he was tired. After a time, he excused himself, stretched out, and closed his eyes, trying to sleep.

But there was no blinking the new reality of his situation. When he and his party had checked into their hotel in Hartford, Tsongas met in his rooms with Kanin and his wife, Carol, who had come in from Boston for a rare chance to be with him. The mood was ashy. Tsongas went straight to the only question on the table—whether he shouldn't just get out of the race and go home.

There were more arguments for quitting than against. He was short of cash and long on promissory notes, having already borrowed against his Federal matching funds for March and April. Who would write him checks or float him loans now? After Illinois, his campaign wouldn't be raising eighty thousand dollars a day anymore. Could he win Connecticut? Yes, though it would be tough and expensive. If his margin there was less than ten points, would it be interpreted as a Clinton victory in Tsongas country? Probably. Would *any* kind of win in Connecticut help Tsongas in the big New York primary two weeks later? Probably not.

Find out what the debt is, Tsongas told Kanin when they adjourned. He gave no further signal as to his intentions, but a death watch was forming in the staff and the press corps, and when he kept a speaking date that night at Trinity College, it was easy to find the valedictory notes. Tsongas's text was what aides had come to call his Meaning-of-Life Speech. It was one of his standards; still, in the circumstances, it made him sound like a man composing a eulogy for his own funeral. In the speech, he contemplated how he would like his children to remember him when he died. He wanted them to be able to say of him that he had done the best he could—that he had tried to make America a better country and to leave his kids a better chance in life than he had had.

The next day, he went back to Lowell and met again with the Kanins on what to do. Dennis Kanin found himself playing devil's advocate, making the best case he could for staying in the race. "We can downscale the operation," he said; they could dump the campaign plane and put up cheap TV ads, if they used any at all. Clinton was vulnerable—all the polls showed that. The doubts about his honesty had risen to what were, or ought to have been, disabling levels. Tsongas could compete, in Kanin's argument, simply by staying alive. "And it would just be up to the voters to decide," he concluded, "and we would stay in until the convention on those terms."

Tsongas wasn't buying any of it. What if, by some long chance, they won New York—where would that get him? "We'll have won again in the Northeast," he said, guessing the media reaction. They would have to go on from there with no money, no organization, and a growing pile of IOUs; they were already in debt by a half-million dollars, and Tsongas didn't want to go deeper into the red for nothing. Yes, he said, he would be accumulating delegates if he kept on, but not enough to win. The best he could hope to do was stop Clinton short of nomination on the first ballot.

He rested his case and polled the room. Carol Kanin urged him to keep going. Dennis reserved judgment. But the votes that finally mattered—Niki's and his own—were for getting out.

They were winding down when Peggy Connolly, the press secretary, appeared at the door. She had gone home, showered, changed, and rekindled her fighting spirit. "We've looked death in the eye and we've moved on before," she said. But as Tsongas drifted upstairs to discuss things with the children, Kanin called her aside.

"We think Paul's going to get out," he said.

There would be one last meeting later that night, Tsongas listening wearily from his wing chair while his privy council went back over the same ground again. His objections hadn't changed; he couldn't win a first-ballot nomination, and he wasn't in the race to be the man who spoiled it for Clinton. The undercurrent in the conversation was that

Clinton might somehow self-destruct, once people focused in on him as the probable nominee; in that remote event, Tsongas could always declare himself back in the race. Nobody in the room quite believed that would happen—certainly not Tsongas. It was past ten o'clock when he finally said, "Let's do it tomorrow."

A late winter snowfall was turning into a cold rain when, the next day, Tsongas formally "suspended" his campaign. The term was a legalism, a device enabling him to hold onto his delegates in case lightning struck Clinton; as he spoke, his people were completing the difficult process of ensuring him a place on the ballot in New York. But Tsongas did not tease the followers who filled the room with the possibility of his winning. His exit instead had the aspect of a religious passage, the transmutation of the man into the living word. He spoke in nearly mystical terms of the "sacredness" of his mission to redefine his party and the possibility that he might profane it by carrying on a losing campaign.

"The message must live," he said.

"The message has power," he said.

"I will be a player because I am now the message," he said. The obligation of his survival had been met.

Matters of Character

The senior leaders of the Clinton campaign were absorbed in their daily conference call that morning when a wire-service reporter phoned George Stephanopoulos with the news out of Boston. It wasn't official yet, but the Tsongas people had been calling their contacts in the press corps, alerting them that the campaign was about to go belly-up.

Stephanopoulos hung up and rang Clinton.

"Tsongas is out," he said.

"You're kidding," Clinton replied, more surprised than pleased. The initial euphoria around him was already giving way to a sinking sense that it was too early; neither he nor his command was ready for the end to come quite so soon.

He still seemed a bit tongue-tied when Tsongas called around noon, three hours before his formal retirement from the field.

"I've been in the business a long time," Tsongas said, being the good loser, "and you are the first person to beat me."

Clinton mumbled the appropriate niceties. The call tailed off, and Tsongas hung up. The conversation had been *strange*, he told Kanin; it was as if Clinton hadn't known what to say.

In fact, he hadn't. His entire campaign over the past several weeks had been a kind of secular morality play, two characters struggling for the soul of their party and their country. Jerry Brown barely had a speaking part in their script; the action downstage center involved Clinton as the hero of the forgotten middle class and Tsongas as his foil. The contrast between their two plans for the economy, selectively read, had been the main ingredient of Clinton's winning streak. It had bought him shelter from the focus on his supposed deficiencies of character. The doubts about him, to be sure, were rising to dangerous new highs in the polls. But for a time, people seemed to suspend their unbelief in him and to vote their fears about what life might be like under Tsongas.

In their last days in Chicago, Clinton's handlers supposed that they could get by for the moment with more of the same. They hadn't figured out how to deal with the character question anyway; they couldn't even say with any precision what it was. It could wait, so long as they had a winning formula and a suitable fall guy in Tsongas to run against. Their more pressing concern, indeed, was getting the candidate to Connecticut for the next round. The primary there was only a week away, but the Clintons were determined to head for Little Rock instead for a couple of days off.

The idea of taking a furlough in the middle of a war tried James Carville's dwindling reserves of patience; you couldn't just cede the field to the enemy and let them keep up the attack without answering. "The media is looking for evidence it's hurting us," Carville said the day before the two big midwestern primaries. "If we do poorly in Connecticut, the press will say, 'Ah hah! It's finally beginning to hurt him.'"

"You've got a candidate who's absolutely whipped," Mickey Kantor protested. "He's starting to spin off into outer space. To take two days off is better in the long term."

Two days off sounded dangerous to the others. The issue of character wouldn't stay submerged forever. Brown was sure to raise it in Connecticut, and Clinton's handlers still hadn't figured out what to do about it other than let people see him close up and decide for themselves. One camp within the campaign was arguing even then for a big-bang solution—a press conference or even a Nixon-style Checkers speech in which Clinton spoke more openly than he had so far about his marriage and his personal values.

But most of the players in the war room that afternoon thought they had the luxury of a little more time. "We don't want to solve a problem that isn't hurting us electorally," Mandy Grunwald said; they needed first to understand it better and, if it *was* a problem, work out a long-haul solution that would serve Clinton through the fall campaign. The economic contrast had served him well as a primary strategy against Tsongas. With certain alterations, it could be used against Brown as well; he didn't even pretend to have a plan. "Does that erase the queasiness?" Grunwald asked rhetorically. Maybe; they didn't know. Did they have to deal with the problem at all? They needed to find out. "Stan," she suggested, "should look at this in his polling. Come back to either Michigan or Illinois and see what happened."

"If you start the general election," Carville said, "and ask people, 'Is there something about Bill Clinton that doesn't sit well,' and 65 percent agree, and you also ask, 'Bush doesn't care about you,' and 65 percent agree, I'm not sure which is worse. Give Stan four weeks to play with this."

Could they wait that long? Greenberg himself wasn't sure. "The character issue is on the table," he warned. "Jerry will put it there week after week."

"I just remain skeptical that the way to deal with the character issue is to deal with the character issue," Carville said. Could you prove you had values by saying you had values? Would anybody believe so scarred a man as Clinton? "When we come out of this," Carville worried, "we may have more of a problem with Slick Willie than womanizing."

"I disagree," Greenberg answered. "Slickness can be fixed. I'm not sure adultery can be."

"It may be that we find that is our problem, and we have to live with it and win in spite of it," Carville said.

The flutter over Hillary's finances interrupted them that day, but when they resumed on primary morning, they were still picking at the problem as they might at an incompletely healed wound. It underlay a decision to have Clinton skip his usual victory lap around the morning TV talk-show circuit.

"They'll be all about Hillary and Gennifer Flowers," Grunwald said. "All process, like, 'Are you electable?'"

"Because they *always* steal his victory," Stephanopoulos added.

"Let me say this," Carville put in, "I'd rather be in Connecticut for one event than be on the morning shows. You are gonna take a toll in Connecticut being out of the news cycle for two days. It ain't a good idea."

"You're wasting your time," Kantor said. The Clintons were dead set on going home, and it was always hard budging them once they had made up their minds.

Unhappy looks flickered around the room. They wouldn't have the candidate in Connecticut till late in the week, and they wouldn't have a lot of paid media, either. They had planned all along for Clinton to come out of Illinois and Michigan broke but happy, with the nomination effectively locked up. They had got only the first part right; the Clinton war chest had been emptied before the war was over. Until the cash started churning again, there wouldn't be enough to put up a real ad campaign. For the first forty-eight hours in Connecticut, Clinton would be all but invisible.

"Look at what mistakes we've made," Stephanopoulos said. "Every time we were out of the cycle, we lost."

"The table is set on these things by Friday," Carville argued. "I'm still haunted by the weekend we left New Hampshire. I still wake up in the middle of the night and think about it."

The talk maundered on some more, dwelling on the nuances of what Clinton should say and do once he did get back on the road. The meeting was a big one, bigger than Carville liked; the more people in a room, the blurrier the focus. So far as he could see, they were putting together a schedule without a rationale.

"What I'm curious about," he said, his voice sharply edged, "is what is our core philosophy? What's our *message?*"

"It's a heavily substantive message," Susan Thomases, the lawyer and FOH, replied. "Big. Education, foreign policy, urban."

"If we don't do that in a sexy way, we will be eaten alive," Grunwald said. The press pack in New York was a carnivorous beast; Jerry Brown would be feeding them stuff every day, and if Clinton didn't do likewise, the media would be feeding on him. "If we don't toss them big things—*big* things—we're dead," she warned. "There's going to be fifty mikes in his face asking if he slept with rabbits last night."

"If you don't know your message going in, you've got a problem," Carville said. "I'm not from New York, I'm from the South. But my guess is, people there want to close the book on the '80s, too."

Closing the book on the '80s had worked only too well against Paul Tsongas, whose economic plan could be made to seem a kind of Dead Sea scroll washed up from the Age of Ron. But with his withdrawal, the terrain was shifting under Clinton's feet, and for a long while thereafter, he and his strategists would have trouble finding their bearings. The view from outside was that the race had effectively ended the day Tsongas got out. When Ron Brown wanted to call a press conference and say so, the Clinton team had to dissuade him. It wasn't seemly to declare victory with the primary season little more than half over.

The prospect from inside the movable war room looked less clear.

The suspicions about Clinton's integrity were real and growing, and he didn't have Tsongas to kick around anymore as a means of diverting attention from his own battered person. The last man standing in his path instead was Jerry Brown, and Brown in possession of the Clinton File was like an urban terrorist with a nuclear device. He was running against an entire order of politics and didn't mind blowing up any of its exemplars who got in the way.

II.

The Doom Crier

If the Marquis de Sade had written the climactic scenes in the story of Bill Clinton's march to the nomination, he would have been hard put to invent a torment more exquisite than Jerry Brown. For months, Brown had been the antimatter candidate in the race, largely invisible to what the analysts of our politics suppose to be the real world. His occasional victories had been minimally noted in the press, like the scores of Division III college football games, and Clinton's handlers had never really bothered with him in their strategic planning. But Brown had outlasted everybody else in the field, and when Clinton arrived belatedly in Connecticut, Brown was already there, choosing among his implements of pain.

The usual rules of war in late presidential primaries hold that you don't unduly bloody the probable nominee of your own party—not if you want a future in politics. But it was in the very nature of Brown's candidacy to break the rules, since he was running against the club that had written them, and Clinton, in his view, was its embodiment. They were opposite men, so unlike that, by the end, their differences of mind and spirit appeared to have taken physical form. Clinton, a junk-food junkie, had picked up a layer of McFlab in his travels and was in danger of swelling up into a Thomas Nast cartoon. Brown more nearly resembled a prophet rendered by El Greco; a regime of jogging and fasting had burned away forty pounds and left him sunken of belly and hollow of eye.

The contrast suited his mocking definition of the race; it had come down finally to the 800-pound gorilla against the 800-number guerrilla, he said, and so far as he was concerned, the hour of the guerrilla was at hand. He had never had a real chance to win the nomination, and the possibility that he might stop Clinton had shrunk to the vanishing point the day Tsongas packed it in; it would have taken the two of them, campaigning actively, to deadlock the process and open the convention to somebody less tarnished than the favorite. The media were in the process of declaring the race over and were treating

Clinton as the nominee. Brown begged—or, more accurately, demanded—to differ. In his apocalyptic vision, a party rotted by money, apathy, and cynicism was on the verge of a suicidal choice: an old-time "scandal-a-week" politician who had little hope of getting elected and less of governing if he did.

What Brown promised instead was radical change, beginning with an electoral process that could produce such an outcome. His own candidacy was his model for the revolution. Its symbol was the $100 limit on contributions, his warranty that he couldn't be bought; its nerve center was what his people dubbed Electric City, a wonderland of new political technologies and reinvented uses for old ones. Long before Ross Perot discovered the power of a toll-free telephone number and Bill Clinton became a regular on the gab shows, Brown had done it all and more. By the time he got to Connecticut, he had built the first interactive presidential campaign—an electronic two-way street between the voters and the people who proposed to govern them.

The founder and mayor of Electric City was a bright, skinny young volunteer named Joe Costello, who had caught Brown's eye and Pat Caddell's with his ideas about where the next frontier lay in media politics. The unlikely source for his inspiration was the television ministry—those late-night salvationists who booked time on cable channels, put up their 800 numbers, preached their hellfire sermons, and waited for the checks and the decisions for Christ to roll in. They were offering eternal life, but it was their marketing that interested Costello, not their theology. It struck him that a politician could do just as well with a phone bank, a sound stage, and a satellite hookup; if his message was powerful enough, people would respond.

At his most fevered, he argued that old-fashioned politicking was dead—that television was the new grassroots politics and all the rest of it was a waste of time. Why bother speaking to a thousand people at a rally in Concord or Manchester, he wondered early on, when you could invite yourself onto a radio talk show and reach fifty thousand free? Why even send Brown to New Hampshire at all? *Fuck* New Hampshire, was Costello's advice; the candidate's time and money would be better spent staying home in Los Angeles, getting on television and satelliting his image, his ideas, and—most important—his 800 number from there to the rest of the country. You weren't real until you got on television anyway. Television, Costello said, was where people got their information. Television was what people believed.

In the event, Brown did go to New Hampshire and submitted to the usual things candidates do there—the rallies, the coffees, the strolls through diners and shopping malls. But he flogged his 800 number at every stop, and back in Electric City, the phone lines came alive with pledges of support and money. For months, nobody noticed, except, perhaps, the most dedicated viewers of C-SPAN; it was as if Brown existed in a parallel reality invisible to the respectable media. In the national press and the network newscasts, his eclipse was near total; he wouldn't do sound bites or quickie interviews, and no one thought him worth pursuing at greater length. He existed instead in the crannies largely ignored by the other candidates, on talk radio and cable TV. The costs were cheap, the exposure was free, and the message could get out intact.

What Brown had discovered was something new in American politics: the populism of the airwaves. For a bargain price, a mad-as-hell electorate could buy into a revolution against big-time, big-money politics, and in surprising numbers, people did. The campaign would never get rich by modern standards; the $100 limit precluded that. But telephone pledges kept coming in to the nation's best-known 800 number, and roughly half were followed by checks, an extraordinary success rate in mass-market fund-raising. An early event at Brown's home, telecast by C-SPAN, brought in commitments totaling $20,000. A guest turn on Larry King's radio show in September, before the campaign had been formally launched, generated $20,000 more. A return engagement with King, this time on TV, gridlocked the phone bank for nearly twenty-four hours; those callers who got through the busy signals promised $125,000.

As a candidate, Brown would never quite catch up with the forces he had set in motion. He had always been a bit jangly for television, and his skills had further rusted in the nine years since his last stump speech as a candidate for office. On his best days in the fall and winter, he tended to overheat, like a latter-day Jonathan Edwards on the trail of the spiders of hell. At his worst, he verged on incoherence. At the AFL-CIO convention in November, he instructed the barons of labor that special-interest money—by implication, money like theirs—was "the umbilical cord . . . eating away like a cancer of the Democratic Party." His shrill pitch and his mangled metaphors betrayed him. The unions, once his friends, seemed uninterested, and the press—perhaps mercifully—forgot he was there.

"I don't think it went very well," he told his part-time counselor Mike Ford afterwards. He sounded as if he were talking about somebody else. Ford told him it didn't really matter that time—the entrenched labor leaders were part of the problem. But Brown had it right. He had done badly indeed, and if he didn't get better fast, he would never be heard.

Ford was in some pain, caught as he was between his belief in the message and his growing concern that Brown was losing it in the translation. He had never deluded himself that Brown was going to win; for Ford, that wasn't the point. There was something stirring in the land, a level of disgust with politics he had never seen before, and Brown's candidacy was a way to make it count for something real. If you had a friend or family member who had slipped into a persistent vegetative state, Ford thought, you at least had to try to wake him up. That was Brown's duty to his party and the country; it was his mission in the race to catch that inchoate anger and give it political form, skillfully and powerfully enough that the old crowd in charge could no longer sleep through it.

But Brown's skills seemed to have deserted him. The guy wouldn't talk about his own past as the two-term governor of America's biggest state or about his plans for the future, if he had any; he had become, in Ford's view, the rebel without a clue. After the labor meeting, Ford sent him a memo invoking the lesson of Plato's Cave, the teaching parable about a group of slaves who have been imprisoned in a cave so long that they come to mistake the shadows on the walls for reality. One of them—Brown, in Ford's updated version—escapes to daylight, then comes back to tell the others what he has seen. Nobody wants to believe him; the lot of them—the party, the press, the labor leaders— are too heavily invested in the shadows. "We can't go back into the cave and stridently tell these people they have a corrupt view of reality, even though it is true," Ford wrote. "It must be told with a little more gentleness and put into historical perspective."

Brown seemed too consumed to do either; it was like telling the prophet Jeremiah to lighten up. In his public and often his private person, he could be a distant, humorless man, self-absorbed to a point where only the most devout of his volunteers felt any psychic income from serving him. "I have to work on the happiness quotient," he said one day when the morale problem was called to his vagrant attention. By then, it was too late to fix it.

Neither could he be induced to crack a smile, let alone brighten his act with a little comic relief. In November, all the candidates were dragooned into one of those silly rituals of politics, a roast for a New Hampshire congressman named Dick Swett. Ford, a man of sharp, earthy wit, saw the occasion as a chance for Brown to be funny—even to laugh at himself a little. But when Brown read through a batch of one-liners Ford had written for him, he called and bounced them.

"I don't like jokes," he said. "I don't like to tell jokes. I'm not Jackie Gleason."

Ford's heart sank, less out of pride of authorship than at learning that Gleason was the most current comic Brown could think of. The dude had missed maybe twenty or twenty-five years of pop culture. The roast was looking riskier than Ford had thought.

"If you can't do the shtick, don't go," he told Brown. "The only thing you can do is confirm right before their eyes that you're still an asshole. Don't do it."

"No, no, it'll be all right," Brown said. "I can do something funny."

He couldn't. He lost most of the jokes on the way to the podium, along with whatever passed for his sense of humor; instead, he was still screaming at the bondsmen in Plato's Cave, questioning the whole idea of serious people getting together to raise money and tell jokes when they ought to be talking about the fate of the nation. The effect on the room was deadening. Ford had been right: Brown shouldn't have gone.

Ford continued the rehab effort anyway, in memos and late-night phone calls. His design in these tutorials was to get Brown to humanize himself and to move beyond just talking about the rot in the system; the sorry state of our politics was indeed the core issue, but the message had to grow into a call to power by a man with the mind and the relevant experience to make it work for people again. "We have to inspire action as in, 'Take Back America,'" he wrote in November. "We must make clear that we offer first a challenge—a challenge to people who have seen no real choice—to become active by taking it back themselves. We are an instrument, not a Deus ex Machina. OUR CANDIDACY MUST BE SEEN AS THE ONLY REAL CHANCE FOR REAL CHANGE."

Nothing happened; Brown was still the itinerant doom crier with a hole in his message where the heart belonged. In December, with the first nationally televised debate coming up on NBC, Ford sat down at his word processor to try again. His tone this time was magisterial, his language unsparing. Brown, he said, had to get out from under his hardening image in the press as being for term limits and campaign-finance reform but not much more. "Our message is diminished in power because it is unconnected to assuaging fear, only to stimulating anger," he wrote. "We are not dealing with the economic panic or pain out there. We are talking about a flawed system, not people. We offer no solutions. Some people are indeed accepting our invitation to dinner, but we have no food to offer them."

The NBC debate was Brown's chance to put something on the

table, with the season's biggest audience looking in. To the few professionals in his eccentric orbit, it became a major event—maybe, Pat Caddell thought, the whole damn campaign—and they game-planned it like coaches preparing for the Super Bowl. Brown would talk about himself at last; he would be the most experienced guy up there and the most innovative as well, somebody who had actually created jobs and made change happen. He could distinguish himself from the rest of the pack; they were politicians, he wasn't—not anymore. He could go after Clinton frontally—zap him for promoting a New Covenant for America when the only thing wrong with the old one was its corruption by politicians like him.

And Brown could advertise his 800 number free to the entire country. The idea made NBC queasy, and after some false starts, Tom Brokaw, who would be emceeing the show, put in a call to Ford. Ford was a Washington guy. He had to be sane. Maybe they could work something out.

"Can you get him off this 800 number?" Brokaw asked. "It's really stupid."

"Well, we'll do our best," Ford said, amused at being thought the voice of reason in the campaign; it was a little like calling Che Guevara an agrarian reformer. Brown, in his view, could not only use the toll-free number but could make a free speech issue of it, and the louder Brokaw squawked, the better. It would be living proof that the pols and the press were allied in defense of the status quo.

Over several days of prep sessions, everything had been anticipated—everything except the possibility that the candidate would be as nervous as an ingenue on opening night. At first, he resisted the idea of prepping at all, and when he finally submitted, he wouldn't pay attention. He seemed distracted. He complained about the lines his people had prepared for him. He couldn't memorize things, he said.

"You're not supposed to memorize," Ford answered. "*You* are the speech. These are the sutra." They were meant, that is, as cues to his own memory; it was a device the Hindus had figured out before the birth of Christ. "When Bill Clinton talks about change," Ford said, "the response just comes to you."

Brown wasn't interested in the sutra. His flirtations with Eastern religions gave way, under pressure, to his training as a lawyer. He demanded "bullets"—short, punchy bites of information.

By the day of the debate, he looked to his coaches as if he was losing his grip. Ford led him into the bedroom of the hotel suite they had hired for the prepping.

"Look, I don't know why you're bothered," he said. "You're the only guy who's won a presidential primary. The only guy, y'know what I mean? They're rookies. You're the only pro in camp. You're big time, y'know? Arkansas? Little place. Smaller than West Los Angeles. Fucking *relax.*"

"Yeah, yeah, you're right," Brown said.

But Ford's pep talk didn't help, and neither did a jog before airtime. Brown's friend Jacques Barzaghi delivered him to the studio in rocky shape, and he got worse as he plowed into his opening statement. He looked tense, angry, a little crazy. Some of his sentences didn't parse. In the press room upstairs, reporters were snickering at him.

At home in Annapolis, Ford was staring at the show in disbelief. Caddell was back in the hotel suite, doing the same. An open phone line connected them, two normally verbal men reduced to stunned silence.

"Maybe it's a body-snatcher thing," Ford said. The real Jerry Brown had somehow been replaced by a gibbering amateur.

He did get the 800 number in, over Brokaw's objections, but nothing else seemed to work; he kept missing opportunities to rough up his opponents and drive home his case for himself. The epiphany came when the camera caught him leaning back in his chair reading a newspaper, as if he had got bored and tuned out of the debate entirely. The paper, as it happened, was a copy of the *Philadelphia Inquirer* with a long, devastating report on what had gone wrong with the American economy and how the power elite of politics had let it happen. Caddell had given it to Brown to wave on camera: Exhibit A for the prosecution. Instead, he looked like a man at a breakfast table waiting for the coffee to be poured.

"Definitely the body-snatchers," Ford said.

The show was a disaster for Brown, so bad that several past donors to his campaign called the 800 number and asked for their money back. He knew he had done badly, but he phoned Ford and Caddell anyway, fishing for reviews. Caddell screamed at him and told him he was finished. Ford wouldn't take his call. Over the next forty-eight hours, the two strategists played semiseriously with the idea of having Caddell go to New Hampshire and file for *vice* president. If Brown couldn't get the message straight, Pat could, and the sheer audacity of his doing it would draw attention to what he had to say.

They finally dropped the venture, but their relationship with Brown and the campaign would never be quite the same. Professionals like the two of them always been a bit out of place among the believers, like agnostics at a camp meeting; the fact that they were themselves working as unpaid volunteers was never sufficient proof that they were pure of heart. Even an old trooper like Brown, in the spell of his new gospel, was ambivalent toward them. "What are you guys anyway, spinmeisters?" he demanded one day, catching Caddell and Ford talking to some friends in the press corps. In his pre-Copernican universe, everything revolved around him; the proper business of advisers was not to presume to speak for him but to be near their phones whenever he chanced to call for counsel.

He seemed to prefer the unquestioning company of the groupies who had always followed him and who now, in middle age, gave his latest campaign the aspect of a superannuated Children's Crusade. He put them on short rations of warmth and gratitude; their allegiance instead was to the word and to the austere new style of politics Brown embodied. His $100 limit on gifts in itself made a powerful unifying symbol for his believers. It imposed its own discipline on the campaign and fostered a kind of mystique as well—a through-the-looking-glass perspective in which poverty was somehow cleansing and amateurishness a virtue. "We couldn't spend money," one aide, Mike Bourbeau, said. "We had to create a myth." They did, and for his tribe, at least, Brown was its hero; the repentant power broker had come down from his tower, put on a hair shirt, and become one with the people.

His metamorphosis was complete, though never adequately explained. Brown answered to the great nineteenth-century critic John Ruskin's description of a contemporary as a man who thought by infection, catching opinions like colds. His latest rebirth was like his earlier passages, from seminarian to politician to pilgrim to politician again; they simply happened to him, without visible transition. This New Jerry flew tourist. He bunked free in the homes of supporters, like a mendicant friar. He fasted. He jogged. He advertised his brief sojourn with Mother Teresa, tending to the needs of the dying. His fancy Italian suits were retired to their hangers back home; he took up lumberjack shirts and union windbreakers instead, most often worn over white turtleneck sweaters. His pale, thin face above the white collar took on a priestly look. "I'm a Jesuit monastic," he said one day, when somebody told him to slow down; campaigning for president, for him, had become the equivalent of having to say ten million Hail Marys.

His support troops mirrored his style. They resembled a new-age commune, an idealized world with all the usual titles but no real hierarchy. His campaign manager, Jodie Evans, a wealthy art collector and sometime fund-raiser for Brown, presided over the drab headquarters suite like a Zen den mother. "Everybody walks in with a different gift," she said, and she saw that everybody got to speak up, even the greenest volunteers. The arrangement was warm, fuzzy, familial, and deathly slow at getting anything done. In November, Ford had flown out, planning to stay a month and help get things set up. He lasted three days in the Land of the Brownies and fled. "THERE IS NO DEFINED ORGANIZATIONAL STRUCTURE OR MISSION AND NO DISCIPLINE," he warned in a memo once he had got safely home. "There are too many cooks in a campaign with so few diners."

Not much changed, even after Electric City got up and running and brought a certain measure of budget-class prosperity. "Our campaign transcends understanding," Jacques Barzaghi said airily. For people accustomed to orderly process, it did. But measured by the mere fact of its survival into spring, after everybody else had dropped out, it could fairly be said to be working. All but unnoticed, Brown had stolen victories from the big boys in Maine, Colorado, and Nevada and had kept springing little surprises elsewhere; his silver medal in Michigan was only the latest and splashiest among them. He had already picked off perhaps 130 delegates, with richer opportunities yet to come to him in his new role as the last alternative to Clinton. He would have enough, at the very least, to kick up a row at the convention—to show up at the gates of Madison Square Garden with a blowtorch and put it to the feet of the party and its presumptive nominee.

He had become, at the end, the unlikely vessel for all the fear and loathing Clinton had excited on his way to the nomination. A believer in destiny or irony might have been tempted to think that the two of them had been fated to meet in the final battle. Clinton had always wanted to run as the outsider in the race, but the fall of the cards had made him the inside man instead, a play-by-the-rules politician in a year of revulsion with politics. In what ought to have been his hour of triumph, his campaign had lost its footing. The papers were feasting daily on the untidier passages of his life and works in Arkansas; his honesty was suspect to nearly half the voters of his own party. And now he was about to face his last trial: a one-on-one struggle with an opponent whose announced intent was to bring down the political system—and whose planned first step toward that end was Clinton's destruction.

Bill's Day Off

Afterward, James Carville would call it "the most expensive fucking golf game ever played in American history." His client Bill Clinton had held to his resolve to take a couple of days off at home and, after a luxurious night's sleep in his own bed, had done what members of the local gentry do for daytime recreation: he had gone off to the Little Rock Country Club for a round of golf. It seemed not to matter to him that the club had no black members, or that the press had already made inquiries about why he sometimes took his ease there, or that the Connecticut primary was less than a week away. In the glow of victory and the grip of fatigue, Clinton had become the boy prince of Arkansas again, cavalier of habit and careless of appearances. With his day at the club, the game of gotcha between him and his pursuers moved to a higher level of risk, and this time, he got got.

As he usually did in a fix, Clinton would have plenty of ex post facto explanations for his behavior—that he was only an honorary member of the club, as a perk of being governor; that he had gone there that day as somebody else's guest; that the club was in the process of screening black candidates for its rolls. But the mere fact of his outing in its hitherto lily-white precincts made his talk of racial healing sound hypocritical, and the accompanying news photo compounded the damage. Front pages across America were abloom with the likenesses of the governor and a similarly pale, similarly overweight crony lolling in a golf cart like two young planters on a tour of their fields.

The image was particularly unfortunate for Clinton in the Northeast, where southern politicians as a class were regarded with some suspicion. In fact, his gubernatorial record on racial matters was strong, and he had made the reconciliation of blacks and whites a powerful theme of his campaign. But on holiday, he had slipped back into the arrogance some of his people thought they detected in him—an air suggesting that he was above reproach on such questions and, in any event, could do as he pleased in his own duchy on his own time. His protestations that it wasn't his club missed the point. The question was why, after due warning, he had gone there at all.

He could hardly have done Jerry Brown a larger favor on the eve of their first one-on-one encounter. Brown had been quicker in any case at adapting to life without Paul Tsongas; while Clinton tarried in Arkansas, his last surviving competitor was busily laying an ambush for him in Connecticut. The state was Brown's kind of place: small, white, affluent, cheap to campaign in, and mad as hell at the condition of American politics. If he did well there, moreover, it would resonate across the state line to New York, the next big theater of war. Nobody had to draw him any pictures of the possibilities. By the time Clinton finally showed up, Brown had been around for two days, mocking him as just one more of "the good old boys of yesteryear."

The sages and scribes of politics were well along by then in the process of anointing Clinton the nominee. His face beamed forth from the covers of four national magazines that week, and the press was already speculating about his choice of a running mate. But the aura of inevitability can be a dangerous condition in politics. Clinton was like an out-of-shape fighter, ripe for embarrassment, and Brown was spoiling to oblige him.

"This race ain't over yet," he told Ron Brown by phone that week. "I know," the party chairman replied.

For a heady time, Spaceship Jerry seemed finally to be getting airborne. Its lift-off was fueled partly by the raw power of its message and partly by the politics of default; if you were a Democrat and you didn't like Clinton, Brown was all there was. The effect of this revelation bordered on the magical. JERRY BROWN IS HOT, HOT, HOT, a sign at headquarters proclaimed, and for once, a placard there could no longer be lightly dismissed as a work of naive art. The 800 number was engulfed with calls and pledges, more than the operators could handle; one woman in Kentucky tired of trying to get through, flew out to California instead, and worked for a week as a volunteer. It was Clinton, with his mighty money machine, who had to worry about where his next dollar was coming from. Brown was raking in $40,000 a day.

He was, moreover, doing it his way, flying below the radar of the press and the political establishment. "We will need a bigger plane, we will need a bigger plane," Jacques Barzaghi fretted, anticipating a fresh wave of attention to his friend the candidate and, perhaps, to himself. In fact, a bigger plane was the last thing Brown needed. The media weren't interested in him or, for that matter, the small-stakes game in Connecticut. Reporters went home to rest up for New York, two weeks later, and their inattention gave Brown, for the last time, the kind of protective cover he thrived on. To Joe Trippi, who had lately signed on as media consultant, the campaign till then had consisted largely of Brown wandering around banging on pots and pans and yelling "Change! Change! Change!" at the top of his lungs. Up close, it looked ragged and sounded awful, but in those states where he had camped out long enough and banged hard enough, the message had somehow got through.

The enterprise would not have stood up to inspection on the usual measures; it more nearly resembled a human-potential retreat than a presidential campaign. Callers needing a decision from its manager, Ms. Evans, were sometimes told to ring back later—she was chanting at a staff meeting and could not be disturbed. Anything that smacked of a top-down structure was discouraged, even the term "national headquarters." Experience at the game was suspect; in bad times, the word "betrayal" flew about, usually aimed at anyone who, like Ford,

Caddell, or Trippi, had ever worked at politics as a livelihood. Staff meetings had the flavor of a summer camp for old flower children. Everybody was invited and everybody came, some standing, some occupying chairs, some sitting cross-legged on the floor.

"What works?" Evans asked at one such gathering, with the Connecticut primary just three days away.

"The hundred dollars," somebody said.

"The discipline to stay pure to the message," somebody else offered.

"That we don't do things the old way," a third voice piped up.

Evans sat taking notes, as if wondrous new insights were unfolding before her. It was, she thought, the best campaign she had ever been around—less like a campaign, indeed, than like a huge family coming of age together.

"What are the obstacles?" she said.

"The press."

"The money."

"The political establishment."

"Our lack of experience," a volunteer said.

But wasn't that an asset, too? They talked about that awhile, with Evans scribbling notes, and concluded finally that it was.

"What are the values that the campaign represents?" Evans asked.

"It's not about personalities."

"It's about quality. And ee-quality."

"Courage."

"Truth."

"Compassion and caring."

Evans took more notes, getting it all down.

"Creative."

"Vision."

"Devotion."

"A touch of magic."

"It's a movement!"

The "chant," at the end of staff meetings, was more accurately a college cheer, a bonding ritual Evans had encouraged starting early in the primary season. At her bidding, a staffer would rise and lead the mass incantation:

> If not now, when?
> If not him, who?
> We the people, me and you,
> Vote President Brown in '92!
> Call 1–800–426–1112!

> If not now, when?
> If not now, when?
> Governor Brown, Governor Brown—
> President Brown in '92!

The price of its perfect democracy was a certain incoherence in making anything actually happen; it was as if time and tactical necessity didn't exist. Ads were slow getting on the air at all in Connecticut, and when they did, they were slotted for the wrong times on the wrong stations. Matching spots with audiences is an advanced art, in politics no less than commerce, and Trippi's wife and buyer, Katie, was gifted at it. She went to work buying time for Brown on shows with strong appeal to educated suburbanites—abandoned Tsongas voters who didn't much like or trust Clinton and were looking for a new home. It was, as she soon discovered, a waste of time. The campaign was calling the stations a step behind her, canceling her orders and substituting its own.

Trippi, in a lather, phoned Evans in Santa Monica. "What's going on, Jodie?" he demanded. "Tell me what you did."

The campaign, she replied, didn't want to pay the commission charged by media firms like Trippi's on any TV time they bought; it didn't seem right when so many true believers were working for nothing. Headquarters already had a perfectly good starting point: the manifest of programs they had advertised on in Michigan. Evans had turned it over to a volunteer with instructions to replicate it, show for show, in Connecticut.

"Jodie," Trippi said, "our targets in Michigan were blue-collar workers. We're not going after the same people here. You know, there's a *reason* we do this for a living."

Evans was unmoved. The buy went forward her way. Factory families got a saturation dose of Brown that weekend. Upscale voters had to be channel-slumming to catch him at all.

The mind of Jerry Brown was as undisciplined as his campaign. He was still groping for an affirmative message, something he was *for,* and with no resident brain bank to serve him, he often accepted the advice of the last person he had talked to. A couple of supply-side economists had sold him on a flat income-tax rate of 13 or 14 percent for everybody, with an accompanying value-added tax of 13 percent or so to make up any lost revenue. The concept was at least arguable on the merits; the tax code as it existed was a multivolume record of deals, some benign, some shady, with special pleaders, and a flat tax was a way to clean it up at a single stroke. The problem was that it had a snake-oily sound. Brown hadn't thought through the details when he offered the idea and so had trouble defending it when, inevitably, it came under attack.

It was an opportunity for Clinton, but he was slow seizing it. His vaunted campaign was adrift, his own compass suddenly unsure. If Brown's operation looked and acted like Camp Jerry, Clinton's was, in the words of one of its senior hands, like a goddam Quaker meeting: everything had to be done by consensus. There was no strategy, another member of the general staff complained; everybody was obsessed instead with the tactics of keeping Clinton alive from one week to the next. The mere fact that he had got as far as he had was in contradiction to one of James Carville's hard rules—that you couldn't win an election answering questions about yourself. Clinton *was* winning, Carville mused one day, because he had money in the bank and a weak field to run against. But his longer-term situation was precarious. After all those weeks and all those battles, people still didn't know what he wanted to do as president.

In Connecticut, he and his team weren't even managing the rudimentary business of survival very well. Brown had come into the state with high negative ratings, but so had Clinton. The matchup accordingly came down to which man was the lesser evil, which suited Brown's purposes fine; the trump card in that game was to rail against politics as usual and make the other guy the horrible example. Clinton seemed at a loss for where to go and what to say in reply. His late arrival had cost him two days on television, and when he finally did show up, his scheduling was a shambles. Over the decisive last weekend, he did two events for blacks, a small fraction of the state's electorate, and only one for working-class ethnic whites—his prime target audience.

Neither had he figured a way to redefine the race, as he had done so effectively with Tsongas. The flat tax looked like the best available weapon; they had begun using it against Brown in Michigan. But the real measure of its destructive power didn't come clear until the night before the primary, too late to help. Stan Greenberg and Mandy Grunwald had slipped into Manhattan that evening to see what a couple of focus groups made of Brown's big idea and Clinton's critique of it as one more beneficence to the very rich. The results were devastating for Brown. The voters in both groups turned on him and his contrivance when the fine print was spelled out to them.

"*Toast!*" Grunwald whooped, high-fiving Greenberg in their booth behind a one-way mirror.

"It's done," Greenberg said.

"We can demolish this guy," Grunwald added.

But could they levitate Clinton at the same time? The first group, all women, flocked to him at the end of the session. The second, all men, seemed resistant to his charms, except that he seemed well-spoken and had survived a lot of bashing; he was, one said, "the best of the worst." The arguments for him didn't work. One man bridled visibly when Clinton's face came on a TV monitor, and most were prey to one or another of the familiar litany of doubts about him.

"It's not the affair that bothers me," one said. "It's that he would lie about it."

"Same old stuff repackaged," another said.

"Didn't do such a great job as governor," yet another thought.

"A little flashy," a fourth said. "Maybe a little insensitive to minority issues."

That one was a new entry on the ledger, and it troubled Greenberg; one round of golf, he thought, had got in the way of Clinton's whole message of racial healing.

And there was more:

"The letter about the draft."

"Too much tinsel. I would never buy anything from him."

"I don't have trust or faith in him."

The women had wound up ten-nothing for Clinton. The men listened to the best case for him and still split down the middle, five for him, four for Brown, one undecided. Behind the looking glass, Grunwald glanced at Greenberg.

"That's a little scary," she worried.

"Sure is," Greenberg said. They had their attack weapon, yes, but Clinton's own message still couldn't be heard above the static about his character and his past. Nothing he said had connected, Greenberg thought unhappily. Nothing.

Their worries were confirmed when Connecticut voted the next day. Clinton had wakened to a new scandal, this time a report in the *Los Angeles Times* that he had personally lobbied to award a multi-million-dollar state bond contract to a man known to be the target of a cocaine investigation. The connective tissue in the story was loose, and it was effectively shot down within twenty-four hours. But there was no such thing as a harmless hit for Clinton anymore; the residue of all the character stories, fact or fiction, was the supposition that he must have a character problem.

The gloom among his troops was compounded when the day's first exit polling in Connecticut had him trailing Brown, 42-35. Paul Tsongas was siphoning off 19 percent, and he wasn't even running anymore.

George Stephanopoulos went numb. "We're going to lose," he said.

"It just means we've got a two-week, breakneck campaign to beat his ass," Begala told him.

Two weeks was what they had left till the New York primary, and Clinton convened his war council in his rooms at the Sheraton Manhattan to talk about what to do there. His spirits were low, his manner touchy. He's *frightened,* one close adviser thought, and as often happened on bad-news days, his tone was edged with rebuke.

"We're getting burned in Connecticut," he said with visible disgust, "because we ran an unresponsive campaign. It was arrogant to think we can go in and win with the same old stuff on the air where they've been told I was a low-life S.O.B."

Greenberg reminded him that Brown had beaten him into the state by forty-eight hours and that his scheduling, once he got there, had been poorly managed. "We had two black days," he said, "and we didn't do enough blue-collar."

"It was a weird week," Grunwald said. "We were half in, half out; half looking at Bush, half looking at Brown. The key thing is, starting tonight, this thing is serious with Brown, and we've got to kill him here."

A newscast playing low in the background underscored her warning. Clinton's negative rating in New York was nearly as bad as Brown's, and 45 percent of the state's Democratic voters expressed doubts about him—as high a number as he had encountered anywhere.

"We have to have the battle with Brown set on our terms," Greenberg said. "We have a lot of ideas to kill him. *Kill* him."

"What are they?" Clinton asked.

"The flat tax," Grunwald answered. "We've got to launch a big salvo at him on this flat-tax thing."

How to launch it was another question. The television budget was too small, Begala argued.

"We don't have any money," Clinton said drily.

"I know," Begala answered, "but we're going to be pounded on character."

"All these people know about me is I'm a jerk," Clinton said.

"They want to know what you stand for," Greenberg told him.

The talk ran on, and as the focus shifted to what they *could* do in New York, as against what they couldn't, Clinton's mood seemed to brighten a bit.

"So you don't think it's a cesspool?" he said.

"This city?" Grunwald, a longtime New Yorker, joked. "It's *always* a cesspool."

"But not zillions of people who will never vote for me?" Clinton asked.

"I think there are some," Grunwald said, "but not zillions." The trick, she told Clinton, was to do to Brown what they had done to Tsongas: kill him, yes, but in a way that made people want to vote for you. "New Yorkers have a higher political bullshit meter," she counseled. The only way to reach them was to do "a real people's schedule" and speak to them in a language they could hear and understand above the noise. "Things you can shout out a taxi window," Grunwald said.

Clinton left for an event, feeling better. The others hung back in the suite with their worries. They had to scratch up more money for TV, "or," Begala warned, "we will lose this thing." They had to clean up the schedule—get Clinton out of the standard round of labor, black, and Jewish organizations and put him in situations of risk and courage. And they had to recreate their wounded candidate yet again, this time by contrasting him to Jerry Brown. They had a good ad ready comparing the two men, but it wasn't the home run they were looking for. How could they make it better?

"Let's talk about who we are," Greenberg opened. "This is not a complicated strategy."

"Serious change for serious times," Begala said, thinking lines aloud. "Brown's another gimmick."

"Another gimmick that screws average people," Greenberg went on. "We have the rap on Brown—the rap is, he's a slogan and a gimmick. We've got to decide who *we* are."

"Gimmick is not strong enough," Susan Thomases said. "It's a cruel hoax."

"Jerry's Tax," Stephanopoulos dubbed it at another point. They could use that; it had just the right note of derision.

They had just got a fresh exit-poll report from Connecticut when Carville arrived, late for the gathering. The race was a dead heat. Close wouldn't be good enough for Clinton, not by the time the pundits got through interpreting the results. In their stressed-out state, his advisers could still fantasize his somehow losing the nomination—or alternatively, sustaining so much damage that he would be easy prey for Bush and Perot in November. Brown couldn't win the big prize, but he could make serious trouble for Clinton, and he was going to get a bump out of Connecticut—a *big* bump, Greenberg said worriedly.

And Clinton helped blow it, Carville brooded, with one expensive fucking round of golf. "In the focus groups," he went on, "people ask, 'Why are you talking to us about race?'"

"We're so goddam damaged by our own mistakes," Harold Ickes,

Clinton's New York manager, said. Ickes was a lawyer of sound pedigree—his father had been FDR's secretary of the interior—and excellent connections, both Clintons among them.

"We're damaged by our fuck-ups and our lack of strategy," Carville said.

Could they recover with a smart-bomb attack on Jerry's Tax? Greenberg was worried; it wouldn't be enough in itself to drag Clinton out from under the freight of negatives weighing him down.

"Right now, we're hemorrhaging," Carville said. "We better stop some bleeding. We do have to define ourselves. We have serious, serious problems we have to deal with. But right now we just got beat in Connecticut. We have the dope dealer. The golf game. We've got to change the focus over to Brown and get us back on our feet."

"Do we have anything on the other side?" Greenberg asked. Something positive to say about Clinton?

"I hope we do," Carville said, "but starting tonight and through the weekend, we got to define Brown. Hammer him on everything."

"And every surrogate we have should be saying this," Grunwald agreed. "Let's give ourselves until Sunday to single-mindedly hammer him."

Carville didn't like the schedule; it was too diffuse. "I don't think people understand the strategy," he said impatiently. "We have to knock Jerry off his game and off his message. To do that takes unbelievable focus and concentration. We are faced with a grave danger. This bastard's coming to New York with the kind of thing people like here: he's anti-this and anti-that. We have to fight that son of a bitch in the trenches."

And on the air, if they could find a way. "The irony is that Brown may have more money than we will," David Wilhelm worried.

"Jerry Brown will be on the air more than we will," Greenberg said. "If he puts a tough negative ad up on us in New York . . ."

The thought trailed off. Greenberg smacked his hands together. The sound was as sharp and final as a gunshot. *Bang*, it said. You're dead.

"I Didn't Inhale"

"I think we're in a crisis," Mandy Grunwald was saying four nights later, "and we're not acting like it." Her disembodied voice, over a conference line connecting the scattered general staff of the Clinton campaign, was dark with impatience. They had indeed lost Connecticut to Jerry Brown, and while the final margin had been a single percentage point, it was a deep embarrassment; nearly two-thirds of the state's Democrats had preferred somebody other than their nominee-apparent. It was Brown who was riding a wave now, and Clinton who was wandering New York from one pointless event to another, Bubba in the Big Apple, dogged by hecklers and battered by the press. He wasn't focused, Grunwald complained. He didn't know what to say, and his handlers were in no frame of mind to help him figure it out. "I don't care about delegate numbers," she said. "If we don't win New York, we're gone."

That Clinton's team could still imagine him losing, after having come so close to the prize, was a measure of the state of entropy that had stolen over the campaign. The note of gloom and rebuke in their conversation that evening was in part simply exhaustion talking. They could barely remember their last day without a crisis or their last decent night's sleep, and now they found themselves, stressed and groggy, in Handlers' Hell—an urban brier patch where the tribes were noisier, the tabloids meaner, the vanities larger, the power brokers more cynical, and the undercurrents deeper and trickier than in any other polity in America. The secret to surviving New York, as one of Michael Dukakis's men had put it four years earlier, was stepping around the bullshit, and Clinton had arrived there with no grander strategy than that. Survival, a top hand said, was his single imperative.

But even that modest goal seemed suddenly in doubt to his people in their melancholic round-robin that evening. They took small comfort in the mathematical evidence that Clinton would be the nominee—that his harvest of delegates had passed the point where anybody could catch him before the convention or deny him once he got there. That was the forest, and they were lost among the trees. Their talk was suffused with a sense of their own futility, the feeling that they had already said everything they had to say and yet had been unable to do anything. Some kind of inertia had got hold of them, Stan Greenberg said from his home in Connecticut, some failure of purpose and execution. Drift was a losing strategy, he continued—a *big*-time losing strategy. Time was running out. The showdown in New York and the same-day primaries in Wisconsin and Kansas were less than two weeks away.

"My gut feeling is that it's slipping away," Greenberg said. "*I'm* having trouble figuring out a reason to vote for us."

"This is a campaign in trouble," Mickey Kantor added. "We will be written off. I think it is Armageddon in New York."

"We said that three weeks ago," Greenberg snapped. It wasn't as if they didn't know what to do; as he had summed up the consensus in a strategy memo a couple of days earlier, the key to victory in New York was a sharp, aggressive campaign that "marginalizes Jerry Brown and reintroduces Bill Clinton as a fighter for the middle class." But that wasn't happening. The schedulers still hadn't got with the program; they had Clinton paying the usual house calls on the usual organized constituency groups, events too easily drowned out by the clamor about *him*. The aimlessness of it seemed to Greenberg to have infected the candidate; that steady guy, comfortable with people and comfortable with himself, wasn't there.

"Everything's a measure of how damaged Bill is," Harold Ickes said.

"Because of these hits," David Wilhelm said. "You can't take all these hits and survive. Story after story after story. It is very hard."

"Greenberg says we're in danger of free fall," Kantor told Ickes, who had plugged into the discussion late.

"No, we're not in danger," Ickes replied. "We *are* in free fall. No one believes him about Gennifer Flowers. No one likes him on the draft, although they're willing to let him slide on it. No one believes him on the segregated golf club." They had to take some risks, maybe challenge Brown to a whole series of debates and go at the character questions head-on. "It's a real roll of the dice," Ickes said, "but these thirty-second spots and these events ain't going to do it. We are in the fight of our life. If we lose this state, we are gone. It is fucking over. It is goodbye, Sally."

The possibility that Brown, of all people, might be the agent of Clinton's undoing made it all the more galling. "He's an empty vessel," Wilhelm said, "but it's dangerous, because Brown is running against a flawed candidate. It's really about us. Clinton is running against himself."

If so, he was not making a very good job of it; even if he had been on his game, which he wasn't, the press wouldn't let him be heard. A certain competitive madness had fallen over the media, with Clinton's head as its trophy; even the respectable papers were shooting first and asking questions later, and the tabloids seemed to have gone more than normally blood simple. The epitome, for Clinton's people, was an issue of the *New York Post* splashing a large photo of one of his rumored girlfriends, a former beauty queen. The accompanying text reported her denial that they had ever had an affair, but the choice of illustrations was like a large, lascivious wink at the readers.

Carville, furious, suggested over a Saturday night dinner with

Stephanopoulos that they make the whole campaign about the press—hold up the offending issue of the *Post* and say, "Don't let this be about someone who said, 'I never slept with Bill Clinton.'"

Stephanopoulos, who dealt with the media every day, was fighting down his own rising bile against them. He wasn't sure he saw any way around the problem.

"We don't got no option for error," Carville told him. "We're going to win. James Carville is telling you we're going to win. You don't know the power of will."

"That's what I was afraid of today—that he had lost his will to fight," Stephanopoulos said. Clinton had done another of his non-events, a speech at Harlem Hospital, and had been ambushed by a leftist minor-party candidate, Lenora Fulani; she had stood on a chair and screamed abuse at him till he finally gave up and walked away. "It's New Hampshire again," Stephanopoulos added, sliding toward darkness. "I really thought we were out of it."

"We've got to go to our strength," Carville said, "and Bill Clinton's strength is his heart."

His weakness of the moment was his jaw; it had turned to glass, and starting with his holiday in Little Rock, he seemed to have been leading with it. The mere sight of the picture of him and his chum at the country club had sent Brown's media man, Joe Trippi, into a state he called negative-spot euphoria—a transport induced by the scent of spilled blood and the means to draw more of it. Trippi was a bright, tough pol of thirty-five with a chessboard mind and a warrior heart. He and his young partners were even then working on a reputation as the bad boys of their business, and Clinton's people were about to discover why.

While Carville and Stephanopoulos were brooding over dinner that Saturday night, New Yorkers tuned in to TV got their first glimpse of a wicked little attack ad skewering Clinton with his own self-indulgence. After a bit of fluff about Brown, the golf-cart picture came up, freeze-framing two southern good ol' boys indolently at play. "Governor Clinton's Arkansas," the voice-over said. "A right-to-work state that ranks dead last in worker safety. Its wages among the lowest in the country. And while Bill Clinton plays golf at a restricted all-white club, Arkansas remains one of only two states with no civil-rights act." The screen, all the while, had been going black, leaving only Clinton's face inside a shrinking circle. "Now that's slick," the voice went on, "but we want real change." The circle around Clinton was down to golf-ball size; with a *whoosh* and a *whack,* an invisible club knocked him off the screen.

It was the tough negative ad Greenberg had worried about; it hit home, and Clinton tried to recoup in a speech at a black church in Queens the next morning. His people had urged him in a memo to get confrontational with Brown and the tabloids; being pushy was the only way to get noticed in New York. They didn't know whether he had absorbed or even read their advice, but he showed up for the event with that withdrawn look he wore on his best days as a performance artist. "He's got his game face on," Carville told Stephanopoulos. "He's going to *whale* this thing."

He did, so powerfully that a couple of his handlers were wiping away tears in the back pews. He *had* digested their script and had improved on it, suffusing it with a passion they hadn't seen for several weeks. His day at the country club, he admitted, had been "a foolish mistake," but it didn't seem to him to warrant the fuss being made over it. "I have seen myself turned into a cartoon character of an old southern deal-maker by the tabloids and television, in a total denial of my life's work," he said. "This is not a race about whether we have all done right, but whether we can do better." He spoke bluntly to his black audience about black-on-black crime and about welfare dependency; no president, he insisted, could do anything for anyone that they would not do for themselves. It was uncommonly straight talk for a white politician in a black neighborhood, and the congregation liked it. "I think," Carville said afterward, "we're on our way back."

The high wore off before the day was out. The next stop was a free-form television debate on WCBS, and Clinton got there near exhaustion, as if his Sunday morning sermon had drained off the last of his adrenaline. While a makeup woman powdered and painted him, trying to cover the fatigue in his face, Stan Greenberg went to work on his spirit.

"There's been no real surge to Brown," Greenberg told him. "You're still the only one who can be president."

"I'll be lucky to do well," Clinton said. "I'm really tired, and I don't feel well."

"Sometimes when you finish a question, you smile," Stephanopoulos cautioned.

"Don't?" Clinton asked.

"Just don't," Stephanopoulos said.

Clinton started well, flaunting his more detailed understanding of public policy and keeping his smile in check. In their holding room, his handlers began their celebration early. "The more they're both on the same stage, the better," Greenberg said. But they had warned Clinton in a briefing memo that the debate would be "a knife fight," and when the blades started flashing, he impaled himself.

The subject was drugs, and the cutting edge was the stock answer he had been giving for years—that he had never violated the drug laws "of my country." The formulation was too nice by half; it invited the belief, shared by most of his own people, that he must at the very least have dabbled with marijuana during his years at Oxford. His team had talked about it often among themselves, knowing Clinton would sooner or later have to explain himself. Carville, in these conversations, didn't even need to put his concern into words; instead, he would slit his eyes, purse his lips, and pantomime dragging on a joint. But he and his comrades had never pushed Clinton to go beyond his pat answer, and he, miraculously, had not been challenged—not until one of WCBS's panel of interrogators asked him if he had ever broken any drug laws *anywhere.*

"When I was in England," Clinton answered in a sudden access of candor, "I experimented with marijuana a time or two, and I didn't like it. I didn't inhale and never tried it again."

A nervous silence fell over the crew in the holding room; the candidate had just told the world more than he had ever told them. They believed him, even the gratuitous add-on about not having inhaled; the line would become a national joke overnight, but for people who knew him, it was consistent both with his medical history as a man of a thousand allergies and with his psychological profile as a gregarious sort hungry to be one of the boys.

"I think it was the best presentation of the truth," Greenberg said guardedly.

"It was honest," Stephanopoulos said. "He was asked a direct question, and he had to answer it."

But their hearts were not in their rationalizations. For one thing, his new answer made his old ones sound like Slick Willie talking. For another, the semipermanent garrison of investigative reporters in Little Rock were even then chasing rumors that some of Clinton's friends had used drugs at the governor's mansion, perhaps with his knowledge.

"This gives them an excuse to do drug stories," Stephanopoulos said.

"That's all there's going to be," Carville added. "They'll look up every answer he's ever given and say he was slippery."

"Is there any chance this isn't bad?" Stephanopoulos said. "No."

The debate ended, and Clinton joined them. He seemed almost giddy, talking about how badly Brown had done. Nobody mentioned the drug question until he did.

"Listen," he said, "I may have given you a heart attack on that deal. But I thought it was time, and this was the first time I was asked that question directly. And that's the spin you have to give."

"No cocaine use?" Greenberg asked nervously.

"Never," Clinton said. "There is no problem there. Let me tell you something—I've got a lot of problems. That isn't one. Wipe that out of your minds." He knew, he told them, that he had got himself into a box with his cuteness, making it sound as if he might have had more than a couple of tokes to hide. He had been handed an opportunity to clear the air and had grabbed it; it was as simple as that.

"I just decided, why let this become an issue in October?" he said. "Just do it."

The handlers trailed him out of the studio and watched him head into a thicket of reporters. "I'm not saying we did the wrong thing," Carville told the others. "I'm just saying that we're blocked out again for a couple of days."

"It cuts against being slick," Dee Dee Myers said wishfully. "He was asked a direct question and he gave a direct answer."

But slickness was indeed the issue; the questions flying at Clinton had less to do with his having smoked dope than with why he had been so cagey about it for so long. While he cleared the gauntlet of reporters and escaped to his next event, his people walked the two blocks back to their hotel, reassuring one another that everything would be okay.

"He's up," Carville said. "The thing is to keep your eye on the prize. If he's up and he's performing, he'll come through. And *he's* up, and that's why *I'm* up."

"I'm dark again," Stephanopoulos answered. "I'm very dark."

"Don't be dark, Georgie," Carville urged, flinging a skinny arm around his smaller, younger friend. "We'll be okay. It's always darkest just before the dawn."

They found Kantor and Wilhelm in the war room at the Sheraton Manhattan, doing their own damage assessments. Kantor's was hopeful. "I really don't think this is going to hit us," he said.

A television set was tuned to CNN. A fresh news cycle was beginning. The handlers looked up. The lead story was what they had feared: a hard-edged piece contrasting Clinton's confession that he had smoked pot to his dodgy past answers on the subject.

Slick Willie was back in town. Wilhelm looked grim. "I think we just hit our low point," he said.

Jerry's Tax

So had Jerry Brown, though he and his constant companion Jacques Barzaghi were too spaced out on momentum and fatigue to know it.

The ripples out of Connecticut had become a wave, and if its driving force was more anti-Clinton than pro-Brown, it didn't seem to matter. The early polls showed Brown leading in Wisconsin—that had never happened to him before—and close behind Clinton in New York. Money was cascading in, $150,000 one day, $200,000 the next; there would be enough for a million-dollar media blitz in the two key states. Even Mario Cuomo flashed what looked like a flirtatious wink in Brown's direction. "We haven't even begun to think about how Mario will fuck us," one of Clinton's strategists had fretted going in. The suspense was short-lived; in two days' time, the governor granted Brown an audience in Albany and declared his view that, no matter what anyone said, the race was still "wide open."

Clinton seemed, moreover, to be bleeding from self-inflicted wounds—first the country-club outing, then the awkwardly done confession that he had smoked dope. On the Oscar night telecast that week, the host comedian, Billy Crystal, had only to utter the words, "I didn't inhale," to get his biggest laugh of the evening. The papers had something new on the guy every day, and when the broadsheets ran out of real stories, the tabloids spun their own. To Joe Trippi, the Clinton campaign had the look of a car skidding around a corner on two wheels; all it would take was one more thing, one little push, to tip it over and total it.

But Brown and his odd-lot crew were no better prepared to ride the tide they had loosed or even to understand how perishable it was. The first thing he needed to do, his few professional advisers thought, was come off the road to rest up—he hadn't had a proper day off in months—and to plan strategy for the new world in which they found themselves. "We really need to sit down," Joe Costello, the electronic whiz, warned Jodie Evans. "We need to get everyone grounded. Things are going to blow up." But Brown was reluctant, and when the pros pushed the idea too hard, Barzaghi interposed his black-clad person between them and him. "Everybody I know is yelling, 'Stop, stop, stop,' except Jacques, Jacques, Jacques," Mike Ford complained.

The meeting the professionals wanted never happened; Brown kept up his manic schedule, and when his energy drooped, Barzaghi was there to flog him on. Two days after Connecticut, Ford flew out to Milwaukee to talk to him and was appalled by what he saw. Brown looked cadaverous, his skin pale, his cheeks sunken, his eyes dark-rimmed from too many twenty-hour days. His fast had been going on since January, and when Ford suggested breakfast, Barzaghi brushed him off.

"We do not eat breakfast," he said. "We are fasting."

"Well, you *oughta* eat," Ford told him, "'cause he's gonna *die.*"

Argument, as usual, was unavailing with Barzaghi; his influence on Brown had always been great, and with his jealously guarded access to the candidate, he was becoming the final arbiter on strategy. He had no visible gift at it, but in this campaign that was a virtue, and his word took on some of the force of law, for Brown and everybody else. It did little good for Ford to protest that Brown was a sprinter, not a marathon man, and that he might not wear well with overexposure. Barzaghi ignored him. The mad chase around the landscape continued, and when Brown fell behind in his rounds, Barzaghi scolded him: "You are late all the time. What is *wrong* with you?"

What ailed Brown most acutely at the moment was exhaustion, to a point where even he finally complained. "Why are we keeping this schedule, this macho death march?" he asked on the road one day, dashing by car from one event to the next.

"Because it is on the schedule," Barzaghi said.

Barzaghi's growing authority was a source of distress to the pros, who found themselves unable to get at Brown alone; Jacques was always there, protecting the candidate and the movement from contaminants. Ford took to calling him the Man from Remulak, for his resemblance, in flesh and otherworldly spirit, to those intergalactic travelers, the Coneheads. But Barzaghi was only the embodiment of the Dionysiac side of a deeply schizoid campaign; the true Brownians made a mystique of their artlessness and resisted professional advice because it was professional. They reminded Trippi of addicts who longed to try pure heroin, knowing it would kill them if they did. The consultants were the milk sugar in the mix, the adulterants you needed if you didn't want to die. On bad days, you were glad to have them. In high times, the necessary evil didn't seem so necessary anymore.

Barzaghi, as body man and best friend, became the high priest of the campaign—the man whose self-ordained mission it was to defend the purity of the movement against the artifice of the handlers. At one point, Costello lined up three hours of studio time in Wisconsin, to be used to beam satellite interviews to nearly every TV station in New York state. The potential audience was seven or eight million, but Barzaghi thought it more important for Brown to keep a date with a dozen black ministers, and he scrubbed half the booking; the place of a people's movement was with the people, not on TV.

Neither, in his mind, should it resort to the usual negative tricks. When Brown finally did get to the studio, Ford handed him a copy of the *New York Times* reporting the latest dig into the underside of Clinton's record in Arkansas. To the pros, holding up the story on camera was a way to document what Brown had been saying all along about Clinton and the system. To Barzaghi, hovering close at hand, it was an offense to the sanctity of the campaign.

"No!" he said sharply. "This is not the way we won Colorado."

"You're right, Jacques," Ford answered, "it's *not* the way we won Colorado. But they're very much the same, Colorado and New York."

Irony was lost on Barzaghi. He stood his ground, elevating a quarrel over a stage prop into an issue of principle. Brown dithered; in his cosmos, Jacques against everybody else was a tie, and he couldn't decide what to do.

Ford watched him stew, then lost heart for the argument and slipped out into the control room. He found Costello there, steam coming out of his ears.

"Joe," Ford said, "what's the burnout factor in this campaign? About twenty-four hours?"

"Yeah," Costello said. Like Ford and the other professionals, he was almost there.

The flip side of purity was chaos, a collapse of the order required to run any enterprise larger than a mom-and-pop shop. All campaigns take on some of the personality of the candidate, and Brown's was the lengthened shadow of one of the most disorganized men in our public life. Ads got stuck in the pipeline. Scheduling was a stew of events that conflicted with one another and with the basic antipolitical message of the campaign. Sometimes, Brown would be handed three different schedules for a single day; Barzaghi would choose whichever suited him, and off they would go. The whole thing was turning into a big, shapeless blob, Ford thought. They wouldn't even be able to say afterward that they had at least fought the good fight, because they hadn't; they had fought a dumb fucking fight and had done every fucking thing wrong.

The mistakes only began with a fundamental misunderstanding of the structure of the race in New York, one in which a shadow campaign for Paul Tsongas offered a third choice for people unanchored either to Brown or to Clinton. The floating vote consisted disproportionately of Jews, who usually made up a third of the Democratic primary electorate. But Brown seemed to go out of his way to offend them. One day, he journeyed to Wall Street to call the roll of "moneychangers" who had given money to the Clinton campaign; he had got well down the list before he realized, too late, that practically all the names on it were Jewish.

At another juncture, egged on by Barzaghi, he chose America's most Jewish and least forgiving city as the place in which to pursue a long, unrequited flirtation with Jesse Jackson. Don't do it, the pros argued. It didn't make sense politically to cozy up to a man who had once got caught referring to Jews as Hymies and to New York as Hymietown.

"This is something we are going to do," Barzaghi said, cutting off dissent. "There is no question. We have to do it."

Brown did, crashing a Jackson rally outside the board of elections and proclaiming the reverend his first choice for vice president. He hoped for Jackson's endorsement, which never came. What he got instead was the appearance of a liaison with a man whose blessing, for much of the New York electorate and most of its penny press, was the kiss of death.

Brown was equally unadept at defending the flat tax. It had come under withering fire, and not just from Clinton; the press was picking it apart, and Senator Daniel Patrick Moynihan said it could mean the ruin of social security. Brown didn't have the answers, and his support troops had neither the time nor the resources to provide them. In some desperation, his Wisconsin state chairman, Ed Garvey, called what passed for a research department in Santa Monica. He was getting a lot of questions about the tax, he told the director, Sheila Starr, and if he was going to respond adequately, he needed to know its intellectual basis.

"There isn't one," Starr told him. Its rationale, so far as it had one, existed in Brown's mind.

Brown seemed unable, under pressure, to make its charms clear to anybody else. He had let himself get suckered into accepting Clinton's challenge to a series of debates in New York. The pros, once again, were dismayed; the debates tied the campaign down in a city where it was fast wearing out its welcome and pitted their underprepared candidate against an opponent whose great gift was argument. The encounters gave Clinton a chance to pummel Brown face to face, and where he left off, his TV ads took over, lampooning Jerry's Tax as a gift to the rich.

The response from the Brown camp was mostly silence. Joe Trippi had to beg permission to make an ad defending the flat tax and counterattacking Clinton. He finally did, but his work never ran. The campaign chose instead to use a spot cobbled together by Pat Caddell with a couple of his Hollywood connections, Carroll O'Connor and Rob Reiner, recreating the television roles that had made them famous; there they were, Archie and Meathead, talking tax policy in a presidential campaign. "This is powerful," Barzaghi, the wannabe filmmaker, said when he saw it. It was also late; by the time it got on the air,

Clinton had been beating up on Brown and the flat tax for ten un-answered days.

Brown thus found himself in the shoes once occupied by Paul Tsongas; he had been artfully repainted as one more politician for whom honesty was a shtick and change a new way of socking it to the middle class. He needed to get upstate, where there were votes to be mined, and to Wisconsin, where his lead in the polls was evaporating at a rate of a point a day. Instead, he seemed transfixed by the bright lights of the big city, particularly the little red lights that told him a television camera was pointed his way. As Clinton's campaign tight-ened in focus, Brown's got looser, louder, nastier, and more self-centered. His movement, We The People, had taken on a first-person singularity; he talked less about "you and you and you" and more about himself as "the voice of the voiceless."

To Mike Ford, watching from an increasingly unhappy distance, Brown was beginning to sound like Father Coughlin, the Thirties radio demagogue, on speed. His high pitch was alienating people, even Clinton-haters, and if enough of them found their way to Tsongas, Brown was dead. "WHAT HAS HAPPENED," Ford said in a memo, "IS THAT WE ARE NO LONGER THE UNDERDOG. . . . WE HAVE BECOME ONE OF THE BOYS." It was a metamorphosis for which Brown had himself to blame. "You are far too hot," Ford wrote. "You must soften yourself. Lighten up." Just for starters, he needed to be more civil toward Clinton and less sanctimonious when he was asked whether he would ultimately support the nominee of the party. "Treat Clinton like a man," Ford counseled, "not a turd."

Brown read the memo on a flight in from Washington and, as often happened with the last advice placed before him, he agreed with most of it; he had to calm down, had to get out of the city, had to return to his message about the breakdown of the political system. But once he deplaned in New York and plowed back into the media mob, his determination to do better melted away faster than new year's resolu-tions in a chocolate shop. The danger signals from Wisconsin were faint and distant as against the clamor of New York; Brown seemed transfixed by the attention, and Barzaghi was at his elbow with The Schedule, by now crowded with debates.

One of the close encounters was to be on MacNeil-Lehrer on Wed-nesday evening, six days before the primary. In a conference call that afternoon, Ford, at his home office in Annapolis, argued for bagging it and sending Brown to Wisconsin instead. "We're losing ground there," he said, "and it was one of the places we could win. Whenever Jerry goes there, he gains ground. When he isn't there, we're getting killed."

Others joined in, and Jodie Evans finally agreed to the plan: Brown would call a press conference, pull out of the debate, and head for Wisconsin. But when word reached Barzaghi, in the van with Brown, he reversed the decision. Wisconsin was off. The debate was on.

The conference call was still in progress when Barzaghi came on the line. Ford made his case one last time. They were letting Clinton run their schedule. They had to get Brown out of the debate.

"Oh, no," Barzaghi said. "We are doing it."

They needed to get Brown to Wisconsin, Ford insisted.

"Give me one rational reason why we go to Wisconsin," Barzaghi said.

"Because if you don't go," Ford replied, "we lose."

"No," Barzaghi said. "We do not need to go to Wisconsin. We have already *won* Wisconsin."

The crossfire continued for a time, and Ford, a man of humors, had a harder and harder time hiding his despair. "Look," he argued at one point, "do We The People have to be stupid?" He got nowhere. The war was over. Jacques had won. He was running the campaign.

"So," Ford said finally, "the decision is not to go back to Wisconsin."

"That is correct," Barzaghi said.

Ford quietly hung up. The campaign was in entropy. It couldn't be fixed. He walked downstairs from his third-floor office and headed for the front door.

"I'm going out," he told his wife and partner, Sally.

"What do I say if anyone calls?" she asked.

"Tell 'em I've gone out to kill myself," he said.

His friend Trippi did phone that night, trying to coax him back aboard. The two of them had been working on an idea for an ad in which Brown would make what amounted to a Shavian case for electing him in spite of himself. The setting would be a burned-out patch of the South Bronx, where a generation of politicians had posed before him and offered up their empty promises to rebuild the inner cities. Yes, Brown would concede, he was "a flawed vessel," abrasive and hard to love, but maybe you had to be unpleasant to effect real change in a debased political order. The script was a daring one by the usual standards of the craft; candidates usually called attention to the other guy's defects, not their own. Trippi had sent it to headquarters with faint hope, assuming that, as with most of his and Ford's ideas, the Brownians would either bounce it or lose it.

For once, they didn't. Jodie Evans approved the spot, and Trippi called Ford excitedly with the news.

"It's over," Ford told him.

"No," Trippi said. "Hang in there, bro. Go to New York with me. We're going to get it done."

"Joe," Ford said, "if you go up there, it's going to break your heart."

It nearly did. Trippi flew in late from a meeting in Atlanta and walked into a snakepit of contending cliques with competing agendas. The shoot had been delayed past midnight and moved indoors, into a studio in downtown Manhattan. War parties were everywhere, shooting at and hiding from one another. On one floor, Barzaghi was trying to get the Ford-Trippi script killed. On another, Pat Caddell rewrote it. In his version, the mea culpas were gone. He preferred Brown in his apocalypse-now mode, sounding, unsurprisingly, just like Caddell; he called on the voters to "take back our government from the check-bouncers, out-of-touch politicians and corrupt special interests," and "their hand-picked candidate."

Trippi, from long experience, knew when to hold 'em and when to fold 'em. It was no good arguing with Caddell in one of his fits of creation, not, certainly, with the meter running. Instead, he went looking for Brown, gave him the revised script, and proceeded with the shoot; they called the spot "Making History," which was what Pat's Jerry immodestly proposed to do. But while Trippi was editing the footage in one suite, a crew of Brown aides was at work in another, making the spot Caddell *really* wanted: a series of man-on-the-street encounters with New Yorkers talking about Clinton's alleged private vices and public failings.

Their ad could have been called "Making Trouble," beginning with their decision not to tell Brown what they were doing. He had left the studio at two in the morning under the impression that "Making History" was it—that there would be nothing else new on the air for the closing days of the campaign. But once he and Barzaghi were out the door, Caddell took over. He wanted the two spots shipped to stations around New York, he told Trippi, and he wanted 80 percent of the air time for "Man in the Street."

It took all night, but Trippi and his firm got the ads out, and he was feeling suitably heroic when he sat down to a red-eyed late breakfast at his hotel. A hostess beat his oatmeal to the table. There was a call for him, she said, and it was urgent.

Trippi dragged himself to a phone. Tom Quinn, one of the rump group who had made "Man in the Street," was on the line.

"Joe," Quinn said, "Jerry is adamant that he never wants it to see air."

"*What?*" Trippi exclaimed. He glanced desperately at the time. It was five past ten on Friday morning. The stations had the spot and were getting ready to close their books on traffic changes for the weekend.

"We just showed it to him," Quinn said, "and he doesn't want to see it aired, so you'd better not let it air."

"Tom, you *made* it," Trippi said. "What the hell are you talking about?"

"It was Pat's idea," Quinn protested.

He was still backpedaling when Brown, in a rage, grabbed the phone out of his hand. A couple of people in the spot had alluded to the sex and marijuana stories about Clinton. Brown insisted he didn't care about that stuff, and if he did, he would speak for himself; he wasn't going to hide behind some anonymous citizens on a little square box. "I want it off!" he told Trippi. "I want it off right now!"

Trippi hung up and dialed his office. His people were still celebrating their heroics.

"Take it all down," he said.

They did, but a copy of "Man on the Street" leaked anyway and got on the air as news. The story gave Clinton a chance to be pious—he called the ad the sleaziest he had ever seen—and required Brown's people to explain it away as the unauthorized work of "volunteers."

The campaign by then had fallen into that state once memorialized by a blues singer: if it wasn't for bad luck, they wouldn't have had no luck at all. The air at its scattered bases of operations was acrid with hard feelings, the pros and amateurs blaming one another for all that had gone wrong. At headquarters in Santa Monica, Jodie Evans sat alone in her office for a time, wondering where the magic had gone. Then she slipped away to a bakery, bought a cake, and brought it back to share with her staff of believers.

"It's over," she told them wanly. "We've lost our way."

Not Yet, But Soon

It was one more debate in their endless series, but Brown arrived at an urban forum at the mayor's residence, Gracie Mansion, in an impish humor. He signed the guest book first and, in the space for addresses, wrote, "1600 Pennsylvania Ave. *Age Quod Agis."*—Latin for "Keep doing what you're doing." When Clinton signed in, he saw Brown's inscription and smiled. He, too, gave the White House address as his own, adding in English: "Not yet, but soon!"

Soon was a long and treacherous distance away for Clinton; it wasn't time yet to be sorting swatches for the Oval Office. But while

Brown seemed indeed to have lost his way, Clinton recovered his, at least through the thicket of primaries directly in front of him. It was plain by the closing days that he couldn't do anything to stop the riot of rumor and accusation about himself. Instead, in ads, speeches, and chat-show appearances, he changed the subject whenever he could to what he wanted to talk about: the need to elect a man with a plan for the economy and the concomitant folly of wasting a vote on Paul Tsongas or Jerry Brown.

His reintroduction to America was by no means perfectly done. It consisted rather of a series of tactical improvisations to get himself out of the larger strategic bind he found himself in—the situation of a man trying to talk issues when the press and the pols were obsessing on whom he had slept with and where he had played golf. The danger was illuminated for Mandy Grunwald when she slipped away to Alaska for a day to watch some focus groups in a Senate campaign she was working on. When the presidential race came up, a woman in one of the groups spoke in language almost identical to Clinton's about moving beyond the "brain-dead politics of the past." But when she was asked about Clinton himself, she slammed the door in his face. "I don't think he has an idea in his head," she said.

Grunwald's mind wandered back to the time—it felt like an eon ago—when Clinton had been criticized for having too *many* ideas. He needed to be that guy again, and on the long ride back to New York, she thought through the basics of a new spot. On-screen, Clinton's plan would appear, with its catchier proposals highlighted; that was Carville's touch. Off-camera, a voice would say: "Looking for a different candidate for president? Someone who actually has a serious plan to move this country forward and put people first?" The announcer ticked off some of Clinton's ideas about investing in jobs, upgrading schools, reforming health care, healing racial divisions, moving people from welfare to work. "That's the plan of a different candidate," the voice said. "His name? Bill Clinton. Yes, the *real* Bill Clinton."

The ad made a kind of framing statement for the final week of the New York race: a declaration that politics ought to be about the great concerns of the day and not the rowdier interests of tabloid journalism. The odd bifurcation of his polls suggested that Clinton and his strategists were on to something; sizable numbers of people who didn't trust him were prepared to vote for him anyway. The appetite for scandal was less powerful than the deeper hunger for change, and when Clinton did Phil Donahue's talk show on his frenetic rounds, that longing was made dramatically plain.

The date was a calculated risk, given the fixation on sex common to the daytime chatmongers, and, in this, Donahue did not disappoint. For nearly half the show, he pressed Clinton with the shelfworn Gennifer Flowers story, demanding to know whether he had ever had "an intimate relationship" with her.

"Gennifer Flowers's story is not true," Clinton answered, his voice hoarse and angry. "I've said it repeatedly. I have nothing else to say."

Donahue kept probing, but Clinton stood fast behind his general rebuttal, refusing to be drawn into details. "We're going to sit here a long time in silence, Phil," he said. "I'm not going to answer any more of these questions. I've answered them until I'm blue in the face. You are responsible for the cynicism in this country. You don't want to talk about the real issues."

The gallery burst into applause, and when Donahue invited questions, the first person on her feet was a young Republican named Melissa Roth. "I think, really, given the pathetic state of most of the United States at this point—medicare, education, everything else—I can't believe you spent half an hour of air time attacking this man's character," she said. "I'm not even a Bill Clinton supporter, but I think this is ridiculous."

The house exploded in claps and cheers. Clinton smiled a tight smile of vindication. Donahue backed off.

There would be one more scare for Clinton and his handlers, set off by a *Los Angeles Times* story alleging that he had actually got an induction notice while he was at Oxford in the spring of 1969. He had never mentioned that before, and people inclined to think ill of him didn't buy his claim that he had forgotten all about it. The notice became, for them, fresh evidence that Clinton had been consciously draft-dodging when he signed up for the ROTC that summer and then withdrew in the fall.

The story afterward would seem trivial, one more detail in a thrice-told tale. But it was magnified for Clinton's troops by their exhaustion and by their anger at having been blindsided yet again by something the candidate had neglected to tell them; in their spent state, it looked like the One More Thing that could ruin him. The core group labored through the night assessing the damage, then met with Clinton at six on Sunday morning for what was to have been a prep session for his last debate with Brown. They found him annoyed, incredulous, and, as one senior hand put it, full of denial. The story, for him, was one more irritation he could talk his way out of.

His people tried without success to persuade him that it could be serious. Afterward, several of them retreated to Carville's room. Carville and Stephanopoulos headed for the bed and slipped under the covers. Grunwald stretched out beside them. The three of them lay silent, too numb with fatigue and despair to speak.

Clinton sailed through the debate, shrugging off the draft notice and soaring, Grunwald thought, on the big stuff. His victory glow, coming off stage, cheered his troops but did not diminish their anger with him. He was scheduled to fly on to Washington for an abortion-rights rally that afternoon. Only Frank Greer among the consultants volunteered for the trip, and his attitude, expressed to his colleagues, was mostly good-soldierly: "Fuck it. I'm going to take whatever line he feels comfortable with, and I'm going to sell it." No one else wanted to be around Clinton, though Grunwald was prevailed upon to make the trip. The others felt betrayed by him and compromised by having to hide their misgivings from the press.

The storm blew over quickly, and the bruised feelings with it. The real damage, Carville guessed accurately, would be long-term, but nobody seemed very interested for the moment—not enough, anyway, to hurt Clinton's chances in the decisive primaries. Over the last weekend, his favorable ratings were on the rise, and Brown's were sinking out of sight. In a business where people were paid to worry, the last torment for Clinton's people was not Brown but Tsongas. He was skimming a lot of Jewish votes, and Brown, inexplicably, was helping out, urging people who couldn't stomach him to vote for Tsongas rather than Clinton. A big vote for a noncandidate could be a serious embarrassment for the presumptive nominee of the party.

"Scenario One," Grunwald said when the core group gathered in Carville's room on primary day. "Clinton 43, Tsongas 25, and Brown collapses."

"We thank the people of New York," Carville said, "but it shouldn't be Comeback Kid II."

"What if it's 40-35-27?" Grunwald asked.

"Grab a baton and be a drum major," Carville said. "This is a parade running you out of town. Get in front and *lead* it."

Exit-poll numbers drifted in through the day, pointing to another sweep for Clinton. But his lead in New York was shadowed, as his people had feared, by a strong showing for Tsongas and a deep vein of doubt about him. Barely half the electorate thought he was honest enough to be president.

"As long as we win by more than ten points and stay above 40 percent," Clinton said, "it doesn't matter what Tsongas gets."

He was calling in from Arkansas, where he had detoured for the funeral of the discount-store billionaire Sam Walton. It wasn't till they overheard him placing an order that his staff realized he was at a Taco Bell, fueling up for the road. Everybody laughed.

"You know—first things first," Clinton said, sounding sheepish.

Mickey Kantor gave him Tsongas's home phone number. Tsongas was upset over a botched attempt to get his endorsement; the message, conveyed through third parties, was that there would be something big for him in a Clinton administration but not the vice presidency. A little flattery from Clinton himself wouldn't hurt, once the results were clear.

"What do you think I ought to say?" Clinton asked.

"That his message is important," Kantor said.

"He had the guts to get out there when no one else did," Stephanopoulos said.

And in his victory speech?

"I think we ought to be real nice to Tsongas tonight," Clinton answered. "And we should say something nice about Brown empowering people with his 800 number. I need to find a way to be real humble and grateful for what happened."

It was the voice of the winner talking, the all-but-certain nominee planning the obsequies for his fallen enemies. "Bill, before we forget, congratulations," Kantor thought to say; they were all too shell-shocked to celebrate.

"Let me tell you some bad news," Clinton said suddenly. "Or at least some sobering news."

There was a hush at the New York end of the line. Bad news, in the Clinton campaign, usually meant the next scandal.

"The doctor says I have to take a week off now," Clinton said. "That if I don't, I risk permanent damage to my voice. He saw something that really disturbed him. He scared me. That would be like being a basketball player without legs: I can't play."

The relief among his aides was palpable; at least it wasn't some new plot twist in the story of Bill and the draft, another little embarrassment he had neglected to tell them about. More primaries lay ahead, and the harder labor of preparing for the fall campaign, but Clinton's handlers no longer had to begrudge him a few days off.

Neither did they have to worry about Brown anymore; Spaceship Jerry had blasted off, flamed out, crashed, and burned, all in the brief span of two weeks. In New York, he ran a disastrous third, fifteen points behind Clinton and three behind Tsongas. In Wisconsin, the alchemy of neglect had transmuted his early lead into a three-point loss. In Kansas, he managed to finish fourth in a two-man race; he couldn't even beat Tsongas or "uncommitted."

Brown limped on after that, a ghostly figure banging his pots and pans as he had at the beginning of his campaign. That so many people responded to so flawed a candidacy with money and votes was a measure of America's discontent with the state of our politics and with the choices it had produced; one Democratic primary voter in five across the country preferred a shrill political eccentric to anyone else their party had offered them. But neither he nor his odd-lot movement was built for distance. He limped home to California the weekend after his rout and encountered another of Caddell's Hollywood pals, Warren Beatty, at a fund-raiser. "Jerry," Beatty told him, "you've got to do two things: get fatter and get funnier."

Both options were beyond his powers, and it was too late in any case for repairs. The professionals in the campaign had tired of being scapegoated for its failures and had mostly gone away mad. "This whole thing," Ford wrote Caddell, "has become a self-indulgent, pious, whimsical, purposeless, conflicted attempt to play at politics." His own role thereafter was reduced to answering Brown's phone calls, and his advice grew increasingly pessimistic. The next major stop was Pennsylvania, a demographic nightmare for Brown with its aging population and its hard-time economy.

"Pennsylvania is pretty much your last shot," Ford told him.

"Yeah," Brown said. "After that, it's probably ridiculous, isn't it?"

"Yeah, it is," Ford answered. "You're out there yelling, and there's no cameras anymore."

So it played. The rest of the primary season was a long victory lap for Clinton—a romp with just enough opposition to keep him in the news, not enough to spoil his progress toward the nomination. But he had the bruised look of a survivor rather than a victor's glow. The prize had come to him by the triumph of tactics, money, and will over a weak field of rivals. He had won without really having been heard.

There was accordingly something hollow in the attendant celebrations—for his handlers and, apparently, for him. His campaign was becalmed, his image tarnished, his message blurred. He was running behind George Bush and the upstart Ross Perot in the polls. He was, de facto, his party's nominee. Now came the hard part: the reinvention of his candidacy at midpassage in his campaign.

12.

The Manhattan Project

Through the long spring, Clinton sank deeper and deeper into that dark mood his people referred to tactfully as self-absorption. The field was his at last, but to aides exposed to his flashes of temper and fits of brooding, nothing else in his situation seemed to please him. In what ought to have been the crowning moment of his lifetime in politics, he turned inward, cultivating his sense of victimization by the establishment and, most particularly, its propagandists in the press.

The warm gaze and the rueful smile survived only for public consumption. Off-camera, Clinton was cranky and hard to be around. He upbraided his management team for being too traditional, too bureaucratic, too slow. He complained about being overscheduled when what he really needed was time on the ground to read, think, talk policy, and work on his speeches. He called a senior aide one night and flew into a paint-peeling fury at his media strategy—or, as he felt, his lack of one. He dawdled over the hard personnel decisions he would have to make to get his message out and to impose peace on the quarreling power centers within his campaign.

What he could not seem to acknowledge was the possibility that the problems began with him—that his quest for the presidency would go under if he didn't somehow allay the unresolved doubts about himself. When he addressed those questions at all, his tendency was to blame the questioners, to rail against a process whose apparent objective, he said, was to chew up all the candidates and spit them out. At an event in Florida one day, a couple of students asked him to explain his claim that he had once tried marijuana but didn't inhale it, and he exploded. "There is no trust issue," he said, "except the press once again trying to make a mountain out of a molehill. . . . I think I've done a pretty good job being an imperfect person who tried to follow the real moral obligation of life, which is to do better tomorrow than you did today. What you're seeing is what you get, and if you don't want it, vote for Bush. Because this is *crazy*. Vote for Bush and vote for four more years of America going down the tubes."

The issues he raised needed airing; politics and political journalism in our time had too often become search-and-destroy operations, aimed at anyone with the audacity to seek public office. But anger at the process, for Clinton, was not an adequate response to his problems, not with the hot light of the general election just ahead. His moods became a matter of active concern within the campaign; he was, one senior operative said, "the most bitter man I know right now," worse than outsiders could ever imagine, and it wasn't doing him or his cause any good. Robert Reich, a key economic adviser, wrote him a letter urging him to let go of his sense of personal grievance, and Stan Greenberg, always the bravest of his strategists, scolded him to his face. "You're feeling sorry for yourself," he told Clinton bluntly on primary day in Pennsylvania. "You're too self-absorbed. People aren't going to vote for someone to bring about change unless it's for *them*, not for *you*."

Clinton's message by then had become a blur, a rote series of things he said when he wasn't obliged to defend himself. His idea of a New Covenant between government and the people had been good enough when he floated it, a token that he had a coherent sense of where he wanted to lead the country. But it had always been a bit abstract for the hurly-burly of a campaign, and it had got lost in the tactical scramble to get him through the primaries. He had emerged from that struggle, one aide lamented, with no overarching philosophy, not even a villain to run against. Instead of a clear rationale for his candidacy, he had a bunch of programs and a freight car's worth of baggage weighing down his forward progress; he couldn't get any message across until he and his people better understood and addressed the questions about him.

And so was born what Mandy Grunwald dubbed the Manhattan Project, a top-secret program of research aimed at Clinton's resurrection as a viable candidate. Its first mission was to probe the doubts about him and look for ways to allay them; only when they were sure that people would listen could they profitably move on to the question of what he should say. Like the quest for the atom bomb for which it was named, it sought the means to victory in the arcana of science—in this case, the dimly understood complexities of opinion research rather than the knowable laws governing nuclear fission. And like the encampment of physicists, chemists, and engineers in the New Mexico desert half a century earlier, Clinton's strategists were racing against time. They had roughly three months, from the New York primary to the party convention, in which to find a cure for what ailed him—and a message powerful enough to carry him past Bush and Perot.

They had got their go-ahead on primary day in New York, when Carville, Greenberg, and Grunwald approached Mickey Kantor in his rooms at the Sheraton Manhattan and laid out their proposal. For formal purposes, they called it the General Election Project, which sounded less dramatic than its nickname and therefore less likely to attract the interest of the press. They would ask the Democratic National Committee to pick up the $100,000 bill for the effort, presuming, accurately, that the party would see its interest in Clinton's rehabilitation; nobody of sound mind there would be eager for a rerun of the electoral disasters of 1980, 1984, and 1988. They would invite opinions from outside experts at politics and policy, but their principal research tool would be that staple of modern marketing, the focus group. The recurring complaint about Clinton was that nobody knew why he wanted to be president. Now, they needed to hear from the voters themselves what it would take for him to break through.

Kantor signed off on the plan, and the first focus groups were convened in mid-April in Allentown, Pennsylvania. They started with ten middle-aged, middle-class white women, all independents or shaky Democrats. Five were for Perot going in, three for Bush, and only two for Clinton. The reasons were instantly plain. They couldn't think of much to like about Clinton, but when they were asked about their doubts, it was like opening a spigot.

"Trust!" one woman exclaimed.

"Two-faced," said another.

"Only in it for the glory," said a third.

"Like JFK and Ted Kennedy," a fourth put in, and she wasn't talking about statesmanship.

Was he strong?

"He just goes with the flow," somebody said. "If you asked his favorite color, he'd say, 'Plaid.'"

That one hurt; for a long time thereafter, when Clinton fudged on an issue, his people would say he had gone plaid.

But there was more. Did Clinton care?

"Not about things in my life."

Was he trustworthy?

"He wouldn't steal, but he would shade the truth."

What about his morals?

One after another, each of the women said it wasn't a problem for her—and then added, tellingly, that it probably would be for most other people.

Greenberg had a hypothesis he wanted to test—that people would like Clinton better if they knew more about him than they had read or seen through the filter of the media. He had reduced the candidate's life, times, and public record to three dozen bits of information—that he had been born in a small town in Arkansas and raised by a lately widowed mother; that he had stood up to his drunken stepfather and made him stop abusing the family; that he had worked his way through college, won a Rhodes scholarship, and then come back to Arkansas to try to make a difference in people's lives; that, as governor, he had fought to improve education, reform welfare, and create new manufacturing jobs at ten times the national rate; that he had once allowed the arrest of his own brother on drug charges rather than use the power of his office to get him off.

It was a pointillist portrait, an assemblage of dots done only in the colors most flattering to Clinton, but it began turning the tide in the room.

"Sounds like he has a lot more morals than the papers give him credit," a woman said. "And ethics."

"I feel cheated and manipulated by the media," another commented.

A third held up her copy of Greenberg's list. "I would like this person to be my president," she said.

Not all were so quickly won over, but as they were given more information and shown some ads and video clips, their resistance melted. By the end, Clinton had moved from last to first choice in the room; the count was seven for him, two for Bush, and only one for Perot.

The women left, and eight men from the same demographic slice of life were ushered in. They, too, leaned heavily to Perot at the outset; five supported him, to only one apiece for Clinton and Bush and one abstention. And they, too, reacted cynically to the first mentions of Clinton's name:

"He's a politician, and a politician is going strictly for the job and power."

"He'll do anything to get your vote."

Did he say what he meant?

"Slick Willie," someone said.

"He plays both sides of the street."

"I don't believe Clinton is dishonest, but he sure as hell tries to stretch it."

The men had been less moved than the women by the stories of Clinton's morals; each spoke of having had problems in his own life, and none was prepared to judge Clinton for his suspected deviations from the path of righteousness. Neither were their reservations so grave as to shut out new information. Once they had got the treatment—the biography, the film clips, the ads—they, too, dramatically shifted ground; six were for Clinton, one for Perot, and none at all for Bush.

The people in the focus groups had been captive audiences; in the real world, you couldn't just bombard people with your side of the story and shut out all the dissonant noise. But those first exercises in deconstruction did give Clinton's handlers a clear and somewhat scary view of what they were up against. His character problem no longer had much to do with the particulars of the case against him: the suspicion that he was a philanderer, a draft-dodger, or a long-ago dabbler at dope-smoking. It was the residue of all of those things, and it was worse than any of them. Clinton was, in the public mind, a politician—one more smiling hustler who would promise anybody anything to win and could not be trusted thereafter to act on his word.

He had, that is, become his cartoon, the Bill Clinton rendered by Paul Tsongas, Jerry Brown, and the unfriendlier caricaturists in the mass media. What his handlers saw through the one-way glass between them and the focus groups was how little people actually knew about him or what he stood for—and how much of what they thought they knew was wrong. To the extent that they were aware of his background at all, they had fastened on his student days at Oxford and Yale and concluded that he must have been the son of privilege, a playboy whose way up in the world had been greased for him by money and family connections. It was an easy leap from there to the belief that nothing about him was authentic, and that nothing he had to say could therefore be worth listening to.

The diagnosis was in, and in the days thereafter, Greenberg sat down with his notes, his polls, and his instincts to draft an interim report for the project team. At forty-seven, he was a product of the academy, a political scientist before he became a political operative; he looked a bit out of place in the raffish culture of his new trade, as if he had just wandered in out of a carrel in the library. But his donnish past and his elfish look were deceiving; more than once, Carville had watched him scold Clinton to his face and had told colleagues, reverently, that the little motherfucker had balls. Greenberg's advice, in the memo, was characteristically blunt. Nothing would do, he told Clinton, short of "a fundamental remaking of your campaign . . . to address the debilitating image that is dragging us down. We believe the campaign must move on an urgent basis before the Perot candidacy further defines us (by contrast) and the Bush-Quayle campaign defines us by malice."

The heart of the matter, the problem they had to address, was the impression that Clinton was "the ultimate politician"—a suspicion too often reinforced by his own presentation of himself. The worst aftereffect of the scandals was the uncandid sound of Clinton's response to them. As he existed in the minds of the focus groups, the memo said, Clinton "is not real. He is 'packaged,' created by image makers." Under pressure, he turned evasive, all fast talk, handy lists, and equivocal answers. He wouldn't look you in the eye and tell you the truth—a charge more devastating, in the jaded politics of 1992, than the most lurid tattlings of Gennifer Flowers.

The mistrust in his word had short-circuited everything else he was trying to say and do. The litany of citizen complaints about him went to the very heart of his candidacy: "[Clinton is] weak—controlled by the political establishment, 'the powers' and the money people. . . . Clinton's for himself, not people. . . . Clinton cannot be the candidate of change." It was implicit in the memo, indeed, that he was doomed unless the campaign took radical steps quickly toward a single end—to so "depoliticize Bill Clinton" that people would give him a hearing.

The idea was not to reinvent him; no officeholder who had served as long and published his ideas as widely as he had could be turned into somebody else so late in the game. But he could be *repositioned*, using the raw materials of biography and public record that were already there. Clinton had to go back and start over again, Greenberg thought, by telling America the story of his life. Once people heard it, they stopped speaking of him as a politician and started using descriptives like "self-made . . . down to earth . . . honest, hard-working man . . . no silver spoon . . . the opposite of Bush." His story was the means of his transformation, Greenberg wrote, from a self-seeking careerist into "a human being who struggled, pulled his weight, showed strength of character, and fought for change"—and the updraft it created for him in the polls was "extraordinary."

He had to change his own demeanor as well, "from self-absorption," Greenberg said, "to caring about people." He needed to stress his record of commitment in Arkansas, standing up to the narrow interests and winning. He had to barnstorm the "counter-political" media—talk shows and town meetings that showed off his gifts at human connection and not his fascination with political analysis. He had to persuade people that he had a plan, not just a jumble of proposals, and that its heart lay with the neglected middle class. And most of all, he had to reassert the most basic premise of his campaign. "Clinton's candidacy will not catch on unless voters come to understand what Bill Clinton wants to do to change America," Greenberg said. "Right now, they have no idea what he wants except to get elected."

The campaign had to square up as well to the fact that Hillary, through no particular fault of her own, had become part of the problem. She was less well-known even than her husband and was therefore the prisoner of assumptions people made about her, her marriage, and her political ambitions, which were presumed to be lustier even than his. "In the focus groups," Greenberg wrote, "people think of her as being in the race 'for herself' and as 'going for the power.' She is not seen as particularly 'family-oriented.' More than Nancy Reagan, she is seen as 'running the show.'"

The perception might be "remarkably distorted," as the memo tactfully put it, but it was out there, and it was contributing to Clinton's politician image; if she was that power-hungry, he must be, too. They needed to get Hillary out of sight for "a short pull-back period," Greenberg thought, while the process of reintroducing Bill was going forward. She would not reemerge, in this scheme, until after the primaries and then would do more family-plan campaigning—joint appearances with her husband, a new emphasis on their affection for one another and for their daughter, a series of Bill 'n' Hillary "dates with the American people." In the process, the two of them would have to spell out what her role would be as First Lady, if it came to that. "Ambiguity looks like a power game," Greenberg warned. "It is very important that voters feel comfortable with Hillary's role and not see her as an empowered Nancy Reagan."

Clinton was already in a grumpy mood when Greenberg, Carville, and Frank Greer brought him their findings in the bedroom of his suite at the Warwick Hotel in Philadelphia. It was primary day in Pennsylvania, and his vital signs were looking strong; he was winning the state and the day by better than two-to-one over Jerry Brown and four-to-one over the ghost of Paul Tsongas. They found him angry at his campaign, but not because it had no message. His complaints of the day were rather that his schedule was crazy, his strategy was all over the papers—and oh, by the way, there weren't enough women and blacks in visible positions of authority in the campaign.

It was then that Greenberg chided him for his self-pity. Clinton was silent at first, suggesting to his visitors that he got the message. When he spoke, it was plain what really had been bothering him. He had been doing his own obsessive reading of the polls and had been brought up short by the latest spike in his unfavorable rating. Was it so high, he asked, that he could not be elected in the fall?

Greenberg filled him in on the *good* news from phase one of the

Manhattan Project and watched his mood brighten as they talked. The voters hadn't finally closed the door on him, the pollster said. He could work through his troubles, and the project findings pointed the way. It was a matter of America's getting to know him as he was, not as the tattlers of politics and the press made him out to be. If he could just get his act together in time, he would be all right.

"What Are We Waiting For?"

Was there time? Mandy Grunwald wasn't sure. The problem seemed to her obvious enough in the blanket of polls and memos spread out over her worktable in Washington, and so did the countermeasures the campaign would have to take. As it was, she thought, people saw Clinton as a yuppie—a young climber with no past worth remarking outside the gossip columns and no important achievements to show for his long run as governor of Arkansas. As a media consultant, Grunwald would be a key player in the attempt to change that perception. But it couldn't be done with television ads—the money wasn't there—and alternate routes kept dead-ending somewhere in the top layers of the campaign. Thanks to the Manhattan Project, they knew what would work. Making it happen was something else. It was daunting. If people still didn't know the basic facts of Clinton's life, his career, and his message by the end of the convention in July, Grunwald thought, he was toast.

As she spoke, Clinton's candidacy was ten weeks away from the toaster, and knowing how to avoid it didn't seem to help. His complaints about the campaign's dulled reflexes were well taken, though he and Hillary were in some degree to blame; it was they who had ensured their own command authority by refusing to trust it to anyone else. The result was a diffusion of power among too many camps—the staff, the consultants, the FOBs and FOHs—and an onset of creeping paralysis at the top. Egos collided. Alliances and enmities formed. The Little Rock cadre griped that the campaign had got too consultant-driven. The consultants regarded Little Rock as a bureaucratic nightmare. "You know that old saying that Willie Mays's glove is where triples go to die?" one of them groused after a particularly trying day at the office. "Well, this campaign is where ideas go to die."

It fell to David Wilhelm, as manager, to hold things together. He did, with generous applications of civility and plain talk; wars were settled, walkouts averted, flashes of temper doused. The price was a pattern of rule not by decision but by consensus. Wilhelm and his deputies were compromised by what one colleague called "Bill and

Hillary's schizophrenia"—their habit of undercutting their own command structure, such as it was, and relying instead on themselves and their formidable network of friends. "We may not be ready for a presidential campaign," this aide worried aloud one day in May, "but neither are they. They're not ready for anything but a governor's race."

In the view of their strategists, they wouldn't be ready until they began implementing the findings of the Manhattan Project. "We need a maniac driving this forward every day," one senior hand said, but no one emerged, and nothing seemed to happen. Carville withdrew into his anger, like a snapping turtle into its shell; several times, he had to be talked out of quitting. Once, the entire consulting team considered going on strike, just to get the attention of the Clintons and the Little Rock crowd. Grunwald stewed while the plan to blitz the talk shows languished without a yes or no. "What are we waiting for?" she and her senior partner, Frank Greer, bristled in a memo to headquarters in late April.

The high cost of stagnation was only too clear when the Manhattan Project team opened a second round of focus groups, this time with ten middle-aged, college-educated women in the New Jersey suburbs. Of all the demographic groups in the campaign's polling, women like them had been the most resistant to Clinton all along, but Greenberg and Grunwald were stunned by the depth of their hostility; the group was the most negative either consultant had ever seen. Not one of the women could think of a good thing to say about Clinton. Half said they wouldn't even consider voting for him. It didn't help that most of them were at least equally unhappy with Bush; their first alternative was not Clinton but Ross Perot.

Once again, the moderator probed at the roots of their dislike. Was Clinton too much a politician? There were yesses around the table. Could he be trusted to keep his promises? This time, there were noes, sometimes with subliminal echoes of the Flowers scandal. "If he's not ethical in one area," a woman said, "he's not ethical overall." What was he about? No one seemed sure. "I don't even know who he is," one member of the group said suddenly. "It's kind of sad—he's running for president, and I don't even have a sense of the man."

What would it take for him to break through? The consultants knew they couldn't make him up; instead, like mosaicists, they gathered up the disparate bits and pieces of Clintoniana already at hand and rearranged them into three one-page attempts at a Message. The first was a reworking of the themes he had started out with—the argument that both the rich and the idle poor had been getting something for nothing while "real people" found their lives stalemated. Clinton's New Covenant would reverse all that, creating opportunity and demanding responsibility. He would move people from welfare to work. He would reward companies that generated new jobs and punish those which exported them overseas. There would be no more tax breaks for corporate polluters, no more free rides for deadbeat dads who didn't make their child-support payments.

A few of the women in the room seemed to like what they read. Still, they remained skeptical, and the others were unmoved.

"Can I ask where this is coming from?" one demanded. "Why haven't I heard this before?"

"This is almost a wish list," another said.

"He can say anything he wants and it doesn't matter," a third said, "because we don't believe him. We don't believe anything he says."

"I think it's just words. He's just saying what we want to hear."

"Actually, it's very insulting. It's like blaming the victims. It's disguised in 1992 jargon, but it's almost like Hitler."

Behind their one-way glass, the consultants were dumbstruck. Grunwald laughed hysterically. Greenberg dipped his head to the tabletop before them and moaned.

The second message track fared just as badly. It was called "Fighting for the Forgotten Middle Class," a war Clinton would wage with "an end to welfare for the wealthy," tax cuts for workaday citizens, and a restructured health-care system. The reactions ranged from cool to ice cold.

"This is baloney," one woman said.

"*Baloney!*" another echoed.

"Propaganda," said a third.

"Everything is 'Clinton *wants*,'" a fourth criticized. "But how is he going to do it? There's no *how* anywhere."

"And here's a lie," a fifth said. In a mock southern accent, she read a line about Clinton's having been reared in a small town in rural Arkansas. "He went to *Oxford!*" she exclaimed. "Did he grow up with *sharecroppers?*"

They moved to track three, "Putting People First." The message was old-shoe comfortable for Clinton, the formulation he had worked on for years and had used to win the primaries. Its premise was that the policies of the Reagan-Bush years had put people last, feeding the national debt and starving investment in the public good. Clinton, in this formulation, would reverse all that—would spend less on defense and more on the health, safety, education, and general well-being of the citizenry.

"I just don't like Bill Clinton," one of the women said, "so nothing he says will change my mind."

By then, the two consultants had tuned out, unable to watch any more. The management of the facility had thoughtfully left some desk toys in their observation room. Grunwald attacked a puzzle. Greenberg played with a bright purple Slinky. On the far side of the glass, the group was telling them what they already knew—that people would listen to Clinton only if they got to know him better. It was depressing, Greenberg thought, and not a little frightening. Clinton might as well have been trying to address America through a wall of thick plate glass. He was moving his lips, all right, but if he couldn't break through the barrier of mistrust between him and the voters, it didn't matter how elegantly he framed his message; no one would ever hear what he had to say.

The campaign by then had a profile in rare depth of a candidacy in some trouble, along with some strong clues as to how to fix it. But Greenberg wanted to carry the exploration even deeper with a tool that had been much favored by Ronald Reagan's polling team: the dial group. The technique involved assembling twenty or thirty people in a room, showing them a video presentation of ads and speeches, and asking them to register their responses by turning a dial on a handheld electronic meter. The needle on the dial covered a range roughly equivalent to that of a thermometer, from a frigid zero to a hot, hot, hot one hundred. Reagan's team had used dial groups to keep refining his stock speech until it consisted entirely of applause lines. The puzzle for Clinton's strategists was harder: finding a message so compelling as to make people suspend their disbelief in him.

Their laboratory, this time, was a hotel room in Dayton, Ohio, and their sample consisted of twenty-six moderate to somewhat liberal white women. Most of them looked on Clinton with feelings ranging from apathy to strong dislike; only six owned up to thinking kindly of him. At least some of the ads he had been using—the ones with flags and rallies—drove the needles down; just as he himself suspected, they made him look like a common politician. The test confirmed that Hillary wasn't helping, either. The women didn't like her—not, at least, as they imagined her to be. The readings fell precipitously at the mere sight of her face on-screen.

But there were things that worked for Clinton. Direct answers helped; he fared best when he skipped the politics and cut straight to the heart of the matter at hand. People liked it when he said things like "no more something for nothing" and when he advanced some of his New Democratic ideas. When he talked about keeping children in school, the collective response on the meters hit 60. Improving access to college pushed it past 70. Getting people off welfare and into jobs after two years produced spikes to 75 and 80.

For two hours, the moderator bombarded the group with positive information about Clinton, then polled them again on their preferences. "If we can't move them after all this," Carville said, "shoot—we ought to all quit." That, as it turned out, wouldn't be necessary. Clinton won the straw vote against Bush and Perot this time, and his favorable rating popped past 60, while they remained stuck at 45 apiece. At the beginning, he had scored badly on a list of attributes people wanted in a president. By the end, the women saw him as strong, determined, caring, in tune with their values—and presidential.

"Jesus," Greenberg said, "look at the favorables. We know we can make a difference. We just need a message and a way to communicate it."

A few days later, Carville and Greenberg met with Clinton at a Holiday Inn in Charleston, West Virginia, and showed him a copy of the video. A trend line had been superimposed over the pictures of himself, tracking the collective ups and downs in the reactions of the dial groups to what he was saying. He watched it transfixed, eyes glued to the screen; he always wanted to be the best student, one of his handlers said, and here he was, watching people grade him.

He resisted some of what the tape had to tell him. When the line nosed downward with Hillary in the picture, he guessed that she had had a bad hair day; he could not admit to himself that she was unpopular. But he plainly got the message that his depoliticization would have to begin with his presentation of himself. He doted on politics and loved talking about it, when people really wanted to hear what he would do about their problems. Months of nagging by his own team and by various outside advisers hadn't reformed him. It took a line across a TV screen, dipping sharply whenever he sounded or looked too political, to drive the point home. Talking politics, in an antipolitical year, was indeed a turnoff. Maybe he and the Manhattan Project hadn't found the ultimate answer yet, that elusive forumulation known in the trade as a message, but for a time, at least, he seemed to know what *not* to say.

In Search of Magic

Toward the end of May, Clinton's generals convened in Little Rock for one more go at reframing the rationale for his candidacy. The ingredients were all there in public record and rhetoric, but after a month of

research, the Manhattan Project was still struggling with high concept, still looking for something as simple and as powerful as Reagan's
pledge in 1980 to get the government off the backs of the American
people. "We have a Bill Clinton problem," James Carville worried at
the eve of the conclave, and for a change, it didn't come from the case
file on his past. It was figuring out what he could possibly say now to
get himself seriously considered for president.

In their latest report, the Project team had reshuffled the deck and
expanded the number of possible message tracks from three to four:

- *The People First,* investing in the American people to secure
  the economic future;
- *Opportunity With Responsibility,* stressing no more something
  for nothing.
- *The Middle Class,* a populism of the center, not the left.
- *Reinventing Government,* not a revolution but a plan to
  make the system work for you.

But no single one of them had put big numbers on the scoreboard
in the research, and in the absence of the right formula, the campaign,
like the candidate, had got too absorbed with the tactics of staying
afloat. "Ask yourself how much time we spend communicating our
message versus politics," Carville lectured an opening session of two
dozen or so Clintonians in the basement of the governor's mansion.
"We are too concerned with inside politics. This is the sign of a campaign in trouble."

The real question, in his view, was easy to frame and hard to answer:
"What will we tell the people?" He liked the *People First* message best
of the four on the table, with a heavy infusion of *Responsibility.* But
whatever they settled on, he said, had to be *big.* Suppose Clinton was
talking to a paradigmatic voter, a divorced mother who had questions
about eight specific areas of concern in her life. There were those in
the campaign, Carville said, who would offer a "particularist" response, addressing each of the eight issues in turn. "If you add them all
up, you don't have a message," he said. "If you say all eight things,
does she hear *anything?*" Carville doubted it; he argued instead for
that lean, "universalist" approach more often referred to as a Vision.

As it turned out, Clinton was on the same wavelength. He and
Hillary sat up late that night discussing the problem, and when the
meetings resumed next morning, she jumped in.

"Bill, before we start," she said, "tell them what we talked about
last night."

"I've been thinking about the message," he told the group, and his
thoughts had been running along universalist lines. He had always

been uncomfortable with the populist underpinnings of the *Middle-Class* manifesto, and *Reinventing Government* was too hard to explain; not even the people in the message group had been able to reduce it to sound-bite size. The *Opportunity/Responsibility* thing was too small for Clinton's tastes, once you got to the details; he did want to stress responsibility in the campaign, but a strong message required a big-time villain to shoot at, and he didn't see one.

"Here's what concerns me," he told the group. "I *love* this stuff, but I can't run against deadbeat dads."

What he had in mind sounded more like *People First* than anything else, though he worried that that didn't have a villain, either. He wanted an economic message, he said, something that drew a sharp contrast between himself and George Bush. He was much taken with the ideas of his economic adviser Robert Reich on the need for an activist government investing *up* to create jobs and promote growth rather than waiting for wealth to trickle down from the top. But the presentation would need work, and so would the economic ideas he had set out with in the fall. The world had changed since then, he said. Some of the assumptions he had started from were no longer valid. He needed time to rethink his proposals and to talk them over with the experts he trusted, idea men like Reich and Ira Magaziner. *Saying* "people first" was fine, but there had to be substance behind the slogans.

The economic retreat was quickly laid on for the following week, but what pleased the handlers most was that they had Clinton's attention. They left that day's meeting on air, Mandy Grunwald thought. After a long, lonely passage of flailing around, they were at last thinking strategically, not just about how to manage today's crisis or survive next Tuesday's primary. The campaign was focused, the candidate engaged. Grunwald could almost feel things beginning to move.

They all knew it was no more than that, a beginning. The terrain of politics had changed with the astonishing rise of Citizen Perot from his countinghouse in Dallas to the top of the polls in three months. Without him around, they could have run a simple, bipolar race: Clinton as the agent of change against Bush as the defender of the way things were. But Perot complicated everything. Clinton himself had watched his progress with growing agitation and not a little anger at having his own role as the outsider stolen from him. Could they get that back by somehow yoking Perot with Bush as the inside men? Or should they ignore him and embrace what some people in the campaign were promoting as The 38 Percent Solution—playing to the traditional Democratic base in the hope that it would be enough to prevail in a three-way race?

The consultants mostly leaned to Plan A, and on a Friday in late May, Carville and Grunwald joined Greenberg in his room at the Capital Hotel in Little Rock to think through the new dynamic of the race. They would be leading a meeting with the Clintons the next day, a summit conference on strategy, and they wanted to be on the same page when they got there.

"In the end, doesn't Perot *have* to be part of the problem?" Greenberg asked rhetorically. "He didn't make his money by investing in people—he made it by getting government contracts."

"If the press ain't done this son of a bitch in by Labor Day, we're going to have to do some work," Carville said. But not yet; in his view, they had to deal with their Clinton problem first, designing a message and keeping him on it.

"I don't expect to beat up Perot for months," Grunwald said.

"We can't beat him up right now anyway," Carville agreed. Perot had too much money. If they attacked him, he could blow them right off the air.

"He could literally have his own evening news show," Grunwald said.

They studied the new positioning problem like chess players, looking for unseen opportunities to tie Perot to Bush short of a frontal attack. Perot didn't have the patience to take on long-term problems, Greenberg said, trying out one possible line, and Bush didn't have the core beliefs he would need to solve them.

"That's why I like the idea that there's no quick fix," Carville answered. "Stanley, Perot doesn't have much fight in him. I'll guarantee one thing—he's got a glass jaw."

They started working on lists of the distinctions they could draw, taking off from Greenberg's notion. Clinton was committed to solving problems; the other guys weren't. Perot had no patience, Bush no beliefs. Clinton had made the system work for people; Perot had made it work for himself, Bush for his rich and powerful friends. Clinton was warm and compassionate; the others were cold. Bush just didn't get it, and Perot was rigid and ruthless.

"Ruthless is okay if it's done on behalf of people," Greenberg warned.

"Yes," Carville began, "but ruthless in the drug war . . ."

"Right!" Grunwald said. "There goes the constitution. Boom!"

A second list evolved from the first, positions that Clinton had to contest and those he might as well concede. He couldn't, for example, be more of an outsider than Perot or more the embodiment of change.

"He can't beat Perot as Perot," Carville worried. "But he wants to *be* Perot so bad. His instinct is to try to beat Perot exactly where he can't."

"Part of our job tomorrow," Greenberg agreed, "is to say that us being Perot is deadly. That we can only be a milktoast Perot, just like we were a milktoast Jerry Brown."

Then what *should* Clinton be? Greenberg offered yet another run-up at a message. The '80s were the problem, a time when values were out of kilter, good jobs were lost, and the economic security of the people was threatened. The solution was investing in people. A real plan. Making America work. "If this is our message," Greenberg said, "what's the one-sentence description? What's the message that is going to win this election for us?"

"'Working together again,'" Carville answered. "We've got to take this work thing and drive it so hard up those Republican asses. We need to mention 'work' every fifteen seconds. By Labor Day, people are going to know we value work."

"By the end of the convention," Grunwald said, warming to the idea, "what do we want people to know about Clinton? That he worked his way up. That his life's work has been in education and investing in people. That he values work. That he has moved people from welfare to work. That he has a national economic strategy to put America back to work."

"The word 'work' works for us," Carville said. "'There's no quick fix, no hoaxes, no easy answers. We have to work our way out of this mess.'"

They still didn't have that single magic sentence, the words that could capture Clinton in a sound bite or on a bumper sticker.

"We need elements of moral language," Grunwald said. "'They did America wrong.'"

"'Put America right again,'" Greenberg suggested.

"There you go," Grunwald said. "'Do right by our people.'"

"'It's time to do right by our own people,'" Greenberg said. "I like it."

They broke for the night with the feeling that they were at last getting somewhere. But when they reconvened over breakfast the next morning, Carville was worried. There was no real flash point in their formulations separating Clinton from Bush and Perot on the economy. "Something we're for that they're not," he said. "Something where people say, *'Yeah!'*"

"Well, we can't *not* lead off with economics," Grunwald said.

Still, Carville was concerned. "Let's don't convince ourselves we have something with an edge," he warned. "We don't. Let's don't convince ourselves we have something that's radioactive. We don't. And let's understand that we have learned a lot with this Manhattan Project, but what we've got ain't nearly there. I want something George Bush will attack the next day. Because my humble opinion is that if we don't get an idea out there—"

"—then we're out of the mix," Grunwald said, and they could just about kiss Clinton's chances goodbye.

"We're at Zero"

Bill Clinton was at the bottom of the polls looking up when he and Hillary received their senior strategists at the governor's mansion that afternoon, and his discouragement was plain in his impassive face and his long, somber silences. He was *afraid,* one senior adviser guessed during that spring of Clinton's discontent; too afraid to believe in his team or his prospects anymore. It was as if he no longer wanted to win—as if winning ranked about eleventh on his wish list, the aide said, and finding someone to blame for his reduced state was number one.

The mission of his team that May afternoon, his man said, was to begin the process of making him a messenger with a message—a clear, holistic statement of who he was and what he proposed to do as president. He had a window of time in which to reintroduce himself, Greenberg told them, opening the meeting, but the Manhattan Project research had pointed up a couple of basic problems he would have to overcome. "One is we're too political," he said, "and the second is people don't know what we care about." Clinton had to do something fast to remedy that or risk being defined wholly by contrast to Perot. If that should happen, Greenberg said, "it creates what was created in the primaries with Tsongas and Brown. They ran on honesty. The opposite of that is dishonesty. It highlights our negative. We've got to break that by moving very quickly to establish who we are and what we care about."

He didn't pretend that this Manhattan Project had invented the secret weapon that would win the war. But their research had isolated some of the components. The buzz phrase "investment in our people" was one; it made a nice umbrella for Clinton's ideas about jobs, schools, and health care. "Welfare and work" was another—not just moving the poor from the dole to jobs but putting the whole country back to work. "Getting us together" had power after the greedy '80s. So did talking about "responsibility" and governmental reform; that went straight at the wall they needed to knock down, the perception that

Clinton was just another promise-'em-anything politician. If he didn't achieve that, Greenberg warned, nothing else would work: "They don't listen to the rest of the story."

Carville, next up, warned the Clintons that a message, in politics, was always a work in progress. "Like a kid playing with a piece of putty," he said. "You're always playing with it, you're always shaping it, you're reshaping it, you change something, you move something around. You can always make it better." It had to be clear, it had to be real, it had to have a villain, and above all, in Carville's rules of war, it had to be optimistic. "Democrats tend to be too pessimistic," he said. "Always *terrible* out there. We have to explain to people that something's wrong with the country, but in everything that Bill Clinton exudes, he smiles. He's an optimistic guy. People just have to sense we can turn this country around. We can get back on our feet. There is an answer."

He had brought along his list, by now swollen to eighteen dimensions of mind, belief, and background on which the candidates would be examined and judged. "You can't contest everywhere," he said. "If you contest everywhere, you literally contest nowhere, and nothing gets through." The point instead was to meet the enemy on the ground most favorable to yourself. "You fight a war," Carville said, "you have certain kinds of weapons. Like if you have a strong navy, you want to fight at sea."

He started down his inventory. Grunwald jotted the entries on a sheet of chart paper as he spoke. The composite picture they drew was not encouraging for Clinton; they confirmed his fear that Perot was stealing the ground out from under him. Of the eighteen areas of contention, only five went on the scoreboard as Clinton strengths:

> Bring America Together
> Cares about People like Me
> Help Education
> Improve Health Care
> Environment

Bush had the edge in three dimensions:

> Keep America Strong
> Family Values
> Experience

Perot was strongest in seven:

> New Ideas
> Take Action
> Values Work
> Represents Change

Not a Typical Politician
Independent
Get Economy Moving
Three more looked up for grabs:
Committed
Has Real Plan for America
Makes System Work for People like You

Clinton would have to do battle for these last and recapture some of the ground he had lost to Perot as well. The determining question, Carville said, was where he could win. "Can we beat Ross Perot on '*Not A Typical Politician?*' No. Can we beat Ross Perot on being independent? No—we're a Democrat."

"'*New Ideas?*' Yes," Clinton said, speaking for the first time.

"Yes," Carville agreed.

"'*Take Action?*' Yes," Clinton said.

"'*Take Action,*' yes," Carville agreed.

A new list began taking form, the points Clinton had to fight to hold or win:

New Ideas
Take Action
Values Work
Committed
Makes System Work for Me

"Big one," Carville said as that one went on the board. "Biggie."

Has Real Plan
Improve Health Care
Get Economy Moving

"This is a big one," Carville said. Clinton couldn't just go out and say, "Jobs, jobs, jobs," but the economy would be the heart of the matter. "This is the one, as much as anything, that will drive the election," Carville went on.

"But we don't want to have an argument about '*Change,*'" Grunwald said—not with Perot in the race.

"As much as that is a natural contour," Carville said, "we will let '*Change*' speak for itself. We don't mind ending up a little behind on that. We don't want to get into a thing where my change can be as drastic as yours."

The message had to be value-driven, he went on, and it had to be broad. "You will hear a lot in this campaign about the so-called 38 Percent Strategy. Bush is hearing the same thing. 'Look, don't worry about TV—get your core base out. Get the black vote out. Get the liberals out. Work through the unions.'" Carville's eyes narrowed in disdain. "That is not a strategy," he said. "That is crazy thinking. You can energize a core constituency a lot more with a message that is relevant to them than you can with a phone bank."

"Right, right," Hillary said. Till then, like her husband, she had listened in opaque silence.

Next came Grunwald with her assigned piece of the puzzle: how Clinton could run against Perot/Bush as if they were twins joined at the hip. At the moment, she said, Perot was setting the terms of engagement; he was the outsider in the race, the living embodiment of change. "We are never going to be more for change than Ross Perot," Grunwald reminded them. "He's not part of the political system. If we continue to let that dynamic be what this is about, we're going to lose."

What they had to do instead was cut the deck and deal again, hoping for better cards. *Commitment,* for example—Clinton had shown it all his life; the others hadn't. "What do we know about George Bush? Photo op president, never follows through, doesn't really care about anything, won't stick with it." And Perot? "He cuts and runs. He loses patience. There is no lifetime commitment there to ideas and principles and things he cares about."

There was a "cold-cold-warm" dynamic as well, Grunwald said. In the focus groups, Bush came across as distant and cool, Perot as hard-edged and cold, even scary. "One of the great strengths of Bill Clinton," Grunwald went on, "is that he is all heart and warmth. That is a strength we have that they will never get." Neither could the others match his feeling for ordinary people and their problems. The frequent complaint about Bush in the research was that he just didn't get it. The nagging suspicion about Perot was that he was ruthless; maybe he could take an idea and drive it through, Grunwald said, but "you might get driven right over."

Her last card was the one about how the system had been exploited during the Reagan-Bush years; Bush had made it work for the corporations, Perot for himself. Clinton had a large target to shoot at—the suspicion that in the '80s, the system had been "rigged," Grunwald told them, "for a few people who made out like bandits." Clinton needed to suffuse his speeches with some moral indignation, not just a promise to do better. In his presidency, he would put a stop to the fast practices that had too long favored the few at the expense of the many.

Carville flipped the chart to what they had come up with the day before: IT'S TIME TO DO RIGHT BY OUR OWN PEOPLE. "It's something that people can understand: we did wrong to our own people," he said. "And ours is more a right-wrong argument than it is a new-old argument."

"There are a lot of other dimensions we could go on," Grunwald added. "We are saying it should be about wrong and right."

For Carville, it was about work and commitment, and not just as ·elements of the message; they had to be watchwords for the Clinton campaign itself. If there was a quick fix for their own problems, he said, "that is the answer we don't have. We think we do have an answer to win this campaign. But is there something that, by the Democratic convention, we're going to be at 42 percent in the polls and people all over the country are going to be immediately loving us? No, there's not." What Clinton had to remember was that no one else had the answer either. "It would be a terrible mistake," Carville cautioned, "to try to go from one short cut to another, one stump speech to another, trying something for a week and then saying this doesn't work. This message has to demonstrate commitment over the long haul. The idea is that it says something larger about the candidacy and is about something bigger than the person. And," he said, drawing out the words, "it . . . means . . . leaving . . . things . . . on . . . the . . . ground."

"It meets all your criteria for a message," Clinton said. "I'm not sure there's a villain."

"Oh, yes," Carville said. "Oh—the shortcuts they took. Oh, yes, we're going to set them up *good.*"

"The people who made the system work for the few—that's what was wrong with the '80s," Grunwald repeated. "That is what we attack. *Those* are the villains."

"It also hangs Perot," Clinton nodded. "Nobody knows Perot made all his money from the government."

"We're not going to be the ones who tell them about Perot," Grunwald said. "At least, *you're* not."

"And me neither, I guess," Hillary laughed.

"When you're asked about your life and bio," Grunwald said, "you worked for everything. When you talk about your record, it's a lifetime of commitment. It's doing right by people. You can tell the story of what you've done in Arkansas a thousand different ways. This is the filter by which you do it. When you talk about what they did wrong in the '80s, they did it the wrong way. They didn't value work. They didn't invest. They went for the shortcuts. What is the solution? Doing right by our people. Valuing work. Having a plan."

"At least I can see the positioning," Clinton said tentatively.

The session by then had crossed the line between show-and-tell to tutorial, an effort to get Clinton not just to understand the message but to begin feeling it in his bones. It was plain to the handlers in the room that he wasn't there yet.

"This is not a class argument," Greenberg said, knowing Clinton's aversion to running as a populist. It was about the neglect of the middle class in the '80s, and in the popular imagination, middle class meant everybody—all but the very rich and the very poor. The answer for the '90s had to be a plan to do better. "A plan means you're real," Greenberg said. "A plan means a contract. It's not 'read my lips.'"

Begala, the resident wordsmith, got up and did a two-minute synopsis of a new stump speech—one the handlers hoped the Clintons would embrace as their own. "We have to make America work again," he began. We tried an experiment in the '80s. It worked for a few, but it failed for the rest of us. It didn't honor, reward, or encourage work. It did not invest in our people. It took us twelve years to dig ourselves into this hole, but we can get out if we have a commitment and a plan to do right by our own people. Investing in our people means education, health care, cutting the bureaucracy, taking on the insurance industry and the drug companies. Rewarding work means saying to the long-term welfare poor, "You'll get education, job training, health care, but after two years, you'll get a job." But responsibility also applied to CEOs who paid themselves outrageous salaries while their companies went down the drain. We have to build a whole new economy, create millions of jobs in high tech, biotech, fiber optics, short-haul aircraft, high-speed rail. And we have to come back together as a society. If we don't, "we are doomed to fail."

Clinton listened attentively. But when the group turned to the money they would need to get the message out—$1 million was a fair guess—his discontent began bubbling to the surface. He was supposed to redo his plan *and* run around rattling a tin cup, and he didn't like it.

"We have to have the discipline to let me stay here and work on this thing," he said.

"We're the worst scheduling sluts I've ever seen in my life," Carville agreed.

"If we need the million dollars," David Wilhelm said, "we have to raise the money."

"That's right," Clinton snapped, "and because this campaign is not perceived to stand for anything, I can't raise money unless I haul myself all over the country raising it."

At one point, Carville tried to humor him by telling a story on himself, about the first TV spot he had ever made. "It was awful," he admitted. "I showed it to the client, and he said, 'I don't know what this spot is supposed to say.' And the fella I was working with said, 'Gee, do you want the opposition to know what we're thinking?' And the client said, 'I never thought about that.' Well, we want everyone to know what we thinking here. We're trying to tell 250 million people. This is not a secret—all this is, is a start."

Clinton retreated into his shell for a while more, but as the meeting wound down, he stood up and cut through the rhetoric like a buzz saw through balsa wood. They had won the nomination, he told them, "without standing for anything, without anyone knowing what we stood for. Everything we did failed." It was Ross Perot who had the momentum, and if they sat around waiting for him to self-destruct, Clinton said, "we're full of crap." He was not exactly swept away with what he had heard that day. It was fine, really good, he conceded a bit grudgingly, but it sounded to him like a forty-five-second rehash of his announcement speech. They should have started using it seven months ago. Now, after all this time, it was all they had, "and," he said, "we're going to get murdered if we don't do it."

Or be reduced to irrelevancy at the very hour of his nomination. "So far as I'm concerned," he complained, "we're at zero. We're a negative. We're off the screen. We don't exist in the national consciousness. We might as well have been like any member of Congress— just kissed every ass in the world that the Democratic Party has. And if you look at the way we allocated our time and resources, you can make a compelling case for that." It had all been futile, and it fed his tragic view of his piece of the human condition. "I don't think you can minimize how horrible I feel," he said, "having worked all my life to stand for things, having busted my butt for seven months, and the American people don't know crap about it after I poured $10 million worth of information into their heads. That is a devastating thing for me to live with."

When he finally ran down, Carville tried to redirect his anger outward, back onto the battlefield. "It's like what you teach infielders," he said. "Every time the ball is hit, you want it. 'Come *my* way, come *my* way.' You have something to tell the American people. You're right— you spent $10 million, you spent all your life fighting for things, and they don't know anything. You oughta be like, 'Damn it, I want to get out there and tell people what the hell I'm about. I've got something to tell these people, and I'm pissed off that here I am in May, and all they think they know is that I'm sort of a bag of hot air out there drifting around the country. I'm proud of what I've accomplished, I'm proud of the plan I put together, and I'm damn pissed off that people don't know about it, and I want to tell them about it.'"

The rudiments of the message were there, and so was the plan to get it out; they were planning to buy time for an ask-Bill town meeting on network television and to sit Clinton down with every talkmeister from David Brinkley to Arsenio Hall so he could speak his piece his way. "Your attitude," Carville told him, "has to be, 'I'm tired of people having these misconceptions. I've got all these so-called god-dam bright people around me, and they haven't come up with nuthin' but a forty-five-second version of what I started with. And I'm for doing that. Let's get out and do it."

Clinton looked grim. "We don't have an option," he concluded, "I think we will lose this whole election if we don't."

13.

The Man from Hope

As May gave way to June, Clinton slogged on through the last big round of primaries in California, Ohio, and New Jersey. The news that Tuesday was good on its face, as it had been every primary day since his stumble in Connecticut; he swept the board and picked up the last delegates he needed to guarantee his nomination. But it didn't seem to matter, to his own battered morale or to his prospects in November. The press was all but ignoring him. His campaign was shot through with internal tensions. He was still third in the polls; winning primaries wasn't so much fun when a quarter to a half of the electorate in your own party said in the exit surveys that they would have been happier voting for Ross Perot.

"So I've struggled through all these primaries," he groused to Frank Greer one day, "and all I get for it is that I'm in third place."

Greer tried to persuade him that being third was a blessing in disguise—that it sheltered him from an air attack by the Republicans at a point when he had no money left with which to fight back.

"So being third after all these primaries is a plus instead of a minus," Clinton said. He sounded unconvinced; where he came from, third place was third place.

He didn't see a clear way up from under; on the contrary, he was having an attack of what he might have called buyer's remorse over the new message elements his people had laid before him. Privately, he complained to his friend Bruce Lindsey that too much of it came from focus groups and people meters as against the years of study he had done preparing himself for the race. It had all sounded okay at a two-hour meeting, but after a couple of days of reflection, he wasn't sure anymore. His discomfort showed in his speeches, which seemed, if anything, to be busier in detail and fuzzier in conception than ever. "We were playing Moses out there," one senior adviser said after a particularly bad show in California. Clinton was wandering all over the desert, adrift from theme to theme.

The Manhattan Project task force kept trying and, by mid-June, came back around to a variation on an old primary theme: "putting people first." In its new form, it owed importantly to the work of two of Clinton's favorite idea men: Robert Reich, the lay economist, and David Osborne, a swami-in-residence at the Democratic Leadership Council's public-policy think tank. Osborne argued that government on the bureaucratic New Deal model had outlived its usefulness and needed to be reinvented. Reich felt that it needed to be redirected as well, into that leaner, smarter style of economic and social activism shorthanded by Clinton as "investing in people." Fused together, their theories became a kind of Populism Lite. It didn't look like the old redivide-the-pie brand, which Clinton wouldn't have stood for, but it did give him a way to identify Bush and Perot with a discredited old order.

In the simple phrase "putting people first," the message meisters believed that they had at last found the philosopher's stone they had been seeking—the three little words that would transform the base elements of Clinton's unruly public offering into gold. Its first premise, Stan Greenberg wrote in the Manhattan Project's final memo to the candidate, was that Washington had failed ordinary Americans in the Reagan-Bush years, when public policy favored the rich and let the rest of the country slide downhill. Its objective was to reestablish Clinton as an outsider who identified with the popular rage against Washington and who stood for something new: the promise that government would be of, by, and for the people again.

Greenberg's latest poll had presented the argument this way:

> Americans are fed up with their government, and for good reason. It consumes more of our tax dollars yet delivers less value— producing worse schools, unsafe neighborhoods, more welfare, and less affordable health care. But for the wealthy and big corporations— the top 1 percent—it is producing massive tax cuts, deregulation and the S & L bailout. All the while, the middle class is shrinking. The trickle-down experiment is failing. Government is failing. Our leaders have let things get out of control and demanded little in return for the country. America needs a new economic strategy that invests in our own people, that puts people first.

The message had lit up Greenberg's computer screens like a video arcade at the mall on Saturday afternoon. Three-quarters of the people agreed with it, and when it was coupled with a tough negative assault on Perot, it propelled Clinton from last place at the start of the poll to a tie for first by the end. "This is a message capable of changing the dynamics of the race," Greenberg wrote, and the beautiful part was that it didn't require Clinton to change a thing he had been saying all along. It was simply a matter of fitting his ideas into a rebuilt conceptual frame.

It struck Greenberg, moreover, that Clinton could make himself heard once he got over the "personal hurdle"—a delicate way of describing the whole constellation of doubts and questions about him as a man. It seemed not to work when he addressed those questions directly, claiming to be of good character. In a new dial-group study in Chicago, the trend line bent downward when people saw him talking about the problem; putting Hillary in the picture didn't help, either. But the specifics of the case against Clinton seemed to count less than Greenberg had imagined they would. People didn't see him as a scoundrel or a rake. They thought of him as a basically good person who shaded the truth about himself, and with the right dosage of information about his life and record, Greenberg thought, that could be fixed.

The door was otherwise open for Clinton to walk through. The good news from the dial groups, Greenberg reported, was that Bush was "in deep trouble" with the people. The sight of his face alone was a turnoff; he was no longer credible as president or, as he claimed belatedly to be, an agent of change. There were opportunities for Clinton as well among the Perot voters in the study. They were strongly anti-Bush, and they were getting uneasy with Perot's refusal to be specific about what he would do. They didn't like Clinton, to be sure, when he sounded or looked political. But when he spoke about rewarding work and investing in people, the Perot fans were at least willing to listen.

To get anywhere at all, Clinton had to impose some order on his own house; too many promising ideas were being smothered in bureaucracy or caught up in the tensions among the various chieftains and tribes grouped uneasily under his banner. Squabbling was constant, and threats to resign were as regular as April rain. Not even primary night in California, the night Clinton won it all, was enough to revive the seabed-low morale among the troops. To the contrary, Stephanopoulos counted it one of the worst nights of the entire campaign. We *lost,* really, he thought. Everybody hates everybody. No one's in charge.

For a long time, Clinton resisted playing referee or even engaging with the problem. The psychic scars of growing up in a warring household had bred in him the habit of avoiding conflict as much and as long as he could. He was instead a born conciliator, preferring reasoned argument and honeyed words to raised voices—except, occasionally, his own. The peacemaker in him gave him an edge in governance, the art of the possible. But it could be a crippling disability in elective politics, the far more ruthless craft of seeking and seizing power.

At his most passive, he let a barracks revolt fester to a point where it almost blew up his campaign. Its immediate target was his onetime statehouse chief of staff, Betsey Wright, whom he had installed in a low, concrete building next to headquarters known as The Bunker. Her assignment was to answer questions about his past. Clinton was right to want her around; no one knew more about his life, times, and public record. But she was a moody and controlling sort, given to sudden, teary storms at what she took to be slights by her colleagues. She wrote complaining memos about them and refused serially to report to any of them—first Stephanopoulos, then Wilhelm, then the newly named chief of staff, Eli Segal.

During one such blowup, Clinton tried to make peace by naming her deputy chair in charge of all research operations, answerable only to Mickey Kantor. The trouble was that he didn't tell the others of his plan and didn't realize how affronted his nominal managers would feel at Wright's promotion. In fact, she was received in her new role as warmly as Lucrezia Borgia at a wine tasting. The entire oppo (for opposition-research) staff quit rather than work for her, leaving no one behind to assemble dossiers on Bush and Perot for the fall. Wilhelm, whose even temper and steadying hand had helped get the campaign through past internal crises, was at the point of following them out the door.

In the end, nobody quit; the squall blew over, and in its aftermath, something like a coherent command structure began to take form. Segal, a publishing millionaire and a longtime FOB, was given the decision-making authority he needed to keep the trains running on time. Stephanopoulos had been called in off the road and put in charge of communications, with a mandate to get the stalled new message strategy off the ground and onto the talk shows. Grunwald, a favorite of the Clintons dating to the long-ago night when she stood up to Ted Koppel on *Nightline,* was promoted ahead of her partner Frank Greer to run the ad team—the first woman ever to reach that eminence in a presidential campaign. The oppo staff was persuaded to come back. The scheduling mess would eventually be turned over to Susan Thomases; the senior aides who thought up that move meant it as a way to contain her random kibitzing about everything else, but she turned out to be good at it, bringing a new and sharpened focus to the business of moving the Clintons around.

And James Carville started on his rise to primacy as chief strategist of the campaign. Through his own long mopey period, his leading allies, Grunwald and Greenberg, had been after him to take on a larger role. It didn't come to him, and when he tired of waiting and brooding, he finally made an opening for himself. The franchise he volunteered for was, on its face, modest enough; he had decided, he said in June, to move to Little Rock and take over the surrogate program, which seemed painfully maladroit at getting outside speakers on the road to defend Clinton and attack Bush and Perot. But the charter he envisioned for himself quickly broadened to include the command of what would come to be known as the War Room—a quick-response unit built to address new issues and answer fresh charges as they came up in the rough-and-tumble of the race to November.

Carville's friends at court understood that what he really was attempting was a putsch. "And you know what?" one said. "Thank God. He's the only one who knows how to play in this league." Not everybody was so enthusiastic; the idea of a war room with James in charge met with instant resistance at headquarters, from the FOBs and some of the staff. But Grunwald ran interference, meeting privately with Clinton and urging him to do more—much more—with Carville. The organization wasn't ready for what lay ahead, she said; it was drifting in a no-man's land between two camps, accomodationists in one, warriors in the other. Her own heart, like Carville's, lay with the warriors. "This campaign terrifies me," she told Clinton, "because there aren't any people in charge who wake up every morning trying to figure out how to fuck the competition."

The job description was, unsurprisingly, a perfect fit for her friend James. But he needed Hillary's support as well—Clinton ran everything important past her—and Carville presented his case to her in a secret meeting at the mansion one night near the end of June. They spoke alone for a time; then Clinton came in from a film shoot, and the three of them took a walk across the grounds toward the guest house, talking as they strolled.

The Clintons agreed to the idea in principle that night, but it would take one more meeting, during the convention, to close the deal and to cement Carville's standing as main man. He was itchy to get the operation up and running, and with Grunwald and Greenberg in tow, he sat down with Hillary again at midweek in the proceedings in hopes of moving the project along. Clinton came in late and a little scared— this time, for a change, by good news. His poll ratings had shot upward, before he was ready. He would be walking around the country with a target on his back, one aide worried, and his team wasn't organized to defend him properly. Necessity was the mother of invention. It was time to put somebody in charge at long last.

"We want you to take over strategic control," Hillary told Carville. "We want you to run the campaign," Clinton said.

The three consultants floated out of the room and headed for the hotel bar to toast their victory. They had got more than they had dared ask; Carville was not only the autocrat of the War Room but the last word, except only the Clintons, on the conduct of the long march to November.

With the shakedown at the top, things began moving. Clinton gave birth to his new economic plan, an update of the old one with more specifics, sharper cost estimates, and a fresh layering of rhetoric about opportunity, responsibility, and putting people first. There was some talk, goosed along publicly and privately by Mario Cuomo, of packaging the highlights as a "Hundred Days Agenda" and promising to work in close partnership with the Democratic Congress to get it passed. "If you don't do this, you'll lose," Cuomo told Clinton by phone. But Clinton's handlers thought better of the idea and got it snuffed. "[It] potentially puts us in bed with the bad guys," Greenberg wrote in a distressed memo when it looked as if the presentation might actually happen. "We are about to become more political. Help."

The plan instead was presented at a televised town meeting in Atlanta—one in an extraordinary blast of paid and free television appearances that helped revive Clinton's stalemated candidacy. The hope at first had been to buy prime network time for three "Ask Bill" shows, the candidate fielding questions from ordinary citizens. They managed only one, a half-hour on NBC, before the money ran out. It didn't matter. Live candidates had become hot properties on the talk-show circuit, celebrities to be fed into the usual rotation of hunks, jocks, rockers, rappers, and cellulite-busters. In his new job as communications director, Stephanopoulos discovered that he didn't need to *buy* time. He could get Clinton all he needed free.

For a season, it was hard to tune in a program that Clinton wasn't doing or hadn't done. He played *Today* twice, taking questions for an hour each time. He courted the early-bird vote on *CBS This Morning* and *Good Morning America*. He went live with Larry King. He played to Generation X on an ask-me-anything show on MTV. For the night people, he put on his Ray-Bans, got out his sax, and played a serviceable few choruses of "Heartbreak Hotel" with the Posse on *Arsenio Hall*. He did regional town meetings and local call-in shows; all he needed to do to get on the air was show up.

His second front in the free-media wars was a return to what his handlers called counter-scheduling—the art of taking an in-your-face position before a particular interest group to impress a larger audience with his independence. His first theater was a meeting of Jesse Jackson's Rainbow Coalition in Washington, and his target was one of his fellow guest speakers, a young rapper named Sister Souljah. She belonged to a venerable African-American street tradition called woofing—talking tough as a deterrent, not an incitement, to war. But Paul Begala had spied a newspaper piece quoting her as saying that blacks should take a week off from killing one another and target whites instead. Taken literally, her words had an ugly sound, and Clinton seized the moment to scold her for talking like a black David Duke.

He was himself woofing for the benefit of white folks, showing, by conscious design, that he was man enough to stand up to a traditional Democratic client group. The calculated risk lay in seeming to diss the reverend, for whom the proper respect was the first price of doing business. Clinton had paid assiduous attention to him through the primary season, meeting with him privately and talking with him frequently by phone. But it wouldn't do for a candidate representing himself as a new kind of Democrat to seem to cater to Jackson, as Fritz Mondale and Michael Dukakis had before him. By chance, Clinton's people had already composed some scolding remarks on Ms. Souljah, for use on an earlier occasion in California. The idea had been dropped then, but at the Rainbow meeting, Clinton tacked the words onto the bottom of what was otherwise, for the audience in the room, a politically correct speech.

Jackson sat stone-faced at his elbow through the presentation. Afterward, on public view, he was cordial; the two men had blocked out some private time together, and the reverend had larger goals to pursue. His staff had drawn up a memo making a case for him as Clinton's running mate, and he brought it along to the meeting. But Clinton stopped him short, informing him point-blank that it wasn't going to happen. Jackson's displeasure with the slap at Sister Souljah seemed in the days thereafter to grow rather than abate. The remarks, he said, had "again exposed a character flaw" in the presumed nominee of his party—a willingness to pander for political gain.

Clinton shrugged off the resulting headlines; they were the price of a larger strategy of "going broad," as Greenberg put it, by reaching beyond the bedrock Democratic base to the disaffected white middle class. There were signs that that effort was beginning to click, and as his prospects brightened a bit, so did Clinton's gloomy countenance. He spent part of a June afternoon stretched out precariously in a hammock with Hillary and Chelsea, posing for the film biography to be shown at the party convention.

"Hold, Bill, for a long shot," the co-auteur, Harry Thomason, called out to him.

"This whole thing is a long shot," Clinton said, smiling what had become a rare off-camera smile.

It *was* still a long shot, as Stan Greenberg reported at a strategy meeting the next morning. "We're at a critical moment in the campaign," he said. "The convention is the last time we have the stage to ourselves." But opening day was precisely two weeks away, and the road to Madison Square Garden still led straight uphill. "We've not been very successful," Greenberg continued. "Our negatives have risen steadily since the New York primary. Half the electorate doesn't like us. Only half are considering voting for us. We have to break that open."

Carville agreed. "If we don't get a whole lot better fast," he lectured his comrades-in-arms, "we're going to get blown off the face of the earth. Your whole life, this is all you will ever be remembered for. The rest of your life, you're going to be tagged as fucking losers." To escape that judgment, they had to act; prayer wouldn't do it. "As they used to say in the Marine Corps," Carville said, "wish in one hand, shit in the other, and see which fills up fastest."

They were still talking when a new ABC News–*Washington Post* poll came in. Clinton had moved up to the top of the heap, and it scarcely mattered to his generals that his edge over Perot and Bush was within the statistical margin of error. First place, spiritually speaking, beat the hell out of third.

With that, even Carville forgot his marine maxim and surrendered to wishfulness. "He's going to get on a fast track," he said after the meeting broke up, sounding more certain than he felt. "It's going to happen."

"They're going to aim their guns at us," his pal Begala reminded him, "and we ain't exactly ready."

Carville's brow knotted. His hands dug deeper into the pockets of his ragged jeans. With his inner eye, he was staring into a future that didn't quite work. They had to get the new message out, get the candidate into gear, get the War Room up and running. "We are light years away from where we oughta be," he said, returning to earth. "We're so far behind."

A Costar Is Born

On a late Monday evening in June, a Jeep Cherokee slipped unnoticed across a darkened Washington, bearing two men from a Senate office building to the Capital Hilton downtown. The driver, a Clinton campaign adviser named Mark Gearan, nosed the car into the loading-dock entrance at the hotel and, with his passenger, sat waiting till the garage door had rolled down behind them. Then the two ascended by separate elevators to a ninth-floor suite booked, for security reasons, in Gearan's wife's maiden name. Gearan left his traveling companion in the sitting room, headed up to the candidate's suite on twelve, and led him back down to nine by the stairs, away from the curious eyes of the reporters prowling the building. It was 10:15 when, with a tap at the door, Clinton slipped into the improvised safe house and began what would run on to a three-hour conversation, communing with the other half of his future in presidential politics.

To some of Clinton's own strategists, the match between him and Senator Al Gore of Tennessee seemed at first an improbable one by all the old canons governing the selection of a running mate—and some of the new ones as well. Gore was a bright, serious man, to be sure, with good breeding—his father before him had been an ornament of the Senate—and sound credentials of his own. He had served with distinction for eight years as a congressman and nearly eight in the Senate, specializing in national-security and environmental issues; both were areas in which Clinton needed some shoring up. Gore had the further advantage of having been around the presidential track once on his own, at least for a couple of laps; he had wilted early in the primaries in 1988 and dropped out. The cost to his pride had been vastly greater than the damage to his standing as a man of size in the Federal City.

Yet even his résumé was something of a mixed blessing in the politics of 1992; he was a member in good standing of the very club Clinton proposed to run against. He offered neither geographic nor ideological balance, coming as he did from a next-door state with a next-door cast of mind. Stan Greenberg alone among Clinton's strategists had been lobbying actively for the senator, precisely because the two men were so much alike; he would reinforce everything the campaign was trying to establish about Clinton as a new kind of Democrat, a southerner with postliberal ideas. The other consultants preferred somebody from almost anywhere else, on the old principle that your ticket-mate should at least bring in a state that you might not otherwise win. The usual criteria included excitement as well, which was not then thought to be Gore's game. Maybe the guy *looked* like Superman, but put a mike and a camera in front of him and he turned back into Clark Kent.

"This guy's wooden," Frank Greer said when Clinton first signaled his thinking. "He's boring. He's from the same region, he's the same age—I'm not sure he's going to add very much."

Clinton shrugged him off; this time, for once, it didn't much matter what the consultants thought. In some measure, he was still the awe-struck teenager in the old photograph, shaking hands with John F. Kennedy; he had never lost his reverence for the institution of the presidency, and he wanted someone who could plausibly succeed to the office if need be. He knew, too, that the choice would reflect powerfully on him, for better or, as Bush could surely attest, for worse. To have his hired tacticians lead the hunt would be somehow to sully it—to make it seem one more in a series of political manipulations aimed simply at winning an election and not at some higher good.

In the event, Clinton took it largely out of the hands of his Hessians and entrusted it instead to a three-person search committee recruited from outside the campaign—Warren Christopher, an attorney and a longtime Democratic wise man; Madeleine Kunin, a three-term gover-nor of Vermont in the '80s, and Vernon Jordan, a civil-rights advocate turned Washington power lawyer. Clinton's first charge to them was to find him somebody qualified to be president, a standard bit of boilerplate that seemed, in his case, to be heartfelt. His second man-date was not to make the usual public spectacle of the process, running candidates past him on open view. "No parade," he told Christopher; there wouldn't be any Noah's ark routine this time.

A first scan produced an arkload of possibilities; when Christopher met with Clinton and a couple of aides in a Tallahassee hotel in April, he brought along a working list of forty names. All the usual suspects were there, the lords and ladies of the Democracy, along with a few wild-card choices from the private sector—men like Bill Moyers, the broadcast journalist, and John Sculley, the head of Apple Computer. To Clinton, the selection was a bit heavy with incumbent officeholders and light on daring. He directed Christopher to go find "three more Sculleys"—people of talent and vision who had made their reputations outside the government.

In the meantime, he pruned the working list quickly from forty names to fifteen. Sculley and Moyers made the cut. So did Gore and five fellow senators—Bill Bradley of New Jersey, Bob Graham of Flor-ida, John Kerry of Massachusetts, Sam Nunn of Georgia, and Jay Rockefeller of West Virginia. There were three sitting governors, Ann Richards of Texas, Barbara Roberts of Oregon, and Roy Romer of Colorado; one former governor, Bruce Babbitt of Arizona; one con-gressman, Lee Hamilton of Indiana; and one mayor, Maynard Jackson of Atlanta.

But the man who stirred the most excitement was General Colin Powell, the black super-achiever from Harlem who had served in the Reagan-Bush years as national-security adviser to the president and, more recently, as chairman of the joint chiefs of staff. His role explicating the Gulf war on television had made him a star overnight. He offered the perfect complement to Clinton in color, background, style, military service—he had had a wartime command in Vietnam—and experience at world affairs. No one knew his party preference and, in the heat of the moment, nobody cared. The idea had history written all over it, and Vernon Jordan, a man of great tact, was assigned to see if Powell was available.

The approach, as it happened, was not the first. In the spring of 1991, a delegation of Republican senators led by minority leader Bob Dole and his Kansas colleague, Nancy Kassebaum, had tried to interest the general in supplanting Dan Quayle on the Republican ticket for the good of the party. At a nod from him, they said, they were prepared to mount a draft-Powell movement and try to make it happen. The nod never came; as Dole told it later, Powell was all grins and smiles at being thus flattered, but he wasn't interested.

Jordan's feeler didn't tempt him, either, and his name was crossed off the list. Others soon followed. Bill Bradley was intrigued enough to meet with Christopher, a date he kept secret from his own staff; he walked around the idea, then said no thanks. So did Jay Rockefeller, whose wife, Sharon, was reluctant to give up her day job in public television. The real John Sculley was scratched when the search party discovered that he had been married three times; the hunt for others like him went on, without notable success. Other contenders were dropped or shuttled around among the A, B, and C lists. In this case, C could easily have stood for convenience; it was a parking space for people who *had* to be included for reasons of politics or affirmative action.

A team of lawyers did memos on each of the live prospects, the thickness of the dossiers varying according to their place in the standings; Gore's filled fifteen single-spaced pages, to one apiece for people on the C list. The search committee graded each candidate on several criteria, then bound the research into notebooks and forwarded it to Clinton. Within the next ten days, he sent back a stripped-down A list with four old names and three new ones: Al Gore, Bob Graham, Lee Hamilton, Sam Nunn, Mario Cuomo, Paul Tsongas, and Senator Harris Wofford of Pennsylvania.

Of the new lot, Cuomo was the most titillating to Clinton's people. They hadn't thought to include him at first, for all his high rank among the princes of the Democratic church; they simply presumed that his vanity and his staticky history with Clinton would make it next to impossible for him to say yes. But with his addition to the list, a boomlet stirred up in the ranks, one to which Clinton himself was not wholly immune. "I'd love to pick Cuomo," he said at a meeting with his senior staff in June, "for one reason—if you let me be in the room when they tell Dan Quayle."

It didn't work out; Cuomo said no and was duly struck from the short list. As in all important matters affecting himself, he was ambivalent, and, a bare five or six days before the choice was to be announced, he tried to get back into play. His agent in this was Ron Brown, who phoned Clinton from party headquarters to say that Cuomo was willing to be considered after all. But he didn't want to go through the same intensive investigation required of the other finalists, and even if he had been willing, there wasn't enough time. A thorough job would take more than a week, Christopher told Clinton, effectively ending the dalliance.

The list would stay fluid nearly to the end of the process. Tsongas took himself out of the running. Sam Nunn was dropped; his record on women's issues troubled Governor Kunin, and his lukewarm defense of Clinton in the Georgia primary had not been forgotten. Dick Gephardt, the House majority leader, and Senator Joseph Lieberman of Connecticut each floated briefly across the screen. Ann Richards, who had fallen off the list, got back on for a time. So did Bob Graham, a close friend of Clinton's; this time, he would last to the final cut. Bob Kerrey somehow crashed the party. Even Christopher got a look; the searcher, for a moment, became a searchee.

By late June, the shuffling and reshuffling had left what amounted to a Final Five for Clinton's scrutiny: Al Gore, Bob Graham, Lee Hamilton, Bob Kerrey, and Harris Wofford. Clinton, who pretended not to like polls but gobbled them up like Big Macs, had commissioned one on who could help him in the fall and who couldn't. The results were suggestive, though not so strongly as to tilt the table one way or another. Gore did well. Hamilton fared poorly, Graham not much better. Kerrey's numbers were only fair. Wofford, among the finalists, hadn't been included in the questionnaire; to insiders, his subsequent audience with Clinton had the look of a courtesy to a friend rather than a serious size-up for the vice presidency.

Within the campaign, a consensus was forming by then around Gore, who had been in Clinton's private top tier all along. His own presidential ambitions were well-known, and when Christopher first asked him if he was interested in being considered, he begged twenty-four hours to think about it; he had some fast calculations to make as to how his decision would affect his future prospects. His yes-look-me-over reply didn't allay all the doubts. Some of Clinton's people wondered whether Gore could *ever* adjust to playing second banana to another New Democrat from the New South. "Would he look in the mirror every day," one staffer wondered, "and say, '*I* should be president?'"

No problem, Gore insisted when the question was put to him; he ducked his head and labored on through the rigors of the screening process. The ground, mercifully, had been well plowed during his own campaign four years earlier. He submitted written answers to a dozen pages of questions about his finances and his medical history and endured a three-and-a-half-hour grilling by a squadron of lawyers. It was during that session that the gumshoes raised what had come to be known as the Eagleton Question, after the former Missouri senator who had neglected to inform *his* patron, George McGovern, that he had had electroshock treatments for depression. "Is there any problem you want to tell us about?" Gore was asked. His answer, unremarkable for so straight an arrow, was no.

Decision day was less than two weeks away when Gore was spirited down from the Hill to his secret meeting with Clinton, the first of the pretenders shown into the presence of the crown. Aides left them together and bowed discreetly out into the bedroom to wait. At midnight, the phone rang, and one of the staffers stepped into the sitting room to pass the message to Clinton. He found the two men afloat in wonk heaven, happily comparing the names of their favorite economists; they were plainly getting along just fine.

In the days that followed, the remaining contenders filed through the suite to stand inspection. Clinton himself was uncommonly tight-lipped about the process in his encounters with the press, and he instructed Gearan that he didn't want any of the candidates hung out on public view. The comings and goings were accordingly played out like scenes from a bad spy movie; the last time Lee Hamilton had seen security measures so tough, he told Gearan, was when he met with Colonel Muammar Kaddafi in a bunker in Libya.

The press, as it turned out, was more resourceful than the colonel's enemies. Only Gore slipped unseen through a tightening media cordon around the hotel; all the rest were spotted and recognized. By the time they arrived, the ladies and gentlemen of the press had staked out every entrance and exit, including the loading dock. It didn't take the posse there long to figure out the drill. Each time the garage door lowered behind Gearan's Jeep, reporters peeked underneath, checking out the shoe styles of his mystery guests. Failing all else, they could always cruise the hotel studying the feet of departing dignitaries, look-ing for the tell-tale Guccis.

The rank order of the finalists was roughly visible in the length of their respective audiences; Gore got three hours, Graham and Wofford two apiece, Hamilton one. The last in the procession, Bob Kerrey, had to follow Clinton to Little Rock and was booked for a sitting at the governor's mansion after midnight one night. Hearts sank among his well-wishers when they heard the time of his visit; the later the hour, the spacier Cosmic Bob tended to be.

The train by then was leaving the station anyway, with Al Gore seated alone in the first-class car. Clinton went over the paperwork on the contenders again and spoke several times with Christopher, one on one. Then, after dinner on the eve of the planned announcement, he and Hillary sat down with Christopher, Gearan, and Bruce Lindsey in a conference room in the mansion to review the bidding. The group shared Clinton's warm feelings for Senator Graham, but he remained the second choice; the night belonged instead to Gore. He made a comfortable match for Clinton in intellect and ideology. Hillary liked his deep commitment to environmental issues. A pairing of two men in their forties had strong generational appeal, and an all-southern ticket might just work, the old rules to the contrary notwithstanding; in a three-way race, the South would be a prime battleground.

The talk ran on till 11:30, when Clinton finally closed it down. "Okay," he said, "let's get him on the phone."

History still had to wait a moment; Lindsey said they had to have a photo of the occasion, and Clinton dashed upstairs to get his camera. One of the group dialed Gore's home in Carthage, Tennessee. The senator's wife, Tipper, took the call in their bedroom. Clinton asked apologetically if he had wakened her. He hadn't; the Gores, it turned out, had been sitting up waiting for the phone to ring.

When Gore came on the line, Clinton didn't pop the question immediately; instead, he tiptoed up to it with a long soliloquy about all the things he wanted to do if he won. "I just think you could be a wonderful president," he said suddenly; if it came to that, he wanted somebody who could carry on after him. Would Gore join him on the ticket? The instant answer was yes, and plans were laid to get the Gores to Little Rock in the morning.

What neither they nor anyone around them could have predicted was the raw, lightning-in-a-bottle electricity they would generate as a team. Four days before the party convention, they walked out onto the veranda of the mansion and stood side by side in the brilliant summer sunshine, with their wives and children—one Clinton and four Gores—

arrayed in a serried blond rank behind them. The tableau itself was a message, a potent visual promise of rejuvenation and change, and it set a charge of excitement coursing through the big crowd of spectators on the mansion grounds. It was as if one plus one somehow added up to four, a Clinton aide thought; the costars had more force together than either had ever had running alone.

The choice could have been called an inspired one, had anyone reckoned beforehand on its impact. No one had; even the pros in the crowd were brought up short by the power of the moment and by its instant impact in the polls. There was a marked movement of voters to Clinton, even before the weeklong glitzbath in Madison Square Garden. Choosing Gore, Mandy Grunwald thought in some wonderment, was the booster rocket that kicked Clinton's troubled candidacy to a newer, higher level. Only a few weeks before, he had seemed hopelessly earthbound. Now, if only the convention went according to plan, he could soar straight out of the Garden into orbit.

A Garden Party

A party convention, in modern politics, is like the dinosaur room at a natural-history museum—a reliquary of the life forms of a bygone age. With each new election year, the courtiers and scribes of politics wove their dream scenarios of deadlock on the floor and nominations brokered in back rooms. Our recent past suggested that it wasn't going to happen—that the spoils belonged instead to the victor in the primaries and caucuses. By 1992, it had been more than a generation since a convention could be said to have actually chosen a nominee on its own or even to have gone to a second ballot. The role of the assembled delegates instead was to serve as extras in the crowd scenes and finally to arrive at a long foregone conclusion.

But the gathering remained a powerful showplace for the winner, one long infomercial spread over four evenings of free prime television time, and Bill Clinton flung himself at it as hungrily as a starving man at a banquet table. His coronation speech on closing night, as his man Stan Greenberg reminded him in a memo, would be the last time he would have the stage and the spotlight all to himself; he would have roughly an hour in which to recreate his wounded candidacy. Clinton understood the stakes, given all the unfunny things that had happened to him on the way to the forum. He flogged his speechwriters. He bounced draft after draft. He fussed over every word as if it might be his last in politics. "I want this to be uplifting," he told his scriveners. "I want an exciting sense of rhythm. I want this to *hum.*"

In his preconvention memo, Greenberg had accurately described the scale and the importance of the task before them. Clinton was then still in third place, with 27 percent of the vote, but he was closing fast, and he could move up dramatically if the convention achieved two goals. "First," Greenberg wrote, "we must show that Bill Clinton is a man of good values who believes in something. He is not merely a politician who will do and say anything to get elected. . . . Second, we must put our marker down on why we are running for president, how we will change the country. Bill Clinton will put people first again." Everything that happened in the Garden had to serve those two ends. "We dare not miss this opportunity," Greenberg warned. "It will not come again."

Finding a way to convey what he stood for was no longer a problem; they had the makings of a powerful message in the charge that the government had failed the people in the Reagan-Bush years and had put the great middle class last rather than first. The question was still whether people would be willing to listen to Clinton, given what they thought they knew about him. His image had deteriorated since the New York primary, Greenberg wrote; a majority of the electorate "does not now like Bill Clinton very much," and no more than half would even consider supporting him. The Perot vote by then was dwindling, but some of the strays didn't trust Clinton enough to choose him as an alternative to Bush. "We have to give these voters a reason to like and gain confidence in Bill Clinton," Greenberg said. "Right now, Bush enjoys an advantage over Clinton on moral standards, honesty, steady leadership and trust."

The free-media offensive of June had made at least a beginning at Clinton's rehabilitation; in Greenberg's last poll before the convention, he had clawed his way back to a statistical dead heat with his two adversaries, and his choice of Gore had added to his momentum. But the underlying doubts lingered, and the pressure on him and his command to put on a good convention grew accordingly. The show had to be a four-night celebration of Clinton, beginning with who he was and only then moving on to what he stood for. To his own distress, his biography, not his program, became the most important single message out of New York—a token that he was, after all, worth America's attention.

The weeklong buildup to his big moment was the kind of pageant the Republicans had put on in the Age of Ron—a living tableau drained of anything so untidy as suspense or conflict. One by one, the last holdouts, all but Jerry Brown, were persuaded to endorse Clinton as the price of speaking time in the evening viewing hours, when the network TV cameras were on. Tsongas broke off a brief flirtation with Perot and bought in. So did Doug Wilder; while his handlers were making a last, desperate play to get him the second spot on the Perot ticket, he swallowed his ill feelings and his pride and came out for his own party's nominee. Jesse Jackson slipped under the tent, without putting Clinton through the usual ritual of having to beg. Brown's asking price was higher; he wanted not only prime time but Clinton's agreement to a limit on campaign contributions. Clinton refused.

The show America saw was buttery-smooth and even, at moments, moving. Keeping a campaign promise, Clinton blocked out part of one evening for a presentation on the AIDS crisis, with two infected people witnessing to its devastation. One was Bob Hattoy, an openly gay young adviser to the campaign who had lately developed full-blown AIDS; the other, added for balance, was Elizabeth Glaser, who had got the virus from a tainted blood transfusion. Jerry Brown was on the phone haggling with Clinton when Hattoy came on screen. Clinton hung up in mid-conversation, drew up a straight-backed chair to the TV in his suite at the Intercontinental Hotel, and watched intently, chin in hand. "He's doing so well," he said. Occasionally, he wiped away a tear, and when Glaser followed Hattoy to the lectern, great sobs shook his body. In an easy chair nearby, Hillary wept silently. Toward the end, Chelsea came in from her room and curled into her father's lap. She knew Hattoy. Clinton hugged her tight.

"At least I did *something* right with my convention," he told the others in the room.

His own speech obsessed him, occupying his days with a restless search for the words that would somehow win over his chary countrymen. Paul Begala had been put in charge of the drafting process and had steeped himself in the literature, studying past acceptance speeches for guidance. But Clinton never just read a speech handed him by somebody else; it was his habit instead to keep rewriting it up to the moment he was to deliver it, and the bigger the occasion, the more the perfectionist in him came out.

The early drafts displeased him with their heavy accent on populism. "This rhetoric is too clangy," Clinton told Begala and his team on opening day, rejecting their latest try. "It's too class-war. It's too much divide-the-pie and not enough upbeat growth. It's too much about correcting the injustices of the Republicans and not enough about a better tomorrow. There's a lot of blame-placing, and it doesn't have what I've said before—that I don't care whose fault it is, I just want to do something about it." He wanted words that soared. "I know how this rhetoric would go over at the Kiwanis Club in Clarksville, Arkansas," he said, and he didn't mean well.

There were more rewrites, more crumpled balls of paper on hotel-room floors. At one point, Begala gave up for a couple of hours in frustration and walked a few blocks uptown to Saint Patrick's Cathedral; there, he lit a candle and said a prayer. If his hope was for divine intervention, it didn't come, not that day. The speech was still a mess when he dragged himself back to it, and Clinton was going into rehearsals, standing behind a mocked-up podium in a campaign suite without a finished script to practice on.

The ante had gone up, moreover, with the sudden upward spike in Clinton's poll numbers. His bounce from the convention had started earlier and reached higher than anyone had expected. By Tuesday, Stan Greenberg's tracking showed him alone in first place; on Wednesday, an ABC News survey put him at 45 percent, to 28 for Bush and just 20 for Perot.

It was a little unsettling. "Governor," Stephanopoulos said, interrupting a rehearsal, "I've got some good news and some bad news. You're up seventeen points."

Behind his practice lectern, Clinton buried his head in his hands. "I think our people have got to downplay those numbers," he said.

"We didn't pay much attention to them when they were bad," Stephanopoulos said, trying out a line of spin. "We won't now that they're good."

"Though I'd rather be seventeen points up than down," Clinton admitted. A smile briefly lit his face, then faded. "I don't even want to hear that crap," he said. He preferred that the arc of the campaign look like that of a sweet tee shot in golf, starting low, then taking off and streaking skyward. He had been the front-runner once, then had fallen back; so now had Perot, under rising attack from the Republicans and the press. Being out front had its dangers, and Clinton got mock plaintive just thinking about it. "I don't want to be a target again," he said.

His speech by that point was starting to come together, even by his own exacting standards. "It's gettin' there," he had said after a first run-through that morning. "I stayed up all night worrying about it. This is a speech you give on the balls of your feet, not sitting on your butt." He read it again and was even happier. "This speech has got some *legs*," he added. "This is a girl I'll take to the dance."

What pleased him most, predictably, was the issues part; it was as if his people-first economic plan had finally fused with the preachier themes of his New Covenant speeches and come out one coherent whole for the first time. He was less thrilled with the passages of personal revelation, which kept creeping upward from the bottom of the speech toward the top. Until he declared for president, he had never had to talk in public about having grown up in a troubled family, and he still felt uncomfortable with it; it seemed to him "narcissistic" to go on so about himself. "Go back to Roosevelt," he complained. "Or John Kennedy—he didn't talk about *his* life."

The game, of course, had changed since then, as Begala tried to tell him. The old wise men of journalism, sages like Joseph Alsop and James Reston, had been tastemakers with a more rigorous sense of the public interest. But they weren't setting the rules of play anymore. The new arbiters of our public life were Oprah and Phil, *People* and *Geraldo* and *Hard Copy*. Their business was the private lives of public figures, and if you didn't get personal about yourself, they would do it for you—or, more accurately, *to* you.

Intellectually, Clinton understood all that; he recognized that people would have to get to know him before they would trust him with the presidency. But his unquiet with it remained and to a degree even spoiled his pleasure in the film biography that would precede him to the stage on closing night. The movie was the work of Linda Bloodworth-Thomason, an old Arkansas friend who had made it big in the TV sitcom business as the creator of *Designing Women* and *Evening Shade*. She had shot hundreds of hours of interviews with the Clintons and their circle and had stitched together a rich court portrait of the nominee, one that powdered over his warts but did not try to hide them. It opened with a grainy black and white shot of the old railroad station in Hope, Arkansas, and came back there at the end. "I still believe in America," Clinton's voice said, "and I still believe in a place called Hope."

As political propaganda, the film was a three-hankie masterwork. "Wow!" Hillary said, previewing a rough cut through flooded eyes. Clinton, too, was moved to tears when he caught up with it. "It's *good*," he said hoarsely. "That's *stout* at the end." But partly on his objection, a segment on Vietnam was edited out, for fear it would simply reopen the whole subject. He was nearly as troubled by the references in the movie to his difficult boyhood and to the problems in his marriage; it was all so personal, so invasive, when what he wanted to talk about was the ills of America and their solution. "I hate all this stuff," he complained. "This is not what American politics should be about."

Still, he resigned himself to it and, from the distance of his hotel suite, watched the march of the convention toward the hour he had dreamed of all his life. He had got Mario Cuomo to place his name in nomination, with yet another big assist from Ron Brown. As in all things, Cuomo was hesitant, giving in only when the party chairman made it a personal matter. "You were my law professor," said Brown, who had studied under Cuomo at Saint John's University in the '60s. "You were my *mentor.*" He was calling the chit for himself and their party, and Cuomo finally relented.

His intentions were another matter; his relations with Clinton had been scratchy, and there was no telling what he might do once he got to the rostrum. The advance word, relayed by an aide who had once worked for Cuomo, was that Clinton would be very happy with the speech. But Cuomo wouldn't send Clinton's people an advance copy for vetting, and the jitter level in their command bunker remained high. What would Mario *say?* Would he sound enthusiastic, as if he really meant it? Would he try to undercut Clinton on some policy question on which they disagreed?

There was a tingle of anxiety in the Clinton suite that evening when Cuomo came on. Tom Caplan, an FOB dating to their student days together at Georgetown, had sent for champagne so they could toast the moment of Clinton's formal nomination. The feast of celebration consisted otherwise of standard room-service fare, pasta for Hillary, a side of fries for Bill; his friend Bruce Lindsey had eaten the accompanying burger, thinking it was his. The also-rans of spring were on TV, doing their valedictories and their obeisances to the winner. When Tsongas finished, there was applause in the suite. Paul, Clinton said, was "a class act."

Then Cuomo came on, and as he began speaking, the people in the room began to breathe again. The speech was a barn burner, as promised, and its adulation for Clinton was unrestrained; at the thought of the wonders he would work, Cuomo exclaimed, "I want to clap my hands and throw my fists in the air." When he placed Clinton's name in nomination, applause once again filled the hotel sitting room. At its center, Clinton sat shaking his head in silent wonder. "I never thought I'd live to see this," he said; he was a roll call away from his dream.

One of his advance parties found Cuomo afterward on the Garden floor and put him on the phone to Clinton.

"Oh, Mario," Clinton said. "Thank you."

"I gave it just the way you wrote it," Cuomo joked, "except I left out the part about how handsome you are."

Clinton laughed. "God, it was wonderful," he said. "I'll never forget it."

"I'm a good lawyer, like you," Cuomo said. "I can make up a case when I have to. Tonight I didn't."

As the balloting began, all three Clintons left to look in at a party of Arkansas supporters at Macy's and to walk the two blocks from there to the Garden for the final votes putting him over the top. The "impromptu" visit had been dreamed up by a Hollywood producer, Mort Engelberg, and had been meticulously planned by Clinton's handlers, down to the positioning of camera crews to capture every step of the stroll on live TV. The national party fought the idea; it just wasn't done—not, anyway, since John Kennedy paid a call on his convention in Los Angeles in 1960—and the logistics of getting Clinton safely to the hall looked daunting. But the campaign finally got its way. The photo op was irresistible, a walking apotheosis of the young prince and his family. The network night was flooded with images of their royal progress, intercut with pictures of the crowd inside the Garden cheering their coming.

Clinton wakened early the next morning and went for a jog in the muggy heat; his voice was disappearing again, and the exercise, along with copious amounts of water, seemed to help. Then he returned to the dining room in his suite and went back to work on his speech, still dressed in his red shorts, blue T-shirt, and running shoes. He was in his usual mortal combat with his writers, wanting to cram in more ideas on more issues than one speech could hold. The one restraining voice he would listen to in such circumstances was Hillary's, and she occasionally gave a little tug on the reins.

He was still pushing words around when Carville burst in, flushed with excitement. "AP is reporting that Perot is dropping out," he said.

The news was not a total surprise; a friendly television journalist with good sources in Perot's circle had alerted them early in the week that it might be coming and had warned them against including anything harsh about Perot in the speech. Still, the suddenness of it was heart-stopping. The whole terrain of the race had changed, and they were like strangers on it, trying to find their way around.

"*Damn!*" Clinton said, not wanting it to happen so soon. "Ross Perot is my main man."

"Just hammer this speech home and they'll *all* drop out," Carville told him.

"Whoa, whoa," Clinton said. "If he drops out, we've got to make a special appeal to his voters."

The two of them began working on language.

"God, this is awful," Clinton said, this time with the bare beginnings of a smile. "I don't want Ross Perot to drop out."

They were still contemplating their good fortune when the latest numbers from Greenberg's tracking poll reached them. Clinton was smashing Bush, 58-38, in what was now a two-man race.

"If I get up twenty-one points," Clinton said, by now laughing, "I can drop as far as Dukakis did and still win."

They moved into the living room to watch Perot's press conference. More aides drifted in. Clinton stood in front of the TV set, gazing from his own new eminence at the tableau of defeat unfolding on the screen.

"He looks like he's in a lot of pain," he said.

"Butter him up, baby," Carville crowed. "He's *toast!*"

"Shut up, Carville," Clinton said. Perot was going out with style, in part, he said, because the Democratic Party had "revitalized" itself in New York. All around Clinton, people were clapping. He just stood there, shaking his head. God—it was *incredible.*

"Call him right now," he ordered. "Get him."

Stephanopoulos headed for a phone. Perot was taking questions, speaking again of the great Democratic revivification.

"Yeah!" Clinton said, punching the air with one fist.

"Goddam!" Carville whooped.

Somebody asked Perot if the race had stopped being fun for him.

"Shoot," Clinton said, "it ain't *never* gonna be fun every day."

The press had laid siege to the hotel lobby, clamoring for Clinton's reaction. What could he say?

"No political analysis," Carville warned, stalking around the room. People hated that, coming from Clinton. Better just to put out a statement over his name, a hail and farewell to a rival departing from the field.

"He's a genuine patriot," Clinton said, still watching Perot on the screen. "I am very moved. I'm deeply impressed by what he said. I am going to reach out to his people."

"Governor, you're an unbelievable optimist," Carville answered. "He spent $10 million, and he didn't want any more to go down the crapper."

"It's called spin," Mandy Grunwald said of Perot's exit speech.

But Clinton took it to heart; it was easiest for him, as for any politician, to be magnanimous when it was the other guy crying uncle. Yes, he had had some "problems" with things Perot had been saying about him, but, he said, "I got to tell you—I was pretty touched."

Stan Greenberg walked in. The press pack downstairs had worked itself into a frenzy. They would have to say something.

"Paper, no faces," Grunwald said, seconding Carville's warning. If they sent a live body down to the lobby, the mob would demand political answers to political questions.

"No human beings," Mickey Kantor agreed. "We're about to give the biggest speech of our life. This is not our story."

The suite was crowding up with aides and advisers, most of them wandering the living room in a communal daze. Only Hillary seemed to have her eye firmly fixed on the prize. "Okay, gang, we can't do anything about *Pea*-row," she said, pronouncing the name as the Perots had until Ross Frenchified it. "The speech is more important. Their leader told them this is a revitalized Democratic Party. We got to show them what it means."

Stephanopoulos, still working the phone, found Al Gore and put Clinton on. "You were my choice in a three-person race," he said, teasing, "but in a two-person race, I've got to go with Cuomo."

Next on the line was Perot. Clinton took the call in the living room, sitting on one arm of a couch. The Texan was gracious, extending his congratulations.

"I was really moved by what you said," Clinton told him. "No one in American history ever moved as many people as you did—no one running an independent campaign." He suggested that he and Gore come down to Dallas for a visit—"if you'd let us," he added quickly. "I just don't want you to lose your interest in being involved in this process. I still think we have a chance to transform this country this year."

"I got to get away from this for awhile," Perot said. That meant no face-to-face meeting any time soon; instead, he suggested that Clinton go directly to the Perot voters and volunteers, state by state, and invite them to join him. But he seemed oddly unconfident that any of it would come to anything, given the scale of the problems facing the country. "My one fear," he said, "is that you're going to win, and this economy will collapse next year. It took twelve years to get into this mess, and it's going to take twelve years to get out."

Clinton seemed touched by the conversation. "He's emotional," he said afterward. "You can imagine—he's human, too."

Hillary finally got him back to his speech; as his aides had long since come to understand, she was the only person around who could make him do something he didn't really feel like doing. He gathered his writers and labored through what would have to be a last draft. Hillary gave him a new closing line, echoing the coda to the film biography. "'I end tonight where it all began for me,'" she said. "'I still believe in a place called Hope.'"

When they had finally finished, Clinton and his entourage headed for the Garden and the touched-up locker room where he would wait to go on. An aide set up the nebulizer that followed him everywhere, and he sat hunched over it, breathing in steam to revive his whispery voice.

"So, George, did you think we'd be here tonight?" he asked Stephanopoulos.

"I've got to say, governor, I didn't," Stephanopoulos said.

"Who'd you think would win?" Clinton asked.

"Kerrey," Stephanopoulos confessed.

"I thought I would win if they didn't take me out," Clinton said. "I knew they couldn't beat me head-up."

On TV, the band struck up Paul Simon's "You Can Call Me Al," and Gore made his entrance. Clinton clapped in time with the music and beamed at the big crowd response in the hall.

"I did good," he said. "To have someone who is smart, who thinks like you, who has done something—it's a big deal. I'm so proud I did that."

His own speech ran overtime, unsurprisingly for him; he spoke for nearly an hour. But this time, he didn't wander off-message or lose his audience. According to plan, he started with a walk through the story of his life, using it effectively for the first time as a prelude to and a matrix for his campaign promises. "In the name of all those who do the work, pay the taxes, raise the kids, and play by the rules, in the name of the hardworking Americans who make up our forgotten middle class, I proudly accept your nomination for president of the United States," he said. "I am a product of that middle class. And when I am president, you will be forgotten no more."

His public offering was "a new approach to government" unlike anything people were accustomed to hearing from more traditional Democrats. "We've got some changing to do," Clinton told his party. "There is not a program in government for every problem. And if we really want government to help people, we've got to make it work again." He hit the notes he had been tickling all year—opportunity, responsibility, community, a New Covenant between the government and the governed—and this time made a chord of them. "We offer our people a new choice based on old values," he said. "The choice we offer is not conservative or liberal; in many ways, it's not even Republican or Democratic. It is different. It is new. And it will work."

Measured by the polls, as all things are in modern politics, the show and the speech were grand successes. It was as if, by some magic of validation, Slick Willie had died in New York and Clinton had been born again. For the first time in months, his favorable ratings were higher than his negatives; by majority verdict, the New Clinton was Middle America personified—a steady, sincere family man who had worked hard for everything he had achieved in life and could be trusted to lead the country. Hillary, too, was borne upward on the tide; her image crossed the line from negative to positive and would stay there for the rest of the campaign.

The triumph was one of art, not yet of substance. It troubled Stan Greenberg that Clinton's new popularity had everything to do with who he was and hardly at all with what he proposed to do as president. There was time, of course, to get his ideas out, and a sizable majority of voters were now willing to grant him their attention. But Clinton himself wore the aspect of a mountain climber who had labored for a year just to get to Base Camp One. Before he left New York, he and Hillary watched a video strung together by Linda Bloodworth-Thomason in comic celebration of his victory. The players on-screen were all the politicians and pundits who, at various times in the primary season, had confidently pronounced him dead. The background music was the voice of Frank Sinatra, crooning, "Who's got the last laugh now?"

Laughs came hard to Clinton in his exhaustion; he managed only a weak smile. "I'd feel a lot better if this was the last day of the election and I saw that," he said. Instead, it was only the first day, and, Clinton realized, "it's going to be awful. Those people don't want to give up power."

A game of cards: The Clintons on a campaign flight. *(Ira Wyman)*

A council of war: George Stephanopoulos, Stan Greenberg, James Carville, Paul Begala. *(Ira Wyman)*

The golden boy: Bob Kerrey courting voters. *(Larry Downing/Newsweek)*

The olden boy: Tom Harkin prospecting for air time. *(Jacques Chenet/ Newsweek)*

The rebel: Jerry Brown on the trail. The guru: Jacques Barzaghi in
(*Jacques Chenet/Newsweek*) gear. (*Larry Downing/Newsweek*)

The shadow: Uncandidate Mario Cuomo receiving candidate Brown.
(*Jacques Chenet/Newsweek*)

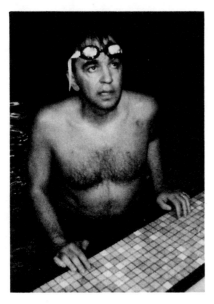 

First in: Paul Tsongas in the swim. First out: Doug Wilder in thought.
(Jacques Chenet/Newsweek) *(Ira Wyman)*

Forty winks: Tsongas catching a nap on his charter jet. *(Jacques Chenet/ Newsweek)*

The visiting professor: A campaign stop in a schoolroom. *(Jacques Chenet/Newsweek)*

The road warriors: Brown, Clinton, and Tsongas at a debate. *(Jacques Chenet/Newsweek)*

The Ragin' Cajun:
James Carville in
full battle dress.
(Ira Wyman)

A strategy session: Clinton with Stephanopoulos, Carville, Greenberg, Frank Greer, and Dee Dee Myers. *(Ira Wyman)*

A civics lesson: The candidate lecturing Phil Donahue on sticking to the issues. *(Ira Wyman)*

On tour: A walking talk with Paul Begala and George Stephanopoulos. *(Ira Wyman)*

Off stage: A corridor huddle with Stephanopoulos and Mandy Grunwald. *(Ira Wyman)*

III

The President

*What is the use of being elected or reelected
unless you stand for something?*
—Grover Cleveland, to his
handlers, 1887

14.

Where Was George?

The president was dressing for a speech to a $1,000-a-chicken-breast fund-raising dinner in Houston on Halloween, 1991 when his press secretary, Marlin Fitzwater, sent him a story from the day's harvest of wire-service cuttings. Bush scanned it. He had taken yet another partisan shot, this one from Senate Democratic leader George Mitchell, for his seemingly untroubled view of America's economic distress. The charge that he was doing too little to put things right was routine stuff, even for a man as thin-skinned as the president; the bolder of his advisers were telling him as much, in terms more polite but no less urgent. What put Senator Mitchell's comments over the top was that he had likened Bush to Herbert Hoover.

Till then, Bush had ignored repeated warnings to come out fighting for his presidency or risk losing it; it was a measure of his resistance, and his team's growing frustration, that they felt it necessary to use guile to move him where open diplomacy had failed. This time, the ploy worked. The president was steaming nicely when he and Fitzwater encountered one another an hour later in a holding room at the Sheraton Astrodome hotel.

"Well, Marlin," Bush said, his smile veiling his anger, "you're trying to cause trouble by showing me this before dinner."

"I was trying to get you fired up, sir," Fitzwater answered, smiling back.

"One of these days, we're gonna have to get into this," Bush said, heading for the dais.

By "this," he meant politics, and he did get into it for one rare time that night, to electric effect. The event, before he went on, had bordered on disaster. The night was cold, the local economy sour, and enthusiasm low for writing checks to the homeboy president. A large empty space yawned at one end of the ballroom, where a dozen tables had gone unsold, and the open display of passion was as wanting as at a symposium on semiotics. The audience barely feigned interest in the warm-up speeches. "It's called quiet confidence," a young advance man wisecracked unhappily, but the silence was nearer somnolence. Even Dan Quayle, normally a fair speaker on partisan occasions, seemed bent on wet-blanketing the crowd with the thoughts of "two of my favorite historians—Will and Ariel Durant."

Desperate eyes met across the White House staff table. Forget that the president was at least nominally a local hero; the first fund-raising event for Bush/Quayle '92 was a distinct dud.

"When I clap, you clap," Fitzwater whispered to a colleague in the mausoleum hush. "We've gotta start this baby moving."

They couldn't; it was Bush, to their surprise and delight, who started it moving without any help. He came on forty minutes late, and his hold on the language was, as usual, insecure; speaking of one piece of pending social legislation, he complained that the Democrats "want to ram it down my ear." But in the end, his sulfurous anger saved the day. He junked most of the flaccid script his handlers had written for him and proceeded to scorch the sauce jardiniere with a shrill, podium-thumping attack on the "small-bore" partisan criticism he had to endure every day. "Come on!" he cried. "We have a responsibility here. I have a responsibility to lead, and I'm not going to let Democratic, liberal carping keep me from leading." Why, if he had followed the advice of handwringers like Ted Kennedy, he said, "Saddam Hussein would still be in Kuwait. . . . Thank God I didn't have to listen to these carpers telling me how to run that war!"

His scheduled ten-minute speech ran on to thirty, much of it delivered at a near shriek. The crowd loved it. "Guess *I'm* gonna have to be the nice guy in this campaign," John Sununu, the famously unnice White House chief of staff, joked to his tablemates; the president plainly would supply the anger.

"Marlin, you made me do it," Bush told Fitzwater afterward.

"No, I'm innocent," Fitzwater protested.

"I just got tired of being a placid punching bag for those guys," Bush said.

The Least Happy Fella

The president's ardor for battle cooled again in the days thereafter, as if it had been no more than a twenty-four-hour virus and he had got over it. Bush had never been a very happy warrior anyway. Politics, to him, was what broccoli had been in his boyhood, something you had to get through if you wanted dessert. His small appetite for it had been further dulled by the pasting he had taken for the nastiness of his 1988 campaign; it had become one of the trials of his presidency to be so often reminded of how meanly he had won it.

His distaste for an encore was an open secret, even to relative strangers. "Are you a glutton for punishment?" he asked one surprised campaign-management recruit who had been marched round to meet him during the summer of '91. "I'm not looking forward to this." Thanks to Bush, there was not then a campaign to be managed. He much preferred holding office to the grubby business of seeking it. There had been days in all his campaigns when he had the air of a rich man slumming and not enjoying it very much. By start-up time for 1992, dislike had become dread, or so it appeared to his friends. Merely to declare his candidacy, in his mind, was to cross the line from statesman to beggar, and he refused to be rushed into it. "Everybody's always in a hurry," he complained one day. Everybody, that is, except him; it was important to his self-esteem to be thought a steady man, even when steadiness meant paralysis and became a vice.

There had been a time when he had wondered seriously whether he should run at all—whether his continuing in office would impose too large a burden on his family. Several of his brothers and sons had come under scrutiny for their business dealings, and while his wife had become a kind of national icon, their life at the top had not been entirely easy for her. She had watched the office age Bush, as it did all presidents. She had been witness to the daily slights and disloyalties directed against him and had taken them hard—harder, some thought, than the president. She had endured the whispers that he had been unfaithful to her, a tale that had shaken the markets for a day during the 1988 campaign on the mere rumor that it was about to see print. Her feelings about it and its effect on their marriage were her secret, but in the new world order of journalism, there was no guarantee that it would not be raised again in 1992.

Her larger reservations about a second term were well-known to her friends. She could, as she often told them, live just as easily without the perks or the cares of the White House. Her ambivalence had deepened when, in the spring of 1991, Bush's heart had gone into a scary and briefly disabling flutter. The problem was quickly traced to Graves' disease, a thyroid condition she too suffered, and the pills that remedied the problem overcame her last line of resistance. Running again had always been George's decision, not hers, she told her chums. She had deferred to his wishes in business and politics all their lives, and she wasn't going to meddle now. His choice would be okay with her, either way.

Bush had always known that she would be with him; his misgivings

centered on his children. An old friend who had joined him trolling for
bluefish off Walker's Point in Maine one sunny morning in 1990 found
the president's mood curiously out of joint with the beauty of the
setting and the brilliance of the day. What had set him off, he said, was
an ugly story in a Texas paper questioning his motives for mobilizing
to drive Saddam out of Kuwait. The article implied that he was doing
it because his eldest son, George W., had business interests in Bahrain
in need of protection from a widening war.

But his more urgent concern was for his third boy, Neil, who had
got entangled in a messy savings-and-loan scandal in Colorado. The
press had pilloried him, and the legal fees had cleaned him out.
Would that have happened if he weren't the president's son? Bush
didn't think so.

"The Neil thing is really bothering me," he said. "My heart aches
for my son."

His companion protested that Neil seemed to be getting his life
back together, and that Bush in any case had a higher duty to his
country to run again.

Irritation flashed in the president's eyes. "It's my flesh and blood
whose life I'm affecting," he said.

The issue was settled that Christmas, when Bush gathered the clan
at Camp David and polled them informally about his seeking reelection. "Dad," his second son, Jeb, told him, "the world needs you."
There were no dissenters, not Barbara, not Neil. The family consensus
was, go for it.

Even then, the president dawdled. Active planning for Ronald Reagan's reelection had begun a year and a half before Election Day, and
the outcome then had been a nearly foregone conclusion. Bush, by
contrast, had let the seasons slide away without so much as beginning
to put together a campaign command. He missed the people who had
run the show for him in 1988—Lee Atwater, the demon attack strategist, dead of brain cancer at forty; Roger Ailes, the ad man, reduced at
his own wish and his wife's to kibitzing by phone from New York;
Jimmy Baker, the boss of bosses, busy elsewhere being secretary of
state and securing his own place in the presidential line of succession.
A new set of handlers—suits, as Ailes used to call them—would materialize once Bush announced, and he dreaded their arrival. Just be
yourself, they would tell him, except—ah—the vacation time in Maine;
it reminded people too vividly of his blue bloodline and their own
travail.

Through the summer and early fall, aides and friends did what they
could to get him engaged with the reality of his situation; the first and,

some thought, fatal mistake of his candidacy was his tardiness getting it started. An old pal encountered him one day on a receiving line at the White House. It was August. The clock was running. Nothing was in place. Not even Bob Teeter, the putative top hand, had had what he called The Conversation with the president.

"Are you about ready to give us some work to do?" Bush's chum asked.

"Sooner or later," Bush replied. "I don't see any reason to do anything now. Do you?"

The unspoken answer was yes, but not even intimates found it easy to be blunt with a president. Instead, they entered a conspiracy of indirection, a flutter of hints, leaks, and discreet soundings of his moods and humors. The caballing was transparent, and Bush saw through it. At cocktails one evening, a longtime confidant asked him—innocently, as it happened—if he had been giving any thought to the campaign.

Bush studied his friend over the rim of his martini glass. "Who put you up to this?" he demanded.

His own plan, stubbornly held, was to field an organization in January and to declare his candidacy a month later. When he submitted to a midsummer day's political retreat at Camp David, it was, as he let on privately, a way to get everybody off his back; otherwise, they would have spoiled his August getaway in Maine with their tiresome nagging.

For the three dozen people he invited, the half-day conclave in Laurel Lodge was memorable for what didn't get said or done. Bush set the tone and the boundaries up front, indicating that his real purpose was to let everybody ventilate. He had no agenda, or even, at that point, a candidacy to be planned; there was thus no point talking strategy or organization.

"I haven't made any decisions," Bush said. "I wouldn't waste your time if I knew I wasn't running. I expect I will, but I haven't made up my mind yet."

Glances flicked meaningfully around the conference table. Bush's mode was avoidance; he grudgingly agreed to a start-up fund-raising operation, but there seemed to him to be no point war-gaming an election fifteen months away. The economy would be decisive, and in his insistent opinion, it would soon get better by itself.

It didn't, nor did the president's sinking fortunes. By mid-autumn, Bush's job rating had tumbled nearly twenty points in six weeks, and America's unhappiness with itself was rising toward levels unknown in the worst days of Richard Nixon and Jimmy Carter. Only Bush seemed ignorant of the depth of the disquiet. He was sure the people still liked him, and as one of his top aides confessed in the waning days of 1991, no one around him had had the nerve to tell him otherwise.

What he needed to know and didn't, in this aide's view, was that the war in the desert, politically speaking, was over. The economy had become the battleground, and it was worsening. Bush was now the guy who had said "read my lips" to get himself elected and then had raised taxes. He had become part of the problem. The people, as his man put it, were finally pissed off at *him*.

There had been portents of danger in that autumn's by-elections, a wave of revulsion against incumbents of either party. David Duke had run for governor of Louisiana, calling himself a Republican, and had made it to a runoff before losing; the near miss was a profound embarrassment to the president and his party. And with Richard Thornburgh's defeat for senator in Pennsylvania, the tide of antiestablishment feeling had hit frighteningly close to home. Thornburgh, the challenger, had been perceived as the incumbent in the race—and as a close enough match for the president in thought and style to have been his clone.

Bush's responses to adversity had the look of panic; for a time, it was almost as if having read his lips was the *least* reliable guide to his intentions. He did dizzying U-turns on civil rights, unemployment benefits, and a Morning-Again-Again economic package put forward by the surviving Reagan revolutionaries on the Hill; he would reject them one day and embrace them, without apparent embarrassment, the next. A long-planned mission to Tokyo and other Asian ports of call was abruptly scrubbed the night Thornburgh crashed and burned in Pennsylvania. The tour reappeared on the president's schedule two months later, but only after it had been clumsily repackaged as a quest for jobs, jobs, jobs back home; the New World Order had become one more casualty of hard times.

The hip-hop dance across the stage of public policy made a bad start for Bush's campaign; it reinforced a new complaint, beginning to be heard from voters in Steeper's focus groups, that maybe the president *did* change his mind too much. His numbers were still sliding, to a level ten points lower than where Bob Teeter had hoped and thought they would be on the eve of battle. His own people were muttering darkly that, as one put it, they could *lose* this thing if the president didn't get the fuck in the game.

Bush finally did begin to sense his jeopardy and to understand that he could not hang back much longer. But there was a painful matter he had to address first, a canker of discontent that had bedeviled his presidency and was stalling his campaign. He had to do something about John Sununu. Nothing was going to happen until Bush squared up to the problems Sununu was causing him, and as he was reluctantly coming to realize, the only way to fix them was to make them go away.

Invitation to a Hanging

Bush had always hated confrontation, and when he finally moved on Sununu, he did it his way: with dragging foot and hidden hand. The device he chose after much delay was a letter, privately dispatched on the last day of October, 1991, to the eight or ten men who made up his privy council in politics. "I have asked son George to very quietly make some soundings for me on 1992," he began. "I'd appreciate it if you'd visit with him on your innermost thoughts about how to best structure the campaign."

Their responses would be held strictly confidential, he promised; he had instructed young George, the most politically adept of his four sons, not to communicate their views to anybody but him. "My plan," he went on, "is still to wait—defer final campaign structural decisions until after the first of the year at least; but there seems to be a fair amount of churning around out there." He hoped his friends would speak freely, though he would understand, he said, if some had qualms. What he needed, he said, was "the unvarnished, frank views of my most trusted political confidants" about what had to be done to get his earthbound campaign off the ground.

Bush had chosen his words carefully and had made sure that Sununu was included on the eyes-only distribution list; on its face, the letter looked like a routine request for advice. In fact, it was more nearly an invitation to a hanging. The president didn't really need to be told how his people felt about Sununu; half the cabinet had been intriguing for months to get him fired, and the core members of the Bush-Quayle campaign-to-be were muttering that they didn't want to work with him. But the president preferred not to have his signature alone on the execution warrant, if there was to be one. He was in effect soliciting a vote of no confidence, a don't-blame-me consensus of the troops that Sununu had to go.

Using his son as channeler was his way of providing cover for himself as well. People sometimes had a hard time being frank with him, he told an old friend over drinks a couple of weeks after the letter went out. He was accordingly depending on George W.'s reconnaissance tour to get them talking.

"I think I can use that as my rationale to do some things I need to do," he said.

"If you're comfortable with John Sununu," his friend told him, catching Bush's drift, "we're all ready to help him. If you're not comfortable with John, you should not spend another day agonizing."

Bush said nothing. But his growing discomfort with Sununu was well-known among his people; they counted it a sign of progress that he was willing to entertain advice to do something terminal about it.

Getting to that point had in fact been a long, unhappy journey for the president. He had been Sununu's protector long after the bond between them had frayed to a last thin thread of personal loyalty. By the end, Sununu had no other friends who mattered. John was smart, even brilliant; everybody had to concede that. He had come down from New Hampshire after six years as governor wearing his genius IQ on his sleeve and his 1988 campaign ribbons on his chest. But he was widely regarded in Washington as the poster boy for that locally pandemic disease called the arrogance of power. His approach to management appeared to have been modeled on Caligula's, and so did his appetite for the trappings of power. His frequent use of Air Force planes for personal trips had become a public scandal, and when he was finally grounded, he had made matters worse by taking a chauffeured government limousine on a shopping trip to a stamp auction in New York.

For their first two years together, the president had actively defended Sununu. The heavyweights in the cabinet—Jim Baker at State, Dick Cheney at Defense, Nicholas Brady at Treasury—had each counseled Bush to get rid of him. The answer, each time, had been no. Sununu had his uses, as a lightning rod if nothing else, and besides, he had earned those medals he flaunted so proudly. Bush's candidacy had been near death in the '88 New Hampshire primary when Sununu stepped in and showed him and his panicky troops how to win. The president owed him for that, and while his warmth had diminished with time, his sense of debt had not. By mid-1991, his confidence in Sununu was gone, one cabinet member guessed, but Bush still couldn't be induced to send him packing.

At critical moments, Sununu seemed bent on handing his enemies a whole armorer's stock of swords. There had been the time, for example, when the president needed a new Republican national chairman and asked Sununu to sound out two veterans in Bush's service about taking the job. One, Rich Bond, a key operative in the 1988 campaign, was actively interested. The other, Craig Fuller, who had been Bush's vice-presidential chief of staff, was a good deal less enthusiastic; still, he was willing to swallow his misgivings if the president really wanted him.

But Sununu, jealous of his own standing at court, told Bush that both men had said no. In time, the truth reached the president, who was not pleased. Bond eventually got the job he coveted. Sununu had placed his own more deeply at risk than ever.

He had had the further bad sense or bad luck to offend Barbara Bush, who had been his second strongest defender after the president. The Bushes had laid on a pep luncheon at Camp David for a dozen blue-chip corporate CEOs who had agreed to raise money for the president's America 2000 initiative on alternative schools. The group ego massage was going nicely till Sununu came on, spoiling the day for the executives with his patronizing tone and his dismissive response to their ideas. Appalled, the First Lady plucked him aside afterward and asked sotto voce if he hadn't been a little hard on their friends. Sununu didn't think so. Mrs. Bush did, and his next-to-last vote at his patron's dinner table was at hazard.

Through the summer of 1991, the strains between the two men grew harder to hide. When the Soviet old guard mounted its coup attempt against Mikhail Gorbachev, Bush pointedly excluded Sununu from the list of aides he summoned to Kennebunkport to help him deal with the crisis. Sununu came anyway, on his own motion, but was never a major player.

Not long thereafter, he showed up unannounced at Walker's Point once again, interrupting Bush at tennis.

"Why are you here?" the president asked.

"I just wanted to talk to you about something," Sununu said. He mentioned a pending problem of state.

"I solved that yesterday," Bush said tartly, turning on his heel and walking off toward the horseshoe pit.

Sununu started after him. They continued past the pit to the house and disappeared inside. Five minutes later, Sununu came out alone. Without a word to anyone, he got in his car and was driven back to his own home in New Hampshire.

The insurrectionists who watched the scene or heard about it afterward took silent satisfaction in it. The president, one said, just didn't want the guy around anymore and had all but said so to his face.

Neither did it help Sununu's cause that the sedition had spread to the unborn reelection campaign. He had put it about that he himself would be directing the effort out of his White House office. The idea had worked nicely for Ronald Reagan in 1984, but Jim Baker had been chief of staff then, and people had *wanted* to work for him; he could be as tough and demanding as Sununu, without leaving bruises. Sununu commanded no such affection. Several key designees for the campaign team were near mutiny at the prospect of his being in charge, and their leading man, playing Fletcher Christian to Sununu's Captain Bligh, just happened to be one of the president's best friends.

His name was Bob Teeter, and his hard feelings dated to the days when Sununu had muscled him out of a serious management role in the Bush White House. Teeter's wounds had not mended with time. He usually masked his emotions behind a stolid midwestern reserve, but his unfondness for Sununu was apparent, sometimes explosively so. He didn't like the man or trust his word, and—while he could not bring himself to say so directly to Bush—he didn't want to chair the campaign if it meant reporting to Sununu. He had done six presidential campaigns, he told friends that fall. He didn't need a seventh. He might not be there at all.

He needn't have worried; Sununu was well along in the process of destroying himself. On Election Day, 1991, he convened the political group in his West Wing office to discuss how to put the best face on Dick Thornburgh's defeat in Pennsylvania. Afterward, Sununu turned to the matter of the president's scheduled trip to Asia, leading the others to believe it was still on.

It wasn't. Sununu adjourned the meeting at 6:00, then walked down the hall to the Oval Office. At 6:30, word went out to the networks and wire services: the trip was off till after the first of the year.

The political people were thunderstruck. The decision, in their eyes, was a wretched one politically—an invitation to the media to picture Bush as Chicken Little the day the sky fell. Worse, the president's most senior campaigners hadn't even been asked what they thought. On the contrary, they had been lied to like hired help who couldn't be trusted with a secret.

They were, predictably, furious. One of them, Charlie Black, who had sided with Sununu in the past, cornered him afterward and demanded to know why they had been misled.

Because, Sununu answered airily, he couldn't count on them not to leak the story to the press.

The insult was bad, the timing worse: Bush's tell-it-to-George letter had gone out only five days earlier, and Sununu, with his obsessive secrecy, had handed his enemies one more atrocity tale for the dossier. The coup plotters composed their lines for George W.'s imminent visit. Dan Quayle, till lately a friend and apologist, began saying privately that Sununu would have to go. Jim Baker made a last solo run at his friend the president, trying to hurry the process on terms particularly pleasing to him; his suggestion, this time, was not merely that Bush remove Sununu but that he bring in Dick Cheney from the Pentagon to take over.

Baker's idea had a certain surface plausibility, given that Cheney had been Gerald Ford's chief of staff in the 1970s; he knew his way around the White House and was a man of nearly universal respect in the capital. But Baker was not without guile, and his proposal included certain barely hidden fringe benefits for himself. It would, for one thing, spare him being dragged back to a job he had held in Reagan's first term and, in the bargain, would diminish a potential rival for the presidency in 1996.

Bush was not blind to the subtext; his response to Baker's démarche was no thanks. But there were few contrary voices left to plead for Sununu's survival. His last friends at court belonged to the president's family—among them, ironically, the man assigned to gather the hanging case against him. George W., known widely and inaccurately behind his back as Junior, had been invited only two months before to join the cabal and had refused. "Sununu is loyal to George Bush," he had replied, "and that counts for more than you think."

The day it stopped counting for Junior came in the wake of the president's idle proposition, in a speech, that the interest rates charged by banks on past-due credit-card payments be lowered. The idea, while popular, was a nonstarter as a business proposition; the interest charges were an important source of profit for the banking industry, which was already operating close to the edge, and the markets had bellywhopped badly the next day at the mere suggestion that they be trimmed. Bush's embarrassment was deep enough when the world thought he had been reading some ghostwriter's bad idea from a prepared script. But his chagrin was made worse when Sununu went on TV and announced, "The president ad-libbed."

The seismic rumble that followed was the sound of people surnamed Bush deserting Sununu en masse, the First Lady and all five of their children among them. One of the plotters, knowing of Junior's impending trip up from Texas, called to tell him about Sununu's act of lèse-majesté.

"We have a saying in our family," Junior said. "If a grenade is rolling by The Man, you dive on it first. The guy violated the cardinal rule."

The responses to his formal canvass, begun two days before Thanksgiving, were devastating. The White House and the campaign were in disarray, and in the nearly universal view of his colleagues, Sununu was the problem. Nobody quite had the nerve to say what several had threatened privately: that they would jump ship if Sununu stayed. But Jim Baker once again urged his removal. So did Bob Teeter, who was to run the show as chairman, and Bob Mosbacher, a Bush family friend slotted for a more ornamental role as general chairman. Even the president's campaign manager-to-be, Fred Malek, casting a lonely vote for keeping Sununu on, did so with the stipulation that his wings be severely clipped. The plea was not for mercy but for its appearance; it would make too much of a mess, in Malek's view, to sack him outright.

Junior's call on Sununu was an amiable quarter-hour visit, not much longer or less civil in tone than that Washington social ritual called a drop-by. There were pleasantries about the Bushes' affection for Sununu, and his for them. But the reports Junior had been hearing from the troops were troubling.

"John," he said, "a lot of people are saying the problem is you."

His tone was unjudgmental, his language guarded. One way to solve the problem, he counseled gently, might be for Sununu to consider leaving. But he stopped well short of making the suggestion a demand. What Sununu did need to do, Junior said, was go have a frank talk with the president.

Sununu was visibly shaken. On the evidence of Bush's letter, he had expected to be asked how the campaign should be structured, not to be told by indirection that he might want to freshen up his résumé. He agreed to speak with the president. But when Junior left, the man Sununu phoned was Charlie Black. Charlie was a friend, for all the strain Sununu had put on their relationship. Maybe he could help again, as he had in the past.

Black couldn't, not this time. "John," he said in his soft Carolina drawl, "the Indians are outnumbering the cowboys. Maybe you ought to consider getting out of here."

Sununu brooded for two days, concluding, finally, that he would rather fight than quit. "Look, I've got some support," he told a friend. "The president is only hearing from people who are against me. I'm having some people call him."

"Don't overdo it, John," his chum warned. "If he thinks you're running a campaign, it's going to hurt you."

It did. Junior, as it happened, was not the first to his father's door; the day he paid his call on Sununu, Roger Ailes, the ad man emeritus, had dropped by the White House for drinks with the president and had been asked what he thought about the Sununu question. Bush expected a defense; Ailes and Sununu had always seemed to him to be friendly. What Ailes told him instead was that Sununu had alienated everybody—himself, Mosbacher, and, most dangerously of all, Bob Teeter. If Sununu stayed, Ailes warned, Teeter would be out the door.

There were no pleadings to the contrary; Sununu was having a hard time making his counteroffensive work. One of the men he tried to enlist had flatly refused to carry his case to Bush. Another had agreed to try, but when he put in the call to the Oval Office and got through to the president, he told him Sununu ought to go. Three of the chief's senior deputies begged an audience, under instructions from their boss to say how much the staff all liked him and wanted him to stay on. But the cue cards somehow got lost on the way to the Oval Office. The three aides presented themselves instead with studied neutrality and asked the president, "How can we help?" Bush told them all the bad things he had been hearing. They got the picture; all three concluded that Sununu had to quit for the president's good and his own.

Sununu's own meeting with Bush had led nowhere. The surmise among the president's men was that he wanted Sununu out but had been unable to pull the trigger; the guy, one former aide said, had never been particularly brave about firing anybody. The next morning, Sununu wakened to find himself on a political respirator, barely alive but still breathing. He went to see his sometime pal Dan Quayle, pleading for a stay of execution.

Quayle listened noncommittally, then briefed the president over lunch that noonday.

He's resisting, Quayle said.

Bush appeared to be in pain.

Afterward, Quayle walked into Sununu's office, closing the door behind him. Sununu played his last card. The staff wants me to stay, he said.

He didn't get it, and Quayle tried, gently, to explain. The president was anguishing, he said. He simply couldn't bring himself to fire an old friend. Sununu would be doing himself and Bush an enormous service by standing down.

Fifteen minutes later, a chastened Sununu appeared in the Oval Office and offered his resignation. It was an awkward moment, and Bush, not wanting to face it alone, buzzed Quayle in for company. The three spent a half-hour working out the details, including a face-saving farewell tour for Sununu with an important-sounding new title as a figleaf.

Sununu was carrying a longhand copy of his letter of resignation when he boarded Air Force One for a trip to Mississippi next day; the measure of his fall, or so his enemies believed, was that he had photocopied it himself. Bush showed it to members of his road party, along with the reply he had drafted in green ink on a legal pad. There was to be no more sniping, he said, whispering so Sununu wouldn't hear. "John's been really good about this," Bush instructed his troops. "He's written a gracious letter, so be kind to him."

The last impediment was gone, and the Bush-Quayle campaign was rushed into being, a step or so ahead of the president's legato schedule. The victors in the coup claimed their spoils at headquarters on Fifteenth Street, with Teeter, Malek, and Mosbacher occupying the executive offices. Secretary of Transportation Samuel K. Skinner, who had coveted Sununu's White House job for months, finally got it. Even the president began preparing, unenthusiastically, for the coming struggle. He would do whatever he had to do to win, he said in a television interview one night. The line, in the morning papers, looked like a threat, but its tone on delivery was nearer resignation.

By then, reality was closing in. A Draft Buchanan committee was in the field in New Hampshire, with its hero's blessings, preparing a way for his imminent entry into the race. The air, there and elsewhere, was aflame with insurrection. The mood that had so worried Fred Steeper in early autumn was turning more sullen and more dangerous by the month. In the standard polling measure of discontent, three-quarters of the citizenry thought the country was off on the wrong track. The "recovery" then arguably in progress had neither generated jobs nor restored hope.

Not even a man as resistant to bad news as Bush could completely shut out the portents. Soon after Sununu's departure, the president called around to some old friends, receiving congratulations and asking advice.

"Mr. President," one of them told him, "your problem isn't John Sununu. It's the economy."

"I know," Bush answered wanly, "I know."

President Pangloss

Two days after the midterm elections of 1990, Bush had invited a dozen of his outside brain trusts to the White House for lunch, bonhomie, and some postmortem political counsel. The Republicans had taken some light but painful hits at the polls; two governors, one senator, and eight congressmen had been lost. There had, moreover, been a first wave of "no" votes against officeholders of both parties, punishing them simply for being there. The portents were not comforting for Bush as First Incumbent, and as his guests attacked the marinated chicken and the chocolate-orange soufflé, he asked them, "Where can I improve?"

Most of the answers were the usual rote chat about message and communications; it was easier to talk the talk than to complain about John Sununu, who was then still aboard and was sitting at the table. But a couple of brave souls told Bush as frankly as they dared that he was getting bad advice from his economists. Their rosy forecasts were all wrong. Times were tough. People were scared. Jobs were disappearing. Unemployment lines were getting longer. The economy was in recession, no matter what the bar graphs said, and it was getting worse. If Bush didn't acknowledge it and make a show of trying to deal with it, it could be his undoing.

"I'm not sure there is a recession," Bush replied.

He was, in this, the embodiment of what the liberal economist John Kenneth Galbraith has called "the culture of contentment"—the shared conviction of the fortunate in a society that, since *they* were doing well, the existing order of things must be sound. A voting majority of Americans had held that belief for most of the '80s, many of them against the evidence of their own stalemated lives. It was a piece of the popular ideology that had sustained Ronald Reagan for most of his eight feel-good years in office and had raised Bush to the presidency as Reagan's chosen heir.

But the politics of contentment had died in the Georgian America of the '90s, the casualty of a sagging economy and the deepening alienation of the people from their government. The boom years were over. The growth rate in the Age of Bush had been the weakest since the Great Depression, and the what-me-worry smile that came so naturally to the president was no longer playing in Peoria. By the time he could fairly claim that a recovery was in progress, not one American in ten believed him. The rest, in one published poll, were evenly divided as to whether what they were enduring was merely a recession or a full-blown depression.

For more than a year, only Bush and the closed circle of economic advisers he trusted seemed blind to that psychic reality. It was not for want of warnings; soon after his postelection luncheon in 1990, the president got a long, eyes-only memo from one of his guests, Fred Malek, an old government hand who had gone on to make a success in the private sector, as a senior executive at Marriott and an entrepreneur in the airline business among other ventures.

The memo was gently done, framed in the flatteries thought to be due Bush as a perquisite of his office; Malek had learned how to address presidents in his years at the courts of Nixon and Ford. But his implicit message was blunt: it was on the economy that Bush would finally be judged, and if he didn't get a grip, quickly, his survival was anything but assured.

America "is indeed in a recession," Malek wrote, and while its impact on various regions was mixed, it had "the clear potential of becoming deeper, larger and more destructive" than the heavy economic turbulence Reagan had had to endure in 1981–82. The crisis, as Malek sketched it, was one of belief as much as numbers, and Bush's serene approach to it had become part of the problem. "There is a serious fear, bordering on paranoia, developing among the American people," the memo said—a fear of the future made worse by "a sense of government apathy, unawareness, or insensitivity to the growing problems."

The president was not without means to respond; he could, for example, press for lower interest rates and looser credit, and he could work with business leaders on the particular problems of the hardest-hit industries. But first and most urgently, Malek wrote, he had to recognize the real anxieties abroad in the land; there could be no solution to the problem until Bush owned up to himself that there was one.

It would help if he expressed concern about a rising wave of corporate layoffs, "which to date," Malek remarked as politely as he could, "you have not really addressed." It would be better still if he used his coming State of the Union message to float a set of recovery measures, if only to show that he was in command. It would be best of all, though Malek did not put it quite so baldly, if the president showed the people that he cared about their pain. "They need you as a 'father figure,'" Malek wrote, "to take them by the hand, acknowledge times are tough, and offer hope for the future."

The president's only response was a polite thank-you for an interesting submission; Malek would find himself making essentially the same arguments in a shorter, sharper memo nine months later, with heightened urgency and similarly limited effect. The new missive closely followed Bush's half-hearted summer political retreat at Camp David, which had been haunted by concern over the economy and how it might affect the coming campaign. "A double dip back into recession is a distinct possibility," Malek's confidential MEMORANDUM FOR THE PRESIDENT said, "and you are perceived as somewhat detached from the problem." His prescription was that Bush spend much of his time in September and October "personally getting into the issue and developing your own firm convictions on the depth of the problem and possible solutions."

The implicit message to Bush was sobering: to be urged so late in the day to go get some convictions was to be told that one didn't have any—not, at all events, on the issues that mattered most to the voters. Partly as a result, the president's support had already begun crumbling. But the alarms rising around him ran cross-grain with his own deep optimism and with the reinforcing counsel of his house economist, Michael Boskin; his budget director, Richard Darman, and his secretary of the treasury, Nicholas Brady. Their collective wisdom was that the economy would fix itself—that all the elements necessary to a recovery were in place and that discretion dictated leaving well enough alone.

Bush's belief in his troika was no longer widely shared in his party. They had fallen from favor both with centrists, who found them rather too calm about the state of the economy, and with conservatives, who felt they had sold out the Reagan Revolution by acquiescing in the tax rise of 1990. The right had made Darman the particular object of its loathing. He was a pragmatist, a sin akin to heresy in their eyes, and was intellectually a bit flashy besides; his brilliance and his irony were all too commonly mistaken for arrogance. By late autumn, Bush's sons George W. and Jeb had joined the anti-Darman sedition, lobbying their father to get rid of him.

Bush had refused, partly out of loyalty to Darman, partly in the serene belief that the economy *was* getting better. He had never liked being thought the creature of his handlers, in politics or in policy; the advice he had been getting had prevailed because it so neatly suited his own cast of mind. Prudence had always been a higher virtue than daring for Bush, and his compass tended to flutter anyway in the deeper thickets of domestic affairs. To be told that a recovery would happen without his intervention was, for him, welcome counsel. George really didn't know what he stood for, one outside friend and adviser said privately, so the easiest thing for him to do was nothing at all.

Denial thus was elevated to public policy: Bush would announce from various venues, including, imprudently, a golf course, that there was no recession, or that if there was one, it was blowing over. He sounded on these occasions like President Pangloss, and nobody was buying it, not even the big-money boys who dependably supported Republicans with their votes and their money. Some had already quit the Eagles, a club for big givers to the party, and formed their own informal countercaucus of the aggrieved. What bound them together was the belief that they and their businesses literally could not afford a second Bush administration.

Some heavy hitters who hadn't actually deserted him were, as one of Bush's own men put it, really pissed at him. He seemed to them not to be living in the same world they saw daily on their balance sheets. *His* world was mapped for him by his house cartographers, backed up by the blue-chip economic forecasters they relied on as their chorus. George's problem, a business crony said, was that he was taking his cues from those thumbsuckers with their computer models instead of his real friends who were out there running businesses, meeting payrolls, and trying to ride out a storm he seemed not to see.

A roomful of them got to tell him so, in more politic tones, at a fund-raising reception in California in September, 1991. The economy, they said, was in trouble, and it was past time for him to do something about it.

Bush seemed surprised and finally annoyed. "What a bunch of fucking crybabies," he grumped as he left the affair.

He meant the businessmen, but he might have been speaking of the more nervous attendants at his own court. His view of what was happening in that strange land known to people within the beltway as Out There remained impermeably calm. Bush, like his predecessor, seemed to understand pain when he saw it close up but not in the large. The numbers that quantified it remained abstractions to him even when they had begun to undermine his credibility as president.

His mood was accordingly serene when he called an old friend one day in mid-autumn and asked, "What's new?"

A national poll had just come out, his friend said. Bush's job-approval rating had fallen to 55 percent and was headed due south.

"Hell," Bush said, "that means the staff will want to panic over the economy."

In fact, the panic button had long since been pushed. It was a source of some distress to Bush's political people when he jetted off to Madrid in October to open the Arab-Israeli peace talks; the voters by then were holding his preoccupation with foreign affairs against him, and the trip seemed literally to fly in the face of their anxieties.

The day he got back, he sat through a White House meeting on the economy, a burden for him even when he was rested and the news was good. The advice was, as usual, dissonant. His political people, as usual, wanted him to send Congress a recovery plan, the sooner the better. His economic people, also as usual, argued against it. If Bush sent up a recovery package, the Democrats would junk it and substitute some inflationary confection of their own.

The head handwringer this time was Dan Quayle, a man whose vague look and Veep Lite reputation masked a shrewd native instinct for politics. With his own future on the line, Quayle had taken up with the younger post-Reagan conservatives in the party and had become an advocate of their ideas about stimulating growth and opportunity by getting the tax codes and the bureaucrats out of the way. He had not got far selling their blue-sky agenda to the president, but, he argued heatedly, Bush had to propose *something*. People thought he had abandoned them, and it would be far better to fight and lose than to do nothing at all.

But to Quayle's undisguised dismay, Bush sided with his more traditionalist court wizards. The talk then current in the press and the business community was that America was sliding into phase two of a double-dip recession. The advice of Bush's economic team was, in effect, to forget it. The downturn had ended and the recovery begun sometime in the spring of 1991, in their view, and Bush would be riding into the general election in the sixth straight quarter of slow but real economic growth. There was no point getting agitated in the meantime. They would wait till the president's State of the Union message in January, nearly three months down the road, to propose whatever further fine-tuning might be needed.

The decision was risky and, in the event, a costly one. But Bush could not be budged from it, and his patience for further debate was near an end. A deputation of frightened Republican congressional leaders descended on him next morning for a meeting in the Cabinet Room, a session described later by one participant as a verbal food fight. Phil Gramm, chairman of the party's Senate campaign committee, ignited it with an intelligence report on the Senate by-election in Pennsylvania, then just five days away. Dick Thornburgh was a goner, Gramm said. He was viewed as Bush's man, and people were going to be reading all kinds of invidious meanings into his defeat.

"I think it's very important for everyone in this room to understand that next week could very well be the worst week of your presidency," Gramm said. "We better get our game face on."

Bush was silent.

"You need to get engaged, Mr. President," Newt Gingrich, the House minority whip, chimed in. "Your reelection is not assured. You've got to do something to show we understand the impact of this."

Gingrich had long been an irritant to Bush, a Reagan revolutionary who did not seem to understand that that war was over. He had raised an intraparty mutiny against the great budget compromise of 1990, in which Bush had had to surrender on taxes as the price of a deal to reduce the deficit. Bush had never forgiven Gingrich and did not gladly suffer being lectured by him.

"I'll lead the charge," the president said, "but when we get there, I don't want to look behind me and see all you guys with bent spears peeking out from behind the bushes like last time." It was in fact too soon, he said, to be charging at all. "I've been here before," Bush told him. "I was there with Reagan during the '82 thing. I heard all the same stuff then."

The babel of advice to the contrary rattled on until, after forty-five minutes, Bush cried for mercy. "Part of the problem," he complained to his callers, "is you're all saying different things. I feel like I'm in the middle of a hurricane, and I can't hear anything."

Hearing nothing, he did nothing. "I don't think there's anything wrong with this situation that two points of growth wouldn't cure," he told a nervous member of his political team with the onset of winter. It was as if he expected them to materialize by an act of God—not, heaven forfend, by his own intervention.

At low tide, he suggested to a group of reporters that the problem was not so much economics as public relations, persuading America that the seeds of recovery were real and would soon bear fruit. The remarks made him sound like a dentist telling a patient undergoing a root-canal procedure to think about something other than how badly it hurt. The ensuing headlines were devastating, a portrait in collage of a president inhabiting his own alternate reality. In a season of change, one old Reagan-Bush hand worried, he was becoming the candidate of the status quo. People wanted something done, and all they heard from him was what he couldn't, wouldn't, or shouldn't do.

Events finally forced him at least to acknowledge reality, if not to take arms against it. The last weeks of 1991 had brought a firestorm of layoffs; corporations were downsizing at a rate of 2,200 jobs a day, and just before Christmas, General Motors, that monument to a rusting industrial past, announced plans to cashier 74,000 workers. A contagion of angst long familiar on factory floors was spreading through white-collar America as well. By the time Marlin Fitzwater was propelled forward to concede on Bush's behalf that, yes, the economy was in recession, the collective anxiety attack had reached epidemic levels.

Yet even then, to the despair of the president's men, the decision to do nothing remained the order of the day. The president's approval rating was below 50 percent for the first time since the war and was still nosing downward. A first fund-raising letter had gone out over his signature to a list of tested Republican givers and hadn't even raised enough to cover the mailing costs; the word on the street was that it had actually lost $500,000. Bush's enemies had the field to themselves, and not just the Democrats. Pat Buchanan had finally hit the ground in New Hampshire and was raising his revolutionary brigades for the coming war against the man he derisively called King George.

The portents were ugly when, just before Christmas, Roger Ailes called one of his friends in the campaign command to convey his alarm.

"We're managing a disaster, boys," Ailes said. "It's time to get on the offensive."

The warning was relayed to Bob Teeter on Fifteenth Street. Ailes was right, he said, but they were stuck with the president's determination to wait for the State of the Union and to hope in the meantime for visibly better times. Teeter sighed heavily and waved in the general direction of the White House. His friend's presidency was at stake, but so far as he could tell, the people over there didn't even understand they had a problem.

15.

The War against the Crown

The day was uncommonly warm for mid-November, but the invitation-only gathering at Pat Buchanan's place in McLean, Virginia, sat damp and uncomfortable in blue-wool power suits in deference to the gravity of the occasion. The fifty guests were the Lost Boys of the farther American right—the prophets, pamphleteers, and activists whose access and influence in Washington had been sorely reduced when Ronald Reagan left town. They had been looking ever since for a way back inside, and as they helped themselves at the bar and found seats in the living room, their sense of anticipation was high. They knew, or could guess, the revolutionary purpose Buchanan had in mind: bringing down George Bush's presidency from within his own party—or, at the very least, embarrassing him so badly that he would have to listen to them again.

The vehicle Buchanan offered that steamy afternoon was himself: he was indeed on the verge of challenging the president in the Republican primaries, and he wanted his soul brothers of the right to hear about it first. A scant three years after Bush's election, he told his guests, the Reagan Revolution was over; its inheritor had betrayed "the most successful political movement of the second half of the twentieth century." The president had knuckled under repeatedly to the taxers, the spenders, and the social engineers. Only that morning, he had signed the Civil Rights Act of 1991, a measure known to conservatives—and, till lately, to Bush himself—as a "quota bill."

"George Bush, if you'll pardon the expression, has come out of the closet as an Eastern Establishment liberal Republican," Buchanan said. For the first time in a decade, the conservatives had no alternative of their own within the party, and the president seemed to know it. "George Bush," Buchanan went on, "has sold us down the river again and again."

He was accordingly ready to take a year out of his life, as he put it, to give the Republican right a choice. His plan of attack, he told his friends, was to "fly over" Iowa—its season-opening caucuses were too easily rigged by the party regulars—and to begin his war of rebellion on the friendlier ground of New Hampshire. His showing there would determine whether it would be realistic for him to go on. But, he insisted, he wasn't out to put on a one-state protest demonstration and then head home. He would be running to win.

He knew that his chances were slight—that earlier mutinies against sitting Republican presidents led by Teddy Roosevelt in 1912 and Ronald Reagan in 1976 had come to grief. He felt, he said, like a rookie running back on his own goal line, with the great linebacker Lawrence Taylor coming at him like an all-pro avenging angel. He thought he could see a seam upfield, he said, an opening he could slip through to the nomination and perhaps even the presidency. But he did not deny that he was asking his guests to buy into a dream they might not share.

"You may not feel comfortable endorsing this campaign," he said. "The odds are Bush is going to get reelected, and then you guys have to spend four more years working with this administration. But to those of you who can't endorse me publicly, I would ask you not to damage us."

In a season for insurgency in American politics, Buchanan thus proposed the ultimate act of rebellion—the equivalent of an attempt by the courtiers against the crown. The thought alone was seditious in a party as famously royalist as the Republicans; its customs dictated that you took your Tak-A-Chek number and waited in line for your turn. But the slow disintegration of Bush's support all that autumn was itself an open invitation to the right to repudiate him—a signal, to Buchanan, that the old order was in crisis and that its timorous rules and manners no longer applied. America under Bush was in danger of losing what it once had had, he thought, and if somebody had to lead the mighty hosts to Armageddon, he was ready.

His formal credentials for the presidency were not obvious, even to his friends. He had spent most of his adult life as a paid provocateur—a trafficker in print, TV, and after-dinner commentary as subtle, he once said, as a barbed-wire enema. His main experience at presidential campaigning had been writing combative speeches for other men. He had worked in the White House, having followed two of his patrons there. But he had been more or less effectively quarantined once he got inside, by Richard Nixon's Prussians during his first tour and by Nancy Reagan in his second. His battle station in the Reagan Revolution had been a windowless office, where he spent much of his tour churning out memos to nowhere.

He was further burdened with more baggage than Imelda Marcos might have packed for August in Cannes. Offstage, Buchanan was a genial, gregarious soul, much valued for his company over drinks or dinner. But in his public person, he became the street fighter he had been growing up in Blessed Sacrament parish in the forgotten far north end of the Federal City. Among the several sects of modern Republicanism, he was closest in spirit to Nixon's, class-conscious and resentful. He believed, like his mentor, in whipping heads and taking names, and had made a small fortune at it.

He preached and practiced politics as the great turn-of-the-century historian Henry Adams once defined it: the systematic organization of hatred. His father had taught him that anger was the only emotion worth harboring, and he had turned the aphorism into a career. His life was a waxworks tour of retro Republicanism, from his boyhood heroes, Robert Taft and Joe McCarthy, to the patrons of his grown-up years, Nixon and Reagan. He was, spiritually, their godchild. His platform was his own: isolationist in outlook, nativist in hue, and warlike in spirit.

The business of being outrageous had bred a certain recklessness in him; he had, as one TV colleague put it, developed the habit of saying unnecessarily interesting things. His incaution would have destroyed most pretenders to the presidency before they had so much as declared for the job. At various times in his recent past, he had ridiculed the Gulf war, called Hitler a man of courage, diagnosed AIDS as nature's retribution against gays, and spoken harshly enough of Israel and what he called its "amen corner" in Washington to raise the published charge, denied by him, that he was anti-Semitic. Even the slogan he chose for his candidacy, America First, was an incitement of sorts—a battle cry borrowed from a movement that had been at best indifferent and at worst friendly to the rise of Nazism in Germany in the '30s.

Yet the mere fact of his availability had a certain appeal for the guests at his audition in McLean; win or lose, Pat would be a useful blunt instrument for reminding Bush that they were still around. His own ambitions were higher, as they well knew. He had flirted with the notion of running in 1988 but had dropped it when the Republican right embraced Jack Kemp instead, robbing him of whatever base of support he might have had. Only his timetable had changed, not the dream. In the winter of 1990–91, he was back, encouraging a short-lived draft-Buchanan boomlet in New Hampshire and elsewhere. The modest flutter of interest it stirred up had blown away on the winds of war in the Gulf.

His rekindled interest a year later smelled like personal ambition to some of the more purist ideologues in the room. Was Pat serious about

1992? Or was he, as some of his guests suspected, trying to steal a march on the competition for the hearts, minds, and votes of the right in 1996? Doubt lingered. But the doubters did not question Buchanan openly as to his wisdom or his motives. It was plain that he was about to jump in, with or without leave from his friends, and no one raised a voice to discourage him.

He had in fact come only slowly and timorously to the idea. It had been raised that fall in hushed family discussion with his sister and confidante Angela (Bay) Buchanan, who had served as treasurer of the United States under Reagan and had run for state office in California herself. She was tougher than her brother, by his own admission, and was gung ho for his running. He was trepidatious; as their conversations got more serious, he scrubbed his TV commitments for two weeks, flew west to California to be near her, and, in his word, mushed the subject around through a series of spirituous evenings and sleepless nights.

What frightened him, he finally realized, was not so much defeat as humiliation—the possibility that he might make a fool of himself. But it got somehow less scary when he framed it as a scene from one of his head-full of movie memories. If I get beat by the president of the United States, he thought, what the hell—he's still the heavyweight champ, but I'm Rocky. What mattered was not the punches you took or the blood you spilled. It was the fact that you were game enough to have fought at all and tough enough to have survived.

The role appealed to the brawler in Buchanan, and he had finally decided to go for it. With a nod from him, Bay leaked word first to the conservative *Washington Times* that he was close to a decision to run. The stir he kicked up surprised him. When he called a press conference in the Capitol, ostensibly to come out against a pending foreign-aid bill, he found a dozen TV cameras and forty or fifty print reporters waiting for him.

"Jesus," he muttered, seeing them, "look at this."

His first attempts to find professional help were another matter; to aid and abet a challenger to a sitting president of your own party could be, for political handlers, the business equivalent of hara-kiri. Buchanan's head-hunting for somebody to run the show led him early on to Ed Rollins, a tough, street-smart pro who had managed Reagan's 1984 campaign but had fallen out of favor at Bush's court. Rollins, an old friend, offered Buchanan advice—mainly to get organized—but not consent. He was not interested, he said, in piloting any suicide missions.

Buchanan had better luck trawling at the margins of the trade, hiring younger guns who, in some awe, called him Mister Buchanan and saw his candidacy as a cause, a career opportunity, or both. But the campaign would never really outgrow its beginnings as a family business run by Pat as candidate and Bay as chairperson. Their brother-and-sister arrangement struck Tony Fabrizio, one of the few well-seasoned pros on their payroll, as a recipe for disaster. No candidate, he thought, should place his fate in the hands of someone who couldn't or wouldn't tell him when he had said something dumb.

Fabrizio's repeated entreaties to them to hire a real manager got nowhere. "Our campaign is quasi-organized and disjointed," he wrote in a last magisterial memo late in December. "[It] cannot and should not be run as a 'Mom and Pop' political campaign." By then, he and his two-headed client had got tired of the bickering and of each other. A friend had warned him when he signed on that the Buchanans were never wrong or, in any case, would never admit it. The Pat and Bay Show was still playing when Fabrizio quit in January as a part-time, all-purpose consultant and walked away wondering why he hadn't heeded the warning in the first place.

In a year for outsiders, Buchanan's amateurishness had a certain street-level appeal. But it carried a price as well. His candidacy was born with no team, no plan, no polling, and no cash on hand except his own $50,000 check to himself; he had simply said one day that he was running, and that was that. When Bay asked Brent Bozell, a prominent young movement conservative, to come aboard as finance director, he imagined that the job would be easy. He had heard Pat say several times that "people" had been after him to run. While he never named them, Bozell simply assumed that he meant people with money.

"Let's look at our assets," he told Bay. "Who are the backers?"

"Nobody," she said.

"Surely some people have committed?"

"Not yet," Bay said.

"Okay," Bozell said, "now we're in trouble. How about a list of Pat's contacts in the financial community?"

There were none, Bay told him.

There had to be, Bozell answered; anybody as famous as Pat had some rich friends. "We'll see in his Rolodex that he's connected to people with bucks."

"You don't know Pat," Bay said. "If you look in his Rolodex, it's all conservative hacks that he knows. It's not the hoi polloi and the money set—he never hangs around with that gang. He'd rather have a beer than a cocktail."

Buchanan's on-the-ground operation in New Hampshire was only marginally more imposing. He had found a credible young field director for the effort in Paul Erickson, who had been a youth organizer for the party and later for the Reagan-Bush reelection campaign; the state had been one of his assignments. He had retired from politics soon thereafter at a tender twenty-two, discouraged after five unrewarded years of trying to save America, and had gone off to make money trading in real estate and producing action movies.

His twin careers were going nicely when Buchanan came along, and it took some persuasion to tempt him back into the trenches. He liked Buchanan's politics but not his approach to the hard labor ahead of him. Buchanan seemed to have formed his notions of what it would take in the low-energy Nixon campaign of 1968 and to have learned precious little since; he believed, for example, that he could spend three or four days on the road and then go home to McLean for a long weekend to collect his thoughts. His attitude, Erickson thought, was bad—very bad. But the cause and the command assignment were heady to a twenty-nine-year-old, and he had finally let them overcome his doubts.

The glow had dissipated quickly when he arrived in Manchester, just eleven weeks before primary day. Headquarters then was a bare suite of offices on Elm Street tenanted by Paul Nagy and Chris Tremblay, two activists recruited from a threadbare right-wing political action committee. The campaign's assets consisted of two chairs and a folding table. With Erickson's arrival, they would have to borrow a third chair from a neighbor down the hall so that the three of them could meet sitting down.

The prospects looked daunting, and Erickson had stood at his hotel-room window for a long time the night he hit town, gazing down over the depressed cityscape. It was below zero outside. Snowflakes danced on an icy wind. There was no Buchanan campaign, Erickson thought, except what he had brought in his briefcase. In the morning, he would have to start building a revolution from nothing. He was thinking, "What have I done?"

His guess that Buchanan needed a catch-up course in modern campaigning proved well-taken. The candidate was as green as his team and, as he acknowledged to one of them, as prone to rookie mistakes. He had to be talked into delaying his announcement for a week, against his own impetuous instincts; it would be crippling, Erickson advised him, to declare for president of the United States without at least the appearance of an organization arrayed like a Potemkin village behind him.

It was sweaty-palm time for Buchanan when the big day finally came. At his hotel in Manchester that morning, he seemed so visibly agitated that Erickson wondered whether he was having second thoughts about running at all.

"This is your last chance," Erickson told him. "If you're going to change your mind, you better do it now. As soon as you walk out this door, you're unleashing a tidal wave."

"Let's do it," Buchanan said, leading their little entourage off to the elevator and downstairs to his van.

They passed the half-hour ride to the state capitol in Concord in uncommon silence. But the clouds darkening Buchanan's brow parted when he saw the mob of reporters and camera crews waiting for him, a crowd so dense that he and his party had to fight their way out afterward; Erickson would lose a shoe in the crush. Buchanan's hand-done speech was a powerful manifesto for conservatives in the post– Cold War era, a summons to "a new patriotism where Americans begin to put the needs of Americans first." Bush was a gracious and an honorable man, he said, "but the differences between us now are too deep. He is yesterday and we are tomorrow."

The usual problem in presidential campaigns is finding a message. Buchanan had too many; he was like a small boy turned loose in a video arcade with a fistful of quarters and a houseful of hot buttons to jab. He tended to load up his speeches with his whole repertoire of causes and crotchets, and when he first took his show on the road, the habit kept getting him into trouble. He suggested in various forums that the more noisome homeless ought to be jailed for vagrancy; that the constitution should be amended to permit not only prayer but religious instruction in the public schools; that the way to stop illegal immigration from Mexico was to build a 200-mile "Buchanan Fence" along the border—and that even legal immigration might need re-thinking if it required America to assimilate a million Zulus, say, as against a million Englishmen.

His hip-shooting made him sound intemperate or worse and led him far from the heart of the matter: the weak state of the economy and Bush's complicity in it. He was to presidential politics, his man Fabrizio thought, what Howard Stern was to talk radio: his metier was shock, and he seemed unable to shrug off a question or walk past a fight without saying something incendiary. Fabrizio bombarded him with memos, four in a single day in December, advising him in effect to shut up about everything except "the Bush Recession." One, titled "Things We Wish We Never Said," reminded Buchanan bluntly that their enemies already had "a virtual treasure trove of 'Buchananisms' to use against us. And quite frankly," Fabrizio wrote, "we don't need to be providing them any more."

The argument was well taken; the insurgency started clicking when Buchanan found ways to connect it with New Hampshire's pain. The state was in its third year of recession, its high-tech boom times of the '80s gone ingloriously bust. Half a dozen banks had bellied up in a year, the number of personal bankruptcies had nearly doubled, and new applications for welfare were coming in at the highest rate in the nation. People were losing their jobs, families their homes; one downtown Manchester restaurant renamed its bar the Foreclosure Lounge and papered the walls with front-lawn sheriff's-sale signs.

Sitting in Washington writing speeches and columns about the recession was one thing, Buchanan would reflect later. Seeing it firsthand was another. He stopped at a paper mill in the North Country one bitterly cold afternoon just before Christmas for what was to have been a routine photo op, the candidate pressing the flesh during a change of shifts. He and his party were feeling chipper after a good couple of days on tour. But the company had chosen that morning to lay off 350 people. As Buchanan arrived, the day-shift workers were lined up for their free Christmas turkeys, a traditional beneficence from the management. Many of them still had their pink slips in their hands.

It felt to Buchanan's embarrassed party as if they had intruded on somebody else's private grief. For so public a man, Buchanan was oddly shy among strangers, and he didn't know quite what to do. None of the second-shift workers punching in seemed to know who he was, or to care.

"Pat, go shake their hands and introduce yourself," Erickson told him.

"What do I say?" he asked.

"Say, 'I'm Pat Buchanan, I'm running for president,'" Erickson said, shoving him toward the line.

Buchanan tried it. The response was polite but perfunctory at first, all touch handshakes and manufactured smiles. Then a man in the queue moved close, head down, studying the frozen ground.

Buchanan took his hand. The man glanced up.

"Save our jobs," he said.

The mood was somber in the van as they headed for their next stop. "What do you do for a guy like that?" Buchanan kept asking.

No one in his party had an easy answer. He turned to his wife, Shelley. She had been crying.

"We're going to come back here," he said, "and we're going to make things happen."

Things did start happening, at least for Buchanan. His speeches hammered at his newly populist message and locked onto its prime target, the president, like a smart bomb in the Gulf war. In his attack mode, Buchanan was the schoolyard bully beating up on the rich kid in class, a sport in which he seemed to take an almost feral delight. He had had the state to himself for a month and had used the time well; he tweaked "King George" daily for having become the biggest taxer and spender in American history and guessed that the only unemployed person *he* knew in New Hampshire was John Sununu. His punches, to his further delight, were drawing blood. When he gathered his staff in McLean one Sunday near the turn of the year, the tastiest bit on a full plate of good news was that Bush had finally laid on a trip to New Hampshire in mid-January—a fair sign that he had been stung badly enough to be scared.

Buchanan's own mood that wintry day was high. His crowds everywhere had been big and warm. His bank balance was looking less anemic, thanks in part to a begging letter he had done himself on his home-office computer. His hired experts were aghast at its homemade look, but it brought in $650,000, six times what they had advised him to expect. His poll numbers, once stuck in the teens, started moving upward. By Christmas eve, Bush's lead had narrowed from forty-eight points to twenty in the published polls, before Buchanan had put a single TV spot on the air. His fear of looking silly was behind him. People are taking me seriously, he thought, contemplating the newest numbers. He would remember the day afterward as one of his happiest in the campaign.

There had been days when he let his imagination run even further, days when he would ask Fabrizio if it were possible that they could take the whole ball of wax. Fabrizio had told him no. If they were lucky, he said, they might knock Bush on his ass in a couple of states, and New Hampshire probably wasn't going to be one of them—not if knocking him on his ass meant winning outright. A more realistic view, Fabrizio wrote in one of his final memos, was that Buchanan would do well to hold Bush under 55 percent of the vote there and to score somewhere between 30 and 45 percent himself.

If Buchanan was disappointed, he didn't show it. In private conversation with his people, he himself had regularly predicted that Bush would be reelected. But politics can be an opiate for the most hopeless candidates, and Buchanan was not wholly immune to its addictive power. Even 30 percent would be a moral victory, he believed, and anything much higher might be the stuff of history. His unlikely role model in these reveries was the antiwar liberal Eugene McCarthy, who had got 42 percent in New Hampshire against a sitting president in 1968. McCarthy had finished second, but the press and the political community had declared it a victory, and within the month, the actual winner, Lyndon Johnson, had dragged himself broken and bleeding from the race.

"Message: I Care"

With the turn of the year, George Bush summoned his campaign command to the Oval Office for one more walk around the Buchanan Problem. His people had brought him some good news for a change, better, indeed, than what they really believed was happening on the ground. Pat was in the low twenties in their latest polling in New Hampshire, they reported; the president was still beating him three to one. But the numbers did little to brighten Bush's visibly dark mood. Buchanan was up there bashing him every day, and he was getting tired of it—tired of the punishment and tired of their own defensive reaction to it.

"Why aren't we accentuating the positive?" he demanded. "Why aren't we using some of my strengths?"

"We've got to take care of this perception problem first," Bob Teeter, his campaign chairman, delicately replied.

The perception problem was the one that had dogged Bush for much of his job-hopping public career and now was undermining his presidency: the suspicion, widely held, that he brought no real sense of purpose or direction to the job. He was then still scoring high on what polltakers call the Boy Scout battery of virtues; people thought he was kind, honest, trustworthy, likable, sincere, and, no doubt, reverent, and they were finally coming to believe that he cared about their problems. But their fondness for him as a man was no longer enough to offset their collapsing faith in him as a leader. The lion of Desert Storm seemed to the voters, one year on, to be out of touch with his own country and flummoxed by its economic problems.

There had been ample warning that Buchanan could make trouble in New Hampshire, feeding on precisely those weaknesses. He wasn't even in the field when former Governor Hugh Gregg raised the alarm in Nashua one early autumn evening over dinner with the president's sister, Nancy Ellis.

"People are frustrated with government, they're mad at bureaucrats, they're out of work, and they're going to blame George," Gregg said. The Buchanan challenge was still a rumor then, but Pat would be a formidable opponent if he did jump in.

"Hugh, you're all wet," Ellis replied. "They love George in New Hampshire. We're neighbors."

"Nancy," Gregg said, "they do love George, and they'll vote for him in November. But they won't vote for him in our primary. It's so bad he could get beaten up here by *anybody* unless somebody starts paying attention."

Nobody did; the campaign seemed chronically afflicted with what one White House staffer privately diagnosed as "reality denial." At the first Bush/Quayle '92 staff meeting in early January, Fred Steeper, the polltaker, reported that 36 percent of the primary electorate might cast protest votes—an uncannily accurate measure, as it would turn out, of how much potential Buchanan actually had. But the campaign command seemed transfixed instead by Bush's 60–20 lead in a head-to-head trial heat against Pat. The margin seemed to them to foreshadow a landslide.

The prospect made them several shades too comfortable, to a point where Dan Quayle complained privately to the president about their low intensity level. The key players in the Bush command were almost too accustomed to winning elections. They had the air of machinists for whom all problems were soluble by referring to their user's manuals and following directions—laying on another phone bank, say, or flinging a few more operatives into the field. They were technicians, one White House official complained, when the real problem was the president's policies. People didn't like them. It was as simple as that.

The tranquility of the bunker blinded Bush and his staff to that possibility and led them to a series of strategic miscalculations. The first and deadliest was not to do anything dramatic about the economy or the miseries it was causing. The nondecision stemmed not just from Bush's own enduring conviction that a recovery would simply happen but also from a want of anything particularly dramatic to do. Kibitzers in his orbit and snipers outside volunteered ideas—offering up some or all of his economic advisers as human sacrifices; flinging together some sort of growth package and jawboning Congress to stay in session till it passed; doing something, anything to recapture the initiative and show that there was something Bush was for.

But as a senior White House staffer peevishly replied, they had nothing meaningful on hand or in the pipeline to play offense with. You couldn't go much further lowering interest rates, which had already been cut fourteen times in a year with modest effect, and you couldn't spend your way out of the slump in the ancient and honored tradition of presidential election years when you were already running a $300 billion deficit. The nasty fact was that public policy was in checkmate to debt and divided government. What few new ideas were around were being husbanded for the State of the Union late in January. In the meantime, Bush's man wondered, what were you supposed to do—go out and announce that the economy was shitty?

Having already done that, though in less vivid terms, they drifted on, and Bush's slow downward spiral continued. There were times in his aimless passage when doing nothing came to seem a better idea after all than what he actually did. His trade mission to Japan, when it finally happened, was a case study in the workings of Murphy's law: what could go wrong did, and the hee-haws echoing down off the slopes of New Hampshire were the sound of Pat Buchanan laughing.

The first mistake had been the five-alarm decision to postpone the Asian trip, which had greatly offended the Japanese. The second was repackaging it as a kind of economic prayer pilgrimage, the president leading a troop of American corporate CEOs in quest of trade concessions and jobs. The result was a public-relations disaster. Bush threw up and passed out at a state dinner; the automakers in his entourage upstaged him, grumbling openly about how little he had achieved; his hosts sent him home with their sympathy instead of the favors he had come to beg. He returned to Washington annoyed with his new management for their clumsiness. "I think our political people panicked a little bit," he told a friend, but it was he who took the heat and the further punishment in the polls.

Their confidence that they could effectively destroy Buchanan in New Hampshire had by then become the political equivalent of faith healing. Bush's manager, Fred Malek, was conceding privately that there wasn't a prayer of holding Pat under 30 percent. The number, though an embarrassment, would not be life-threatening if they could cap him there; a 70-30 finish, in Malek's view, would be better than a passing grade. But the campaign's private polling showed that only 40 percent of the voters of Bush's own party were solidly for him. To get from there to 70, it wouldn't be enough for him just to hold all his own softer supporters and peel away some of Buchanan's. He would have to win back practically all of what might be called the express-mail vote—the angry Republican loyalists who saw in Buchanan no more than a cheap, fast, and efficient way of sending the president a message.

Bush would have to accomplish all that, moreover, without going after Buchanan directly. The choice was in large part his own. To attack Buchanan, he knew, would only offend conservatives he would need in the fall, and there would be nasty stories in the press about how, in desperation, he had once again reverted to his Willie Horton mode to save his own skin. Having been burned once, he was reluctant to begin his last campaign by going negative, and a decision was taken early on to ignore Buchanan rather than go nuclear against him.

The problem, as some of his people conceded among themselves, was not so much Buchanan anyway as Bush himself. The state that had saved his candidacy four years earlier had fallen out of love with him long before Pat showed up. His handlers, knowing it could bury him this time, wrote what amounted to a three-act scenario for his revival. Act I called for Bush to go there, a promise he had made in 1988 but never kept, as a token that he really cared about New Hampshire and its woes. Act II, set in Washington on State of the Union night, would prove that he had a plan to heal the economy after all. In Act III, he would return to New Hampshire to close the sale: if you like my plan and want it passed, he would say, don't waste your votes on a protest candidate—give them to me.

The scenario, like much of what Bush tried in his long fall from grace, looked better on paper than it played on the road. He did not take punches well, and by the time he got to New Hampshire for what his people called the Reconnect Trip in mid-January, he was feeling more than a little sorry for himself.

"Those guys have been up there for weeks beating on me," he told his people the day before he left. "Now it's my turn."

He might have done better skipping it. The trip was an orgy of verbal wackiness begun when he threw away his prepared speeches— he thought they were blah—and kept only his shorthand talking points. He got them all in with a vengeance. He mentioned Barbara every chance he got, deferring to her higher ratings in the polls, and did repeated promos for his State of the Union speech. But what he had really brought New Hampshire was what amounted to a presidential CARE package, a word he uttered at least two dozen times in a single day. At one point, reading his note cards verbatim, he said, "Message: I care." At another, he upped the ante: "The answer: Barbara cares and I care."

Mostly, Bush stayed in that state of hyperkinesis that often seized him when he went unhandled; the tour was a throwback to his 1984 vice-presidential debate with Geraldine Ferraro, when, as one of his best friends remarked at the time, George looked as if he were being electrocuted. "Don't cry for me, Argentina," he told a gathering of bewildered insurance men in Dover. He quoted a country song popularized by the Nitty Gritty Dirt Band, but spoiled the man-of-the-people effect by calling them the Nitty Ditty Nitty Gritty Great Bird. He stumbled through his mea culpas about the economy, declaring it to be "in free fall"—it wasn't *that* bad—and blaming himself a bit extravagantly for not having noticed it sooner. His traveling party winced openly at his words.

The only happy man on the plane home was Bush himself. His conversation, tense and perfunctory on the way up, turned joky and relaxed; he always felt better breaking free of his handlers, even when it made them feel worse. His mood was reinforced by a quickie state poll showing, in effect, that New Hampshire appreciated his having come to visit. But his pleasure was short-lived. His standing in the horse race with Buchanan didn't improve, and the national press—a tribe he regarded as warmly as Rome had the Vandals—made him the object of sport for days.

The failure of Act I raised expectations for Act II impossibly high. "Is there anything I can do or say to play down the hysteria on the State of the Union business?" Bush wondered aloud one day. The answer was no; he had said and done too much to stir it up with his repeated hints that he would be proposing something big to rekindle the economy. In fact, he had no such intention. To put forward a truly ambitious package would, in his view, be a lose-lose proposition: he would look weak if it got shot down by Congress, and it might overheat the economy if, miraculously, it passed. "I just don't want to do anything stupid," he told his political people, which meant to them that he wouldn't be doing anything much at all.

For a time, he seemed to be under the delusion that he might actually get by with the minimalist approach he had in mind—that the Congress might just be induced to put the national interest ahead of politics and go along. His men Teeter and Malek put that oddly romantic proposition to a gathering of what one participant called the loudmouth Republican consultants—a mix of old Reagan hands and young neopopulists who had been shut out of the Bush-Quayle campaign. The objective was to get them inside for a night, all singing from the same song sheet when the media went hunting for quotes for the next morning's papers.

Instead, the loudmouths lived up to their name, informing Bush's men heatedly that the Democrats weren't about to make him look good with the presidency on the line; a better bet was that they were getting down on their knees every night praying for the recession to continue right up to Election Day. The Democrats, one of the dissidents said, were in a campaign mode, while Bush, God bless him, was trying to be presidential. His posture was an invitation to his enemies to hang whatever negatives they wanted on him. It was like being fitted with a lead suit, layer by layer, and discovering too late that it was more weight than you could carry.

As a unity rally, the session was a disaster. Teeter and Malek crawled out of the meeting, by eyewitness account, taking their happy talk with them. The message from the loudmouths was that, if Bush didn't put on his game face and come out swinging, he was through.

In fact, some of Bush's own men were themselves having second thoughts about his decision to hold off till the State of the Union instead of having put forward a recovery package in, say, November or December. The argument for the waiting game, advanced by Dick Darman among others, was that rushing out something called a Bush Program overnight would have looked like flailing—an empty and desperate response to the yearlong erosion of his standing. There had been a time in the wake of the Gulf war, Darman thought, when a big-bang package might have worked. In a series of memos through the summer of 1991, he himself had argued for an OPERATION DOMESTIC STORM!—a blitz of domestic initiatives launched with all the intensity and focus Bush had brought to the deliverance of Kuwait.

But the moment had been lost, and Darman had become an advocate of patience. The best course, in his view, would have been to build incrementally toward the State of the Union address, showing in a disciplined, orderly way that the president knew where he wanted to go and had some fresh ideas about how to get there. An off-the-shelf Bush Plan would have been dead on arrival on Capitol Hill anyway. A speech to a joint session of Congress, with its august setting and its national television audience, would have far greater effect as politics and as theater. In a State of the Union, Darman argued, you resonate.

The buildup had never happened; a single speech had been invested with almost totemic healing powers, and as the magic night drew near, the view spread among Bush's people that he and they had blundered—that no amount of eloquence was going to reverse his slide. Their confidence was further drained by the realization that, at the end of the day, there wasn't going to be a plan worth bragging about. After a three-month tease, the measures Bush had agreed to were mostly retreads—a cut in capital-gains taxes, for one especially roadworn example—and bits of creative book-cooking. His chefs had thrown together a stew of table scraps and called it an economic program. The sell would have to be in the presentation, the triumph of style over substance, and the reinforcements called in to help were the show-people of politics. Roger Ailes, a master of stagecraft, did a brief return engagement to help relax the president for his big night, and Peggy Noonan, the poet laureate of Republican speechwriting, holed up at the Jefferson Hotel downtown for five days to doctor the script.

What the president needed most was to recapture his lost aura of leadership, as one of his people made so bold as to tell him over lunch the day of the speech.

"You've got to be the George Bush of Desert Storm," the aide said. "I hear you, I hear you," Bush impatiently replied.

Noonan's prose was written to suit. She was not without her detractors in the president's command group; one unreconstructed male chauvinist among them complained that she made Bush sound like a girl. In fact, her words were vastly more muscular than his ideas. The echoes of the Gulf war were there, according to plan. The commander in chief twice said of the recession, as he had of Saddam's invasion of Kuwait, "This will not stand." But the splashes of heightened color from Noonan's palette clashed with the pale hue of her client's program. When Bush laid down a March 20 deadline for congressional action on his package, it was recognized on both sides as artifice—a dab of makeup meant to simulate the bloom of strength and health in a sickly presidency.

The president's own spirits were incongruously perky afterward, despite the flat notices in the morning papers. "I've been in tough spots before," he said at a senior staff meeting, trying to perk up his rattled troops. There was plenty of time; the economy would turn around, and so would his fortunes. "I know all of you are nervous," he said, "but don't be. I'm not worried. I don't want to seem overconfident, but I'm absolutely convinced we're gonna win this thing."

His pep talk brought them some cheer, and so did a brief period in which the speech seemed to have stopped the bleeding. The economic package, such as it was, stirred a flutter of approval in Steeper's focus groups in Chicago; the question of why it had taken Bush so long was, at least for the moment, a muted undertone. Fred Malek moved a sales force of surrogates north to New Hampshire to drum up support, and the theme of Bush's television advertising was changed according to the playbook, from "I care" to "I have a plan."

But there was no effective follow-through; the president himself soon deserted to Camp David to meet with Boris Yeltsin, raising yet again the suspicion that his heart wasn't in the package he had just announced. Buchanan was hooting at him. So were the Democrats. Not even his own men seemed dependably with the program. His secretary of housing and urban development, Jack Kemp, who had his own rosy economic ideas, dismissed some of Bush's as "gimmicks." The president's private response to that was thermonuclear.

In New Hampshire, where it counted most, he got only a modest bounce from the speech; whatever faint momentum it might have generated seemed to stall out within the week. But Bush's most senior command remained in a state of calm bordering on lassitude, exhibiting the confidence of men who, like Teeter at the top, had seen the movie before and were simply waiting for the happy ending. Some of the younger hands in the White House and on Fifteenth Street grumbled that the old guard were too cautious, too reactive and risk-averse. To one of them, the Great Bush-Quayle Reelection Machine looked more like a large, lumbering elephant, slow in responding to anything.

They needed a wake-up call, one of the warhawks thought; maybe a little bad polling from New Hampshire would stir the campaign to life. In early February, they got their wish: Bush's lead over Buchanan suddenly contracted from forty or forty-five points to thirty. Nothing happened. Buchanan was scoring heavily with ads mocking Bush's broken promise not to raise taxes. The president's men had seriously underestimated the power of the issue, resisting private entreaties from Hugh Gregg and his son Judd, the current governor, that Bush take the pledge again and this time promise in blood to honor it.

Bush declined, accepting the word of his team over the advice of his allies on the ground. The tax issue hadn't come up strong in the campaign's polling, and they let Buchanan have it to himself. The effect was devastating. It was hard to turn on a television set and not see one of Pat's ads, skewering the president with his own ill-chosen words. Even schoolchildren in the state were doing serviceable impressions of Bush saying, "Read my lips! No new taxes!" Bush's men briefly considered a counterstrike, then decided against it. They still felt themselves on track to the 70-30 victory they had talked themselves into thinking possible.

But the serenity of the executive suite on Fifteenth Street was no longer matched in the field. "It's smelling like Thornburgh up here," an operative calling in from New Hampshire told his superiors at Bush-Quayle headquarters. In the political metaphor of 1992, he meant the odor of comfort, overconfidence—and, if they weren't careful, defeat.

Send Him a Message

The night was bitter cold, and the crowd that greeted Pat Buchanan when he showed up to speak was of a size that advance men sometimes get fired for, smaller in number than the forty or fifty reporters and cameramen who were paid to be there. But Buchanan would look back fondly on the rally at what once had been Pandora Mills in Manchester. It was a kind of media-age epiphany for him—the moment when he knew that his uprising against the president and the entrenched power of the government was finally coming together.

Pandora had been a lonely survivor among the shuttered mills that had long ago made Manchester's riverfront the largest textile center in the world. George Bush had paid it a call in 1988, using its defiant bustle as a backdrop for his free-media campaign. But the company had not lived past midpoint in his presidency. It, too, had shut down, and Buchanan had seized on it as a symbol of another, darker sort—a ruin of recession and neglect. While he spoke outside, a map of the state unfurled on the factory wall, and a beam from a rented klieg light probed the night sky. The light, the challenger said, was Buchanan's Beacon—a guide back to New Hampshire in case Bush had forgotten how to get there.

The media event, in one sense, followed a standard rule from the playbook for challengers: make the race a referendum on the incumbent you chance to be running against. But in the mutinous climate of 1992, Buchanan was riding a vastly larger wave of discontent with what he had begun referring to as one-party government in Washington. His dissidence on the Republican right was becoming what Jesse Jackson's had been and Jerry Brown's would be on the Democratic left. It had begun as a sectarian rumble and was becoming a citizens' insurrection. Buchanan was challenging not just a particular incumbent but the idea of incumbency—the rise of a professional governing class with no principle larger than maintaining itself in power.

His weapons, as always, were words, and in his hands, they were as subtly administered as truncheons in a police state. He had been careful at the beginning not to get personal; he had referred to the president regularly as "my friend George Bush" and had spoken condescendingly about what a nice man he was. But his efforts at politesse had got fewer and more perfunctory with time. The media ignored them anyway, preferring red meat, and Buchanan was more than happy to oblige. He promised to end the reign of "Skull and Bones International"—his derisive label for Bush's new global order—and to get Washington thinking about America's problems again. "President Bush wants to be president of the world," he said. "I want to be president of the United States."

His strategists were not displeased. They had come to believe that Bush was the issue—that his policies and his compromises were merely symptoms and could not be separated from the man. The tactical question was how best to target him. The usual course in politics was to do a poll and see what might work, as Tony Fabrizio had frequently counseled. Running a campaign without one, he wrote in one of his memos, was like driving from New York to Brownsville, Texas, for the first time without a road map.

But the Buchanans looked on polltakers with something like the terror hypochondriacs felt for germs: they were contaminants in an ideologically pure crusade. The campaign was an old-fashioned one, in Bay's design, and she meant to keep it that way. She thought of Washington consultants as a worthless lot, a crowd of charlatans who brought nothing but high prices and inflated egos to the table. She and Pat could do quite nicely without their scripts and their numbers. When she finally did hire Frank Luntz, a promising young man of twenty-nine with an Oxford doctorate and a newish polling business, she made it clear to him that his role would not be large. Nobody, she informed him, told Pat Buchanan what to say.

Their mistrust complicated the search for ways to reduce Buchanan's Gatling-gun assault on Bush to thirty-second rifle shots on paid TV. They were flying by wire when, in mid-January, they met back at Pat's place in McLean to figure out the central themes—the "lunch," as the newly hired media man Ian Weinschel called it—for the coming ad campaign. After much debate, they settled on a two-course menu. The appetizer was the claim that the loyal Buchanan, not the faithless Bush, was the rightful heir to the estate of Ronald Reagan. The entrée was taxes. Bush, a man of expedience, had raised them. Buchanan, a man of his word, would not.

But when Bay grudgingly agreed to test-market the strategy in a poll, it became plain they had got it all wrong. The first thing they needed to know, Luntz reported at a tense staff meeting the night the numbers came in, was that Buchanan wasn't going to win New Hampshire. He was starting from a base of 18 percent, simply by showing up. He could build from there to something between a fourth and a third of the vote—perhaps, at the outside, to 40 percent. But it would take an act of God, Luntz said, to get him much higher than that. They were talking about a moral, not a mathematical, victory.

They weren't even going to get that far, in Luntz's analysis, by trying to ride the Gipper's coattails. "Reagan is not the god we thought he would be," he told the group. "In fact, he's barely mortal." The Reagan magic appeared to have expired with the Reagan boom. Even Bush in his diminished state was more popular among Republicans than his old patron, and there was little advantage for Buchanan in lighting votive candles to a fallen idol.

Neither could he reach very far beyond his own bitter-end conservative base with the tax issue alone. That was an argument for true believers, the conservatives who actually thought and hoped that Pat would win. Its appeal widened only if you made Bush's broken vow a metaphor for a broader, deeper disappointment in his leadership, especially on the economy. The sad fact was that only a minority of the people attracted to Buchanan really wanted him to be president. Twice as many saw a vote for him as a way to send Bush a message, and it wasn't about whether he had kept his campaign promises—it was about the recession and the president's seeming unconcern with it.

The numbers went to the strategic dilemma at the very heart of Buchanan's campaign. Should he play to the right and settle for making an ideological statement? Or should he widen his appeal and try to win? Luntz wasn't an ideologue, but he found himself arguing for the conservative approach as a matter of simple political realism. Buchanan was never going to beat Bush outright, in his view, but he could take a third of the vote, which would be no small achievement against a sitting president. There was no point wasting what little advertising money they had chasing a victory they couldn't win; it would be smarter and safer, Luntz said, to fire up the solid-for-Pat voters they knew they could get and turn out enough of them to make a statement.

But Bay, decisively, disagreed. "Give us a strategy that will get us 50.1 percent and we'll make that stretch," she said. They would reach out for the send-him-a-message vote and go for broke.

Weinschel retired to his farm near Dulles airport in the farther Virginia exurbs and went to work. His wife, Betsy, the time buyer in their family business, had already begun lining up an ad schedule and had found it as easy getting the slots she wanted as shopping in an empty department store; the Bush campaign, in its torpor, hadn't even started making its buy. Ian, a prickly sort who had gone into the season hoping to work for Bush, was just as happy savaging him. The spot he created had the raw look of a late-night cable ad, all hot colors and tabloid type. "Read my lips," the president was seen saying in grainy video flashback, to which an off-camera voice replied: "Bush betrayed our trust. He raised our taxes. . . . Send Bush a message. Vote for Pat Buchanan for president."

It was a devastating first strike in what would prove a one-sided air war. The president's spots were relentlessly nice, while Buchanan's stayed negative nearly to the end of the campaign. His people had begun with a classic challenger strategy, which did not aim for or expect overnight conversions; you first had to give people reasons for voting against the incumbent, and only then explain why they should vote for you. But Buchanan's people kept postponing part two of the formula. His attack ads were moving the numbers, chipping votes away from Bush, and as long as they were working, Weinschel and Luntz argued for keeping them on the air. Buchanan's virtues could be advertised on radio and in his speeches. Bush's sins made better TV and, to the extent that the medium had devoured the process, better politics as well.

Some of Buchanan's ground troops in New Hampshire didn't like what the ads said about the direction of the campaign; there had to be a purpose larger than making life miserable for Bush. The locals were hearing complaints from friends and neighbors about the sheer savagery of the air war. Even the state chair, Chuck Douglas, a one-term former congressman, was pestering headquarters to take down those obnoxious read-my-lips commercials and put up a positive spot showing Pat at work in his White House days—a way of saying he was more than just a talk-show personality making noise.

The gripes sounded like coffee-shop wisdom to Bay Buchanan. But she too thought it time to start selling what was good about her brother; he hadn't made so much as a cameo appearance in his own ad campaign, let alone put forward a case for himself. Bay pushed for a fifty-fifty positive-negative mix for the last two weeks of the campaign. The media team held her off; the more attack ads Buchanan ran, their polling showed, the better he did. When a mostly positive spot finally did get made, it stayed in the can for several days. The primary was only a week away when the sweet-and-sour blend Bay had wanted finally went on the air.

By then, Buchanan's people all sensed that they were on a roll—that they had rocked Bush back on his heels and were a punch away from a technical knockout. The president's response time seemed slow and his care-mongering ineffective. Buchanan, with nothing else to do, had got good at the touchy-feely politics required of candidates in New Hampshire. His Hermes ties and manicured nails seemed not to come between him and the people; when he worked an unemployment line, his pain was visible and unfeigned. Bush, by contrast, appeared to have lost the personal touch that had revived him in 1988. On one of his intermittent sallies northward, a woman thrust her unemployment-insurance ID booklet at him, the evidence of her suffering. Bush thought she wanted his autograph. He signed the booklet and handed it back.

He did cause the Buchanan campaign a few days of heartburn with his State of the Union speech, for all its poor reviews in the press. Buchanan watched it in his rooms at the Holiday Inn in Manchester, taking notes on a legal pad and looking vaguely ulcerous. What had worried his people most was that Bush might use the forum to apologize for his perfidy on taxes, thus robbing them of their prime line of attack. He didn't; apology did not come easy to the president. But Buchanan's scribblings seemed to him the record of a preemptive shift rightward on Bush's part—an attempt to paint himself as a lonely warrior against Congress for lower taxes, a freeze on spending, and less federal regulation.

When the speech was over, Buchanan adjourned to his bedroom with a couple of aides, then reemerged with his critique. Bush was trying to steal his positions, he said; it kind of made you wonder who had been in charge for the past three years. But his jaunty smile masked serious concerns. The speech and its follow-up ad, exhorting New Hampshire to send Congress a message by voting for Bush, struck at the rationale of Buchanan's campaign.

Luntz spent a sleepless night worrying about it, and there was little to cheer him in the polls for a few days thereafter. Bush's favorable ratings were edging up. Buchanan's momentum had stalled.

"Why aren't our numbers moving?" Bay demanded. "Why isn't the advertising working?"

"You have to give it time," Luntz told her. "This doesn't happen overnight."

A more prophetic answer might have been to give the president time: he had dependably played into their hands before and soon would again. The conservative New Bush of the State of the Union was upstaged within days by the crypto-moderate Old Bush, hiding between the lines of his budget message. The document turned out, on close inspection, to include sizable increases in both taxes and spending. The lonely warrior had surrendered yet again, without a fight.

Worse still, when the president sent Congress a stripped-down, fast-track version of his growth package, it was missing its one small tax break for the middle class: a $500 increase in the exemption for children. The omission was bad enough, but the damage was multiplied when an anonymous aide told the press that the whole idea had been politics—a throwaway meant for the New Hampshire market. The Buchanan camp, jubilant, flung together one last, crude negative ad for the final weekend. "New Hampshire, don't be fooled again," it said. "It is George Bush himself that's taxing and spending your future away."

The counterattack they had expected never came. Bush made a final two-day swing around the state, some of it lost in the imposing shadow of his traveling companion, Arnold Schwarzenegger. When he did manage to steal back the spotlight, it was mainly to defend himself against Buchanan's charges of betrayal. The Big Mo, as Bush might have called it, was all on the other side. The three houses Buchanan's people had rented for volunteer canvassers had run out of sleeping room, even on the floor. The rallies they laid on for the last three nights were explosions of noise and animal energy; bands played, balloons dropped, speakers blared "We Will Rock You," and placards in the shape of Bush's lips bobbed in the crowds. "Come Tuesday," the candidate promised, "Buchanan's brigades are going to turn in to the hollow army of King George and cut them like butter."

Buchanan woke on primary morning feeling bullish, on no evidence better than his own unpracticed fingertips. In fact, the first batch of exit polls showed him far behind Bush, with an anemic 20 percent of the early vote.

"This is insane, don't even tell Pat," Bay commanded when she heard the numbers.

He didn't need to be told; he knew from her silence over breakfast that the news must be bad. He had raised an edifice of dreams, and now he felt as if he were waiting for it to fall, the bricks tumbling down around his head. He was, he thought, going to have to put on a brave face just to make it through the day.

But the polls kept improving as the hours slipped by. "You're going to do damn well," Frank Luntz told Buchanan when he and his entourage left their hotel for a jog at midday. At the running track, a reporter told him he was only four points behind Bush. When he got back to his room, he was, fleetingly, two points ahead. The lead would prove illusory, an artifact, as pollsters call their mistakes. Still, for a tingly moment, Buchanan found himself thinking that the edifice was still standing—that he might actually beat Bush.

So did some of his staff. A couple of his young aides came by at five o'clock to talk about his speech.

"Look, the exit polls have been as high as 49-49 all afternoon," one of them told him. "It's difficult to believe, but you really have to entertain the notion that you may win."

Buchanan was silent for a moment. Then he looked up and laughed his thin, whickering laugh.

"What the fuck are we going to do?" he asked.

16.

The Last Inaction Hero

All primary day, the president sat steaming in the Oval Office, furious with Buchanan for having challenged him and with his own handlers for having underestimated the threat. His lead, so they had told him, had never been less than twenty-eight points in their day-to-day tracking polls; he still had a shot at the 70-30 victory they had been promising him. But their hopes and his calm started melting when that ugly last ad went up, the one about his forgotten promise of tax relief for the middle class. Pat was distorting his record, questioning his integrity, calling him a liar. The more Bush thought about it, the hotter he got. So foul was his mood that, when Buchanan briefly passed him in the exit polls, not even his old friend Bob Teeter was brave enough to bring him the news.

That he finally won, 53-37, was no comfort at all—not when he and his people tuned in the late-night news and read the morning papers. The press was writing off a sixteen-point landslide as a defeat for Bush, and only partly because the boys and girls on the bus had begun framing their stories when the exit polls still pointed to a much closer race. The nasty fact was that nearly half the Republicans in the season's first primary had preferred voting for anybody else available. Some who couldn't stomach Bush or Buchanan wrote in a Democratic interloper, Paul Tsongas, who ran first in his own party and third in the president's.

Bush had thus lost what had become the real battle in media-age politics, in which the actual results counted less than what the experts made of them. It did no good for his spin doctors to claim that he had, after all, won the primary or to blame New Hampshire's acute economic distress for the thinness of his vote. The real question was whether Bush could afford many more such victories in what amounted to a yearlong referendum on his presidency. New Hampshire had been a bad beginning to that process. His narrow escape had laid bare all his weaknesses: the squishy shapelessness of his record, the rising dissatisfaction of the voters with him, and the suddenly glaring inadequacies of his reelection team.

The surprise of his handlers at being ambushed was itself a measure of their overconfidence—a hubris born, in some of them, of having won too many presidential elections too easily. Their faith in their 70-30 dream scenario had endured until the weekend before the primary and had faded only when Buchanan's attack ad on taxes went on the air. Bush saying he had a plan, one of his people admitted, was no match for Buchanan responding, "Hey, he's lying again."

Yet even then, Bush's command missed the steep trajectory of his fall. On primary eve, they told him he would still win by better than thirty points. Their confidence washed away on the early waves of exit polling. At the White House, Marlin Fitzwater, the president's press secretary, locked himself in his office, announcing that he would see no one unless the numbers turned around. On Fifteenth Street, Mary Matalin, the campaign's tough young deputy manager, got a call from an old pal wondering how things looked. "Like your worst nightmare all day," Matalin answered grimly.

Somebody had to make an embarrassment sound like a victory, and the task was assigned to Charlie Black and Jim Lake, two smooth and seasoned pros who had gone on to make their fortunes lobbying an administration they had helped to elect. They had substantial personal stakes in Bush's success; their access to power was not the least of their attractions to the multinational client lists they were still servicing while they worked part-time for the campaign. But as they set out for Manchester, the portents looked bad. They had called Teeter from Dulles airport and heard the news that no one had dared tell the president—that the early exits showed him losing. The ground-to-air bulletins had brightened by the time they touched down in New Hampshire, but their spirits had not. Bush had popped ahead by eleven points; still, it wasn't going to be easy pretending for public consumption that they were happy with a less than presidential win.

"It's gonna be a rough fuckin' night," Black said.

Lake smiled back, thinly. "Well, Charlie," he replied, "it won't be the first time."

The night would be roughest of all on Bush, simmering alone in his office. Even when the numbers bumped up from catastrophic to merely bad, his mood kept souring. At one point, when they had finally got up the courage, Teeter led a party into the Oval Office to tell the president that the race was neck and neck.

"What about all those polls saying I was gonna win big?" Bush demanded.

Teeter said they hadn't exactly promised that, though they had expected it. They had instead covered their bets, he reminded Bush, by giving him three possible outcomes: a twenty-point win, a narrow win, or a narrow loss.

Bush said nothing. He turned away from his visitors, wheeled his chair over to the French doors near his desk and, for what felt like a full minute, gazed silently out at the Rose Garden. He seemed, in the stillness, to be ineffably sad.

Finally, he turned back. "Well," he said in a small voice, "we'll just have to work a little harder."

His seeming fatalism did not soften his anger. His people had cobbled up some suitably gracious remarks for him, praising Buchanan for having run a strong campaign and reassuring America that he had got the message. The plan was for Bush to descend to the pressroom and read the statement in person. But that idea had got less attractive to his handlers as his ill humor deepened through the day, and when he emerged from a 6:30 dental appointment with a newly replaced bridge, they abruptly called it off.

"He's got a mouthful of novocaine," Teeter told headquarters. "He can't do this."

The truth, as Teeter knew, was not that he couldn't but that he wouldn't. It was Bush's pride that hurt, not his jaw, and he was in no mood to be nice to Buchanan.

"I won by thirty points," he told his handlers, stretching it some, "and that's what I want to say."

Their draft statement was accordingly discarded, and Bush typed his own, with a facility practiced over a half-century of writing bread-and-butter notes. He was, he said, "delighted tonight to have won"—a reading of the results in which he was practically alone. He conceded that there was "dissatisfaction" in New Hampshire over the economy; the primary, as a result, had been "far closer than many had predicted," and he understood why. But he offered no apologies for his own record and no gracious words for Buchanan—not even so much as a grudging mention of his name.

His spin merchants were left to put out the line that Pat, after all, had spent ten weeks and $2 million in a state with a particularly high misery index and had "only" got 37 percent of the vote. If he couldn't win there, so the party line went, he probably couldn't win anywhere, and the press would soon lose interest in his insurgency. There was more merit to the official optimism than the people retailing it knew or felt at the time; Buchanan would never make quite so big a splash again. But the sunny-side-up approach sounded a bit tinny when a sitting president had been repudiated by so many voters in his own party. One middle manager on Fifteenth Street looked at the returns and concluded, with a clinical air, that a lot of people out there hated George Bush.

The verdict did have its salutary effects, not least of them scaring the reelection team into a seven-day work week. To some of its veteran warriors, the enterprise *felt* like a campaign for the first time since its sputtery launch. But it reminded one senior White House official of what has come to be called, in the cant phrase of the day, a dysfunctional family—one in which the parents are too weak to maintain control and the children have to try to make things work on their own. They couldn't, and they fell to blame-mongering instead. Everybody was mad at somebody and said so, usually anonymously, to the press. The talebearing got so bad at one point that Fred Malek, as manager, declared it to be "an act of treason" against the president and directed that it stop forthwith.

The spill of information and insult into public view tapered off thereafter. The finger-pointing within the family did not. Campaign people referred to their peers at the White House as "weenies" or worse. The White House crowd lamented the chronic indecision on Fifteenth Street; they missed what one staffer called the "crazy courage" that a Roger Ailes or a Lee Atwater had brought to past campaigns. Both sides were also divided within, the hired hands against their bosses.

"Get ready for a tough couple or three weeks," Sam Skinner said at a White House senior staff meeting the morning after New Hampshire.

"At least Sam got *something* right," one of his less than loving colleagues jeered afterward.

The noise level, moreover, did not stop with the usual barracks bitching about the line officers. You knew there was trouble, a White House official said, when the handlers started bad-mouthing the candidate. That they did, and even Bush's generals joined in; Bob Teeter and Sam Skinner were heard complaining privately that the president had no vision, that he didn't pay enough attention to domestic problems, and that he tended to go goofy if you put him in front of an audience without a script.

The bad feelings, to a degree, were reciprocated by Bush. Like most candidates, he looked around him for other people to blame when things went bad; on his list, his own managers were up there with Buchanan, the Republican right, the Democratic left, the press, and the fates as the objects of his unconcealed displeasure. Both he and Barbara were having a particularly hard time finding a comfort level with Skinner, a man of strong ego and diffuse management style. But the president's larger complaint was with the sheer cacophony all around him—the difficulty his team seemed to have reaching a consensus on anything. It galled him to a point where even his old chums found him cranky—"as cranky as I've ever seen him," one said. "He's no fun to be around these days."

He was, moreover, taking his irritability home to the East Wing after work. A crony who came by for a purely social visit one evening was drawn aside by the First Lady for a private chat.

"My friend," she said, meaning her husband, "is not happy with the way things are going."

Bush himself tried to say so, mostly by indirection, over a casual dinner of pasta and salad with his inner political circle the Sunday night after New Hampshire; they had to listen between the lines to understand that he was telling them to get their act together. His single open show of peevishness with them came when they presented him a tentative decision they had reached on a policy question affecting the campaign. Bush said okay, but he was reserving the right to change his mind later.

"I agree," one of them said. "But if you get the urge to do that, maybe we should talk about it some more."

"All right," Bush answered tartly. "I heard you. I appreciate your counsel. But remember, *I'm* going to make the decision—all right?"

His irritation otherwise was directed mostly at Buchanan, and it was mixed with bafflement as to his motives. That Pat might actually want to be president, this time or next, seemed beyond Bush's ken.

"Why is he being the way he is?" he asked. "What the hell is he after? What does he want?"

Nobody had a sure answer. A campaign is nearly always the lengthened shadow of its candidate, and Bush's handlers were, like their client, pragmatic men. They had no real feeling for movement conservatism beyond the cosseting it required at election time. For them, the doctrinaire right was like a petting zoo where you showed up once every four years, stroked the animals for a while and then went home to the world of affairs. What Buchanan represented to them was not a cause to be parsed or a soul to be plumbed. He was an inconvenience to be removed—the sooner, in their view, the better.

"We know how to beat this guy," Teeter told the president, "but you're going to have to campaign like hell the next three weeks."

"Fine," Bush said. "Whatever's necessary."

There was little sentiment then for the president's going after Buchanan directly. The postmortem judgment on New Hampshire was that staying positive had probably been a mistake; the command group, flogged by Bob Teeter and Charlie Black, was moving toward a decision to slam Pat hard and try to run him out of the race. But as the campaign turned west and south, Bush's people weren't yet sure that it would be wise for him to dirty his own hands.

Bush agreed. "He's trying my patience," he said. "If this goes on much longer. . . ." He paused for a moment, as if fantasizing a terrible revenge. "When somebody hits me," he went on finally, "I want to strike back. But it's below the presidency to answer such nasty attacks."

Nothing else of consequence got settled that night—not even a final decision as to whether or how the campaign ought to go negative without the president's active help. After New Hampshire, the campaign had entered what one player called a hurricane of meetings—a most apt metaphor for the level of wind, noise, and scatteration they seemed to produce. A first flight of negative TV ads went up attacking Buchanan's quirky views on the issues. But they did little to shore up Bush's own standing or to bring the strays back home. In South Dakota, where Buchanan was not on the ballot, 31 percent of the primary electorate chose an uncommitted slate—a vote, in effect, for anybody except Bush.

"What do you recommend?" Dan Quayle's brainy chief of staff, William Kristol, twitted Teeter. "That we put up negative ads against 'uncommitted'?"

Teeter granted Kristol his premise—that there was probably going to be a protest vote of 30 percent or so no matter what the president did. "But you've still got to knock Buchanan down," he said. "You've got to get him out. You have to make him an unrespectable vehicle for that sentiment."

Bush didn't like bickering among his wartime consiglieri, not, anyway, in his presence. The recurrent squabbles they brought to him were the kind of thing his friend Jim Baker used to settle for him out of court, but under the new crowd, they kept happening. There was one loud scene in the Oval Office about whether or not he should attack Buchanan openly in a speech in South Carolina for running an "extreme and nasty" campaign that could only damage the party in November. Teeter, who had labored for a day and a half getting the tone to his liking, argued vehemently for using it. Dan Quayle was as heatedly opposed; he thought the president should be going after the Democrats and would look small and whiny if he picked on Buchanan instead.

Bush, caught in the crossfire, finally sided with Quayle and decided against using the material. But that, to his great annoyance, didn't stop the infighting. The day of the speech, the boys on Fifteenth Street shipped a revised text to him on Air Force One with the offending language only slightly toned down. Quayle, off campaigning on his own, was furious when his staff called to inform him of the end run. He phoned the White House to register his protest and demanded that it be made known to the president. It was, and the passage was finally scissored out. The only residue of the quarrel was more bad feeling in a campaign that had all it could use.

There was further discord over the frenetic schedule the campaign proposed for Bush—twenty-two cities in twenty days between New Hampshire and Super Tuesday. Quayle and his people once again were among the dissenters, arguing that, as one put it, the president would lose the glow of the Oval Office if he ran around the countryside like a congressional candidate grubbing for votes. It would be better, in their view, for him to sit tight in Washington, governing the country and battling the Congress, than to show up somewhere Out There with nothing much to say.

Bush himself was inclined to agree. "Why am I doing this?" he asked his chief scheduler, Kathy Super, singling out a couple of particularly dubious stops.

Skinner had put them on the schedule, Super said.

Bush sent for Skinner and repeated the question.

"Teeter thinks it's important to go everywhere," Skinner said.

Bush didn't, but his manic mystery tour continued, and so did the steady diminution of his standing in the polls. The sad fact was that he *didn't* have much to say when he showed up somewhere, no message of his own and none his people could divine with any clarity in his record.

"You guys are the architects and I'm the construction engineer," Skinner's miscast deputy, Henson Moore, told the campaign group at a White House strategy meeting one morning. "Tell me what I'm constructing."

No one knew. There were no blueprints near at hand to build from; as it had been all his public life, the House of Bush was less a work of architecture than an assemblage of daily improvisations. There was nothing permanent in its structure, nothing visionary in its design. Bush's art instead was eclectic in the extreme. He had built his presidency with found materials, and if one piece or another came to displease him or his critics, he simply took it down and threw it away.

There were days in his frantic travels through the South, indeed, when his only immutable principle seemed to be his mutability under fire. When Buchanan charged that the National Endowment for the Arts was funding pornography, Bush fired its director. When a prospect for the top environmental job in the Justice Department came under conservative attack, Bush dumped him and chose somebody of less Greenish hue. When word got out that the Internal Revenue Service wanted churches to identify their big givers by name, Buchanan raised a ruckus, and the plan was held up for a prolonged "reevaluation."

And when Bush's acquiescence in the tax increase of 1990 at last became too burdensome to carry any longer, he abandoned that, too. His political people had been nagging him regularly to repent of ever having agreed to it, and Bush had as regularly said no; he and his economists felt that it had been a necessary trade-off to rein in the deficit and get the economy percolating again. But Buchanan had made what had been an act of pragmatism look more like a Faustian bargain, and the president's handlers warned him that if he didn't disown it, he would still be carrying it like a millstone around his neck on Election Day.

Bush finally yielded; it was only when necessity became mother to invention, always a suspenseful process in his hands, that things started going awry. His managers advised him to wait till the March 20 deadline he had laid down for passage of his economic package. Congress naturally would reject his proposals, and Bush could slip something appropriately rueful into his response—an aside to the effect that accepting a tax rise hadn't worked out as he had hoped and that he wouldn't make the same mistake again.

But he contrived to get both the timing and the content wrong. Instead of waiting, he did his act of contrition in a newspaper interview on the eve of the March 3 primary in Georgia, and managed in the process not to sound contrite at all. "Listen," he said, "if I had that to do over, I wouldn't do it. Look at all the flak it's taking."

His field operatives in the conservative South were ecstatic. His strategists in Washington were not. The only way to neutralize the issue, in their view, was for Bush to admit that he had been wrong on substantive, not political, grounds; the point had to be that the tax increase had been a bad idea in principle. "We really need to put this on a policy basis," Teeter told him gently, after the fact.

The damage by then had been done. Bush had put his mea culpa on a political basis, making it sound as if his reputation and his survival in office were all that really mattered to him. The value of his repentance was accordingly debased; he had made himself neither leader nor sinner but victim, upset mainly at being held accountable for his campaign promises. A *New York Times* editorial rechristened him President Noodle, scolding him for an "appalling lack of conviction," and some of Bush's most loyal lieutenants had to agree that that was the impression he had left.

"I guess I screwed up the tax thing," Bush himself told a friend afterward.

No one around him had the brass to tell him so directly, but he had.

The showdown in Georgia was already the source of some anxiety among Bush's generals, who saw in it the potential for panic if Buchanan did really well. Their strategy was to go for an early knockout—to punish Buchanan in the South, starting in Georgia, and drive him from the field as soon as possible thereafter. But the president had played into Pat's hands with his clumsy handling of the tax question; as one of his most trusted aides remarked, it made him seem willing yet again to tack left or right for no apparent reason larger than the political needs of the moment. There were days, indeed, when Bush seemed to have become Buchanan's caricature of him as a man without principles—none, anyway, for which he would risk his career.

Pat's Excellent Adventure

Me and Teddy Roosevelt, Pat Buchanan had thought when he went to bed still sky-high on primary night in New Hampshire. Like TR, he had mutinied against a sitting Republican president and had bloodied him badly—maybe badly enough to bring him down, as Roosevelt had helped topple William Howard Taft in 1912. It was only the beginning of a long march, but the way he and his sister Bay had been spinning it at the victory party, they were going to beat Bush somewhere in the South and light a firestorm that would blaze across the country. And even if it didn't happen, he had already achieved something big, something permanent. Me and Teddy, he was thinking. Pat Buchanan was in the history books alongside the greatest rebel Republican of them all.

But he and his war party woke up in an oddly dark mood the next day, a collective hangover having little to do with the victory toasts they had raised to one another the night before. New Hampshire had exposed Buchanan's vulnerabilities as glaringly as it had the president's. He would be heading south with no message, no polling, no field organization, and only a half-done semblance of a schedule, much of it putting him in the wrong places at the wrong times. What passed for a strategy for the weeks ahead had been thrown together by his team on primary day at a back table at the restaurant in their Manchester hotel.

In the cold light of morning, Buchanan's page in history thus looked less like Teddy Roosevelt's than like Gary Hart's—not the pleasure seeker of 1987 but the overreacher of 1984. Hart had actually won New Hampshire and still was undone; his momentum, as Ed Rollins had reminded Buchanan early on, had simply outrun his meager resources on the ground. Pat, at the time, hadn't seemed much interested in going beyond New Hampshire anyway. His intent, as Rollins understood it, was to make a splash there as a prelude to a real race in 1996. The problem was that the splash, when it actually happened, looked at least fleetingly like a wave, and Buchanan, like Hart before him, was utterly unprepared to ride it.

He had proclaimed Georgia the New Hampshire of the South, but Patrick the Unready spent his earliest days in Dixie wandering South Carolina and Florida instead; no one had thought to book him into his prime target state. Even his flight southward on an aged Convair turboprop had been a horror show of slack advancing and long delays, including, at the far end, a lost half-hour roaming a Marriott hotel in Tampa in search of the audience he was supposed to address. It took his overwhelmed party that long to figure out that the crowd was waiting for him at another Marriott.

By the time Buchanan finally got to Georgia, he had just eight days in which to achieve what he had spent ten weeks building in New Hampshire. The hour was too late and the state too large for his surprising new skills at retail politics. Georgia, as he mused one day in his travels, had ten media markets and six and a half million people. If you went somewhere and shook fifty hands, so what?

What he had was his gift of polemical gab, and he used it efficiently, belaboring Bush in ads and media events with the wedge social issues that had helped elect him president in the first place. One devastating spot, tailored for the Bubba market, showed idyllic scenes of children at play—practically all of them white—and charged Bush with "closing doors to their future" by having surrendered on racial quotas. Another featured a group of gay men frolicking in leather S&M gear, a scene from a movie indirectly financed by the National Endowment for the Arts. The taxpayers were subsidizing pornographic and blasphemous works, the ad said, and it wasn't enough for Buchanan that Bush had made a human sacrifice of the head man at NEA. Elect me, he said, and the whole hellish place would be padlocked and fumigated.

The Bush campaign returned fire this time, forking up some tasty bits of Buchaniana out of their ample opposition-research files. But combat was Buchanan's game, and he was as intoxicated as a heavyweight title contender by the roar of the crowd and the scent of Bush's blood on the air. Even his public rhetoric smelled of the locker-room at Stillman's Gym in the '50s. He had put Bush on the canvas once in New Hampshire, he said, and if he decked him again in

Georgia, the whole thing could be over; people were going to start counting the president out.

So Buchanan kept swinging. His attack in the South was tailored to the Christian right. Its big-name lay leaders and divines, men like Pat Robertson and Jerry Falwell, were with Bush for their own reasons of realpolitik, but their followers were there for the plucking, and Buchanan played to them with a relentless stress on social and moral values. It was when he and his campaign succumbed to an attack of the heebie-jeebies in the last days that they threw up their ad attacking Bush on quotas. The spot was, as one of his people said, a conscious pitch to "the hidden racist vote"—the 5 or 10 percent who never seemed to show up in the polls but who dependably voted their skin color on Election Day.

In the end, Buchanan couldn't quite deliver the knockout punch. He came close, or thought he did; his 36 percent split of the vote in Georgia was a fresh embarrassment to the president, and so were his 30 percent showings the same day in Maryland and Colorado—states where he hadn't even campaigned. "We can win the nomination, we can win the nomination!" he crowed that night in Atlanta, and when he wakened the morning after in Shreveport, Louisiana, his next stop, his fantasies took on even brighter hues.

He was smiling seraphically when Frank Luntz found him in his room at the Holiday Inn, sipping a glass of orange juice and reading his notices in a stack of morning papers. If he had a worry, it was Super Tuesday; he was afraid he might do well in one state, maybe even win it, and still lose the day by running badly everywhere else. But his mood was already up when Luntz arrived, and as they went through a closer reading of the Georgia numbers, it reached dizzying new heights. A hefty share of his vote, Luntz said, had come from Democratic and independent crossovers—mostly southern white conservatives who had been voting Republican for president at least since Reagan. Bush was losing them and, without them, would lose the White House as well.

"George Bush is unelectable," Luntz said. He was turning into Jimmy Carter. He would lose in the fall, big-time, and take the party down with him.

The Carter analogy had been meant only for that most perishable form of political communication, the message of the day. Luntz had tried it out on Greg Mueller, the press secretary, in the hotel bar late the night before, and Mueller, with nothing better in hand, had asked him to run it past Buchanan. It clicked only too well; a sheet of Kleenex, in Buchanan's hands, somehow became a tapestry. The president, he said at a press conference that morning, was losing Reagan Democrats in droves to a man who only twelve weeks earlier had been no more than a television commentator. "George Bush should step down," he said. "He's in danger of becoming the Jimmy Carter of the Republican Party."

The commentary in the days thereafter fastened less on his analysis than on his hubris—the possibility that, as Marlin Fitzwater acidly put it, Pat had gone Looney Tunes. Maybe King George's reign was shaky, but Buchanan's rebellion against the crown had in fact reached its flood in Georgia and was already beginning to recede. His claims to have won without winning, plausible to the arbiters of opinion after New Hampshire, would grow harder to sustain if he kept losing by two to one or worse everywhere else.

With the approach of Super Tuesday, moreover, the degree of difficulty was about to get exponentially higher. As he had feared, Buchanan had reached that point where the sheer sprawl of the landscape and the exorbitant cost of covering it were more than his fly-by-wire enterprise could handle. Bay had given in only grudgingly to polling in the South and, when it came in, had paid little attention to it. She was too busy trying to do everything herself, and she preferred her own instincts anyway, though they were highly changeable and sometimes hard for the help to follow. In Mississippi, Buchanan's prime target state, she changed the ad schedule five times in a single day and threatened to find a new buyer if the Weinschels couldn't keep up with her whims.

At that point, Buchanan became the political equivalent of a migraine headache, not so much a threat to the president as a source of recurring and debilitating pain. The fear he had caused Bush's reelection team subsided. Their determination to smash him did not. Even the doves began coming around as Buchanan got meaner and, in the process, kept undermining Bush's candidacy. It would only make the president look weak and vulnerable to the swing voters he would need in November if he let Pat rough him up all spring and summer without swinging back. As one of his strategists said, he had to show people that he was willing to fight for—well, whatever it was he was willing to fight for.

The plan that emerged was to punish Buchanan—to give him so bad a shellacking across the South that he would have to find an early and graceful way out. Some mutual friends of the two campaigns warned the president's men that their early-kayo strategy misread Pat's real intentions. The guy didn't give a fuck about '92, one old

Reagan-Bush warrior told a buddy on Fifteenth Street; he was making a name and a base for himself for '96, and as long as there were camera crews trailing him around and adoring crowds urging him to screw Bush, he would keep going. But the advocates of a blitzkrieg strategy prevailed. They wanted Buchanan dead, politically speaking, and circled March 17—primary day in Illinois and Michigan—as an appropriate day for the last rites.

Whatever was left of their fastidiousness about attack ads got lost on the road south. One new spot chided Buchanan for his opposition to the Gulf war; another for having once written that women were "less equipped psychologically" than men to succeed in the workplace; yet another for driving a Mercedes—his wife's, Buchanan said—in preference to an American-made car. When inspiration flagged at one meeting on scripts, the insuperably mild Bob Teeter went into what an aide called his *Boss* Teeter mode, impatient and curt. "What this spot has to do," he said sharply enough to cut through the fog, "is tell voters that this guy's the goddam president and the other guy's a goddam typewriter pusher, and the toughest thing he's had to do in his life is change the ribbon on his Olivetti."

The flak attack worked, and so did the president's superior resources for fighting a multifront war. A pattern was taking form in polling for the Super Tuesday primaries and beyond: a fourth to a third of the Republicans in any given state were sore enough at Bush to vote against him, whether or not Buchanan showed up to campaign or was even on the ballot. There was not much the president's men could do about that, but they could lower the ceiling over Buchanan's head, and with negative campaigning, judiciously applied, they did.

Super Tuesday, indeed, would prove the beginning of the end of Pat's excellent adventure. He lost all eight states in play by margins of two, three, or four to one. He did worst in Mississippi, to which he had committed heavily, and best in Florida and Rhode Island, where he had barely campaigned at all; it was at least arguable thereafter that the Buchanan Revolution had little to do with Buchanan and might in fact be better off without him. He did keep slogging on to the finale in California, but his percentage of the vote drifted downward through the twenties into the teens and lower. At a point in his decline, he found it useful to his own future in Republican politics to moderate and finally quit his direct attacks on the president. He had by then become no more than a nuisance to Bush's men, a household pest who, at some modest expense in time and money, had to be kept under control.

"Our Worst Political Nightmare"

It was in the nature of things that there would one day be a reconciliation scene—a prime-time tableau of unity, probably, at the party convention in Houston. But Bush, in his continuing pique, directed his people not to make any overtures to Buchanan. "Look, I don't care whether he speaks at the convention or not," he told them, "but we're not asking him." Bush had spent a political lifetime trying to please the Republican right, against his own pragmatic instincts, and was not about to reward the ultimate act of ingratitude. If Pat wanted any favors, he was going to have to come begging.

The president's spirits had been raw even in his hour of victory, his anger with Buchanan redoubled by the latest evidence of his own sinking fortunes. His mood made Super Tuesday a curiously joyless day in the White House, and his people could not cheer him with the news that the exit polls were coming up roses—that he was winning everywhere. The only poll he seemed to care about was a new national survey in the morning paper recording a further downward slide in his approval rating, to a sad-sack 39 percent. If the election had been held that day, Bill Clinton, battered though he was, would have won by five points.

Bush was seething. You guys have had me all over the place for two weeks, he told his managers, and everything's worse.

His people were silent. He looked at them, tight-lipped.

"Why are the numbers going down?" he demanded.

"You're not getting the message out," someone was brave enough to reply.

"Why am I not getting the message out?" Bush asked.

Resolve melted before his rancor. There were mumbled excuses about the media's fixation on Buchanan, the deficiencies of Bush's own speechwriting shop—anything anyone could think of at the safe outer margins of their concern. What several believed but none dared say was that Bush himself was the problem. You couldn't get the message out if you didn't have a message.

And so the quickening erosion of the Bush presidency went on unchecked. Fred Steeper's Super Tuesday had been spoiled by his own latest polling numbers, and not just because of Bush's shrunken approval rating. What troubled him more was the sullen and vengeful mood abroad in the land. It was out of character for Americans to be pessimistic, Steeper thought, but the majority who felt that the country was on the wrong track had swollen to a stunning 78 percent. The gloom level was the worst he had seen in his twenty years in the polling business.

This time, it was Bush who was in the crosshairs; his situation, Steeper wrote in a bleak mid-March summary of his findings, was "about as bad as it could be." The good news was that the president still had some important plus factors working for him: his experience, his credibility, his show of resolve in the Gulf war. The residue of Desert Storm, in Steeper's data, was the enduring belief that Bush was a strong leader—or that he could be "once he decides to put his mind to it."

America's quarrel with him was that he appeared not to have put his mind to the problems that mattered to the unrich, unseen majority of the country; for them, he had become the Last Inaction Hero. "They think if he had been on top of things," Steeper wrote, "he would have done something last summer." Bush hadn't, not so far as the voters could discern, and the recession had been allowed to run on unaddressed. The president's show of passivity through the fall and winter had compounded what was "a huge problem" for him politically. His belated claim in the primaries that he had a plan seemed only to have irritated the voters, reminding them of how little attention he had paid to their travail until it mattered to his own survival.

It was true, as Steeper noted, that people were inclined to blame Congress more than the president for having brought on the ills of the economy. But running against the crowd at the far end of Pennsylvania Avenue had built-in limits for Bush, since he and they stood together in the dock. *All* Washington insiders were in trouble, as the protest vote for Pat Buchanan and the early demise of Senators Bob Kerrey and Tom Harkin in the Democratic primaries suggested. On his blackest days, Steeper could imagine the election turning into a kind of political Jonestown for incumbents: a mass immolation ending with a Democrat in the White House and a Republican majority on Capitol Hill.

The only means of salvation he could find in his numbers was a back-to-square-one strategy—a belated effort to "rehabilitate" Bush by accentuating the positives in his domestic record, such as they were, and loosing a flurry of new economic initiatives to freshen up his portfolio. That meant getting past the intraparty catfight with Buchanan and arming for the real showdown against Clinton or Tsongas in the fall. "We are moving to a situation where it will be a choice of one of their 'plans' against our track record," Steeper wrote. "If there is no recovery, this choice is not a good one for us."

His findings still bore heavily on him when, at a campaign staff meeting just after Super Tuesday, he was called upon to recite. His tone was as dry and abstract as a pathologist's on reporting a bad biopsy.

"If the election were held thirty days from now," he said, "we would lose."

The room was silent for a moment.

"That's bullshit," Charlie Black said, his soft Carolina drawl dark with rebuke. "In thirty days, we can run a better campaign than they can. In thirty days, the people in this room are better and smarter than Clinton's people."

"Presidents with 40 percent approval ratings don't get reelected," Steeper said. "Presidents with recessions that aren't stopping don't get reelected. Presidents facing an electorate who want a lot of change don't get reelected."

"Clinton's not gonna get elected with 55 percent negatives," Black replied.

The quarrel was the collision of men under stress, one thinking the campaign needed a wake-up call, the other fearing the damage to its already low morale. It lasted a minute, no more, and soon blew over on a momentary gust of good news. The economy seemed for a time to be perking up, the Clinton campaign had sailed back into stormy waters, and the Buchanan revolt was entering its long, slow fade.

But as the primaries had exposed the president's weaknesses, the wrangle among his own men was a window on the difficulties still before him. All Steeper had intended was to alert his comrades that they had become the underdogs; as he wrote in a follow-up memo to Teeter and Black a few days later, they would have to wage a high-risk campaign and "do some things we would not normally do" if Bush was to have any prayer of winning. Steeper's view of the landscape had not changed, and he offered no apologies for it. The outcome, he wrote, would seem obvious to the most impartial observer: "We face a twenty-month recession, a 78 percent 'wrong track' number, and a Southern Conservative Democrat. In my mind, this is our worst political nightmare."

Black was not blind to the realities of the president's situation or to the need for an aggressive, catch-up campaign. He was the nearest thing to Lee Atwater's heir in the campaign, the tough guy with a back-channel line to Bush; the president had entrusted his fortunes to Doctor Jekyll, in the person of Bob Teeter, but he still liked talking down and dirty with Mister Hyde. The polling available to him and his counselors that spring was indeed the profile of a loser. Steeper's prescription was to rehabilitate Bush. Black's was to save him by blowing up Clinton.

"The guy's a liar and a draft-dodger," he said at a staff meeting during the spring. "There's no reason we can't play with it as hard as we want."

His side of the argument would ultimately prevail. The economy didn't really improve, not in a timely way, and neither did the president's numbers. By summer, Bush would seem beyond rehabilitation. All that remained to him and his men was the politics of destruction—the attempt, combat-tested successfully in 1988, to make your guy look better by making the other guy look worse.

17

"He Doesn't Get It"

One day in the spring of George Bush's decline, a man of cabinet rank in the government and impeccable loyalty to the president sat sadly cataloguing all the things that had gone wrong in his friend's campaign. Most of them were the obvious ones. Buchanan had damaged Bush. So had Ross Perot and the tidal wave of anti-incumbency he was then riding. Bush's own late start was a continuing handicap. His staffing was weak. He had no message, no agenda for prosperity at home to lay alongside his prodigies of peacemaking in the world.

"But his biggest single problem," the president's comrade said, "is that he hasn't persuaded anyone he has any convictions."

A visitor asked why not.

"Because I don't think he *has* any convictions," his friend replied softly, almost sadly. "If you asked him why he wanted to be reelected, he'd have to look at his note cards. That's the fundamental problem at the core."

It was a season of despair in Bush's service, and while recrimination was its common currency, the trail of blame most often led back to the empty space at the center of the enterprise. The sustaining hope had been that a rousing recovery would render a Vision Thing unnecessary. The reelection effort, Fred Steeper said, would then have become a no-brainer—a race so easy that it wouldn't much matter whether Bush seemed to stand for anything or not. But as the economy limped along at stall speed, his people found themselves counting more on a wounded Clinton to lose the election than on the president to win it.

Bush had left them no other option; neither he nor they had come up with a positive rationale for his candidacy, a compelling argument for reelecting him beyond his blue-chip curriculum vitae and his re-assuringly familiar face. His speeches, during the spring, had taken on a certain hangdog tone—an air of helplessness that reminded Dan Quayle, for one, of the late days of Jimmy Carter. The veep showed up for lunch in the Oval Office one day in April with a copy of Carter's famous lament over the Great Malaise of '79. For effect, he had underlined some of Carter's damper language: *I will do my best, but I will not do it alone. . . .*

Quayle waited while Bush scanned the text. Then he handed over Exhibit B—a draft speech for the president's own campaign. The language was depressingly similar.

Bush got the picture and, two days later, sent the malaise speech off to Fifteenth Street with a covering note in his own hand. "Bob Teeter," it said. "We must avoid the kind of handwringing that Carter conveyed to the nation in this speech. I'm sure you agree with that. . . . Just 'FYI,' y'all."

Figuring out what he *should* say remained a harder puzzle. The elders of the campaign looked on the message gap, as on most problems, as a matter of political mechanics. Bush was still the guy people wanted to vote for, in their view, and a combination of clever repackaging and a weakened opponent would ultimately provide them the reasons. But Bush's younger middle managers longed for a flag of brighter colors to rally round. The campaign reminded one of them of a dog-food company worrying about squeezing better gas mileage out of its delivery trucks when the real problem was the product: it was purple, and dogs wouldn't eat it.

The Voice of the People

The Bush team took comfort where they could find it that spring, most often in faith. It was frequently said among them that the formula for getting the president reelected wasn't something you could plot on a graph—it would simply happen. Bush himself seemed briefly cheered by his prospects, once Buchanan had been safely neutered and Clinton had been roughed up in the Democratic primaries. When the president complained one April morning about all the damn fundraising events on his schedule, his people took it as a sign that he thought he was winning. It was only when George was looking into the abyss, one old Reagan-Bush strategist said, that he would shut up and do as he was told.

Faith is, of course, a perishable thing in politics; the business is governed by numbers, and Bush's had been trending steadily downward since fall. At the beginning of May, the believers did find a bit of hope amid the usual bad tidings in Fred Steeper's polling. The mood Out There was still bad, and so was Bush's job rating. But in an election, you run against somebody, and the president was then beating both Clinton and Perot by margins approaching two to one.

By the first of June, even that faint glow was gone. A new public poll showed Bush in free fall, down fifteen points in a month, and he was no longer number one—he had fallen behind Perot and was a scant four points ahead of Clinton for second place. His plunge set off one of the recurring anxiety attacks that had afflicted his team from the beginning and raised the level of recrimination among its factions and generations; the guys at the top, one young warhawk complained, could have run the Brezhnev campaign. The press was once again full of anonymous sniper fire, some of it directed at Bush himself by men he had imagined to be his friends. Their ingratitude for his past kindnesses was a breach of his gentleman's code; people who owed him ran for cover and trashed him as soon as the weather turned hot, and, an aide reported, his feelings were hurt.

His spirit turned sour, his manner abrupt. Staffers who brought business to his attention were greeted with sharp looks, clenched fists, and curt just-the-facts-please responses. He believed himself badly served by the help, and Sam Skinner, as chief of staff, found himself increasingly the target of his boss's annoyance. "If you're so smart," Bush demanded of him one day, "why aren't you president?" But his displeasure was directed at Bush-Quayle headquarters as well for its tardiness at producing a strategy to stop the bleeding, let alone win the election.

"I've done everything you've asked me to do," he complained at one council of war, "and I keep going down in the polls."

His situation in fact was worse than the raw numbers showed or than Bob Teeter had been willing to tell him. In late April, Steeper's polling shop conducted a series of focus-group studies among 1988 Bush voters in suburban communities in California, Michigan, and North Carolina and were stunned at the ferocity with which they had turned on a president they had helped to elect. The only good news was that Clinton had become the object of their contempt; they used words like "liar" and "scum" to describe him and, as Steeper wrote in a summary of the findings, appeared to be "dismissing him from serious consideration as president." The real race for their hearts and minds, so it seemed then, was between Bush and Perot, and the bad news from the focus groups was that Perot was winning it, three to one. Among swing voters, Steeper said in a less guarded separate memo reflecting his own pessimism, "Perot is a major threat to the president; Clinton is not."

What Steeper had tapped into was the undertow of discontent with government and its recent history of failure. The voters, one of his several memos on the study said, "are disgusted with politicians, partisan politics and government gridlock. . . . They see the country facing enormous domestic problems—the deficit, crime, health care, education, and a weakened economy—and a political system incapable of offering any real solutions." And, he wrote, they were scared, not just about their own lives but about the state of the American Dream. "Everyone agrees," he said, "that today's generation will be the first not to do better than their parents."

Their dismissal of Clinton was cold comfort, given their deep disappointment in Bush. They were not open to the standard arguments for him—that he was good at foreign policy, or that he had been stymied by Congress, or that he was reengaging with problems at home. They thought of him as "the absent president," uninterested in their problems, Steeper wrote. Anything he put forward so late in the day would be seen as a catch-up attack on "yet another problem he should have taken care of before he faced reelection." Neither were they taken with a theme line then under consideration by the campaign: *The man who changed the world will change America.* As Steeper drily put it, "They are critical of the premise (he didn't change the world) and the logic (he should have changed America first)."

So discouraging were the results that Teeter pruned the distribution list for any such studies in the future from a dozen to two, himself and Fred Malek. It would, he thought, be imprudent to spread any further gloom through an already demoralized campaign. But the command group did splice together a twenty-minute highlight tape from the focus groups for the private edification of the president. He had to be shaken from his rescue fantasy, the dream that Desert Storm and a reviving economy would save him, and his people had no more potent medicine than the video. One aide, previewing it, looked around the room for a window to jump out of. Another stared at the screen and muttered, "President Perot. President Perot."

Bush himself was nearly as shocked, watching the tape one May weekend at Camp David. "There is a consensus that George Bush is at his core a kind and compassionate person, well-meaning and sincere," the covering memo said, summing up the findings as politely as possible, "and his presidency is not dismissed outright as a failure. What is lacking is the perception of actions and results in the issues important to people today."

The unfiltered voices on the tape were not nearly so gentle with their president:

"He doesn't get it."

"Out of touch."

"Doesn't care."

"Doesn't have a clue."

"Haven't seen him lately."

"We don't think he's paying attention."

"More interested in foreigners than America."

"He doesn't understand how bad things are out here."

The drumbeat went on and on; its cumulative effect was overwhelming, and Bush had no real rebuttal, no credible road map suggesting that he could find a way out of the woods. At a campaign show-and-tell session in the Roosevelt Room not long thereafter, a Bush-Quayle staffer talked about satellite TV transmission as a cheap and effective way for the president to reach large numbers of voters in widely scattered media markets; it had cost only $15,000 for one recent "Ask George Bush" event.

A senior Bush operative scribbled out a note and sent it to a colleague at the far end of the room.

"If only we could spend $15,000 and get a message," it said.

"For a message," the return note replied, "I'd sacrifice my first-born child."

The Adults and the Kids

The quest opened a generational divide within the campaign between factions who came to be known as The Adults and The Kids—the pragmatic senior hands and the thirtysomething young bloods who thought of themselves as reform conservatives. Dick Darman, who owned and flaunted the most formidable intellect among The Adults, was no longer sending DOMESTIC STORM! memos down whatever black hole in the Bush firmament had been devouring them. Nothing had come of them, and Darman no longer believed that the president could credibly descend from a mountaintop one morning with a vision. The hour was too late, and the negative perception that he didn't have one was too deeply embedded for that. The only way to work through it, Darman thought, was to fashion one incrementally, proposal by proposal, like an artisan of old patiently fitting bits of colored tile into a mosaic.

But The Kids believed that the president actually could be recreated at age sixty-eight as the champion, if not the creator, of young ideas—a post-Reagan reform agenda seeking nonbureaucratic solutions to a wide range of public concerns. One of the leading Kid theoreticians, James Pinkerton, a gangly towhead of half Bush's years, had wrapped the concept a bit fancily as "The New Paradigm" and proposed that it could be applied to problems ranging from health to day care to air pollution. Fighting taxes and communists had carried the Republicans about as far as it could, Pinkerton believed and argued when he could find a forum for his views. The party's future lay in what he called "a platform of domestic reconstruction," challenging old interests with new ideas.

His audiences tended to be more scholarly than political. He had begun promoting his reform agenda as one of Bush's White House policy planners, a job description as meaningful as photo editor at the *Wall Street Journal*, and had carried it with him when he was reassigned to Fifteenth Street. There were kindred spirits in both shops, intellectuals like Bill Kristol in Quayle's office and activists like Mary Matalin at campaign headquarters. But they were outranked and outnumbered, and Pinkerton, by spring, was finding it hard dragging himself to his desk in the mornings. There was, he told friends, a senescence about the operation—an exhaustion of purpose beyond the personal and professional interests of its leaders in having helped reelect a president.

It wasn't as if the older crowd didn't listen to his ideas; they did. But nothing seemed to happen except nods and smiles, and when his frustration reached a low boil, Pinkerton—Pink, to his friends—announced at a senior staff meeting that the campaign reminded him of the Union Army in the Civil War. "We're big, slow, well-funded, and not all that tactically adroit," he said. "We have more than our share of careerists, opportunists, cynics, and profiteers. But there is a moral core, a moral thread running through what we're doing here. It's bigger than all of us. It involves the liberation of our fellow human beings, and we'll win if we don't lose sight of that."

The lecture made Pinkerton feel better but changed little else. The White House and the campaign remained securely in the hands of The Adults and their orthodoxies, chief among them the view that there was nothing wrong with Bush that a mending economy and a nuclear assault on Clinton wouldn't cure. Bush, in their model, was the man of stature in the race. Give him a real and timely recovery, The Adults said, and his reelection was secure; Clinton's negatives alone, matched against Bush's standing as president, would kill him.

The Kids countered in vain that a dangerous new dynamic was at play—that decades of failed government had rendered *all* politicians suspect and most of politics irrelevant to the problems of everyday life. What people cared about, one of The Kids said, was whether their children could walk to school without getting mugged and how they could pay for nursing homes for their parents. They hated Washington and its inbred folkways—hated them so much that they would elect a convicted baby-killer, let alone a man of Clinton's lesser alleged misdemeanors, so long as he wasn't part of the system.

The only way for Bush to stay afloat on the tides, The Kids argued, was to restyle himself as the real agent of change in the race, not as a man running merely to cling to power. He had to become the advocate of what Pinkerton, in a speech at the Kennedy School, called a Fourth American Revolution—a reheated version of The New Paradigm under a more tradable name. The president had to have what amounted to an out-of-body experience; the quintessential pillar of the establishment had to become, persuasively, a man of the people.

The idea got nowhere. The Adults found it hard to imagine recasting the president, or, for that matter, themselves, as revolutionaries. The Kids, despairing of further argument, fell back on a movie to try to advance their cause. The film was *Grand Canyon,* Lawrence Kasdan's look into the lives of decent people, black and white, trying to cope in a world falling apart around them; it was, in The Kids' eyes, a vivid introduction to the real world and its worries about crime, homelessness, and social disintegration. They tried to have the picture screened for Bush at the White House and, failing that, pestered Teeter relentlessly to go see it himself. When they asked him periodically whether he had, he would roll his eyes and change the subject.

The president did do a brief turn as Mr. Reform, one of a series of personae he tried on like wardrobe changes during his long descent in the polls. It worked no better than his earlier tour as the Man with a Plan, and while he held onto some of its particulars—court reform and term limits on members of the House of Representatives, for two examples—he soon dropped it as a form of holistic medicine for what ailed him. By fall, Bush as reformer would give way to Bush as victim, a helpless hostage to Congress and an unwilling prisoner of the status quo.

Not even when events demanded it of him did he seem able to articulate any higher sense of national purpose. When the black quarter of South Central Los Angeles went up in flames in the spring, Bush's first instincts were of the kinder, gentler sort he had once promised to govern by—not simply to put down the rioting but to address himself to the economic poverty and the social anomie at its roots. He suddenly rediscovered the forgotten agenda put forward by his own housing secretary, Jack Kemp, for rescuing the inner cities. He even considered apologizing for having made a subliminally racial campaign issue of Willie Horton in 1988.

But the impulse yielded to his own unease with big ideas and to the political realities outlined for him by his managers—mainly that it would offend the white male voters who were a major part of the base he had inherited from Ronald Reagan. A moving first draft of his speech to the nation about the riots accordingly gave way to a red-meat second version, with most of the compassion edited out and a heavy helping of law-and-order ladled in.

Bush, unable to choose between the two versions, passed the buck to Skinner. "You decide, Sam," he said.

Skinner did, siding largely with the hard-liners; the final version, while justifiably tough on the need to restore order, was otherwise one more reminder that Bush had no idea what to do once the burning and looting had been put down. When he subsequently borrowed Kemp's agenda as his own, it was with lukewarm embrace and little follow-up. One of the few black senior officials in his government attended a meeting on the package and left in tears. He had come, he said, hoping to see the George Bush of Desert Storm and instead had found a man paralyzed by the latest polls.

Prognosis Negative

What the polls of spring and summer were saying was that America was losing faith in Bush, not just as president but, for the first time, as a man. The campaign's own soundings showed that more than 40 percent of the voters looked unfavorably on him—a level at which, by his late friend Lee Atwater's rule of thumb, a candidate was all but unelectable. So deep was the disaffection that Bush's strongest positive of all, his conduct of foreign policy, was turning into a negative for him, and not simply because he had spent so much time at it. His claim to have brought peace to the world had become one more argument for his early retirement, with thanks for a job well done.

Outside assessments were no more cheering. In early July, Dan Quayle breakfasted with three Republican polltakers not directly affiliated with the campaign. The veep himself was under no illusions as to the state of affairs; the White House and the campaign were both in terrible shape, he had told friends, and the frightening part was that they didn't realize it. But even he was jolted by what his breakfast guests had to say. Clinton's big surge out of the Democratic convention hadn't even happened yet, and Perot was beginning to wilt in the heat. Yet Bush kept falling. He would be lucky, the pollsters said, to get 42 percent of the vote.

Afterward, Quayle, still numb, retired to his West Wing office and called Teeter in for a briefing. Neither man could argue with the basic assessment, or with the problem at its heart.

"We're not telling the American people what we want to do for the next four years," Quayle said.

Teeter agreed. The two were at once too loyal to blame Bush and too realistic to believe that he could be changed. But something had to be done, starting, they both believed, with Sam Skinner's unsure management at the White House.

Quayle said Bush was resisting changes.

Teeter thought the latest unemployment figure might change his mind. It had bumped abruptly upward to 7.8 percent, the highest since the Reagan recession. Bush had been shocked by the number, Teeter said. The day it came out had been a watershed in his awareness of how bad things were and what he had to do to fix them.

What remained of the president's own optimism seemed to fade with the daily assault of bad news and worse numbers. He had indeed been stunned and angered by the sudden spike in unemployment, the more so for having been told yet again by his economists the day before that the seeds of recovery would soon be sprouting. He had believed and repeated their reassurances all winter and spring, urging his political people not to panic. When the pols in turn confronted him with the latest polling data suggesting that he no longer had any credibility on the subject, he had brushed it aside. "This may all be true," he said, contemplating the numbers, "but it's all gonna turn around."

The unemployment figure was the splash of cold water that wakened him from his reveries, and he was furious. "Goddamit," he exploded, "I had a forty-five-minute economic briefing yesterday, and nobody told me this would happen. They all said it was gonna get better." It hadn't, and in his anger, he turned on his advisers; for the first time any of his people could remember, he blurted out his belief that Boskin, Brady, and Darman had failed him.

The strongest remaining prop to his and his team's psyche by then was what they had come to call the last-man-standing theory—the belief, doggedly held, that Perot would go away and that America would never elect Bill Clinton president. But even that bit of comfort was battered by a new public poll recording Bush's fall to third place, behind both men. Two-thirds of the country had chosen sides against him.

"We had a pretty good week last week, and then this," he said heavily at a strategy meeting that morning. He pursed his lips and made a sputtering noise, a *brrrrp* like the sound of a baseball card in the spokes of a moving bicycle. It was, his people understood, the sound of a fatalism bordering on despair.

His own passivity had by then become a contributing factor in his decline and Clinton's resurrection. In the days before the Democratic convention, Bob Teeter argued for a flight of attack ads aimed at driving Clinton's numbers down before they got unmanageably high.

Jim Baker was for it. So, from his seat in the grandstand, was Roger Ailes. Bush was not, and when Teeter pressed him too hard, he took his refusal public; he was not inclined, he told the press, to get into a "campaign mode" just yet. In the aftermath, Teeter would blame himself for not having run the spots anyway. The president, he imagined, would have grumbled at his insubordination, but that would have stopped once Clinton's numbers started falling. That was hindsight, though. At the time, Teeter had acceded to the president's wish in the matter, and the campaign was once again prey to the curious diffidence of its candidate.

With bad fortune, Bush's sense of grievance deepened, and its targets multiplied. The media were against him. His people weren't defending him fiercely enough. Perot was getting a free ride. Skinner kept causing problems. Teeter couldn't make decisions. The First Family was suffering unfairly, especially Neil; the guilt Bush felt for his son's misfortune had not gone away. Meeting with a few close associates in the Oval Office one day late in the spring, he spoke yet again of Neil's near ruin and suddenly started to cry.

"If it weren't for me in this office," he said, tears flooding his eyes, "this wouldn't have happened to him."

Bush was normally an exuberant man, but the charm and affability natural to him in social settings took on the look of a mask imperfectly in place. Irregulars in his presence wondered if he was feeling well; rumors began circulating that he was not. Intimates worried about his curious passivity; the energy you might expect of a man in a fight for his political life and his place in the history books seemed to several friends to be almost totally absent in him. So open was his distaste for the subject that one close chum stopped trying to talk politics with him entirely. It seemed to him only too plain that the president had never really had his heart in the campaign.

Similar doubts were endemic in Bush's circle as the campaign maundered through the spring and summer. It struck his devoted press spokesman Marlin Fitzwater early on that a critical spark was missing from the enterprise—that nobody, not the president or his managers, was hungry enough to win. Nothing Bush said or did suggested otherwise. His enduring inability to say why he ought to be reelected made some friends begin to question whether he really wanted to be. At least one of them, a member of the Bush cabinet, sensed that he did not. It was time, the official told colleagues, for somebody who cared about the president to suggest gently to him that his presidency was over—that he should drop out of the race while he still could.

18.

The Quayle Hunt

For most of four years, the men around George Bush had looked on his alliance with J. Danforth Quayle in the manner of relatives regarding a bad marriage in the family; it was, in their eyes, a mismatch that could not be undone and so had to be endured. But with the president's swoon in the polls, the search for an offering to the gods began, and Quayle, the butt of a million late-show jokes, was by far the most tempting. By summer, Bush was hearing from party leaders, Richard Nixon and Gerald Ford only the most prominent among them, that he needed to find somebody better to run with. "Boy, there sure are a lot of people against Quayle," the president said in private wonderment during a road trip in July.

There were, among them the president's son George W. and, covertly, the senior leaders of what was nominally the Bush-Quayle campaign—and they came nearer than the world would know to winning the president around to their cause. Bush entertained and finally even invited suggestions that he pitch the vice president overboard and replace him with someone of greater stature—someone, say, like General Colin Powell, or Senator Bob Dole, or Secretary of Defense Dick Cheney. During the month between conventions, the president seemed to people privy to his deliberations to be at the point of giving in. What finally saved Quayle was not so much the president's faith or loyalty as his fear of the consequences. He could not bring himself, in the end, to tell the vice president that he was off the ticket, though that was what Bush wanted. Instead, he clung to the forlorn secret hope that his protégé would fall unbidden on his sword.

The irony was that Quayle's rehabilitation seemed till then to have been making some progress. He could not change his pale eyes, which looked like windows into an unfurnished room, or his accident-prone tongue, which rivaled Bush's own; together, they were to the language what Thelma and Louise were to male chauvinists or Bonnie and Clyde to small-town banks. Neither could Quayle easily make the sages of Washington believe in him or his long-term prospects. Even his friends guessed privately that the only way Dan would ever get to be president was if something bad happened to Bush.

But Quayle was a clever and ambitious politician, and he had surrounded himself with a strong staff—a bright, young, ideological group who thought of themselves as "Fort Reagan" defending the faith in occupied territory. They had kept the veep supplied with ideas from their reform-conservative agenda, and his own interest in policy questions had deepened—a catch-up education, one intimate said, for a sometime gentleman-C student hitting the books a bit later in life than he might have. By spring, the *Washington Post* had run a series of stories suggesting in encyclopedic detail that he was not after all an unserious man, and a senior White House aide was telling colleagues to face it—Quayle, not Bush, was the star of the reelection campaign.

Murphy Brown Meets Mr. Potatoe Head

It was even possible for Quayle and his people to imagine, in the spring of their content, that his war with the TV sitcom heroine Murphy Brown had done the ticket some good—that it had at least changed the subject from the economy and the polls to the safer Republican ground of family values for a few days. The vice president had been doing speeches on the subject for months, seeing it as useful to Bush's shaky prospects in 1992 and to his own possible candidacy of the right in 1996 or beyond. His homilies on the importance of whole families and the linkages between crime, poverty, and broken homes had gone nearly unnoticed. But the Los Angeles riots had thrown the subject into high relief, and Marilyn Quayle, a woman of strong will and fiercely conservative beliefs, saw the permissive attitudes of American popular culture as part of the problem.

"We have to fight the entertainment industry," she said one night aboard Air Force Two, en route home with her husband from a campaign event in New York. "Look at all these shows on television." She paused for a moment. "And then there's *Murphy Brown,*" she said.

Quayle, as it happened, had never seen the program. But he had heard enough about the studio hype to know that Ms. Brown, the fictional TV anchor played by Candice Bergen, was having a child out of wedlock and that several real-life newswomen would be doing cameo turns on one episode as guests at a baby shower. To Quayle, as to his wife, the mere idea of glamorizing illegitimacy was bad enough; having the superstars of television news join the celebration made it worse.

Quayle tucked the idea away for the moment, but it floated back to the surface one morning not long thereafter when he breakfasted with the conservative sociologist James Q. Wilson, a further session in his ongoing cram course on what he had missed in college. Wilson had given him an earful on the causal relations between illegitimacy and poverty, arming Quayle with fresh data for his repertoire. That noonday, the veep talked with his own troops over a working lunch about a speech he was to do in San Francisco. It would be his first trip to the Coast since the riots, and, he said, he knew what he wanted to talk about: the breakdown of family, personal responsibility, and social order—and *Murphy Brown*. It was cavalier, he lectured, for some Hollywood scriptwriter to romanticize unwed motherhood when so many fatherless children were growing up poor and wild.

No one at the table said no. Quayle's people liked the allusion precisely for its shock value, and when they pruned it from three sentences to one in the final draft, their only purpose was to make it a crisper sound bite. They thought briefly of clearing the text with the White House, but they weren't required to do so unless Quayle was talking foreign policy, and Quayle himself decided against it; the speech, one aide guessed from experience, would have come back reduced to rice-pabulum crap. The White House, as a result, first saw it four hours before Quayle went on—too late to do any damage. The campaign got its copies with an hour to go, along with a covering note saying, with some understatement, "We may make some news."

They did. The speech as a whole was a serious conservative reflection on what Quayle called "a poverty of values" underlying the riots. But the newscasts that night splashed his one-bite attack on Ms. Brown for "mocking the importance of fathers by bearing a child alone and calling it just another lifestyle choice."

Quayle's party went to bed euphoric, pleased that he had at least attracted some attention; they were already planning the next rounds in his newly declared war on Hollywood's "cultural elite." Their pleasure lasted till morning, when a Quayle aide, Al Hubbard, emerged from a White House command meeting and called chief of staff Bill Kristol on the road.

"They're worried about *Murphy Brown*," Hubbard said.

Panicked might have been a more apt word, given the run-for-cover response back in Washington. Nobody objected to Quayle's thematics; Republicans had been winning presidential elections with social issues since 1968, and "family values" had a piquant extra dimension in a race against a man of Bill Clinton's rumored appetites. But for the veep to pick on Murphy Brown was the equivalent of a Democrat attacking Ozzie and Harriet in their prime-time prime. Ms. Brown was, as deputy campaign manager Mary Matalin remarked, the second most popular woman in America. The first, it went without saying, was Barbara Bush, and she was, if anything, unhappier than Matalin with what the Quayles had wrought. Her affection for them had more to do with their loyalty to her husband than with their political judgment. The potshot at Ms. Brown was, in Ms. Bush's word, *ridiculous*—a sappy display of pandering to the right when what the president needed most was to win back the center.

The judgment was widely shared. Quayle had violated a fundamental rule of politics, which was never to quarrel with somebody who bought printer's ink by the barrel—or videotape by the mile. The empire struck back; Quayle was once again a staple of the midnight monologues on television, and the answering laughter gave the campaign a collective case of the williwaws. The younger hands on Fifteenth Street in particular questioned whether the vice president ought to have made a target of a sitcom character in the first place— particularly a pop icon of their own generation.

"It makes him look like a joke," one of them said at a staff meeting. "It resurrects all the lightweight stuff."

Maybe, Charlie Black replied, but the speech itself made strategic sense. "It's a damn good deal for our base," he said, meaning the party's conservative hard core, and the base, in a three-way race, might conceivably be enough to save the president. The bit of business about *Murphy Brown,* in Black's view, was simply a problem of spin control. All they needed to do was play up family values and play down Ms. Brown's alleged offense against them.

The script got to the White House too late. Its notion of spin looked more like a 180-degree gyration, from backing Quayle to praising Ms. Brown for the strong family values *she* had shown by choosing to have the baby instead of aborting her pregnancy. News of the cave-in reached the Quayle party in a holding-room in Los Angeles, where the vice president was having a VIP breakfast. His man Kristol, normally a witty and mannerly sort, reached for the phone in a fury and began punching up numbers at the White House and the campaign. A colleague, seeing his anger, thought it best to clear the room so Bill could scream in privacy.

His passion did no good.

"I think the vice president should praise her decision to have the baby," Bob Teeter told him.

"There *is* no fucking baby!" Kristol exploded. "It's just a scriptwriter!"

He was still simmering when he joined Quayle in the limousine bearing them to the day's next photo op and reported on his telephone canvass.

"They're squishy," Kristol said. Their White House friends, as a colleague back home had put it, were moonwalking backwards.

Quayle picked up the car phone and rang Bush. The president was in a meeting, and the vice president, while he waited, was put through to Sam Skinner instead. Skinner, in deep squish, argued for caution—they were, after all, taking on a very popular show.

"Hey, this is a winner, believe me," Quayle said.

"That's a minority view around here," Skinner replied.

The minority turned out to include the president, as Quayle learned when they finally connected. Bush said he had read the speech and thought it was terrific. Quayle hung up, smiling. "As usual," he said, "the president is better than his advisers."

His master's voice was sustaining, and so were the early returns from his assault on the cultural elite. As Black had predicted, Quayle's message was a bull's-eye hit with its target blocs of political and cultural conservatives—people for whom Murphy Brown had always been an alien from Planet Hollywood. Reports from campaign operatives in the field were happy, for a change: somebody in the campaign had finally seemed to stand for something.

But gratitude, in politics, is fleeting, and so was Quayle's redemption. It ended the day he did a media event at a grade school in New Jersey and spelled the word "potato" with what nearly proved to be a terminal "e." The flub endeared him anew to stand-up comics—he was by actual count the most joked-about person on American television—and armed his antagonists at the White House and the campaign with fresh ammunition to use against him.

In Search of a Hanging Brief

The vice president's enemies at Bush's court had always been more numerous and better positioned than his friends. The ticket had barely been elected when Lee Atwater, a favorite of the president-elect, ventured in several private conversations that Quayle would have to be replaced the next time around. Atwater had nothing against Quayle's deep tilt to the right; on the contrary, he advertised himself as a conservative. But his real ideology was winning elections, and he had been at it long enough to believe that he knew a losing hand when he was dealt one. The vice president, to him, was like a lone deuce in draw poker—a card to be traded, if necessary, in hopes of something better. "If we screw up and Bush is in deep shit," Atwater told a friend at the

White House as early as February, 1989, "Quayle will have to go." It would have to be done surgically, he advised another comrade in Bush's service, and that meant early—no later than 1991. The wingers would howl, he said, but if you built in enough time for them to ventilate, the storm would blow over early enough to avert a scene at the convention.

Whether he confided his view directly to Bush was a secret buried with him; he was gone, and the president was too discreet to tell. But a close confidant of both men had reported Atwater's views to the president. The dump-Quayle party had got transfixed for much of 1991 by Bush's swollen popularity ratings and so had missed the witching hour proposed by their old comrade in arms; if you believed the polls, it was hard to make a case for changing the ticket. It was not until the spring of 1992 that one of the antis, a mutual friend of Bush and Atwater, approached the president and ventured that maybe Quayle ought to go. The response, he thought, might have been scripted by Lee's ghost. Forget it, Bush said; there was an appropriate moment for considering such a change, and it had long since passed.

His resistance didn't end the sedition, which only gained force as his own situation got worse. The signs at his campaign headquarters said Bush/Quayle '92, but the principals there and at the White House had regarded Quayle from the moment of his anointment as one of the president's worst ideas, and he had done little since to improve their opinion of him. Their lack of confidence had gone from chronic to acute as they read the glowing notices Clinton had got for choosing Al Gore as his running mate. Comparisons were inevitably drawn and were mostly unflattering to Quayle. The main rap against Gore was that he was, if anything, *too* serious. Nobody had ever said that about Dan Quayle: his late-blooming sober side had been hopelessly compromised by his bent for saying silly things.

The faction most powerfully drawn to the idea of his removal from the ticket was led by Bob Teeter and Fred Malek, the two top operating officers of the campaign. Early on, Teeter had considered shrinking Quayle's name on the official Bush/Quayle '92 bumper sticker, so little did he think of what the younger man brought to the ticket. By spring, Malek's thinking had taken the next great leap forward. He began lobbying Teeter, as the president's best friend in the campaign command, to use his ready access and make the case for dumping Quayle outright. Teeter finally did, though with gingerly step and carefully chosen words; the gist of his argument to the president was that this was something they ought to consider. The time was not ripe; Teeter bumped into Bush's sense of obligation and his regard for the proprieties. The president, in those days, was resisting all such suggestions; his response, when he was approached, was that he liked Quayle and was happy with the way he was going about his job.

His feelings in fact were more mixed than he let on to any but his closest associates. Both he and Barbara *did* like Quayle; they appreciated his hard work and his good-soldier fidelity to the president, even when it ran crossgrain with his more conservative beliefs. Until his own situation reached critical mass, Bush refused even to countenance advice that he find a new number two. "How's Quayle doing?" he asked a friend in the summer of 1991, when he still had the time and the popularity to do as he pleased about the situation. "So many people are dumping on him to me."

His guest, like so many callers on the president, did an equivocal shuffle-step. On the one hand, he said, Quayle was controversial; on the other, the conservatives seemed to like him.

"Well, dammit," Bush said, "he's been loyal to me. I'll never consider getting rid of him."

But as time went on and his own fortunes ebbed, a pro forma quality crept into Bush's defense of his vice president, an unenthusiasm in his tone and, sometimes, his conversation that betrayed his real feelings to his intimates. Quayle, they knew, had been a disappointment to the president—so much so, one well-positioned friend said, that Bush no longer valued his advice or considered him a real partner in the government.

His complaint, confidentially expressed, was that Quayle had become the captive of and the mouthpiece for the party's farther right. Bush himself had been accused of pandering to what he called the "nut fringe" during his career in national politics, most often during election years. But even by his own elastic standards, Bush thought that Quayle had been overdoing it, as if he really believed what he was saying. Among friends, the president put some of the blame on Marilyn Quayle for her husband's surrender. Marilyn was too shrill, too hard-core, Bush said. Her influence was bad for Dan politically; on hot-button issues like abortion, the president thought, he had let her push him too far right. Bush had had to rebuke him several times for saying things that had been politically or diplomatically damaging, and Barbara, in less open ways, had made known her dismay. "Can you believe what our vice president said today?" she asked staffers after what she considered a particularly primitive utterance on AIDS.

The grievances by themselves were not enough to move Bush to drop Quayle; his code of loyalty had given under strain in other situations where his own survival was in peril. His sense of face was another matter; he preferred living with the vice president to confessing error or exposing himself to attack by the conservatives or the press. He had singlehandedly created Quayle as a national figure, raising him up out of the deep back benches of the Senate in 1988 against the judgment of his closest advisers. To drop him now would be seen not merely as an act of expedience but as a confession that he had been wrong—that he had elevated a mistake to within aspiring distance of the presidency. Maybe Quayle was a drag on the ticket, Bush told friends defensively, but only a mild one. Removing him was simply not worth the risk.

There was no way to budge the president, the plotters knew, without compelling evidence that Quayle might actually cost him the election, and Bob Teeter went looking for some. In the early summer, he and Malek made another run at Bush, this time suggesting that they do a poll on the Quayle question. Though he seemed unenthusiastic, the president, tellingly, did not say no. "I'm not persuaded it's going to make any difference," he told his men, "but if you want a poll, that's fine." They did, and Jim Baker, then still at the State Department expecting and dreading Bush's call, was interested enough to go along. He and Teeter had a series of questions about the vice president inserted into three of Fred Steeper's national polls in July and August. Their purpose was to measure whether Quayle was indeed a deadweight dragging the president down—and, if he was, to confront Bush with the potential cost of being loyal to a loser.

The fishing expedition didn't quite work out. The hyper-secret returns, though intriguing, were not nearly conclusive enough to carry forward to the president. On a first sweep, in early July, voters were asked whether they would be more or less likely to vote for Bush if he dumped Quayle. Half said more likely; only a fourth said less. At first glance, the two-to-one tilt against keeping the vice president was pleasing to his enemies. But a closer reading suggested that the numbers were swollen by Democrats who would never vote for Bush anyway and by Republicans who would finally come home to him, even if they did prefer some other second banana.

The most you could make of the poll, Steeper wrote in a memo in mid-July, was that losing Quayle might conceivably be worth four to six points to the president. "[There] are fairly large numbers on both sides of the issue," Steeper wrote. "Vice President Quayle generates a lot of strong opinions, more against than for." The reading was like the kiwi-and-arugula salad in a nouvelle-cuisine restaurant, attractive to the eye but unfilling on the stomach. It wasn't enough, and Teeter sent Steeper back for more.

The second and third courses, delivered in late July and early August, were a stew of mixed portents. On what pollsters call a "thermometer scale" of 0 to 100, Quayle's mean rating was 25—the rough equivalent, weatherwise, of a sleety day in February. Dick Cheney scored a tepid 34, Jim Baker a warmer 51—and General Powell, a secret favorite among the plotters, a mellow 57. But in a series of trial heats, Bush fared only a point worse against the Democrats with Quayle on the ticket than he did in a one-on-one matchup against Clinton alone. Only Baker among the pool of substitutes made an appreciable difference, closing the gap from 21 points to 14. The finding, while it tickled Baker's vanity, was not enough to tempt him into volunteering for veephood—or to warrant a switch even if he *had* made himself available.

The further returns were no more encouraging to the putschists. The worst they said about Quayle was that he was still stuck inside his caricature as a man playing cards with something less than a full deck; a solid majority of voters thought he wasn't qualified to be president and that Bush should therefore offload him for the good of the country. But an even larger number thought that dropping him would reek of fear, a response to no civic need larger than Bush's own collapse in the polls. Conservative voters were particularly offended at the idea of losing one of their own at the president's court. The party right had never much liked or trusted Bush anyway, for all his lip service to their agenda, and they felt better with Quayle beside him than with any of the alternatives.

There was thus no hanging brief to lay before the president, as Teeter and Baker agreed in their informal back-channel talks about the problem. No matter how you crunched the numbers, they still supported Steeper's initial guess—that there was no better than a four-to-six-point profit, if that, in dropping Quayle. In a close race, that might have proved decisive. But in the dog days of midsummer, the Bush camp was looking at something nearer a blowout—a defeat so punishing that a few points one way or the other would not make a meaningful difference.

Et Tu, Jimmy?

Teeter pressed ahead anyway. Baker, at first, hung back. It wasn't that he shared what he regarded as Bush's bizarre affection for Quayle; on the contrary, Baker had been appalled by the choice in the first place and had seen no reason since to feel better about it. His wish, privately expressed to friends, was that the vice president simply go away without having to be asked. But no one who knew the Quayles believed that he would quit voluntarily; Marilyn, a friend said, would *never* let Dan do that. He would have to be removed forcibly, and Baker, who abhorred messes, thought it would do Bush more damage than it was worth. When the two of them talked about it during the summer, Baker ventured his view that it was a bad idea, and Bush quickly agreed.

Prudence ranked as high on Baker's scale of values as on Bush's, and for a time, he held to his view that it was best to leave bad enough alone. But he never quite closed the door to arguments to the contrary. He knew he would be shanghaied into the campaign, like it or not, and as a precaution, he assigned two of his top guns, Robert Zoellick and Dennis Ross, to work up a memo blueprinting what would have to be done for Bush to win. Their sense of the terrain was as bleak as Baker's own. The president, in their view, was finished unless he did something so dramatic as to change the basic perception of the race and persuade Americans that everything would be different in a second Bush administration. One possibility was to put forward some flashy new domestic-policy initiative. The only live alternative they saw was for Bush to dispose of Quayle—and to draft General Powell to replace him on the ticket.

The idea was not a new one among Bush's circle of friends and advisers. Fred Malek had first raised it in the spring, as part of his quiet intramural lobbying for a change of running mates. Malek was widely acquainted among Democrats and had heard from several of them that a swap of Quayle for Powell was the single stroke they most feared; its shock value alone could buy Bush a second look and perhaps alter the course of the race. The timing was wrong when Malek first raised the possibility, but he never let go of it and never bought the verdict of some of his colleagues that their polling did not provide ample grounds for dropping Quayle. A poll, in his view, was a laboratory exercise, as distant from the real world as a culture in a petri dish; it could not measure the impact of two or three weeks of saturation media coverage of Bush having traded up for a new vice president.

The moment was more propitious when Powell's name came up again, and his attractions were obvious, to the Clinton and Perot camps as well as Bush's; he was the only person known to have been short-listed for vice president by all three campaigns. His credentials as a military man and a White House adviser were impeccable, as his champions among Baker's boys pointed out. But it was the color of the general's skin that pushed the idea into the megaton range as a political weapon. Powell would be the first African American ever on a major-party ticket—a fact that would assure Bush a place in the history books under profiles in courage and would threaten Clinton's biracial base of support in the bargain.

The general himself might have admired so exquisite a flanking maneuver. It had its downside, as Baker's longtime aide, adviser, and confidante Margaret Tutwiler warned in their running conversations. She liked the idea in principle, having never disguised her own low regard for Quayle or her belief that he should be jettisoned like spoiled cargo from a ship. "Mr. Bush doesn't want him around any more than we do," she told her colleagues in Baker's circle. "He knows he's a liability." But she was herself a native Alabamian, and she worried how a Powell nomination might play with conservative white voters in the South, an indispensable building block in the Reagan-Bush coalition.

Her influence with Baker was large, and he took her concerns seriously. His particular reservations about Powell echoed hers; it could put Bush's own white conservative base of support in jeopardy. But he was prisoner as well to his larger doubts about changing the ticket so late in the game. At one point, he told Tutwiler impatiently to stop pushing the subject so hard—it wasn't going to happen, period. The cost, in his view, would be yet another wave of stories about Bush the flip-flopper; the Democrats and their buddies in the press would portray him as a weak and desperate man willing to do anything to get elected.

There was no certainty in any case that Powell would be available, and considerable ground for suspecting that he would not be. At the height of the buzz in Washington about what a wonderful choice he would be, the general himself called Quayle to say that the talk wasn't coming from *him;* he was, he said, neither interested in nor bucking for the vice president's job. The task of getting him interested was further complicated by the absence of a warrant from the president; no official approach could be made to Powell without Bush's say-so, and the plotters had no such grant of authority.

But politics is a clubby business, and an unofficial emissary appeared providentially in the person of Stu Spencer, a sharp, salty California pol with a place in history as one of the inventors of modern campaign consulting and with a chestful of ribbons from the Reagan-Bush wars of the past. Spencer, by wry coincidence, had managed the Quayle-for-vice-president tour in 1988 and had been frank even then about his low regard for his candidate's gifts—a bit too frank for the tastes of his superior officers. His out-of-school comments on the subject had got him frozen out of the reelection effort, but he had friends in high places in the campaign, and, by happy chance, was on good terms socially with General Powell as well.

Spencer was smart enough at the game to know that, whatever signals he had picked up in his conversations with old chums at headquarters, a run at Powell would have to be a solo operation, without formal commission; the rules of play in such matters required deniability all around. His secret meeting with the general at the Pentagon was undertaken without Bush's knowledge and was carefully indirect, a discussion of the *idea* of a Bush-Powell ticket; it was something people were talking up, and Spencer, for purposes of the conversation, was curious as to what Powell made of it.

Powell's response was a not-quite-slammed door. He gave the strong impression that he would accept a place on the ticket if it were offered to him and if he were certain that the tender had come straight from Bush. But he was emphatic about not wanting to be asked. He was flattered to be thought of, he said; it was just that the moment was all wrong for him. His distinguished career as a soldier was near its end, and, he said, he felt obliged to serve out the remaining year of his term as chairman of the joint chiefs of staff—the highest station ever achieved by an African American in the military. Then, after thirty-five years in uniform, he needed time to make some money and collect his thoughts on what to do with the rest of his life.

He wondered further whether the people promoting him for the job really knew who he was, politically speaking. He had been scrupulous to a fault about keeping his views to himself on any issue outside his official duties, narrowly defined. Even his party preference, if he had one, remained his secret; like Dwight Eisenhower forty years before him, he found himself pursued by both parties, each assuming that he was, or might be, one of theirs. But he *had* opinions, and, he told Spencer, he imagined that some of the people promoting him for vice president might change their minds on hearing them. He was carefully unspecific about where the problems might lie. Some of Bush's people thought they had at least one fair guess; they supposed that the general's feelings about abortion might be more tolerant than the official pro-life militancy of the party.

Under the rules of play, Spencer could not formally give the campaign a report on the sitdown. But he and Powell both had friends in the network of Republican power politics in Washington, and news of the general's reluctance made its way quickly back to Fifteenth Street. The caballers felt finally obliged to respect his wish to be left alone. But their hopes burned on, and the tides of politics were bringing Jim Baker slowly, inexorably their way. Baker was a master of inside moves, and as his reading of the president's chances darkened through the summer, his tactical positioning shifted subtly from anti to neutral on the larger issue of dumping Quayle. If Jimmy wasn't actually promoting a coup, one friend said, he wasn't standing out there waving a stop sign, either; on the contrary, he allowed and even encouraged Quayle's antagonists to play through. He listened to repeated entreaties from Zoellick and Ross, never once cutting them off. He received the news that George W. Bush had joined the dissidents, sharing with them—and with his father—his opinion that Quayle ought to go. And when Jerry Ford called one day in July to say that he, too, favored a change, Baker urged him strongly to phone the president directly and make known his views.

Ford had come to his judgment slowly and reluctantly. Sixteen years earlier, he had let himself be talked into dumping a politically inconvenient vice president, Nelson A. Rockefeller, in favor of Bob Dole and had regretted it ever since. Ford had always liked Quayle and thought him underrated, both by his enemies in the press and by his supposed friends in Bush's circle. But he had concluded sadly that the effort to rebuild his image had failed. Quayle, he believed, had become a liability to the ticket, and soon after his conversation with Baker, he rang up the president.

They missed connections at first, but when Bush called back from Air Force One, Ford was characteristically blunt. "George," he said, "the campaign is dead in the water. You could lose unless there's some new spark." The only way to strike it, in Ford's view, was to get Quayle off the ticket. But it had to be done delicately. Someone irreproachably loyal to Quayle would have to go to him and persuade him to walk the plank for the good of his president and his party.

Bush wasn't buying. Yes, various of his friends and retainers had been after him to make a change, but, he told Ford, he didn't think Quayle was as big a problem as they did, and he didn't like the idea of doing a public flip-flop on something so important. He thanked the former president for his advice and said he would mull it over some more. He promised no more than that, and, he told Ford, he didn't think that he would be changing his mind.

In fact, the idea of replacing his running mate had begun to grow on Bush, far more than he had let on to Ford or anyone else. He was hearing practically nothing else from the people he normally looked to for advice. Even his long-ago patron, Nixon, had sent word through an intermediary to the campaign that Quayle had to go; given the state of the economy, the former president said, he had become a luxury Bush could no longer afford. Bush had already lost Teeter and Malek to the anti-Quayle party, and as his situation worsened through the summer, he was finally losing Jimmy Baker as well. Baker had known for some time that he would be running the campaign. His own reputation and his future would be on the line with Bush's, and the more he stared into the clouds boiling up on the horizon, the more expendable Quayle came to seem.

With just two or three weeks left till the convention, Baker chaired a meeting of his own people and the senior campaign leaders around the dining table at his house on Foxhall Road, and the Quayle problem inevitably came up. The rough consensus among them was that the vice president *was* a problem and that the best solution would be a scenario not unlike what Jerry Ford had proposed: sending somebody Quayle knew and trusted to persuade him to stand down.

But who would be the messenger of doom? The question was not a new one among Bush's inner circle; several of its members had approached him individually, volunteering to be the bearers of the bad news to the vice president. Bush had declined their offers, and they could not go forward without his say-so; they knew that Quayle would never go for the idea that he leave unless he was dead certain it came from Bush himself. The group around Baker's table worried the question one more time. Baker himself fit the profile they needed; the problem, apart from the dignity of his high station, was that his disdain for Quayle was only too well-known, to the vice president and everybody else, and for the moment, nobody had a better idea.

The group parted that night without a solution, but they kept talking, and, after much spirited discussion, came up with what they were sure was the perfect choice. Their nominee was somebody who genuinely like Quayle, despite the occasional problems he caused, and who unquestionably spoke for the president. Her name was Barbara Bush.

It was Baker who carried the idea to his friend the president—and who soon came back with the president's flat no. The plotters comforted themselves that he hadn't objected in principle to the idea of doing Quayle in; he seemed rather to be saying he didn't want his fingerprints on the weapon, not even by proxy. It was inappropriate, he told Baker, for Barbara or anyone else in his family to serve the death warrant—a blanket refusal that took his sons Junior and Jeb out of play as well. The plotters flipped their mental Rolodexes back to card one and resumed the search for the right bearer of bad tidings. They never found one, not, anyway, in Barbara's league, and another scenario died for want of the right casting.

Smoke Signals

There were, of course, other, more subtle ways to deliver messages in Washington, and finding themselves without a live emissary, Quayle's enemies resorted to one of them: sending him anonymous smoke signals in the press that he had become a liability to the president and was no longer wanted. The story of the campaign's secret polling mysteriously leaked, in a form calculated to damage the vice president. He was hurting Bush, it was said, and his place on the ticket was not assured.

The plain intent of the leakage was to get him to go quietly. The effect was just the opposite; he decided to make a fight of it and enlisted those allies he could find, mostly on the party right, to back his play. His people activated a claque of conservatives to speak up for him, and Quayle himself put in chummy, what's-doing phone calls to some of his old Republican colleagues in the Senate. Some of the senators on his list, he had been accurately informed, were in fact quietly intriguing against him. While he did not raise the subject of their perfidy with them, his calls could at least be taken as his sign that he knew.

But the story of the poll was an open wound, and in the absence of any other rebuttal, one of Quayle's men informed a higher-up on Fifteenth Street that they were going to knock it down themselves; the campaign, after all, had assured them that no such survey existed.

No problem, the campaign official said; go right ahead and deny it. But an hour later he was back on the line to Quayle's man, sheepishly suggesting that maybe going public wasn't such a hot idea after all. "It might be better," he told Quayle's man, "for you to say that we don't discuss our polls."

Quayle's people realized that they had caught the campaign in a lie—a fact soon confirmed to them by a mole on Fifteenth Street who had seen the secret data about Quayle. The vice president's man Al Hubbard confronted Teeter with the discovery. Teeter shrugged him off. Nobody was trying to dump anybody, he said. The polling had been a precaution, nothing more; it was simply a matter of seeing that the president knew everything he needed to know.

Quayle's paranoia, as it happened, was well-placed; all that stood between him and termination with extreme prejudice, at that point, was Bush's squeamishness about pulling the trigger. The argument that there was no other way to preserve his candidacy had finally got to the president by late July, after much pounding by aides and friends; by the end, he was not only receiving but soliciting advice from them as to whether he should cut Quayle loose. One of them, a man not aligned with the cabal, concluded after several such conversations that the president had made the leap intellectually from resisting the idea to embracing it. Teeter, among the coup leaders, seemed to sense as much. "There's movement on the Quayle front," he told one of his allies. The president was coming around.

Bush was in fact at the point of yielding to temptation when Quayle himself, having got wind of the maneuvering, tried to force the issue during one of their regular weekly meetings. One aide privy to the president's views on the subject described him as "desperate" by then to make a change, had he only been able to figure out how. All that stayed his hand, this source said, was his fear of getting caught, by the press and the party right; he could not bring himself to be more than a passive actor in the drama, hoping against hope that Quayle would jump without his having to push. Some of Quayle's edgier aides would claim afterward that he had volunteered to stand down if it would advance the president's fight for survival. He hadn't, not quite. If he *had* offered to go away, the president, by authoritative account, would have accepted on the spot; indeed, one of his most senior couselors said, he would have been the most relieved man in America.

Their encounter that day instead was a shadow play of things not said and meanings not apprehended. The Quayle-must-go stories in the press, the vice president said with less than total confidence, were ridiculous. Bush had agreed, or seemed to. He did tell Quayle that some important people had been urging him to consider a change; at least some of his men took that to have been his awkward way of inviting the vice president to quit the ticket on his own motion. But Quayle didn't take the hint, if it was one, and Bush eased back from the brink. The stories *were* ridiculous, he told Quayle. The best thing to do was to ignore them.

Quayle seized on this last as his reprieve. "There's nothing to worry about," he told his people afterward. "He's in good shape."

But his team sensed something less than confidence in Quayle's demeanor, and something less than final when, at a photo op that morning, Bush said in response to a direct question that the veep's job security was "very certain." Quayle's men, some of whom had gambled their own futures on his, wished the president had sounded a little more definitive and a lot more enthusiastic.

"He didn't really close the door," one of them complained to Marlin Fitzwater later in the day.

"You don't understand," Fitzwater said. "*He* thinks he closed the door."

Both camps toiled like medieval scholastics over the metaphysics of The Door. Was it half closed or half open? Quayle's people suspected the latter and plotted a high-risk strategy for their man; to get it unmistakably slammed, they believed, Quayle himself was going to have to open it first. He was booked for an interview on *Larry King Live*, the new arena theater of American politics, and in an afternoon prep session, he and his coaches rehearsed his lines. He would say that he was prepared to stand down in an Indiana minute if he really believed that he was hurting the president. But, he would add, he had concluded after much soul-searching that he was an asset to the ticket and so would be staying on.

It was guts poker, and when the deal went down, Quayle got only the front half of his bluff on the air—the part about his willingness to disappear if it would help Bush get reelected. There was no follow-up, no chance to accentuate his positives; the stories next morning made it sound as if he were bending his neck to the blade. He was still vulnerable, as he and his people agreed over an uneaten breakfast that day. Maybe Bush was aboard, but the media scented blood, and it was important to get the president to abort the feeding frenzy before it got out of control.

His antagonists had beaten him to Bush's door. Baker, by now a wholehearted convert, and Teeter, a believer from the beginning, had pushed the case for change in separate meetings with the president that very week. Bush had seemed to be open to the question and intrigued by the latest alternative they laid before him: Senate minority leader Bob Dole. There was no love lost between the two men; they had waged a famously bitter fight for the nomination in 1988, a class war in miniature between the scion of privilege and the son of hard times. But Dole was well-known and widely admired in Republican Washington, and he had been under the media microscope before, having run two prior national campaigns. There were no undiscovered embarrassments in his past, and no automatic giggles for comic monologists at the mere mention of his name. His potential impact was strong, in Steeper's polls and others; in several battleground states in the Midwest, his popularity ran twenty points higher than Bush's. The vice president, by contrast, didn't help the ticket anywhere except in his native Indiana—and, as one senior aide said, if Bush couldn't win Indiana without Quayle, he wasn't going to get reelected anyway.

For a suspenseful moment, the plotters believed and Quayle's men feared that Bush might capitulate; both sides would agree afterward that Quayle's future on the ticket, and as a viable national politician, had been perilously close to ending at the hand of the man who had made him. It was not till the last minute that the president finally decided to keep him on, and even then, it was less a vote of confidence than an act of caution. "I think the press would murder me if I did this," Bush told his disheartened privy councilors. The issue for him had reduced itself to the single question of how it would look if he dropped Quayle, and for a man so concerned with appearances, the case was closed.

Quayle didn't know that when he dropped by the Oval Office to make one last pitch for the president's formal benediction. The press was still going crazy speculating about his future, he told Bush. He wanted to do something to stop it. There was a way, of course, and the president still clung to the hope that Quayle would take it—that *he* would resolve the whole unpleasant matter by heading for the exit on his own. But Bush would not say so, and Quayle would not step forward without being asked. He chose instead to ignore what had gone unspoken between them; the fact that the president hadn't come out and suggested that he step aside could be interpreted, or at least spun, as a token of approval as against a failure of nerve.

"Don't worry, the door's closed," Quayle told his staff afterward. He seemed actually to believe it; still, to make sure the world saw it that way, his chief aide, Bill Kristol, leaked a story of imaginative weave to the *Washington Post* for its next morning's editions. The story strongly suggested that Quayle had expressed his willingness to go away and that Bush had told him never mind—he was still on the ticket.

Quayle's people would claim afterward that the leak had been authorized by the president. In fact, when Bush read the story, he was furious. Nothing in it squared with his memory of the meeting—not the offer to leave and not the invitation to stay. "He never said anything to me," the president complained to his people. "This never happened. Why do they think they have to do this?"

The only plausible answer was that they had been bluffing, and that it had worked. The plotters would cling to their dreams and schemes to the very eve of the convention, but the public speculations quieted and would never again reach that critical mass necessary to force a change. Quayle had weathered the crisis. The storm, one of his men said, had turned out to be raindrops.

The outcome was not quite what the Bush command had hoped for. Marilyn Quayle guessed as much; her antennae were at least a match for her husband's, and her sense of grievance lay closer to the surface of her skin. Her anger at Bush's managers was well-known within the campaign—Baker was at or near the top of her enemies list—and so was her belief that the media were willing parties to a plot to lynch her husband. His survival through the summer had not eased her suspicions. With the convention almost at hand, she worried aloud that Dan might still be in jeopardy—that Baker and Teeter might yet find the words to persuade Bush to dump him.

Her suspicion showed when, late that last week, the vice president's staff came around to his residence to run through his convention schedule. At one point, Quayle stepped out of the room, and a junior staffer, making conversation, said, "It's great all that flap is over."

"Don't be too sure," Marilyn said. "It's not over until he gives his speech."

She was wrong only about the realpolitik of his situation, not the wish of his enemies. They had carried on their Quayle hunt all summer, and had given it up only out of despair. Even as the Republicans gathered in Houston, Jim Baker was still talking wistfully among friends about what might have been if Quayle had only had the sense and grace to catch Bush's meaning and bow out without having to be shown the door. Baker's preference for a bloodless coup did not reflect a concern for the tender feelings of the vice president, whom he held in some contempt. It was rather that dumping Quayle forcibly would have made one more mess for him to clean up when, at the command of his friend the president, he had finally to step in and try to save the campaign.

19.

The Return of Little Brother

That James A. Baker III would be called in to rescue Bush's failing presidency had always been inevitable—a matter not of whether but of when. Though they were old and close friends, neither man was happy with the idea, and they put off confronting it as long as they could. Baker greatly preferred his role as global statesman, building one of the best résumés in modern history for his own possible run for president in 1996. And Bush in turn was reluctant to concede to the world that he couldn't win without the man he sometimes called Little Brother—a term of affection with visible trace elements of sibling rivalry.

But his presidency *was* failing, dragged under by a dismal economy, a chaotic infrastructure, and the seemingly irreversible collapse of his support. His approval ratings had started down after Desert Storm, slowly at first, precipitously with the onset of winter. Nothing since had arrested the slide, not the State of the Union, or the spring Sitzkrieg with Congress, or Bush's undefeated run through the primaries—not even his historic arms-reduction agreement with Boris Yeltsin. He hadn't had a single popular success all year, one aide lamented, or a single week in which his numbers went up instead of flatlining or worse. The embarrassing last chapter of the dump-Quayle story had been a wave of suggestions, whispered and published, that perhaps it was Bush instead who ought to be dropped from the ticket.

His wish scenario all along had been that the economy would perk up, whereupon his glories of international statecraft would kick in and carry him to victory. Realists in his command had argued to no avail that they could not assume a real recovery and in fact had to plan as if it wouldn't happen. The surprising summer uptick in unemployment had been the splash of cold water on Bush's daydreaming, and the indices only got worse thereafter. A high-level presidential adviser sat morosely over a single day's headlines, reading them aloud: "83,000 Jobs Lost in August . . . Job Losses Cripple U.S. Recovery . . . 167,000 Jobs Lost in U.S. Businesses." People voted their pocketbooks when they were scared, Bush's man knew, and the numbers gave them ample ground for fear.

There was, moreover, nothing Bush could say to make things better. His credibility on the economy, an aide said, was so low that it hurt him even to mention it. But he could not ignore it either; to do so would suggest either that he didn't care about it or that he hadn't a clue as to what to do. Neither could he change the subject to foreign policy. Two ads promoting his successes overseas got what one witness called a big Bronx cheer from a focus group in Cleveland and were quietly shelved; the rest of the world didn't matter as against the contingency of everyday life at home. Even Desert Storm, in the campaign's soundings, had metamorphosed from triumph to failure—an act of bellus interruptus that had left Saddam Hussein alive and well in his bunker in Baghdad.

By midsummer, America's mood bordered on clinical depression. A record 80 percent in a campaign poll thought the country was on the wrong track, and the president's approval rating had sunk to a level a bare point or two higher than Jimmy Carter's had been at his lowest ebb in 1980. His showing in trial heats was equally dismal, once Ross Perot had left the field. Bush seemed frozen at 38 or 39 percent in the popular vote; a nearly equal number said they wouldn't vote for him under any circumstances.

"These are the most negative numbers I've ever seen," Bob Teeter said, scanning the returns, and the color-coded maps festooning the war-room walls on Fifteenth Street were no more comforting; they had the look of a Democratic landslide in the making. There were no blue-for-Bush states at all till late August, when dependably Republican Utah was tinted in. The rest, when polling was available, were all Clinton red.

If he was discouraged, the president did not show it, not, at least, in the presence of the help. "I don't care if anybody else is down," he said in early August at one of the outsized campaign meetings that had grown up under Teeter and Skinner. "I'm up! I'm convinced I'm gonna win. Compared to what the polls look like, I feel good."

But his cheerleading did nothing to quiet the intimations of mortality spreading through the White House and the campaign. The chat in the corridors was grim—"We're not in sync with the national gestalt," one bull-turned-bear said grimly—and the air of morbidity nearly spoiled Dan Quayle's pleasure in his own deliverance. Quayle's size-up of the situation, by midsummer, was politics reduced to prayer, for a major Clinton screwup, say, or for the timely demise of Saddam. "Even if we run a perfect campaign," the veep told a friend, "we can't win unless we get a break."

Twin Peaks

Quayle in fact had been worrying aloud since winter about the breakup of the team that had put together Bush's victory in 1988—the loss of men like Jim Baker, Lee Atwater, and Roger Ailes. He even missed John Sununu, though his own fingerprints were on the murder weapon. The old crowd had brought an unsparing discipline to their work, an order and focus backed up by the president's complete trust in Baker's gifts of command. What had grown up in their place four years later, by Bush's own design, was an organizational shambles—a two-headed monster run by men who, as if in conformity with the Peter Principle, had been elevated by Bush to levels beyond their obvious capabilities.

Sam Skinner and Bob Teeter, sitting atop the twin peaks of authority, were both well-liked and well-pedigreed men, and Teeter was Bush's close friend as well. When the two lobbied vigorously for the big jobs at the White House and on Fifteenth Street, it had been hard for the president to say no. But nothing appeared to be working under their bifurcated command. They had what one colleague, speaking scatologically, called a reverse Midas touch, and by summer, the president had lost confidence in both of them.

Teeter's problem, as even friends conceded, was his notorious prudence—a seeming inability to decide anything quickly or crisply. His curriculum vitae was impeccable, after six presidential campaigns, and he seemed to have survived them all without enemies. There were those who thought that that might be part of his problem in his new role—that he was, for example, too nice to be the bearer of bad news to anybody including his principal client. Being a gentleman was unfortunately low among the desiderata for campaign managers, on a plane with collecting Steuben glass or re-reading Proust. The premium rather was on toughness, which was not Teeter's style. Bob was a great guy and a real pro, Ailes once said, but how could you spend twenty-five years in so nasty a business and not have *anybody* dislike you?

The consensus that formed with time was that he had simply been miscast. His real profession was polling, and his habits of mind were more academic than managerial; he tended to see and to convey ambiguity, whether reading the latest survey data or running a strategy meeting. Even his sharpest critics within the Bush entourage conceded his gifts at understanding the currents of popular opinion and at finding tactical advantage in them for his clients. Their quarrel with him was that his politics tended to be a picture without a frame. Teeter was one of these *modern* Republicans, one of his more conservative colleagues on Fifteenth Street said, by which he meant a campaign technocrat not burdened by strong ideological convictions. What Teeter was about was winning elections, and over a long, largely successful career, he had come to believe that you won more of them by stressing your candidate's best personal qualities than by selling his positions on the issues.

Teeter's Law was arguably a dangerous one in the close political atmosphere of 1992, given America's hunger for straight talk about real problems. It hadn't worked for Dick Thornburgh, a Teeter client, in the Pennsylvania Senate by-election, and by summer, it was plain even to its author that it wasn't working for Bush either—not with the people blaming the problems on him. But Teeter had little stomach for the alternative course, which was to win by destroying the opposition. He had been a dove in the year of Willie Horton and was again in the season of Gennifer Flowers and Inspector Perot. No less a critic than Richard Nixon had puzzled aloud in the spring as to why George had put a goddam pollster in charge in the first place. If you were looking for a great political analyst, the former president said, send for Bob. But if you wanted to kick somebody in the balls, which more nearly described Nixon's view of how the game was played, you'd better get somebody willing and able to do it.

The answer to Nixon's bafflement was simple. Teeter had got the job because he wanted it and had bucked hard for it, making it known that he might not play at all if he wasn't in charge. He figured that Bush/Quayle '92 would be his last campaign, unless his friend Dick Cheney happened to run the next time around, and Teeter didn't want to spend it as numbers runner to somebody else. He had played that part too many times before.

There were questions as to whether so gray and ambivalent a man was up to a job requiring the managerial gifts of a Fortune 500 CEO and the reflexes of a quarterback reading defenses and running audibles from the line of scrimmage. One of the doubters was George W. Bush; he had argued early on for somebody of proven executive talent—somebody, for example, like the then secretary of transportation Sam Skinner. His father had disagreed. Teeter was the president's friend and, to a degree, his security blanket after their several campaigns together. So what if he wasn't a born manager? A corporate type like Fred Malek, as number two, could make the planes fly on time. Teeter had earned his shot at being number one.

Skinner was rather less admired among Bush's retainers; it was only after he was gone that they began to eulogize him as a straight, honest, good-hearted soul and to describe his fall as a tragedy. He had promoted himself for chief of staff when Sununu was fired. His troubles had begun almost as soon as he got the job he had so openly coveted. People liked him well enough, or professed to, but a judgment quickly formed that he was in over his head trying to handle government, politics, and an increasingly cranky president all at once. His approach to his work struck one senior colleague as "pure scatter"—all chaotic motion with no focus, no organizing principle. At times, he seemed almost to agree. "I don't have time to fix anything," he complained to a pal early in his tenure. "I'm fighting fucking fires everywhere."

By spring, Bush's faith in him, and Skinner's in himself, seemed near collapse. His defenders said he was never given the authority he needed to do the job right, including, first of all, the power to hire and fire. It was true that Bush had instructed him not to make wholesale changes; it was likewise so that when Skinner tried a couple of retail moves, he showed an uncanny aim for the wrong targets. At a dinner meeting with the campaign team at Bob Mosbacher's house early in his tenure, he announced his plans to replace Dick Darman as budget director and to move Ron Kaufman, the White House political liaison, to the Republican National Committee. What he missed was that official Washington was a city of markers—of private debts and old connections—and his stack was no match for those held by the men he was trying to dispose of. Kaufman was a favorite of Bush's, and Darman a friend of Jim Baker's. Their patrons intervened to save them, and Skinner was left to his custodial duties, the chief of staff as maître d'.

He had no alliances that mattered; his friends were vastly outnumbered by his detractors. He had even contrived to offend Barbara Bush by trespassing on her turf, as when he contacted her one afternoon in Kennebunkport and told her who would be coming to her house for dinner that night; the maître d' had exceeded his brief. By summer, the president had grown to regret his choice and even to wax nostalgic for John Sununu. "In the old days," Bush complained, in the tone of a White Russian émigré mourning the time of the czars, "I used to know who did what around here."

Skinner's own spirit seemed to have been broken by his slide from favor, which softened his manner—senior colleagues found him more deferential—but did not help his performance. He had been perhaps 70 percent up to the job when he started, a White House topsider said; the problem was that, as it engulfed him, he seemed to shrink rather than grow. It was a benchmark of sorts when he left town for a long weekend without informing Bush of the sudden bump in unemployment to 7.8 percent. The president's upset at the news was compounded by his having been blindsided by it. The oversight struck Skinner's associates as the product of stress rather than dereliction of duty. Sam, it was said around the White House, wasn't looking or acting himself; he sometimes seemed to doze off at meetings or to lose track of what they were about.

It was plain by then to everybody, the president included, that the machine he had built was a lemon. The bipolar structure had been a bad mistake; decisions got stalled for days between the dithering on Fifteenth Street and the muddle on Pennsylvania Avenue. There was no discipline, no clarity of message or direction. Reaction times were slow. Speech texts were chronically late. Scheduling was ragged. An all-star media team recruited by Teeter on Madison Avenue was having trouble producing anything airworthy. Their early works included a summer flight of ads with Bush in tight close-up, talking earnestly to the camera. "The president as elevator music," one of the men responsible for them said drily. "'He's alone, he's there, he's a nice guy who just doesn't get it.'"

There wasn't even a campaign plan, normally a start-up requirement for a serious run for president. The form was more an intellectual exercise for handlers than a playbook to be read and followed literally; the best-laid plans were usually overtaken by events, but the mere act of producing one was useful as a way to force attention to the basics of what a candidacy was all about. The Teeter regime on Fifteenth Street never got that far. Its nearest approximation, finished in early June, was a fifty-page working paper to get the president through the summer. A twenty-five-page executive summary was produced for him, so as not to tax his famously short attention span.

As an essay on strategy, the plan was not a threat to Clausewitz or Sun-tzu. Its most important advice was what amounted to a 38 percent solution, a rough guess at what it might take to win a three-way race. In the circumstances, it would behoove Bush to concentrate on shoring up his base vote—the political, economic, and social conservatives who still needed persuading that he was one of them; for once, there might be enough of them to elect a president. The document was otherwise remarkable mostly for its bleak implicit message to Bush—that his reelection would be unprecedented in our history for a time when so many Americans so clearly wanted change.

Seeing the danger was one thing, squaring up to it quite another. The Bush command, both in the White House and at the campaign, appeared at times to be paralyzed by caution. Bill Kristol left one summer staff meeting furious at a decision not to fight for Bush's recovery package in the Senate. His elders had decided that it was a lost cause anyway—that pushing it would only open the president to attack by the Democrats on the issue of its fairness to the middle class.

It was the notion of surrendering without a fight that set Kristol off. "The American people won't be impressed by talk about our growth agenda when it's not backed up by fighting for it," he wrote in a scorching memo to Skinner and Teeter. "As for the 'fairness' issue, is fairness the reason we're down by almost thirty points? I suspect the poor economic record of the last three years, and our perceived passivity and failure of leadership, have far more to do with our problems." The president had a chance to show some boldness and conviction, Kristol said, "but our discussion proceeded as if we were twenty points ahead and the economy were doing fine. We're not, and it isn't, and conflict avoidance doesn't strike me as the way to go."

Kristol never got an answer. Skinner and Teeter didn't *have* a way to go, and as spring gave way to summer, the pressure for radical surgery grew. Fifteenth Street came in for a full ration of blame; there were too many suits there, Ailes complained from his sideline seat in New York, and not enough people willing to kill or die for the president. The bolder dissidents argued that Teeter had to go; even with a seasoned corporate executive like Fred Malek around to carry out his wishes, a White House official said sourly, Bob couldn't organize a two-bicycle parade.

Teeter in fact was an unhappy camper, quite apart from the increasingly nasty whispers about him. The president had promised him total control of the show, but things never really work that way when incumbent presidents seek reelection. There were competing power centers in the White House and the office of the vice president, and Teeter, with his gray manner and his ruminative mind, was overmatched in the tug-of-war among them. Even in his own shop, he had been arguably superseded by Charlie Black, the lobbyist and counselor without portfolio, as the president's chief strategist. Some campaigns had been fun for Teeter. Bush/Quayle '92 was not; the stress level was too high, the odor of death too powerful. There were days when, for all his practice at masking, he could not conceal his anxiety—days when he tensed up like a turtle in a shell, a staffer said, and avoided making eye contact with anyone.

But no one who knew his relationship with the president thought he was really in danger; no matter how deep Bush's disappointment, he would never fire so close a friend. The man at ground zero instead was Skinner, who did not have Teeter's history with the boss and so made a more exposed target. One senior colleague called him and his team the worst White House command group in the postwar era;

another said he had seen junior-high-school student governments function better. Barbara Bush, exposed one day to Skinner's jumpy attention span, asked aloud if he was *always* that excitable. Dan Quayle, himself bleeding from a thousand cuts, found it hard hiding his contempt for a man with a thousand and one. In his view, privately expressed, it was a mistake to speak of the president's chief of staff; he didn't have one.

"It Isn't Working"

In the circumstances, Jim Baker became a kind of cult object at the White House and the campaign—a distant magical figure who, if the right prayers were uttered, could be induced to return from his realm in the middle air and put the world right. Teeter himself, in conversations with Bush, was an early advocate of his recall. So, ironically, was Skinner; he raised it with the president in April, in one of their serial discussions of why the machinery was malfunctioning.

"It isn't structured right," Skinner said. "It isn't working."

Bush asked what could be done.

"We may need to get Baker back," Skinner said. "With this economy, we have no choice."

Both Skinner and Teeter imagined till the end that they could survive a putsch with their titles and authority intact. It was Teeter's assumption, indeed, that it was Skinner they were talking about superseding, not him, and he became an active supporter of a coup. He couldn't move frontally, even if it had been his way; the president himself had told him that Skinner was staying, and Teeter was reduced to seeking surrogates to help make the case. At one point, he asked Quayle to use his entrée to Bush and press for a change of command at the White House. At another, he tried to enlist George W. Bush to lobby his father.

As it happened, neither man had to be persuaded that the president needed Baker if he was to survive. For Junior, the tie was almost familial; for Quayle, who didn't like Baker, it was strictly business. But each man hesitated at pushing the president to draft his old pal. Bush seemed bent on trying to make the existing arrangement work; it wasn't *that* bad, in his stubborn view, and if he started making changes so late in the day, he said, everybody would paint it as panic. It was always hard changing his mind when he was in his Cool Hand George mode, the one calm man in the eye of the storm, and both the vice president and the first son told Teeter no. "I don't have the brass," Junior said, "to tell my old man how to run his White House."

The president's view of the situation, by early summer, was a lonely one. He was running third in the polls behind an issueless billionaire and a saxophone player, as Roger Ailes described the opposition, and most of his circle had defected to the anti-Skinner party. Several of his outside friends—the Republican national chairman, Rich Bond, among them—breakfasted with Quayle one morning in July and bitched loudly about both the White House and the campaign; the consensus was that Baker had to be brought in. At almost the same moment, a deputation of ten old Reagan hands sat down at the White House mess for a similar conversation with the Bush command group, its tone muted only by the fact that Teeter and Skinner were at the table.

"Either Baker or Cheney has to come over here," Frank Fahrenkopf, who had been Republican chairman during the Reagan years, said at one point.

There was a pregnant silence; people felt embarrassed for Skinner.

"I don't mean *here* necessarily," Fahrenkopf said, faltering. "Maybe the campaign."

There was another awkward pause, this time for Teeter.

"Maybe we don't have to *replace* anybody," Fahrenkopf said, by now desperate, but he still felt somebody had to come in.

Skinner and Teeter pretended not to have heard.

The tattooing continued, and not just from Baker's admirers at the table. A surprising vote for his recall came from the Gipper's pal Paul Laxalt, the conservative former senator from Nevada. The two had been fierce rivals in the Reagan years, each jealous of the other's access to the president and suspicious as to how it might be used. But Washington was a city of strange bedfellowships; it mattered less whether you *loved* your partner of the moment than whether you respected him afterward, and Laxalt respected Baker. "I've had my differences with him," he said, putting it mildly, as the breakfast broke up. "But he's gotta come over here and take charge. You guys need him here."

Bush finally had to give in to reality, and so, reluctantly, did Baker. Their relationship, while close, had always been a more complex affair than it seemed to outsiders. They had come up together in the worlds of money, society, and politics in Texas; they had been in one sense competitors, however friendly, and the bond between them had inevitably been tinctured by their old rivalry for prestige and pride of place. Baker was the more at ease in the world in which they had finally arrived, and the more obviously gifted at its gamesmanship. He was boardroom smooth where Bush was hopelessly gawky; he was the master manipulator of the press to his own advantage, where the president tended to look on reporters only too openly as bees at a picnic.

And yet Baker had always remained the junior partner, the man on whom Bush relied in election years and who in turn depended on Bush for patronage. They were a brotherhood bound together not just by affection but by mutual need, and with Bush in trouble, they both knew without having to say so that there was no alternative to Baker's return. Baker had postponed it as long as he could. By summer, he had run out of excuses; on a fishing holiday at his getaway spread in Wyoming during the Democratic convention in July, he said yes at last to the president's plea for help.

His surrender was an act of pain, but as one man privy to his thinking described it, the SOS was an offer he couldn't refuse. It wasn't just that the two of them had been close for nearly thirty-five years or that Baker owed the job he loved to Bush; it was simply that, as a purely practical matter, he wasn't going to *be* secretary of state anymore if the president didn't get reelected. It required a leap of faith to believe that Teeter and Skinner were going to work that particular miracle unaided; it might even be beyond Baker's own part-real, part-mythic powers. The saving fact for him, in his friend's reading, was that he couldn't lose either way. His strategically late arrival assured that nobody could blame him if Bush were defeated. And if, mirabile dictu, he won? Baker would return to the state department in glory, the hero of 1992 and the early front-runner for the nomination in 1996. It was a win-win situation—the equivalent, his confidant said, of buying IBM at a dollar a share.

Baker did make a last, forlorn effort to come back halfway—to take a leave of absence from State and oversee the White House and the campaign as a "counselor" on temporary loan to the president. The arrangement would have been a sop not just to him but to the two men he was displacing; it would have permitted Skinner to keep his title and Teeter the appearance of command rank on Fifteenth Street. It wasn't till the day of the announcement that Bush broke the news to Skinner that the lawyers hadn't been able to make the scheme work; Baker would be coming in as chief of staff, and Skinner would be shipping out to the Republican National Committee as something called general chairman.

"I wish we didn't have to do it this way," Bush told him.

"It's no problem," Skinner answered, swallowing his pride. "Whatever it takes. We've got no margin of error."

"Sam," Bush said gratefully, "you're a broad-gauged guy."

The coup was accomplished, and Baker moved smartly into his new role, bringing with him four favorite colonels from his past commands. One of them, Margaret Tutwiler, had scouted the terrain for him in advance, interviewing people they knew and trusted about who was good, who was furniture, who had been frozen out, and what needed fixing. The scan served the double purpose of gathering intelligence and creating a de facto fifth column, a network of people in the campaign who were in effect working for Baker weeks before he was piped aboard. Tutwiler's twenty-page sum-up became his blueprint for a peaceful takeover. The cadre of his occupying army was already on the ground.

Baker could not disguise his unhappiness at his assignment or his understanding of the odds against his and Bush's success. "We may not be back next year," Baker had told a European head of state months earlier. By then, some of his closest aides had already begun amusing themselves with speculations as to where in the private sector they would find work starting in 1993. Nothing since then had parted the clouds; it was quickly evident to colleagues that Baker and his team had the good sense to be scared.

In time, his misery would show, in his demeanor and, some thought, his performance on the job. But his arrival alone was tonic for a demoralized campaign, the cavalry charge at the end of the movie. The day the deal went down, Junior started packing for a fishing trip back in Texas. His dad didn't need him anymore, he told friends; everything would be under control the rest of the way. The buzz on Fifteenth Street was that somebody real, somebody *formidable*, was finally in charge. If Bush lost now, one elder there said, it would be the zeitgeist that had brought him down, not the abject failure of his own management team.

20.

This Way to the Jihad

In the normal course of events, the renomination of a sitting president is as formal and as stylized as a tableau vivant at the court of
Louis XIV—a set piece meant to flatter the once and future king. But
the convention ratifying George Bush's candidacy for a second term
was nearer Grand Guignol as political theater. It began with a mistake—
a deal making Pat Buchanan the de facto keynote speaker—and ended
with a pasted-up acceptance speech including practically everything
except poetry, promise, or hope. The acts between got mostly negative
reviews for their shrieky tone. For four nights in Houston, it was as if
the melancholy state of the union counted for little as against the
scarlet sins of liberals, lesbians, Democrats, feminists, congresspeople,
gays, Greens, trial lawyers, single women who had babies, all women
who aborted them—and, at the head of their advancing columns, Bill
and Hillary Clinton.

The show in some measure followed the normal thermodynamic of
party conventions: the cooler the voters to your own man, the higher
the heat applied to the opposition. But some of Bush's handlers conceded afterward that they had let the brimstone quotient get out of
hand. They had arrived in Houston with four strategic goals: first,
to humor the party hard core with large helpings of red meat; second,
to tiptoe around the abortion issue without anybody noticing; third, to
put forward a credible domestic agenda; and, fourth, to showcase
Bush as a leader with a vision for a brighter tomorrow. They succeeded
only at the first of these goals: the red-hots, a campaign topsider
gloated afterward, were white-hot now. The rest of the screenplay
somehow got left on the cutting-room floor.

The die had been cast with the decision, after the primaries, that
Buchanan had to be appeased—that he and his brigades of the right
could wreck the convention if they were not made part of it. Bush
himself was a quadrennial red-hot, ever willing to treat with the party
right in election years; he had magically got over his initial nausea at
the idea and had authorized Charlie Black and Jim Lake to enter

negotiations with the Buchanans. His impulse was by no means unanimous in his councils. Sam Skinner, then still in charge at the White House, was against doing Pat any favors, and so was Rich Bond, the party chairman, for whom politics was a slightly higher form of demolition derby.

"The guy has no base," Bond argued at a meeting in Bush's hideaway work station off the Oval Office one day in July. Only a small fraction of Buchanan voters had actually voted for *him;* the rest had meant only to send Bush a message. Why reward Pat with podium time at the convention? "We owe him nothing," Bond said. "He's already screwed us, and his message is one we don't want to associate ourselves with. I think we oughta go tell him to take a flying leap."

"I don't feel comfortable with this whole situation either," Bush answered. "But let's see what Black and Lake come back with. I want to know what Pat's willing to do for us."

Bond found himself in a minority; the consensus followed one of the oldest rules of the game, that it was better to have the enemy inside the tent pissing out than outside the tent pissing in. Buchanan was in the hospital recovering from postseason heart surgery when his wife, Shelley, got a call from Fred Malek wishing them both well. The gesture was the first in a familiar minuet of politics—a choreography of painted smiles and exaggerated bows leading to a loveless final embrace.

The point man in the truce talks was Lake, a smooth persuader on part-time duty as a senior counselor to the campaign. He and Black had been the butts of a particularly nasty Buchanan ad, one that made much of their continuing day jobs as lobbyists for foreign interests. But their attitude toward the give and take of politics was like the Corleone Family view of the occasionally necessary murder: it was only business and was not to be taken personally. Lake had known Bay Buchanan for years, and while he warned her up front that some of his colleagues still harbored grudges against her brother, he proposed that they sit down and try to work out a reconciliation.

They met for the first time in perhaps the safest setting in America for two Republican conspirators seeking privacy: at a Sixth Avenue deli in Manhattan during Democratic convention week. Bay's bill of demands was surprisingly short and mostly easy. The single problem was that Buchanan insisted on speaking in prime time in a year when the traditional big-three networks were rationing convention time to an hour or two a night. That would take some working out, Lake said. But Bay made it clear that it was the price of Pat's endorsement; no prime time, no public blessing.

The demand set off a shudder of paranoia in the Bush command. Teeter and Skinner thought they smelled the makings of a double cross—at best a tepid endorsement; at worst, a network-television reprise of all the mean things Buchanan had said about Bush in the early primaries. When talks with Bay resumed a week later in Lake's offices in Washington, he and Black offered a slot for Pat at 9:30 Tuesday, the second night of the convention; they had checked around and learned that at least two networks would be starting their coverage early enough to pick up the speech. But there was a price. Buchanan would have to come out for Bush in some public setting up front, at a press conference, say, or on *Larry King*. Or, Black said, he could book time at the National Press Club and bless Bush a month before the convention.

The Buchanans thought about that for forty-eight hours and said no. Buchanan thought it better as theater to draw out the suspense to the last moment—an impulse reinforced in him by a phone conversation with his old patron Richard Nixon.

"I talked to the Old Man," Buchanan told a pal at Bush-Quayle headquarters one day. "He agrees we ought to have some mystery."

Bush's generals were furious. The passion of Buchanan's embrace was becoming a fixation for them, to the exclusion of anything else he might say.

"We've got to see his remarks," Teeter said. "I want to be sure his endorsement is real."

Lake dutifully carried the message to Bay.

"We're part of the team," she said. "You can trust us."

Lake did, but his principals didn't, and he was obliged to press their concerns as if they were his own.

"I'm really goosey about this," he told Bay one day in early August. "We haven't seen the words."

"You'll see them before the convention," Bay said.

Teeter's anxiety wasn't allayed. Pat was trying to waffle on the endorsement, he said, and his suspicions seemed to him confirmed when he saw the text of a letter Buchanan proposed to send to the eighty thousand people on his mailing list over the weekend before the convention. Bay had presented it as a token that her brother was in earnest about being a team player; the bottom line, indeed, was his recommendation that his followers vote for Bush. But the letter, in some passages, seemed less than wholly enthusiastic. Teeter hated it and demanded some changes. To his astonishment, Buchanan made them.

What he wouldn't give up was his moment in the klieg lights, and when he was slotted between Jack Kemp, the new-age conservative icon, and Senator Phil Gramm of Texas, the keynote speaker, on Tuesday night, the deal almost came unstuck. All three were ambitious men, and each had a jealous eye on the others. Kemp didn't want to share the evening with Buchanan. Gramm wasn't happy costarring with either man. Buchanan didn't like being the filling in a sandwich; in his nightmares, the networks would cut to the anchor booths while he was on, leaving him to preach to the faithful inside the hall when he wanted the whole world watching.

In retrospect, Bush's managers recognized that they would have served their client better by standing on their original offer to Buchanan: Tuesday night or nothing. But the impulse to get his benediction for the ticket had progressed from wish to obsession, and obsession, as often happens in politics, begat mistakes.

The first was the suggestion by Craig Fuller, the old Bush hand running the convention, that Buchanan be reslotted into prime time on the first night instead of the second. The evening was to be a night of nostalgia for the Reagan years, starring the Gipper himself, and Fuller proposed that Buchanan open for him. The attractions for Buchanan were obvious, not least of them the likelihood that a big audience would be tuned in for Reagan, and he seized on the offer. No one reckoned on the possible consequences; the imperative was closing the deal, and permitting Pat his opening-night showcase was its apparent price.

The second and larger blunder was the campaign's blindness to the damage Buchanan could do the party and the ticket, even if he nominated Bush for beatification. All Teeter and Skinner cared about was what he might say about the president, and from the beginning of the two-month round of shuttle diplomacy to the end, they remained locked into their fantasies of betrayal. With the terms of Buchanan's surrender finally set, the negotiators set up a pro forma meeting in Washington so that everybody could shake hands on the bargain. The night before, Skinner and Teeter phoned Lake. They were sure Buchanan was up to something treacherous. They wanted to call the whole thing off.

"If Pat makes a deal, he's gonna keep the deal," Lake told them. The guy was honorable, and even if you didn't buy that, he was no idiot; he was smart enough to know that he was dead as a Republican if he embarrassed Bush from the podium.

In the end, the meeting came off as scheduled in Teeter's suite at the Jefferson Hotel, a few blocks up Sixteenth Street from the White House. Buchanan, having muscled his way onto prime time, couldn't resist tweaking his former adversaries one last time on the president's swan dive in the polls. "Why are you guys so down in the mouth?" he asked mischievously. "When *we* hit 30 percent, we broke out the champagne."

But as Lake had predicted, Pat had come to play. He had always meant to endorse Bush, he said, and to campaign aggressively for him in the fall. As a token of his good faith, he fished up a personal letter he had written the president and asked Teeter to deliver it. Teeter, with Buchanan's leave, read it and stopped twitching. It was a mash note, or near enough to quiet his suspicions. That afternoon, Teeter forwarded it to Bush, with a covering memo suggesting that he call Buchanan to seal the agreement.

"We Are America"

And so the dance ended as it had begun, in an exchange of manufactured pleasantries between two men who at once despised and needed one another. Bush phoned the next day, inquiring solicitously about Buchanan's health. Buchanan said he was fine, thank you, and was excited about his impending return to the fold at the convention. Bush said he appreciated the help and was delighted Buchanan would be speaking; he hoped they would see each other in Houston.

Even the Buchanans were surprised by their victory; Bay had forced the game like a poker player holding a low pair and had won. "You won't believe this," she told a friend. "They're giving us prime time!"

Bush's men were under the illusion that *they* had won and were still congratulating themselves when, as part of the deal, the Buchanans hand-carried a copy of his text to Craig Fuller's trailer at the convention hall. It was a sermon addressed to the choir of the fundamentalist right, but Fuller and Lake each read it with a cycloptic eye, seeing only what it said about Bush. To their relief, Buchanan's praise for the man he had ridiculed as King George was, as promised, unrestrained. When they saw the goodwill, one player in the events would confess later, they tuned out. Measured against a strong endorsement, nothing else mattered.

"This is terrific," Fuller told Buchanan.

Lake thought it a bit ripe around the edges, but he, too, waved it through without a change. He called the White House, where Teeter was briefing Bush on arrangements for the convention. Teeter told him to send a fax copy, ASAP. Lake did. Teeter read it quickly, butterflies still fluttering. Then he passed it to Bush.

Minutes later, Teeter called the trailer.

"This is fine," he said. He liked it. So did the president. The deal, and the speech, were on.

The marvel was that nobody in the loop asked the next question: how it would look to America to tune in for its first glimpse into the future in a second Bush administration and to be told that it would be consumed by a cultural and religious war for the soul of the nation. In the aftermath, some of the president's shamefaced handlers would try to spin the story that Pat had double-crossed them after all—that he had preached his Monday evening sermon without clearing it with them. In fact, everybody who mattered, including Bush himself, had seen it and stamped it APPROVED. All the president required of Buchanan was flattery, and having got it, he and his handlers were too pleased and relieved to notice that it came wrapped in an invitation to a jihad.

The first consequence of their negligence was the ruin of what was to have been Unity Night in Houston—a pageant in which two conservative heroes celebrated Bush as their kind of Republican. Reagan did his part; the old stager softened his rhetoric with a smile and spoke up for his successor as if he really believed his lines. But Buchanan had unilaterally proclaimed disunity night before the Gipper went on. In his vision of "a nation that we still call God's country," the Lord of Hosts would be voting Republican. The Clintons—Hillary was a particular object of Buchanan's scorn—had thrown in with the criminals, deviates, baby killers, and career women who made up the armies of the night.

The speech opened the proceedings on a note of intolerance, a smallness of spirit from which they never wholly recovered; the convention would be the most narrowly sectarian since Barry Goldwater's conquest of the party in 1964. Even Dan Quayle complained privately that Pat had been far too harsh. The war on Murphy Brown was one thing, Buchanan's screed another; the tone it set, in Quayle's view, was jarringly at odds with the president's need to recreate himself as a man of broad and generous vision.

In fact, both Quayles joined the chorus of the scolds, along with Pat Robertson and others of the secular and religious right. Reagan's turn on Monday was a museum piece; Jack Kemp's, on Tuesday, was a futurist work, a bit sky-blue for the tastes of the audience in the hall. The music otherwise was martial, the rataplan of Christian soldiers marching as to war. Long after it mattered, Rich Bond would lament his party's celebration of what he called "the stale ideas of a dead and dying past." Inside the hall, he was one of the celebrants. The big-tent Republicanism once envisioned by his predecessor, Lee Atwater, had the steamy air of a revival tent instead—a judgment seat where sinners, broadly defined, were cast into darkness and only the saved were made to feel welcome. "We are America," Bond, caught up in the spirit, had crowed then. "These other people are not America."

The show was less than pleasing to Jim Baker, who, by choice, had signed on too late to stage-manage it and so watched it from the shadows at a secure distance from blame. He was by no means squeamish about tooth-and-claw politics; he had been party to the brutality of the 1988 campaign, though Atwater and Ailes, among others, had taken the fall. His own view of the field of battle was much as it had been then—that there was no nice way for Bush to prevail.

"You've got the hard part," Charlie Black teased him one evening on the convention floor. "You get the president's positives where they need to be, and I'll get Clinton's negatives where they need to be."

Baker laughed in agreement. Redoing Bush *was* the hard part, perhaps impossible in the ten weeks remaining. For the president to win reelection, Clinton would have to be destroyed, and to the extent that the torchier rhetoric in Houston had focused on him, it had served a useful strategic purpose.

But Baker and his circle worried that the people who ran the show had pandered *too* much to what pragmatists like themselves called the full-mooners of the Republican right. Playing to them might get you to 40 percent of the vote, one of Baker's lieutenants said, but they were probably with you anyway; 40 percent, indeed, was roughly what Bush was getting in the polls. You still needed 50 percent to win, his man said, and you couldn't pick up those last 10 points mounting a crusade to eradicate sin from the world. You were more likely to drive them away.

In his private assessments, Baker himself was most visibly bothered by the one-note stress on family values as defined by men who appeared to have overdosed on reruns of *Father Knows Best*. He figured the president had problems enough with women voters over the issue of abortion without having his friends invent new ways to alienate them—connecting feminism with witchcraft, say, or recasting Hillary Rodham Clinton as Lady MacBeth with permanent PMS. When he took over, the stress on family values would all but disappear, except for narrowly targeted audiences. Its demise as a main theme of the campaign was marked the day Dan Quayle sent Murphy Brown a note and a stuffed elephant to show his tender regard for single mothers.

But Baker had come in too late to save the convention from its own lax management, and he took some hits afterward for his tardiness. He himself had set the standard in such matters in Ronald Reagan's reelection campaign in 1984; at his insistence, as one old colleague remembered, the last word on who said what and when they said it had reposed in his office and was ruthlessly applied. The straw bosses nominally in charge of the show had gone around as usual doing their private deals with this faction or that warlord, promising them favorable time slots and freedom of speech. The markers had only that value Baker and his tight circle chose to give them; at a word from them, texts were bounced, time slots juggled, and deals undone where necessary to ensure the perfect setting for the Gipper's ascent to glory.

In Baker's absence, his man conceded, that sort of discipline had collapsed. His successors had left the convention to conventional Republicans, party men whose habit it was to let the full-gospel fundamentalists out of their cages once every four years and allow them to holler themselves hoarse. There was nobody to undo the deals this time, certainly not men so chary of giving offense as Teeter or Skinner. The stage managers instead had been allowed to run the show, and they had too easily yielded control of the podium and the platform to the scorched-earth ideologues of the right. Their client was a man who had spent much of his career having to prove his credentials as a conservative, and their impulse, like his, was surrender.

They had accordingly neglected the usual drill, which was to screen every speech both for its own content and for its contribution to the ensemble effect. The breakdown had only begun with their misbegotten deal with Buchanan. Their tolerance throughout bordered on tone deafness; as one of them would admit afterwards, they missed the cumulative impact of the convention until the curtain had come down and the bad reviews flooded in.

The Search for the One True Bush

The failure of quality control only intensified the pressure on Bush himself to deliver what the brokers of expectations in the press were saying would have to be the Speech of His Life. He had been widely credited with having done just that four years earlier, even if he had since had to eat some of his words; his muted eloquence then had burnished his reputation for rising to the big occasions. But the demands on him this time were immeasurably larger, given the crisis of confidence in him, and neither he nor his management could meet them.

To succeed would have required his overnight metamorphosis from the in-box problem solver he was by nature into a national leader of clear purpose and coherent views. No such transformation would have been plausible, a member of his strategic inner circle said; the president had been operating at too low an energy level for too long, and at far too high a cost. By convention time, in this analysis, his months of seeming passivity had carried him into a danger zone well beyond the old question of whether he cared about domestic policy. He seemed not to care about *anything*, even getting reelected; people had begun asking again whether he was well and whether he really wanted to be president anymore.

In the circumstances, this aide thought, the minimum goal for the speech would be to show a president fully engaged with the campaign and the issues and ready to do battle with Clinton for territorial rights to the American future. He would have to rough Clinton up a bit, his staffer said, though not quite so violently as some of the earlier speakers had done; he had to persuade voters that, no matter how bad they thought he was, the other guy would be dangerously worse. But the president would have to retouch his own portrait as well—to present himself at the very least as a safe, sane, and reassuringly familiar alternative—and Baker's group thought they saw a way for him to dab in some bolder colors. He would say that he had been preoccupied in his first term with the great questions of war and peace in a world turned upside down. That wouldn't be necessary the second time around; he was home from the wars now and ready to take on the economy as vigorously as he had dealt with Saddam Hussein.

What Baker's shadow management didn't think profitable was to send the president out with a formally packaged Bush Plan for the salvation of America. His earlier stabs at presenting an agenda had got nowhere, and they didn't have a big-bang idea for him anyway. They had toyed at some length with a proposal for a radical reconstruction of the entire tax system, downsizing the income tax on ordinary citizens and small businesses and imposing a tax on consumption instead. The idea had worked for the Germans and Japanese and could be sold as a way to increase productivity, as they had done.

But Baker's people had finally backed off. They feared, for one thing, that the Jack Kemp wing of the party would bolt the hall at the mere mention of a new tax; in the acid view of one White House aide, they didn't believe you had to pay for *anything*. The command group was tormented as well by its secret doubts that Bush would be believable proposing anything so dramatic so late in the day. The yearlong search for The Plan, in their chastened view, had taken on the aspect of the quest for the Holy Grail in Arthurian times—a vain enterprise grounded, finally, in a belief in miracles. It wasn't a "plan" people wanted of Bush, his men told themselves. It was some sign that he was paying attention to their problems and was at last committed to finding solutions for them.

Even that modest set of signals got scrambled in the writing process; the speech, when it finally emerged, answered accurately to the old definition of a camel as a horse put together by a committee. Peggy Noonan, the gifted ghostwriter who had produced most of Bush's big lines in 1988, had jumped ship the second time around. Her scripts had always been a bit emotive for the president, whose taste in prose, as in tailoring, ran to shades of gray. When her successors ran up something in purple for him to say in sympathy for the dispossessed victims of a hurricane in Florida that summer, he bounced it. "This is Noonanesque," he said. "I don't wanna do this poetry stuff. People need *wood.*"

Still, the big occasions called for *some* poetry stuff, and in Noonan's absence, Bush enlisted Ray Price, once the kinder, gentler speechwriter in Richard Nixon's stable, to try his hand. Price had sent the president a personal note suggesting some theme music for the speech and had in turn been invited to produce a full-length draft. Price accepted, but he appeared, at sixty-two, to have slowed a bit at short-order cookery since his days making Nixon sound nice. He delivered his offering a bare week before Bush was due on the rostrum and did not pretend even then that it was really a draft. He called it "preliminary thoughts" instead. Bush's men didn't like it, and, with the clock running, they mounted a frantic salvage operation.

The men in charge were a badly matched pair. One, Bob Zoellick, Baker's trusted lieutenant, was a smart but deadly serious policy wonk. The other, Steve Provost, Bush's chief speechwriter, was a word merchant trading in crowd-pleasing prose. The two got on personally, but the shotgun marriage of styles was a bit like installing Placido Domingo as lead singer with the Grateful Dead. Zoellick, working with Dick Darman and his deputy, Bob Grady, produced a draft heavy with domestic-policy initiatives. Its intent was to show that Bush was really on the job. Its effect on its first readers was leaden. The political boys hated it—Roger Ailes pronounced it as exciting as a mattress tag—and the president himself was less than pleased. He had arrived in Houston for the Speech of His Life without so much as a working script to begin practicing on.

"We'd better start from scratch," he grumped, not troubling to hide his displeasure.

The convention was already in progress when Baker finally stepped in and dragooned Provost and Ailes to juice up the speech. They rather overdid it, at least in Zoellick's eyes; when he saw their rewrite, *he* was appalled. "You wouldn't believe these guys," he told one of his comrades in Baker's circle back in Washington. "They're playing to the hall and not the country. It's a bunch of one-liners strung together."

In fact, neither draft worked, and there was not enough time to start from scratch on a new one; the only solution was to feed everything they had into a Cuisinart and see what kind of puree came out. While Bush stewed in his rooms, his people wrote, rewrote, scissored, pasted, and bickered among themselves about priorities. What they created was a kind of rhetorical sandwich—a mostly refried policy agenda wrapped in mostly negative prose. Shots at Clinton were liberally salted in. So were the obligatory nods to God, country, and family—and, at the close, the debut of George H. W. Bush in *Harry Truman II: The Sequel,* declaring war on a "gridlock Democratic Congress."

The process was slow, the delivery schedule ragged. Bush was kept waiting in his suite at the Houstonian Hotel, the voting address he called home but rarely tenanted. His mood darkened as the days slipped by. He had been complaining for months about the chronic tardiness of his speechwriters on the most routine occasions. Now, with his presidency on the line, the problem had got worse instead of better. He and Ailes, his speech coach and ego masseur, were forced to go into rehearsal the day before the event with major sections of the text still in the sausage grinder. The president, as an aide delicately put it, was upset.

His performance, in the end, was better than his script. The speech was prosy, cluttered, and long—longer, even, than Clinton's marathon celebration of himself in Madison Square Garden in July. What Bush needed most to do, one of the parade of writers said, was to communicate a sense of *coherence* in his presidency—some unifying frame for what he had actually achieved in his first term, against partisan resistance in Congress, and for what he proposed to do in his second. He had had three and a half years to do so and, the aide admitted, he had failed. The only rationale he had conveyed for his reelection was, in effect, that he was there.

His speech did little to fill in the large blank spaces in America's understanding of what he stood for. His wordsmiths appeared to have despaired of finding the One True Bush and to have tried instead to assemble one out of whatever component parts lay at hand. The Bush they pieced together was a figure of grievance rather than hope—a president libeled by a liberal opponent and thwarted by an obstructionist majority on Capitol Hill. Blame was the most conspicuous element in his speech. Coherence was the least; it was as if he had emptied a truckload of bricks on the podium and said they were a house—or would have been if only Congress would let him assemble it.

Bush himself had made known his wish for something in broader strokes, not the sort of legislative shopping list thought appropriate to State of the Union addresses. But a list was what he got, long enough to produce nationally broadcast yawns in the network anchor booths. He did offer a couple of catchy Darman-and-Zoellick ideas—a check-off box on tax returns for people who wanted to help pay down the national debt, and an across-the-board tax cut pegged to equal reductions in spending. The proposals were all but lost in a catalogue of mostly recycled goods and were quickly abandoned in any case when critics began calculating the cuts they would require in such off-limits programs as social security and medicare.

In the aftermath, Bush's handlers would argue that the speech had at least shown his fighting spirit and that the convention as a whole had helped shore up the party's restive conservative base. But it did little to move the men and women in the middle—the moderates, independents, and Reagan-Bush Democrats who had made the Republicans a de facto majority party in the past three presidential elections. The campaign had assembled a dial group of forty-five swing voters in Arlington Heights, Illinois, to watch the president and indicate their reactions to his address on electronic meters. The needle jumped smartly when Bush spoke out against crime, lawyers, and big government and for term limits for members of Congress. But his pledge to cut taxes bombed, and so did the miscellany he called a plan for economic recovery.

The dial group suggested, and the postconvention polls affirmed, that the miniseries emanating from Houston had failed in its larger mission: the rehabilitation of George Bush. The bounce he got from four nights' exposure was small and fleeting, the product mainly of partisan Republicans coming home. But they had never added up to a majority in a two-way race, and little that happened at the convention was calculated to widen Bush's following. The jury was still out on Clinton, and his numbers moved up and down with each transitory shift in public perception. Bush's did not. He still seemed stalled at or around 40 percent in trial heats with his rival, and his low job rating was like a dead weight anchoring him in place.

The bad news undermined some of the hope that Baker's arrival had brought to the cause. The president seemed to one troubled campaign official to be running not just against Clinton or the economy but against karma, as if it were his fate to lose and any effort to change that outcome would be futile. In the days following the convention, Bush's handlers got hold of a page of talking points dispatched by the Clinton campaign to its employees and friends, and Fred Malek brought it to a staff meeting.

"This thing is full of falsehoods," Malek said with mixed surprise and anger.

Everybody laughed. Politics was politics, a game of overstatement. Maybe Fred had been off in the private sector too long.

"No," he protested, "this goes beyond what we would *ever* do."

"Yeah," David Carney, Bush's field director, wisecracked. "They want to win."

So, of course, did Bush's people. What they lacked was not the will but the way.

Bush himself thought he saw one, or so he told the well-wishers he had received in his rooms at the Houstonian during convention week. He could sense the fear behind their bright chatter and their good-luck smiles; some of them, he noticed, were having trouble looking him in the eye. The president, by contrast, seemed almost preternaturally calm. The tonic he recommended to his visitors was David McCullough's highly praised new biography of Truman, particularly the parts about how old Give-'em-Hell Harry had come back from the dead and won reelection in 1948 by running against an obstructionist Congress.

"Start reading at page 653," Bush advised. The story of Truman's resurrection began there, and, he said, "that is what I'm going to do."

The strategy, like most of its predecessors, was equal parts wish and desperation. The president's own strategists were saying that a Truman scenario would not be enough to save him, and as summer faded away, so did some of the president's optimism. "This is gonna be the worst two months of my life," he told an intimate a few days before his kickoff tour over Labor Day weekend.

It seemed plain by then that he wasn't just talking about the wear and tear of a campaign on a man of his advancing years. He knew that his presidency was in peril, and, in unguarded moments, an uncharacteristic fatalism crept into his conversation. He believed he was going to win, he told a chum in the waning days of August, but if he *should* lose? Hell, that had happened to other people, he said, and they had survived it; life would just go on.

His confidant was surprised, not by the odds—he knew that they were prohibitively long—but by the president's flagging spirits. Bush was the kind of competitor who would do anything to win a game of horseshoes, let alone a presidential election. Till that day, his old friend had never heard him concede even the possibility of his defeat.

The unhappy warrior: Friends wondered if Bush's heart was in his last campaign. *(John Ficara/Newsweek)*

The miscast manager: Aides complained about Sam Skinner's short tour as chief. *(David Valdez/The White House)*

An American icon: Barbara Bush outpolled her husband. *(Larry Downing/Newsweek)*

A family Christmas: The president read a story to his grandchildren at Camp David. *(Susan Biddle/The White House)*

The exile: John Sununu left at gunpoint. *(Larry Downing/Newsweek)*

The general: Bob Teeter managed by meeting. *(John Ficara/Newsweek)*

The fall guys: Economic advisers Richard Darman and Nicholas Brady found themselves in the bull's eye. *(Larry Downing/Newsweek)*

The pollster: Fred Steeper kept worrying. *(Courtesy Cathie Steeper)*

The deputy: Mary Matalin kept running. *(Larry Downing/Newsweek)*

The A-team: Fred Malek and Bob Teeter ran the show on Fifteenth Street. *(Wally McNamee/Newsweek)*

The reluctant dragon: Jim Baker watched his friend's campaign from the sidelines as long as he could. *(John Ficara/Newsweek)*

One man's opinion: A sermon from Pat Buchanan. (*John Ficara/Newsweek*)

Two for the road: On tour with his wife, Shelley. (*Larry Downing/Newsweek*)

Three little words: A celebratory headline in the *Manchester Union Leader*. (*Larry Downing/Newsweek*)

The unready reserve: The Quayle hunters wanted Colin Powell. *(Larry Downing/ Newsweek)*

The unwilling sacrifice: The vice president refused to bow his neck to the blade. *(John Ficara/Newsweek)*

The spokesman: Marlin Fitzwater.
(Larry Downing/Newsweek)

The campaign command: The president with Fred Malek, Mary Matalin, and Bob Teeter. *(Larry Downing/Newsweek)*

IV

The Billionaire

He has lived all his life in the idea that there was a time a long time back when everything was run by high-minded, handsome men wearing knee breeches and silver buckles or Continental blue or frock coats, or even buck-skin and coonskin caps, as the case may be . . . who sat around a table and candidly debated the good of the public thing. It is because he is a romantic, and he has a picture of the world in his head, and when the world doesn't conform to the picture, he wants to throw the world away. Even if that means throwing out the baby with the bath. Which . . . it always does mean.

—Robert Penn Warren, *All The King's Men*

21.

Citizen Perot

In plain Texas talk, as Ross Perot might have put it, the whole thing might never have happened if he hadn't returned a cold call from a total stranger named John Jay Hooker one November morning in 1991. Hooker was just one more in a long line of good people who had been after Perot for years to run for public office—people who had fallen hard for him or, more often, for his legend as the last of the great cowboy capitalists. There had been so many of them for so long that his assistant, Sally Bell, usually spared him the trouble of having to say no himself. Mr. Perot had heard it all before, she would advise callers to his corporate tower in Dallas, and had never been remotely tempted.

But neither she nor her boss had ever run into anybody quite so persistent as Hooker, or so persuasive when in the throes of one of his visions. Hooker, at sixty-one, was a large, idiosyncratic man with a shock of white hair, usually crowned by a Panama hat, and a roughly matching white Cadillac. The day he punched up Perot's number from his sixth-floor apartment in midtown Nashville, he had a mission as well: to save America from impending ruin. Hooker, a liberal Democrat, had himself failed in three tries at elective office; he had done better in business, from fried-chicken franchising to newspaper publishing, but had never given up his dreams of changing the world. He had a knack for putting rich men next to big ideas, and this idea was his biggest ever. He had decided that Ross Perot should be the next president of the United States.

"Oh, he's not going to do that," Ms. Bell told him, laughing.

"Maybe he'll say no," Hooker said, "but let me just ask him."

"You're wasting your time," she said.

"Just get him to call me," he insisted.

Within a half-hour, his phone rang. "Hello, John," a reedy voice said. "This is Ross. How you doing?"

A Game of Catch

The introduction began a yearlong conversation between the two men—a dialogue that began as game of catch, Hooker thought, and ended in a messianic challenge to the entire American political system. Hooker was not the first of the rainmakers to find his way to Dallas in the drought season of 1991–92. He wasn't even the most exigent; a retired Florida financial planner named Jack Gargan, who had become a full-time agitator against all incumbent politicians, was already at work on his own freelance draft-Perot movement. But for a critical time, Hooker was to Perot what Falstaff had been to Prince Hal in another time and another accent: a man of spirit and appetite whose lot was to help prepare his charge for a larger destiny and then to recede from view.

It had hit him that November morning, sitting in his blue easy chair, that there was nobody else—that Bush wasn't doing anything and that none of the contenders from his own party was worth a damn, either. What the country needed was strong leadership, and when Perot called back, Hooker wasted as little time on pleasantries as the chivalric codes of the South permitted.

"The reason I'm calling," he said, "is I want you to run for president."

"Look," Perot said, "people over the years have talked to me about that, and that's the one thing I know I *don't* want to do. It'd be like putting a square peg in a round hole."

Hooker was a salesman, and he lived by the laws of his trade—first, that a "no" answer was never personal and rarely final; second, that the trick was to keep the prospect talking. "Let me ask you a couple of questions," he said. "Number one, do you think the nation is governable? Here we've got all this $4 trillion in debt, got all this racism still exists in this country—is there *anything* anybody can do?"

"Yeah," Perot answered. "I think it's governable."

"That's very encouraging," Hooker said. "Let me ask you another question—if you were president, what would you do?"

Hooker had, as he sensed, said the magic words—the open-sesame to thoughts Perot quite obviously had been thinking without having to be prompted. "The first thing I'd do is get at this economy," Perot began. You had to *grow* it—use the resources at hand to increase sales, expand trade, make and market the goods that the rest of the world hungered for. The soliloquy ran on for twenty minutes, itself a good sign. Perot would have to be played slowly, Hooker thought, but he was interested.

"I'll call you back tomorrow," Hooker said.

Perot didn't say no.

They spoke the next day, and again a few days later; by December, they were talking three or four times a week. The courtship, Hooker thought, was a bit like dating a shy and somewhat bookish girl: Perot kept saying no to the will-you question, but he obviously liked being pursued for his mind.

"You know what?" Hooker told him one day. "I believe you're going to run."

"I told you I'm not going to run," Perot said.

"Well, let me ask you a question," Hooker said. "How can you *not* run?"

"What do you mean, how can I not run?"

"Well," Hooker said, "if you are who you say you are, if you are a patriot, I believe you have a sense of duty, and I think that that sense of duty is going to *require* you to run." Hooker was winging it, stitching the threads of biography he knew from the papers into a tapestry of Perot as Cincinnatus hearing his nation's call. "I just think that you're destined to do this," he said.

"That's mighty nice of you," Perot answered, "but I'm not going to do it."

"I tell you what," Hooker told him. "I'll bet you a dollar."

"That's like throwing a dollar away," Perot said.

"Well," Hooker said, "I've always wanted to add to a man's wealth who already had two or three billion. I'll give you one more."

Perot laughed and took the bet. Sally Bell got in for a dollar, too. So did one of her office colleagues; nobody who had witnessed Perot's stubbornness at first hand could resist what looked like a sure thing.

The Man in the Myth

It was precisely Perot's reputation as a man of iron will that drew so many suitors to him at a time when American political life seemed governed by timidity and drift. Hooker knew practically nothing else about him; neither did Jack Gargan, the maverick Tampa coupon-clipper who ran an outfit called THRO (for Throw the Hypocritical Rascals Out) and had actually beaten Hooker to Perot's doorstep by a year. Like uncounted others, they had bought into the Myth of Ross Perot, a work as carefully cultivated by its proprietor as the formal gardens at Versailles. At its center stood the ultimate self-made man— a tough, determined, and often lonely warrior willing to take on politicians, bureaucrats, industrialists, financiers, third-world dictators, or anybody else who got in his way.

People encountering Perot for the first time were often surprised by the person inside the persona. There was nothing particularly heroic about him to look at or listen to; he was, at sixty-one, a banty rooster of a man with question-mark ears, a mangled nose, a barber-college haircut, and an East Texas drawl as thin and sharp as wine gone to vinegar. His real trade was not hero but salesman, Willie Loman with a hundred-megahertz product line and an imperial fortune. There were, in his portfolio, two or three billion reasons why attention had to be paid to such a man.

He had got in on the ground floor of the computer-systems business when it was new and hot and, even by the up-tempo standards of the Sun Belt, had become one of the superrich in record time. He was not your typical Texas billionaire; he was a free enterpriser at play in the welfare state, with a burgeoning government health-care bureaucracy as his principal customer. His success was built on other people's ideas—young men, usually, with white shirts required and military backgrounds preferred. His gift was merchandising their work. His secrets of salesmanship ran far beyond a shoe shine and a smile; he could be rough, even cutthroat in competition for a big job.

But the Myth of Ross Perot was of more epic dimension, in large part because so many strands of the American Myth had gone into its weave. The parts that didn't fit got left out; his life as presented in his official self-portrait was, as he often said with unconscious irony, too good to be true. He was the Horatio Alger hero who had earned his first dollars riding a paper route on horseback on the wrong side of Texarkana. He was Jack Armstrong the All-American Boy—the Eagle Scout, the Annapolis middy, the young officer who had joined the navy and seen the world, the family man who got all misty when he said he had married way above himself and fathered the best kids in the world.

And he was the most romanticized American businessman south of Lee Iacocca—the object of a recurring longing for a can-do chief executive who knew how to make a decision, meet a payroll, close a deal. The Perot of the Myth was Huck Finn as entrepreneur—a simple country soul who started his company with one thousand dollars of his wife's rainy-day money and his own American know-how. He was the wildcatter who found his black gold in software instead of oil and got richer quicker than any Texan ever. He was Rambo in a business suit, whether sending in his private commandos to get two of his employees out of jail in Iran or fighting for twenty years to bring the last missing boys home from Southeast Asia. He was the Little Guy who took on General Motors, Wall Street, and the United States government, and if Goliath kept winning the battles, it didn't matter in the Myth. What counted was that Perot, as David, had dared to stand up and fight.

Practically the only part of the larger myth he *hadn't* played was "Mr. Smith Goes to Washington," which was exactly what his pursuers had in mind for him. There had been a lot of them over the years, admiring businessmen, old soldiers, ordinary citizens drawn to his aura like moths to bright light. When Jack Gargan, the warrior against the ins of both parties, bearded Perot in his seventeenth-floor executive suite in Dallas in May, 1991, he was only the latest in a very long line. The trip was, for Gargan, the journey of a pilgrim to a shrine. He felt himself captured not just by the man but by the museum he inhabited—by the personal memorabilia, the Norman Rockwell paintings, the Frederic Remington bronzes, the Gilbert Stuart portrait of Washington that popped right out at you when Perot flicked on a light. To a quasi-unsophisticated guy, as Gargan styled himself, it all seemed so classy, so patriotic, so *well done*. It was understated elegance, was what it was.

As Hooker would later, Gargan stated his business bluntly: he had concluded that only Perot could save the country and that he was therefore obliged to run for president. "I'm just a businessman," Perot protested out of long habit. "I really don't think you need to pursue this anymore." But he let the conversation run overtime—a good buying sign, Gargan thought—and he kept taking Gargan's calls thereafter. Before long, he had agreed to keynote a THRO meeting in Tampa in November.

The meeting was, politically speaking, a honey trap. The quasi-unsophisticated Gargan arranged for a quasi-spontaneous demonstration, with preprinted ROSS FOR PREZ signs, and Perot responded with a fire-eating speech—a summons to a discouraged electorate to take up their shovels and "clean out the barn." The crowd of three thousand went unspontaneously wild, waving their placards and chanting, "Run, Ross, run!"

The day was Perot's first experience of the most intoxicating rush in politics—the mass adoration of strangers—and it did nothing to stiffen his resistance to John Jay Hooker's more artful sell. The game of catch was getting serious, the more so as Bush and Clinton both ran into turbulent weather.

"I'm begging you on behalf of the American people," Hooker told Perot in one of their frequent talks. "*Begging* you."

"I'm not going to do it," Perot said, "but it *is* very interesting, isn't it?"

Hooker was a lawyer and a litigator's son; he knew all the organ stops of argument, and the next one he hit was shame.

"You know, Ross," he began one day, "I got a postcard one time. It said, 'Greetings. You have been selected to serve in the United States Army.'" The card hadn't asked whether it suited him, or his family, or his business; it had simply commanded him, along with millions of other young men, to report for duty. "Now I'm giving *you* one," he said. "I'm telling you, Ross, 'Greetings. I'm drafting you on behalf of the American people to run for president of the United States.'"

Perot didn't bite.

Hooker tried guilt. He was conversant enough with the Myth to know that Perot thanked his mother for his own sense of obligation to those less blessed than he. Hooker said he hoped he and Ross would meet her in heaven one day.

"Oh, she'll be there," Perot answered quickly.

"Well," Hooker continued, "I want to sit around and listen to you explain to your mother why in this time of great need, you turned your back on your country and didn't run for president."

"You know how to put it on a fellow, don't you?" Perot laughed.

"I'm just warming up," Hooker said.

So he was. He continued their frequent chats and enlisted others to join the siege. Some of his pals in Jimmy Carter's old crowd proposed in the early winter that Perot forget about running as an independent and file in the Democratic primaries instead; they didn't like Clinton and didn't think much of the rest of the field. Hooker dutifully relayed their arguments to Perot, along with his own opinion to the contrary. It was foolish, he thought, to run against more people than you had to. As an independent, you only had to beat Bush and whatever poor soul the Democrats sent forth to the quadrennial slaughter.

But to sell his view, Hooker had to persuade Perot that an independent actually *could* run—that he wouldn't be roadblocked before he began by the difficulties of getting on the ballot in every state. Could he do it? Hooker hunted up an expert on ballot access, a Californian named Richard Winger who had navigated those waters for the Libertarian Party. Winger's answer, in effect, was that it could be done; the first state deadline for filing petitions wasn't until May, and that, fortuitously, was in Perot's own Texas. Triumphant, Hooker fed Winger's state-by-state rundown into his fax, with his own scrawled message across the top: "Ross—Let's go! We have plenty of time. John Jay."

The First Talk-Show Candidate

The communiqué lit no fires in Dallas—not, anyway, in the belly of Ross Perot. Hooker, undaunted, went back to his long game, marshaling new arguments and new pleaders. He was calling everyone he knew, and the trail through his black book led inevitably to Pat Caddell in his exile in California. When Hooker wanted to run for senator in 1976, Caddell had first tried to talk him out of it, then had done his polling. Hooker had liked both his candor and his work in a cause he considered hopeless, and they had been friends ever since.

"What do you think about Ross Perot running for president?" he asked Caddell when they connected.

"It's ironic that you called," Caddell replied. He had just finished haranguing a gathering of handlers and reporters in San Diego about what he saw as the deepening crisis of the American order—the disaffection of millions of people from a political system that had failed them. He might as well have been preaching Calvinism to the college of cardinals; he had been doom crying for years, and, as his audience reminded him, the republic still stood. Caddell's response had been a desperate improvisation. Forget Jerry Brown, he said, though Brown was his candidate of the moment. "This message cannot be shut out," he warned. "Wait till you get someone like Ross Perot."

In fact, Caddell cared little about the identity of the messenger. He was something of a Platonist in politics, a man who carried the picture of an ideal candidacy in his head and had been shopping for years for somebody willing and able to act it out. A whole train of hopefuls had disappointed him, as Brown inevitably would. In Caddell's possessed view, time was running out on America. Somebody had to rouse the citizenry to assert their rights and take back their country, and if Jerry Brown wasn't up to it, as he seemed not to be, Ross Perot would do at least as well and maybe better running from the outside. Maybe the system *couldn't* be challenged from within one or the other of its two corrupted parties.

The idea of Perot seemed to grow on him in the ensuing weeks, and when his ardor reached a ripe maturity, Hooker arranged for the prophet and the billionaire to meet. In late January, Caddell flew to Dallas. Perot showed up alone at the gate and drove him to a hotel near the airport, where they sat down to lunch in a conference room. They were not a match made in heaven. Perot was a fastidious sort, razor-creased and spit-shined. Caddell was not. He was big, shaggy, and unpressed, with hot eyes, matted hair, and a wide, white stripe down one side of a dark beard; he might have stepped out of the pages of a Dostoyevsky novel. The man was smart, Perot would say later, but he talked too fast and jumped around too much from thought to thought without transition. His presence alone seemed to make Perot uncomfortable. Caddell guessed that it must be the beard.

Still, he plunged ahead with his vision, with Perot replacing Brown at the center. "*Someone* should run for president this year," he told Perot. "*You* should run."

"I'm not going to run," Perot said. "Absolutely, I'm not going to run."

Caddell didn't get it; why agree to a meeting if the answer was no? He tried a different tack. The movement was the important thing, he said, not the candidate. Perot could use his voice and his resources to help get it launched, then step back and let a people's convention draft a people's nominee. The idea was a set-up, a recipe for getting Perot into the race somewhere down the road. But it permitted him to speak out loud about it without having to commit himself to anything, and he climbed aboard for the free ride. The two men talked animatedly for an hour or so about how such an enterprise could be put together. The line between movement and campaign seemed to Caddell to blur in Perot's mind; the guy obviously had been thinking hard about the country, and about himself as president. At a point, Perot asked how a hypothetical third-force challenger could get on the ballot. No problem, Caddell assured him; most of the legal impediments had been cleared away during John Anderson's maverick campaign in 1980.

When they broke up, Perot drove Caddell back to the airport. "Something has to happen," he said. "I'm not a guy who sits around thinking about it. I'm going to do something soon."

The session went into Hooker's ledger as a big plus. Perot still wouldn't bite; their game of catch was beginning to sound to Caddell more like a form of phone sex, and he told Hooker so. But the attention seemed at the very least to please Perot, and the dialogue went on. Hooker wondered aloud in one of their conversations if he shouldn't be consulting others close to Perot as well—his lawyer, Tom Luce, say, or his corporate alter ego, Mort Meyerson.

"You talk to *me*," Perot said. He hadn't even mentioned Hooker's name to them; he was like a boy with a secret too scary to share.

The secret was that he was warming to the idea. For Hooker, the first sure sign came when, in February, Perot flew to Nashville for a radio call-in show he could have as easily done by phone from his desk in Dallas. Hooker, elated, picked him up at the airport and put it on him in earnest, starting in the car and continuing for four solid hours at Perot's hotel downtown. The game of catch till then, Hooker thought, had been a warmup, a matter of getting Perot to the point where he could look in a mirror and see himself as a national leader without laughing. He was there now, and Hooker, in a room with his quarry for the first time, threw all hard balls.

It was Perot's *duty* to run, he said, just as it had been Dwight Eisenhower's forty years before; the old soldier hadn't wanted to be president either, but the country had needed him to clean up the mess in Washington, and he had answered the call. This time, Hooker said, the mess wasn't just one party's doing. This time, half the country hated *both* parties and their candidates, and once you had that *anti* vote on you, there was no way to get it off. People wanted a third choice. If Perot would only say yes to a draft, he could be the next president.

Nobody's drafting me, Perot said.

You haven't let folks know you're available, Hooker replied.

Well, Perot said, finally relenting, he'd do it—but only if the people, acting on their own, put him on the ballot in all fifty states. It wasn't going to happen—but if it did, he would run.

Hooker was ecstatic, but he was an audience of one; he had to figure out a way to get Perot to tell all America the same thing. The local call-in show the next morning was one blown opportunity, and an impromptu news conference afterward was another. When Perot finally did say the magic words, to a reporter from the *Nashville Tennessean,* he hit the fifty-state threshold a bit too hard. "If it's forty-nine, forget it," he said. He sounded grudging, and the paper seemed unexcited by its scoop. Its story was a five-paragraph shrug headlined, skeptically, PRESIDENT PEROT?

Nobody noticed, and, as Perot had predicted, nothing happened. Hooker, frantic, redoubled his telephone canvassing, trying to generate ideas and build a claque. Most of his contacts in politics, business, and the press seemed to like the idea, but not well enough to get engaged. Even Pat Caddell was fazed by Perot's insistence on a fifty-state draft. "Holy shit," he told Hooker, "that's unnecessary. I understand what he's trying to do, but that seems pretty extreme."

Hooker agreed; he had himself begun to wonder if that wasn't an attempt by Perot to make the whole thing go away. But his own faith was undiminished, and he set about trying to get his man to offer the same challenge in a larger forum. He pushed Caddell hard to reopen *his* dialogue with Perot. Caddell was more than willing; his head had been buzzing with the things he should have said but hadn't when the two of them were in a room together, and he set down some of them in a long, impassioned "Dear Ross" letter to his new best friend.

The nine-page cri de coeur was dated the day before the New Hampshire primary. Caddell's other candidate, Jerry Brown, was at least nominally a player there, but he was doing poorly, and Caddell's allegiance was not personal in any case; it was to his vision, and if he had to look elsewhere for somebody to star in it, so be it. His argument to Perot came straight from his personal Book of Lamentations. The two parties, he wrote, had become one, cynical, self-seeking, and indistinguishable from one another. In combination with their support troops—a pygmy army of hacks, PACs, lobbyists, journalists, and buck-hustlers—they had brought America to the brink of a steep decline. Only a real leader could stop the downhill slide, and Perot was uniquely suited to the part; it was, Caddell said, a matter not of choice but of duty that he accept it.

The letter arrived in the midst of Hooker's campaign to get his dream in front of a national audience. Whether it influenced Perot—whether in fact he even read through it, given his famous impatience with long memos and fancy talk—was known only to him. It barely mattered. He had already got halfway across the Rubicon on his own, and with Hooker's further prodding, he arranged an invitation to appear on *Larry King Live*. The booking, on CNN, had vastly greater powers of amplification than a press availability in Nashville. If Perot repeated his dare to the people to draft him, he would almost certainly be heard.

The timing of the interview was fortuitously perfect, two days after New Hampshire. Bush and Clinton had limped off the battlefield bleeding, the one an unpopular president, the other a scandalized challenger; together, they were what the old politics had come to, and what Perot seemed at last poised to challenge. But would he say the word? Not even Perot was sure, so friends would say afterward, and Hooker, knowing his diffidence, did what he could to prevent another misfire. Along with some of his claque, he called King before the show to prime him on what questions to ask and on the need to keep asking them.

He and Caddell watched the program in a hotel room in Beverly Hills, where Hooker was visiting. Caddell still seemed sure that they were about to see history happen. Hooker did not. He was in a state of high agitation, and it got higher as Perot kept saying no, so often that King finally changed the subject.

"Don't worry, John Jay," Caddell said. "He's going to do it."

Perot did, sort of; it took King five tries over fifty minutes to extract a yes from him, or, more accurately, a yes-if, festooned with what sounded like impossible conditions for his running.

"Number one, I don't want to," he said.

"I know, but is there a scenario?" King asked.

Perot said something evasive about how lucky he had been in life and how a lot of less fortunate people—"all these everyday folks that make the world go round"—had been writing him all these begging letters in painful longhand urging him to go for it.

King cut him off. "Is there a scenario?" he asked again.

It turned out finally that there was one. Perot wasn't encouraging anybody to do anything, mind you; what he seemed to envision instead was a kind of a priori politics, a candidacy declared not by the candidate but by the people. If all these nice folks begging him to do it weren't willing to organize and get him on the ballot in all fifty states, he said, then "this is all just talk. . . . I want to see some sweat." It was their choice. If they did their part, on their own, he would do his. He would seek the presidency as their humble servant.

With those words, he had become the first serious candidate ever to put himself forward for our highest office on a television talk show. Not even he knew that yet; he understood neither the meaning of his commitment nor the excitement it would stir up. His wife, Margot, was more than a little surprised when he got back to their hotel in Washington that night; he hadn't said anything to *her* about running for president.

"Don't worry," he told her breezily. "It'll never happen."

But when they got back to Dallas the next morning, the phone lines at Perot Systems were flooded with calls from well-wishers. By the close of business that night, his operators had signed up a platoon of virtual strangers to chair petition drives in twenty-eight states. A candidacy was being born around him.

"We got it going there, didn't we?" John Jay Hooker said when he got through the gridlocked switchboard to Perot.

"This'll die out in four or five days," Perot answered.

"Ross, I'm telling you," Hooker insisted. "You better get ready. It is coming."

"We'll see," Perot said, "but I don't believe it."

"You'll see," Hooker told him, smiling a wide Falstaffian smile.

22.

The Age of Innocence

For an intoxicating time, it was if a cult had been born—a kind of American Shinto in which leader and followers alike sought the innocence of a lost ancestral past. Never mind that that innocence had never really existed in our public life; never mind either that the gnomish man offering himself as redeemer was utterly unprepared for what he had got himself into. Ross Perot had been transformed overnight into a shaman for the television age, a healer who proposed to cure the ills of a nation with sound business sense and plain Texas talk. His magic was that he appeared to believe it himself—to imagine, until events taught him otherwise, that innocence not only could compete with experience in the fallen state of our politics but could finally prevail.

Perot was an intuitive genius at self-promotion, but his surprise at the ruckus he had kicked up with his nonannouncement was unfeigned. He hadn't even mentioned to the men closest to him that he was going on the King show, let alone what he meant to say when he got there. His lawyer and friend of twenty years, Tom Luce, tuned him in only by accident, flipping channels during a workout in his television room at home. When he heard the curtain line, Luce nearly fell off his treadmill. What Ross appeared to be telling America was that if they built a candidacy, he would come.

"What the hell are you doing?" he demanded when Perot got back to town. "Why didn't you tell me?"

"Aw, don't worry," Perot told him. "Nothing will come of this."

Luce asked if there was any research he should do, any people he should call. He had run for governor of Texas himself two years before, and while it had worked out badly—he ran third in a three-man Republican primary—he had made some good political connections.

Perot said no—the whole thing would blow over in a day or two.

It didn't. Perot and his shapeless populism had tapped into a vein of history literally as old the American nation, the revolt of the burghers against a distant and unfeeling crown. He had been driven in part by his disdain for George Bush; he spoke of the president privately as a whiner and a handwringer and, by published account, had once called him a rabbit to his face. But Bush hadn't come from nowhere, and neither had Bill Clinton, the unloved front-runner in a weak Democratic field. Perot's larger complaint had to do with the shallowness and venality of a process that could produce such candidates for our highest office—a feeling he shared, if the polls were to be believed, with a mad-as-hell majority of his countrymen.

The response to his tease was a fresh measure of their alienation. Far from blowing over, the storm of calls kept growing; Perot's offices were a bedlam of ringing phones and backed-up messages from people wanting to help. The press didn't know what to make of it; in an age when everything in politics seemed programmed, the common guess was that Perot must somehow have planned the whole thing long in advance. In fact, his ploy was neither as calculated as the media imagined nor as spontaneous as it looked in the version he would incorporate into The Myth. The idea *had* been gestating in his mind for months, nurtured by Hooker among numerous others. But his brainchild, when it was born, was a preemie; he was at once pleased with the notice it brought him and unready for the consequences of parenthood.

For two or three weeks after the *Larry King* show, he seemed immobilized, watching the tides of passion rise around him and doing nothing at all to ride them. The Perot campaign, to the extent there was one at all, consisted of Sally Bell and her office staff answering calls and taking names. From Nashville, Hooker turned up the pressure; he and Perot were talking practically every day. Nothing came of the dialogue. In conversations with friends, Perot seemed torn between the siren song of ego and the wish that somebody else would save America instead.

"You're a Democrat," he told one chum, Richard Fisher, a Dallas investment manager and a onetime trade official in the Carter administration. "Who's gonna make it work? Tell me. Give me a Democrat that's capable."

"We had one last time—he was just on the wrong end of the ticket," Fisher said. He meant Senator Lloyd Bentsen of Texas, a man he and Perot both greatly admired.

"Okay, I'll grant you," Perot said. "If Lloyd would run, I wouldn't even think about this. Tell me one who's willing to play the game."

Fisher was doing some issues prepping for Clinton, without believing wholeheartedly in him. "I can't think of one," he said.

"Well, give me a Republican," Perot continued. "You know all these guys." He mentioned Senator Richard Lugar of Indiana, a sometime navy officer who had served with honor in the Senate for going on sixteen years.

"No, it's too late," Fisher said. A man as little known nationally as Lugar could never create a national candidacy that quickly. Fisher's pick of the litter on the Republican side was James Baker.

"Jim Baker," Perot said, lighting up like a Nintendo game. "If Jim Baker would just step up to the plate, and the president would step down and say, 'Jim Baker's my favored successor,' I wouldn't even think about it."

They both knew that wasn't going to happen, and Perot threw his line back in the water one last time. "C'mon, Richard," he said. "Give me a name. Give me anybody. *Name* somebody. Who's going to lead?"

There was nobody, not in their shared view; whether Perot had been looking for a way out or a way in, the catechism ended as one more argument for him to run.

What was plain was that the phones weren't going to stop ringing, as he had imagined. With no further encouragement from him in those early weeks, the traffic kept growing, and his reticence got harder and harder for him to defend. He had been saying for years that nothing would change in America unless the people got involved; they had to take the country back from the pols, the lobbyists, and the interests and put it in the hands of *real* leaders whose only imperative was to do the right thing. Now, old friends were quoting his sentiments back to him, and total strangers were giving them flesh. It was as if he had offhandedly invited America to a revolution, and everybody came.

His conversations with Hooker took on a practical edge, a businessman's concern for the bottom line. He didn't talk about how to get there; that would be Tom Luce's lookout, if it came to that. What preoccupied Perot instead was whether there was a real chance for an independent to win. It wasn't merely losing he was worried about; it was the possibility of doing just well enough to convulse the country. What if he got a plurality of the vote but threw the election into the House of Representatives, say, or tipped it to one of the other candidates in the electoral college—somebody the country really didn't want?

Hooker turned to his pal Caddell again; Pat had done some electoral-vote studies in the '80s, and while he had gone a little rusty on the subject since then, he got out a legal pad and began teasing scenarios out of the election results of the past twenty years. His labors led him to a counterintuitive conclusion: a third-force candidate with a narrow plurality of the popular vote would be able not only to win but to win big in the electoral college. The trick, he wrote in an eighteen-page memo to Perot, was to draw votes away from the Republicans and the Democrats in roughly equal numbers. To do that, an independent would have to run straight down the middle, positioning himself as the alternative to *both* parties, but it could indeed be done.

Perot seemed surprised; he had two feasibility studies in hand by then, one informing him that he could get on the ballot everywhere, the other proposing that he could actually be president. He didn't jump, not just yet. But he called in Luce to help him get a handle on the whole messy situation, and Luce in turn began seeking more expert advice, just in case. He took it to be his duty as Perot's friend and counselor to start looking hard at the pros, the cons, and the how-to's of a campaign without having to be asked.

One of the people on his list was Pat Caddell. It was a chance call; Luce didn't know that the two had already been talking, but he caught up with Caddell's communications to the chief and invited him down to Dallas for a talk. Once again, Caddell found himself in a meeting room at an airport hotel, making the case for a Perot candidacy to Luce and another of Perot's friends, Liener Temerlin, a Dallas ad man. Luce wore his skepticism on his sleeve, Caddell thought, but he asked good questions, running the range from the zeitgeist in broad strokes to the problems of ballot access in petit-point detail. In his enthusiasm, Caddell swept all doubt aside. The thing was already happening, he said. With only the slightest coverage from the national press, a movement was building from the ground up. The question was how to nurture it, and ultimately, Caddell said, that would mean bringing in some pros.

They would have to be pros of the right sort, he hastened to add; if they *acted* like handlers, they could smother the volunteer spirit of the campaign, the raw citizen energy that would give it its force. There weren't many, Caddell said, who could adapt to movement politics, but there were a few. At one point, he seemed to be describing himself.

"So you'd run it?" Temerlin asked.

A look of something like terror crossed Luce's face; Caddell's volcanic reputation had evidently preceded him to Dallas. "No, I'm not in the business," he told Temerlin quickly. "This thing ought to be homegrown. My role is to help engender the movement. I got out of politics to get away from campaigns."

Luce looked relieved, and when the meeting broke up after five hours, he asked Caddell to do a strategic plan for a campaign that didn't yet exist. The assignment, in effect, required juggling two campaigns—Jerry Brown was building toward his crest in Connecticut—and a couple of weeks went by before Caddell could get to it. By the time he did, something had clicked with Perot, some inner toggle from his passive to his active mode. He hadn't *exactly* become a candidate, but he was ready to commit himself and his substantial resources to the aid of the citizens' movement trying to make him one.

In early March, while the seers and shakers of politics were preoccupied with Super Tuesday, Perot called together a half-dozen employees of his companies—the Original Six, as they would come to call themselves—and parceled out assignments. It was a typical Perot Group start-up, an act of energy and will rather than technical expertise; you threw a bunch of young tigers at a problem, he liked to say, and told them to go solve it. Volunteer committees were springing up in the states; they would need some quality control and a lot of advice and hand-holding. The press was beginning at last to hear the rumbles of rebellion; someone would have to field their inquiries. The corporate switchboards were near meltdown from the overload of calls from citizens; the movement would need a phone bank of its own.

Within days of their deployment, the tigers had acquired that new appurtenance of politics, an 800 number, and had wired a rented floor in Perot's tower on Merit Drive with sixty new phone lines. One of the Original Six, Darcy Anderson, was working the phone-bank area one night in mid-March when Perot called in from Washington. He was on the set of Larry King's radio talk show, ready to go on. "Are we ready for the number to be made public?" he asked Anderson. They were; thirty of the phones were covered, and within seconds after Perot's first mention of the toll-free number, they were all ringing. The deluge ran on till one in the morning, started up again the next day, and never quit till Perot did.

The phone bank grew to a hundred lines, which still weren't enough. The King show was only the first stop in a heavy free-media offensive. Suddenly, Perot's face and voice were everywhere, along with his phone number, and his boiler room on Merit Drive was overwhelmed. The Perot Petition Committee, as the noncampaign dubbed itself, had to do a deal with the Home Shopping Network for twelve hundred more lines, and Perot's tigers trained volunteers in shifts to handle the traffic. Every last line would be needed; in one ten-day stretch, there would be a million calls, mostly from volunteers for what looked like a second American revolution.

The View from the Front Porch

For a time that spring, it was all grand fun for Perot, a warm bath of adulation from The Volunteers and a bounteous feast of attention from the talk shows. It was, as he might have said, just beautiful; the people *did* care, and they were inventing a campaign themselves, out there on Main Street U.S.A. He mixed and mingled with the folks working the phone banks. He took some calls himself. He spoke of spending $100 million or more, a number that set the two major-party front-runners trembling; at that level, his stake would be as big as their two put together. He traveled the landscape alone in his corporate jet, almost always to rallies celebrating his having got on the ballot in yet another state. The events reinforced the irresistible view that The Volunteers were America and that he was the embodiment of the nation's will.

But his real milieu was what would become the first electronic front-porch campaign, a media-age throwback to a time when it was considered vulgar for candidates for president to go out on the road begging for votes. Perot despised politics as he saw it on the newscasts, a five-a-day aerial circus of photo ops, tarmac touchdowns, and empty one-liners. He refused up front to play that game, or even to spend more than one night per trip away from home. "No one is going to tell me where to go," he informed his people, or what to say when he got there. The road, for him, was the information superhighway, and he traveled it from one radio or television talk show to another. The air time was free, the inconvenience minimal, the questioning usually friendly, and the demand for specificity low.

He was, moreover, a master at the game—as folksy as Will Rogers and as cocky as a riverboat gambler with the biggest stack on the table. His ease at the medium was such that he spoke seriously of running the government by electronic town meeting, confident that Washington's gifts at obstruction were no match for his at salesmanship. "I won't sound-bite it," he would protest when an interviewer pressed him on a complicated issue. But his offering was in fact a montage of sound bites, including that one. He had no defined public philosophy, no studied positions on the issues, not even the usual retinue of experts who attach themselves to men of power. Most of what he knew about policy and politics was what he didn't like. His believers otherwise had to imagine Ross Perot for themselves.

What he did have, at least for a time, was a nearly perfect ear for the vernacular and the anger of that vast America beyond the Potomac; suddenly, *somebody* was saying what the aggrieved middle classes wanted to hear in terms they could understand. How bad was the economy? "We are now in deep voodoo," he said. Did he regret having opposed the Gulf war? "Just trying to give you an occasional Super Bowl with smart bombs going down air shafts on cable news, forget it," he answered; you wouldn't find *him* sending American boys and girls into battle to prove his manhood—a position that suggested, by implication, that that was what Bush had done. Wasn't he trying to buy the election? "I'm buying it for the American people," he claimed. What would he do if he won it? "In plain Texas talk," he said, "it's time to take out the trash and clean out the barn."

For a season, he and his sample case of home remedies were the hottest items in the marketplace of politics. Early on, he let his people talk him into hiring a pricey Manhattan polling firm to do a survey for him. It was an idea he gagged on in principle—polls, he said, were part of what was wrong with politics—and liked even less when he got the $180,000 bill. The returns gave him just 10 percent of the vote going in, but he had plenty of growing room once America got to know him and his message better.

The survey was accurate as to his prospects; with the beginnings of spring, his path upward would cross Bush's and Clinton's going down. By April, he was at 26 percent in a public poll, gaining on Clinton for second place. In late May, he hit 35 percent, and was leading the field. With his name in play, the turnout in the party primaries kept shrinking, and among those who did vote, the percentage who wished there were somebody new on the ballot grew from a third to a half. By the grand finale in California, that somebody was unmistakably Perot; he stole the show from the day's nominal winners, Bush and Clinton, by winning the exit polls in both their parties.

The problem was that Perot was riding a homemade rocketship without a captain, a crew, or a flight plan—with nobody at the controls, indeed, except himself. Its central operating principle was that his candidacy, if it came to pass, was going to be different—that he wasn't going to play by the settled rules and conventions that governed everybody else. He didn't even want to start campaigning in any formal way until fall; he had always been troubled by the spectacle of grown men spending a year or two chasing a four-year job. In some alarm, his friend Tom Luce did some research into voting patterns in 1988 and got up a pie chart showing that four people in five would have made up their minds by October; if Perot waited that long, he would be playing for no more than 20 percent of the vote. Along with his Rockwells and Remingtons, pie charts were usually among Perot's favorite works of art. This one didn't move him—not enough, anyway, to make him change his course.

Neither was he eager to surround himself with people who made a profession of winning elections in the old, manipulative ways. It was in the nature of the man and the enterprise that he would resist running a traditional campaign, with the usual retinue of handlers, spinners, leakers, and what he called cosmetologists; that was precisely what he was running *against*. But what he had wrought, with The Volunteers, was an unruly army put together in the manner of a garage sale. Its field officers were mostly self-selected; they were, typically, the people who had got to the phones fastest and had been awarded state and local chairmanships on a first-come, first-served basis.

In that age of innocence, the me-and-The-Volunteers arrangement seemed to suit Perot just fine. He didn't need or want outside professionals telling him what to do; he preferred building his campaign as he had his businesses, on a light-infantry model, with people he knew at the top and SWAT teams of buttoned-down young men borrowed from Perot companies to execute their orders. The man he ultimately asked to oversee the enterprise was his longtime counselor Tom Luce, who had at least run for something once. His choice to direct The Volunteers was his chief security man, Mark Blahnik, who had no political experience at all.

What Luce quickly discovered was that he was in over his head; the fire Perot had lit at the grassroots was burning out of any possibility of control by his little cadre of amateurs in Dallas. Luce had had misgivings about the whole venture at first and, out of his sense of obligation, had said so. "Don't do this," he had told Perot; no one could run for president from a standing start in March and expect to get anywhere. But Starship Perot was already off the pad by then, and as Luce worked the phones and watched the progress of the petition drive, he found himself becoming a believer. A movement had come into being, not with slick ads or voter-targeting software but with card tables in shopping malls. To sign up for Perot, in the spring of 1992, had become a talismanic act—a blind and even desperate leap of faith in the cleansing powers of a man nobody really knew.

Luce was a bright and thoughtful man, but his single season in Triple-A politics had not prepared him for the challenge he had been handed: reshaping the unmanaged energies of an all-volunteer petition drive into something resembling a real presidential campaign. Amateurishness seemed not to matter greatly at first, when nobody in Perot's circle, possibly excepting Perot himself, really believed he could win; his people thought of his candidacy instead as a kind of wake-up call to America, a protest against the debasement of politics by fat wallets and empty talk. But as Perot kept rising in the polls, Luce and his team found themselves up against what would become the central paradox of his campaign: the wide and finally unbridgeable divide between the innocence of its beginnings and the experience required if it was to go all the way.

The Soul of A New Machine

It was Luce's unhappy lot to try to reconcile those imperatives—to build a new machine whose soul would match Perot's but whose working parts would somehow get him elected president. It was plain that the early circle of believers who had helped egg Perot into running wouldn't do; for one reason or another, he no longer wanted them around. Jack Gargan, the anti-incumbent agitator, opened a draft-Perot office in Washington before Dallas was ready. Luce shut it down and froze Gargan out of the campaign. Pat Caddell submitted his strategy paper, but he, too, found himself bumped out of the loop; Perot had taken against him and his spiky manner. Even John Jay Hooker's easy access was reduced to an occasional long-distance conversation. In April, Perot showed up for a rally in Nashville, Hooker's hometown, but didn't take the time to see or call him.

Finding the *right* people was a great deal harder, given Perot's iron determination to reinvent presidential politics and his habit of running things himself. The scent of money is an intoxicant in campaign seasons, and there were applicants aplenty to help Perot spend his $100 million; one Republican firm sent in a $5 million bid for the polling contract alone. Luce found himself in a thicket, trying to separate the hustlers from the believers willing to lay aside their old playbooks and put together something truly unorthodox. For Perot, the process was achingly slow. He had promised a world-class campaign, and while he had no idea what one looked or felt like, he knew that what Luce had put in place by spring wasn't it.

The sign of his impatience, so his people thought, was the day his sometime corporate CEO, Mort Meyerson, started showing up at campaign meetings. The core group at that point consisted of a chairman, Luce, with an oh-and-one lifetime record in state-level politics; a press secretary, Jim Squires, a former newspaper reporter and editor who had covered campaigns but had never been in one; and a pollster, Frank Luntz, late of the Buchanan team, who had had to be smuggled aboard like an article of contraband without so much as an introduction to Perot. Meyerson himself was a wholly apolitical animal, a cultivated man who cared more for his collection of modern paintings than for the performance arts practiced in Washington. But he knew organization, and he was closer than any of the others to Perot—close enough to tell him, after a quick look around, that he needed professional help.

The pro then nearest at hand was Hamilton Jordan, who had been political guru and White House chief of staff to Jimmy Carter. At forty-seven, Jordan was out of politics and was working for Whittle Communications in Knoxville when Perot first popped onto the radar screen. He wasn't interested, not then; his natural home was the Democratic center, and like others of the Carter alumni club, he was back-channeling advice to Paul Tsongas at the time. But with the passing weeks, he found himself drawn to Perot and to the explosion of citizen energy he had loosed on a stagnating political system.

In March, Jordan had called Luce. "I know you don't know who I am," he began, as if he shared some dusty corner of American history with the Antifederalists and the Know-Nothings. As it happened, Luce did know who he was and was pleased by his offer to help out in a quiet, background kind of way. At his invitation, Jordan became a periodic weekend commuter to Dallas, an unpaid counselor without portfolio to what was then still a campaign-in-waiting.

His advice was welcome, the more so because he seemed to understand that the campaign would have to be styled to suit what was different about Perot; most of the consultants Luce had been talking to had it the other way around. But Jordan's early take on the state of things was not entirely sanguine. Knowing how little Perot and his organization men liked paper, Jordan showed up at a meeting in late March with a good news–bad news chart on a two-by-two square of posterboard. The chart was as neutral in tone as a spreadsheet, but its implicit message was that the good news was mainly history and the bad lay just over the horizon.

Under POSITIVE, Jordan had written:

Perot's noncandidacy continues to demonstrate enormous strength and philosophy.

Under NEGATIVE:

Lost control of the campaign.

Under POSITIVE:

Perot has dominated the political press in the last 20 days.

Under NEGATIVE:

Pressure to define Perot has increased proportionally.

Under POSITIVE:

Press has been overwhelmingly positive. . . .

Under NEGATIVE:

There'll be a day of reckoning. . . .

Under POSITIVE:
Survey results have made Perot for the short term the most viable 3rd Party candidate since Teddy Roosevelt.
Under NEGATIVE:
It's fragile and lacks definition. Half of Perot vote is anti-Clinton, anti-Bush.
And finally, under POSITIVE:
Opportunities abound.
Under NEGATIVE:
What do we do next? . . . What is our plan and our strategy?

The questions were the heart of the matter. The short answers were that nobody knew; there was no plan or strategy, and no cadre of pros to put one together. Jordan himself kept kicking in ideas, on matters ranging from scheduling to stage-managing an announcement. At one point, he proposed a sixty-day hiatus from the front-porch campaign, with Perot retiring to the front parlor to study the issues. Most of his suggestions were well received by Luce, Meyerson, and—so Jordan was regularly told—Perot. But nothing much came of them. The uncandidate seemed to prefer things as they were.

Finally, Jordan tried to pull everything together in a mock-up schedule for May, presented first to Luce and Meyerson and then to what passed for a strategy group. The program was light on travel, out of respect for Perot's distaste for fly-around campaigning. He would do two Volunteer rallies a week, plus a couple of listen-and-learn events with groups of experts on a particular subject or maybe just with concerned citizens. His briefing time would be bulked up and his talk-show bookings cut back; Jordan worried that his act was underdone in substance and overexposed as theater. Instead of freelancing around the chat circuit, Perot would do two major speeches on paid TV to fill in his sketchy public profile. One would be a Who-I-Am oral history, delivered in Texarkana and synchronized with ten thousand Volunteer house-parties around the country. The second, two weeks later, would be a What-I-Believe manifesto, defining at last what he stood for besides change.

The response, again, was enthusiastic. The results, as usual, were minimal. The sixty-day study period was declared and as quickly forgotten. The two defining speeches never got made, nor were the ten thousand house parties laid on; once having filed their petitions, The Volunteers were given nothing to do, not even serving tea and cookies. The orderly timeline came unglued; Perot kept making the rounds of talk shows and Volunteer love-ins, doing his own breast-pocket scheduling without troubling to tell anyone where he would be.

Neither was a team coming together—the corps of skilled artisans who, as Luce and Meyerson were coming reluctantly to realize, would be necessary to an enterprise as dauntingly large and complex as a presidential campaign. Nobody really liked the idea of bringing them in; even Jordan, himself an old pro, thought it ran against the revolutionary grain of the movement, and Perot was stubbornly opposed. His men saw no other choice. They could still run an untraditional campaign, Luce told Perot, but they needed *somebody* around who had been there before.

It was Meyerson who, in mid-May, came up with the design that finally prevailed—a bipartisan structure with matched pairs of Republicans and Democrats in each of the major occupational specialties. He called the vessel Noah's Ark. But to the true believers, Perot among them, the plan had the smell of a Faustian bargain about it: a deal in which innocence would be bartered for knowledge—and, ultimately, would be the doom of the campaign.

23.

The War of the Worlds

The day he and his prospective shipmates on the Ark met in Dallas over the last weekend in May, Ed Rollins wondered why he had come—why, indeed, he had been invited in the first place. After a month's courtship, he and Hamilton Jordan were ready to sign up as full-time co-chairmen of the campaign-to-be and had flown in to close the deal, first with Tom Luce and Mort Meyerson, then with Perot. But at the Saturday preliminaries in Meyerson's office, everything Rollins threw at Perot's two guys about what needed doing seemed to make them nervous, even suspicious of his intentions. Their partnership hadn't even begun, and Rollins was already feeling as welcome as an atheist in a convent garden.

There had been signals from the beginning that he was walking into a collision of cultures—the pro-am civil war that would help destroy the first Perot campaign within six weeks of the day Rollins arrived. He was, on his record, everything that Perot was running against. At age forty-nine, he already had a secure place in the handlers' hall of fame, for having lasted twenty-five years in the business and having managed Ronald Reagan's postcard-pretty landslide in 1984. He even looked different from the smooth, clean-shaven corporate men Perot favored; he was a taut, thick-chested ex–prize fighter with a beard, a fringe of receding gray hair and an air of contained, almost dangerous energy. The uncandidate himself had been wary of the match from the beginning, a view reinforced by some of the purists who had his ear.

"I got some questions whether Rollins would fit," Perot had said at one point in the long mating dance. "Does he understand this type of campaign?"

The most accurate answer might have been yes and no. Rollins was what he seemed, a tough, combative, anything-to-win professional. But he did not fit the stereotype of the handler as a man without beliefs except in his own ever-rising net worth. Like others in his trade, he was fed up with the aridity of American politics and had found himself powerfully drawn to the raw, up-from-under energy of the

Perot movement; he had never seen anything quite like it. His disaffection was well-known in the political community. Pat Caddell had mentioned him to Perot's men; so had Hamilton Jordan. At a distance, he sounded as though he might make a good fit, and Tom Luce had called him in April. Would he be interested in helping put together a Perot campaign?

"Tom, I really can't," Rollins had said at the time, with real regret. He and his wife, Sherrie, both had new jobs, his with a powerhouse New York–Washington consulting firm, hers in Bush's White House. Rollins would be jeopardizing both their careers and his own future in the party he had worked in all of his life in politics. He was willing to help out, he said, but only in the shadows, chipping in ideas and helping find good people.

The contacts had continued, the parties drawn inexorably together like mismatched lovers into a bad relationship. At one point, Rollins had sent down what amounted to a ten-page manual on how to assemble a presidential candidacy, from announcing to putting up TV ads to finding a plausible running mate. But as he elaborated on it over a clandestine dinner date with Luce and Meyerson in mid-May, he was surprised at the sales resistance, given what seemed to him the ardor of their pursuit.

"You know," Meyerson told him, "this all makes great sense, page by page. But then when I finish it, it's a truly conventional campaign, and this is not a conventional candidacy."

"Mort, I understand that," Rollins had said, "and you can never do anything to undo the volunteer effort. But sooner or later, if you're serious, you're in a traditional campaign. You have to do the things everyone else does. You can't just do it going on the *Larry King* show and talking to your own voters at volunteer rallies."

Meyerson hadn't been persuaded. To him, the plan sounded like a replay of Ed's Greatest Hits, the kind of image politics that had elected Reagan and Bush. It was what the people were rebelling against.

"I'm not trying to run 1984 or 1988 all over again," Rollins had protested. "There are just certain things you do in a campaign. You get a field organization, you advertise, you have a convention, you pick a vice president."

"Well, this thing is different," Meyerson had said.

They had arrived at an impasse, Perot's men torn between their distaste for what Rollins represented and their need for his technical expertise. Need had finally won. Rollins appeared by then to have got over his worries about what his wife, his employers, and his party might think; once he had decided that he wanted the job, he pitched hard to get it, mixing flatteries for Perot and the movement with some low-key bragging on his own unique qualifications to run the show. He was in the business of persuasion, and Luce and Meyerson had fallen under his spell; they had convinced themselves that the middle-aged tiger across the table could actually change his stripes to suit what Perot was trying to do.

In the manner of men accustomed to buying what they want, they had asked what it would take to get Rollins aboard. He had rehearsed his misgivings one more time, but the money looked good, and so did the cause; it was a chance to lead an assault against a political order he had been part of and in some measure had come to despise. He could deal with whatever problems it caused him, he said. He was available and eager to play.

By Memorial Day, the Arkwrights and their chosen cocaptains had had a first get-acquainted meeting in Jordan's offices in Knoxville and had worked out a rough division of labor. Jordan would do the big picture stuff—strategy, message, and media—while Rollins would oversee hiring, budgeting, and the day-to-day business of the campaign. The four had parted amicably, exchanging vows of secrecy, and agreed to meet again in Dallas the following weekend for the closing.

But Rollins was to newsprint what Michelangelo had been to the Sistine Chapel ceiling: he understood it to be his job to fill blank spaces with his art. Within two days, the story of the billionaire's dalliance with the gunslingers had leaked to the *Wall Street Journal*. It hadn't mattered to Rollins's new employers that the press had bought his spin, treating the advent of the pros as a grand coup for Perot. Spin, in their view, was part of the old way of doing business, not Perot's way. For Rollins and his pros, a leaked story, artfully told, was part of what they called The Game—the daily jostling for an edge in the way the media saw and reported a race. For Perot and his amateurs, *that* game was over; the people were fed up with the tricks and illusions of conventional politics, and they would have no place in a Perot candidacy.

On Merit Drive, the *Journal* leak had revived all the repressed doubts about Rollins; he was incorrigible after all, an old-school pol who couldn't keep a confidence and couldn't adapt to a new kind of campaign. A gale of I-told-you-so's had blown through the corridors at headquarters. Only a gunpoint apology and a promise to button up in the future saved Rollins that time. Perot was furious; he had to be talked out of calling off the deal before it had been closed.

The Mercenaries

The alliance of innocence and experience went forward as scheduled, but a cloud of mistrust and misunderstanding lingered over the end-of-May sit-down in Meyerson's conference room. From Rollins's vantage point, what was to have been a final laying on of hands turned into a feinting spell, all smiles and no delivery on matters he had thought already resolved. He tried to be reassuring; he understood, he said yet again, that Perot could succeed only by being different. But there were some basics that *no* campaign, however untraditional, could avoid. You had to advertise. You had to schedule the candidate in ways that helped get his message across. And you had to keep feeding the press; it would be necessary, Rollins said, for him to go on the talk shows and speak for the campaign.

"Is Ross going to go batshit," he asked, "if he sees me on TV talking about his strategy? That's all part of what you have to do."

The men across the table bridled. One of the beefs they had heard about Rollins was that he loved attention too much, and here he was nominating himself for spokesman in chief. They didn't like the idea and didn't think Perot would, either. Ross, they told Rollins, had never let anybody speak for him before.

Rollins was bemused. Meyerson had assured him during the courtship period that Ross, like any Texan, knew what happened if you swam halfway across a river and stopped; once he had jumped in, he would do whatever was needed and spend whatever it took to be viable. But he found himself talking into a void between their two views of how things ought to work—between his insistence on what he saw as the bare necessities of a campaign and their manifest unhappiness with anything that looked or sounded traditional.

In fact, Perot's men hadn't come prepared to discuss strategy or tactics at all. Their concern instead was with the chemistry of the brew they were concocting; they were genuinely unsure whether Jordan, whom they trusted, and Rollins, whom they didn't, could run the kind of anticampaign Perot wanted. They had gone way out on a limb just getting Perot to entertain the idea of hiring handlers and had finally had to resort to the metaphor of sports to persuade him; if you were buying a pro football team, Meyerson had said, you'd have to get somebody who knew something about blocking and tackling. With much grumbling, Perot had bought into the idea and accepted the further word of his old friends that Rollins and Jordan were right for the job.

But as Rollins laid out his ideas, they began to wonder, and so did he; it was as if they were commissioning a bricklayer to build the Taj Mahal. To them, originality and purity of design were central purposes of the campaign. To him, politics was a series of tasks rather than a question of metaphysics; the objective was victory, and there were things that had to get done to get you there, whether they were orthodox or not. He spied a greaseboard, picked up a marker, and wrote: 156 DAYS. That was how long they had to elect Ross Perot president of the United States, and, Rollins said, "every single day matters. It all ends up being a one-day sale in November, and you can't lose a day."

Everybody agreed on that, and, with some misgivings, Perot's men said they would carry Rollins's ideas forward to the boss. But there were some things he had to understand about the relationship. This wasn't going to be like working for Ronald Reagan. In this campaign, Perot was the final arbiter and the chief spokesman; it would be his way or no way. Did Rollins *really* want to join up? He had been divorced once before, Meyerson reminded him, and now, by his own account, he was straining his second marriage, putting his career ahead of his wife's. Was he willing to take a chance on becoming a two-time loser? And what about his health? He had had a slight stroke ten years before. Was he up to the rigors of a campaign?

Rollins brushed off the sudden concern for his well-being; his health was fine, he said, and his marriage sound. But the questions troubled him, and he went back to his room at the Omni in a down mood. First, he put in a call to Sherrie—she was in Los Angeles on a trip with Bush—and told her not to worry. He would hang around and meet Perot the next day, he said, but he could tell the thing wasn't going to come together.

"Quit worrying," he said.

"Go home," she advised. "Don't meet with him."

"I can't leave without meeting him," he answered.

"No, your instincts are right," she said. "It's not going to work. Get the hell out of there."

He couldn't do that, he said. He had to do the meeting.

Afterward, he went out for drinks with Charlie Leonard, a protégé who had preceded him to Dallas and was already in trouble for his pushy New York manners. Tom Luce had brought Leonard down to do a Campaign 101 seminar for a gathering of forty or so of Perot's green young field staffers. The session had gone badly; Leonard had made too little of what the amateurs had accomplished and too much of the intent of the new crowd to professionalize the campaign. Perot's young tigers were offended, and so was their designated leader, Mark Blahnik, a man Perot literally trusted with his life; the two spoke, on the average, six or seven times a day. The result of Leonard's elbow-throwing had been another blowup. Perot had been upset with him, and he had barely escaped with his job.

It was nearly eleven on a Sunday night when he and Rollins set out from the Omni, looking for a bar. As they wandered the deserted streets, Leonard spoke of his troubles, and Rollins replayed his meeting with Perot's men. He seemed particularly bothered by the inquiries into his long-ago medical and marital problems.

"What's strange about that?" he asked Leonard rhetorically.

"How come they know you've been married before or that you had the stroke," Leonard said.

"Right," Rollins replied. As it happened, Meyerson had heard about the stroke from Jordan in casual conversation and had guessed on his own that Rollins was on his second marriage. He was himself a man of a certain age and had meant only to be solicitous; running a campaign was, after all, a high-stress undertaking. But the inquiry had spooked Rollins. Someone must have checked him out, he guessed. There was probably a dossier on him.

"Do you think they're following us now?" Leonard asked, only half kidding.

"Who knows?" Rollins said.

They found a bar, walked in, and ordered drinks. They had sipped their first sips before they noticed there were no women in the place—or, so far as they could tell, any other heterosexual men.

"Well," Leonard said, "if he *is* following us, Perot's first report is, 'Leonard and Rollins meet at midnight and go to a gay bar together.'"

Rollins's suspicions went on hold when he and Jordan met with Perot the next day. He found himself charmed, even smitten. The Perot he saw wasn't the little autocrat you read about in the papers. The guy was an American original, a political naïf who clearly believed in what he was doing and seemed wide open to professional advice. Jordan did one of his chart presentations, a timeline of what had to be done when. Perot agreed with it all. The TV show and the ten thousand house parties? He adored it. The two-headed organizational structure they had agreed on? Fine. The need to get started, do some polling, get cracking on ads, define himself and his positions? No problem.

The guy could flat-out communicate, Rollins thought in some awe; he reminded you of Reagan with his gift of gab and Nixon with his quick, reductionist mind. But did he know what he was letting himself in for? The question troubled Rollins, whose own future was on the line with Perot's, and he found himself delivering a cautionary homily on what lay ahead. "Ross, this is like war," he began. It wasn't going to be a cakewalk, Perot and The Volunteers marching arm-in-arm to victory, and it wasn't going to be a draft, either. Elections were about power, and, Rollins told Perot, "we're going up against the whole power center of the free world"—a capital city in which everybody had a stake in the system as it was and everybody was going to be against him.

It was going to get ugly, Rollins warned; nobody would get killed, but the weapons of modern politics were lethal in their own way, and it would take more than plain talk to win—it would take the organization and discipline of an army in combat. Amateurs in politics tend to be true believers, in themselves or their heroes. Professionals are agnostics; you start a race by figuring out how you would run against your own guy, and Rollins knew exactly what he would do to Perot—paint him as some kind of nutty little billionaire with paranoid delusions.

"Ross," he said, "there's two words I want you to write on your mirror every morning. One is KOOK and one is HOPE."

Perot flinched. "What do you mean by that?" he asked, sounding defensive.

"Every single day," Rollins said, "your opponents are going to make you into a kook. If they make you into a kook, or if anything *you* do makes you into a kook, you lose. The second thing is, every single day, you've got to go out and be the candidate of hope—the person who can change the direction of this country. If you can keep focusing on hope and not let them drive you the other way, you can win this thing."

Perot had to remember as well how important the race was to the American people—how deep their disillusion was and how much deeper it would get if he lost his resolve. He couldn't quit, Rollins said, nor could he, once committed, retrieve his political virginity by firing the pros. "If you're going to back off and not do this the right way, you're going to turn these people off more than ever before," Rollins told him, "and you're going to have that on your conscience for the rest of your life."

Perot nodded. He still wasn't going to be *handled,* but he seemed willing to entrust his campaign to people who knew how to run one. "This is the team," he said.

Rollins left the session sky-high. Maybe the guy *was* naive, he was thinking; maybe he didn't have a clue about how politics worked. But he just might be the next president of the United States.

The euphoria was fleeting. The public debut of the copilots was well received, stealing the headlines from Clinton and Bush at the moment they wrapped up their respective nominations. In private, Perot found ways to make his lingering ambivalence plain. In the official announcement, he tried to take Jordan and Rollins down a peg from cochairmen, the title they had all agreed on, to comanagers. Rollins protested, and the release was redone his way. But Perot absented himself from the confirmation ceremony. In the world of handlers, pictures mattered, and Perot belonged in the frame, his presence confirming their authority. In his world, the attendance of the proprietor was not required at the hiring of, say, a couple of new plant superintendents; he skipped their piping-aboard, leaving it to Luce to emcee the show.

The mixed signals did little to improve Rollins's mood when, within the week, he reported for work in Dallas. He should by rights have been happy: Perot had just crested at 39 percent in a CNN poll, eight points ahead of Bush and fourteen up on Clinton. But his spirits were oddly low. His wife had quit her job at the White House and was sore at him. His candidate was running dangerously far ahead of the campaign. There was no strategy, no plan, not even a team; Perot's new headquarters on the LBJ Freeway was a ghost town of closed doors concealing empty offices. Walking around, Rollins felt lonely and oppressed by the calendar. The number of days left had shrunk to 148. He was thinking he had just made the biggest mistake of his life.

White Shirts and Hired Guns

Staffing up, relatively speaking, was the easy part. Some of the Republican operatives in Rollins's Rolodex had already got calls from Bush's chief enforcer, Charlie Black, and his button men, warning them in effect that they would be lucky to get state assembly races to run if they deserted their president. But Rollins had set a powerful example, and Perot provided the cause, the money, and the polling numbers required to tempt good people aboard at whatever risk to their futures.

By mid-June, forty pros, mostly Rollins's draft picks, had occupied the vacant warrens at headquarters and the rental apartments provided by the campaign nearby. They had all accepted up front that it wouldn't be the kind of campaign they were used to, with press planes, spin doctors, and made-for-TV media events. What they weren't prepared for was their own reduction from court magicians to office help in what amounted to one more Perot Group company—a fifty-state chain-store operation in which The Volunteers owned the franchises and Ross Perot was not merely the product but the CEO.

The war of the worlds began with their arrival and would not end till they had all been sacked and sent home. Perot and his circle never stopped regarding their coming as a contamination—like introducing some kind of bacteria into a system, Jim Squires, the press secretary, thought; once inside, they started devouring their host. Antibodies formed almost immediately, to a point at which it was hard getting anything done. Days started routinely with what was called a management-group meeting but was more nearly a tutorial, Jordan and Rollins explaining the ABC needs of a campaign to Meyerson and Luce and waiting while they consulted Perot. The wait was often a long one, and the reward was seldom a go-ahead. To the pros, Perot's management style seemed to be to resist or postpone; in time, Luce and Meyerson had become the tutors, instructing Rollins and Jordan in what their candidate wouldn't do.

In frustration, Rollins and his troupe sought advice from people closer to Perot than they and were told not to worry—his cantankerousness would blow over in due time. "He'll be right in your face for thirty days," Bill Gayden, a longtime Perot finance officer, told them, "questioning every single decision you make and wanting to know why. It's Ross's style. And then once he becomes convinced that you know what you're doing, he'll say, 'Okay, you run this thing.' He'll go away and he won't bother you."

The day never came. Perot, when he was in town, was a hovering and sometimes invasive presence. No matter was deemed too trivial to warrant his attention; at one point, a plan to move a minor functionary's office was put on hold till Luce could clear it with Ross. But Perot's larger concern was with how his money would be spent, a zone of natural interest for the man writing the checks without always understanding what they were buying him.

"You keep building the Pentagon here," he told Rollins one day, complaining about the scale of the headquarters operation. Why did they need so many desk officers when they had The Volunteers?

"Ross," Rollins answered, "there are fewer people here than in the Clinton or the Bush campaign—probably a third of the people they have. You've got some of the best professionals in the country."

"Well, they oughta be," Perot said sourly. "I'm paying them enough."

The budget was an early and constant source of contention, under his suspicious eye. Like most successful consultants, Rollins had worked for rich clients who, like Perot, had talked about spending a lot of money and then had developed palsy of the pen hand when the bills came in. He asked Meyerson and Luce up front whether they wanted a *real* budget or a bullshit version, lowballing what they would actually need if they were to make Perot competitive.

Ross wants whatever it takes, they assured him. Give him the real deal.

But when Rollins sent forward a $147 million first draft, it bounced within an hour; the word from Perot was that he was never going to give his mercenaries license to spend that kind of money. New drafts were done. Bar graphs and footnotes were added. Euphemisms were coined; the two polltakers already on the payroll were hidden under "market research"—Perot didn't see why you should pay for polls when you got so many free in the papers—and voter contact became "Volunteer activities." A $2 million line item for issues research had to be hidden where no one could find it. All it produced, so far as Perot could see, was a bunch of big, fat briefing books when a couple of pages would do him just fine.

The campaign, viewed from within, was something less than an advertisement for a Perot presidency. His appearances were amateurishly advanced, without regard to pleasing camera angles; at a stop in Hartford, he was posed facing the state capitol, not backed up against it, so *he* would have something nice to look at while he was speaking. His beloved Volunteers were growling among themselves and at their masters in Dallas—not just the hired guns but the paramilitary Perot Group "white shirts" assigned to oversee them.

Decisions piled up in Perot's in-basket; Mr. Can-Do had somehow become Mr. Can't-Say on when and how to declare his candidacy, what to do to match or top the major-party conventions, how to go about finding a plausible running mate, and what kind of media campaign to put on. Dates shifted. Deadlines slid. Memos went unread, or at least unanswered. John White, a sometime Carter administration official assigned to work up Perot's plan for America, could barely get in to see him, let alone trade ideas; in White's first month in Dallas, they met twice. Rollins, in frustration, ordered up a one-page catalogue of the problems of the campaign. The list of ills began badly— NO STRATEGY—and got worse. Perot said he would think about it. Nothing happened.

The bottleneck was caused partly by the resolve of the amateurs not to do *anything* in the usual way; their view, summarized by Luce, was that the process sucked and that it was a major part of Perot's mission to change it by his refusal to play along. The believers put a premium on what they liked to call "thinking outside the box," and Rollins seemed to them hopelessly trapped inside it. After all their warnings, he was still trying, in their view, to replicate the 1984 Reagan campaign. Rollins in turn would regularly protest his own purity of heart and his understanding of what Perot was attempting to do. But he was who he was, the product of his own experience, and whenever he drew on it, he seemed to give Perot's men fresh ground for offense.

It was as if the two tribes had descended to Earth from separate and distant planets, one political, one corporate. Each excited the other's paranoia, and the boys from Planet Rollins didn't ease suspicions with their brassy attitudes, their fat salaries, and their adherence to the old tricks of their trade. On Planet Rollins, it was part of a manager's brief to front for his candidate on TV, and Rollins insisted on doing so. On Planet Perot, company rules applied; only the proprietor could speak authoritatively for the firm. On Planet Rollins, scheduling mattered; you moved the candidate around in ways that reinforced his message with words in the papers and pictures on the nightly news. On Planet Perot, the candidate went his own way; he didn't do airport stops, photo ops, or sound bites composed for him by other people. On Planet Rollins, campaigns ran in an intuitive, quick-response mode, the players playing The Game from day to day. On Planet Perot, you started with a detailed business plan for any new enterprise, with precise goals, deadlines, and cost estimates, and Rollins couldn't or wouldn't produce one.

That the two cultures were incompatible was evident at one of their earliest meetings as a team in June. Rollins arrived in his full I'm-in-charge-here mode, ticking off all the things they would have to do. Most of his recipe was familiar but unobjectionable; everybody at the table knew they would have to get ads on the air and impose something like coherence on Perot's schedule. Rollins's mistake was his reliance on Reagan '84 as his example. His manner was that of a connoisseur remembering a 1961 Lafite Rothschild. They had won forty-nine states, he said. It had been the perfect campaign.

"It may have been perfect," Jim Squires said, "but you had a robot for a candidate."

"This is the only way to do it," Rollins shot back.

"It may be the only way to do it," Squires said, his temper rising, "but it is going to be the most difficult way for us to do it." Squires had never wanted Rollins around; the guy, he had told Meyerson at the time, was the embodiment of the old politics—a handler of the most conventional sort. Nothing since had changed Squires's mind. Rollins didn't know Perot or the kind of campaign he proposed to run. You couldn't make him go flying around the country, reading somebody else's speeches and mouthing somebody else's idea of the message of the day. "I've been fooling with him for two months," Squires told Rollins, "and *I* know he feels strongly about these things."

The flare-up exposed a rift that would torment Perot's managers for the rest of the campaign. Luce kept the peace that day, mostly by maintaining a scrupulously neutral boardroom manner. He agreed with much of what Squires was saying; it struck him that Rollins was trying to refight World War II. But it was in Luce's nature as a man and a lawyer to try to compose differences, not inflame them, and he chose not to take sides. He sensed as well that he and Meyerson had trumped themselves with Ross—that they had sold him on the idea that you could hire professional handlers and still run a new kind of campaign. Luce was stuck with his own idea and felt obliged to try to make it work. He had to reconcile what was irreconcilable in the interest of holding his ill-sorted management group together.

What he could not do was heal the fundamental split between the two camps on the very nature of political communication in a modern age. To Rollins, a campaign *was* communication; everything you did—the ads, the events, the travel, the give-and-take with the press—had to serve the single purpose of winning voters and getting them out on Election Day. To Perot and his men, the end was indisputable, but the means, as Rollins outlined them, were somehow unclean; you would never get Ross to go along with the games handlers play. "Eddie" wouldn't understand that *this* campaign was different, Squires complained privately. Eddie only knew one way.

For a time, Luce kept the peace, or at least a basic civility around the table. The strains remained; the price of harmony was a chronic inconclusiveness, born in part of trying to get everybody to agree to everything. The willfulness of the pros bumped into a kind of vanity among the amateurs, the hubris—shared by Perot himself—of having soared too high in the polls too soon. If one thought of the handlers as bacteria, the etiology of the problems afflicting the campaign seemed obvious and the recommended cures irrelevant. "All you big-shot experts," Squires scoffed one day soon after Rollins's troops rolled into town. "We're sitting on top of the goddam polls."

The feeling was exacerbated by Rollins's chesty way of doing business. To the inhabitants of Planet Perot, he seemed to be breaching all the limits he had agreed to. He leaked stories. He did TV. He poached on Jordan's franchise, the media, and Squires's, the press. He tried to undercut Luce and the other old soldiers, suggesting to Perot that they didn't know what they were doing. For him, it all had a purpose: winning. For them, he was addicted to the sport of politics like a junkie to drugs. The provocations finally multiplied to a point where Meyerson approached him one day and warned him of a "theory" circulating around headquarters that he was a double agent—that the Republicans had sent him in to sabotage the campaign.

Once again, Meyerson had meant his words as a kindness to Rollins, a heads-up alerting him to a potential problem; he hastened to add that he didn't believe the talk himself. But Rollins took it as a message from the top, and he flared. "Mort," he said, "that just goes to show your ignorance. I've got a reputation for integrity. I'm blowing up my life. I'm putting my marriage at risk. I'm putting my career at risk. I'm here because I believe in the cause."

The irony was that people on both planets agreed in principle on what needed doing. The question was how; the consensus broke down in the often scholastic bickering over what was and what wasn't unconventional. All campaigns go through start-up pains, Jordan told Luce, speaking from his own experience as Jimmy Carter's top gun; Carter and his troops had made plenty of mistakes and still had won the presidency. But Carter had had plenty of time to fix things. Perot didn't; to Luce, it felt as if they had dropped into the Super Bowl in the fourth quarter and were still trying to get their uniforms on.

In fact, Perot's honeymoon trip was ending even then. The media were beginning to get on him, first for the great gaps in his knowledge of the issues, then for his allegedly frequent resort to private eyes to spy on people—even, in one published account, his own children. The Myth was in danger of coming unraveled. Citizen Ross was metamorphosing into Inspector Perot, the scourge of striped shirts, bearded jaws, over-the-collar haircuts, and two-timing husbands. This Ross Perot was a man of authoritarian mind and lurid conspiratorial fantasies, the kind who probably kept an enemies list and cared little for the Constitution. If he had had his rent-a-cops spy on his kids, as the papers claimed, what might he do with the FBI and the CIA at his disposal?

Perot seemed bewildered by the turn of events. His denials accomplished nothing; neither did blaming the Republicans for spreading lies about him. His standing in the polls started to melt. His pride was wounded, his sense of betrayal intense.

"You know, I never got bad press until I hired you and Jordan," he told Rollins one day.

"Well, Ross, it might be because no one took you seriously," Rollins said.

In a Faustian bargain, there was always a price, and Perot was paying it. The day he signed up the mercenaries for his general staff, he had crossed the line from folk hero to candidate, and from war games to war. And yet he seemed oddly unprepared to fight it. To his hired soldiery, it was as if he had already seen victory in the worshipful eyes of The Volunteers and, instead of engaging with his enemies, was waiting for them to surrender.

24.

Point Counterpoint

In George Bush's mind, the shooting couldn't start soon enough.
Like Bill Clinton's handlers, his people had spent much of the
spring tiptoeing gingerly around Perot, frightened off by his rising
numbers in the polls and his seemingly bottomless pockets. But Bush
had been building up a head of steam at least since mid-May, when he
came into possession of a videotape of a Dallas TV interview with the
Plain Texas Talker talking about him. As he screened the show, Bush
alternated long, smoky silences with muttered complaints about this
slap shot or that dodge. It was not until Perot charged him with
having brought on the Gulf war by coddling Saddam Hussein that the
president finally exploded.

"That's a lie!" he snapped at the screen. "My instinct is go fight
that little guy. When do I get to take him on?"

It would take some time for his impatience to overcome what he
saw as the timorousness of his own troops. If they had only known it,
Perot was an easy target—a man who regarded image as a dirty word
and so hadn't done or authorized a thing to protect his own. But to his
opponents that spring, he was something new and dangerous, a billionaire populist riding a squall line of white middle-class discontent
with the old political order. Handlers, who ply a trade learned only by
experience, had never seen anything quite like the Perot phenomenon
before. Their reflex accordingly was to hunker down like islanders in
the path of a hurricane and pray that, with a little help from the media,
it would blow over.

Clinton's people were particularly eager to avoid, or at least postpone, a fight. The national Democratic Party's oppo man, Dan Carol,
did set up a covert lunch with David Tell, his counterpart at Bush-
Quayle headquarters, to see if they could swap dossiers. Carol called
for Tell at his office, wearing a false beard as a joke. Then they adjourned to a Chinese restaurant near Dupont Circle, away from the
usual haunts favored by political operatives, and talked in a general way
about what sort of goodies each might provide the other.

The approach came to nothing; the Republicans were far ahead of the Democrats in stockpiling ammunition for use against Perot, and the Clinton command wasn't ready to pick any fights with him anyway. It was the president who was spoiling for war and was disappointed that so few of his generals stood with him.

His initial response to the Perot challenge had been genuine perplexity: what, he kept asking, was the guy up to? Like many of his handlers, Bush assumed at first that the venture wasn't real—that Perot, whom he knew, had neither the will nor the temperament to see it through to the end. His scorn was plain when, during a spring meeting in the Roosevelt Room, he raised the subject with his friend Rich Bond, the Republican chairman.

"So, Rich," he asked lightly, "how's your friend Perot?"

"Well, Mr. President," Bond replied, "the last time I looked, he was in first place."

Bush detonated. "You're the national chairman," he said heatedly. "You of all people should know this guy's *crazy*. He won't go anywhere in this race. He won't be taken seriously."

Bond sat unhappily at Bush's elbow, staring straight ahead. His blank stare gave away his wish that the president were finished. He wasn't. "You people don't understand," he said. "You're spending too much time and focus on Perot. He's a big media celebrity, but people are gonna realize that he's never gonna go the distance. He is *not* a serious candidate for president."

At the time, Bush was under the spell of his command group, most of whom presumed that Perot would simply go away. Teeter's early guess had been that the guy would get no more than 10 percent of the vote, and even when he soared to two or three times that level in the polls, nobody panicked; the consensus among the president's advisers was that the whole thing would soon implode. Their placidity comforted Bush for a time, but as Perot's attacks on him sharpened, he turned on his generals like Lincoln on McClellan. The little SOB was riding high at *his* expense, taking bites out of *his* backside, and it was time they did something about it.

"I don't seem to have many people standing up for me," he grumbled when his war council reconvened at the White House one afternoon in early June. He fixed his top hands, Teeter and Fred Malek, with a meaningful stare.

Teeter protested that they had dozens of surrogates in the field, constantly pleading his cause.

That wasn't what Bush had meant. "Why isn't anybody taking on Ross Perot?" he demanded. "We're letting this guy sail smoothly, and

I think we oughta knock him down. Maybe I'm gonna have to take him on myself."

Not now, Charlie Black said. Not yet.

"I'm getting a little impatient," Bush said. "*Somebody* ought to start taking the little bastard on." He didn't like Perot accusing him of having invited Saddam into Kuwait. "That's a bunch of bullshit," Bush said, "and he knows it." And all those simple little home remedies for the deficit? The president ripped a page from a legal pad and slipped into a fair imitation of Perot's scratchy East Texas twang. "Gimme a clean sheet of paper," he mimicked. "Gonna balance the budget!"

Black still favored holding back. If they attacked Perot, they might only provoke him into attacking back, at thermonuclear levels they couldn't match; the campaign's private calculation was that Perot could put $10 million a month on the air starting immediately, trashing Bush's reputation and spending him broke if he tried to retaliate. If you only had a couple or three bullets, Black said, you had to think twice about shooting at someone with an unlimited supply. The better course was to leave the Ross-bashing to the media and to Clinton. He, after all, was the guy in third place. Sooner or later, he would have to go to war.

"Perot is not an outsider," Black said. "He's a phony, and there's a fifty-fifty chance the news media will do a good enough job on him to *convince* people he's a phony. Let's let the press do their thing for a while."

"If my message isn't getting through anyway," Bush said, this time with less conviction, "maybe I ought to take the little bastard on. I'd love to debate the little son of a bitch right now."

"We need to dust him up a little bit," Black suggested. "Maybe we can goad him into making a mistake. But you should stay out of it for now."

Bush did; the dusting-up was left largely to surrogates and to periodic feeds to the press from the thousands of pages of Perotiana in the campaign's oppo file. The air was suddenly acrid with name-calling, the expletives ranging from "demagogue" at the gentler end of the scale to "monster" and "wacko with a capital W" at the harsher. By mid-June, Dan Quayle, a leader among the warhawks, had diced and sliced Perot as "some temperamental tycoon who has contempt for the Constitution of the United States."

Red lights began blinking in Bush's command bunker. It was always risky to go negative in a multicandidate race; mud sticks to the attacker as well as the attackee, and voters begin looking for an alternative to either one. The danger of shock politics could be compounded if one's aim was untrue, as the assault on Perot had turned out to be. In June, Fred Steeper tested the particulars of the case against him in focus groups made up of people who had voted for Bush in 1988 but had gone soft this time. What he discovered, a colleague said, was that there was no magic bullet, no one thing that seemed to work. The campaign was shooting blindly at Perot with a scattergun and was looking more than a little desperate as a result.

What was missing from the picture was a frame, and the man who provided it was the beleaguered White House budget director, Dick Darman, a man whose own survival hung tenuously on Bush's personal loyalty and on his own subtle mind. Darman was a policy maker by calling, but he had a keen sense of politics as well, and he had been warning for months that Perot would be a problem. In his view, heatedly expressed, Bush's analysts had to start reprogramming their computer models for a three-way race, and not on any traditional assumptions, either. The prominent third-force candidates of our recent past—George Wallace, say, or John Anderson—had been effectively undone by money problems; their angels had lost heart when the going got tough and had quit writing checks. That wouldn't be a problem for Perot, as Darman noted. Perot could finance himself, lavishly, to the end.

He had the ego, too, Darman thought; one could read his life back to his boyhood days in Texarkana as preparation for a run for president. Darman, who believed in meticulous preparation, had picked up a popular biography of Perot and had combed it for clues as to what made him tick. At the time, most of Bush's strategists were writing him off as a rich adventurer and were predicting his early demise. Darman wasn't so sure. In his reading, he had come upon the story of how Perot, in 1968, had bought back his family's old house from its more recent owners and had set about restoring it to the way it had been when he was growing up. Its brick walls had since been repainted white and couldn't be sandblasted back to their original color. Perot was unfazed; he had had all the bricks taken down, numbered, reversed, and reassembled, with their pristine red inner sides facing out.

The story fascinated Darman; it read to him like an act of prospective pyramid-building by a man who dreamed of being president and was preserving his boyhood home for posterity just in case. There was plenty in Perot's history to support the argument that he wouldn't last to the end—that he had a way of folding his cards and quitting when things didn't go his way. But Darman thought it dangerous to underestimate the will of a man so driven as to make a museum exhibit of his own past. You had to calculate that he would be around for a while—and, in Darman's view, you had to take the appropriate measures against him.

Darman's alarm had grown with Perot's rise toward the top of the standings. The man was riding a tide of white-collar grievance against the political order and had chosen the president as the special object of his wrath. To the degree that his campaign was becoming an anti-Bush movement, he was dangerous, Darman said, even if you did assume his ultimate collapse. He was going to pass Bush *and* Clinton in the polls, and you couldn't let him sit up there unchallenged for weeks or months on end, lobbing grenades at the White House and making an already weakened president look even weaker. The guy can do us a lot of damage, Darman told his colleagues. We can't let that happen.

The question, in his view, was not whether to go after Perot but how. The usual cut and thrust of politics wouldn't work; Perot was a black-belt master at judo, turning attacks back against his attackers. The answer came to Darman one spring morning as he leafed through a magazine story on Perot, written when his darker side was just beginning to come into view. Three words in the text popped out at Darman, and he circled them: "scary," "dangerous," and—a label applied to Perot by one of his own ex-employees—"dictator." They were the words that would do Perot in, the alchemy that would take a Bush weakness—his sometimes immobilizing caution—and turn it into a strength. Perot had been selling himself as the bold risk-taker, but if he were seen as scary, dangerous, and dictatorial as well, a man of caution might not look so bad.

Darman had made his case for weeks, with Steeper's active backing and polite nods from practically everybody else. But by mid-June, Perot *was* on top of the polls, and Darman, having invited himself to a strategy meeting, found a suddenly more attentive audience.

"The general theme," he said, "should be that Perot has an authoritarian, fascist personality. That means he's scary and dangerous as opposed to merely risky."

Risky, as it happened, was the term of art they had been using, and Teeter preferred sticking with it. Their strategy, he said, should be to paint Perot as a man who operated outside the rules.

"This year, people *want* to take a risk and don't mind somebody who operates outside the rules," Darman said. They had to go the next step and paint Perot as a kind of homegrown Mussolini—a man who would trample on the Constitution, move toward a police state, and turn loose the investigators on anyone who didn't conform with his narrow beliefs and values.

Teeter was hesitant. Wouldn't they just scare Perot's more liberal supporters into Clinton's arms?

Steeper thought not. He had tried out fourteen different points of attack in his focus groups by then, and the only ones with any legs at all had to do with whether the Constitution would be safe in Perot's hands. "This goes beyond the ACLU," he said. "*No* American wants a dictator."

The session ended, after two hours, in a kind of split consensus. Perot had to be bloodied, just as Darman and Steeper had argued, and the chosen buzzwords resembled theirs—"scary," "intolerant," and "tampering with the Constitution." But the direct attack would continue to be left to surrogates and would be muted; as one aide remarked, the campaign literally couldn't afford to get Perot too worked up too soon—not when he had his rumored $100 million in mad money lying around waiting to be spent. The media were fully in the hunt by then anyway, sometimes working leads provided by the Bush campaign, sometimes doing their own deep and richly rewarding dig into Perot's idiosyncratic past. All the president's aides had to do was keep a clipping file and, in Darman's word, reaggregate the facts into the shape they had agreed on—a portrait of a potentially dangerous martinet.

They didn't have to wait long for the press to do the reaggregating for them. First, the *New Republic* reported that Perot's hired gumshoes had spied on his own children; then, the *Washington Post* alleged that they had been on Bush's case for years and had investigated the president's kids, too. The stories were less than perfectly riveted, but their inaccuracies mattered little as against their effect. They fit the emerging cartoon of Perot as a dotty billionaire with a private army of private eyes, an addiction to conspiracy theories, and a particular animus toward the president of the United States.

It was the assertion that his house dicks had spied on Bush's sons that put the story over the top. No one in the Bush-Quayle campaign had to say anything about so flagrant an act of lèse-majesté, but everybody did—including, this time, the president himself. He was suitably shocked, *shocked* by the story "if it's true," he said, though he had ample ground for believing that it was not. His certitude seemed to increase in the days thereafter, along with his dudgeon. "I don't think that's particularly American," he said, no longer bothering with the qualifiers. "Leave my kids alone, I say."

Perot and his men insisted that there was nothing to the stories—that he had used private investigators no more than three or four times in his life and then only for legitimate business reasons. But denials got him nowhere, and his insistence that the stories came from Republican opposition-research files seemed only to dig the hole deeper. Rollins tried to steer him away from that line of defense. The oppo shop, he said, was "a bunch of kids sitting around digging up crap from newspapers." They weren't the problem; the papers and the networks were.

"From what I hear," Perot said, "the Republicans dig this stuff up out of the files of the government. Then they leak it."

"The press can get anything it wants from government files," Rollins reminded him. Congress had seen to that when it passed the freedom-of-information act.

Perot was undeterred; he went right on asserting that the "dirty-tricks crowd" at Republican headquarters was after him and had been since he first signaled his willingness to run. This time, his gifts at judo had failed him; he seemed only to have provided his enemies fresh evidence of his conspiritorial cast of mind, and the Bush campaign went into a state of what one aide described as testosterone overload making fun of him. Mrs. Bush called him bizarre. Marlin Fitzwater said he was paranoid. Rich Bond phoned him on *Larry King Live* and demanded that he prove his charges; Perot made the mistake of saying that he could, in good time. It was all great fun while it lasted, but after two or three days, Fred Malek quietly put out the word to the troops to tone it down. Perot didn't need any help; he was doing a sufficiently damaging job on himself.

The Inspector and the Character Cops

The wonder, to outsiders, was how ill-prepared Perot was to deal with the flak. The pros he had let under the tent had warned him from the first to stick to his theme of fundamental change and not get caught up in The Game, the daily war for advantage in the media; that was best left to others in the campaign. But Perot did not suffer criticism gladly, and he kept wandering off course in his speeches and talk-show appearances, answering the latest charges by the opposition and the press. In desperation, Jordan picked up a blank sheet of paper one day and drew an arrow across it, from the left edge to the right. The arrow was the message, he told Perot, a straight, true line from that moment to Election Day. Everything else was irrelevant.

"Ross, you gotta stay on that message," Jordan said. "If you don't spend your time chasing down stories and arm wrestling with the papers, you win. You get pulled off your message by the press, by the Republicans, by the Democrats, you lose. Let everybody else talk about The Game."

But Perot could not resist temptation, nor would he license his hired handlers to speak for him; the whole idea of The Game remained anathema to him, and Rollins's repeated misdemeanors against the new code were part of what had poisoned relations between them. Rollins didn't *know* Perot well enough to be speaking for him, not in Perot's eyes, but he kept going on television anyway, spinning his own idea of the line. It was message-of-the-day politics, a particular object of Perot's loathing, and Ed sometimes got things wrong; the others, including Perot himself, kept having to sweep up behind him. When Perot finally agreed to let Luce and Meyerson do the talk shows, it was in part a surrender to necessity and in part an attempt to get Rollins off the air.

Perot was in fact his own best salesman, after a lifetime of practice at self-promotion. He saw himself as something of a revolutionary as well, a commonsense rebel against the artifice and cant of politics in the contemporary manner; his resistance to handling and his insistence on speaking for himself were matters of conviction as well as ego and pride. But his billions and the power they had bought him appeared to have spoiled him for the war of succession as it was waged in modern America, with attack ads and anonymous slanders instead of guns and knives. He was particularly bewildered by the hostility of the press, having grown accustomed to its flatteries of the past. "When I was in business," he complained one day, "these guys just wrote down what I said and wrote the story the way I told it to them."

It didn't work that way in politics, not in the age of reporters as character cops. The habit of the new political journalism was not to celebrate seekers after public office but to assume the worst about them and then go out and try to document it. There were ways to survive the assault, mainly by creating news yourself and dominating the coverage. Clinton had grasped that reality. Perot had not; he was only too obviously unprepared for what was happening to him.

To the pros around him, men in the business of winning elections, his conduct under fire bordered on unilateral disarmament. He was doing practically nothing to define himself or to explain exactly what he was attempting with his one-man war on the conventions of politics. He seemed instead to be clinging to the fun parts of his campaign; he kept repeating his set speech at Volunteer events, to ever-diminishing coverage, and making the rounds of the interview shows, to ever ruder and more personal questions.

Neither would he bend to entreaties from the pros to spell out what he stood for, beyond his one-liners; the sworn enemy of image politics was running on his image, or, as he preferred, his principles. "The

American people don't *care* about issues," he would answer when his strategists pressed too hard. "I've talked to my people, and they don't care."

In fact, they did care, greatly. Jordan confronted him one day with yet another of his visual aids, a blowup of a graphic from a *Newsweek* poll. Its message was sobering; not even Perot's supporters felt they knew enough about him. To present so blank a page to the world, in the view of both the pros and the amateurs around him, was an open invitation to his enemies to portray him as they chose. Events bore out their concern; the stories that did make the papers and the newscasts usually had to do with Inspector Perot defending himself against yet another I-Spy charge—and with the steady rise of his negative ratings in the polls.

The pros were frantic to get some ads on the air, if only to stop the bleeding and start bringing some definition to the campaign. What they preferred was a bio reintroducing Ross the Good to America; the more people got to know him, their focus groups suggested, the better they liked him, no matter what anybody said about him. "That means television now," Rollins's shop argued in a new campaign plan at the end of June. "We must sustain our paid advertising buy through the election."

But the air attack never got off the ground. Perot flinched at paying the bills for what he didn't like, which was practically everything the professionals put in front of him. His ardor for Jordan's early brainstorm—the paid TV special and the ten thousand Volunteer house parties—had cooled with his calculation that he could get the same bounce free. "Why do I want to pay for this," he asked, "when I can go on *Larry King?*"

Some of his handlers presumed that he was one more rich guy backing away from the table when he saw how much it would take to play. In fact, there was method in his meanness; he was trying to show that campaigns did not have to be as expensive as they had become in his lifetime. But Perot's quarrel with the plans before him had to do with their content as well. He detested a style of politics that sold candidates like soap, with heart-tugging imagery and soaring music; he wanted *his* TV to be plain and direct, a no-frills presentation of the candidate and his ideas. Before the pros had even arrived, his own people had cooked up an extravaganza of precisely the sort he didn't want: a live-from-Texarkana announcement speech with a bio film by the television producer David Wolper as a frontispiece. Perot hated the package from the moment it was presented to him.

"How'd Wolper get involved?" he asked Squires.

Perot's friend Liener Temerlin had recommended him, Squires said. Temerlin was an ad man. He said Wolper was the best there was.

"We don't want to do this the way Hollywood does," Perot snapped. Perot didn't want to do it the way Ronald Reagan had, either. In early June, Tom Luce had interviewed Hal Riney, the creator of Reagan's soft-focus Morning-Again-in-America ads in 1984, for a possible role in the campaign. Rollins was delighted, and he pushed hard to close the sale. Luce warned him that Perot would reject anything slick. Not to worry, Rollins replied. Riney was the best in the business, an artist so slick that he knew how to be unslick.

The management group finally yielded, in part because nobody had a better idea, and asked Riney to do some ads on spec. The arrangement never had a chance. Perot and his men saw Riney from the first as Rollins's guy, an impression inflamed when word of his "hiring" leaked to the press; the presumption was that Rollins had blabbed again. Riney never got out from under the burden of guilt by association, nor could he get any clear guidance as to what it was he was expected to do. There was no polling to work from and no clear design for an ad campaign. Perot was still waiting for a written media plan, with concepts, delivery dates, and cost estimates set forth in clear, linear fashion. Rollins had never produced one and didn't see the utility in it, given how little time they had.

"Ronald Reagan never saw the commercials till he saw them on television," he told Luce.

"Ed," Luce said, "this isn't Ronald Reagan."

Riney thus found himself flying blind. His only order, straight from the top, was to go out and start shooting rallies; the boss wanted pictures of himself talking to The Volunteers and of Volunteers saying nice things about him. Riney did as he was told, without much heart or much luck; the footage, he reported to Rollins, was garbage. The whole purpose of an ad was to get your message across in thirty or sixty seconds, in a way that would make people want to watch it more than once. Maybe C-SPAN could just turn on a camera and a microphone and let people talk, but you couldn't make an effective spot that way—not by the accepted rules of the business.

"Ross, here's how we normally do it," Riney told Perot one day. "We draft scripts, we talk about concepts, we bring story boards, we shoot footage, and then we edit it. We don't run out and shoot for the sake of shooting. That way, you waste a lot of money."

Perot brushed him off. He didn't like what Riney represented, and he didn't have the patience to sit through a lecture on how the image makers of politics had always done it in the past. He had seen Riney's reel of ads for past campaigns and had detested it. For him, his adoring Volunteers were the heart and soul of the campaign. He wanted them featured, and he wanted ads fast.

"I don't understand why I can't get good commercials," he told Rollins. "The whole problem with this campaign is, I'm used to hiring twenty-one-year-old people, and they get the job done. Why can't I get commercials made tomorrow?"

"If you tell me you want a commercial in twenty-four hours, great," Rollins said. "But I'd like to also have something that has quality and that pleases you."

It was plain by then that Rollins had set himself an impossible task. Nothing the pros did was likely to please Perot. The gulf opening between them was already too wide.

In the House That Ross Built

They tried anyway, and on the last morning in June, Jordan and Meyerson set out with some trepidation for Perot's office to show him what they had. Riney had roughed out eleven spots from his rally footage, intercutting between Perot and The Volunteers, and the campaign had commissioned a five-minute bio by Andrew Wilson, a young Dallas filmmaker. Perot's men had warned Jordan by then that Ross had good days when he was approachable and bad days when he was not—when it was useless trying to get him to decide anything. "That's crazy," Jordan had said. "If he gets to be president, that won't work." But that was Perot, and when they arrived at his aerie on Merit Drive, they found him at the bottom of a bad day.

Nobody loved the Riney ads, not even Riney; he had already decided to go off on his own, with or without formal authorization, and make some spots the way *he* thought they ought to be. The bio was in better shape, and Jordan and Meyerson screened it first.

Perot sat watching the images roll by, his anger rising frame by frame. He hadn't wanted a bio in the first place; his people had gone ahead anyway, and this was what they brought back. He didn't like the way they had lit his wife, or interviewed his sister, or left out whole chapters of his story, or added banjo music in the background as if he were some kind of hillbilly.

"This is *crap!*" he said. "You guys don't know anything." His voice was rising, almost to a shout. "You're supposed to be a pro," he told Jordan. "You tell me this is supposed to be world-class, like you know what you're doing."

Jordan was stunned. His last candidate, Jimmy Carter, had been a notoriously fussy detail man, but not like this; Carter had understood that *his* job in a campaign was to get out there and deliver the message, not to waste his time on the mechanics of advertising and scheduling. Perot was different. He had no rigor, no discipline, no willingness to listen and learn. Like a lot of self-made men, he could be tough to argue with and tougher to cajole. Jordan tried a little of each, without success.

"You've got form confused with substance," he told Perot. "Nobody cares who does your film. What people care about deeply is knowing where you stand on the issues. Who are you? What do you believe in?"

Perot wouldn't budge.

"Ross," Jordan said, with as much good humor as he had left, "I'll bet you five dollars that if you get any twenty people in this office to watch this film, they'll like it. And by the way, it's your money I'm betting you."

"I don't care if they like it or not," Perot said. "I'm not going to pay for it."

"You're not going to take me off my bet," Jordan teased.

"I don't care if everybody in this building likes it," Perot said.

Jordan slipped Meyerson a note asking whether it was worth pressing on. Meyerson signaled back that it wasn't, but it was too late; they were two men in a foxhole, pinned down under hostile fire. "What the hell do I need you for?" Perot was yelling when Rollins and Luce slipped into the room, arriving late from another meeting.

Jordan looked shaken. Rollins tried to explain that the ads were rough cuts, that they could be edited into shape.

Perot didn't care. "Who authorized spending this money on this crap?" he demanded. "*On this crap!* You've just wasted my money. *My money! On this crap!* Who authorized it?"

"Well, I guess I did," Luce said.

"Goddammit, I never authorized you to spend that money," Perot said. In fact, he had; after much delay, he had finally signed off on a short-term, second-quarter budget earmarking $7.5 million for advertising through July. But it was no good arguing with him, not when he was in one of his moods. His four visitors packed up their reels and their arguments and left.

"I'm out of the media," Jordan told Rollins.

He was shaking as they cleared the building, and by the time they got back to headquarters, he looked ghastly. He had gone ashy pale and was gasping for air. He had had a siege of lymphatic cancer some years before, and while he had fully recovered, his comrades were frightened for him. Rollins thought he might be having a heart attack. Jordan said no, it was just stress. It had happened once before. It would pass.

The seizure did. The pain didn't. The irony was that Jordan had warned Perot early on to be skeptical of advice from the pros, including himself. "This ain't the Jimmy Carter campaign," he had said, "and it ain't the Ronald Reagan campaign." He had had a motto printed on a sheet of paper for Perot, words for him to live by in the weeks ahead. "Beware of generals fighting the last battle," it said; it had been Jordan's token that he was one with the spirit of the campaign. But Perot was treating him instead as part of the problem; he had finally crossed the line between skepticism and abuse, and Jordan felt wounded by it. Nobody had ever talked to him that way before. He had given up a lot to come to Dallas; his friends, even his wife wondered what the hell he was doing there. He was humiliated. They were *all* humiliated.

"This is horseshit," Jordan said. "I'm getting out of here."

He walked into Charlie Leonard's office, dropped into a chair, and talked about the meeting. Leonard kept moving paper and taking phone calls, half-listening to the account.

"How are we going to get out of here?" Jordan asked.

Leonard looked up from his paperwork and gestured at a greaseboard behind him. Rollins had written FORT ALAMO on it.

"There is no way out," Leonard said.

"I think he's going to let us all go," Jordan said. Perot didn't want them, didn't think he needed them. "I think we're all going to go out together," he repeated.

Leonard shrugged and went back to his paper. Jordan headed for his own office. Rollins found him there.

"What are you going to do?" Rollins asked.

"I don't know," Jordan answered. "I can't go by myself. Will you go with me?"

"I can't go," Rollins said. "This *is* the Alamo for me. I can't get the hell out. I've hired forty people here. I've got nowhere to go."

"This is the biggest mistake I've ever made," Jordan said.

That day, he wrote a letter of resignation, then disappeared for a couple of days. Once, he and Perot spoke by phone. Perot's spirits had recuperated, but he was still down on the ad and on the "high-priced professionals" who had brought it to him. He wasn't going to budge, and Jordan returned to Dallas in some despair. No one was going to talk to him that way again, he said, and he wasn't going to keep on beating his head against the wall, either. He spoke first with Luce and

Meyerson, then with Perot. He was looking for an honorable discharge, a way to leave quietly without damaging the campaign.

"Ross, this thing is not working," he said. "Nothing's getting done. I'm not sure why you brought us here. I don't wish you any harm, but I really want to go back to Tennessee."

"You might be right," Perot said, without apology. "It might have been a mistake to bring you guys in."

In fact, Perot liked Jordan, in his fashion, and hoped he would stay. It was Rollins who had come to symbolize his larger doubts about having gone pro. "I don't trust Ed," he said. "Ed's got Washington disease." He didn't have any loyalty to Perot or the cause; he was looking out only for himself.

In the end, Jordan hung around, for want of a graceful line of retreat; he continued showing up at morning staff meetings, and he told Rollins he would do what he could to help, on the fringes. To prove something to Perot, or perhaps to himself, he gathered one group of white shirts and another of Volunteers and asked them to grade the bio film. Everybody loved it except Mark Blahnik, who knew Perot's feelings about it; he rated it only average. Perot himself showed it to a gathering of state Volunteer leaders. They stood and cheered.

The tests changed nothing. The only Perot campaign that mattered was going on in the mind of its master, where he and his beloved Volunteers were being subverted by the enemy within their walls. It was the pros, in his fancies, who had spoiled everything. He felt, one aide said, as if he had put together a Frankenstein's monster out of hopelessly mismatched parts. His creation had turned on him, devouring his money and trying to make him do things he didn't want to do. He resisted; not even the evidence that he was alone in the matter of the ads could induce Perot to put them on the air.

Jordan watched the spectacle with growing sadness. He was no more than a shadow presence in the campaign by then. Rollins was living on borrowed time, under a direct threat from Perot that he would be fired if there was one more leak to the press. Even Luce and Meyerson had slipped from grace; in Perot's mind, so far as his people could read it, they were men of suspect political judgment who had got seduced by the pros and were allied with them against him. He was a man entrapped in a rickety building. With not much more than a huff and a puff from the Bush campaign, the improbable House That Ross Built was about to come tumbling down.

25.

The Long Goodbye

One day near the end of his first campaign, Perot sat talking with Ed Rollins across the vast canyon of misunderstanding and mistrust that had opened between them. His tone was almost wistful.

"Is this ever gonna get fun again?" he asked.

"Fun?" Rollins repeated. The word was not in his working vocabulary, not during a campaign.

"Yeah," Perot said. "When I started, this thing was fun."

"Campaigns are *never* fun," Rollins answered. "It's like war. It's miserable. Running for office isn't fun. *Winning* is fun."

"What about the presidency?" Perot asked. "Is that fun?"

"The only time the presidency is fun," Rollins said, "is the day you get inaugurated and the day you dedicate your library. If you're going to do what you're setting out to do, it isn't going to be fun."

In fact, by early summer, it had long since stopped being fun for Perot, his organization, and his public. His numbers were crumbling, his negatives rising. He had slipped back to second in the polls, with Clinton, in third, on his heels. His campaign was fragmenting, at war with itself and, on some issues, with him. His plan to redeem America from corruption and debt was late coming together in a way that suited his demanding tastes. His press had turned brutal, a daily battering for his business practices and his allegedly promiscuous gumshoeing; he seemed unable to change the subject back to anything that mattered.

Even his jealously guarded family life was under scrutiny. With the turn into summer, the media were chasing a report, put in play by Bush's men, that he had sicced his private eyes on one of his daughters, Nancy, and a man she had known in college—a lit professor whose offenses were alleged to have been that he was older and a Jew. There was, even in Perot's own telling, a kernel of fact inside the story. He had always thought of his children as natural targets for the bad guys, given his money, and when Nancy was robbed at gunpoint, he said, he had put her under surveillance for her own protection. Her friendship with the professor had come up only as an incidental blip on the screen. But the more lurid versions in circulation made Perot sound like the master of a private ministry of fear, with his own offspring among its targets.

The stories were deeply wounding to him. The Inspector, it turned out, could not abide inspection, not of himself and certainly not of his world-class wife and children; that was the last straw on an already insupportable load.

"It's a sign of success," Jordan said, trying to sound optimistic. It meant that his candidacy was being taken seriously by the opposition and the press.

Perot asked what would happen if he won—could he ever have a normal family life again?

"Ross," Jordan told him, "you think *this* is something, you wait until you get up *there.*"

The prospect bore heavily on Perot, and his spirit seemed to be breaking under its weight. "I just don't want this job that much," he told his son-in-law, Clay Mulford, who was general counsel to the campaign, and he could no longer hide his unhappiness. A camera crew working on yet another new batch of television ads shot him speaking to his state chairpeople one day in early July, trying to capture the old Perot energy on film. What they recorded instead was its deterioration. The guy was drawing back, thought Paul Maslin, the Democratic half of the polling team aboard Noah's Ark, as he sat watching the footage with the media boys. Perot wasn't the same. He wasn't *there*. Maybe he wasn't going to make the race at all.

His days in fact were numbered, at least in the odd hybrid candidacy he had created; if the campaign was indeed Frankenstein's monster, it appeared to be coming apart a limb at a time. At one pole of the splintering enterprise was Perot himself, cranky and refractory. At the other was Rollins, trying to apply his old mechanics to a new machine. Jordan floated between the two, at ease with neither, half-estranged from both. Luce and Meyerson led what amounted to a corporate party-within-a-party, the Perot Group regulars and their frequent ally, Jim Squires; they were struggling to build something that would at once please the boss with its newness and inspire him to do some of the old-style things you had to do to win. Groupings shifted from day to day and issue to issue. Some days, on some issues, it was everybody against Perot. Most days, on more issues, it was everybody against Rollins and his gang of forty.

With summer, the Rollins tribe had been put in a kind of de facto quarantine, isolated from the others by a wall of mistrust; if they couldn't be relied on to keep a confidence or to act in untraditional ways, it was simplest and safest to ease them bloodlessly from the center to the periphery of the campaign. Inside the cordon sanitaire, they kept pushing their plans for the announcement, the television ads, the Volunteer effort, the selection of a running mate. It was motion rather than action; they had alienated practically everybody with their style of doing business. Even when the others agreed with Rollins on basic objectives—getting ads on the air, say, or rationalizing Perot's schedule—they differed irremediably on the means. Rollins's ideas looked conventional to Perot and his people, and in spite of numerous warnings, he had never mastered the art of communicating them to the boss in clear, corporate, bottom-line English.

The boys from Planet Rollins had become the equivalent of an animatron exhibit at Disneyland, a lifelike representation of how campaigns used to work. Their energy was high, their movement constant, but their proposals kept disappearing somewhere between their diorama on the LBJ Freeway and Perot's desk on Merit Drive. Rollins wanted his talented chief of advance, Joe Canzeri, to run the scheduling operation. The leaders of the Perot party were happy enough with Canzeri's work, but he was old school, and they put Mort Meyerson in charge of travel instead, in part as a way to shut Rollins out; Mort at least understood the imperative of letting Perot be Perot. Rollins had brought in a second pollster, Paul Maslin, before the hiring window slammed shut and had ordered up a series of focus groups. It was a pointless exercise, given Perot's scorn for the whole idea of letting twelve people in a room dictate what he should or shouldn't do. Nobody bothered telling Rollins no; they let him have his groups, adding further to the campaign's rising pile of unwanted and often unread paper.

The problem was that the Perot crowd hadn't yet invented a better way—not, at least, to the satisfaction of the one man who mattered. Perot had set out to shatter all the existing assumptions about how presidents are elected; the campaign going on in his mind was all grassroots passion and no artifice, no blue smoke and mirrors. But the real campaign he had suffered to be built around him was like a car constructed from scratch in a chop shop, its parts and colors all clashing with one another. What was intended as revolutionary came off as merely incoherent, a Babel effect that became grist for still more negative stories in the media. Tom Luce harbored the radical idea that Perot should explain to America exactly what he thought should be done to change the electoral process, step by step, and then go out and do it. The proposal got nowhere; Luce's colleagues in the oxymoronically named management group were against it, and he himself still felt too compromised by his complicity in the mess to take it forward to Perot on his own.

By then, Perot's private state of entropy had begun to show in his demeanor around headquarters and in his sallies out on the road. His energy was depleted. He wouldn't commit to anything that mattered, regardless of which of his warring tribes it came from. The increasingly worried talk at staff lunches was whether they had a candidate or not.

"Tom, what do you think Ross *really* thinks?" Jordan asked Luce in a moment's frustration.

"Goddamit, Hamilton, I don't know," Luce said, and *he* had been Perot's friend for twenty years.

"A World of Setups"

The issue that finally brought matters to critical mass was, fittingly, the ad campaign. Perot was even more a creature of television than his major-party rivals; he had once been romanticized in a miniseries about his commando raid in Iran, and he had waged his candidacy almost entirely on talk TV. But he dragged his feet when his war counselors urged him to put up a first flight of ads before the Democratic convention. In their eyes, it was a last chance to rehabilitate himself and to slow Clinton's gathering momentum. In his, it was the old game, slick, expensive, and empty. His economic plan was nearing completion, and he wanted it featured in a spare, simple way in his commercials, with him looking dead into the camera and explaining it to America. Days passed. Deadlines slipped. Clinton rose. Perot fell— and still nothing happened.

For the space of a single day, the impasse seemed about to break. Hal Riney had recut his first rough spots of Volunteers talking about Perot, this time with the art and the emotive warmth that had made his reputation as an ad man. Everybody liked them—even, to the astonishment of the campaign command, Perot himself. "These are first-class commercials," he said. They weren't the Perot-to-camera issues ads he had wanted; still, he seemed ready to put them on the air—and, in a suddenly mellowed mood, he agreed to a new try at a bio ad as well.

But his resolve melted when he met with his state chairpeople in Dallas the next day. His heart had always been with them, since theirs were so unquestioningly with him; when they had complained about the professionals at headquarters, Perot had taken their side, wondering aloud why he needed to pay anybody when The Volunteers had such good ideas. By the time he screened the ads for them, his own mood had shifted. It seemed not to matter to him that most of the chairpeople liked the spots. A few objected that they were the usual bullshit, the kind of stuff you might expect from Clinton and Bush, and Perot was an easy mark for their critique. He didn't defend the ads; instead, he listened in moody silence, with the complaints ringing louder in his ears than the compliments. The ads didn't look so first-class anymore.

When the show was over, he sent for Riney. It was too late, he was told. Hal was on a plane home to San Francisco. Perot, by now boiling, ordered him back.

Two days later, Riney found himself on the carpet, along with Luce and Rollins. Perot had recaptured the lead in a newspaper poll that morning. The finding was at war with his own polling, which showed him second and slipping, but he liked it better; it reinforced his sense that he had been paying good money for bad advice. His complaint that morning, indeed, was with Riney's production bills, $125,000 a spot. Perot had asked around and had been told that was much too much. Riney offered to cut his rates. Perot wasn't interested. A friend named Murphy Martin, a retired Dallas newscaster, had said he could do the ads for $2,500 apiece, and Perot had believed him.

"You're a Rolls-Royce," he told Riney. "All I need is a Volkswagen."

Riney's spots had been scheduled to go on the air that night. He and Rollins went back to headquarters, at Perot's order, to try to work something out. Luce followed an hour later. He had been trying to reason with Perot, but, he told Rollins, it wasn't going to work. Perot's order was to pull down the spots and fire Riney.

The issues were real to Perot, but Riney in a larger sense was a noncombatant in a drive-by shooting—the casualty of a bullet meant for Rollins. The purists by then had thoroughly demonized Rollins and anybody associated with him, including Riney; Perot had referred to them acidly as "you and your people" so often that Rollins had finally marched on him and told him to cut it out. *They* weren't the problem, Rollins said. Perot was. His lead and his magic were slipping away. He had three options left, Rollins told him. He could get out of the race. He could fire the pros, run as an amateur, and wind up with 12 percent of the vote. Or he could run a *real* campaign and just possibly win.

Perot seemed receptive, for a change. But the Democratic convention was almost upon them, a big free ride for Clinton, and they had nothing to answer with—no ads, no ad maker, and no airtime. In desperation, Rollins reached out to Perot's son, Ross, Jr., whom he had been cultivating, and sent him home with the latest bad news from the polling shop. Perot's negatives were higher than Clinton's and were still rising; his mean score on a scale of one to ten had fallen below five for the first time. They *had* to get ads up, Rollins said, and they had to be good ads, not somebody's $2,500 home videos.

Young Ross pleaded the case over dinner with his father that evening. Perot was livid. It wasn't the first time Rollins had approached members of his family, trying to use them, Perot thought, to get at him. The latest attempt failed, as the others had, but Perot's last reserves of patience were gone. His response was delivered by Meyerson to Rollins at the next morning's strategy meeting in one curt sentence: "Don't you ever use my son against me."

In fact, *everybody* agreed that they had to put some ads up fast, before Clinton's coronation party in New York stole the last of Perot's flagging momentum. Only Perot hung back, and, as a consequence, his air war remained as invisible as Saddam Hussein's over Kuwait. In the run-up to the convention, Clinton had the screen practically to himself. America's principal glimpses of Perot that July weekend came from two disastrous day trips into the wilderness of our politics. His willingness to take them had been celebrated by his circle as signs of the birth of a New Perot. Their pleasure was premature; the two outings would prove to be watershed moments of quite another sort for Perot—the further evidence, in his mind, that his campaign as it stood was broken beyond repair.

The trips had been designed and sold to Perot as examples of the way things ought to work—the way they *had* to work, indeed, if his candidacy was ever to get real. The first took him to Lansing, Michigan, for a speech to his Volunteers. His coaches had talked him into injecting a little substance into his usual pep-rally thank-you to the troops. He was under growing pressure to get specific on the issues, and a topic was chosen to suit the venue; he would talk about using trade policy to restore Detroit to its old eminence as the number-one carmaker in the world.

The speech went well enough; the problems began when Perot presented himself at the airport afterward for a press availability. Doing it at all went against all his antipolitical instincts. He didn't like airport events, which only tied things up for people in the terminal, and he didn't care much for news conferences, either; it had been weeks since he had met the press formally in any number larger than a talk-show panel. But Meyerson and Squires had persuaded him to break his rule. It would be a way to quiet the rising rumble in the media that he was hiding and to make some news on the issues, for a change. The press couldn't just ignore his speech, Squires said; they would *have* to ask him about his promise to put Detroit back on top again.

Perot gave in, but his recalcitrance was plain from the moment he hit the tarmac. Joe Canzeri had advanced the stop and had taped an "X" on the ground for Perot to stand on. Perot glared at it and chose his own spot, somewhere else; as one aide would remark later, you could practically see the chips rising on his shoulders. He was primed for questions about cars and trade. None came. Topic A instead was his attitude about gays in government and the military.

Perot had opened that particular can of worms himself, remarking in a television interview weeks earlier that he probably would not knowingly name a gay to his cabinet. The outcry from gays and liberals had been immediate; the campaign had had to rush out a statement "clarifying" what Perot had meant to say—that he had misgivings about putting a gay person through the trauma of the confirmation process. His only reservation had to do with gays in the military, and he was reserving judgment on that. The statement had only opened a new front, and gay groups had laid siege to the campaign. Meyerson had opened a long, talky series of negotiations and got Perot to sit down with them as well. Perot called the sessions "brain surgery"— his term for what he had to do to get anywhere with people he considered intractable.

After weeks at the table, Meyerson had come up with a statement he believed both right and politic: a declaration reaffirming that Perot was against discrimination and adding that he didn't mind gays serving in the military after all. Nobody else in the management group had liked it. Neither had Perot when Meyerson brought it to him; he had struck the reference to the military. What remained of the statement had been no more than a rehash of his old position, which had satisfied no one; it was too little for gays and too much for veterans, some of them prominent figures in his own campaign. Perot had felt ill-used. His own pal Meyerson had led him down the garden path, and now he found himself pinned to the tarmac, answering inquiries about gay rights when he wanted to talk economics.

His patience ran out after two questions; he closed down the press conference and stormed back to his private jet. The first person to fall under his angry gaze was his traveling press secretary, Sharon Holman, who, only four months before, had been selling real estate for one of his companies. She was a novice at politics and had had nothing to do with planning the trip, but Perot scolded her so roundly that she burst into tears. "Never again!" he raged as the jet scrambled aloft and nosed south toward Dallas.

He was still smoking when he took off again the next day, this time for Nashville and the annual convention of the National Association for the Advancement of Colored People. Rollins, who had come up with a plan to blitz the event with black entertainers, sports stars, and military leaders who supported Perot, had sent an operative to Dallas to set things up. The idea was too showbizzy for Perot; he called it off, and the advance man was ordered home. Squires tried his hand at writing a speech, a call for understanding and caring. Perot ignored it. Luce had an assistant pull together some ideas, culled from Perot's own sentimentalized store of memories about how well he and his family had got on with black people back home in Texarkana. "Perot can't tell those damned stories," Squires protested; they would make him sound patronizing and out of touch.

But Perot was on strike against his handlers, no longer distinguishing between the pros and the amateurs. He spoke to no one before he left for Nashville and took no one with him, not even Ms. Holman; he was alone when his Tennessee state chairman, Steve Fridrich, picked him up at the airport for the drive into town.

"They've been hammering on you a little bit," Fridrich said.

"I can take it," Perot replied.

His date with the NAACP would exceed his threshold of pain. His speech was an improvised stew of the boyhood stories that had so alarmed Squires, garnished with repeated references to African Americans as "your folks" and "you—your people." In the audience, John Jay Hooker sat with his head buried in his hands. The tales were redolent of the plantation, and the chill was palpable under the polite spatters of applause. Only Perot missed it; he didn't realize how insulting he had sounded until some reporters chased him to his car and told him. "I didn't realize I upset anybody," he said. "I apologize."

It had been his first campaign trip into the galaxy beyond Planet Perot; he had let himself be talked into appearing before an organized interest group, against his own rules, and the event had wound up in shambles. On the jet ride home this time, he seemed aggrieved—who *were* these people, he wanted to know—and finally depressed. He had meant well, but now, he fretted, a black person might look at him and think he was a racist. He called a friend from the plane to share his mortification and to complain about the toils and snares of campaigning.

"I live in a world of setups," he said.

The End of the Line

Perot's people would wonder later why they hadn't seen the end coming—why they hadn't added up all the funks, the quibbles, the tantrums, and the stalled plans and figured out that the captain would sooner or later scuttle the ship. The loss of his and his family's privacy obviously troubled him. So did the cost, in money as well as purity, of having rung in the pros. "This could all end at any time," Mort Meyerson, who knew Perot better than any of them, had repeatedly warned friends at headquarters. But the hired hands missed the warning signs. Like Sisyphus, they kept pushing the boulder up the hill. This time it was about to roll back down over them.

Not even the men closest to Perot saw it coming. Two days after the NAACP fiasco, Meyerson and Luce told Rollins that Ross wanted him and Jordan to stay. But it would be on his terms, not theirs. From now on, he was going to do things his way. "He's not going to quit," Meyerson said. "He's not going to abandon The Volunteers. But he's not going to do what you wanted. There has to be some in-between."

Rollins was adamant. Perot would sink like a stone if he didn't entrust the campaign to people who knew how to run one. "There's no in-between," he said.

"There has to be," Meyerson argued. They could simply fire the pros and announce what amounted to an anticandidacy: no handlers, no ads till fall, no more speeches to interest groups—nothing that smacked of politics as usual.

"You can do all that," Rollins said, "but you're going to wind up at 12 percent of the vote."

They fenced some more, getting nowhere. Their two worlds were galaxies apart.

"So what you're telling us," Meyerson said at length, "is that there are only two ways. We do it your way, or we quit."

"Yeah," Rollins answered.

Luce and Meyerson went off to see Perot—the campaign had long since been reduced to shuttle diplomacy—and came back with what Rollins mistook for a hopeful response. If they were going to go his way, the two asked Rollins over lunch, what was it going to take? Perot was a businessman. He hadn't built his fortune flying by wire. He needed things spelled out to him. He wanted a timeline, a media plan, a detailed strategic explanation of what he was supposed to do and why.

It wasn't the first time they had asked, but the request came from Perot this time, and Rollins took it as a go sign; the campaign, he told himself, was back in business. When he got back to the office, he started punching buttons, and by the end of the day, a plan had been flung together to something like Perot's specifications. Ads would go up by the weekend, after the Democrats had struck their tents in New York. Perot would declare his candidacy the following Monday and, ten days later, would follow up with a filmed prime-time speech disclosing his economic plan. His answer to the conventions would be a late-summer unconvention, a giant red-white-and-blue picnic, maybe in the Rose Bowl, maybe on the Mall in Washington. It would be a Norman Rockwell painting come to life.

Rollins delivered the plan to Luce that evening, starting it up the chain of command. The next day, he sat in his office waiting for a response; there was not much else left for him to do. The Tuesday morning command meeting had been canceled. Perot was around headquarters, but was plainly avoiding him. When visitors did drop in, the tidings they bore were usually unhappy. Perot had fallen back to 20 percent in Paul Maslin's overnight polling. He was back where he had begun, in third place.

Rollins's humor was further darkened by the collapse of one of his last, desperate operations to jump-start the campaign: a negotiation, conducted through proxies on both sides, to get Governor Wilder of Virginia on the ticket as Perot's running mate. The idea had begun as a gleam in the eye of Joe Trippi, who had been media consultant to Wilder's own aborted run for the Democratic nomination and had been quietly promoting him for vice president ever since. One door closed the day Clinton chose Al Gore for his ticket, without having given Wilder so much as a look. But Trippi sensed another opening. He called Maslin, a comrade from past campaigns, and told him Wilder might be available to run with Perot. His tone was light, as if it were a joke; he was half afraid the feeler might be taken that way.

It wasn't. Rollins and his people had been agonizing for weeks over the need to find a person of size for the number two spot; Perot had promised a world-class choice, but neither he nor his men, Luce and Meyerson, had got very far with the search. An early working list of a hundred possibilities included at least one dead man, which, as a Rollins man smirked, should certainly satisfy the demand for somebody unconventional. Other names flew back and forth among the tribes like shuttlecocks in badminton: Jack Kemp, Bill Moyers, Paul Tsongas, even Cokie Roberts of ABC News. None got past the talk stage; the selection process was bobbing dead in the water the day Maslin came forward and plopped Wilder's name on the table.

Wilder was an incumbent politician, which was strike one in the

Perot campaign, and was a figure of controversy in his own state and his own party as well. But he was not without attractions as a complement to Perot. He was certainly different—a black maverick Democrat who governed a major state and knew how to balance a budget. The mere fact of his office would bring Perot a certain added legitimacy, at a point when not many prominent ins of either party were eager to be associated with him. Rollins and his deputy, Charlie Leonard, loved the politics of it; to Leonard, it was like the rush in a pinball game when you hit all the right bumpers and start collecting bonus points.

Their enthusiasm alone was not enough, given the isolation chamber they had been sealed into; Rollins had been effectively cut out of the search, on the suspicion that he could not be counted on either to think original thoughts on the subject or to keep the selection process secret. But this time, Tom Luce, to his later regret, let himself be drawn partway into the game. His sense of urgency overcame the reservations he felt about Wilder, and he authorized Maslin to keep the talks going. At one point, Luce himself joined the pursuit; he called Wilder in Richmond and proposed, with careful indirection, that the two of them meet and talk about "something important."

The scheme was doomed from the start, in part by its origins on Planet Rollins, in part by the tyranny of the clock. In three days' time, Wilder was due to lead the Virginia delegation to the Democratic convention, where he would be under enormous pressure to endorse Clinton. If he was to bolt his own party, he needed an answer fast, and it couldn't be maybe; at the very least, there had to be staff-level talks early in the week to review his background, the prelude to a formal laying-on of hands. "Those guys are in a bunker now," Maslin warned Luce; the story had leaked, and the heat on Wilder was rising dangerously. But Luce was having second thoughts by then, and when he took the question to Perot the day the convention opened, the answer was no. He wasn't going to let Wilder or anybody else force his hand like that.

Maslin called Trippi in New York and told him the verdict. "If you guys issued a Sherman statement today," he said, "nobody here would blame you. But Rollins says to gut it out as long as you can. He says, 'The old man doesn't know it yet, but Doug Wilder is the only choice he has, and he'll know it in ten or fifteen days.'"

Trippi was incredulous. "You want us to gut this thing out for ten or fifteen *days?*" he said.

"No one here will blame you if you don't," Maslin said. "But gut it out."

Trippi dutifully carried the message to Wilder's people, knowing that it was impossible. Wilder, who loathed Clinton, endorsed him anyway and used the noise about his flirtation with Perot as further leverage to get himself slotted for a speech to the convention in prime time; at least some of his aides guessed that that might have been his intent all along.

The deal was dead, and with it, so far as Rollins and his men were concerned, an opportunity for Perot to reignite his foundering candidacy. Rollins brooded in his office. Maslin came in. "I think it's going fast," he said. "I'm not sure it can be salvaged anymore if we don't move quickly."

By then, nothing was moving at all. The next morning, Charlie Leonard picked Rollins up at his apartment.

"I think this is our last day," Rollins said.

"If not today, this week," Leonard said.

"No, it's today," Rollins insisted.

It was. Perot's demeanor was conspicuously sunny that morning, even excited. His people presumed it was because his economic plan was finally ready. The delay in getting it done had been one of his sorest disappointments in the campaign, given how much he cared about it; the plan was to be his legacy to America, a monument that would endure whether he won or lost. Its slow fruition owed at least partly to his own quirky stewardship of his campaign. Its principal author, John White, had had to build it from scratch with no staff—he had only a volunteer national network of graduate students to draw on—and only infrequent access to Perot himself. When the two men did get together, it was as if they were talking past one another, in different languages. White spoke and wrote in the gluey lingua franca of economics. Perot's native tongue was Texarkana homespun; at one presentation, he told White, "Goddamit, get it *simple.*" White thought the plan should set forth what *could* be done in the real world of politics and compromise. Perot wanted to talk about what *should* be done; his single, irreducible goal was to balance the budget in five years, no matter what it took.

The process had been at an impasse for weeks; the low-pain, low-gain formulations White sent forward were intercepted before they got to Perot's desk and were sent back with orders to get tough. White finally had. His final version was red with the blood of sacred cows, among them defense, social security, medicare, medicaid, and farm subsidies, and it required some tax increases as well. But it promised a balanced budget on Perot's schedule.

"Jesus Christ," Jordan said, contemplating the carnage at a preliminary run-through, "where are we all going to work if this thing goes through?"

"I don't know about you," White said. "I'm going to be an organic dairy farmer."

The finished product answered Perot's demands for a hard-truth package, and his calendar had been cleared so that he could go over it with White, Jordan, and some of his own men. The prospect pleased him, but it was more than a day in the sandbox of public policy that had brought his smile back to life. He had come to a decision on the Rollins question, and while he tinkered with his pie charts, his people arranged a lunch with Rollins to execute his orders.

Ross had changed his mind since their last conversation, Luce and Meyerson said as the three sat down to their last meal together. He wanted Rollins gone, and his forty guys with him.

Rollins said he, too, had been rethinking his situation and had decided that he didn't want to stay anyway.

Perot's men blamed him, as Perot did, for the latest leaks—especially the embarrassing story about how Jordan had almost quit. It looked to them like a power play on his part, and they said so.

"Wait a minute," Rollins objected.

"Who has a vested interest?"

"Listen," Rollins said, "I didn't want Hamilton to quit. I've hand-held Hamilton every goddam day for three weeks. He's my only backup. I don't want him out of here. There's no power play—hell, I had it all."

Perot's men were unmoved. In Luce's eyes, leaks were to Rollins what drinks were to an alcoholic; he might *tell* you he had sworn off, but he hadn't and probably couldn't. The Jordan story had to have come from him.

"You guys are nuts," Rollins said. There were a lot of people who could have leaked the Jordan story, Jordan's own friends among them. But the larger point they needed to understand was that politics wasn't like business—you *had* to talk to the press.

"Ross hears that when you go back home on weekends, you go to dinner parties with these reporters, and you're bad-mouthing the campaign," Meyerson said.

"Wait a minute, Mort," Rollins said. "I've been home two goddam nights since I got here, and neither night did my wife and I go out to dinner parties. It's just fucking absurd." *He* wasn't the one who had tried to quit, he reminded Perot's men. "I have been in this fucking city thirty-three out of the last thirty-five days. I've seen my wife two nights. Every single goddam day, I've gotten up and I've come in here and I've tried to win this campaign, no matter how shitty it's been. And every goddam night, I've walked out of here depressed because I haven't been able to accomplish anything. I've got up the next morning knowing that I'm the leader, that I *couldn't* be depressed—I had to get my troops back up. Every single day, we came in here and put plans on the goddam table and tried to move this son of a bitch forward. There's not a day that I have been here that I haven't been trying to win this thing. I just resent this horseshit."

"Oh, it's just a thought process," Meyerson said.

"It's a fucked-up thought process," Rollins said.

They went back to headquarters. Rollins started making the rounds, alerting his men to the descending blade. At least one person he encountered thought Rollins had been crying.

Luce retreated to his own office to organize a press conference and start calling in the Rollins people on the hit list. Perot was there with him when Jordan walked in.

"Rollins is gone," Perot said. "I know you want to go, too. I hope you won't."

"Will the next four months be like the last three?" Jordan asked.

"I'm not going to let y'all handle me," Perot said.

Jordan asked for time to think.

"I hope you'll stay here," Perot repeated. "But in fairness to you, I want you to know I may pull the plug on the whole thing."

Afterward, Rollins found Jordan. "I'm out of here," he said. "Are you ready to go now?"

"I don't know," Jordan answered. The economic plan was coming along—a tough package of the sort that had drawn Jordan to Dallas in the first place. Perot had agreed to ads promoting it. He seemed serious about running a stripped-down, no-bull candidacy of the sort he and the purists had been talking about, a campaign not just to elect a president but to reform the process by example. Jordan felt torn.

"Hamilton," Rollins urged, "for three goddam weeks you've wanted to get out of here. I'm going. Everybody's going."

"Well, I don't want to get caught up in everybody leaving," Jordan said.

"What better time is there?" Rollins asked.

Just about any time, Jordan thought; he wasn't about to join Rollins's bunch, going out under a big, dark cloud. "Can I have an hour to think about it?" he asked.

"Shit, Hamilton, it's been announced," Rollins said. "We're gone. We're outta here in an hour."

He was stunned to learn at his own public execution that afternoon that Jordan had agreed to stay on as manager. Perot had absented himself from the event, as he had from Rollins's hiring; it was left to Luce and Rollins to make it sound like an amicable divorce. Luce said the campaign would carry on. Rollins read a terse prepared statement, then took questions. "I will spend the next thirty years of my life," he said, "with my wife saying, 'I told you so.'"

When it was over, he moved through headquarters one last time, thanking The Volunteers in the phone room and counseling his own men. The corridors were aswarm with security guards, shutting down offices, unplugging computers, and cutting off phones. "What is this, Nazi Germany?" Joe Canzeri was yelling. "The train for Buchenwald leaves at five." Outside, TV crews found parking tickets on their vans; somebody inside had called the cops.

The scene was surreal. Rollins spoke with Jordan again.

"Jesus Christ, you're not going to last two days here, Hamilton," he said. "What do you think—this is a game? Did you talk to Perot?"

"Yeah," Jordan told him. "He said I could stay."

"*Getting* to stay and *wanting* to stay are two different things," Rollins said. "Did Perot say he was going to change the campaign?"

"No," Jordan said. "He isn't going to do it our way."

Rollins left. Jordan stayed behind and, at six o'clock, convened a meeting of the survivors. "We've still got a campaign," he told them. "We've still got a field operation, and we're going to look forward." Not everybody looked convinced. Jordan tried a bit of gallows humor to lighten the mood. "I've always said we were better off if we were behind in the polls in the late summer," he joked, "and by George, we've done it!"

In fact, Perot was within hours of deciding to throw in his last cards. The TV newscasts were already alive with speculation that he was quitting when John Jay Hooker called from Nashville and asked if it were so.

"No," Perot said. "But I've got to see some sunshine."

There was none. His still undeclared candidacy was in ruins. His market share of the vote was in a nine-G nosedive, dropping ten points in four days. Clinton was back from the dead; he would be nominated that night and beatified the next by his victory-starved party. The dirty-tricks crowd at Republican headquarters was at it again, or so Perot had heard from his shadowy private network of connections. The word was that they had pasted up a fake photo of one of his daughters, purporting to show her in a compromising position with another woman. The plan was to sell it to the tabloids.

It was sometimes hard for outsiders to measure where fact ended and credulity began in the mind of Ross Perot. What mattered was that he seemed genuinely to believe the story, and to be horrified by it. His dream was coming undone. He went home to his compound on Strait Lane that night, close to the end of his tolerance for pain. Luce and Meyerson came by at eight o'clock.

I'm getting out, Perot told them. He had already canceled appearances in Minnesota and Virginia in the next two days.

Luce argued for staying in. The polls were volatile; look how Clinton had turned *his* around. Perot would bounce back once he put his economic plan on the table and reopened his campaign for business, this time as his own man on his own terms.

But Luce had used up his chits by then, and Meyerson's size-up of the situation was as unhappy as Perot's. He had lost whatever heart he had ever had for the race. He no longer thought it was winnable.

I think we need to cut this thing off, Perot said finally. A press conference had already been scheduled for ten the next morning. Perot would take Luce's place at the lectern and would drop out of a race he had never quite put himself in.

The word was already buzzing around headquarters when, a few minutes after ten, Perot appeared in the pressroom. He looked tired and gray. He praised The Volunteers for having reawakened both parties to reality, but, as he spun out his rationale, they had done their work all too well. "The overriding change was the revitalization of the Democratic Party," he said. With their revival, it had become all but certain that the race would be deadlocked if he stayed in and that the next president would be chosen by the House of Representatives. Such an outcome, he said, would be disruptive for the country and impossible for him. He had known all along that he had no chance if the election was settled in the House; he would have had to win a clean majority of the electoral votes if he was to win at all.

The explication came as news to Rollins, watching the valedictory on TV in his apartment. There was Ross up on the screen, a wounded man cutting his losses and wrapping the decision in civics-book reasons. His troops, his friends, even his family knew that his real motives were personal, some mix of discouragement with his progress and concern for his wife and children. With them, he had never made a major issue of his fear of deranging the country or its institutions; he seemed to them to have crossed that bridge before he ever put himself in play.

The announcement done, he walked away, to go back to work, he said. He left Luce behind to thank The Volunteers at headquarters; Perot didn't want to face them or their disappointment in him. His fear was well-grounded. His switchboard was alight again, some callers begging him to get back in, some suggesting various anatomical impossibilities he might want to try. At Boston headquarters, a local Volunteer leader fed Perot petitions into a paper shredder. "I feel like I've been stood up by a hooker," he said. In Ventura County, California, campaigners pulled down an eight-foot statue of the Plain Texas Talker, draped a noose around its neck, and forklifted it into a Dumpster. In East Los Angeles, a twenty-three-year-old campaigner faxed Perot a note. "My parents taught me respect for my elders," it said, "but under this situation, if I was in a room with you, I would kick your ass." At Dallas headquarters, a surviving staffer watched Perot explaining himself on *Larry King Live* the next night and shouted at the screen, "Fuck you, Ross—why don't you shut up and go home?"

Yet there were those who wondered even then whether Perot had really quit or had just taken a furlough from the wear and the abuse that had become his daily lot. Hooker had phoned again that morning, and after the news conference, Perot, faithful as ever, returned the call.

"We need you," Hooker said. "What happened? Why? What has changed?"

Perot repeated what he had told the world, about not wanting to do anything disruptive.

"Is there any possibility you would get back into it?" Hooker asked.

"I'm still in the stadium," Perot said. "I'm on the sidelines, I'm not in the game, but I am still here."

"Are you going to continue to be registered in all fifty states?"

"Yes," Perot said.

"So if you're going to be registered in all fifty states, you're still in the stadium, then we'll see," Hooker said. He was smiling again as he rang off, promising to call back. The first Perot campaign was over, but the game of catch was on again, and Hooker was betting his throwing arm that Ross, having stayed in the stadium, would sooner or later get back in the game.

The Plain Texas Talker: Ross Perot led a grassroots uprising against the political order. *(Ira Wyman)*

I'm Ross, you're the boss: The Volunteers turned a Perot rally into a two-way laying on of hands. *(Jacques Chenet/Newsweek)*

The mad-as-hell vote: A Perot supporter hoists a placard twitting the vice president. *(Jacques Chenet/Newsweek)*

Flying solo: The anticandidate preferred running for president his own way, alone. *(Jacques Chenet/Newsweek)*

Coming aboard: Ed Rollins and Hamilton Jordan started a short, unhappy run as handlers. *(David J. Sams)*

The Spirit of '92: Perot's office in Dallas was a museum of his own and his country's past. *(Gerald Schuman/ZUMA)*

V
The Choice

Something happened.
—Geoffrey Garin, Democratic polltaker,
December, 1992

26.

The Boys on the Bus

They called it the First Thousand Miles, the beginning of the long, arduous journey to Election Day and, if fortune smiled on them, the White House. Its planners started from the premise that Michael Dukakis had lost the presidency in the weeks after his nomination in 1988, going home to Massachusetts to brood for the rest of the summer while a nineteen-point lead melted away. Whatever the larger merit of their claim to be Democrats of a new kind, Bill Clinton and Al Gore weren't going to make *that* mistake again. The day after their debut as a ticket, they and their wives climbed aboard a chartered bus, cranked up Bonnie Raitt on the sound system, and headed westward out of New York into the heart of small-town America.

Like most successful exercises in our politics, the tour was an act of artifice—a showpiece put together by a Hollywood producer, Mort Engelberg, from an original idea by a campaign manager, David Wilhelm. But it was an undeniable masterwork of the form, its brilliant imagery of youth and purpose evoking real passion from real people. For six days, the caravan rolled like a rock tour over wide concrete interstates and back-country blue highways in Indiana, Illinois, and Missouri. Clusters of townsfolk and farmers stood by the roads, waving at their hopes going by. Families watched from lawn chairs in their front yards. Small children lit sparklers and held them in the air. Three men stopped their combine in a field and draped a giant Clinton-Gore banner across it.

The bus delivered the nominees to places long neglected in an age of jet stops in major media markets, and big turnouts greeted them everywhere. Some people had come to cheer, some just to gawk at the latest celebrities from Back East. It didn't matter; the crowds became part of the theater of the tour, the extras populating an unrich, un-poor, un-urban American midland that Democratic candidates had been flying over for years. At every stop, the Clintons and Gores waded into the crowds, shaking hands and signing autographs. Gore would speak first, warming up the audience. Hillary and Tipper would smile, wave, and hug like sorority sisters. Then Clinton would bend into his stump speech, an emotive sermon on putting people first again. The connection between the company on stage and the crowds before them was real and powerful. When they played Vandalia, Illinois, hours behind schedule, candles lit the night, and ten thousand people sang "God Bless America."

The effect on Clinton himself was intoxicating, to the distress of his handlers; euphoria, in their trade, is a forbidden drug to be ingested only on winning election nights. But after the serial punishments he had endured on the way to the nomination, Clinton found it irresistible. His throat was raw, and his hands were cut and puffy from too many handshakes, the stigmata of his new success. It was campaigning as he had always hoped and dreamed it would be, a love feast centered on him and blotting all the bad news out of the media coverage. And if the road show was contrived, well, that was in the very nature of popular democracy. Clinton was something of a Lincoln buff, and the leg of the journey through Lincoln country had appealed to the realist as well as the romantic in him; even Honest Abe, he liked to say, was one of our more calculating presidents.

The trip began a sunny time for him, short but deliciously sweet. He and Gore ought naturally to have been rivals, two princes of similar age and ideology from adjoining states. Instead, as one staffer remarked, they were acting more like siblings reunited after a long separation—the good brother, Gore, and the mischievous brother, Clinton, swapping stories, sharing memories, spinning ideas, learning from one another. The synergy growing between them seemed even to affect their performances, as if style were something catching. Gore, usually wooden, lightened up. Clinton, often rambly, buckled down.

He seemed to gather renewed physical strength as well, borrowing energy from his crowds—"October crowds," he bragged, "in July." To friends, he *looked* better than he had since the heavens opened on him in New Hampshire; his eyes were less baggy, and he dropped some of the junk-food poundage he had picked up on the road. There was a note of wonder in his voice when he spoke of the numbers of people who came out to see him and the intensity he saw in their eyes. One day in Seattle, he did his speech and worked the crowd as usual, then came back to his hotel suite just before dusk to catch his breath. His shirt was soaked through with sweat, but he stood gazing out over Puget Sound for a few moments, thinking aloud about the feelings he had stirred and the responsibility they placed on him. The weight of it was awesome. People brought him their problems and actually *cried*.

"You look at their faces," he said, "and they're allowing themselves to do something they haven't done for a long time: believe again."

The polls, in that honeymoon season, seemed to confirm the evidence of his eyes; the news they brought him was almost dangerously good. With Perot out of the way, the dynamic of the race was back where he and his strategists had wanted it all along. The issue was the economy, and the choice was change versus more of the same. Stan Greenberg did a three-day national survey in late July, with the convention fresh in memory and the bus tour still on the road. Clinton was burying Bush by twenty-two points, at 56-34. The convention and the buscapade had transformed his image, from "too slick" in April to steady, honest, trustworthy—even, by overwhelming vote, a family man who shared the common values of the people. Voters thought Clinton had an economic plan. They suspected that the president didn't, and only 38 percent were even considering voting for him, a devastatingly low ceiling on his future.

"Bush is cooked," Mike Donilon, a new recruit on the media team, said when he saw the numbers.

"I'm framing this," Greenberg said. "It cannot get better than this. It cannot."

Clinton's team knew it could get a great deal worse. "The worst thing they can do is turn us back into Slick Willie," Mandy Grunwald fretted one day. It didn't take an astrophysicist to know that the Republicans would try precisely that; they would come at Clinton on the issue of his trustworthiness, rubbing salt in all his old wounds, and it would require the most rigorous discipline on his part and theirs to keep the choice framed to his advantage.

That meant that Clinton had to use the month between conventions, not squander it as Dukakis had. The summer, in Grunwald's view, was a season of opportunity—a time to soften up Bush for an all-out fall offensive built around the interwoven themes of people-first economics and change. She proposed to do this by raising a trust question about the president, for a change, portraying him as "a typical politician who broke his promises." But driving home a message in a campaign requires a relentlessness bordering on monomania. The Clinton of the bus tour wasn't delivering that, or anything much more, indeed, than stunning visuals on the evening news. His handlers worried that he was out there getting *too* high on crowd noise—that he was wandering off his message and basking instead in the sunshine of his unaccustomed popularity.

He came in still aglow from Saint Louis, the last stop on the First Thousand Miles; thirty thousand people had shown up there for the grand finale. He found his people waiting for him with incongruously long faces. Greenberg had followed up his good-news poll with a second survey testing the damage potential of the incoming rounds they could expect from the Bush campaign and rehearsing various defenses against them. At the beginning of the poll, Clinton was leading the president by nineteen points. Then, the polltakers read respondents a broadside assault on him as a thinly disguised liberal who had proposed billions in new taxes and spending; who had ducked the draft in wartime and now wanted to weaken the nation's defenses; and who had embraced a left social agenda favoring gay rights, abortion on demand, and condom distribution in the schools. The attack, unanswered, cut Clinton's margin almost in half.

There was some comfort in the poll, mostly borne in on a rising tide of antipathy toward the president. Specific answers to specific charges did Clinton's cause some good, but the best defense proved to be a good offense. "This is just more of the same old 'read my lips,' Willie Horton–type politics from George Bush," one test response read. "Instead of doing anything about the real problems facing this country, like the economy and health care, George Bush would rather sling mud. . . . The American people just cannot afford another four more years of the same old politics from George Bush." The formulation worked; when people heard it, Clinton's lead over Bush ballooned back out from ten points to seventeen.

Still, some of the particulars did hurt Clinton, especially those having to do with his record in Arkansas. The deadliest was the charge, already afloat, that he had raised taxes 128 times as governor. The number was bad enough by itself and worse in the context of his claim to have been a successful governor. It made people wonder what he had bought with all those increases, given Arkansas's low rank among the states on most measures of public well-being, and it reinforced the suspicion that he would be back at it again as president.

"No wonder they have that big sign out in Houston: 'Failed Governor of a Small State,'" Grunwald said when the strategists gathered to review the poll. "What do you think the chances are that the opening line of their spot will be quoting Clinton—'Come on down to Arkansas'?"

"'We went down to Arkansas, and here's what we found,'" Frank Greer said, continuing the script.

"If we can't keep the focus on Bush and the economy and not being able to afford four more years, and they get the focus on us, they can *kill* us," Grunwald concluded. That had to be their line of attack right through to Labor Day.

"We've got a lot of work to do," Greenberg said. "If we were running against Clinton, I could find a strategy in this data."

"We've probably lost ten points this week," James Carville guessed, in spite of all the excitement over Bill and Al and Hillary and Tipper on the bus.

"Momentum is not a message," Grunwald said.

"Mandy, that is a home-run point," Carville said. He was worried about the way things were going—about a certain cockiness he sensed in the campaign and in the candidate. "My main concern is that Clinton is not being disciplined enough," he said. "That he's returning to his old ways. He really never got out of them."

There *had* been some slippage in his polls by the time he got back to Little Rock. "It's the soufflé settling," Grunwald said; that, anyway, was how they were spinning it to the press.

The line was not comforting to Carville. Greenberg's new poll was sobering, he thought, a window into how vulnerable Clinton really was. The Republicans had only been picking around the edges so far. Sometimes, soufflés collapsed.

"The answer is the economy," he said.

"Over and over," Grunwald said. "I don't want him to coast. He's pulling his punches."

"I agree with that," Greenberg said. "The message for most of the week was bus, crowds, and stunned reporters when people actually liked him."

Their gingerly recommendation to Clinton, when they got his attention, was to put a populist frame around his message and stick to it no matter what. They weren't trying to change him into Tom Harkin or Jerry Brown, Grunwald said; he wouldn't have to change a single policy position to make the frame fit. It was simply a matter of emphasizing things that were already there—his promises to invest in people and protect the middle class—and giving them a populist edge. You couldn't *be* too populist in the political climate of 1992, Grunwald argued. Much as he hated the word, populism was the booster rocket that could propel Clinton to the presidency.

This time, the advice took; Clinton headed west the next day, and his speeches were precisely on target. "I believe you are here because you want to change your country, because you want to take your country back," he told a big crowd on the Spokane riverfront. Greenberg's polling warned Clinton away from calling Bush a "failed president," a bit too strong a phrase for popular taste. But it was okay to say that the country had spent the past twelve years "in the grip of a failed *idea*" called trickle-down economics—a rationale for an order in which the rich controlled 90 percent of the wealth and the middle class declined. It wouldn't work that way in a people-first economy, Clinton said; there would be more jobs, better schools, affordable health care for everybody. The crowd loved it, and him. "There's no sign of the Slick Willie problem," a local TV reporter gushed. "This is where Bill Clinton is the best."

For a brief time, the president seemed almost to be conceding that judgment without a fight. Clinton's handlers regarded their opposite numbers on Fifteenth Street with an edginess bordering on dread. The top guns on the Bush team had been winning presidential elections since 1980; none of Clinton's generals had even played the game at so high a level. The special object of their concern was James Baker, then still barricaded in his office at the department of state. It was accepted as a given that Bush would draft him to run the show, and Clinton's team awaited his arrival in the manner of a sheriff expecting Billy the Kid to show up in town. Baker was a gut fighter with the face of a deacon. Carville practically alone among Clinton's handlers doubted that the guy was as good as his reputation, and even that appraisal was tinctured with envy; the mere fact that he *had* the reputation told you something about his gifts at spin.

In the view from Little Rock, the wonder was how slow the president's handlers were at engaging Clinton and how faltering their step was when they did try. It certainly wasn't a want of ammunition that held them back. As a way to rouse the troops, Greenberg did a make-believe "Memo to George Bush" from Bob Teeter, the campaign chairman, outlining how Clinton could be undone. "If the election is about the economy, we lose," he wrote, affecting Teeter's voice. Bush had to change the subject to what was wrong with Clinton—knock him off the pedestal he currently occupied and redo him as a weak, dangerous liberal who had failed as governor and couldn't be trusted as a man. "Bill Clinton must be made unacceptable," the fake memo said. "After Clinton has been tarnished, voters will be looking for a way out of this malaise, and we must be ready to make George Bush the answer."

The memo was deadlier than anything then emanating from Bush-Quayle headquarters; the president's vaunted team was still groping for a coherent attack strategy. The greater danger to Clinton was the overconfidence spreading in his own campaign, a climate of contentment so pervasive that Carville threw one of his calculated tantrums to try to jar his people awake. "Some of you think Republicans are just like us—that they just have a different philosophy," he raged at a staff gathering. "They're not. They're seasoned. They're professional. They're *ruthless!* And they're *rotten!*" He glanced around the room with slitted eyes, then got up and walked out.

The blowup had something like the effect of shock radio in drive time, strong but transitory. The campaign seemed then to be humming along nicely on cruise control. It was summertime in Little Rock and life was a beach; by mid-August, Clinton's lead had widened to twenty-six points in Greenberg's latest sounding, and the other side had only just begun to fight.

In the War Room

This time, when the attacks did start, Clinton's generals were ready. Dukakis once again was their model of how not to act; he had frozen under enemy fire, cowering in his bunker when he should have been shooting back. The Clinton campaign didn't believe in bunkers. Its command post instead was the War Room, and at its center sat James Carville, his stringy frame hunched behind the outsized conference table that served as his desk, his dais, his meeting place, his conning tower, and his come-to-Jesus tent. Greenberg, Grunwald, and Stephanopoulos all had their assigned workstations nearby, but Captain Carville was in charge, his commission from the Clintons reinforced by periodic orders, threats, insults, and sermons to his young staff.

"Run, don't walk!" he would command.

"I'm going to erupt sometime very soon," he would warn.

"At the minimum," he said one day, gesturing toward the Associated Press ticker, "I'm going to really embarrass someone and at a maximum, *fire* someone if that wire isn't watched every minute, and we get asked about something on it."

"I'm going to be irritated all day," he said another time, when somebody proposed holding more staff meetings. "This ain't no job for the fainthearted, y'know? You're talking about *talking* more. I'm talking about *thinking* more. I'm not your mama. I'm not your daddy. I can't think for you every part of the day."

Under his lash, his War Room fairly pulsated, even when not much was actually happening in the outside world. Its mission was equivalent to that of the Patriot missile in the Gulf war, shooting down enemy rockets before they did significant damage. Its weapons were the paraphernalia of high-speed modern communications; the command group worked to a background cacophony of clicking keyboards, grunting copiers, droning television monitors, and the incessantly chattering AP wire. Its overriding imperative had been reduced by Carville to three words and pasted on a wall where no one could miss it, ever. THE ECONOMY, STUPID, the sign said. Nothing else mattered; nothing else could be allowed to get in the way.

Under that battle flag, the War Room succeeded to a remarkable degree in hijacking the agenda for the fall campaign. Staffers tracked every stop made and every word spoken by Bush and his surrogates, and dug out whatever damning material they could find to rebut them. An overnight crew monitored the news and got briefing papers ready for Carville and Stephanopoulos when they rolled in each morning at six o'clock. A satellite dish at headquarters pulled in events as they were happening. If he saw something that troubled him, Stephanopoulos would ring Begala on the road with Clinton and trigger an instant reply. No charge was to be left unanswered, no thrust unparried, no claim unchallenged—not even for the duration of a single news cycle. By fall, so the other side complained, you couldn't read a favorable story about the Bush campaign without encountering George Stephanopoulos somewhere around the third, fourth, or fifth paragraph, saying it wasn't so.

The first real test of the operation, Clinton's team knew, would be the Republican convention in mid-August. It was sure to be a festival of Bill-bashing, and Carville put the War Room on a war footing; he wanted an answer to every line in Senator Phil Gramm's keynote speech, he said, no more than an hour after it was uttered. The presumption was that Bush's men would try to beat Clinton as they had beaten Dukakis, by incinerating him. "They have no other choice," Grunwald said, not with the polls looking the way they did. The strafing began, indeed, in the week before the convention, and as the War Room crew sat waiting for the opening gavel, the tension was palpable in the air. Only Carville, surveying his domain from behind the vast plain of his worktable, seemed calm contemplating what the Republicans might pull.

"They're just screwed up," he told his edgy colleagues. "They're not that good. We're freaked from the last go-round."

He had shown up for work on day one of the convention in his usual jeans and a fatigue jacket stenciled SEABEES. Someone handed him bootleg advance copies of the two big opening-night speeches, by Pat Buchanan and Ronald Reagan; they had been faxed to the War Room by a friendly reporter in Houston. The Gipper's appearance on the program wasn't a worry; he had always had a way of making Bush look smaller by comparison, and now his presence connected his successor to a no longer lamented past. Carville scanned Buchanan's text, with its summons to a holy war for America's soul and its slap shots at "Hillary" as a radical feminist bomb thrower. "Do they talk about problems?" Carville said, getting an early start on the night's spin. "No—they attack the spouse."

His own first agenda item was, in his phrase, to screw around with their day, and his pal Stephanopoulos found a way—calling Bush on a pledge to fire anybody on his side who raised the issue of Clinton's marital problems. The president's friend Bob Mosbacher, general chairman of the Bush-Quayle campaign, had done precisely that; so had a senior administration official. Would Bush sack them? Stephanopoulos dropped the challenge into a press briefing and was surprised at the furor he set off.

"Now I'm a little worried," he told Carville afterward.

"Shoot, what are we trying to do?" Carville told him. "Screw around with them. You went down there and got it done."

He was right. The story led the evening news that night. Bush's day had been satisfactorily screwed around with.

"It worked," Stephanopoulos said, sipping a pre-dinner martini at Doe's in Little Rock late that night.

"And you were panicked," Carville teased.

"We're in for a great week," Stephanopoulos said. "They chanted 'Four more years' ten times in the beginning of Reagan's speech."

Greenberg laughed. "Four more years is the voters' greatest fear," he said.

There would be a brief flutter of anxiety in the War Room at midweek, when Clinton's lead withered to six points in one poll and eleven in another. "Not too good," Carville muttered. But Greenberg massaged the numbers and counseled calm. Bush was just getting a normal convention bounce, he told his colleagues; the important thing was that Clinton's favorable rating had held steady through three days of nonstop bombardment. "It's no free fall," Greenberg said. "It's pretty stable."

Still, a tingle of nervousness lingered in the air when Carville assembled his young grunts for the last night of the convention. "On your tippy-toes," he told them; the president would be speaking that night, going for a home run, and they would be trying their best to spoil it for him. The command team saw their opening in an advance text of the speech, nestled among the attacks on Clinton as a man who couldn't be trusted anywhere near the tax code. Bush was actually promising to lower taxes and balance the budget at the same time, a juggling trick of the sort he himself had once ridiculed as voodoo economics.

"The president said he'd do anything to get elected," Stephanopoulos crowed, rehearsing *his* lines for the evening, "and he obviously meant it. This makes 'read my lips' look responsible. He's trying to buy the election."

As it happened, Clinton's own issues team had put together briefing papers testing just such a proposal and concluding that it couldn't be done without major cuts in social security, medicare, and other sensitive programs. Stephanopoulos faxed copies of the documents to the networks and the major print media that night. Greenberg convened a quickie focus group to see how typical voters would react to the plan. They laughed at it.

"What a gift!" Stephanopoulos whooped. "It's a disaster for him."

Carville strode into the War Room, closely followed by two gofers lugging a case of beer. Bush was just was going on the air. "Have we got a tax hit?" Carville yelled. "This means the end of social security. Can you *believe* this crap?"

A corporal scurried off to mobilize the American Association of Retired Persons against the package. A research team gathered around a computer, framing a critique; copies of it were faxed to the network anchor booths in Houston before Bush had finished speaking. Stephanopoulos worked the phones to the major dailies, trying to steer the coverage away from the assaults on Clinton and toward the president's economic sleight of hand. He got through to a *Washington Post* reporter, did his spin, then hung up.

"Pretty good," he said.

"What'd he say?" Carville called out.

"Bush is going to get killed on the economics," Stephanopoulos said. "He's going to have a great night tonight and a world of hurt for the next two months."

Carville turned back to his staff. "Count up!" he commanded. "Anything that costs money—the tax cut, health care, school vouchers." He wanted to see Bush limp out of his own convention with reporters on his heels, demanding to know how he was going to pay for all the wonders he had promised. "The biggest thing we can do tomorrow is wire up the economists," he said. "The fewer politicians we have commenting on this and the more experts we have, the better. Never has a politician promised so much to win an election. He didn't promise the moon—he promised the *universe*."

Clinton already had the perfect forum for a rebuttal, a speech to the Economic Club of Detroit the next day, and his team adjourned to Stephanopoulos's office for a conference call on what he should say. Carville sat on the desk. The others crowded around. There was a riot of suggestions, everybody talking at once.

"We can say five hundred things," Carville interrupted. "The question is, what is the *one* thing we're gonna say?"

"The theme to gingerly underscore," somebody suggested, "is that they've been in charge for twelve years."

"We've got the whole campaign to do that," Carville said. "What I'm talking about is the one thing we do *tomorrow*. I want to put pressure on them all weekend that it's all gimmicks and it's all bullshit."

"It's not gimmicks, it's promises," Stephanopoulos said, and they came from the same politician who had sworn in the same forum four years earlier that he would tolerate no new taxes.

"We just need to say one thing," Carville repeated. "If you want to say something other than what I just said, fine—just don't say more than one thing. It's impossible to do all of what he said he would do. Keep the pressure on—then we can force him to produce the plan."

Their go-get-him manner hid an undercurrent of worry about some of what Bush had said about Clinton—questioning his fitness to be commander in chief, for example, and challenging his claim to be a new breed of Democrat. "I think his remarks diminished us a fair amount," Greenberg said. "It was very ugly. *Effective* ugly."

Carville knew it; the speech was tough, and it sharpened his own appetite for the attack. After work that night, he stopped for drinks in the dark, paneled bar of the Capital Hotel with Mike Donilon and Mike's brother Tom, a veteran operative who had joined up for the fall campaign.

"The next forty-eight hours are critical," Mike Donilon said. "We need to organize an all-out assault on the credibility of Bush's proposals. Go straight at him."

"We got to knock them off stride," Carville said.

"We've got to knock them right out of the box," Tom Donilon said, "because if we don't, it changes the whole dynamic of the race. Who's going to be against a tax cut?"

"We've got to beat this thing back," Carville growled. "*El pronto.*"

Waiting for the Big One

The world looked brighter to Clinton's people in the morning; it was a clear day, and you could see the White House again. "We're going to be okay," George Stephanopoulos told himself. The attacks that had sounded so scary the night before no longer troubled him greatly; the speech reminded him of Dukakis's to the Democrats in 1988, great for the hall but lousy as strategy for the months ahead. Bush would live to regret his promises on taxes and the budget. "We're going to *destroy* him on the economics," Stephanopoulos mused. "This is Tsongas Redux. We know how to win this race."

An overnight Greenberg poll, taken before and during the speech, reinforced Stephanopoulos's sense of comfort. Bush had got his bounce, no question about it; Clinton's lead had narrowed briefly to six points. But it would jump back to eleven in a matter of days, and his favorable rating was a solid 51 percent, exactly where it had been before the missiles started flying his way from Houston. Bush matched him for a day or so, then fell back. Before the convention, there had been some talk among Clinton's handlers about rushing an attack ad on the air, aimed at countering whatever the president and his propagandists might throw their way. Afterward, it no longer seemed so urgent; they had got the desired effect for nothing.

"Boy, the War Room worked last night," Stephanopoulos said.

"That's one of the reasons for not panicking," Carville said. "We're up and running. We're ready."

An unexpected fringe benefit was a sharp rise in Hillary Clinton's favorable ratings. She had been a favored target of the oratory in Houston, starting with Pat Buchanan's screed on opening night; the scenarists had made rather too much of her bad polls and had portrayed her as a hot-eyed radical feminist who would destroy the American family if she had her way—as, in a Clinton administration, she probably would. The shots had boomeranged badly. "The Republicans did for us what we could never have done," one of Clinton's strategists said. "They made her a sympathetic figure."

In fact, she was already well along with her own rehabilitation. Among friends, she admitted that she had not been fully prepared for the transition from Arkansas politics to the crueler rigors of a national campaign, and her husband's managers had done little to help her find her way around. Instead, she had had to improvise and had made a bad start of it with her tart tongue and her sometimes sharp-edged speeches. A cartoon Hillary had emerged, a power-hungry climber who would function as co-president if her husband got elected—and not necessarily as his junior partner. That wasn't who she was, she said. It was just that people didn't know her, so they had made her up for themselves, she guessed, drawing on what little snippets of information were available to them.

She would insist afterward that she hadn't really recreated herself. But, in consultation with her own informal circle of friends and advisers, she did submit to a bit of cosmetic surgery on her style. A costuming consultant from her friend Linda Bloodworth-Thomason's show *Designing Women* helped her pick a softer wardrobe. Her signature headbands disappeared in the process; a pricey Hollywood hair stylist redid her in a more modish, easy-care look. She learned to watch what she said in public and to reduce her thoughts to sound bites when the cameras were on her. If people were going to judge her on a series of fleeting signals, she wanted to make sure they were the signals *she* wanted to put out.

The press reported her changes, sometimes in mocking tones. Feminists charged her with selling out to advance her husband's career. Even her friends worried that she was suppressing part of herself—that, as one put it, she couldn't clearly say "who I am" anymore. In fact, she was enjoying herself as the New Hillary, after a lifetime spent with small regard for the whims and currents of fashion as against the demands of running a household, making a career, and counseling her husband. The only part of the remake she regretted, she confided to chums, had been having to cut her hair.

Her transformation in image paralleled Clinton's own, from riverboat swiftie to potential president. His passage out of his Slick Willie period was more remission than cure, a willing suspension of disbelief on the part of voters looking for somebody acceptable for the job. Perot was gone, and as Greenberg found in a poll between conventions, three-quarters of the electorate thought that Bush was doing a bad job as president. So intense was their desire to turn him out of office, Greenberg wrote, that they *wanted* to lay aside their negative feelings about Clinton. In the new atmosphere, people were beginning to say that he was an average guy after all, somebody who might just be good for them and for the economy. When Greenberg tested Clinton's people-first approach to economics, it scored three times higher than the counterproposition that he was just another tax-and-spend liberal of the old Democratic school. People still weren't sure what was in his plan. They were beginning a leap of faith in *him*.

But the ghost of Slick Willie lay in an unquiet grave, ready to be reawakened at a fresh hint of scandal or a further show of equivocation. Clinton couldn't simply waltz to the White House on blind confidence that he had a plan, Greenberg warned; the campaign would have to run "guerrilla attacks . . . [to] keep the president from turning this into an election about character" and to reassure voters that their newly positive picture of Clinton was real. The stability of his lead and his favorable ratings after the Republican convention could not be taken as evidence that he was bullet-proof. The single most vivid lesson of his rocky passage to the nomination had been that there was always one more thing.

Alarms accordingly sounded in Little Rock with the word that the press was poking around in the draft story again. Clinton had tried to lay that one to rest in August with one of the guerrilla actions Greenberg had written about, a speech to the annual convention of the American Legion. It was to be his "last" explanation of what he had and hadn't done to stay out of the war twenty-three years before. If people were still sufficiently bothered, he said, so be it; he could only wish that they would make their votes about the future and not the distant past. His appearance was warmly received, thanks in part to an accompanying cornucopia of promises to the veterans. "That was like passing a kidney stone," Carville said at the time; the Clinton team felt as if they had got a source of pain out of their systems at last.

But it never stopped haunting Clinton's handlers, in part because the subject seemed to spook *him* so badly, in part because they didn't know why it did. They guessed that he felt conflicted, even guilty about what he had done in the summer of '69 to stay out of the war; he had spent so much time since then rationalizing his behavior and justifying himself, in this theory, that he was no longer sure what the truth was. The problem for his team was that the hypothesis was only that, a hypothesis. Both Clintons had dismissed the fear that his draft history would be a problem in their earliest planning meetings in the mansion, and he had not been wholly forthcoming with them since.

Clinton himself knew that he had misunderstood the power of the issue and as a result had mishandled it from the very beginning. His plea, when pressed about it, was that he had thought it all settled long ago, when he first ran for Congress in 1974 and for governor in 1978. All of it had come up then, including the question of whether he had used his commitment to the ROTC to avoid serving in the war and then had welshed on it when he was no longer in harm's way. It was he, he said, who had sent reporters to talk to Colonel Holmes, the ROTC man who had signed him up. Holmes had told them at the time that, while he couldn't remember all the details, he was sure that there had been no wrongdoing.

That had closed the case, or so Clinton imagined; when he was preparing to run for president, he said one day during his first bus tour, he thought through just about everything he could be attacked on *except* the draft. Now, a decade and a half later, it appeared to him that somebody had got to Colonel Holmes—had "refreshed his memory in a way that was just flat-out wrong." Clinton's implication was that he was the victim of a dirty trick, though he had nothing but surmise to go on. Mainly, he said, he had felt "floored, just *floored*," by the colonel's turnaround so long after the fact. The hit had blindsided him, and he knew he had sounded both vague and defensive in his responses to it.

He had, by his own account, been innocent to the point of naïveté at the discovery that, once he stepped up to national politics, he wasn't in Arkansas any more. He had been surprised, he said, by the degree of media interest in his past and by its adversarial tone. It was as if his life had begun, for the press, on the day he announced for president, and the burden of proof was on him to justify everything about himself, no matter how long ago it had happened or how thoroughly it had been hashed over back home. If he had seen the draft story coming, he said, he would have swept up whatever letters and papers were still around as a way to refresh his own memory and get out in front of the story. Instead, he had handled it reactively and grudgingly, reneging on a promise to release those documents he had.

His rattled response to the issue baffled friends who had watched him sail through the Gennifer Flowers uproar with keel steady and smile in place. He himself seemed a bit bemused by the lacunae in his story, given the pride he took in what he called his steel-trap mind. He could remember and recite the phone number of one of his boyhood pals from the days when they were both nine years old, yet he kept drawing blanks, or claiming to, on a subject of far greater consequence to his young manhood and his adult ambitions. Could he *really* have forgotten so much about it? People repress traumatic memories, he said, and the Vietnam era had been an occasion of intense pain for him, a time when the verities of his southern childhood were at odds with his effort to stay out of a war he opposed. He had been raised on John Wayne movies, he said, and had always imagined himself fighting for his country. It had been a troubling time for him, very troubling, and as he had learned, "facts do slip way"—especially when you were under a lot of stress.

The gaps in his recollection posed a delicate problem for his handlers. The fresh stirrings of media interest in the story confirmed what they secretly suspected, that they had not yet laid it to rest. On the contrary, the Republicans had seen the signs of discomfort it caused Clinton and were using it like an electrical probe, trying to stir the Slick Willie in him back to life. His team was handicapped by its sense that only two people in the campaign knew all there was to know about Clinton and the draft. One was Clinton himself, with all the odd gaps in what he could or would remember. The other was Betsey Wright, and she held her knowledge as jealously close as a miser hoarding gold.

Wright's role in the campaign was clear enough; she functioned as the archivist of Clinton's past. Her place in his firmament was other-wise something of an enigma to his troops. They had first connected in the McGovern campaign in 1972; for most of the 1980s, she had served as Clinton's statehouse chief of staff and, in election years, his campaign manager. Her dedication to him was obviously fierce and sometimes stormy. But her wire-taut manner offended legislators, and Clinton himself had finally wearied of her tight, compartmentalized way of running his office. In 1989, he had forced her out, a difficult act for him even in less charged situations. People close to both of them said it had been, professionally, the equivalent of a divorce.

Her return to his service in 1992 had been difficult and sometimes disruptive. She reigned in isolation over her bunker next door to head-quarters, behind concrete walls and glass doors covered over with brown paper. It was nicknamed the Department of Defense, and she seemed to take the commission literally, guarding her store of Clinto-niana even from her own most senior colleagues. They resented her. She in turn felt cut off and patronized by them and made known her feelings in a series of memos, accusing them variously of being sexist, racist, or anti-Arkansas. Once, she tried to have Greenberg excluded from a meeting because he was from out-of-state, and she didn't feel comfortable in his alien presence.

Her zeal in trying to squelch damaging stories about Clinton was unquestioned. Her discretion was not; her secretiveness within the campaign sorted oddly with her sometimes compulsive talkativeness with the press. It was she who coined the impolitic phrase "bimbo eruptions," to describe the recurring rumors about Clinton and women, and it was she who very nearly undid an effort to answer one of the deadliest charges about his record in Arkansas. With great effort, Carville had sold the *Wall Street Journal* on a story debunking the Republican claim that Clinton had raised taxes and fees 128 times as governor—a count supportable only by an over-nice reading of the record. His coup worked; the *Journal* piece set off a wave of similar deconstructions elsewhere and forced Bush's troops to defend their arithmetic when they might have been rubbing Clinton's nose in it.

The authors of the ploy were still celebrating their victory when Wright undercut it and embarrassed them. She had ordered up her own search of the record. It proceeded with a literal-mindedness matching what the Republicans had done for partisan purposes; the *real* count, as Wright inexplicably informed the *Washington Post,* was 127 increases in taxes and fees—just one fewer than the other side had charged to Clinton's account. The Bush camp was delighted. The Clinton command was not. Carville had tried hard to be solicitous of

Wright and to see that she felt involved. Her thank-you set his Cajun blood boiling; in a fury, he disappeared from the War Room, got in his car, and drove around the city alone for two hours, just to cool off. Tantrums settled nothing, not, anyway, to the satisfaction of Wright's unhappy shipmates. Once, an important meeting collapsed when, with no visible provocation, she burst into tears. To the people in the room, one adviser said, it felt as if they had been beamed onto the bridge of the starship *Enterprise* and were exploding into hyperspace. Their complaints were unavailing; Clinton turned them away, reminding them of his debt to her for her years of loyalty and for her return to his service when he needed her. They came to suspect that her hold on him was tighter than he let on—that she was the sole keeper of some back closet with all his skeletons in it. "She's got her finger on the button," one aide guessed. "If he takes her down, she takes him down. It's Mutually Assured Destruction."

Her control over the draft story made her colleagues nervous, with the *Los Angeles Times* and the *Wall Street Journal* renewing their prowls through Clinton's past. But there was no way around her superior knowledge of the facts and her refusal to let them out of her possessive grasp. When reporters questioned Stephanopoulos about the subject, he referred them to her; he had no idea what she knew, let alone what she might say, and he did not want to get caught in any contradictions. At times, she seemed to some campaign officials to be inadvertently keeping the story alive by talking *too* much about it, telling reporters more than they had asked or needed to know.

The *Times* story, when it broke early in September, was less than devastating in itself; it alleged that, during the time Clinton was trying to stay out of Vietnam, an uncle had pulled some wires to get a navy reserve assignment created especially for him. But once again, he got caught in some dodgy answers as to what he knew and when he knew it. The press pounced on him for shading the truth, and the Republicans, fully aware of how the whole subject unsettled him, eagerly fanned the flames.

Clinton was, one aide said, in full denial, a state in which he tended to blame others, sometimes explosively, for his own problems. When he had taken one question more than he could stand on the latest turn in the story, he answered with an ill-tempered counterattack on Bush's veracity. His people groaned, watching the blow-up on television, and braced themselves for worse. In their nightmares and, increasingly, their daytime shoptalk, the draft story was like a match in a powder magazine. It was only a matter of days, they told one another, before the Big One finally went off.

At moments, they let their fear blur their judgment and divert their energies from the central message of the campaign; at times, it was as if the sign that said THE ECONOMY, STUPID had been turned to the War Room wall. In mid-September, there were published reports that Bush planned to go before the convention of the National Guard Association in Salt Lake City and attack Clinton as a draft dodger. In fact, the stories had been planted by the president's more hawkish advisers, hoping to make it happen. It didn't; the doves in his campaign talked Bush out of it.

But the mere rumor brought Clinton's command to the edge of panic—and to a split decision for Clinton himself to chase Bush to the convention to fight back. Greenberg and Stephanopoulos pushed hard for the trip. Carville straddled the fence. Only Paul Begala, on the plane with Clinton, argued against going; they were letting the Republicans bait them off their message and into a trap. Begala was a soft-spoken man, but when he got Stephanopoulos on the phone, he was screaming mad.

"This could cost us the fucking election!" he raged. "This is the stupidest thing I've ever heard. We can't panic on this."

"We have to face this down," Stephanopoulos replied. When the draft story had first surfaced in the winter, Clinton had gone underground and had nearly lost the nomination as a result. "We have to get in front," Stephanopoulos said. "We can't do a repeat of New Hampshire."

The hawks won; the campaign plane was diverted to Utah and the candidate was billeted at a ski resort in the mountains outside Salt Lake City, the only place big enough to accommodate his swollen entourage of staff, security, and press. He was out for his morning jog when Bush went on the next day. The speech they had so feared was as mild as mashed potatoes. Clinton caught the last of it in his room, then headed for the shower while his aides went sheepishly back to work on his text. Its focus shifted from the draft to the economy and to the more conservative of Clinton's values. With the media in a state of heightened readiness, he got more than the usual attention; otherwise, the excursion was a study in lost time and motion.

The Big One never landed, though the Bush campaign kept looking for ways to set it off; the issue receded once again into the background noise of the campaign, constant, irritating, but not quite loud enough to hurt. The deeper doubts it raised, Greenberg warned in a confidential polling memo, were "real and strong enough to cut into our lead." Clinton's softer voters seemed particularly disturbed by it; in focus groups, they would look down at the tabletop and stir uneasily in their chairs when it came up. Yet even those who thought he had been fudging or lying about what he had done appeared to be tiring of the subject, as against their more survivalist concerns. A vast majority in Greenberg's polls said they didn't want to be told any more about it. It was like your sister's sex life, Carville remarked; you knew something was going on, but you didn't want to hear the details.

The larger concern among Clinton's handlers was a certain squishiness in his public offerings. The Comeback Kid had become the Sunshine Boy; he was smiling too much at his rallies and saying too little about how big the problems were and how critical the election would be to America's future. Even his talks about health care, a signature promise of his campaign, had gone fuzzy and platitudinous; he seemed to have lost his nerve for the hard specifics of what he would do and how he would pay for it.

"We're too *soft*," Stephanopoulos said when they all sat down at the governor's mansion in September to talk about midcourse corrections. It was okay to smile *some* of the time, but Clinton needed more edge to his speeches.

"I want to stay right on Bush, right on the fact we're different from him, our economic policies are different," Carville said. "And I really want to make the distinction that we *are* for an activist government— not government intervention but government activism."

Anxiety was not easy to sustain at high levels in a campaign as blessed as Clinton's was then with good fortune and fat numbers. His wide lead in the polls was a bit deceptive, swollen as it was by his support and the president's nose dive in California, New York, and the Northeast. But as Greenberg informed him in late September, he still had "a pretty stable lead" of twelve or thirteen points, for all the relentless pounding he had taken. Bush was collapsing, Clinton riding high. "We cannot lose, and that's a scary feeling," Begala said aboard the campaign plane one day. In the circumstances, it was hard to find anything worse to be worried about.

The Other Guy

In the midsummer of Clinton's rise, his polltakers convened a series of focus groups of swing voters in Georgia and Michigan and got a sobering first look at how perishable his lead really was. Greenberg and his partner, Celinda Lake, had embarked on the study in a euphoric mood, expecting to find that the convention had laid to rest a lot of the questions about him and buffed up his scarred armor for the fall campaign. It hadn't, not nearly as much as his strategists had hoped.

The race, at that early stage, was barely about *him* at all; it was instead a referendum on George Bush, and the president was losing it, badly. The great American middle still didn't know Clinton very well or trust him terribly much. His place in their hearts, to the extent he had one, was as the Other Guy in the equation, the one who wasn't Bush. He was, for the moment, the only alternative they had to a president they no longer wanted around.

The depth of their dislike was evident from the first mention of Bush's name to one group of ten women voters in Macomb County, Michigan, the suburban laboratory where Greenberg had done his seminal studies of what made blue-collar Reagan Democrats tick. They had almost nothing good to say about a president they had helped to elect as Reagan's heir; his best surviving asset was Barbara, and the women counted him lucky to have her. Otherwise, their reaction to him was a litany of complaint:

"He's not a strong leader."

"He doesn't know what to do."

"'Read my lips.'"

"I feel cheated."

"Our unemployment is terrible, and he doesn't seem to care."

"He's off fishing and golfing instead of being in the White House, taking care of the country."

"I don't think he knows what it's like to live on $20,000 a year."

"He's done nothing for me."

But Clinton was a long way from winning their hearts and minds for himself. The convention and the bus tour afterward *had* helped connect some of the dots in his unfinished portrait. The women knew, now, that he had come up from mean beginnings, and they sensed that he had not forgotten them; they spoke of him as a good family man who knew what it was like to struggle in life and who hadn't lost the common touch. But there had been a price for the heavy stress on his life and times at the convention. The women in the room still weren't sure what he stood for, if anything, and they harbored nagging doubts about his makeup—his honesty, his integrity, his ambition. When the moderator asked what worried them most about a Clinton presidency, one member of the group said, "Everything about it."

The echoes of the focus groups were in the air when Mandy Grunwald convened her rapidly growing media team in Washington a couple of days later. The task before them was a hard one. Television ads were a much-maligned art in modern elections, but for ordinary voters not addicted to white papers and policy journals, they were a primary source of information, pro and con, about the candidates and what they believed in. The print and broadcast media were often too absorbed with the odds and the scandal of the hour to dwell much on the content of a race.

What the focus groups told Clinton's ad men and women was that his support was marshmallow soft among the swing voters who would decide the election. People were still nervous about him and would stay that way until they understood the choice he offered them, on his own self-promoting terms. He couldn't count on his summer honeymoon with the press lasting forever. His paid commercials would have to help him show why he was preferable to Bush.

Grunwald took the commission seriously and, on orders from the Clintons, began bringing in outside talent to work alongside her home firm. Her unlikely role model was Roger Ailes, the impresario of Bush's media campaign in 1988; following his design, she recruited a stand-alone team of the pros—political and commercial—she wanted to *make* the ads, but she reserved the last word to herself. Her own strategic design was shaped to take advantage of Clinton's other-guyness, exploiting the fact that he wasn't Bush; in the new two-way configuration of the race, it was the strongest card he could play. At the ad meeting in Washington on the last day in July, she blocked out four main premises:

- This campaign must be focused on George Bush and the country's problems, not on Bill Clinton.
- That does not mean this should be a "doom and gloom" campaign; in fact, hope is a critical part of our message.
- But it *does* mean our advertising must be sharp, almost always contrastive, forcing people to focus on the choice *as we define it.*
- We must not allow the Bush campaign to discredit Clinton to the point where he is disqualified as an alternative to Bush. This does not mean we can allow them to make this race about Bill Clinton—our version of him versus theirs. It must be about the choice as we want voters to see it.

Carville added a fifth imperative, imposed on them by the continuing misgivings about Clinton; the style of the ads had to allay doubt, not reinforce it. "Be aware of being too political," he said, "and be aware of overpromising or being too slick, too good to be true. And watch this 'plaid' problem"—the candidate's own perceived tendency to offer everybody everything. He could be better defined by what he wasn't. "The advertising," Carville said, "should always come back to, 'We can't afford four more years of Bush.'"

"We want this race to be about George Bush," Grunwald said. "We don't want this to be about Bill Clinton." The survey data showed that people didn't think Bush was a bad person, but they did feel he had mismanaged the economy, favoring the rich at the expense of the middle class. The economy had to be the point of unrelenting focus in the ads. "When in doubt, go back to it," Grunwald said. "Even when responding to attacks, we want to return to the economy."

She handed out assignments, and by mid-August, the first ads were ready for testing. Perhaps the most powerful was a negative spot dreamed up by one of Grunwald's draft picks, Carter Eskew, opening with a full-screen close-up of the president's mouth saying, "Read my lips."

"Remember?" the announcer asked in mocking tones.

The ad cut to Bush promising, in 1988, that people would be better off in four years if he were elected.

"It's four years later," the announcer said. "How ya doin'?"

The spot zoomed off the chart in a focus group, but the campaign had decided that its first strike in the air war would be a positive ad on Clinton's ideas about economic change. "All the research shows we *have* to go positive," Stephanopoulos said. "Voters are just starved for information." The question was what to put up. Grunwald wasn't quite happy with the story boards her people had brought in, so she wrote the ad herself, a sixty-second tone poem on change set to pictures from the bus tour. The campaign picked nine carefully chosen target states and invested $1.2 million in what the trade calls a 400-point buy—enough to assure that the average person watching television during its five-day run would see it four times.

In the weeks that followed, that sort of pinpoint targeting would become a hallmark of Clinton's media strategy. The Bush campaign was obliged to go national early, spending heavily on network time in the desperate hope of getting their man competitive *somewhere*. Mondale in 1984 and Dukakis in 1988 had got into the same bind. Clinton did not. He was leading Bush almost everywhere and had the luxury of husbanding his money for where it would do the most good. His campaign didn't buy its first network time until October and then spent only 10 or 15 percent of its media budget on nationwide ads, to roughly 80 percent for Bush.

The work of plotting a battle map had been begun long before by Paul Tully, the large, earthy political director of the Democratic National Committee, and had been refined since by David Wilhelm. When Tully took on the job, doom criers inside the party and out were saying that the Republicans had established a semipermanent "lock" on the electoral college, grounded in the Sun Belt and the West. Tully refused to believe it. He had buried himself in the 1988 returns, looking not just for states but for local media markets in which even the luckless Dukakis had been competitive. The object of his search was a complex new political geography, one in which the Democrats, with the *right* candidate, might actually win.

Was Clinton Mr. Right? Tully, a Kennedy Democrat, had a heartful of private doubts about him but subordinated them to the good of the party; until his sudden death of a heart attack in September, he and his data helped Clinton's strategists decide where and when to play their chips. In weekly meetings, chaired by Wilhelm, states were ranked in various categories according to their degree of difficulty—"Top End" for the gimmes; "Play Hard" and "Play Very Hard" for the gettables; "Watch Very Hard" for states that looked tough but might yet be worth contesting; and "Big Challenge" for those Bush seemed sure to win. The heaviest TV blitzes ran in the "Play Very Hard" states and, in every case, added importantly to Clinton's early lead.

Bush's air marshals rattled them with a pair of tough attack ads on the dangers of putting Clinton in charge of the federal treasury. One listed the tax increases he had signed in Arkansas—a clue, the spot suggested, to how he would pay for the $220 billion worth of campaign promises he was alleged to have made in his run for the presidency. The second ad was even more direct, suggesting that Clintonomics "could" mean higher taxes for anyone making more than $36,000 a year. The Clinton campaign had been testing various lines of attack, at least once using scripts leaked to them by a mole in the Bush campaign, and had seen some danger in the tax issue. As Greenberg warned, it went to the heart of Clinton's assertion that he was something new under the Democratic sun.

The second ad was something of a bust in focus groups; it came from a president who had welshed on his own promise not to raise taxes, and he was no longer a credible witness on the subject. But it infuriated Clinton, given the central place in his politics occupied by the middle class. He sat smoky hot in a tiny makeup room in a hall in Milwaukee, waiting to go on and dreaming of revenge.

"We've got to say he made it up," he told his entourage.

"Why?" Begala asked. "Remember what the dynamic is now. People *like* you. They want to vote for you. They're at the altar, and the minister is asking, 'Any objections?' and Bush is in the back waving his arms. They need reassurance that you're not wild, you're not crazy."

Clinton was not assuaged; the ad was "one of the most totally irresponsible" he had ever seen in a presidential campaign, and he wanted a tough counterattack on the air immediately. "I want to put a fist halfway down their throats with this," he said. "I don't want subtlety—I want their teeth on the sidewalk."

He was demanding overkill. His people had only just conducted yet another round of focus groups, this time in Denver, and had discovered how few arrows Bush had in his quiver. Swing voters had crossed him out, and none of his available lines of attack on Clinton seemed to bring them back—not taxes, not waffling on the issues, not even the draft. Clinton's image had undergone an extraordinary transformation, from country slicker to man of the people; it was based more on hope than real belief, but the hunger for change was stronger than the residual doubts about him—strong enough, indeed, to make them irrelevant.

The draft issue had never stopped worrying Clinton's handlers; under rising fire from the Bush campaign, some of them thought they might have to do an ad addressing it directly. As a test, they showed the two focus groups a film of Clinton telling his side of the story. It didn't move them. The people in the observation chamber had long since concluded that he *had* dodged the draft and that he was lying about it; they just didn't want to hear any more on the subject, from him, Bush or anybody else. "I want to hear about *issues*," one woman said. "I don't care what he did—I want to know what he wants to do tomorrow." The first group, all women, voted seven to one for Clinton. The second, all men, were with him ten-zero.

The talk of doing an ad on the draft tailed off thereafter. There had been a time, Celinda Lake thought, when the issue *had* mattered to people—when it might have been used successfully against Clinton. But Bush's generals had missed the moment and were paying the price. "They really blew it," Lake said with some relief. Their attacks were too cynical and too late, and they were backfiring against the president, reducing him to one more name-calling politician.

Clinton's strategists were prey to larger bafflement as to what the other side thought it was doing. Their dread of Jim Baker and his mighty election machine had given way to mixed amusement and relief at the clumsiness of the Bush-Quayle campaign. The president had made himself a target, not just with his negativism but with the promise-them-anything approach that passed, in September, for a positive campaign. "Bush has walked right into the antipolitical mood of the country," Greenberg wrote in a memo late in the month; *he* had become the politician in the race, a badge of infamy once attached exclusively to Clinton. "The campaign should move quickly to make this an even more indelible impression of Bush," Greenberg wrote, "because his problems here are our best protection on 'Slick Willie.'"

The president's deeper vulnerability, in Greenberg's view, was his low approval rating as president; if the campaign was to become a slanging match, it was Clinton's job over the six remaining weeks to drive that number even lower. "It is important to improve our image," Greenberg wrote. "It is important to raise questions about George Bush on trust. But it is much more important to raise questions about Bush and the Republicans' stewardship over the country." Change remained the magic word for Clinton, the single most powerful talisman he had. To make it work, Greenberg said, he had to make people overlook his "personal failings" by focusing their attention on how bad things were now. "The more we can highlight Bush's failure in office," the memo said, "the simpler our positive task becomes."

The recipe seemed at that point to be working. By the beginning of October, the president's job rating had sunk to 25 percent, and nearly half of adult America said they would *never* vote for him; by any normal measure, he was at the verge of unelectability. Clinton's lead was sixteen points in a public poll, fifteen in his own. The state polls were similarly heartening to his people. If the election had been held on October 1 rather than November 3, it would have been Clinton by a landslide.

Bush was doing what moribund candidates usually do in our politics, trying to save himself by savaging the other guy. But this time, in contrast to the last, it wasn't working for him. The Republicans hadn't done a thing to make Bush acceptable, Greenberg said, poring over his latest numbers. They had based too much of their campaign instead on making Clinton *un*acceptable, which, in Greenberg's reading, misread the real terrain. In the burnout of the Reagan-Bush era, merely to be the Other Guy had become a winning platform. People *wanted* to like Clinton, Greenberg guessed, because they had grown to dislike Bush so much.

27.

The Search for a Silver Bullet

At seven o'clock one evening in late September, a senior staffer at Bush/Quayle '92 headquarters looked up from his paperwork and saw his boss, Bob Teeter, looming in his office doorway. There was no point asking Teeter if he had come with good news, since there never was any. The president was thirteen points behind Bill Clinton in the campaign's polling, and the computer maps on the walls appeared to have been colored in by a child whose blue-for-Bush Crayola had long since got lost. The landscape of America was practically all Clinton red, 397 electoral votes' worth. The deepening gloom had begun to infect everybody, even Bush's own family.

The staff man awaited his orders.

"Find me something," Teeter said.

The staffer, lost in his chores, had only half-heard him.

"Find me something," Teeter said again.

"What?" the staffer asked.

"Find me something that will win the election," Teeter said, smiling wanly and walking away.

The something they were looking for, by that stage, was the silver bullet that would bring Clinton down; it was a given, in the White House and on Fifteenth Street, that Bush was not going to win a second term with advertisements for himself. He had spent a year shuffling identities like a pack of cards, from Lion of the Desert to Man with a Plan to Archdeacon of Family Values to Son of Harry Truman to Man with Another Plan. None of them had worked. Neither had his renomination in Houston, which had brought him only a faint and fleeting bounce. His approval rating in the polls was near Jimmy Carter's historic low for a president seeking reelection, and he still seemed mired at or around 40 percent of the vote in what was then still a two-way race with Clinton. "We're stuck," Jim Baker told a friend in mid-September. "Nothing's happening. It's stagnant out there."

The reelection team had tried fixing Bush, if only as a prelude to his going nuclear against Clinton; it was a measure of his weakness that he had to be somehow made plausible himself before he could start calling anybody else names. The elixir for his revival was to have been a speech to the Economic Club of Detroit, an attempt to achieve a coherence of thought and purpose that had failed him at the convention. In preparation, Dick Darman and Bob Zoellick swept together all his old economic initiatives and added a couple of new ones. They intended to call the repackaging a "plan," but focus groups hooted at the word; they thought Bush incapable of having one. The package accordingly became an Agenda for American Renewal, which sounded more like something that might actually happen.

The work, this time, was skillfully done and well-reviewed, the best case yet for Bush's latter-day laissez-faire economics. Afterward, it was bound up into a handsome, blue-jacketed booklet, so that he would have a policy blueprint to wave around like everybody else in the get-real atmosphere of 1992. It would be hard for him to say that Clinton's plan stank, a senior White House hand conceded, if he didn't have one of his own.

But the impact was minimal—a three-point ripple in his credibility as chief steward of the economy when what he needed was a tidal wave. "We have not made any progress in voter awareness that the president has a plan to improve the economy and is committed to it," an internal memo delicately remarked. The price of stasis was in fact higher than the polite language of interoffice communications let on. Bush, an aide said off the books, was like a repentant womanizer coming home to his wife after a long absence: "She doesn't want to hear that he's going to do better—she just wants to know where the hell he's been for the last three years."

Neither did it help when, after months of pressure, the president finally agreed to dump his beleaguered economic team in a second Bush administration, if there was to be one, and to install the reluctant Baker as his domestic-policy czar. The troika in place—Nick Brady at Treasury, Dick Darman in the budget directorate, and Michael Boskin as house economist—had been under unremitting attack since the tax rise of 1990. The siege, begun by the Republican right, had more recently spread to the center. The most loyal party regulars were looking for somebody besides Bush to blame for the state of the economy and the want of any credible program to fix it.

The president was as usual resistant to abandoning his people under fire. If his wingman had done that to him in combat over the Pacific, he would say when people pushed him too hard, he would never have lived to see the inside of the White House. Boskin wasn't a problem, since he planned to leave anyway. It was the others who caused Bush pain whenever he contemplated a shakeup; Brady was a close personal friend and Darman a brilliant policy man whose single acknowledged ambition was to spend his life at public service. For a long time, the president couldn't face the idea of cashiering them. He did plan to bring in new faces if he won, he had told a visitor in the spring, but not yet—not when the old faces were taking hits for their service to him. "I don't want to hurt anybody's reputation if I don't have to," he said.

With the onset of autumn, his people looked at his worsening polls, concluded that he could wait no longer, and began agitating harder for a housecleaning. What Teeter proposed was that Bush call in letters of resignation from all three men effective at the end of his first term; he could then announce the whole package—their departure and Baker's new assignment—as a springboard into the presidential debates.

Baker liked the first part of the strategy; he had been Darman's friend and protector for years but was perfectly willing to make a human sacrifice of him if that was what it took to win the election. He was less enthusiastic about his own piece of the action and once again had to be shown that he couldn't say no. When he finally agreed to take the job, he did so grudgingly and on his own terms. "I don't want to get nailed down to a time frame," he told colleagues. He would give the assignment one year, tops; then he would go back to his old executive suite at the State Department and to his peacemaking in the Middle East.

The last roadblock was Bush himself. He dithered even when Darman starred in a *Washington Post* series as the lonely hero among the bumblers who had fashioned Bush's economic policies. The chronicle was written by a friend, Bob Woodward, and Darman's fingerprints were all over it; a White House colleague called it "Dick's letter of resignation," whether he had meant it that way or not. But Bush seemed more bewildered than angry at Darman's indiscretion and could not be persuaded that it was a capital crime. If Darman and Brady were to be dispatched, he didn't want to make a spectacle of it— one that would bring discredit to them and, at least in his own mind, to himself.

The president finally did assent to the shakeout, but he botched the announcement in the heat of the first debate. It was to have been his bombshell. Instead, it turned out to be a dud, defused by his own hesitancy and, even with the vaunted Baker in charge, by the weakness of his reelection campaign.

The Man behind the Curtain

Jim Baker had been the de facto deputy president for foreign affairs during the Bush years—a man doing star turns on a world stage and loving every minute of it. Intimates of both partners knew that there were threads of rivalry in the complex weave of their relationship, but they were well hidden from public view and had counted for little in any case when Jimmy was abroad. What had mattered then was the nearly universal presumption that he could and did speak for the president, without having to go through the tiresome business of cabling home for instructions as to what to say next.

The world had seen only their friendship, not its subtle undertones, and had assumed without asking that the two spoke with a single voice. Baker's tour as secretary had spoiled him with the flatteries of heads of state and the adulation of crowds. When he visited Albania after the fall of communism there, a half-million people spilled into the streets, some for the chance to kiss his limousine. When he made his calls on presidents and prime ministers, he was received not merely as the surrogate of his president but as the premier geopolitician of his day.

He was accordingly made miserable by his recall to his old desk at the White House and, worse yet, to the vulgarities of partisan politics. It was a steep fall for him, from his new role as statesman to his old image as fixer, and he wore his unhappiness on his sleeve. One senior aide thought it fair to describe what Baker was going through as a kind of spiritual meltdown. Perhaps his most animated moment in his new incarnation came when, near the end of the campaign, he and his team were killing time on the road, watching a late-night profile of the president on CNN. The piece was routine stuff, but when some file footage of Baker and Boris Yeltsin came on-screen, Baker lit up like Las Vegas at sundown; the gathering turned into a lively seminar on life in the fast lane of foreign policy.

Most of the time, Baker seemed to friends to have withdrawn into his own disappointment. He had gone from being the world's leading diplomat to just another political hack having to worry about balloon drops and spot radio buys, one said, and it was just too much for Jimmy. Psychologically, it was more than he could handle.

His pain had been sharpened by his deep pessimism about Bush's prospects and, therefore, his own. His belief, closely held, was that the election had probably been lost in the months after Desert Storm, when the president had failed either to shake up his team or to expend some of his capital advancing a set of bold domestic initiatives. As early as mid-1991, some of his closest friends had told Baker that his return to the White House was inevitable and that it would be better done sooner than later, while there was still time to put something resembling a recovery program on track. Even if he didn't take over in the flesh, one of his people said, he could at least do a domestic-policy speech, using his great personal authority to get something going.

His response to both propositions had been no. He thought a speech would be a futile gesture, with Sununu and his boys still running the store; they were *jerks*, Baker said, too dim to pick up the ball and run with it. He was even less enthusiastic about returning to the White House, regarding it as a large step backward from the eminence he had achieved at State and the advantage it provided him should he someday run for president himself. "I've given up being chief of staff," he told his early petitioners. "I *did* that job."

The first sign of his distress had been his tardiness at taking over. Some colleagues would never quite forgive him his late arrival; one thought an appropriate epitaph for him and, ultimately, the campaign would be that Jimmy's ego had got in the way. Even those intimates who understood his reluctance wished he had at least taken charge of the convention and cooled off some of the more overheated divines of the Republican church.

His failure to have done so was widely read as his way of escaping blame if the show went badly, a survival skill at which he was one of the Federal City's foremost artists. Baker was famously jealous of his reputation and as notoriously gifted at gilding it, and this time, even his friend the president suspected that Little Brother was at it again. In the days after the triumph of the right in Houston, an old friend called Bush to commiserate and to suggest that heads should roll for having let it happen.

"Well," Bush answered acidly, "you can bet your life Jimmy Baker won't be left holding the bag."

The more charitable of his cronies guessed that Baker, this one time, hadn't been ducking rebuke so much as postponing pain. When he finally did drag himself to his battle station, he attacked the assignment with all his considerable managerial skills. What he could not bring himself to do was feign optimism, though doing so was part of the normal brief of the managers of failing campaigns; the nearest he came was his assertion, often repeated in the presence of the troops, that the race was uphill but still somehow winnable. Neither did he bother pretending to be happy in his work—not, anyway, in the company of friends. "This job is miserable," he complained after having been at it for only a week. "I thought I was past this point in my life."

He had never really been a conceptual genius at politics, for all his superstar billing. He didn't do vision; that came either from the client's heart, as with Reagan, or from the hired wizards and wordsmiths, as with Bush. Baker's gifts instead were focus and discipline, the strengths required to keep a campaign on message once it had one. Fred Malek, who knew one when he saw one, liked to describe Baker as a damned good CEO, which was precisely his approach to his job. With his and his team's arrival, lines of authority came magically clear. Decisions that had taken days were made in minutes and, once made, were treated as commands. Not even the president was exempt from Baker's will. "If I'm gonna do this job," he told Bush on the first business day of his second coming, "I have to have complete control of the schedule, including yours. You can't put one thing on your schedule, including your haircut appointment, without me approving it." The leader of the free world grudgingly submitted.

So did everyone else; Baker's authority flowed directly from the president. The campaign he inherited was the worst-run on Planet Earth, in the dour appraisal of one of its key operatives, and if the new boss was coming in too late to repair it, he could at least bring it a sense of order and purpose that had been wanting in the old regime. The number of people in the room at the twice-daily meetings that really mattered was slashed from a peak of forty-three to a core group of ten. Eight of them were Baker's choices. Bob Teeter was permitted to bring one person from the campaign, usually Malek or Steeper, to the table.

The word "task," under Baker, metamorphosed from noun to verb, as in So-and-so was tasked to do such-and-such. Deadlines for taskees were ruthlessly enforced. So was Baker's First Law of Coherence, which limited the agenda at meetings to a single subject. There were no little speeches anymore, as one regular drily remarked, and no digressions from the business at hand. When Teeter raised a scheduling problem at a session on media strategy, Baker cut him off. "That's not what this meeting's about," he said. "We're here to talk about ads. We'll deal with scheduling at six o'clock."

There was inevitably static between the old crowd and the new. Baker himself had a certain immunity, based on his past heroics and his standing at Bush's court, but his team provoked some resentment for its clubbiness. They were unbelievably insular, a senior officer at Bush/Quayle '92 complained; unless an idea was invented at their table, it was presumed to be without merit. The grumblers were not far wrong in their suspicions. Within a week of their arrival, the Baker Bunch began referring derisively to the old management as the Politburo.

They had produced no strategic design, no coherent message for Baker to shape a campaign around. There was only the bureaucracy in place, or so Baker's people believed; they could make it more efficient, but they couldn't will it to win, and they all knew it.

Baker's own want of illusions had been evident from his earliest days in charge. On Labor Day weekend, he convened a meeting of the old and new command groups around the dining table at his place to size up the situation. The prospect was not a pretty one. At his request, the polling people had worked up single-page summaries of what they had found out about Bush's strengths and Clinton's weaknesses—the foundation stones on which the people at the table would have to build the fall campaign. Baker studied the two sheets. Their net meaning was simple: Bush's supposed long suits—his character, his values, his experience at foreign policy—weren't selling or didn't matter, and he hadn't yet laid a glove on Clinton.

Baker shook his head, then pushed back his chair and walked over to a window. For a long moment, he stared out at nothing. "This just shows what a weak position we're in," he said finally. No one had the heart to argue, either with his assessment or with his all too obvious unhappiness with having to be there at all.

With the passage from summer to autumn, Baker seemed to the people in his circle a changed person, mostly for the worse. At State, he had been crisp, decisive, in charge. In his new billet, he seemed oddly passive, a man hostage to his own discontent. He routinely absented himself from White House staff meetings, turning them over to his man Zoellick to run. When he did show up, he receded into silence and let his people speak for him. Sometimes, he would push back from the conference table in his elegant corner office and pace the floor, his heart and mind continents away. In past campaigns, when Bush had resisted doing something that needed doing, Baker had kept after him until it got done. This time, more often than not, he would make one dutiful run at the president and then quit trying. "Life's too short," he told his people. There were only so many times you could go to the mat, and he had plainly reached his limit in a lost cause.

He was most conspicuous by his nearly total absence from public view. Washington, which feeds on such matters, buzzed about where Jimmy would be seen first—on *Meet the Press* or on the side of a milk carton. He was perhaps the most accomplished spinmeister to hit town since Henry Kissinger, an artist at promoting the boss's interests and, never incidentally, his own. He could have been Bush's strongest surrogate, had he chosen to play the part. One member of his circle thought he should have put himself out front from the convention on, operating almost as a second vice president; at the very least, he would have been more plausible than the man who happened to hold the office.

But Baker preferred staying out of sight and, so he apparently hoped, out of mind. Friends guessed that it wasn't really just another case of Jimmy dissociating himself from a disaster; it was a matter of protecting his own future in the remote event that Bush actually won. Above all else, Baker wanted to go back to Foggy Bottom for a second tour as secretary of state. He would have to be reconfirmed to get there, and, a close friend guessed, he didn't want to show up at his hearings in a power suit soiled with the mud and grime of party politics.

He chose, in any case, to fade into the drapery—to turn down all requests for interviews, invitations to the talk shows, even pleas from his own people to do anonymous background briefings for the press. His response, when colleagues complained, was that heightening his own profile would only feed the perception that the president couldn't govern without him. The Democrats and the press, two groups he saw as one, would have a field day painting word pictures of his role in a second Bush administration as Co-President Baker.

But his disappearing act was less pleasing to others in the president's circle, among them, most prominently, Barbara Bush. The first lady had always had a streak of ambivalence about Baker—wider, friends thought, than her husband's. She had great regard for his talents and for the friendship he brought to Bush's service. Her private complaint was that Jimmy had his own agenda, one that did not always match the president's, and his refusal to take a more public role seemed to her to confirm her suspicions. Baker, she guessed, was deliberately putting daylight between himself and the campaign.

Her upset with him reached a low boil when he refused even to stand up for the new economic "agenda" Bush had laid out in Detroit. The president's speech there was meant as the beginning of his renascence and of Baker's coming out as salesperson-in-chief; he agreed to background reporters after the speech and to do all four of the major weekend chat shows on television. But his loyal-to-a-fault lieutenant Margaret Tutwiler counseled him against it, seeing nothing in it for him. Baker bowed out, and the Bush command was stuck with Nick Brady, the badly bruised secretary of the treasury, as the hardly new point man for what was to be advertised as a new economic program.

With the switch in casting, the interest of the networks visibly declined. "Nobody takes this seriously," the Bush-Quayle desk officer in charge of talk-show bookings reported. "The question is, 'If this is serious, where's Baker?'" Some of his own people were asking the same thing. Bob Zoellick, who had a certain pride of authorship in the new plan, had been distraught watching Brady expound it on CBS-TV the morning after the speech. "These are the people who screwed up the economy," he moaned to a colleague, "and *they're* explaining *this?*"

Baker would default again in the wake of his designation as home secretary in a second Bush administration. His reluctance to take the job was irrelevant; he had had no other choice but to accept it and to go along with the plan to have the president announce it at the first debate. But the plan for him to do a speech a couple of days later laying out just what he would do as czar was dumped at the last minute. A text had been written for him, and the press had been alerted to watch for his emergence from hiding. It never came; by the time the script reached his desk, he had been persuaded that it would make him sound too co-presidential. "I *like* the speech, but the president should be giving it," he told his aides, and that, so far as he was concerned, was that.

Another black mark went down next to Baker's name on Barbara Bush's scorecard. For the First Lady, his disappearance under enemy fire was a kind of betrayal; Jimmy was covering his backside, she told a friend after the Detroit speech, and nothing thereafter changed her mind. When Baker came around to the family quarters in the White House early in October, her company manners were in place, but her dissatisfaction with him showed through. It would be nice, she told him in her nonconfrontational way, if he were more visible in the cause.

"Bar," Bush interrupted finally, swallowing his own misgivings, "get off Jimmy's back."

She did, but her hard feelings toward Baker never changed. He hadn't been there when George needed him; on the last day of the campaign, during what would be their farewell tour of America, she was still speaking bitterly of her husband's best friend as "the invisible man."

Midnight Again in America

It was too late by then for anything but recrimination; before Baker even walked in the door, the president's slide into history had already progressed too far to be turned around. Everything he and his generals set their hands to seemed prey to the exhaustion of a presidency near collapse. His foreign-policy apparatus was pinned down defending its sometimes cuddly past relations with Iran and Iraq. His law-enforcement and intelligence agencies were at war with one another. His response time was tested by a devastating hurricane named Andrew and, fairly or not, was found wanting. His reelection team floated new themes one day and withdrew them the next, at the first puff of flak. Family values were a conspicuous early casualty, to Dan Quayle's disgust. "When they write the history of this fucking campaign," he said on being instructed to drop the subject, "they'll say the fundamental flaw was that it backed down on everything."

In fact, the values issue had been one more loser in the search for a rationale for reelecting the president in spite of the stagnation of the economy on his watch. "It's costing us points," Teeter complained when the public moralizing got too thick. But nothing else was working, either. In the summer, Ross Perot's pollsters drew blank stares when they asked a focus group of Bush voters why they *were* Bush voters; the best reason they could come up with, under heavy prodding, was that they were Republicans. By fall, the Bush presidency was running intellectually on empty, with little left to say for itself. On the evidence of his record and the conduct of his campaign, one of his own senior aides said, the president didn't *deserve* to win a second term.

And so it was Midnight Again in America—a second Bush campaign built, like the first, on the strategic premise that there was no way to elect him except by subjecting his opponent to nuclear attack. In the early planning, the assault was to have been preceded by an attempt at rehabilitating the president at least enough to make him credible when the mudslinging began. Only then would he train his guns on Clinton, moving from his record in Arkansas to the riskiness of his policies and finally to his character. But the foundation crumbled with the realization that, as one high-level strategist conceded, there was no way to change America's perception of Bush as a failure. The effort to make him look good was thereupon all but abandoned in favor of the effort to make Clinton look worse.

The fall thus became what a senior hand called "sledgehammer time"—an unrelievedly negative air-and-ground war aimed at reframing Clinton as a taxer, a spender, a liberal, a liar, a coward, and, in its shabbiest moments, a possible Soviet sympathizer. In the campaign's formative days, two aides to Britain's recently reelected prime minister, John Major, were invited to Bush-Quayle headquarters to tell how *they* had won with a weak candidate, a sickly economy, and an electorate clamoring for change. The experiment in cross-pollination, like most of what the Bush command tried during the autumn, was something less than an unalloyed success. The invitees had not been central players in the Major campaign, according to one man who was, and not all of their advice was brilliant. One suggestion was that the Bush people put up huge billboards in major cities bearing the likeness of Gennifer Flowers and the slogan, AND NOW HE WANTS TO SCREW THE WHOLE COUNTRY.

"We should also say, 'Paid for by Bush/Quayle '92,' right?" one of the president's men said drily.

Another brainstorm was to paper the country with hundreds of thousands of faked photos of "Clinton" as a long-haired hippy with torn jeans, a Mao jacket, and a Viet Cong flag. Even the most warlike of Bush's men knew that they could never pull that one off without getting burned, and they said so.

"Do it late in the campaign," one of the Tories cheerfully replied.

The billboards never went up, and the "photos" never got made. But a couple of Bush's attack ads on Clinton as a binge taxer and spender were borrowed almost frame for frame from the Major campaign, and the overall design the visitors had brought along from London bore a striking resemblance to the president's evolving strategy. Major had won, the visitors said, by relentless daily attack on the Labour opposition—an assault built, as Bush's own would be, on the twin issues of taxes and trust.

Their ideas matched what Bush's generals had already divined: that, merely to get competitive, they had to drive up Clinton's unfavorable rating by five points or so and pray for an equivalent rise in Bush's favorables just by comparison. But getting the media attack airborne was slowed by the chronic muddle in the president's command center and by a split among his mixed team of ad men over first principles, including, most critically, the premise that Clinton had to be whacked mercilessly for Bush to win. In the swirl, it became something of a triumph just to get anything on the air at all, positive or negative, good or bad. The air war had become a casualty of timidity and division on the ground; it was as if Bush had sent his legions to the Persian Gulf in outrigger canoes.

A group of political professionals had made the president's ads for the primary fight with Pat Buchanan. But their work was widely panned as stale and dull, and two high-gloss Madison Avenue ad men, Martin Puris and Clayton Wilhite, were engaged in April to run the $40 million media operation in the general election. Their model was the Tuesday Team, the ad hoc all-star agency that produced Ronald Reagan's "Morning Again in America" commercials in 1984. The new recruits called themselves the November Company, opened offices in Manhattan instead of Washington, and staffed up mainly with hucksters for products ranging from burgers to cars. The Washington pros were salted among their half-dozen creative teams, a warrior minority in a crowd of civilians.

For Puris, running the operation, the experience was a case study in culture shock. He was a product of Ad Alley, a bright, fiftyish man who cut a fine Savile Row figure and carried a big reputation in the industry; it was he who had packaged the BMW as the Ultimate Driving Machine and Club Med as the Antidote for Civilization. But he got nowhere with his efforts to sell George Bush the same way, by finding the "simple thought" that would capture who and what he was and make America give him a second look. His ideas got lost in the spongy mass at the top of the campaign—"the giant thirty-foot marshmallow," he called it—and in the intense counterpressures to go negative against Clinton. By early summer, he was near despair. "Who do I have to sleep with to get *off* this campaign?" he asked a colleague.

Some of the November company's earliest efforts were risible or worse, in the view of the political tribe; they were only too obviously proceeding without a clear road map and were making things up on their own. Their scripts were sometimes amateurish, their "facts" often fictitious. One proposed ad, presented at their first sit-down with the management in May, had Bush holding up a copy of his 1993 budget book, declaring that *it* was the domestic policy everybody had been demanding of him. The responses of the campaign professionals included a muffled giggle, a low groan, and a quick change of subject. Another offering, an attack on Clinton's environmental record, was distinguished mainly by its inaccuracy; every assertion in it was wrong.

The pros suggested reworking it.

"Hey, I'm doing this out of the goodness of my heart," its author replied huffily. "I wanted to be in New York getting rich with my clients today."

Scripts could be doctored. The real and finally insoluble problem was the wide distance between Fifteenth Street and Madison Avenue, in spirit as well as miles. To Puris, the campaign leadership seemed positively obsessed with attacking Clinton at the expense of promoting Bush; it was almost as if the president didn't exist in their war games. "If we don't convince people he's done something useful in the first four years, there's no way to convince them he'll do anything in the next four," Puris argued at a May meeting with the senior campaign staff. He didn't want to make any negative spots at all and had said so, publicly, when he was hired. His contrary advice was that they retrofit Bush with a Vision Thing—a plan, simply framed and easily comprehended, for a new domestic order akin to his vision for the world.

The president, Puris wrote in a memo just before the launch of the

November Company, was generally seen as "a good guy—a decent man—an experienced and mostly competent leader." But he was prey to the antipolitical mood abroad in the land and to the perception that he was part of the problem, a man without a clue as to what to do about the concerns of ordinary Americans. "He is thought to have no domestic vision," Puris wrote. "And in a year when people are genuinely frightened of tomorrow, pathologically worried about America's place in the world and the continued viability of the American Dream, that is a very difficult position to be in."

His proposal was that they seize on Bush's undeniable successes at foreign policy and, instead of using them as an excuse for his inattention, turn them into a proof of the will and the ability he would now bring to the home front. He needed to promulgate "a creative, pragmatic, cohesive, meaningful Domestic Plan" and sell *that* in his ads, instead of just knocking Clinton senseless. His idea was not unlike those already in play among Bush's men; it resembled Darman's proposal for a Domestic Storm of second-term initiatives, and it fit the overarching strategy of building Bush up so that he could believably tear Clinton down. But the giant marshmallow engulfed it, like practically everything else Puris offered up.

At first, he told himself that the boys on Fifteenth Street might be right; they, after all, were the pros at the game, and he was the raw rookie. But he knew something about management and a lot about marketing, and as the weeks slid by without producing anything of note, his crisis of faith in his betters deepened. Teeter in particular seemed to him a man of conventional mind and palpitating heart, incapable of deciding anything. He appeared to be fixated with focus groups, to a point, Puris thought, where they brought the whole campaign to its knees. In commerce, you would never abandon a new product because twelve people in a room in Cleveland didn't love it at first sight. Focus groups were a useful check against doing something truly stupid, but they could as easily deter you from doing anything inventive; their mind-set tended to be negative, chary of new ideas. In Bush's campaign, as in Clinton's, they had a nearly oracular authority. Twelve people in a room *somewhere* hooted at the attempt to link Desert Storm to domestic policy, and the approach was dropped.

Puris's frustration boiled over when, in the spring, rioting swept the black quarter of South Central Los Angeles. First by phone, then at a staff meeting, he urged that Bush fly out immediately and use the war zone as a setting in which to show his new engagement with the unmet needs of the nation. "God has given us something," he told his colleagues in the campaign. "We won't get another opportunity like this before November."

There were skeptical looks around the room.

"Try and look at it as a metaphor for leadership," Puris said.

"What do you mean, metaphor for leadership?" one of the pros asked.

"People don't think he cares about what's happening in the country," Puris said. "This is a once-in-a-lifetime opportunity to fix that."

It was as if he were speaking Urdu. The White House crowd didn't think the rioting was "a Republican issue," Teeter said. They would try it out on a focus group before they did anything rash.

"Don't you think Republicans in Chicago and New York are scared *shitless* over this?" Puris asked, incredulous.

The pros were unmoved. The focus groups were convened, questioned, observed, taped, and analyzed. The riots *weren't* a Republican issue, Teeter concluded. There was no reason for the president to drop everything and go walk through the ruins. He didn't; instead, he let a prudent interval go by, and Clinton beat him to the scene, with its attending photo opportunities, by three days.

Puris plugged on, feeding periodic memos into the marshmallow and watching them disappear without a trace. "I have felt from the beginning that the president's problem is one of articulation," he wrote in June. "We do not present a simple, understandable, memorable product, and that is the essence of successful advertising. Simple, understandable, memorable—and consistent. One basic thought over and over and over again will win the day." The response, as usual, was the sound of no hands clapping. In August, Puris was back, pleading for Bush to announce a domestic "Battle Plan for the 90's" at the convention—then just days away—and to field "an all-star group" of heavyweights like Jack Kemp, Colin Powell, and Dick Cheney to make it happen. "I believe that unless—and until—the president can convince people that he is in charge and that he has a forceful clear plan for this country," he wrote, "no amount of Clinton-bashing or character assassination will get him back to the White House."

Again, there was no response; Clinton-bashing by then was the chosen strategy of the campaign, and Puris's lament was a thrice-told tale, no longer counted worthy of notice. His spirit wilted, and with the convention almost at hand, he told Teeter he had had it. For appearance's sake, he agreed to stay on the roster and chair some media-strategy meetings, but he was finished—and so, he believed, was his client the president.

His frustration with the pols was matched by theirs with him and his Madison Avenue buddies in the November Company; the wise guys on Fifteenth Street were saying that it should be renamed the December Company for its false starts and its poky ways. But even the pros nominally assigned to Puris were chafing under the languid management of the campaign. The Ad Alley boys at least had their amateur standing as an excuse. The crowd at the top were supposed to know better.

As early as spring, four of the surviving Washington consultants on the ad team had slipped into Manhattan for a quiet dinner with the retired rapmaster of attack politics, Roger Ailes, at the New York Athletic Club. Ailes's friends in the campaign looked on him as "our Deep Throat," as one put it; he was still sitting out the campaign, but he remained a back-channel source of advice to his friends among Bush's handlers. There were periodic rumors of his return, usually floated by people trying to bring it about; once, when the buzz got *too* hot, Ailes told Baker angrily that the campaign could tear up his Rolodex card if it didn't stop.

"I'm not coming back," he told his companions that evening before they had a chance to ask. "But I don't like seeing what's happening."

Neither did they, which was why they had sought his counsel. They were gung ho for going negative against Clinton sooner rather than later. The problem was moving anything at all through the pipeline. The November Company was green, squeamish, and slow, but their masters on Fifteenth Street were not blameless. Teeter wasn't giving them any clear idea of what they were supposed to do; it would be said of him by a colleague that his epitaph should read LET'S MEET AGAIN. There was no organization, no direction, the pros complained. Nothing was getting done.

"They'll ignore you until the convention," Ailes told them. "Then they'll panic and come to you. What you need to do is get a budget, don't tell anybody what you're doing, and get eight or nine attack ads in the can so you're ready when the suits panic."

The pros tried the master's recipe, like sous-chefs in a three-star kitchen. It didn't work. Let's wait, Teeter and Malek told them. Their budget request was tabled. Their spots never got made.

The failure at the heart of the media effort was conceptual; neither pros nor amateurs could turn out effective ads without knowing what they were supposed to say. From the president down, the chieftains of the campaign were prisoner to their own incredulity that Bush could lose to a man as flawed as they believed Clinton to be. They were accordingly slow figuring out what to do beyond waiting for him to fall out of the sky. At one point, they turned over their polling data to two academic consultants—experts in the black-box art of making products more appealing to consumers—and assembled the entire ad team in the November Company's conference room to hear them do a presentation on the reselling of the president.

Their findings were discouraging. It wouldn't be enough merely to bash Clinton, they said, nor could the president compete with him at expounding public policy. "Forget the issues," one of the dons lectured in a vaguely Kissingerian accent. "There is no way to fix the issues. They *hate* him on the issues." The key, the pair said, was to raise what they called Bush's Satisfaction Index, by which they meant making America somehow feel better about him. The pros at the table exchanged glances over their half-eaten sandwiches. One thought he had just heard why the president was going to lose.

Baker, sensing trouble, put in his own back-channel call to Ailes in the late summer and asked for advice. First, Ailes replied, bring back Sig Rogich, a Las Vegas ad man and a key member of the Bush '88 media team. Rogich had been rewarded with the ambassadorship to Iceland. It was time to recall him, Ailes said, and put him in charge.

Baker agreed. And then?

"Politics is execution," Ailes said. "Get off the fucking defensive, and get some ads on the air."

Even in the new order, execution was more easily and lengthily talked about than done. A Labor Day meeting on possible lines of attack on Clinton droned on for six hours and wound up without a single negative spot having been commissioned. In the absence of Atwater and Ailes, the campaign was afflicted by post–Willie Horton stress syndrome, a morbid fear of crossing boundaries of ethics and taste and getting caught. But the flow of ads was further impeded by quibbles over everything from high concept to the most finicky production detail. One spot showed "two candidates" on opposite sides of a split screen, taking opposite positions on several issues; their faces were covered by fuzzy blue dots till the end, when both men were revealed to be Clinton in full waffle. To the two women in Baker's political command, the blue dots looked too much like the ones that had been used on television to mask the complainant in the rape trial of Ted Kennedy's nephew, Willie Smith. Time, the one nonrenewable resource in a campaign, oozed away while the debate dragged to a resolution; the blue dots were changed to gray, and the ad went belatedly on the air.

Some promising spots died in the can. In the deepening autumn, the media team schemed up a one-two punch on Clinton's draft record. The opener was meant to be funny, a rapier thrust rather than a hammer blow; that would come later, while people were still laughing. The star was an eleven-year-old schoolboy telling his teacher why he was late with an assignment; while Clinton's contradictions on the draft scrolled up the screen, the boy squirmed through his own series of excuses, finally blurting, "A big dog ate my homework." Everybody smiled except the Baker Bunch, who thought the ad not suitably serious. They sent it back for fixes. By the time it emerged from surgery, it was too late; the spot was never used.

The follow-up punch was, and without the jokey set-up, it came off as merely mean. The visual was a *Time* magazine cover, a sinister-looking photo-negative portrait of Clinton with a headline promising to tell why people didn't trust him. A sonorous voice proposed an answer, or rather, a set of them: the conflicts in Clinton's running account of how he stayed out of the army and the war.

The ad, titled "Time," was not outside the settled canons of the trade, but it bumped the boundaries, to a point where some of the more gentlemanly members of the November Company were made nervous by it. "As an advertising person, I wouldn't run it," one of them told a visitor in early October, while the spot was still under discussion. "It's just too powerful. If it runs, you'll know we're in pretty desperate shape."

Less than two hours later, the campaign core group gathered in Baker's office in the west wing of the White House and screened the spot for the second time. Even they had been hesitant on their first viewing; the press would *crucify* them if they used it, one senior aide said. But Bush *was* in desperate shape, and taste gave way to tactical necessity. There was no dissent; it was time for "Time."

The ad ran, briefly. When *Time* sued and the media tut-tutted, second thoughts prevailed; the doomsday spot was pulled off the air and consigned to an early grave.

The Men from Oppo

The ad was indeed a measure of the growing desperation among the president's men; it was Hail Mary time, a senior hand said, and all they had left to throw was the bomb. Bush was still stalled at or around 40 percent in the polls, with no evidence whatever, in their own analyses, that he could get to 50 without divine intervention. The fitful attempts of his handlers to portray him as something other than the failed agent of an unhappy status quo had fallen flat, and with autumn slipping away, they had all but given up trying. "For the rest of the way, we're going 100 percent negative," one of Bush's generals said late in September. There was no way for Bush to return to the White House except over Clinton's dead body.

The late Lee Atwater had foreseen that the president would come to just such a pass again in 1992 and, as his legacy to his old friend and patron, had provided for it beyond the grave. In his abbreviated tour as party chairman, Atwater had built the opposition-research shop at Republican National Committee headquarters into a state-of-the-art war machine. It was his monument, though he himself had made a deathbed act of contrition for his own uglier adventures in negative politics. The heir to its management was David Tell, a slight, red-bearded young man in his early thirties; he ran the operation through 1991, then packed up his gear and his knowledge and moved over to the Bush-Quayle campaign in a similar role.

Oppo's task was simple: building up dossiers on any rival luckless enough to get in Bush's way. Its data-storage and retrieval technology was perhaps the flashiest in American politics. Its staff, at peak strength, numbered fifty or sixty—a dozen analysts and a bank of clippers working six-day weeks at hourly wages. The size of its budget alone suggested its central role in the Bush-Quayle reelection strategy; it would spend $6 million in two years, by reliable estimate, gathering evidence in support of the axiom that nobody is perfect.

As is the case in most intelligence agencies, Oppo's mode was bureaucratic and its appetite voracious. It gobbled information—most of it from the press and the public record—as uncritically as a hungry shark devouring minnows. Its diggers measured their success by the quantity of material they brought in and were content to let higher authority sort it out. Their aim was only as good as that of their masters, who, being human, were prey to the conventional wisdom. For most of 1991, the Oppo shop invested thousands of hours and hundreds of thousands of dollars researching the life and works of Mario Cuomo on the presumption, then widely held, that he would be the Democratic nominee. When Bush wanted the book on Cuomo's history and style as a debater, Tell's crew punched it up and put it in a memo, accompanied by videotapes of past debates for the president's private viewing. By the time Cuomo took himself out of play that December, the RNC's archive on him had swollen into the hundreds of thousands of pages.

Similar, though smaller, files were developed on the other Democratic candidates and on Pat Buchanan as well, in contravention of the rule that a party remain neutral in its own primaries; in practice, both major parties tend to serve their incumbents first at every level. But with the turn of the year, the men from Oppo had fixed their sights on Bill Clinton and had dispatched operatives to Little Rock to begin the paper chase. They left gumshod footprints around the capital, and their case officers recalled them in February, fearing that they would be charged with poking into Clinton's private life. They weren't, though tales were inevitably volunteered to them and borne back to headquarters. Their mission instead was to find the embarrassing leaves in Clinton's public record.

By the time they were brought home, they had already accumulated thirty file drawers full of statehouse documents. The trove was the heart but not the whole of their archive. Friendly academics passed along a hundred hours of Clinton on videotape, obtained by them from C-SPAN on the pretext that the footage was needed for scholarly research. Oppo had bought up microfilm of the Little Rock and Pine Bluff newspapers for the past twenty years and had subscribed to every daily and weekly newspaper in the state; the clippers combed them assiduously for choice bits of Clintoniana. "I know more about what happened in Arkansas last year than any man should have to know," Tell liked to say. His files were indeed unmatched, and even before the Democratic primaries were over, his colleagues found ways to use them; a senior RNC official, working covertly through third parties, fed information damaging to Clinton to staffers in the Kerrey, Harkin, and Brown campaigns.

What was wanting from their vast storehouse of ammunition was the killer issue, the one story or line of argument that would undo Clinton. His personal affairs, including his supposed sexual adventuring, had been ruled off-limits by Bush's own decree. A presidential memo made it a firing offense to do anything redolent of dirty trickery, and new recruits to the campaign were required to read, sign, and return their copies to certify that they had got the message. "We don't do sex," Tell told his staff, which was true up to a point. Bush's workers were content to let the media lead the chase for them; when a reporter came to them with the latest rumor, they found ways to be helpful without violating the letter of the president's command.

The boys from Oppo, sitting atop their mountain of paper, didn't think it would be necessary to travel the low road anyway to beat Clinton. "This guy has a mediocre-to-poor record across the board," Tell argued in a staff meeting during the summer. "He can be had on the merits." Tell's more senior colleagues at the White House and the campaign weren't so sure. They had watched Clinton's passage through the primaries with mixed awe and trepidation at his gifts for survival under massive assault. "He's not just the smartest of the bunch," one campaign topsider said. "He's smooth and appealing, and he always has an answer for everything."

The Bush command had hoped at first to do to Clinton what they had done to Dukakis in 1988—portray him as a liberal whose beliefs and values were foreign to the American mainstream. They couldn't. There were no furloughed murderers like Willie Horton in the Clinton File, no kamikaze stands against capital punishment or pledging allegiance to the flag in public schools. "I can't figure out a way to run against him from the right," one campaign official said; on social issues, at least, the guy just wasn't that liberal. Neither could he be easily pilloried for fudging the truth—not, anyway, by Mister Read-My-Lips. Oppo had amassed a large file of Clinton's waffles, straddles, ducks, dodges, and fibs. It was mostly wasted paper. "Clinton is a pathological liar," a member of the president's team said. "Unfortunately, George Bush is the only politician in America who can immunize him against that tag."

Even the deadliest bullets in the Oppo arsenal seemed, in the season of Clinton's honeymoon, to bounce off him. The diggers had unearthed one piece of his record that looked to Bush's generals—and to Clinton's—like a potential killer: a successful lawsuit charging the state with criminally negligent treatment of poor and abused children under its care. Clinton had let years go by before acting to clean up the mess; his timing seemed, at least in a partisan reading, to be tied to his national ambitions. But when Bush's people tried out the issue in focus groups, it melted under their will to believe in Clinton as a public man. The sample voters said it would indeed make them less likely to vote for Clinton *if it were so*. The problem was that they dismissed the story as a fairy tale; it sounded too horrible to be true.

What nothing in their yards of files seemed to do was narrow the double-digit lead Clinton had brought out of the Democratic convention. The search for the silver bullet accordingly escalated from wish to obsession and moved beyond the dust-dry work of clipping papers and copying documents to the blacker arts of political intelligence. The Oppo shop wasn't built for that kind of work. Charlie Black was. With Atwater's passing, Black was the last bare-knuckle brawler among the technocrats at the top of the Bush campaign; he made his manicured friend Bob Teeter nervous with the intensity of his will to prop Bush up by taking Clinton down. "We're gonna strip the bark off the bastard," he had been telling his colleagues for months. When they came belatedly to the conclusion that that was needed, Black was there, awaiting his orders.

By summer, he got them, a commission to run his own sub rosa search for the Big One. It was to be conducted off the books, using outsiders as cutouts; if they were found out, Bush and the campaign would still have what was known in the tradecraft of covert operations as plausible deniability.

The spoor kept leading back to Clinton's escape from the war in Vietnam. Only 10 percent of the people, in the campaign's polling, cared seriously about it, far below the 40 percent threshold for an effective attack issue or the 50-plus negative ratings Bush was drawing for his management of the economy. But the mere mention of Clinton's draft history seemed to knock him off his stride, and some of the hawks on Fifteenth Street, Black foremost among them, thought it had a deadlier long-term potential. It could gut Clinton's support in the South because he had ducked out on a war, they argued, and it could damage him everywhere else because of his shifting accounts of how he had done so.

The issue to be drawn, in their view, was not the merit of America's entanglement in Vietnam but the more basic question of Clinton's character—whether so slippery-seeming a man could be entrusted with the presidency. It was the opportunity to advance that attack that drew Black and his fellow warhawks to the idea of sending Bush to the National Guard Association meeting in September. The original invitation had been bucked to Quayle when it came in. The hawks proposed that Bush take it back, go to the convention himself, and attack Clinton straight on for his behavior during the war and his evasions about it in the campaign.

Baker signed off on the idea, and Bush himself was tempted. In private conversations, he railed at Clinton as a draft-dodger and wondered how on earth such a man could even *think* of being president. His younger staffers kept telling him the real issue wasn't what happened in the war years—it was whether Clinton was lying in 1992 to win an election. Bush had his own contrary views, sometimes so harshly expressed that one aide called him "Dole without the Arm"; like Bob Dole and others of their generation, he had answered his country's call when it came, in World War II, and had little charity for those who had not. "I know some of you don't think it's relevant whether he dodged the draft," he lectured a group of aides one day, "but I do. If your country wants you to serve, you serve."

What stayed his hand was a certain reserve, personal and political, about how far he should go. The delicate job of writing a script he would actually follow had been assigned to Baker's sidekick Bob Zoellick. He worked carefully, avoiding the hot primary colors on his palette; the finished work was done in tough but muted tones, using the language of Clinton's long-ago letter to the ROTC colonel against him. Zoellick's draft spoke of the Vietnam era as a testing time for young men, those who went to jail or fled the country to avoid the war as well as those who fought in it; they had all made their choices and had taken personal responsibility for them. Clinton had not; he was, in the language of the speech, trying to have it both ways. "The question is whether someone who has gone to extraordinary lengths to avoid serving can ask our sons and daughters to go to war," Zoellick wrote. "The question is whether someone who 'loathed the military'"—a phrase from Clinton's letter—"can ever be fit to command it."

Unhappily for its author, and for the hawks in the campaign, the text reached the president on the road a bare day before he was to give it. There wasn't enough time for them to make him comfortable with the words or to persuade him that the gambit was not, as one aide put it, some tacky political deal—a violation of his own rule against personal attacks on Clinton. The doves on his flight into Utah reinforced his doubts; they thought it quite enough that they had scared Clinton into chasing Bush into town, thereby knocking him off his message and keeping attention on his draft history instead for another day.

Still ambivalent, Bush canvassed members of his traveling party as to how they thought the speech would play if he did give it.

"Of course," his salty deputy manager, Mary Matalin, told him, "the press is gonna say, 'In a last-minute, desperate, scraping-the-bottom-of-the-barrel attempt to smear Governor Clinton—'"

Bush meditated a while longer, but it was plain to the help that he was losing whatever heart he had for the idea. "Why do I have to do this?" he asked at one point. The clinching argument that he didn't came in the form of an intelligence report to Air Force One from his advance party in Salt Lake City; the conventioneers had booed surrogates for both Bush and Clinton for spoiling a nonpolitical occasion with their partisan rhetoric. A watered-down text was substituted for Zoellick's draft; in it, Bush alluded only obliquely to "the controversy swirling around Governor Clinton," without even specifying which of the Clinton controversies he was talking about.

Another opportunity had been lost, or so the hawks felt; the exchange of speeches with Clinton at the convention was at best a draw at a time when ties were losses for the president. Black pulled in his horns for the moment and bided his time. The issue was a low-grade fever, he said comfortably, and it was going to get hotter for Clinton. There were too many questions the guy couldn't or wouldn't answer.

Bush and his surrogates did begin raising the trust question thereafter, knocking a few chips out of Clinton's repainted portrait. As with everything else, the new line took an achingly long time even to begin sinking in. For one thing, the word trust itself, coming from Bush, had a boomerang effect among swing voters in focus groups: they didn't trust the president's performance in office, either. Without quite telling him why, Bush's prompters suggested gently that he start using "truth" instead of "trust." The substitution was made for a time, to little avail. Clinton's unfavorable rating did rise a few points. The problem was that Bush's did, too.

With his polls looking terminal, the search for the killer issue took on an air of desperation. Most tantalizing of all was the rumor that Clinton, in extremis, had contemplated giving up his American citizenship to escape the draft, a rumor pursued by Bush's men down a bizarre succession of byways. There was, for example, the embarrassing discovery that some of Jim Baker's old political appointees at the State Department had made a frantic search of Clinton's passport records and his mother's as well. The only resulting dirt was what they left behind: their own and, by distant proxy, the president's fingerprints.

When all else failed, Bush himself tried by indirection to paint Clinton as having been a pawn of the Soviet Union in his days as a student antiwar activist at Oxford—a charge of a sort unheard in presidential politics since the Red-baiting heyday of Senator Joe McCarthy in the 1950s. The single supporting prop for the fantasy was that Clinton had toured Moscow, among other European cities, during his Christmas break in 1969. In a series of after-hours speeches, Representative Robert Dornan of California, a fantast of the far right, spun that datum into a picture of Clinton as a real-life Manchurian Candidate—a man who had prepped for politics under the KGB. McCarthy himself might have demanded a slightly higher standard of evidence; the story sounded so far-fetched that, for a time, nobody seemed to be listening.

But Roger Ailes was—and, in a tirade to Jim Baker's command group over a speaker phone in early October, he urged that they pursue the issue. "Go for the red meat," he bellowed. "Get on the fucking offensive!" What was Clinton doing in Moscow anyway? Ailes didn't pretend to know, but he had his suspicions, reinforced by Clinton's own vagueness about where he had gone and whom he had seen. "This guy's hiding something," Ailes said. "He's had to fudge this for twenty years to get elected in Arkansas. Nobody's *that* forgetful."

The group was intrigued, and so was Bush when he received Congressman Dornan and three similarly inflamed colleagues in the Oval Office two days later. Clinton was a traitor, they said, and it was Bush's duty to go after him; if Lyndon Johnson were president, the relevant

CIA files would already be on his desk. Bush replied tartly that he wasn't Johnson. But he was willing to do whatever it took to get reelected, as he himself had said early on. Maybe, just maybe, Dornan *was* on to something useful; it seemed worth pursuing, and Bush instructed his people to meet with the congressman that afternoon to see if he had anything on Clinton besides his own vivid imaginings.

He didn't, as Bush's team reported afterward; not even his chief hit man, Charlie Black, thought there was anything to the congressman's scenario. They still preferred in any case that the president leave the question of Clinton's Americanism alone and keep the assault focused where it would do the most good, on his credibility. "The issue was *candor*, not patriotism," a senior hand said. The central aim of their attacks was to raise doubts about whether Clinton was trustworthy enough to be president, and his conflicting accounts of his antiwar activities during his Oxford years had provided a new opening.

The problem, tactically speaking, was that Bush had his own deep and finally unmanageable contempt for Clinton's behavior; where his handlers saw a liar, one said, he saw "an unpatriotic little worm," and in an appearance on *Larry King* the next night, he all but said so. When King asked about Clinton's trip to Moscow, the president hinted darkly that there had been something sinister in his having gone there at all while the Cold War was still on—and something suggestive in his having forgotten whom he had seen. "I don't want to tell you what I *really* think," he said. But his answer was heavy with innuendo. Clinton had visited an enemy capital and had demonstrated "against his own country" on foreign soil; the suggestion was that the two facts were connected.

Aides winced. As an issue, one said, patriotism was a loser; anybody who held Clinton's draft record against him was probably going to vote for Bush anyway, and to suggest anything darker in his motives was to take the argument over the top. Doing so had been the president's own idea, as his handlers were only too glad to point out in the postmortem finger-pointing. They had often heard him say similar things in off-the-record settings, but he had always bitten his tongue in public, and they had simply assumed that he would do the same on the King show. The notion of challenging Clinton's patriotism hadn't even come up in his prepping.

Bush's own enthusiasm for the mole hunt was undulled by the furor he had stirred up. "Hey, no backing off," he told the troops. "This is a real issue, and I don't want any backtracking." In the widely shared view of his strategists, it was too late to backtrack anyway; the damage had already been done. "The president screwed it up," one of them said. By raising the Red flag, he had strayed from the *real* question about Clinton's character and had raised a three-day storm about his own.

Even then, Charlie Black refused to let go; he smelled blood in the question of what Clinton had or hadn't done during the war, and he put an agent-in-place on the case. His man in England was Gary Maloney, a thirty-four-year-old Atwater protégé who had done opposition research for the president, the party, and a number of prominent right-wing Republicans. By happy chance, Maloney was working on a doctorate at Oxford, which put him in position to do a no-fingerprint look into Clinton's extracurricular activities as a Rhodes scholar. Beginning in the early spring, he had been offering his services to the Bush campaign, for $5,000 and expenses. Teeter's hyper-cautious response had been no.

It was late September when one of Black's cutouts finally called Maloney to see if he was still available. "About damn time," Maloney replied. Bush's numbers were in the toilet by then, and the campaign had come up dry in its own explorations of Clinton's years as a Yank at Oxford; its single interesting discovery was that Bush's resident economist, Michael Boskin, had also demonstrated "against his own country" as a student there. Maloney, who was home working on a campaign between terms, accepted the assignment and made two four-day trips to England in October to see what he could find.

The time was short and the order tall: the campaign wanted photos, film, or videotape of Clinton at the two antiwar demonstrations he said he had helped to organize during the fall of 1969. Maloney slept nights at his flat in Oxford and spent his days prowling newspaper morgues and film archives in London; he skipped the BBC and the Home Office, for fear his cover might be blown. His prospecting brought in ten still pictures for a total outlay of $50 and a videotape of the two demonstrations for $1,700. He pored over his finds for hours, looking for a match with a magazine photo of Clinton in his long-haired, scraggly-bearded student days. He saw several demonstrators who looked like the young man in the picture, but neither he nor a battery of photo analysts back in Washington could make a positive identification.

The campaign paid Maloney $8,000 and expenses for his trouble, writing it off as one more losing investment. Only Black refused to give up. Maloney had brought in a lot of footage of demonstrators waving Viet Cong flags, Mao Zedong posters, and placards with anti-American slogans. Maybe they hadn't found Clinton, but he had admitted having been there, and they could make a lethal ad showing the sort of company he kept. Black proposed a script intercutting shots of the peace marchers with the famous still of Clinton shaking hands with Jack Kennedy. Teeter, ever squeamish, said no, and one more silver bullet turned out to be a blank.

"We're Cooked Meat"

There weren't that many days left to Bush's handlers in which to turn things around, and with the president going into training for the debates, they were about to blow ten days more. Debates put a race into suspended animation, which was itself bad for Bush; he would be frozen where he was, far behind Clinton, till the last arguments had been exchanged and the last judgments rendered. The verdict, when it came, was unlikely to favor him anyway. The best he could do on the merits was a draw, his seconds believed, and the media wouldn't even give him that. "They'll declare Clinton the winner no matter what," Baker said at a Sunday meeting of his core group at the White House late in September, and even a tie in the perceptions game wouldn't be good enough. Clinton would grow in stature just by being on the same platform with a sitting president.

But the form had got institutionalized over the thirty-two years since Jack Kennedy met Richard Nixon on a sound stage in New York. America seemed to have forgotten since then that presidential debates were wholly a creation of the television age; they had come to be regarded as a kind of public entitlement, a spectacle as fixed on the calendar as the Oscars or the Super Bowl. The hype was intense, the sweat profuse, the level of public enlightenment low. Content barely counted, at least in the postgame analyses; contestants won for turning the best wisecrack or lost for committing the dumbest gaffe. The debates survived in important part because candidates were afraid to duck them. The last sitting president who had tried was Jimmy Carter in 1980, and he had been harshly punished for it in the press. In the end, he had had to face Reagan anyway and had been beaten badly. Nobody since had dared say no.

Bush was accordingly stuck with a series of dates he was not eager to keep. When the subject came up, the president would put his game face on and pretend otherwise. "I've done pretty well in all my other debates," he said over lunch with his top guns just after Labor Day. "I think I'll do okay here." His handlers weren't so sure. They guessed among themselves that Clinton knew more about Bush's domestic programs than Bush did and that, as one of the Baker Boys put it, he might well make the president look "silly and irrelevant." When his guard came down, Bush seemed to them to share their concern, and their butterflies. It was, they thought, as if he felt *intimidated* by Clinton's formidable command of the detail of public policy; it would be like going up against a walking *World Almanac,* stuffed to the fingertips with facts and figures.

"I'm not gonna memorize all those statistics," the president told his men.

"You don't have to," an aide reassured him. "It's more important for you to be dignified and presidential."

The irony was that Clinton was hardly more eager to go up against Bush. His ego told him yes, but his political instincts said no, and so did practically all of his advisers. In public, they made sport of Bush for his hesitance, daring him to meet Clinton in single combat. Privately, they feared the debates as much as Bush's men did; the race was going nicely for Clinton as it was, and his team vastly preferred that he cruise to victory without putting himself in situations of undue risk.

Their own approach to the question, devised by James Carville, was a calculated game of chicken aimed at making Clinton look brave and Bush cowardly. When the bipartisan commission organizing the debates put forward its proposed times, places, and rules of play, the Clinton campaign quickly agreed to the whole package and sat back waiting for Bush's response. It was all they had hoped it would be. In an interview on CNN, the president insisted that he *wanted* to debate, but he wasn't sure about the commission's planned format; his people would have to look it over before he gave his reply.

"The wimp!" Carville exclaimed, watching the interview in George Stephanopoulos's office. "He wants Baker to negotiate for him. My debate thing worked."

It kept working deep into September; both sides were stalling, but it was Bush who took the heat for his show of rigidity over the number, timing, and format of the debates. The commission had proposed that one moderator do all the questioning; Bush's seconds held out for the traditional panel of reporters, confident that they would go after Clinton on the draft. The commission's schedule called for three ninety-minute presidential debates, starting in East Lansing, Michigan, on September 22. Baker objected. He wanted two debates—no more, no less—and preferred that they be scheduled as late in the season as possible. As he saw it, Bush would need time to bloody Clinton first, putting him on the defensive before they ever climbed into a ring together.

The demands made some tactical sense. But as September dragged on without an agreement, the champ began to look as if he were afraid to fight the challenger. Demonstrators were showing up at Bush's rallies dressed in chicken costumes, and Clinton ran the old empty-chair game, showing up at the hall in East Lansing at the appointed hour on the twenty-second to wait for the president. A suggestion by Quayle's aide Bill Kristol that the president jet in and show up unannounced in his Air Force One flight jacket had been ignored by his superiors in the Bush camp. Once again, Clinton had a golden photo op all to himself, in a state that Bush had to win.

By the end of the month, Baker practically alone was fighting the inevitable. "I'm tired of looking like a wimp," the president complained, and the more chicken suits he saw at his rallies, the grouchier he got. His crowds were great, he complained to Baker one day, calling in from a whistle-stop tour of the Midwest, but his numbers were still lousy. The debate over debates was drowning out his daily assault and battery on Clinton.

"We've gotta get something going," he said. "Why can't we come up with something?"

His own suggestion was that they up the ante, challenging Clinton to more debates than anyone had then proposed. Baker and his crew still weren't sure; they saw no way for Bush to win, one senior hand said, unless Clinton made some huge mistake.

It was Bob Teeter who argued for once against caution. When the command group met near the end of September, worrying the subject one more time without real movement, he lingered afterward for drinks alone with Baker. They had been counting on the race getting tighter after the convention, Teeter said, but it hadn't. Bush was at stall speed, and Clinton's support, if anything, was hardening. Merely to maintain the status quo was death, politically speaking. They had to do something to change the dynamic of the race before it was too late.

Baker mentioned Bush's idea about challenging Clinton to a whole series of debates, on a schedule approximating the old Friday night fights on television.

Teeter liked it, and so, finally, did Baker. It was a way to reclaim the moral high ground from Clinton and, if Bush should happen to be on his game during the debates, to rough him up as well. If they ever got the guy on the run, Teeter believed, he might just fall apart.

A detailed proposal was put together, and Baker outlined it to Bush over the phone the next day. It sounded good to him, but he wanted to know what Ailes thought. Ailes had been the president's Svengali in such matters in 1988, the last man to speak with him before he went out on a stage with Michael Dukakis. Now, Bush wanted his advice one more time.

An aide hit the phone and pulled Ailes away from a lunch of chicken hash at the 21 Club in New York. Ailes listened to the proposition. Like everybody else, he worried about Bush's prospects in debates with Clinton. In his view, it would be a sixtysomething gentleman against the fortysomething child of an in-your-face generation; the risk was that the younger, more aggressive man in such a matchup would dominate the stage. But Ailes was a warrior spirit, and he liked the challenge for its sheer audacity.

"We're ten points behind," he told Bush's aide. "It's gutsball time. He always rises to the occasion. Let's do it."

His advice was stirred into the mix, one more vote for daring. At a meeting next morning, Teeter asked Fred Steeper if the numbers had moved.

"No," Steeper said.

The president's son George W. was in the room. He winced visibly.

"Should we throw a long ball?" Teeter asked.

"What's the long ball?" Steeper asked back.

"Six debates," Teeter said.

"Sounds good to me," Steeper said.

Within forty-eight hours, Bush sprang his surprise, daring Clinton to debate him every Sunday from October 11 to November 1. The schedule would be reshaped in negotiations. But the gridlock was broken, the chicken suits disappeared, and the president, in a speech, had the last word: "Let's get it on."

"This is either gonna win it for us or sink us," Teeter said quietly, watching the president on CNN.

The question weighing heavily on the minds of the president's team was whether it really mattered—whether *anything* he said or did could change the red tide for Clinton spreading across their computer maps. In a memo to his friends and admirers, Richard Nixon, still a shrewd political handicapper in his eightieth year, guessed near the end of September that Clinton was leading in twenty-eight states with 329 electoral votes—59 more than he needed to win. In fact, that was Nixon's *best*-case scenario for his onetime protégé. His real count, like those on Fifteenth Street, was a good deal more doleful; he had pulled his punches in the memo, not wanting to add to the sum of discouragement in the campaign.

Bush's men comforted themselves for a time with an eye-of-the-needle fantasy in which he would lose the popular vote to Clinton but still win in the electoral college—the first man to do so since Rutherford B. Hayes in 1876. The catch was that he needed to win all of his best twenty-nine states to hit the magic number. By the eve of the first debate, Bush was leading in precisely two of the twenty-nine—and one of those, Texas, had been thrown into doubt by the return of Ross Perot.

Except for the president himself, there weren't many bettors that he could make it; even his boy George W., normally an optimist, had begun thinking privately about life in the terrestrial hereafter. On the night of the first debate, one of Bush's spin doctors stood at the center of a knot of reporters, gamely claiming a great victory for Bush and a "pathetic" third for Clinton. But as he toyed with a steak a couple of hours later at a restaurant near the president's hotel, his forced smile vanished.

"We're cooked meat," he said softly, "and have been since a week after the convention. We all know it." It didn't even matter, he said, that they had run a miserable excuse for a campaign. "People are sick of the president," he said. "They don't dislike him, but they want him gone, and we're powerless to do anything about it."

28.

The Second Coming

Finally, running for president was fun again for Ross Perot. His first try had ended in humiliation for himself—the word quitter leapt to mind—and in disillusion for millions of Americans who had believed in him. His second was what he had always wanted it to be. He had, as he would boast, fired the Pentagon: there were no more handlers, no pollsters, no image makers, no support troops at all except his kin, his corporate whiteshirts, and his decimated army of Volunteers. He had become director, scenarist, and star of our first truly Orwellian candidacy for president—an authority figure who seemed for long passages to exist only as a face and a voice on a television screen and yet represented himself as the embodiment of an entire people.

The style of *Ross II: The Sequel* flowed partly from his real revulsion with the old ways of politics and partly from the ambivalence with which he had got back into the race. It was possible to argue, on a selective reading of the evidence, that he had never really got out—that his withdrawal had been a charade designed to turn down the media heat for a while and buy him time to recreate the campaign his way. The people who knew him best thought otherwise; his disgust with the process and his resolve to get out of it seemed to them genuine, and his reentry came only after a two-month process of fits, starts, doubts, ambiguities, and mixed advice. Even as he laid the pieces in place, some of his operatives were in covert diplomatic contact with the Clinton campaign, looking for a way for Perot to stand aside and still claim a moral victory.

His uncertainty showed from the moment his Volunteer leaders descended on Dallas, on their own invitation, in the days immediately following his abdication in July. Those whose loyalty to him survived his announcement were nearly as angry with him as the larger number who had bailed out. He had always sought their advice and consent before then, but on the biggest decision of them all, they had got the news like everybody else: they heard it on the air or read it in the papers. They felt abandoned, even betrayed, and when the California leadership called for what amounted to a march on Perot, they had no trouble finding recruits. Within twenty-four hours of what they called Black Thursday, grassroots leaders from all fifty states began arriving at a hotel near the old headquarters, bent on keeping the movement going with or without its hero. Some had been up all night working the phones and hadn't had time to pack properly for the trip; one state chairwoman did four days of meetings and caucuses in the dress she had been wearing when she arrived.

Perot seemed both stunned and wounded by the furies he had stirred up. In his cosmology, The Volunteers were the movement, not he; he was surprised that they were coming to Dallas at all, let alone that they felt so aggrieved by what he had done. His first response was a kind of tease, a series of improvised signals that maybe his candidacy *was* over—and, then again, maybe it wasn't. While his state leaders were organizing their pilgrimage to Texas, he was back on the talk circuit, doing interviews with Barbara Walters and Larry King. In both sessions, he seemed to leave the window open to his reentry if he felt the call again. "I don't see a possibility," he told Walters, "unless I thought it was good for the country."

His intimates, even his son-in-law Clay Mulford, winced at that one; they thought, and told him, that he was playing with the emotions of people who had committed some part of their lives to *him*. But the dance of the seven veils continued in his meetings with The Volunteers. With their hotel under stakeout by the press, they had been herded through the kitchen and out a back door for the bus ride to headquarters. Perot met them in the same pressroom in which, two days earlier, he had declared himself out. The place had the look of a house in the path of a hurricane after the occupants had fled; time appeared to have stopped with his departure. Copies of an in-house newsletter lay about, dated the day before Black Thursday. The lead story had to do with the purge of the Rollins crowd. PEROT CAMPAIGN ROLLS ON, the headline said.

The passions in the room visibly disturbed the maximum leader, and his response to it was now suggestive, now merely equivocal. He had left the race, not the movement, he said; he thought it only fair to give the two parties one last chance to get real, and Clinton did seem to be responding. But Citizen Perot wasn't going anywhere very far. At some points, he spoke of an ongoing role for himself on the sidelines as the People's Referee monitoring the contest between Clinton and Bush. "Like the newsman the next day," he said several times; he would do the after-action analyses of whether the candidates had sobered up on the issues of economic and political reform.

At other moments, he was less bashful about getting back onto the field himself. He dropped tantalizing allusions to the possibility of what he called an "October surprise"—a late entry, if The Volunteers commanded it, once Bush and Clinton had beaten one another bloody and alienated the voters in the process. He had often spoken of the budget deficit as the crazy aunt in the basement of American politics, the family secret that nobody wanted to talk about. "Now," he said, "they have *two* crazy aunts in the basement."

His hope, in the meetings, was for something like what Richard Nixon once called a buy-time thing—continuing the petition drive as a way to keep the pressure on the major-party candidates. When his Alabama chairman asked what it would take to get him to run, he said, "I can't . . . I don't think it's the right thing for the country at this time."

"What do you mean, 'not at this time?'"

"Let me finish," Perot said impatiently. "What has happened is that the target is now Ross Perot. The issues are totally lost."

"If we draft you in each state," his Louisiana chairwoman, Betty Moore, asked him, "will you honor our draft?"

He demurred only at the *word* draft, not the idea. "If all the blocks are in place, if the timing is right," he said.

"You'll serve?"

"Yes," he said.

"As a candidate?"

"Yes," he said.

And run?

"Absolutely," Perot said.

In fact, his intent was to postpone a decision, and some of the people in the room were inclined to indulge him; it was enough for the moment, in their view, that they keep the movement going and that he keep signing the checks. But a hawkish majority took charge of the proceedings the next day and, in Perot's absence, passed a motion "declaring" him their candidate whether he wanted to be or not. The words were chalked on a blackboard, and most of the state leaders filed forward to sign their names.

They had barely finished when Perot came in through a side exit, smiling broadly. His eyes fell on the blackboard. The smile evaporated. He took a seat with his back to the words, as if to put the whole matter out of mind. It didn't work. The semicircle of believers in front of him was just as exigent, pressing him for a yes or no.

"I want to know whether you're back in the race," Donna Gilbert, his Alaska chairwoman, demanded. She was sitting on the floor down front, practically at his feet. The motion to draft him had been her doing. It didn't say he had to decide then and there, she told him, "but we need to know: are you in or aren't you?"

"You're really pushing me for an answer?" Perot asked. He seemed tense.

"Yes."

"You might not like it," he said. He needed time to talk to his wife and children. "My family is my weakness," he said, "and if that leaves this room, I'm out."

Gilbert thought he was stalling. She kept crowding him for an answer, to a point where some of her similarly inclined colleagues began getting nervous. They could see Perot's expression darken under the hammering.

"How long can you give me?" he said finally.

"I've got a plane at six," Gilbert said.

Even people who shared her goal were taken aback by her brassiness. Perot ducked out with a few staffers for fifteen minutes, then came back and sat down again.

"I gotta tell you, I'm not going to get back in," he said.

"Any time?" somebody asked.

"It's not good for the country," Perot said. "It's not good for my family. I made a mistake withdrawing. The way I did it, I hurt a lot of people. I don't want to hurt people again by leaving the impression that I am getting back in."

What Perot had envisioned coming out of the meetings was an ongoing political movement, perhaps even a seedling third party; he might be spokesman, banker, broker, even a shadow candidate keeping the big boys honest—whatever The Volunteers asked of him short of actually running. What he had wrought instead was a cult of personality, an unruly and undisciplined lot whose single principle in common was electing him president. He was subsidizing what amounted to a draft-Perot movement with money, support staff, and headquarters space at a point when his own course was uncertain and his viability dubious in any public role. "Here's the problem," Hamilton Jordan would gently warn a subsequent gathering of Volunteers during the summer. "Mr. Perot's name is not good out there."

Before he could sort his options, Perot had to bring his movement to heel, or risk having it settle his future for him. The hotheads had barely cleared town when he and his people began rebuilding the organization, this time from the top down. Old leaders were excommunicated, the more contentious sorts like Ms. Gilbert among them; new chairpeople were installed by the corporate white shirts in Dallas.

The purge was messy, but when it was over, Perot had the kind of organization he wanted, united, submissive, and quiet. The pros were long gone. Tom Luce was back at his law firm, Mort Meyerson at Perot Systems. The Pentagon had shrunk, by Perot's own measure, to shoe-box size; the paid staff numbered around thirty-five, and he was its unquestioned master.

It had a name—United We Stand, America—and a new chairman, Orson Swindle, a sometime Vietnam prisoner of war who had known Perot for years and had chaired his Volunteers in Hawaii. Swindle had emerged as a cool hand among the hotheads in the Dallas meetings, though his aim and theirs were identical. When infighting broke out in one state branch office after his ascent, he suggested getting every-body in a room and writing ROSS PEROT FOR PRESIDENT on a black-board. "That's our goal," he said; he was just more patient than some of his warmer-blooded comrades in the movement. Things seemed to him to be moving inexorably toward their common goal, he wrote his restive troops in August, and would no doubt get there if everybody would just calm down, lay aside ambition and faction, and "ACCEPT THE APPOINTED LEADERSHIP" chosen by Dallas.

What the organization lacked, absent a candidate, was a clear mission beyond a form of political greenmail: trying to get one or the other major-party candidate to embrace Perot's castor-oily economic plan. The chances were slight, given such bitter pills as a fifty-cent-a-gallon tax on gasoline, say, or a five-year deadline for hacking the budget into balance. In book form, his manifesto, *United We Stand: How We Can Take Back Our Country*, shot to the top of the best-seller lists by Labor Day. As real-world politics, its proposed solutions were a drug on the market, and Citizen Perot didn't have the standing to advertise it. You couldn't just buy TV time unless you were a candidate, and some of the friends he canvassed were telling him it would be foolish or worse to try *that* again. "You might get in," Jim Squires warned, "and have to pull out *again*."

But others kept after him to do it, resuming the drumbeat that had helped draw him to the edge of declaring the first time around. His chums in the military were attacking his most sensitive G-spot: his mingled feelings of vanity and patriotic duty. His chief cheerleader, John Jay Hooker, was back on the phone nagging again. So was his friend and counselor John Connally, who had reinvested his own failed dreams of the presidency in Perot. "I wish you'd asked somebody's advice," Connally scolded. "I think you've made the biggest mistake in the history of American politics."

In July, Perot asked his friend Richard Fisher to come by for a chat.

Fisher, the businessman and player in politics, was just back from a lazy vacation, and he wanted to get properly shaved and barbered first.

"Come on up and we can get our hair cut together," Perot joked.

"I'm not *that* loyal," Fisher replied.

But he was true to his belief in what Perot had attempted, and when they did get together, he confronted his friend with the consequences of his sudden withdrawal. "Ross," he said, "think of the signals you're sending to people like me. I'm forty-three, and what you're telling people of my generation is that they shouldn't go into public service. You're saying it's not worth it. Is *that* the signal you want to send?"

Perot kept his own counsel, but Fisher kept pushing, that day and in subsequent conversations through the summer. You couldn't just publish your plan for America, he told Perot, and then walk away without trying to sell it. "To do that, you have to be a candidate," he said. "A book doesn't do that."

The walls were closing in on Perot again. People privy to his thoughts during his summer hiatus believed that his reservations were genuine; his own unhappy experience of professional politics and the assaults on him and his family had brought him to a state of revulsion approaching nausea at the way America chooses its presidents. He had hoped to buy peace with his withdrawal and had got dragged one more time through the muck instead. *Newsweek* had called him "Quitter" on its cover. A newspaper headline dubbed him "The Yellow Ross of Texas." His poll numbers resembled Nixon's in the worst days of Watergate.

John Jay Hooker, having run out of civic arguments for Perot's return to the race, tried pride instead; you owe it to yourself and your children to retrieve your reputation, he told Perot, and the one way to accomplish that was to run. Perot shrugged him off. "I'm just watching the trains go by," he told Hooker more than once during the summer. The salesman at that point had nothing left to sell; Hooker found himself reduced to prayer that Perot would see a train he liked and would climb aboard, this time with a ticket to ride all the way to the end of the line.

George and Bill Do Dallas

The last impediment Perot had set for himself was the possibility that one or both of the major-party candidates would start talking the no-pain-no-gain economics he favored. Little he saw or heard through the summer and early autumn encouraged him to believe that they would; Clinton had got through his whole acceptance speech without

facing up to the deficit, and Bush seemed to have no plan at all worthy
of the name. In his rounds of the talk shows, Perot used his book as a
club over their heads, suggesting that he would have no choice but to
run if they didn't shape up and defer to its higher wisdom. In the
process, he was narrowing his own options, whether or not by design;
the possibility that two such play-by-the-rules party men would *ever*
change enough to please him and The Volunteers was faint to the
point of invisibility.

Perot tried, or, anyway, went through the motions; in the late
summer, he made private diplomatic openings to the Bush and Clinton camps to see if he could interest them in his package or something
like it. Twice in September, he called on Jim Baker at home on Foxhall
Road in Washington. Perot admired Baker, considering him the real
thing in an otherwise counterfeit Texas presidency. But the sessions
were doomed from the start by Perot's low regard for Bush and by the
scars he carried from his first campaign. He used part of his time,
indeed, to complain about his bad press and to allege that the president's son George W. had been one of the dirty tricksters behind it.
Baker denied it and was otherwise unmoved by Perot's presentation. A
colleague asked him afterward what had happened.

"Shit," Baker said. "Nothing."

Bush's strategists were desperate enough in any case to see a silver
lining in Perot's return—even to welcome it. There was risk, to be
sure; his presence could tip some key states to Clinton, only starting
with Texas. But Bush was going nowhere as things were, and Perot's
return had at least the potential to change the higher mathematics of
the race. Dick Darman, for one, had regretted Perot's withdrawal in
July. The objective of the Bush-Quayle summer offensive against him
had been to knock him *down,* not out. The president, in his reduced
circumstances, was better off with Perot in the race.

His return in the fall, in Darman's view, could be useful. The president was having trouble growing beyond 40 or 42 percent in the polls.
The trick was to make that enough, and in a three-man race, it might
be. When Perot got out, his voters had moved disproportionately to
Clinton as the un-Bush in the race. If he climbed back in, he could win
at least some of them back—more, probably, than he could chip away
from Bush. All the president's handlers would have to do to help that
process along was to keep pounding Clinton. If the votes they knocked
loose went to Perot, Darman argued, let them go; it was a risk well
worth taking. The net effect would be to pull Clinton down from the
heights, narrow his lead over Bush to single digits, and *make* people
take a new look at the race.

Clinton's generals, having cast their man as the candidate of change, were a good deal less enthusiastic about sharing the role with Perot and so were more willing to talk. The diplomatic process began with staff-level feelers in July and August, aimed mainly at seeing what it would take to keep Perot out of the race. Some of the inquiries were directed to Jim Squires, the disemployed campaign strategist who had stayed on in Dallas to help out with Perot's book. The apparent presumption in Little Rock was that Squires came from what traditional politicians thought of as the real world and could therefore be addressed in a common tongue. There were intimations, he said, of a job for him and a possible role for Perot in a Clinton administration. Squires's reply to each approach was thanks but no thanks; neither he nor Perot was looking for work.

What Perot did want was to leave some mark on American history larger than his own retreating footprints; it was his program he was pushing, with the implied threat that he would be back if Clinton didn't wrap his arms around it. When negotiations escalated to direct conversations between him and Clinton's campaign chairman, Mickey Kantor, they seemed at times to be tantalizingly close to a rapprochement. Kantor guessed accurately that Perot liked Clinton—better, anyway, than Bush. The issue was whether there was enough common ground between the two men to keep Perot happy on the sidelines. Kantor accordingly stressed the overlap—90 percent, by his measure—between their two platforms.

The problem was that the last 10 percent included most of the tough parts—the bloodletting required to balance the budget in five years—and would finally prove the deal breaker. By the time the two principals finally talked by phone for a half-hour in mid-September, the possibilities of peace between them were all but gone. Perot was under rising pressure from his followers to reenter the race and was running out of excuses for staying out. The conversation was *strange,* Clinton said afterward, but the message seemed to him clear: Perot was about to deal himself back into the game.

The public signals from Perot seemed to confirm the guess, and as they awaited his announcement, Clinton's handlers began planning responses.

"Has anybody analyzed his book?" Stan Greenberg asked one day over lunch at Your Mama's Good Food in Little Rock.

"I guarantee *someone* will," James Carville said.

"I think we've got some bedtime reading for tonight," Mike Donilon agreed. "Do we take on his plan?"

"Shit, yes," Carville growled. They didn't want to alienate the

Perot vote by attacking *him*, but they couldn't let him be the only guy out there with a credible plan.

Their chosen posture for the moment was to wait and see what Perot was up to. In their private geopoliticking, they saw some advantage in his return in a number of important battleground states. It would force the Republicans to fight like hell for the South, Greenberg said, and would heighten the pressure on them to keep shoveling out money for ads on national network television instead of targeting individual states where they might have a chance to win. But there was a countervailing danger in Perot's reappearance in a race about change versus the status quo. "It gets in the way of the message, that's the main problem," Greenberg said. Perot could bracket Clinton with Bush as the old boys and make himself the new Mister New in the campaign.

By then, there was no way to stop him, though the Clinton team would continue to try. All the hurdles Perot had set for himself had been cleared. He was on the ballot in all fifty states. His family was steeled for the process this time, even eager for the fight. Neither Bush nor Clinton was focusing in on deficit reduction, not hard enough, in any event, to suit Perot; America's crazy aunt was still locked up in the basement, out of sight and out of mind. The Volunteers, to whose wishes Perot had always claimed to be willing hostage, plainly wanted him to run. As he moved closer to a decision, he arranged to have his state leaders poll his remaining followers as to their wishes—the equivalent of asking admirers of Elvis Presley whether or not they would like to have him come back from the dead.

The survey was still in the field when Perot called his state leaders back to Dallas for a spectacle unprecedented in our politics: a summons to all-star delegations from both major parties to stand inspection like the boys on the stag line at a debutante ball. Perot had had the brainstorm during a day trip to Washington and had tendered the invitations to Ron Brown, as Clinton's second, and Jim Baker, as Bush's. In his mind, it was a last chance for the two campaigns to make their case directly to The Volunteers and perhaps even come away with an endorsement if they were suitably repentant about the evils of deficit spending and sound-bite politics.

Mulford, among others, reminded him yet again that The Volunteers wanted *him;* some, indeed, were already grumbling that the show-and-tell in Dallas was a waste of their time and America's. Perot insisted on it. The event for him was part civic exercise and part political theater, with himself and his movement at center stage. The two campaigns knew that they were the supporting players in the script; merely to present themselves at Perot's court was to make themselves supplicants for his favor and masseurs for his bruised ego, with little prospect of reward. But both parties feared giving offense to his followers; the show in Dallas amounted to a command performance, and neither star dared tell him no.

The Democrats stacked their nine-member delegation with people Perot liked and admired and sent them west to make one last try at discouraging him from running. Some of the dreamier of Perot's associates saw their agreement to come as the harbinger of a deal, with Clinton embracing the essentials of Perot's plan. Over the weekend before the meeting, its principal author, John White, flew to Little Rock to try one last time to promote a marriage of minds. He got nowhere. Clinton's instructions to his delegation, reinforced twice in phone calls on the eve of the presentation, were not to yield on policy or beg for an endorsement. Their marching orders instead were to appeal privately to Perot's civic sense, with his favorite senator, Lloyd Bentsen of Texas, leading the charge.

Perot greeted them warmly when they arrived at the meeting place, a hotel conference room in North Dallas, and showed them into a holding room off to the side. "It's going to be a real good conversation," he beamed; he himself was just thrilled to death that they had come. The pleasantries were still flying when Bentsen broke in.

"Ross," he said, "I think there's something serious we need to talk about. We need to talk about your decision to get into this race."

"Yeah, okay," Perot answered. His expression said it wasn't okay at all.

The tension was thick. Bentsen pressed on. "Ross," he said, "I've known you for many, many years. We've been through a lot together. I don't think there are two people who love their country more than you or I, or who want change more. But quite honestly, I don't believe you can win any more." If he did poorly, Bentsen said, it would reflect not merely on him but on his message. If he did well, he might hurt the real candidate of change, Bill Clinton.

"Ross," Bentsen said, "I don't think you want to do that."

Perot said nothing.

"Ross," Bentsen went on, "there's another option. You could endorse Bill Clinton. You could seal this election and make sure you and your people are seen as part of the reason Clinton won. When at this stage of an election has one person had so much power to influence the outcome?"

"Those are all good points," Perot said. "Tell them to The Volunteers. *They're* going to decide."

Others in the delegation took their turns. Perot wouldn't budge. "Tell The Volunteers," he repeated. "You guys can get me off the hook."

His intimates would insist afterward that he meant it; if his Volunteers had wanted to endorse another candidate, that would have been just fine with him. But the occasion smelled more like a show trial to his visitors, and Vernon Jordan, the lawyer and sometime warrior for civil rights, finally called his friend on it. Jordan was a person of size in Washington, literally as well as figuratively; he was a tall, handsome, thickset man of magisterial bearing, and he knew how to use his sheer presence in a negotiation. "Ross," he said, leaning into Perot's space until the two of them were almost touching, "I know something about leadership. You're a man who knows something about leadership. Ross, we *both* know enough about leadership to know *you* are going to make this decision, not The Volunteers. *You're* going to get yourself off the hook, not The Volunteers."

Perot changed the subject, closing down further argument. The Democrats went through their paces that morning, once again stressing how much the two men had in common. The Republicans did the matinee, in oddly off-key fashion; some of their hosts surmised, not inaccurately, that Clinton wanted Perot out of the race and Bush wanted him in.

Neither had a chance at swaying The Volunteers, or, in the end, Perot himself; the main effect of their dancing attendance on him was to raise him once again to a kind of parity with the two accredited candidates. The gallery listened politely and attentively to the formal presentations, but when questions were invited from the floor, they were almost unrelievedly hostile; the verdict implicit in them was that *both* parties were guilty of politics as usual. It was as if Perot's people were genuinely pleased to see their high-powered visitors, one of Clinton's delegates thought, but were equally happy for the chance to beat the shit out of them once they were there.

The show closed with Perot summoning his running mate, James Bond Stockdale, on stage along with their wives. Margot Perot looked grim, but the scene was otherwise the traditional tableau associated with presidential nominations. The die, at that point, was unmistakably cast. As a formality, the state chairs were sent home to conclude their "poll," determining, to nobody's surprise, that 95 percent of the 150,000 Perotists they surveyed wanted their champion back in the race. Their word was draft enough for Perot, and three days later, he obliged them. For the first time since the beginning of his great adventure, Ross Perot became a declared candidate for president.

Running for National Huckster

There were just thirty-three days left till the election when Perot stepped to a lectern at the Doubletree Hotel in Dallas and, in the bosom of his family, announced that he was submitting to the will of The Volunteers. The task he had set for himself was a daunting one. His popularity of spring was gone; his share of the vote in the *real* polling universe dropped from double digits to 7 percent the day he announced, though he had dominated the news for most of a week with his slow dance to the starting line. He had no strategy worth the name, no airworthy ads in the can, no speeches or rallies on his schedule, no polling beyond what was in the papers, no certainty that he could crash the debates. One-half to two-thirds of the country, depending on the poll, looked unfavorably on him—a level of ill feeling at which most political professionals would have advised him not to give up his day job.

He did have his ego, his gospel, and his money, great wads of it that he had been hoarding since winter; he instructed his ad men this time to spend "whatever it takes," and they did, at a rate far exceeding $1 million a day on television alone. There would be no road show, not till the very end; what remained of his army of Volunteers became a distant and largely symbolic company of spear carriers, barely relevant to the real action of the campaign. Perot no longer had time for them, however large a space they might occupy in his heart. In his new incarnation, he was like a rock star coming in from a concert tour to cut a new album for a vastly larger audience. His design for his second coming, to the extent he had one, was a one-month binge of TV ads and infomercials—more airtime than his two rivals combined could afford to buy.

The lateness of the hour didn't bother him; on the contrary, it told him that a run for president *could* be a sprint as against a marathon, just as he had been saying all along. His first campaign had been designed according to the old model, top-heavy with generals adept at fighting a long war. His second was built for speed; its small staff and its intuitive style were positive virtues in Perot's eyes, a demonstration model of politics as he believed it ought to be. His faith in it seemed, moreover, to be as large as his regard for himself. People in his circle guessed that he didn't really expect to win, not at first; his reentry, in Jim Squires's view, was a statement and perhaps a warmup for 1996. If so, Perot kept his unbelief in miracles well masked. His new media team, made up of Dallas ad men, called itself the 270 Group for the number of votes required for a bare majority in the electoral college.

Perot thought it should be the 540 Group. He was going for *all* the marbles.

The new crowd around him was similarly unfazed by the odds or by their own inexperience. "This isn't rocket science," Clay Mulford said cheerfully; he and his comrades proceeded instead on the assumption that politics was learnable and that its existing conventions could be overcome by close attention, frank talk, and the sheer force of Perot's personality. What passed for a formal plan was a computer run based on his standing in published state polls at three points in time—in June, when he was leading the pack; at the time of his reentry, when he had touched bottom; and in early October, when he had been back in the field for a week. The synthesis produced a list of twenty-one priority states that could get him the required 270 electoral votes and more. In those where Perot had real growth potential, his ad team would buy local television and radio time to supplement his national media campaign.

That television would be central to the enterprise was a given for a billionaire starting a run for president so late in the day; there were so many voters and so little time. His torment over whether or not to run had not been so profound as to deter him from planning ahead or hiring up. A week or so before his final decision, he approached his friend Liener Temerlin, the Dallas advertising executive, to see if he and his partner, Dennis McClain, would be available. As it happened, they were, though they had scant experience at politics; their vocation was making people feel good about such blue-chip corporate clients as American Airlines. They took the account, and McClain put together his 270 Group to start brainstorming commercials.

From the start, McClain favored an approach known to his trade as relationship marketing—selling Perot as a service to be hired for four years rather than as a product to be bought or passed over at a one-day sale in November. The strategy ran counter to the usual rules of the craft, which centered on prettying up the candidate for the marketplace. Perot didn't hold by that sort of advertising and had been too badly banged up in any case to be sold for his charms; he had become the political equivalent of a fixer-upper in the house-for-sale columns, a good buy if you looked past the cracked plaster and the flaking paint. McClain's strong advice was to stick to the issues and leave the beauty contest to Clinton and Bush.

Perot liked the premise more than the style of the ads McClain had in mind. He wanted to be in them himself, talking directly to the American people about his ideas; anything else smacked to him of the kind of empty image-mongering he was running against. McClain found himself in a position of great delicacy, equivalent to having to tell Frank Perdue to go back to raising his chickens and forget about selling them on the air. The climate was all wrong for the direct approach, McClain said. The race, by October, was already cooking down to a choice of the lesser of two evils, and Perot, with his high unfavorable ratings, would only make it three. "The moment you come on the television," Mc-Clain told him, "people will either turn it off or turn it off in their heads. The messenger will overpower the message."

His alternative scheme was a three-week flight of ads in which Perot would barely be seen, in a smallish still photo at the end, and would not be heard at all. The sell would be the message, not the man; only later, when they had people nodding their heads at what Perot had to say, would they put him on-screen actually saying it. Perot finally bent, and while he tinkered furiously with the scripts, he bought into a level of artifice he might have held unthinkable if it had come from Ed Rollins's boys. His ads were spare but slick, as flossy as anything his rivals had on the air. They described problems, not solutions, in sonorous tones and emotive imagery—a red flag in one, a ticking clock in another, a roiling storm in a third. "The candidate is Ross Perot," they said at the end, with his likeness at last on-screen. "The issue is leadership. The choice is yours."

But Perot's most powerful advertising vehicle was that hybrid called the infomercial, a half-hour or hour's sales pitch dressed up as regular programming. He was, first, a businessman, and in shopping around for a cost-effective way to reach the people, he had settled on a form more commonly used to sell diet supplements and exercise machines. In his hands, it became a revolutionary new instrument of presidential politics. While Clinton and Bush went jetting around the five-a-day circuit in pursuit of local headlines and sound bites, Perot sat behind a desk in a TV studio, talking the talk to the whole nation at a single sitting.

Clay Mulford suggested one day that he might want to get out on the road and appear at some rallies in his priority states.

"Tell me a good reason to do that," Perot replied.

Mulford did a minilecture on what handlers call free media—the art of getting space in the papers and pictures on the newscasts without having to pay for them.

"That's just what everybody does," Perot said. It was politics as usual, and he wanted none of it.

He preferred the politics of the unusual, campaigning almost exclusively on *big-time* television; he seemed to be running for national huckster, so constant were his presence and his voice during prime time. For most of his campaign, the man of the people disappeared in his fleshly person; the nation saw less of him live than of any major candidate since William Jennings Bryan first brought presidential politics down from the front porch and out onto the road a century before. But it was hard *not* to see him on television; no candidate in history had spoken so often at such length to so many people at once.

The miniseries he produced had a homemade look appropriate both to the vanity and the antipolitical instincts of its star. His plan for its debut was to do a fifteen-minute speech and then go to a series of charts illustrating the insolvency of the federal government and its consequences for the economy. His television people cringed at his notion of production values, which was not to have any; they hadn't even wanted him in his spots, and here he was, proposing to go on camera unfiltered for a half-hour at a time. They begged him to stitch in some stock footage of unemployment lines, say, or idle factories— something besides large ears and semi-legible charts to hold the viewer's eye. "We're not going to do that," Perot said. "I'm just going to sit down and talk to the American people."

He did exactly that, with astonishing success. An estimated sixteen million people passed up the usual sitcoms and the major-league baseball playoffs to watch Ross Perot, pointer in hand, ripping through his graphs and charts at a rate of one a minute. As television, the show made C-SPAN look lively. As politics, it worked; Perot had discovered an unmet hunger for hard information and candid talk instead of the usual cant of politics. More shows followed, some lamenting the ills of the economy, some celebrating the life and works of the candidate. His audiences grew, usually beating the competition in his time slots. His Nielsen ratings prefigured his slow but steady rise in the polls.

His role as producer, director, screenwriter, and star obliged him to stay on the ground in Dallas, even if he had been inclined to go anywhere else; it seemed to Mulford that his father-in-law was spending most of his time either at the studio or in his car on the way there. The cost was his near disappearance from the daily stream of news of the race. In standard-issue campaigns, every day is a battle to be won or lost. Perot wasn't even in the field. He had ceded the war of the sound bites to Clinton and Bush, preferring as a matter of principle and of necessity to sit tight in Dallas and work on his made-for-TV monodramas. It would be headline news when, nine days before the election, he made his first in-person appearances at campaign rallies. The uncandidate by then had become the ultimate media politician— the proprietor of his own talk show and, as it would turn out, the scene-stealer in what ought to have been a cameo role in the presidential debates.

29.

Nine Days in October

The first of the debates was just over the horizon, and Bill Clinton was feeling lousy. His mood was cranky. His voice was going again, disappearing into a cracked whisper. His back ached so badly that his aides got him a massage, specifying, discreetly, that it be done by a man. His nerves were as taut as piano strings, in spite of the fifteen-point lead he was carrying into combat. Perot was back competing with him for the change vote, and George Bush was out there zapping him as the failed governor of a Lilliputian state and maybe a Soviet stooge besides. He would have to parry the blows and much, much more. He would be on the same stage as Bush for the first time, selling himself as well as his message of change; he had to make people see him alongside the real article and imagine him as president.

The pressure on him, as on his rivals, was at once enormous and unfair. To Bush's man Bob Teeter, it was as though the entire election were being put into a compactor and compressed into a nine-day series of debates, three for the presidential candidates and one for their running mates. Only Ross Perot was happy with the prospect; for the others, the debates were a high-risk form of low political theater, one in which the reviewers graded the players for their skills at stagecraft rather than the merits of their policies or the force of their arguments. The overriding imperatives were to load up with one-liners, apply the pancake freely before you went on—the darkness of Richard Nixon's jowl undid him in 1960—and try above all else to avoid saying anything stupid.

Yet there was much to be gained in doing well, and each of the three rivals had his own objective. For Clinton, it was to make Bush look like an insensitive bumbler in his management of the economy and to present himself as the agent of change. For the president, as Teeter framed it, the goal was to "change this from a referendum on the times to a referendum on two people"—the only kind of referendum Bush might conceivably win. And for Perot? Merely to have been invited was a victory of sorts, a form of recognition that he was real; he would be up there on a plane with the big boys, saying nuts to both of them and to the decayed political order they represented.

That the debates happened at all owed less to any civic impulse among the candidates than to their common political needs. For most of September, the Clinton command had managed to stall the day of reckoning by hiding behind the debate commission; they had accepted its dates and rules and had refused thereafter to negotiate directly with Bush's seconds about any other arrangement. But the president's belated dare to Clinton to meet him every Sunday for the rest of the campaign had turned everything around. Chicken George had become Captain Courageous overnight; it was Clinton instead who seemed to be stonewalling, and his handlers had no choice but to talk.

Their trepidation was heightened by the prospect of coming face to face with Jim Baker; they believed his glowing notices and assumed that he would somehow contrive to pick their pockets. "This is the guy who negotiated peace in the Middle East," one Clinton hand said. "We will get *killed.*" To their relief, Baker was once again a no-show when the two sides met in Mickey Kantor's law office in Washington early in October for the first of four days of talks. It was Teeter instead who led the president's team, and in his soft hands, the debate over the debates was no contest; the complaint would be heard on Fifteenth Street afterward that Bob got rolled.

The air was tense when the parties sat down, and Kantor made it worse by scolding the president's men for having resisted the commission proposal for so long.

"This really isn't the way to start negotiations, with you making speeches from a moral high ground," Fred Malek growled.

Kantor kept pressing. Malek called him "snide."

"*This* isn't snide," Tom Donilon said, smiling. "It would have been snide if we had come dressed in chicken suits."

Both sides laughed, and the atmosphere lightened a bit. But when they got down to cases, Clinton's team got most of what they had come for. The Bush party wanted a long debate season, a weekly series of sixty-minute encounters winding up two nights before the election; the risks seemed to them outweighed by the desperation of their cause. The Clintonians insisted on a shorter series crammed into eight or nine days in mid-October, ending no later than the nineteenth; that way, there would be two weeks' recovery time if their man stepped into any messes. They won on the calendar and, in important measure, on the question of format as well. The first debate and half of the last would be done the way Bush wanted, with panels of reporters doing the questioning. But the middle round was framed to Clinton's own specifications; it would be done town-meeting style before a gallery of real people, a setting most flattering to him as the Great Empathizer.

Meet Me in St. Louis

The victories of diplomacy did little to improve Clinton's humor; as he lumbered through his first practice rounds, in a hotel conference room in Kansas City, he was mashing his best lines on the economy and wandering through the labyrinth of his draft history like a lost boy at the mall. To the dismay of his coaches, he had devoured his briefing books as if the prize would go to the man who could jam the most boring details into the least possible time. Mr. Propeller-Head was back, spinning out facts, figures, and gluey explanations of what he had and hadn't done during the war. What seemed to elude him was the set of three higher strategic goals his people had set for him—first, to reassure people about himself; second, to hit Bush hard on the economy; and third, to suffuse his answers with hope instead of old-fashioned Democratic gloom and doom.

His first informal run-through, three days before the opening debate in Saint Louis, was a shambles. The winner, on most scorecards in the suite, was "Perot," as played by Congressman Mike Synar of Oklahoma; his success was a first unsettling glimpse into what the real Ross could do now that they had let him under the tent. The more discouraging outcome was that Clinton hadn't even managed to outpoint Robert Barnett, the Washington lawyer standing in for Bush. Barnett was good at the role, having played it in prep sessions for Geraldine Ferraro in 1984 and Michael Dukakis in 1988. But Clinton, achy of back and breaky of voice, seemed to his alarmed seconds to have overdosed on data. A cardinal rule of debates was to say whatever you wanted to say, no matter what you were asked. Clinton had gone suddenly literal, answering questions precisely as they were put to him; he appeared to one handler to be approaching the debate as if it were a final exam.

His people checked a videotape of the proceedings, then sat down with Clinton around a big conference table the next morning. It was Friday. There were two days left, and their gladiator wasn't ready. Tom Donilon, who had been put in charge of the prep sessions, opened diplomatically. "We all think we're making progress," he said, but Clinton had to do better at thinking strategically on his feet. "Ask yourself at the beginning of each question," Donilon said, "can we achieve a strategic goal? You want to take control of the question, not be a *prisoner* of the question."

"There are three points we want to concentrate on," Stan Greenberg said. "First, George Bush means continued economic decline. Second, Bill Clinton is for average people, versus George Bush for the few. Third, you want to draw the contrast between George Bush, who won't do anything, versus Bill Clinton, who will use government to help people. Those are the contrasts, and they haven't changed."

"I'd distill it even harder," James Carville said. "Change versus more of the same, and Bill Clinton is a different kind of Democrat."

The question was whether he could stay on message at all, given the static in the air about his activities during the war years. The draft issue was back, and the president had been trying for several days to escalate it with his sudden excursion into Red-baiting. On the one hand, Clinton's handlers looked on the tactic as an act of borderline lunacy, one that could only make Bush look bad. Clinton himself seemed genuinely puzzled by it. Carville, for whom all colors were heightened, was stupefied. "I got to say, what are they doing?" he muttered. "*What* are they *doing?*"

But Bush kept harping on the subject, and rumors, the hyperinflationary currency of all campaigns, were flying in over the transom. The Republicans were covertly pushing one story that Clinton had gone to Paris during the Vietnam years and had met with representatives of the Viet Cong. Another tale alleged that he had considered renouncing his citizenship rather than serve; the Republicans had got hold of a copy of a letter to that effect, according to the buzz, and Bush might spring it on Clinton in the debates.

The whole subject had become a serious diversion, and when the day's mock debate began, Bob Barnett, as "Bush," was in Clinton's face with it from the very outset. There were, he said, "at least eight unanswered questions about your draft experience," and he demanded answers.

The slap stung, even in rehearsal, and Clinton answered as angrily as he might have at the real thing. By his count, the president had flip-flopped on thirty or forty important issues, including his own role in the Iran-Contra scandals. "You," Clinton said, glaring at Barnett, "are the one with the least room to talk."

"What are the answers to the draft questions?" Barnett pressed. "Maybe we will hear them tonight. What are the answers to those Vietnam protests? I have come clean on what I knew about Iran-Contra. You just have not."

"You have no convictions," Clinton shot back. "How *dare* you talk to any other public servant about constancy and conviction?"

His passion was real, but when Paul Begala, playing one of the panel of reporters, took up the assault, Clinton went off on one of his long, maundering self-justifications, leading nowhere. His coaches exchanged worried looks. "His answers on the draft were horrible," one told another during a break. "He was Mr. Defensive."

They kept him at it for the rest of the day, with only slight improvement. "I want to do all these things with Hillary," he protested finally. She wasn't due in town from her own road tour until late that night, and he did not hide his dependence on her counsel. "I want to go through all these personal things with her," he said.

As it happened, an aide had climbed up into the branches of Bush's family tree and found the perfect weapon to use against him: a statement by his own father, Prescott Bush, excoriating his Senate colleague Joe McCarthy for his commie-chasing excesses of the 1950s. The president's life in business and politics could be read as a flight from his father's shadow, and if he provided an opportunity, Clinton was to cast him right back in it.

"It will drive Bush crazy," George Stephanopoulos said.

"You *want* this," Carville agreed.

What Clinton mostly seemed to want was to be somewhere else. He knew he had been doing badly, and had said as much when Al Gore called from his own training camp one day to commiserate.

"Were you depressed after your first practice debate?" Gore asked.

"God, yes," Clinton answered.

"I came in *fourth* in mine," Gore said—a neat trick with only three people running.

Clinton's answering smile had been fleeting. His throat was a disaster area—his doctor had to be flown in to tend it—and his great skills at argument seemed to have deserted him along with his voice. The practice debate that Friday night was a big one, his first full-dress, gavel-to-gavel rehearsal. Clinton blew it. He wilted under attack on the draft issue, forgetting even to mention Prescott Bush. At one point, Barnett, as Bush, dipped into his pocket and pulled out what he said was a letter Clinton had written during the Vietnam era, discussing the possibility of renouncing his citizenship to stay out of the war. The handlers in the room waited for Clinton to pounce. He said nothing; they gaped at him and one another, horrified at his nonresponse. His answers on public policy, normally his meat, were hardly better; he was in his full wonk mode, as if he were running for dean rather than for president.

When the run-through ended, his senior aides retreated into a tiny equipment room, away from the lower-echelon staff. They were near despair.

"Total collapse," one said.

"There was nothing human, nothing real," said another.

"There was nothing about change. I voted for Perot, and Bush second."

"He never took on the administration."

"And there wasn't a single thing about his life. He didn't tell a single story about his life."

"We've got to go out there and say, 'You won the battle and forgot about the war.'"

The question was how to tell him without destroying what remained of his confidence.

"These are the options," somebody said. "We can go through the tape in an antiseptic way, or we can take him back here and say, 'Look, man, we're not there. We lost ground from last night.' I mean, we've gone through this again and again, and he's not processing it. He's not thinking change, reassurance. He's not personalizing it."

They couldn't give him debate lessons in front of an audience of kibitzers. Carville and Stephanopoulos went off to brace him alone, and the word went out to the more junior staff that they would be watching any subsequent prep sessions on closed-circuit TV monitors, not in the rehearsal room. They had to wean Clinton from his briefing books and get him to concentrate instead on creating "moments," those flashes of drama that would dominate the event and, more important, the coverage. It would take some work to get him there, and it was hard being honest with him with a crowd looking on.

In the end, it was his wife, not his handlers, who got him back on his game. She arrived in town late and headed up to their suite. Stephanopoulos looked in on the two of them after practice that night, bearing the latest dispatch from the front. He found the candidate sitting with a makeshift bib around his neck; Hillary was spooning honey onto slices of lemon for him, a home remedy for his throat. By the time rehearsals resumed in the morning, his voice and his mood seemed greatly improved.

Mandy Grunwald found Hillary in the back of the room, going over some paperwork of her own. "What did you do to him last night?" Grunwald asked. "It's like night and day from yesterday."

Hillary looked up from her papers and smiled.

Clinton did well that day, so well that his coaches had to find something new to worry about; their fret du jour was that he might peak too soon. Otherwise, they had trouble maintaining their professionally saturnine expressions.

"Spectacular," Greenberg said.

"I want to debate right now," Grunwald said.

"Yeah," Clinton said, smiling for the first time in days. "I'll probably screw it up tomorrow."

By Sunday morning, they had encamped at the Ritz Carlton in Saint Louis and had gathered at Clinton's own insistence for one last practice; it was important, he said, for his cornermen to warm him up, even slap him around if they felt it necessary to get him ready. He showed up late in jeans, a plaid shirt, and a leather jacket Hillary had given him the night before for their anniversary; he had sneaked away from his prepping in Kansas City and had picked up a blouse and an antique broach for her. He looked boyish, vulnerable, even a bit scared.

Greenberg tried to pump him up with a report on his latest focus groups, conducted only the day before. "People think you will be president," he said. "They want you to succeed."

Clinton's last workout was on message and razor sharp; his trainers shut it down early to keep him from losing his edge.

"Bye, everybody," he said, heading up to his own suite to change for the big show. "You've all been terrific. If I screw it up, it won't be your fault."

After a while, Carville and Stephanopoulos followed him upstairs for a last word. Don't lose your temper, they told him. Blow up, Bush wins; stay cool, you do. And be prepared for anything. They had practiced against the contingency that the president might indeed spring something on him, maybe even the phantom letter in which he had supposedly considered seeking citizenship in some other country. "They're signaling like crazy that they have something dramatic," Carville said. "But I think it's just a 75 percent chance they're playing a mind game with us."

His guess was right; Bush had no such bullet in his gunbelt, for all the frantic searching by his overt and covert Oppo squads. The debates were his last, best chance to cast the choice between him and Clinton in his own stark terms. The task would be difficult. Teeter had spent his working life reading polls; he knew the voters regarded the president with an anger verging on disgust. What he had to do to turn that around was to remind them why they once had liked him so much—to present himself as the tall, quiet man in the White House who had brought the cold war to a close and had treed Saddam Hussein. The risk in allowing Clinton in the ring had, on paper, its countervailing advantages: a chance for Bush to show him up as too small and too shifty to be president.

The question was how to exploit that opening. The early signs were not encouraging; compared with Clinton's three-day boot camp in

Kansas City, Bush's preparations had all the rigor of a company softball game. He submitted to a series of what his coaches called pepper drills, three-hour sessions in which they flipped through the briefing books and threw questions at him. But the main event, the day before the first debate, was a full rehearsal in Room 450 of the Old Executive Office Building, hard by the White House. Dick Darman paused on his way to the gallows to play Clinton, bringing his mordant humor with him; he showed up with a pair of shades and a $9.99 saxophone from Toys "R" Us, mocking the challenger's appearance on the *Arsenio Hall* show. John Sununu brought a pair of huge fake ears to *his* role as Ross Perot, but the joke soon got tired, and he took them off.

The two stand-ins threw their scripted lines at Bush. He ad-libbed back. After about an hour, Baker got up to administer a therapeutic stroking. "I've been through this many times," he said. "This is the best first run I've ever seen." His colleagues kept their dissenting votes to themselves. The president had seemed to them more than ordinarily tongue-tied, almost incoherent. Their kindest judgment was that, syntax aside, he had made no egregious mistakes. His performance, one coach said, was "flawless but completely unmemorable," which wasn't good enough. Clinton could play for a draw and still win. Bush had to hit a home run—or go to his beanball and try to knock his rival down.

He had neither in his repertoire. He came into his practice sessions still fired up about Clinton's antiwar activities on foreign soil, carrying on about it with a heat that startled his aides. "Anybody have any doubts about my position here?" he asked, seeing their surprise. But when they offered him what they were sure was a knockout punch on the subject, he flinched. Their idea was for him to send a letter to Clinton the day of the debate, demanding that he finally make good his promise to release all his draft records; then, with 100 million people watching, he would announce what he had done and challenge Clinton to come clean. The president considered the idea for a day or so, then backed off. The op-ed sages were already accusing him of McCarthyism, and he didn't want to make his bad press worse.

Neither was he comfortable with his next best weapon—the scheme to have him announce the shakeup of his economic commissariat during the debate. His handlers, Jim Baker among them, had tried to get him to do it beforehand and ride into Saint Louis on a wave of headlines celebrating his clean break with the past. Bush had refused then and was still resisting the backup plan to spring the package on Clinton during the debate, when he would have no prepared answers in his pocket. The president was perfectly willing to talk about Baker's new commission as domestic-policy boss. It was the part about sacking Darman, Brady, and Boskin that caught in his throat; he could not bring himself to subject them to a public hanging.

His handlers improvised something more to his liking. He would announce Jim Baker's role, but his plan to replace his economic team would be veiled by a fig leaf the size of a tarpaulin. He would say he was asking *all* of his senior appointees to submit letters of resignation effective at the end of his first term; if *everybody* offered to leave, nobody who actually did would be embarrassed. The president agreed to that muted variation on the larger theme of change, and his coaches wrote it all out for him on an index card so that he wouldn't forget it.

Clinton's command of facts and figures still haunted Bush, and his anxiety showed in his warm-ups. "We're not electing a budget director," Teeter prompted, "we're electing a human being we need to *trust.*" But the stronger weapon, in combat with a know-it-all, was wit, and Roger Ailes came out of exile long enough to drop off a few one-liners for Bush's use. If there was an opening on trust, he could say, "There is no statute of limitations on character." If the subject of change came up, as it surely would, he could answer, "Governor Clinton is an *expert* on change—he's changed his position several times on just about everything." And if Clinton *did* go into his human-encyclopedia act, Bush could respond, "The last time I heard someone spout that many statistics, he was selling me a used car back in West Texas. It was a lemon."

All three lines were in Bush's debate kit when he climbed aboard Air Force One and flew west for the showdown. En route, he tried out Ailes's used-car joke on Barbara. It wasn't very presidential, she sniffed, and he dropped it. He was down to a couple of one-liners to go with his popgun strategy of attack and his promise to appoint better people if he were only given a second chance. For an electorate hungry for change, it wasn't going to be enough.

The man who had the edge, indeed, was Ross Perot; he was change personified, and he had the further advantage of a near total immunity from attack. "I really would like to go after the guy, but I'm not gonna," Bush said at one point during his warmups; the couple of zingers his people had written for him in case Perot got *really* nasty stayed in his pocket. Clinton's strategists were similarly disposed to let sleeping billionaires lie. Their rehearsals had been a window into the mischief Perot could work, tying Clinton and Bush together as the products of a failed political order. "Perot changes the entire dynamic of the race," Stephanopoulos worried. Still, you couldn't very well go after him for his easy answers to hard problems—not if you wanted to compete for his voters on election day.

The game was made for Perot, and, at least in public, he approached it with ostentatious unconcern. Off-camera, he worked hard at it, for him; he pored over memos and briefing books, canvassed experts by phone, and kicked around ideas with the members of his new all-amateur team. But the mythic Perot wanted it known that he wasn't breaking a sweat. The day before the showdown, he drove to the barbershop for a cut and a round of chat with the boys; it was his first public appearance of his second campaign. On D-day, he was up early riding horseback with his grandchildren across his compound. When John Jay Hooker called to wish him well, Perot laughed at how his rivals were scrambling for credentials to get all their aides and courtiers into the hall.

"Bush and Clinton don't seem to have enough of them," he said. "I'll give them mine. I'm just going to take Margot and a couple other people who don't have anything better to do."

The night, once they finally met on a stage at Washington University, would belong to him; he was the free man in the mix, having nothing to lose, while the others seemed prisoner to their strategies and their ambitions. Bush in particular seemed off balance almost from the beginning. He forgot the rule about making the points you wanted to make, regardless of the question; his best shots got lost, along with most of his meager store of one-liners. Worse yet, he mangled the news of Baker's new role, giving it only a passing mention and neglecting to add that he would be fielding a whole new economic team if he won reelection.

His coaches sat in their curtained-off holding area, exchanging grim looks. The impact of having Bush do the announcement was gone; the purge of the old crowd would have to be explained anonymously by aides in background briefings the next day, reinforcing the impression that no one was in charge. The president's crew was still calculating the damage when a wall clock came loose from its hook and bounced off Dick Darman's head.

"Well," Darman cracked, shaking off the blow, "maybe now the president can announce to a round of applause that his budget director has *died*."

In Clinton's pen, the mood was considerably brighter. His people, who made their livings worrying, had begun the night in their usual state of torment; Stephanopoulos sat on the floor in front of the monitors with his head in his hands. But their man had arrived with his game face on, and when his turn came on the opening round of questions, on the economy, they sat waiting for the kill.

"This is it," Stephanopoulos said.

"Do your moment!" Begala prayed.

Clinton did, following his script to the letter; all his rehearsing paid off in a platinum sound bite. "Mr. Bush," he said, "for twelve years, you have had it your way. You've had your chance and it didn't work. It's time for a change."

Bush was caught flatfooted. Clinton's coaches whooped.

A round or so later, the president took his expected shot at Clinton for his antiwar activism abroad. Once again, Clinton dipped into his database and came up with the ghost of Prescott Bush. "Your father was right to stand up to Joe McCarthy," he lectured the president. "You were wrong to attack my patriotism."

Bush, nonplussed, made a debater's worst mistake. He let Clinton's reference to his father go by unanswered; in a contest in which seconds counted, it would take him and his handlers two days to figure out what to say.

In Clinton's holding area, Greenberg was on an open phone line to an aide at a dial group of undecided voters, getting the readouts and repeating them to his colleagues. The news was almost all good for Clinton, or would have been if he and Bush had had the stage to themselves. "We hit 90!" Stephanopoulos yelped when Clinton did a brisk defense of his qualifications for the presidency. Bush, by contrast, was having a hard time pushing the needles on the people-meters past 50. His trend line nosed downward into the forties at his assertion that he had a plan, and when he repeated his long-standing claim that the economy was "not all that gloomy" anyway, it hit 38. People were tuning him out. They no longer wanted to hear what he had to say.

"He's done," Greenberg said. "He's gone."

But Clinton and Bush *weren't* alone in the hall; after a slow start, Ross Perot was stealing the show from both of them. In theory, Perot was all wrong for television—unpretty, unsmooth, and uncool. In practice, his can-do answers cut through all the rehearsed rhetoric like a breeze through morning mist. "I'm all ears," he said at one point, getting a big laugh; no three words he had spoken all year had done more to establish his humanity. When he was challenged on his lack of experience in government, he knocked that one out of the park, too. "I *don't* have any experience in running up a $4 trillion debt," he said, but he did have some at getting things done.

The meter readers in the dial groups couldn't believe their eyes. The guy was like a jump jet, polltaker Jack Maguire thought, monitoring one such group of 102 voters in his offices in Concord, Massachusetts. In most debates, a strong answer produced a gradually rising line across the screen, the trajectory of a 747 getting airborne and heading for the clouds. Clinton's line usually looked like that when he was on-camera. Bush's was mostly flat. Perot's typically *leapt* upward at the first words out of his mouth and stayed up till he had finished. In the room, the effect was dramatic. In a straw vote afterward, Perot was the overwhelming winner, and his favorable rating quintupled, to 72 percent, in the space of ninety minutes.

His performance cast a shadow in Clinton's holding area, like a lone cloud on an otherwise perfect day. His return had worried both Clintons, Hillary even more than Bill. She had predicted his change of heart almost from the day he had dropped out, and had foreseen the damage he could do to their design for a race against Bush alone. Now, the campaign command was watching her bad dream come true. Perot kept putting seventy-fives and eighties on the scoreboard, almost every time at bat.

"*God,* he's having a good debate," Stephanopoulos said.

"This is worrying me a little bit," Carville said.

"Bothers me," Stephanopoulos agreed.

Bush's handlers were getting similar readings from their own dial group of thirty-two voters in Perrysburg, Ohio. The bulletins from there confirmed their own glum view that the president was not doing well—not well enough, in any case, to change the arithmetic of the race. He couldn't even manage a marketable sound bite; the air would belong instead to his two challengers. His bullets seemed to be bouncing off Clinton, as Fred Steeper would report afterward, and his rose-tinted view of the state of the nation clashed badly with what people felt in their everyday lives. "You lost points," Steeper wrote in a note headed MEMORANDUM FOR THE PRESIDENT two days later, "when you said you took exception to Governor Clinton's position that 'the country is coming apart at the seams. Voters agree with Clinton's assessment. . . . When you argue differently, you hurt your chances."

The private consensus in Bush's holding room, as in Clinton's, was that Perot had won. Clinton's spin doctors, in their pleasure, chose to ignore it. Bush's, in their gloom, tried to use it. "You gotta add this," Charlie Black shouted at Jim Pinkerton, who was typing out talking points for Bush's surrogates. "Clinton came in third."

Pinkerton did as he was told. "Ross Perot had a very good debate," he wrote. "Two mature, experienced leaders of stature and one inexperienced slick politician. Clinton clearly finished third."

The line was gamely merchandised by spinmeisters who knew it wasn't so; the overnight flash polls in the media ranked Clinton even with Perot or close behind, and when he rejoined his handlers, he was smiling his I-won smile. "You guys were tougher than Bush was," he said, sweeping up two of his coaches in a thank-you hug. Perot would be a problem, yes, but the Clintonians were feeling too sky-high to worry.

Bush seemed uncertain of what had hit him. "Boy, that guy was sure programmed," he told his seconds, leaving the stage. They tried to cheer him. It didn't take. Two days later, he met with several of his coaches in the Oval Office, starting preparations for round two. He was feeling discouraged, with his own performance and with the way it had been received in the media; it was still a two-man contest in their minds, and they were declaring Clinton the winner.

"You didn't do badly," Baker soothed. "We've got to make a few adjustments, but nothing major."

Bush waved a copy of *Newsweek* at his old friend. "Read these polls," he said. "They say I got creamed. The people obviously don't agree with you."

World War One-Point-Five

He had raised Dan Quayle out of nowhere in 1988 and had very nearly thrown him back four years later. And now their story was taking its last, ironic turn: the president found himself suddenly depending on his luckless veep to revive his moribund campaign. The strategy going into the debates had been as simple in conception and as deadly in intent as a blast from a double-barreled shotgun: the president was to open the wound, one of his senior aides said, and Quayle was to open it wider. But Bush had been oddly reluctant to get his hair mussed in round one, thinking it unpresidential to mix it up too vigorously with Clinton. Watching on television, Quayle told his own seconds that his patron should have been more aggressive. It would be up to him to draw first blood in the vice-presidential debate two days later, and he was ready for the assignment.

He had always been the lead attack dog in Bush's kennel, partly because the role suited him temperamentally, partly because that was what vice presidents were supposed to do. But his handlers wanted to be sure he had the proper edge, and in their hands, his preparations took on some of the air of a heavyweight fight camp. Al Gore was going to be condescending, they told him, and Bob Grady, the White House staffer who played Gore in rehearsal, lost no time giving Quayle a taste of what condescension meant. "I realize you're no intellectual," he told the veep, "but it doesn't take an intellectual to figure out that this is the worst economic record in fifty years."

It was not in Quayle to back away from a fight; still, his was the voice of restraint in the room. In the days before the debate, Jim Baker had counseled him against pulling any pins out of hand grenades on stage in Atlanta. The press would kill him if he did, Baker said, and the bloodstains would splash back on the president. Quayle did not often suffer Baker's advice gladly; the bad feeling between them dated to the 1988 campaign, when relations between them had verged on civil war. This time, he agreed, if for no other reason than his own self-preservation. His job, he told the more hawkish of his advisers, was to set up attack themes for Bush, not to make himself yet again the object of controversy. "Won't the White House just walk away from that?" he would ask whenever they came up with a bomb for him to toss. It was the plaint of a man picturing himself left to twist slowly, slowly in the wind.

The hardest hit they offered him came out of the fight over the nomination of former Senator John Tower of Texas to be secretary of defense in the first Bush cabinet. Tower, like Clinton, had been dogged for years by a reputation for womanizing and by tales that he was an unrestrainedly hard drinker as well. The Democrats in the Senate, Gore among them, had argued that character counts in public service and had succeeded in killing the appointment. What the hawks proposed was that Quayle read Gore some of the loftier flights of sanctimony from that debate and then ask tauntingly, "Al, do you think Bill Clinton passes the Tower Test?"

The picture of Gore squirming appealed strongly to the pit bull in Quayle. His judgment, and his sense of what the White House might think, told him no, and the idea was dropped from his script. He was not otherwise bashful about tossing darts into Gore's starchy shirtfront. One he liked but didn't get a chance to use was a counter to a possible attack on the issue of women's rights: "President Bush and I have always treated women with the utmost respect, both in our public life and our personal life." Another was the gift of his wife, Marilyn, offered as his dress rehearsal was breaking up. "You've gotta use the phrase 'to pull a Clinton,'" she said. Quayle loved it and carried it into battle with him.

The show unfolded roughly as they had anticipated it would. There was no scene stealer this time, not of Perot's raw star quality; his man in Atlanta, James Bond Stockdale, seemed distinguished mainly at his bafflement and finally his discomfort at being there at all. He came out of Perot's pantheon of war heroes, a retired vice admiral and a survivor of the prison camps of North Vietnam; the bond between them was nearly a quarter-century old. Stockdale was a man of intelligence and craggy dignity, but he was a total stranger to politics and its performing arts. His place on the ticket was pure happenstance, a matter of meeting the legal requirement in some states that a candidate filing for president have a running mate in place. Perot had needed a name in a hurry, and he had drafted Stockdale as a kind of body double till somebody more credentialed came along.

The search had been aborted with his first campaign, and when he launched his second, the admiral was all there was. John Jay Hooker, among others, begged Perot to tell the world that Stockdale was still just a stand-in and that he would be replaced under the Twenty-fifth Amendment should the ticket somehow get elected. Perot's response was angry. "I'm not going to hurt his feelings," he told Hooker. "I'm not going to do that." Stockdale was his man, a *real* leader running against a couple of pretenders. In Perot's book, Gore and Quayle would have a tough time finding middle-management jobs in your average American corporation.

The high price of loyalty was immediately apparent when the second bananas took their places downstage. There hadn't been time to prep Stockdale adequately, though he had read Perot's book and had responded well to what coaching he had. He had barely been seen or heard in the campaign before his one public appearance that mattered, and when the spotlight fell on him, he froze. "Who am I?" he asked, introducing himself to the nation. "Why am I here?" The questions had a certain appeal as a cri de coeur, the response of a rational man to finding himself trapped in a madhouse. The problem was that Stockdale himself seemed not to be sure of the answers. When one or another of his rivals was speaking, he drifted free of his lectern and wandered in little circles. When he was on, he sounded uncertain and looked lost. "I'm out of ammunition," he said at one juncture—the equivalent, in a debate, of pleading no contest and throwing oneself on the mercy of the court.

Gore was the dominating presence in the matchup that counted—knowing, smooth, and programmed. The quickie polls afterward would declare him the winner. But the boys in Quayle's holding room were doing the louder hollering and high-fiving. Their man started badly, yipping at Gore over the first ten minutes or so like a Chihuahua at a Great Dane. One of his handlers, watching on a monitor, remarked early on that Dan was acting a little—well, *dorky*—and he never quite cooled down to that level thought to be presidential. His favorable ratings in the aftermath of the debate actually went down. It didn't matter, except to his own long-term ambitions. His sole mission was to go get Clinton, and he did, attacking him as single-mindedly as a piranha in bloody waters. In his rendering, Clinton was a man addicted to high taxes and fudged truths, and when Gore looked aggrieved, Quayle said, "Lighten up, Al. . . . *Inhale.*"

"Dye his hair and send him to Richmond!" one top Bush aide whooped; the next debate would be there, in two days' time, and the president's second was doing better than the president at the blood sport of our politics.

The wonder, as Quayle himself remarked in the closing moments, was how little Gore had said all night in his senior partner's defense. It was as if he had slept through World War One-point-five; not even the charge that Clinton lacked the honesty and character to be president had seemed to shake him out of his granitic silence on the subject. Clinton, watching the show at his own training camp in Williamsburg, Virginia, was well pleased with Gore's performance until he heard the after-action commentaries. They focused on what the senator *hadn't* said under heavy enemy fire. Clinton began to percolate that night. By morning, he was thoroughly steamed with his running mate—and Hillary, who always took failures harder and remembered them longer, was at an angry boil.

The Battle of Richmond

They should have felt cheery, flying in from Gore's consensus "victory" in Atlanta, but Carville and Stephanopoulos arrived in Williamsburg in incongruously bad spirits. Their candidate seemed off his feed again, scratchy of voice and mood. "I just don't have a feel for this one," Clinton said soon after they arrived. Their response, more delicately framed, was that he had better get one fast. They had accurately read the underlying strategy of Quayle's performance in the vice-presidential debate: he had been playing caddie, teeing up shots for the president to take in his second round with Clinton. "Man, we are headed toward one big showdown," Carville stewed, and Clinton *had* to be ready for it.

The format, this time, favored him, with real voters asking the questions; it resembled the ask-Bill shows that had saved him from extinction in New Hampshire and had sustained his candidacy at moments of need ever since. But the Bush campaign seemed finally to be coming into focus around two words—taxes and trust—and Perot had got a solid bounce out of the first debate. During a break in the skull sessions, Carville, Stephanopoulos, and Greenberg took a walk around the manicured grounds of the Williamsburg Inn, thinking ulcerous thoughts.

"The Perot effect is real," Greenberg said. Perot was making inroads into some of Clinton's target groups, and for the first time since summer, he led both Clinton and Bush in the polls on who could best handle the economy. "That's awful," Greenberg said.

"It's real *now*," Carville said, "but I'm just not sure it will be on November 3." He had sat in on some focus groups in Atlanta; the voters under glass had seemed uninterested in Perot, and Stockdale's weak showing in Atlanta couldn't have helped. Still, Carville was worried. "It doesn't feel right," he said.

"It *doesn't* feel right," Stephanopoulos said. The campaign seemed to him to have gone flat, and the other side finally had a coherent plan of attack.

Greenberg agreed. He had watched Quayle on the morning talk shows, slapping Clinton around some more on the trust question. "It was the first time I winced," Greenberg said. "Because he was good, and their paid media for the first time fits their free-media strategy."

Both tracks, paid and free, were aimed straight at Clinton's character; the Republicans were trying to bury him and resurrect Slick Willie in his place. The old hands in the campaign were prisoners of their history, having spent most of a year dodging bullets with their man's name on them; they expected more to fly in Richmond and were almost obsessive about preparing Clinton for them. Newer recruits like Tom Donilon, the head coach of the prep team, were cooler.

"This is not a crisis," Donilon reassured them. "It's one question."

"But we're going to have a continued assault on character in two more debates," Mickey Kantor countered.

"There's no evidence it's taking a toll," Greenberg said.

"But there are *two more debates*," Stephanopoulos repeated.

"The only thing is," Greenberg said, "that people's minds might be a little more open now because of Perot."

"Tom," Stephanopoulos said, grouchy now, "this is *more* than one question."

"We've got to get more creative," Carville urged. "We've got to pick it up."

"No, we've got to get *sharper*," Greenberg said.

But how? The questions haunted their sessions with Clinton. He was incensed at the free ride Bush appeared to be getting in the media on the skeletons in *his* closet—his see-no-evil defense in the Iran-Contra mess, for one example; his seeming appeasement of Saddam Hussein before the Gulf war, for another. Those were the acts of a sitting president, but the press seemed more interested in what Clinton had been doing as a student tourist in Moscow twenty-two years before. He was itching to raise the issue. His handlers saw it as a second-strike weapon, for use if the president hit him first; he didn't want to be the one launching a nuclear exchange.

"We are waiting for the T-word—trust," Carville said. "Any opening you get, get right to the meat of the coconut. Hit it right out of the chute. Wait for the slightest provocation: 'Mr. President, with all due respect, I'm not going to listen to any lectures from *you* on trust.'" Clinton could tick off some of Bush's equivocations and broken promises, then turn the issue back to the economy and the future of the country. "You deserve a better election than that," he should say, "and I'm going to give it to you."

And if Bush kept at it? "'I've already responded to that,'" Greenberg said, adding to the script. "'I'm going to talk about the *people's* problems now.' Our goal is to have a positive debate."

"No food fight," Donilon agreed.

"We have to liberate ourselves from the cat fight," Carville said. "This tax-and-trust thing they're on is dangerous. They appear to be on it with some consistency. Say what you will, Quayle did a pretty good job on that. Bush will come up with some variation, and the first chance you get, you *smack* him. Not a knockout, but knock him *back*. If we don't, the tendency we will have is to get into a pissing match, and it opens it up for Perot."

Clinton agreed. Back in the spring, when Bush and Perot were doing the cat fighting, he had plodded around the country promoting his economic plan and chastising the others for their schoolyard squabbling. He couldn't fall into the same trap himself, he said, and let Perot have the high ground.

The strategy they settled on was the equivalent of a brushback pitch in baseball, just close enough to the batter's head to knock him off his game; then you got on with yours. "Short of that," Carville said, "I don't see any way we can set the agenda. It's going to be taxes and trust, and Stan and I and George feel that, of all the things they've trotted out in this campaign, that line has the ring of being potentially damaging. We've got 80 million people watching these debates, and we better nip it in the bud. Once you lay the marker down, you don't have to fight him every time. We ought to have the showdown early and get out of it."

It was important as well to make the free-form, Donahue-style format work for him, as it had so often in the past. "You've got to use the audience," Carville told Clinton. It was a matter of connecting with individual questioners.

"You've *got* to," Hillary said.

"Make the audience your friend," Carville said.

"I think tone and body language are important," Clinton said. The personal stuff was history now; he guessed that people had absorbed it and were ready to move on. "They know I'm not perfect," he said. "They want to know if I'm small or if I'm steady."

They were still talking when they got advance word of a new CBS/ *New York Times* poll. Clinton was beating Bush by thirteen points and Perot by thirty-seven. The attack on his antiwar activities was a fizzle; four respondents in five said it didn't matter.

"I'll tell you, the voters are impressive," Greenberg said.

"You think they can hold out two and a half more weeks?" Clinton asked.

"I think they can," Greenberg said.

Clinton wakened to more good polling news the day of the debate; he was leading by ten in Greenberg's latest and by fifteen in a *USA Today*/CNN survey. Clinton's allergies were acting up again, but a two-hour nap at midday seemed to revive both his voice and his spirit. His handlers tossed a last few questions at him on the draft and the antiwar demonstrations. He handled them all, cleanly and crisply.

"Let's do it right now," he said.

"Remember," Carville told him, "when he attacks you on the trust question, use your opening statement like a lawyer. Explain what's going on: he's behind and he's desperate."

Nothing more needed to be said; Clinton was pumped and ready. His seconds yelled and clapped when he walked out of his holding room that night and headed for the stage. Clinton shushed them, but as he pulled the door closed behind him, he flashed a wide smile their way.

"He's totally loose," Stephanopoulos said. They could smell victory in the air.

Bush, by contrast, approached the showdown as happily as a school-boy contemplating a mound of spinach. His seconds thought they had mousetrapped Clinton when they agreed to the town-hall rules of play; the president, too, had used the format often in his campaigns and had almost always done well at it. But when they laid it out for Bush at his dress rehearsal, his displeasure with it and with them was plain. He questioned everything, picking at the smallest details. Why wouldn't there be any lecterns on stage, just three bar-stools for the candidates? Was he supposed to sit on his, or did he have to stand for the whole ninety minutes? Would there be anything to write on? And why had the starting time been pushed back from seven to nine o'clock? Because of the baseball playoffs, his aides explained. The president was unassuaged; he was a five o'clock riser most mornings, and he was worried about wilting so late in the evening.

He seemed nevertheless to have prepared better for the second debate than he had for the first. His vague answers on public-policy questions in Saint Louis had disturbed his handlers and had played badly with Fred Steeper's focus group in Ohio; it was hard to sell the proposition that you had a plan if you had such visible trouble saying what was in it. "You need to improve your presentations of what you are proposing for your second term," Steeper counseled in his summary memo, and at the bottom, under the heading RECOMMENDATIONS FOR THE NEXT TWO DEBATES, he wrote:

> Define your second term.
> Define your second term.
> Define your second term.

Bush had taken the advice to heart, attacking his briefing books with more than the usual industry he brought to domestic-policy matters. His homework showed in his answers; he even navigated the details of his health-care plan without a misstep. But he got nowhere with his second strategic goal, deconstructing Clinton's character. The debate had barely started when the moderator, Carole Simpson, invited the audience of 209 undecided voters to tell the candidates what they had told her before curtain time: that they were sick of personal attacks and didn't want to hear any more. A ponytailed man rose in the gallery and did just that, challenging each of the candidates to limit himself to the issues and lay off the rough stuff. Bush misread the mood and tried to attack Clinton in spite of it. Clinton almost followed suit, starting a variant of the counterstrike he had been rehearsing. Unlike the president, he caught himself in mid-speech and eased off.

Bush never regained his stride. He seemed tired and uninterested in the proceedings. He glanced impatiently at his watch several times, as if he had somewhere more important to be; once, he remarked that Barbara would probably have had an easier time winning the race. In a hotel suite on the road, his blocking back, Dan Quayle, sat watching the show on television and waiting for the president to start swinging. "Here we go," Quayle said at one point, raising his fist in the air. "He's starting." But Bush faltered, not for the first time, and another opening was lost. By the end, Quayle's head was buried in his hands.

Perot did little better, this time around. He, too, was uncomfortable with the informal stage setting. He *needed* a podium, his ad man, Dennis McClain, remarked afterward; it masked his natural body language, the chesty manner of a little guy with an attitude. Without it, he seemed naked. The stool was too tall for him to sit on telegenically in the company of two six-footers; his feet wouldn't have reached the floor. He stood instead, looking gun-shy in repose and aggressive on the move. Neither mode was flattering to him. It was plain as well that he had stinted on his lessons, relying instead on his stock material. At one point, he flubbed a statistic, lighting up the gaffe gauges in the press gallery. Mr. Fix-it had run out of pat answers; his slip-up became his sound bite on the television news.

The night's defining moment belonged instead to Clinton. A young black woman provided the opening, with an awkwardly framed question about how three such powerful and sheltered men had been affected personally by the national debt. She meant the recession, not the debt, but only Clinton was quick enough to catch her drift. Perot, responding first, spoke of the sacrifice *he* was making to solve the problem; the debt, he said, was what had moved him to "disrupt my private life" and run for president. Bush, next up, did even worse. "I'm not sure I get it," he said. The words could have served admirably as the epitaph for his campaign. The trend lines in Greenberg's dial groups nosed toward the floor.

"Bush just lost the election," Carville said. His tone was matter-of-fact, almost clinical.

"That was the whole debate," Stephanopoulos said.

"Can you imagine if *we* had a candidate who did that?" Carville said. "You'd be fanning me right now."

The moment was made for Clinton, with his touchy-feely gifts at human connection. He walked up close to the young woman, made eye contact with her, and spoke affectingly of what it was like being governor of a small state in hard times; he *knew* people who had lost their jobs or their businesses and had been firsthand witness to their pain. The response was a grand-slam home run, and he knew it. Up to that moment, he would tell his people afterward, he thought he had been doing badly, but when Bush foundered, he could feel the tide turn. He *doesn't* get it, Clinton thought. The game was over, and he knew he had won.

Bush knew it, too. His manner had been flaccid, curiously so given the importance his handlers attached to bashing Clinton. "I really don't like all this mud wrestling," he told them; it was beneath the dignity of the office. The problem, in their view, was that he wouldn't *have* the office if he wasn't prepared to fight tooth and claw to hold onto it. The polls confirmed their pessimism; Clinton swept the overnights on who had won the debate, and in the Bush campaign's own soundings, his margin over the president doubled from eight points to sixteen by the eve of round three.

The Clinton dial groups had picked up similar readings. Words like "evasive," "weak," and "defensive" attached to the president. "He has had his four years," one swing voter said. "I just don't get into Bush's ideas any more," said another. Perot had fared better, but it was Clinton who came out the big winner; there were sharp upward spikes in his overall favorable rating and in his scores for honesty and trustworthiness.

"This is a major moment," Stan Greenberg told his colleagues over a celebratory late dinner in Richmond after the debate. "Major things happened tonight."

"This was a rout," Stephanopoulos said.

"This thing is *gone*," Carville agreed.

His dinner companions were startled by his finality. Carville was a famously superstitious man; in one of his past races, he had worn the same underwear ten days in a row when his client was on a roll.

"James," Stephanopoulos asked wickedly, "are you willing to say it's sealed?"

"I'm not willing to *say* it," Carville replied, backing off a half-step, "but if you hooked me up to a thought-o-meter . . ." He stopped and smiled. His comrades didn't need a meter to know what James was thinking.

He's Baa-ack

It was Sunday evening in the West Wing; the line troops had gone home, and the corridors outside the Oval Office were dark. Inside, George Bush sat with a few aides, working on what then amounted to a do-or-die strategy for the final debate on Monday night in East Lansing, Michigan. His mood had been curdled by a *Washington Post* dope story quoting several of his own hired hands, anonymously, as saying that it was all over—that it was time for prudent men and women in the president's employ to start freshening up their résumés. Bush sat listening impatiently to his coaches telling him that, this time, he *had* to go on the attack, early and hard; he had let too many openings slide by in the first two rounds.

"That's not the problem," Bush said, his brow dark with frustration. "I'm ready to do it. The problem is I'm the one son of a bitch around here who thinks I can win."

He was not wrong, though the men in the room protested their confidence in him; most of them were privately resigned to his defeat.

Their advice to him had a clarity born of desperation. He was out of options. He had to cut up Clinton's pretty-boy image and see if he would finally turn out to be the bleeder they had always expected him to be.

The president's preparations, this time, had an ascetic quality about them, the fading champion in retreat to harden himself for his last fight. He complained to Baker that he had been overprepared for the first two debates; there had been too many people in the room and too much conflicting advice in the air. His generals thinned the crowd and tried to lighten the atmosphere at his one formal run-through, with Darman once again playing Clinton and chief speechwriter Steve Provost replacing Sununu as Perot; Sununu had proved wrong for the part. At one point, Darman jabbed hard at the president for his embrace of laissez-faire economics.

"*I* know Laissez-Faire," Provost, as Perot, interjected to much laughter. "He's a French investment banker getting rich off our treasury bonds."

But a final rehearsal was scrapped; Bush packed up his briefing books and went off to Camp David instead to read and rest up alone. His only prepmasters, this time, were Baker and Ailes, the two coaches with whom he felt most comfortable. They blocked out a three-pronged strategy for him: attack, attack, attack. The target zones were to be taxes, trust, and Clinton's record in Arkansas; the underlying objective was to make him out to be a liar. "Forget all the facts and figures," Ailes told Bush. "Forget everything you've learned. Just relax, listen to the debate, and move to the offense as quickly as possible. You *know* what's he's going to say. When he does, come back down his smokestack."

Bush's compunction about the dignity of the office was gone; he knew what he had to do. The question among his aides was whether he had the spirit left to do it. He lunched with Baker and a couple of others at the White House mess that Monday, then made ready to leave for Michigan. Several of his aides wished him well. His eyes were sad. "Thanks—I'll try not to embarrass you fellas," he said, and he was gone.

His intentions were not hard for Clinton's strategists to read. They doubted that Bush would make too much of the personal questions, a course as likely to damage him as Clinton, but they were expecting all-out war on matters of public record: Arkansas, taxes, and waffling on the issues. "I'm scared shitless," Carville said, his thought-o-meter having gone into reverse in the four days since the second debate. "Bush is going to be ready tonight. He's been reading his briefing books. His aides say he's going to have a good debate."

Clinton himself was feeling poorly again; his allergies had sent him back to bed for another long midday nap, and he had wakened with a headache. His aides subjected him to a last prep session, reprising their planned response to character issues if they did come up. The night's format was a Solomonic compromise; there would be a single moderator, as Clinton preferred, for the first half and a panel of reporters, as Bush had asked, for the second. The plan was that if a personal question came from the moderator or the panel, Clinton was to answer it directly. If the president raised it, the order of the day was to fly down *his* smokestack.

"No matter how hard I hit," Clinton said, "I still think I have to come back to those 209 people in Richmond and say to Bush, 'You *still* don't get it. This election is about the people's problems, not my past as a twenty-three-year-old.'"

Bush did come out swinging that night, his manner crisp and combative, his answers well prepared. He admitted that he had made mistakes, the tax increase notable among them, but he gave a spirited defense of his record and wrapped himself in the national honor as the hero of Desert Storm. He fixed his sights on Clinton early on, as his war-gamers had urged him to do, and never let up. This time, moreover, he set the particulars of the attack in context, in the manner of a prosecutor summing up a complicated case. Fred Steeper had provided the thread in his memo on the first debate, warning the president not to lose sight of the big picture. "In our national polling and focus groups," he wrote, "people indicate a problem with Clinton based on his *pattern* of behavior. For some, it is a pattern of his irresponsible behavior; for others, it is his pattern of deceptions and lies." Bush seized on this last and, on stage in East Lansing, accused Clinton over and over again of having engaged in a "pattern" of deception about his public and private life. Could such a man be trusted with the presidency? His implicit answer was no.

There were high-fives in Bush's holding room with each new shot. The trouble was that Clinton was in equally good form and was counterpunching effectively. He got in his line about the 209 voters in Richmond, not once but twice, and when an opening presented itself, he reached for one of those "moments" his people had scripted for him. There wouldn't be any domestic czars like Jim Baker if *he* got elected, he said. "The person responsible for domestic economic policy in *my* administration will be Bill Clinton."

"That's what worries me," Bush retorted without a pause.

A silence had fallen over Bush's aides at Clinton's shot; it was a killer line, one they hadn't anticipated or prepared the president for. But this time, for once, he had taken a hard serve and bashed it back in Clinton's face. His holding room exploded; in a game scored almost exclusively by the number and quality of one's sound bites, the champ had just trumped the challenger.

Both men did well in the postmortems; the problem was that, in some of the first-blush analyses that frame public perceptions, Ross Perot had done even better. He had been furniture in the second debate, the man who talked the most and said the least. In the third, he was playing poltergeist again, the role that suited him best, and Bush was no longer the sole target of his scorn; Perot had become an equal-opportunity maker of political mischief. He scoffed at both men for the timidity of their economic plans as against the "fair, shared sacrifice" he was proposing as the one true path to a balanced budget and a renewed economy. Bush had already struck out, in his view, and Clinton had never managed an economy bigger than Arkansas's.

"We're probably making a mistake, night after night after night, to cast the nation's future on a unit that small," Perot said.

"Why is it a mistake?" the moderator, Jim Lehrer, asked him.

"It's *irrelevant*," Perot said. "I could say I ran a small grocery store on the corner; therefore, I extrapolate that into the fact that I could run Wal-Mart. That's not true." He turned to Clinton, his gaze dismissive. "I carefully picked an Arkansas company," he said.

The thrust seemed briefly to deflate Clinton; nothing in Bush's more detailed attack had been quite so diminishing to him or to his claims of high accomplishment in his home state. His aides contented themselves with his having survived the night and even having won on some scorecards; among the four overnight network polls, two awarded him the victory, a third favored Perot, and a fourth called it a draw between the two of them. But the nine-day war within a war had exacted a price, bringing the case against Clinton into sharper focus for a vastly wider audience. His unfavorable rating, in the manageable high thirties for much of the summer, inched upward into the low forties—a level normally thought dangerous to a candidate's health.

The problem, for Bush, was that *his* unfavorables rose, too, from the low to the middle fifties. His best performance had come two debates too late and was not enough to arrest his slide into history. His campaign had been immobilized for ten precious days with no direct advantage to himself—only another entry on a long list of chances squandered and opportunities lost. "He flubbed it," one of his closest aides said a week after the last debate. "He just flubbed it. He flubbed so many lines. Do you want a list?"

His consolation prize was that Ross Perot had done so well; in the dying weeks of his presidency, Bush's last hope for reelection hung improbably on Perot's success. Perot alone among the three could be said actually to have *gained* ground during the fall forensic tournament; his share of the vote went up from 10 percent before the first debate to 15 percent after the last, and his favorable rating rose from 25 to 56 percent, the best in the field. His strong performance had washed out some of the taint left over from the eccentric course and the abrupt end of his first campaign. He had made himself plausible again with his cocky manner and his blunt speech; his closing statement, an appeal to the people to take back their country from the politicians and the press, was perhaps his most powerful single utterance of the campaign. "The debates made us," Clay Mulford said; in their wake, the Plain Texas Talker came to believe that he could win.

For a wild few days, Clinton's handlers fell prey to a frisson of panic. After his star turn in the second debate, they had begun to think his election bankable and had given themselves to chatter about where they would go afterward to rest up for the transition. The Perot effect coming out of East Lansing sobered them up. Stan Greenberg's latest poll, two days after the debate, gave the Texan 19 percent of the vote, and too much of his growth was coming at Clinton's expense. Clinton's lead over the president had melted down to eight points. If Perot kept growing, he could tip the election to Bush.

"I'm just sick," Stephanopoulos said, staring at the numbers.

"I guess I won't make my vacation plans yet," Greenberg said. "The world changed on us in the last twenty-four hours."

30

To the Wire

Suddenly, in the final weeks, the return engagement of George Bush in his hit 1988 role as the Terminator seemed to be paying off again. The president and his team had put on one of the most unremittingly negative campaigns in our contemporary history, so strident that his own substantial virtues and his newly minted agenda for America were barely afterthoughts to the violence of his assault and battery on Bill Clinton. His handlers called his line of attack T&T, for taxes and trust, and once he finally got his lines straight in the third debate, it began drawing blood. The race narrowed giddily; for the first time since Labor Day, Bush's lieutenants could seriously imagine his winning a second term.

His situation in fact was more nearly remission than recovery, but while it lasted, it was white-knuckle time again in Clinton's War Room in Little Rock—a bungee jump from a double-digit lead to five points in their own polling and to one in the most discouraging of the public surveys. The challenger's team couldn't be sure that he had touched bottom, and a campaign then still being taxed in the press with its overconfidence found itself in a state approaching terror.

"How scared are you?" George Stephanopoulos asked, dropping by James Carville's office one night for company watching the evening news.

"How scared?" Carville replied. "I'm *this* scared: if we lose, I won't commit suicide, but I'll *serious* contemplate it."

It was, ironically, Ross Perot who had set off their latest angst attack with his dominating performance in the last debate. Till then, he had been almost a de facto ally, concentrating most of his fire on the president; the enemy of their enemy had become, to that degree, their friend. But in East Lansing, he had turned on Clinton, bracketing him with Bush as twins separated at birth. The two of them were, in Perot's rendering, the look-alike progeny of a discredited political establishment; neither one had the wit, the plan, or the courage to do what would have to be done to balance the budget, pay down the debt, and revive the economy.

The outcome was what the crew in the War Room had feared in their first anxious reading of the polls. Perot had reestablished himself not just as a serious candidate but as the real agent of change in the race; he seemed to Clinton himself to have won the debate on economics, the only issue that mattered in 1992. He wasn't going to get *elected*, but Clinton's wounds were bleeding again, and Perot had achieved a measure of legitimacy for himself as an alternative. Within days, he was bumping 20 percent in the polls, a level at which Clinton's handlers considered him dangerous. At 25 percent, by their calculations, he could be death.

As usual at critical moments, the campaign had resort to its favorite oracle: focus groups. A fresh round was set up in Macomb County, Michigan, Stan Greenberg's taste-testing kitchen for the whims and humors of that critical swing group called Reagan Democrats. Clinton's people came back to Little Rock alarmed by what they had heard. It wasn't just the spillage of their target voters to Perot that troubled them, though that was heavy. It was instead the echo of Bush's attack themes in their reasons for deserting. They were taking a second look at the entire field, and it was not flattering to Clinton. The character issue was back, "disturbingly" so, Celinda Lake reported in a memo. The people in the observation chambers thought Clinton too smooth, too programmed, too political, and they questioned how he would pay for all his promises without new taxes.

"He's one of the most polished bullshitters I've seen," a man said in one of the sessions.

"He's promising too much," another said.

"I'd like to hear him answer *something* straight out," said a third.

Somebody called him "wishy-washy."

"He's not really," somebody else objected. "He's done good things for Arkansas."

"Yeah," came the reply, "but could he have done a good job in New York? Arkansas is an easy state. Ross Perot could have handled New York."

Perot, indeed, was the direct beneficiary of their disappointment in the major-party candidates. He was bottom-feeding for the votes Bush was chipping away from Clinton. He had become the second un-Bush in the field, respectable again, a way for a switched-off electorate to vote against a president they didn't want and a challenger they didn't trust.

"I'm tired of the two clowns going after one another," a man said in one of the groups. "It's about time someone stood up and talked about the issues."

"He's a hardline guy," another added. "He doesn't take no crap." "Perot says, 'I can make it happen,'" said a third. "The other two are begging for the job."

"He knows what everyone at this table needs," a fourth ventured. "Clinton and Bush are for the corporate interests."

Bush had no friends at all in the room. The mention of his name was like the touch of a probe to an exposed nerve; all the familiar complaints about him spilled forth—"He's status quo," one man said— and not a soul voted for him in the straw ballots at the end of the sessions. But Perot split the no votes with Clinton; he got three out of ten in one group, all women, and five of ten in a second, all men. His presence had opened a seam for Bush, wide enough for him to slip through if Clinton couldn't find a way to block it. "Bush was gone in these groups," Celinda Lake wrote. "Voters were disgusted and had given up on him. Our competition was Perot; our remaining problems are rooted in ourselves."

The immediate question was how to slow Perot's point-a-day rise in the polls. Clinton had come to regret having laid off him in the debates, and Hillary was even more violent on the subject; she agitated within the campaign for taking him down, fast, by any licit means necessary. The media had been slow recognizing the significance of his surge and the anxiety attack it had provoked in Little Rock. "They don't think we're worried sick," Carville said, "but we are." There was risk in calling their attention to the Perot effect by showing too much concern with it. Hillary didn't care; she *was* concerned, and she wanted action.

The others doubted the wisdom of doing negative ads on Perot. Still, the War Room crew played with some attack themes, just in case. For the most part, they shied away from anything personal, in deference to the tender feelings of Perot's supporters. They zeroed in instead on the Perot plan, or, as they preferred in light of the vice-presidential debate, the Perot-*Stockdale* plan; it would damage the economy, so the argument ran, and would come down hardest on the middle class. But when they went back to their focus groups to try out their lines, none of them worked.

"People don't *want* any bullshit about Perot," Stephanopoulos brooded. "All they want to know is who we are, what we're going to do, and how we're going to do it."

Perot remained a nonetheless haunting presence at Clinton headquarters, a bad dream that refused to go away with daybreak. "I can't believe in the end that people will vote for Perot *or* Bush," Carville said over dinner one evening, with the debates still reverberating in the polls. But his fear showed through his profession of faith in popular democracy.

"Is there a natural ceiling to Ross Perot's support?" he asked Greenberg.

Greenberg had been obliged to revise his own estimate upward. "About five points above where he is now," he said. "Twenty-three percent or so."

"If he don't get more than 25, we ain't going to lose," Carville guessed.

"I don't think he will get more than 25," Greenberg said.

Their mood darkened as they watched the new dynamic take form. Till then, Mandy Grunwald fretted, they had successfully made the race a referendum on the president. Now Bush was turning it back on them; a referendum on Clinton's character was not the ground they wanted to fight on, but that was where they found themselves, and the result was depressingly plain in their polls and focus groups. "It's 'he has no spine' and 'all things to all people,'" Grunwald said. "We're going back to where we were last spring."

The press watched the steady narrowing of the numbers and reported it as a surge for Bush. It wasn't; even on his best days, his market share in the polls was still stalled in the middle thirties, about where it had been when Perot first reentered the race. The surge, to the extent there was one, had been away from Clinton; the incessant daily attacks on his character were dragging him back to the pack, and Perot, not Bush, appeared to be winning over the major share of the defectors.

Each new day brought a flutter of polls, some public, some private, some good, some bad; their all-over-the-lot findings set the mood at headquarters bobbing up and down like a yo-yo on a string. One morning less than two weeks before the election, an NBC/*Wall Street Journal* sounding showed Clinton leading Bush by nineteen points. "Too bad it isn't true," Stephanopoulos said morosely. In the next day's harvest, their lead ranged from a comfortable thirteen points to a scary three. Carville and Stephanopoulos, for whom the glass was always half empty, were prepared to believe the worst. "We better get out of denial and get our asses into reality," Carville raged; reality, to him, was a trend line pointing down.

The calm at the eye of the storm reposed mostly in the mind and person of Stan Greenberg; for a time, they were the main props to the morale of the campaign. He never believed that there *had* been a Bush surge, not even when the gap closed to one point in a Gallup poll for CNN and *USA Today* in the last week. His faith was grounded in his own numbers, which showed Clinton with a shrunken but rock-steady lead. Whenever Carville and Stephanopoulos got an attack of the heebie-jeebies, Greenberg would walk them around the terrain one more time and cool them down. "I don't know if our pollster's *right*," Carville said, "but he's ballsy. He's telling everybody not to panic, and we're panicking."

The prime source of his comfort was his state-by-state polling; all their careful targeting and their rifle-shot media buys were paying off in electoral votes, the only kind that finally counted. The tightening in the national numbers was happening disproportionately in Bush's strongest states, which were goners anyway, and in Clinton's, where it didn't matter; his margins in the states on his Top End list were so big that he hadn't even bothered to advertise. The national polls counted only in the battle of perceptions; it was to Bush's great advantage to *seem* to be catching up with Clinton. What both camps knew was that his supposed rush to the wire was illusory. In the battleground states, where the race would be decided, Clinton had got on the air earlier with bigger advertising buys, and he was leading in practically all of them.

Canny though he was, Carville needed to be reminded of that baseline fact from time to time, and Greenberg cheerfully obliged. Ten days out, he said, Clinton was leading by six points in Ohio, not great but okay. He was up eighteen in Illinois, twenty-one in Massachusetts, fourteen in Oregon, seven in Georgia, fourteen in Delaware and so on.

"Whoop!" Carville exclaimed happily. "They're breaking for us, boys, they're breaking for us!"

The fix barely sustained him through the next-to-last weekend of the campaign. On Monday night, with eight days to go, he sat tense and impatient in the dining room at the Capital Hotel in Little Rock, waiting for Greenberg to come downstairs with his latest polling. Carville had guessed that Clinton's lead would be down to five points. Greenberg's guess had been nine.

"It's mixed," he said when he appeared at Carville's table.

"I *knew* it," Carville said. His voice was almost a moan.

"It's nine points nationally, 43-34-20," Greenberg said. "But the *states* are mixed."

The two went through them together. Even to Carville's pessimistic eye, they looked okay.

"That ain't mixed," he said, "that's *good* news. We ain't lost anything since the debates."

His relief again was short-lived. The meltdown of Clinton's margin nationally was still going on, with a nervous-making velocity. It was down to seven points in Greenberg's tracking that evening and five points the next; Clinton was dropping two points a night, and the Bush campaign was out there live and on television trying to complete his ruin. The assault, in the closing weeks, took on a scorched-earth ferocity that surprised and spooked the boys in the War Room. Its epiphany was the president's closing attack ad, picturing Arkansas as a wasteland while a narrator did a savage recital of Clinton's supposed failures there; the closing shot showed a buzzard perched on a barren tree, the sole sign of life on what looked otherwise like a nuclear winterscape.

They called the spot "Vulture" on Fifteenth Street, for its imagery and its intended effect. Like much of what the Bush campaign did, the ad was history repeated as farce. They had burned Michael Dukakis in 1988 with a devastating spot focusing on the pollution of Boston Harbor; the visuals of its filthy waters made mockery of Dukakis's claims to have wrought a Massachusetts Miracle. The Bush-Quayle '92 team found no such compelling metaphor, so they made one up, turning Clinton's Arkansas into something more nearly resembling Stalin's Siberia. Their work was too late and far too loud; the images of devastation were only too obviously overstated, and focus groups laughed them off.

But it was an arrow at the heart of Clinton's self-esteem, and for a day or two, it pained him badly enough to knock him off his winning message; suddenly, he was defending his integrity by attacking Bush's. He found himself at war with his own handlers, who preferred that he limit his counterpunching to the economy and leave the trust issue alone. It made no sense to them to be fighting on the president's turf rather than their own; it was a battle Clinton couldn't win, and when he demanded a spot of his own slamming back at Bush, they tried to talk him out of it.

Clinton was adamant. The more he thought about the "Vulture" ad, during a three-state swing across the South, the steamier he got, and by the time he arrived at the night's last rally in Louisville, he was torchy hot. "Every time Bush talks about trust, it makes chills run up and down my spine," he told the crowd, his voice as near a shout as he could still manage. "The very idea that the word 'trust' could come out of Mr. Bush's mouth, after what he's done to this country and the way he's trampled on the truth, is a travesty of the American political system."

Afterward, he retreated to a holding room and stoked up for his next appearance, on *Larry King Live,* with a grab-and- run dinner. He was pleased with himself. Paul Begala came in from a reconnaissance tour of the press gallery. The reporters, he said, had been asking him what had set the governor off.

"Tell them I got a bellyful of it," Clinton rasped. "Tell them my trusted aides restrained me long enough. The real truth is, I'm sick of it, and I think George Bush is a threat to the republic if he gets reelected."

Begala let him ventilate. Clinton's blowups were a regular part of his response to pressure situations, a kind of safety valve for his psyche; he was always better afterward—as if, one aide said, he had been blundering through a maze with a lot of fits and starts and had finally found a way out. On the *King* show that night, he turned down the volume of his attack on the president. But he wasn't quite out of the maze yet. Intellectually, he knew that it was folly to be presenting *himself* as the aggrieved party; he had got to the finals arguing that the real victims of the Bush presidency were the American people. Emotionally, he had a hard time letting go of his anger. It was *his* character and *his* reputation taking the hits, and when the debate with his command team resumed in the morning, he had not got over the itch to hit back.

His people tried to explain, in rather more respectful terms, that it was *still* the economy, stupid; that was the issue that had got Clinton to the top of the polls and it remained his strongest weapon. It was okay to question Bush's trustworthiness, the War Room command said in a long, testy conference call, but not to make an oh-yeah fistfight out of it; he had to bring it back to the president's failed policies. They had a deadly ad ready, the one recounting Bush's economic promises and asking sardonically at the end, "How ya doing?" Forget Arkansas, they argued. Put up "How ya doing?" instead.

Clinton listened, still simmering at the idea of letting the president's attack ad sit up there unrebutted. "It goes against everything I believe," he said. "I did that once and was beaten in 1980, and I've never allowed that to happen since. I am *very* worried about this."

His handlers never quite *won* the argument; instead, they wore Clinton down, to a point where he simply gave up. He handed his cellular phone over to his road staff. "*You* talk to them," he said. "I've got so much emotionally invested in this, I'm not sure I trust my judgment."

The how-ya-doing ad went on the air, and Clinton recovered his own footing in his stump speeches. "Go out and scare the hell out of them about four more years of George Bush economics," Begala said, warming him up for a rally in downtown Detroit. Clinton did, from that point on. He had discovered his own way of answering Bush's ad hominem attacks, scare for scare; imagine waking up the morning after the election, he said at every stop, to headlines reading FOUR MORE YEARS.

Taxes and Trust, Stupid

For much of the autumn, the president had been running as if on a treadmill to nowhere. Ahead of him was one man he found contemptible; behind him, another he sometimes thought quite mad. He genuinely believed that he was the best of the lot, and yet he seemed stuck in place, unable to gain ground on either one. "I'm gonna win this election," he said one day in September when his own son George W. fell prey to an attack of the glooms. "Make no mistake about it—I'm gonna win." But the game face that had masked his unhappiness all year had become only that, a mask. By October, even he was waxing philosophical, in his rare moments of privacy, about the possibility of his losing the election and the presidency. It wouldn't be the end of life, he said. In some respects, it would be a huge relief.

It was hard for his strategists to look at their reddening battle maps and pretend that his situation was otherwise. They had worked up a secret target list of twenty-nine states, enough for a bare majority of 274 in the electoral college. By mid-October, the president was leading securely in only six and was competitive in seven more; the lot would have given him just 110 electoral votes, to 405 for Clinton, if the election had been held that day. "Kansas and Mississippi are up for grabs, for crying out loud!" a senior campaign operative wailed. Four years earlier, Bush had had the luxury of trolling for votes in normally Democratic states. This time, it was Clinton who was off fishing in what once had been Republican waters.

"Now I know how we made *them* feel in '88," Jim Baker said, his tone matter of fact. "They're playing with us."

To Bob Teeter, it looked like simple cherry-picking, aimed at tying the president down in his own backyard.

"Bob, I don't think he's cherry-picking," Baker said. "I think he's shaking the whole damn tree."

The pessimism all around them was as thick as a fog at sea and as debilitating to the spirit. They were, as George W. put it, running into a ninety-mile-an-hour media headwind—the press had long since written Bush off as a loser—and a recession as well. On a good day, a campaign official put his chance of winning at one in ten. On bad days, which were far more common, the troops scanned the maps and thought they saw shades of Barry Goldwater, the victim of a forty-four state landslide in 1964. "Stop that Goldwater talk!" Teeter commanded them one day. The thought was harder to banish; in Teeter's own analogy, near the end, Bush was a pool player who needed to drop fourteen balls with two shots.

One shot might have done, had it been devastating enough, but the quest for the Big One kept bumping into Bush's code of propriety and Teeter's circumspection at the thought of doing anything rash. The combination placed sex out of bounds as a subject of direct attack on Clinton, though rumors kept flying in over the transom. Not long after Labor Day, Cliff Jackson, the celebrated Little Rock lawyer with a subspecialty in gathering and spreading material detrimental to Clinton, called Charlie Black and told him, "I have some guys here who want to tell you their story." Jackson flicked on a speaker phone and put the "guys" on the line; they turned out to be several Arkansas state troopers claiming first-hand knowledge of their former boss's carelessness of his marriage vows.

"I believe it," Black told them, "but what I believe doesn't matter. Nobody in this campaign can pursue this. You have to go to the press."

When Jackson finally did, it was more than a year too late to help Bush. The troopers' tales would finally see print in the *Los Angeles Times* and the conservative *American Spectator* long after it mattered to the outcome of the election.

Again, in October, a longtime party operative called a member of Bush's inner circle, convinced that he had a line on one of Clinton's rumored amours.

The offer was waved off. "If the girls were willing to come forward," his friend on Fifteenth Street said, "we might have a chance to do some damage. But they won't, and why should they? They're married with kids. Why would you want to admit something like that if you've got a kid in the fourth grade?"

"What *can* I do?" the talebearer asked.

"Go down to your local phone bank," his friend said, "and work like hell to get George Bush reelected."

It was plain by then that Bush wasn't going to help, not if it meant poking around in Clinton's bed linens. Toward the end of the campaign, *Penthouse* magazine bought and published the last scrapings from the bottom of Gennifer Flowers's depleted barrel, in a lengthy text-and-pictures interview. The spread disgusted Bush when a bootleg advance copy plopped on his desk in the Oval Office. "Can you imagine other world leaders reading that before he's even inaugurated?" he said. "I worry about what this means for the country."

To some of his people, he seemed to be conceding out of some inner despair that Clinton *would* be inaugurated. If so, the sacrifice of his chances to his fastidiousness was one he was apparently prepared to make. He ordered his people not to push the *Penthouse* story, and when they came up with an idea for a television spot using extracts from Flowers's taped phone calls with Clinton, the answer again was no. The script had nothing to do with their sexual carryings-on, if any; the idea instead was to scroll through some of Clinton's non-libidinous chat about the importance of keeping their connection quiet if anybody asked. "You read that transcript and you *know* the guy isn't fit to be president," one aide said. But Bush Rules prevailed, and the ad was never made.

The more hawkish sorts in the president's service never gave up their effort to get *something* on Clinton. They relied on the covert track in their intelligence operation and prayed for a breakthrough; their hope was to find and detonate a bombshell and still assure Bush of deniability, even to himself. The sleuthing, done largely through cutouts, continued nearly to the end of the campaign. The Whitewater affair looked then like a dry hole. The target areas instead were sex and the draft, and in the last weeks of the campaign, outside operatives with no traceable ties to the president or his team were pursuing their last suggestive leads along both vectors:

• **The Case of the Preacher's Daughter:** Her name was Naomi, the young black woman said when she rang Bush-Quayle headquarters from a pay phone somewhere in the South one morning in October, and she had a story to tell. It was the day before the first debate. She was weeping. She was, she said, a postal worker in Houston and a devout Christian, the daughter of a Baptist preacher. She had attended a weekend party at her sister's house in Little Rock one Fourth of July weekend in the middle 1980s. A lot of local politicians had been there, Clinton among them, she said, and in a state of boozy concupiscence, they had gone to bed. There were pictures, so she said through her tears. Her sister had been trying without success to contact the Clinton campaign, hoping to sell them the photos for five thousand dollars. Naomi wanted nothing, she said, except that inner peace that would come with God's forgiveness; testifying to her sins before the world would be a part of her atonement.

There had been many calls during the long course of the campaign from women claiming to have had liaisons with Clinton. Most of the callers had flunked one or another threshold test of credibility and had been sent packing. Naomi's tale posed a rather different question for Bush's men—whether it might not be too good to be true. Was the Clinton campaign setting them up, using her as a decoy to entrap them in a dirty trick? They considered the idea, then rejected it. Perhaps it was her tears and her naïveté that persuaded them, perhaps their own desperation; in either case, they *wanted* to believe her, and they did. The aide who spoke with her that morning took down the number of the pay phone—it was easily traced to a small town in Louisiana—and persuaded her to stand by for a return call.

There was a quick scramble to find an outsider willing to serve as her case officer; he rang Naomi back, the first of about ten calls over as many days aimed at teasing her in from the cold. The operation was known to several top officials on Fifteenth Street, though not to the president; the rule, as usual, was that what he didn't know wouldn't hurt him. The plan instead was to reel her in quietly, get her into a hotel room in Washington with a couple of reporters, and have her tell her story and show her pictures to them. To satisfy Bush Rules—or, more accurately, to get around them—it had to look as if confessing were her own idea, not something the campaign had put her up to.

For a time, the plan seemed to be ripening nicely. Naomi's account held up well under questioning; her contact had investigated a number of other bimbo eruptions for the campaign, and had believed none of them until she came along. He offered her a plane ticket and an escort to Washington; she seemed to prefer making her own way there. A second and third cutout retained a lawyer for her in Lafayette, Louisiana, to help her handle any problems she might bring down on her own head. A fourth was enlisted to contact the appropriate reporters; if Naomi's tale should turn out to have been a honey trap set by Clinton's people after all, the Bush campaign couldn't afford to have its prints on the invitation.

Everything seemed to be on track when, the day of the third debate, Naomi phoned one last time to say that she had decided to try to get through to the Clinton camp. She would call back, collect, the next morning, she promised.

She never did.

For a suspenseful day or so, Bush's people sat tight, hoping against hope that she would show up on their doorstep as scheduled. Forty-eight hours slipped by without a word or a sighting. Her case officer was dispatched to Louisiana to hunt her down. He went to every church in the town she had called from, asking for a preacher with a daughter named Naomi. The search led nowhere; all it turned up was

the location of the pay phone, at a combination gas station and convenience store at the edge of town. The operative flew on to Houston,
where he canvassed every branch post office in the phone book without success. The trail had gone cold. Naomi was nowhere to be found.

In their gloom, Bush's operatives guessed that her disappearance
had been begged, bought, or otherwise rigged by Clinton's counterintelligence agents. In practical terms, it didn't matter. They would have
to look elsewhere for the silver bullet. "Naomi" might as well never
have existed at all.

• **The Case of the Gun-Shy Marine:** He was a longtime Bush
loyalist with strong but invisible ties to the campaign, and he, too, had
been enlisted in the search for the Big One. He had spent the evening
of October 15 in front of his television set at home, watching his man
lose the second debate. When it was over, he waved a visitor into the
kitchen and, with an air of mystery, pulled out a legal pad blackened
with hen tracks. "The president is mortally wounded," he said. "He
might pull it out with some miracle. I'm working on the miracle."

The object of *his* attentions, he said, was a man who had gone to
high school with Clinton in the 1960s and had later been a Fulbright
scholar in Norway during Clinton's years as a Yank at Oxford. Their
paths had diverged since, Clinton's into politics, his schoolmate's into
the military; by the fall of 1992, he was a marine colonel assigned to
the Pentagon. But he was said to have carried with him a tale that
could have been, in the words of Bush's man on the case, the game
breaker if it checked out—the lethal scandal they had been chasing so
hard for so long.

The story, as the colonel had told it to at least six acquaintances over
a period of ten years, was that Clinton had pitched up at his place in
Oslo at midnight one December night during his Rhodes years in a
state of high agitation over the draft and the war. In a conversation
that ran on till five in the morning, he said he had decided to renounce
his citizenship and move to Sweden to avoid serving. The colonel, in
this telling, had talked him out of doing anything so rash; his contrary
advice, he said, had been to go home to Arkansas and submit to the
draft, no matter how passionate his feelings about America's involvement in Vietnam.

There were two large problems with the story. First, it clashed badly
with the Bush campaign's earlier portrayal of Clinton as a man who had
been running for president practically since infancy and who had been
obsessed even during the war years with maintaining his "political viability." Second, and more critical to the search, the colonel himself had

changed his tune in more recent conversations—some of them with people friendly to the Bush campaign. His earlier versions, he said, had been a kind of verbal docudrama, fact overlaid with fiction for heightened effect. Clinton hadn't *really* said that he was planning to give up his citizenship, the colonel now insisted; it had never been more than a what-if that he had thought about and had as quickly rejected on his own.

The more suspicious sorts at Bush-Quayle headquarters simply presumed that another source had been somehow got to and silenced. The case officer kept chasing his miracle anyway, hoping, at the very least, for an affidavit laying out the colonel's amended story; it could have been used to connect Clinton to the *idea* of defecting, even if it had never been more than the fleeting fantasy of a young man in anguish over the war. At one point in the pursuit, the campaign—operating once again through cut-outs—enlisted the retired commandant of the corps, P. X. Kelley, to meet with the colonel at a Hyatt hotel in Rosslyn, Virginia, across the Potomac from Washington, and see what he could talk out of him, marine to marine. The colonel agreed to the rendezvous but was skittish about it. At his insistence, neither his name nor his description was given to Kelley; the general reported to the hotel at the appointed time, staked out a place in the lobby, and waited to be approached by a man he did not know.

The minutes ticked away. Nobody appeared. The possibility of a missed connection was negligible; the colonel had informed his case officer that he would know the general by sight. After an hour, Kelley called his contact. The colonel, he was told, had phoned in five minutes earlier and had canceled the date. He had been warned off, he had said, by a source he wouldn't name. The message had been that the other side was on to him and that, if he valued his career in the military, it would be wise for him to break off his contacts with the Bush campaign. The chase was thereupon aborted and the case file closed.

With the failure of their quest for a doomsday weapon, the Bush campaign was forced back to waging conventional warfare with the ammunition that had been there all along. "There are still too many unanswered questions about this guy's character," the president told an old friend, and in the last weeks, he and his surrogates seemed bent on raising all of them *except* sex. TAXES AND TRUST, STUPID, somebody wrote on a conference-room blackboard on Fifteenth Street, flattering James Carville by imitation. The two words were a rubric broad enough to capture all the unresolved doubts about Clinton, the dark undercoat of suspicion beneath his artfully retouched portrait; you couldn't trust his word, Bush argued everywhere, on taxes or anything else.

The final assault had begun in the third debate with the president's repeated allusions to Clinton's "pattern" of deceit; it was a way of using his evasions on private matters to undercut his promises of change in the public arena. Jim Baker, for one, liked the way the line resonated, and in the days thereafter, he sent Bush a memo, urging that he up the ante still more:

> I'd recommend that you follow through with your strong debate performance and put a stress in the stump [speech] for the next few days on Clinton's pattern of either equivocating or lying. I think you should begin with examples of policy flip-flops and evasions (without hitting the draft which just turns people off), and then end with:
>
> "Governor Clinton's got a problem. He's a programmed politician with a pathological pattern of prevarication. Right now, it's just his problem. Don't let it become America's."
>
> That's a paragraph the press will have to use—and it will put Clinton on the defensive if we use policy flip-flops and evasions to get into it.

Bush never uttered the lines; even in his attack mode, it offended his gentleman's code to call his adversary a liar. But he didn't mind leaving that impression in less direct ways, and the message, with endless repetition, finally seemed to be clicking. Clinton's favorable ratings stayed remarkably steady in the low fifties through most of the fall campaign. The punishing effect showed up instead in his unfavorable numbers, which inched up from the middle thirties around Labor Day to the middle forties by the last week of the campaign. The erosion of faith in him in turn prefigured the sudden contraction of his lead. Bush wasn't gaining on him; instead, Clinton was falling back, bleeding from a thousand cuts. "Everything we've thrown at him," a member of Bush's polling team said comfortably, "is coming back to us in the data."

The day Bush's generals dared to start hoping was the day, less than a week before the end, when Fred Steeper showed up for a meeting at the White House grinning. The polltaker had been Doctor Gloom & Doom for a year, but his tracking poll had restored the roses to his cheeks. Clinton's lead had fallen from ten to seven points overnight and was still shrinking.

"I think we could win this thing," Steeper said. "We've had a major shift."

"I guess it *is* over if *you're* smiling," a colleague said.

Bush himself seemed unsurprised by the turn in his fortunes. He had come out of the debates on a nearly manic high, hammering away with his message, if not his syntax, under tight control at last. For days, the only mark of progress had been his own revived relish for the game, on display for the first time all year; he was campaigning as if he actually enjoyed it. Fritz Mondale in 1984 and Michael Dukakis in 1988 had finished on similar rushes of crowd noise and adrenalin; they had heard the sound of the faithful coming home and had persuaded themselves that they were winning. Bush, in his turn, had fallen under the same hypnotic spell. When somebody brought him the news that the gap was down to five points, he slammed his knee with his fist and said, "I *knew* it. I've known it all along."

His people were at pains to keep him pumped up. They did not speak to him about the nearly impossible task of retinting the computer maps in Bush blue. The day Steeper smiled, Bush was still trailing in fourteen of the twenty-nine states on his target list and was leading by five points or better in only two, Kansas and Utah. Several of his must states were gone or going. He was still drawing to an inside straight.

His handlers cheered him instead with the polls.

"Here's how it's gonna go the rest of the way," Jim Baker told him one day, when the race had closed to three points in one public poll. He got a sheet of paper and sketched a line zigzagging daily from plus one to minus two to plus three to minus one.

"On Tuesday," Baker said, sounding more confident than he felt, "it's gonna be one up."

I told you so, Bush's smile replied.

Red Flares in the Sunset

The game was Texas Hold-'em, and for the first time since his hot streak in the spring, Ross Perot was looking at aces again. His share of the vote had doubled over the nine-day course of the debates, and his favorable rating had jumped thirty-five points, from the worst to the best in the field. The china was rattling noisily at Clinton headquarters in Little Rock, and the boys on Fifteenth Street briefly forgot how much they were relying on Perot to do well. With him around, one Bush-Quayle strategist worried, the president could do worse than any major-party nominee since a mercifully forgotten Democrat named John W. Davis polled 29 percent of the vote in a three-way race with Calvin Coolidge and Fighting Bob LaFollette in 1924.

Perot's problem was that he had three enemies as formidable, in their way, as the men he was running against. One was the clock; as his friend Tom Luce had foreseen and tried to tell him early on, he was starting too late to compete for more than a minor fraction of the electorate. The second was the polls; even with his return to respectability, he was still fighting the judgment that he was too far behind to win. The third was himself; having seized the wheel of the campaign from the professionals, the Plain Texas Talker proceeded to steer it over a cliff.

The wonder, indeed, was that Perot was doing so well, given the proudly amateurish mind-set he had installed at the top of his campaign. He still had the money to spend, $40 million of it for advertising alone, and the marvelous gift at vernacular politics he had brought to the debates. Perhaps 40 percent of the electorate had considered voting for him at one point or another in his journey, and his performance on stage with Clinton and Bush had reminded a fair number of the strays why they had liked him. But his resistance to anything that smacked of politics made it impossible for him to get out a coherent message or to defend himself against attack. He and his new crew hated the game too much to play it with rivals who knew how.

His minimalist, twenty-one-state strategy, like his campaign itself, had turned out to be a work of naive art. A more traditional candidate would have invested heavily in what the trade calls face time in his target states, backing up his broadcast ads with live appearances. Perot would have none of it. Having grounded himself in Dallas, he had neither the time nor the will to visit even half the states on his list. To the very end, the populist in the race was only rarely to be found among the people; by election day, he would have ventured out for only eleven rallies all season, five of them in the last seventy-two hours.

His nearly total reliance on paid television was unprecedented even in the age of media politics. He had started well enough with his two chart talks on how bad a pickle America was in and how he proposed to fix it. His overnights in the Nielsen ratings were his last laugh at the network commentators—"the masters of the universe," he liked to call them—who had predicted confidently that a half-hour of straight talk about serious matters was too much for the mass American mind. "Nineteen-point-five million people watched one of the chart shows," he crowed at a rally in Denver. "Win, lose, or draw, we could probably get a TV series going next year."

But like most new series, Perot's had its share of costly start-up troubles. He and his shrunken war council decided, after some argument, that what needed work next was Ross the Man; they had to undo the damage done to his image in his aborted first campaign. They had guessed wrong; it was Ross the Messenger who had captured the debates with his blunt speech and had started upward in the polls without benefit of the usual warm-and-fuzzy advertising about *him*.

His rise caught his campaign unprepared. They had bought up huge blocks of network time and, till the last days, had nothing in the can on issues except reruns to fill it with. They were stuck instead with a series of five half-hour segments glorifying Perot as husband, father, businessman, benefactor, and all-round fine fellow—not as that scrappy little guy with the charts and the answers to America's problems.

Much of the good the miniseries did him was undone in any case in a single network-television appearance on *60 Minutes* nine days before the election—a return engagement of the candidate as Inspector Perot in a world infested by plotters, wiretappers, saboteurs, and even potential assassins. The show's producer, Don Hewitt, had been after Perot for several weeks to sit for an interview on his repeated claims that "the Republican dirty-tricks crowd" had been victimizing him. Their periodic conversations seemed to be leading nowhere till Perot himself brought up the subject yet again in the last of the debates. Hewitt was quickly back on the line, telling Perot that, having raised the charge, he owed it to America to explain himself. The *60 Minutes* staff had been running its own investigation, Hewitt said; he made it sound, at least to Perot, as if they were prepared to put it on the air with or without him as the complaining witness.

Against the advice of his savvier counselors, Perot agreed to appear. The decision was a bad one; he had let himself be mousetrapped into cooperating with what he thought would be a general story on dirty trickery committed by the Republicans in Bush's behalf. The show, for all its brave claims, didn't have enough material to do a story without him. But he contributed richly to his own embarrassment, backing up his dump truck at CBS's doorstep and unloading what bits and scraps of hearsay he had. "Kick the tires," he urged Hewitt up front, knowing that he could not prove his allegations. "Get down under the hood and check the engine." It wasn't till midway through his interview with Lesley Stahl that he realized *he* was in the bull's-eye, not the Republicans; at that point, he ripped off his lapel mike in a fury and had to be jollied into going on with the taping.

He would have been better advised to keep walking. The story as it was finally broadcast was not an inquiry into the black arts of politics at all but an exploration of the darker recesses of Perot's cranium. "Why Did He Quit?" the segment was called, and the proffered answers were not the civic ones he had given when he liquidated his first campaign in July; he had got out, he said, to protect his daughter Carolyn from the dirty tricksters. His detail was lurid, his evidence slight. He claimed to have been told by various tipsters, mostly unnamed, about the alleged plot to spoil her impending wedding by leaking a faked lewd photo of her to the tabloids—and about a further scheme to disrupt the ceremony itself.

He had had no facts to go on, he said, only a series of "red flares" raised by his informants passing along things they had heard. He himself had been skeptical, or so he said. But Carolyn's wedding had then been only a month away, and he had reacted as a father, not as a candidate. "At that point," he told Stahl, "I couldn't prove any of it. I can't prove any of it today. But it was a risk I did not have to take, and a risk I would not take where my daughter was concerned." He had acted accordingly; instead of asking her to postpone the wedding, he had aborted his own campaign.

The interview alone was wounding enough, the portrait of a presidential aspirant so credulous as to believe and act on unsubstantiated rumors no matter how shaky their sourcing. "The son of a bitch is a psychiatric case," George Bush growled after the show, and Marlin Fitzwater was sent forward the next day with the judgment of the White House that Perot was "paranoid." The diagnosis was partisan chaff, but the patient, over the next day or so, seemed almost to be trying to prove it. He steamed into the middle of a testy press briefing at his headquarters the day after the show, bumping aside a battery of spokespeople including his own son, and threw a few fresh logs on the fire. There had been a Republican plot, he said, to wiretap his offices and, fifteen years before, an attempt by the Black Panthers to murder him. When the press questioned him too closely about his sourcing, he cut them off. "It's none of your business," he snapped. "Hey, look, I don't have to prove anything to you people."

It was a measure of America's eroded faith in its political order that some fraction of the electorate believed his accusations; the president's standing in the polls took a fresh dip over the next several days. But Perot's own progress stopped cold, as if a ceiling had been suddenly lowered over his head. In plain Beltway talk, he had strayed off-message and would stay off for days. His share of the vote froze in the high teens, too low even to affect the outcome materially, and his balloon ride upward on the currents of popular favor started abruptly back towards earth; his rating in the authoritative Battleground '92 tracking poll, a bipartisan effort run by Ed Goeas for the Republicans and Celinda Lake for the Democrats, flip-flopped from 56-34 positive to 44-46 negative in the space of five days.

Perot would recover some of his lost ground by the end, filling the airwaves with his ads and infomercials and taking a last untaxing lap around the Volunteer circuit. "I'm Ross, you're the boss," he told his last dependably adoring crowds. But his momentum was gone, and with it, for all but his truest believers, the illusion that he might actually have a chance at a miracle. He had become prisoner to the circular effect of the polls, which at once reported reality and created it. He couldn't win because he couldn't win, and as the impression hardened, Perot found himself crowded back out to the edges of public notice, a sideshow to the main event.

The News from Out There

In that city of mirrors called Washington, the campaign had become a horse-race again in the last days, with George Bush driving to a pleasingly suspenseful finish. But in that strange and distant land called Out There, something deeper was going on, a shift in the tectonic plates of American popular democracy. The party that had all but owned the presidency for a quarter-century was coming to the end of its run, out of ideas and out of luck. In the secret places of politics, the hearts and minds of the 100 million voters who would settle the outcome, a massive vote of no confidence was taking form. The worst thing that happened to Bush, Republican polltaker Ed Goeas would guess afterward, was the published Gallup survey showing him only one point behind Clinton with six days to go. At that moment, the possibility of his reelection became real, and he was doomed.

The office he occupied had become a cruel one in our time, a glass house haunted by impossibly high expectations and patrolled by an adversarial press. Four of its past five tenants had been either forced out or voted out; only Ronald Reagan among them had survived two full terms, and his support was crumbling by the time he had finished his second. But it was Bush's particular bad fortune to come at the end of a dynastic succession, the last prince of a thinned-out bloodline. The kingdom he had inherited had been spent to the edge of insolvency by his predecessor, creating a boom for the rich with money borrowed from everybody else. The bust had happened on Bush's time, and it was too soon obvious that he had no idea what to do about it. If Richard Nixon's sin was the abuse of power, and Jimmy Carter's a clumsiness at using it, Bush's was neglecting it; having little understanding of what ailed that America beyond the Beltway, let alone how to cure it, he chose to do nothing at all.

He would end his campaign as he had begun it, in a state of denial that the economy was in recession. The indices supported his argument that a recovery was in progress, and with less than a week to go, he got a new one: an unexpectedly strong uptick of 2.7 percent in the gross domestic product. Abandoning caution, Bush seized on it as evidence that he had been right all along—that the real economy was coming along fine and that its problems existed mainly in the minds of the press. He might have been Fragonard painting a street scene from Dickens, its harsh edges softened by a palette of pink and gold; the finished work bore little resemblance to the lives he was rendering. Once again, in both parties, the voice of the focus group was heard in the land, and it was angry:

Where are you?

Who cares what the accountants say? Get out in the real world.

Maybe you're not hurting in the White House, but then, you've been there too long.

No single failure of connection so clearly defined Bush's campaign. The issue *was* the economy, far more than any other public concern. Of the voters who would choose the next president, 80 percent rated its condition either not so good or downright poor, and nearly half thought that the government's policies had actually made it worse instead of better; their discontents alone amounted to a mandate for change. But to James Carville, Bush was prey less to the raw economic numbers than to his failure to comprehend what they meant. Franklin Roosevelt had sought reelection in vastly harder times in 1936, Carville remarked, at the depths of the Great Depression. He had promised hope and had won a forty-six-state landslide. Bush had pretended that nothing was wrong and was losing.

Bush had none of Roosevelt's inspirational gifts, of course, or Jack Kennedy's, or Ronald Reagan's. What talents at command he had were best exercised in closed rooms, in the company mainly of middle-aged white men of his own pin-striped cut. His demeanor, even his body language gave away his discomfort with the public arts of leadership. When the candidates came on television doing their stump speeches, the Republican pollster Linda DiVall sometimes watched them with the sound off, watching for the subliminal messages conveyed by a gesture or an expression. To her envious eye, Clinton looked energized, engaged, in full rapport with his audiences. Bush seemed by contrast to radiate disdain for what he was doing. Where Clinton spoke extempore, Bush needed his note cards; where Clinton smiled, Bush grimaced, almost as if he were in pain.

Bush had *abandoned* politics, DiVall thought, and some members of his own circle did not disagree. Their questions as to how badly he wanted the job persisted nearly to the day he lost it; at least a few old and close friends suspected that his heart had never been in it. In fact, his foot-dragging and his complaints were just Bush being Bush, waiting impatiently for America to catch on to Clinton's game. He had never loved the sport of politics or been very good at it, having won only two terms in Congress on his long road to the top; his higher offices had all been achieved by appointment or by right of succession. To one old Reagan-Bush warrior, he appeared to have got fully into his last campaign only in the closing weeks, when it got personal and bloody and his pride was on the line.

His seeming diffidence till then had only reinforced the deadly impression that he was out of touch with the people and that he was unconcerned with their problems. As polltaker David Petts remarked, Jimmy Carter, in similar circumstances, had at least got credit for making the effort to fix a crippled economy; his competence was in question, not his sympathy or his will. The verdict on Bush, in Petts's view, was far more devastating politically: he was seen as a capable man who *could* have done something if only he had cared enough to try.

Bush's domestic presidency could be read, in retrospect, as a record of lost opportunities, dating at least to the winter of Desert Storm. His favorable rating had brushed 90 percent then and had still held at 70 deep into the summer of 1991, before the recession and the spotty recovery dragged him down. No president had ever sat on so lofty a pinnacle of favor for so long. But political capital has value only if you spend it, Democratic polltaker Geoffrey Garin observed, and Bush had not done so; he had put his in the bank instead, thinking to preserve it, and had watched it turn to dust.

One moment after another had been squandered—the afterglow of Desert Storm, the State of the Union address, the I-care offensive against Pat Buchanan, the party convention in Houston. By the time Bush produced something resembling a plan, in his speech to the Economic Club of Detroit in September, it was too late. Clinton's man Paul Begala had had a rare day's home leave that day and had watched the speech with his mother-in-law while she was ironing some of his travel-worn shirts. She was a woman of conservative views, usually most comfortable with Republican candidates, but Bush's words seemed not to be registering with her.

"What'd you think, mom?" Begala asked her afterward.

"Well," she replied, looking up from her ironing, "I don't know how long this recession has been going on, but I know there's an election in a few weeks."

The guy was in trouble, Begala was thinking. She should have been for him, and she hadn't believed a word he had said; it was all empty politics to her, the deathbed conversion of a man trying to get himself reelected.

Her skepticism was widely shared in America in the fall of 1992 and by the end was crystallizing into a final judgment that Bush had failed. His trend line in the Battleground '92 tracking poll was a flat road to oblivion. The most striking single fact in the numbers was that, from Labor Day to Election Day, Bush's average daily share of the vote was 40 percent when he and Clinton were alone in the field and 34 percent once Perot rejoined them. He had never made an affirmative case for his reelection and finally, seeing its futility, had all but given up trying. A hard majority of the country viewed him unfavorably by then, and upwards of 60 percent wanted him gone. He was in contention in the final days only because his two rivals were splitting the vote against him.

So long as Clinton had a corner on the anti-Bush market, he had seemed to be cruising toward a landslide. That he had survived at all, let alone taken a commanding lead, was extraordinary, given the high levels of ill-feeling toward him. By the weekend before the election, his unfavorable ratings were nearly as high as the president's. His lead in the polls was a triumph of hope over fear, of hunger for change over mistrust of its agent. By Election Day, more than half of voting America described itself as concerned or scared at the prospect of a Clinton presidency. To a decisive fraction of the doubters, the risk seemed worth it; they preferred a man they considered a liar to a president they saw as having betrayed a higher trust.

Clinton's ascendancy was a victory as well for a new style of Democratic politics, a shift in the party's center of gravity as it had existed for most of the past sixty years. The strategic genius of his campaign lay in its appeal to the broad middle class, a territory largely unexplored by recent Democratic candidates. The old electoral model had been handed down almost intact from the days of the New Deal. Its base was liberal, urban, and poor; its most dependable support came from households earning $15,000 or less, people at or near the poverty line. That hard core had served the party well through the middle 1960s, but the body of the orthodox Democratic church had fallen victim to a wasting disease. As a train of nominees from Hubert Humphrey through Michael Dukakis had discovered, the votes weren't there anymore.

A new America had been growing up around them, Geoffrey Garin mused, and Bill Clinton had discovered it. In the traditional Democratic imagination, "middle class" had meant people making $20,000 or $25,000, and "rich" began somewhere around $80,000. That was the landscape Kennedy and Johnson had played and won on, but, as Garin remarked, most of the country didn't live there anymore. At a time when two-paycheck families had become the norm, the median household income had risen past $30,000. Clinton seemed at home on the new terrain, having grown up with it and mastered its language as his own. His rewards would be visible on Election Day; he had broadened the party's base to families making up to $30,000 and had fought Bush on even terms for those earning $30,000 to $75,000—a killing field for Democrats for several elections past.

What Clinton and his strategists grasped was the difference between the old world and the new. Its seat was the suburbs, not the cities; its heart was moderate, not liberal; its concerns were vivid and personal, not distant and altruistic. For much of the middle class, the America of 1992 more nearly resembled Clinton's critique than Reagan's fading vision of the shining city on the hill; incomes were stagnant, jobs were disappearing, and the dream of a limitless future seemed at hazard. The central idea of the Reagan Revolution, that government was a bad thing, no longer seemed relevant to reality. The ironic consequence of the Gipper's success was to remind people that the presidency could, after all, be a powerful office. The lesson seemed lost on Bush. He presented himself as the victim rather than the master of fortune; having no discernible ideology of his own, he had accepted Reagan's and was still clinging to it long after its time had come and gone.

Clinton offered something different; his vision of government was activist, and his message was one of confidence, not despair. His reputation had been badly battered during his long march to November, and with it, his authority; he had arrived at the eve of victory known to much of America as a man of suspect word and irresponsible deed. That he should have got so far was less a mark of belief in him than of a loss of faith in the president. It was blameworthy, in the politics of 1992, to address the sins and errors of one's past and say, "I didn't do it." But it was unforgivable to look out at the unmet needs of America and ask, "What's the problem?"

There was an end-of-an-era feeling about Bush's decline—a sense that the powerful coalition that had sustained the Republicans in power for five out of the past six elections was breaking up at last. Richard Nixon had laid its first building blocks in 1968, and Ronald Reagan, a politician vastly more talented than Bush, had held it together by force of personality even after the cracks had begun to show. The illusion of its permanence would be the biggest single casualty of the politics of 1992; a third of Clinton's electoral votes would come from states no Democrat had carried since the epic Johnson landslide of 1964.

The binding principles that had made the Republicans the presidential party in our time had the look of obsolescence in the Bush years. The power of anticommunism as an issue had died with the Soviet Union. The Reagan tax revolt of 1980 had been subverted from within by the Bush tax increase ten years later, when a nation discovered that it had misread the president's lips. The conservative social values celebrated so noisily at the party convention had been overtaken by the recession; it was hard to raise an army to fight a religious and cultural war for the soul of America when people were principally worried about paying their bills and keeping their jobs. Even the Gipper's assault on big government was a spent force, given how much needed doing. "I don't want *no* government," a fiftyish man in one of Ed Goeas's focus groups said. "I want a government that works so well I don't know it's there."

George Bush's failure was to have conveyed only the sense that it wasn't there; it was Bill Clinton's central promise to make it work again in those matters people cared most about. A challenger to a sitting president has the luxury of making up the future to his own visionary design, and Clinton had used the license well. An incumbent, by contrast, is stuck with his past. Popular democracy can be as unforgiving as the God of the Old Testament; the memory of what has gone before—the retrospective look, pollsters call it—is twice as powerful a force in elections as the expectation of what lies ahead, and it did not flatter the president. He was burdened not only with his own record but with Reagan's as well, seen through a revisionist lens; the promised morning in America had given way over a dozen years to an economy in twilight and a governing idea in disrepute.

The unanswerable question was whether the election would mark a real turning point in American political life or merely an interruption in its recent flow. The fall of the ancien regime was as fast and steep as those of 1932 and 1968, measured by the loss of support for the party in power; the analyst Kevin Phillips, present at the birth of the Republican majority, was tempted to see in its demise "a watershed in waiting." Would it ripen to fruition? The answer would shortly lie in the hands of Bill Clinton—in his success or failure at satisfying the hopes he had stirred to life. The task before him would have been daunting even for a man less burdened by public doubt; the dimension of the problems, and the brutalization of the office, conspired against success. The Republicans faced the difficult challenge of rethinking what they stood for as a party besides their opposition to Clinton. The Democrats would have the harder job: delivering on what they had already promised.

They would be trying to do so, moreover, in a climate of deep cynicism about politics and government. The extraordinary success of Ross Perot was only the most visible expression of the distance that had opened between the Federal City and the people Out There. "If once [the people] become inattentive to the public affairs," Thomas Jefferson wrote a colleague just before the dawn of the republic, "you and I, and Congress and Assemblies, Judges and Governors, shall all become wolves. It seems to be the law of our general nature." In 1992, the people became attentive to the public affairs, quite literally with a vengeance. The turnout on Election Day would be the largest in twenty years, and the prevailing mood toward the wolves was punitive.

George Bush was not alone among its targets. Incumbency remained the best single ticket to victory in our politics, but the ride to reelection was the bumpiest in a generation, and not everybody survived it. In the House of Representatives, the mortality rate was the highest since the great post-Watergate purge of 1974. A fourth of the body, 108 members, would disappear, 65 of them more or less by choice, 43 at the hands of the voters. Many of those who would return had to fight harder than they had for years; the average margin of victory for incumbent representatives seeking reelection had fallen five points in four years.

Perot, with all his eccentricities and all his mistakes, had caught the wave and ridden it farther than any third-force candidate since Teddy Roosevelt in 1912. What he had built, in Geoffrey Garin's postmortem reading, was not a coherent movement but a coalition of discontent; *its* binding principle was dissatisfaction, whether with the deficit, or with politics, or with Washington, or with the two major-party candidates. In the end, his candidacy would bump against its natural limits, not least of them the inertial forces of politics and Perot's own idiosyncratic ways. But he had awakened a populism of the mad-as-hell center and had given bravura voice to its unwillingness to take it anymore.

The tendency in the political community afterward was to write off the uprising as a transient phenomenon, a charismatic movement that would wither once its founder and his billions moved on to other, less punishing enterprises. The two-party mind-set of American politics was deep and hard to crack, harder than Perot had imagined. It had been one thing for him to get on the ballot and quite another to persuade people, against the evidence of the polls, that a vote for him would not be "wasted." The gravitational field of our politics drew voters instead toward the two accredited candidates in the election immediately at hand, and the established parties had a gift for accommodating their grievances by the time the next one rolled around.

Third parties, as the great American historian Richard Hofstadter once wrote, "are like bees: Once they have stung, they die." So it had been in our history, since the birth of the third-force Republican Party in 1854 and its ascent to the White House six years later; Know-Nothings and Greenbackers, Populists and Progressives, Socialists and Dixiecrats had all come, stung, and gone. But the bees loosed by Perot were of a rather different strain. Most third-party and third-force movements in our past had been built around a single idea and so were more easily co-opted by the established order. The idea of the Perot movement, beneath its widely varied bill of particulars, was that the established order was itself the problem; it had been corrupted by power and money, protected by its propagandists in the media, and finally paralyzed by that Washington disease called gridlock.

Perot's assault on the system in 1992 finally affected only the arithmetic of the election, not its outcome. The race ended as it had begun, Bush versus Not Bush, and the president was still losing it, 60-40. Perot's reappearance in October had complicated the equation, providing the most disaffected Americans with a new Not Bush who was Not Clinton either. The only movement that mattered in the polls was the division of the Not Bush vote. As Perot got more of it, Clinton got less, and Bush got closer simply by running in place, his share of the vote stuck where it had been all along. Ed Goeas, whose poll had most closely predicted the actual outcome, calculated afterward that Clinton would have beaten Bush by 57-43 or better in one-on-one combat. Other students of politics questioned his arithmetic but had a harder time challenging its bottom line: the direct effect of Perot's candidacy on Election Day was to spare the president the final humiliation of a landslide.

Perhaps that was all there was to it; perhaps, as Republican polltaker Richard Wirthlin suggested, the Perot campaign would be remembered in history more as theater than as politics. But the alienation of some sizable fraction of America from its government had been there when Perot stepped onto the stage and lingered on after his exit. For people who had been drawn to him at one point or another in his passage, the honeymoon attending the election of a new president more nearly resembled a reprieve, temporary and fragile; in their eyes, that class of beings called politicians was guilty until proven innocent. Clinton was closing on his victory not as a hero but as a probationer, the first choice of a wary minority of a nation. They weren't giving him a mandate, his aide Paul Begala thought. They were giving him a chance.

The Final Days

It was the last day but one, and Clinton began it with a visit to a diner in Philadelphia, the first stop in a twenty-eight-hour cross-country sprint to the wire. The vital signs were mostly good, but the polls were still jittery, and as he got into his limousine, they nibbled at the edge of his consciousness. He looked up as Begala slipped into the seat beside him, bearing the latest numbers.

"Governor, Stan's poll is at seven," Begala said.

"Why are all the other polls moving and ours isn't?" Clinton demanded. The question sounded like a complaint.

"Governor, it's a *solid* seven," Begala told him. "It's the day before the election. The day before the 1980 election, Ronald Reagan was up two in one poll and down two in another. This is a winner."

Clinton brooded on that for a moment, then permitted himself a smile and a nod of acknowledgment. The presidency was one day away.

The final days had been a jangly time for him and his handlers, their heartbeats matching the dysrhythmia of the polls. "That old line, the difference between a statesman and a politician is that a statesman lives in the next generation and a politician in the next election?" Carville said in a confessional mood one day. "Shit, man, I live to the next tracking poll." To do so in the tumble of numbers over the last week was to live from hour to hour and from giddy high to despondent low. "We better not sit the fuck back!" Carville spluttered at his War Room posse. "We better make something happen!" It was frustration talking, an emptiness equivalent to what trial lawyers experience when a case goes to the jury and nothing more can be said or done to get them to vote for your client.

It had not been till the Saturday before the election that Clinton himself surrendered to the pinch-me feeling that he might actually win. It had hit him at a weekend campaign rally, a love-bath in a packed high-school football stadium in the Atlanta suburbs. He had got himself back on his message by then, after a time in which, as he would tell his aides, he had almost worried himself *sick* over the president's attacks on him and his record and had too often responded in kind. The basic equilibrium that had governed the race for most of the year was reasserting itself; the focus was back on Bush's record again, not his, and Clinton, in his speech, addressed himself to the last enemy in his path—"whether people had the courage to change." The answering roar of the crowd sent him away in an exultant mood. "That was maybe the most electric rally of the campaign," he told his traveling party.

The resulting adrenalin rush had to fight through the exhaustion of the marathon runner. Clinton had not hit The Wall yet, but his voice had, and when he wound up in Milwaukee that cold, wet autumn night, it was almost gone. He flogged himself through a televised town meeting; then he repaired to a mansion borrowed from a supporter to shoot his coda to his last advertisement for himself, the half-hour closing appeal scheduled to be aired on election eve. He and his handlers sat up late around the dining table, in a pool of light from an ornate sterling chandelier. As he fussed over his script, he sipped herbal tea and began humming to himself, a prescribed therapy for his throat. The song he had chosen for the exercise was "Amazing Grace." The sounds by then were mostly sweet for Clinton.

His mood that night, indeed, was mellow, even charitable toward Bush. His people showed him a rough cut of the film, a celebration of him wrapped around a tough section on the president's broken promises. To Clinton, in his softened humor, the Bush material looked like piling on, and he ordered it excised. The parts he preferred were a sequence showing him and Gore on the bus tour and, even more, a series of testimonials from prominent Republican business leaders who had abandoned the president for him. "This is devastating," he said, watching the parade of defectors flick by.

It was past midnight when he adjourned to the paneled study for the shoot. His reading was perfect, the Great Empathizer at his best. His throat spoiled it. The tea and the humming hadn't worked; his voice was a croak, almost painful to listen to. Watching on a monitor in the dining room, Mandy Grunwald bowed her head to the tabletop. The election, the whole year, could be riding on Clinton's last words to the voters, for all anybody knew, and he could barely get them out.

"This is tragic," Grunwald said.

"Doesn't it sound terrible?" Clinton asked.

"No," Begala said gently, spinning the candidate for a change. "It sounds *serious.*"

Clinton hummed a few bars of "Amazing Grace," then tried again. It took five takes to get it right, and it would be four o'clock Sunday morning by the time he and his roadies arrived at their next stop in Cincinnati in a fog of exhaustion. But Clinton's luck appeared to have turned over the past several days; the same poll that had shown him only a point ahead of the president on Wednesday had him up by seven by the weekend. The sound of Bush's footsteps on his heels had given way, in his mind, to the new worry he had addressed in his Georgia speech—that people might lose their nerve in the voting booth. "Remember the Kennedy election," he fretted aboard his campaign jet; change *was* scary, and JFK, the untested new guy on the block, had watched his lead over Nixon melt nearly to nothing in the last days. The dynamic of 1992 struck Clinton as spookily similar: a challenger arguing that things could be better, the party in power arguing that things could get very much worse.

That had in fact been the heart of Bush's case for reelection, and in the flush of his false remission in the polls, he cranked up the decibel level to a new high. He traveled the country at a frantic pace, as if motion alone could save him, and with each stop, his language got less temperate. He railed at Clinton and Gore as Waffle Man and Ozone, and, one unbridled day, as a couple of Bozos; the First Dog, Millie, knew more about foreign policy, he said, than the two of them put together.

Even Barbara Bush thought this last a bit much, and Bush's handlers chided him for it. "Jeez, you guys, lighten up," he told them. "I was just being funny." They were not amused. The president was, though he accepted their advice to tone it down just a little. When he saw a network analyst predicting a long and suspenseful election night, Bush laughed. "Who would have ever thought this Bozo stuff would work?" he said, twitting himself.

The last days of his last campaign were in fact a declaration of independence for Bush, a deliverance from the tyranny of coaches telling him where to go, what to say, even how to dress. When they worried aloud about what the media might say about his higher flights of Bozo-bashing, he brushed them off. "What are they gonna do," he said, "write *worse* stories about me?" By the end, he was even resisting advice to let his hair grow out—his media man Sig Rogich thought it looked better on television a bit shaggy—and to lose a loud red, white, and blue repp tie to which he alone was partial.

"You're in full-throttle handler revolt," Mary Matalin told him one day, feigning horror. "You're still wearing that horrible tie."

"That's right, Matalin," Bush sassed back, "and I *also* got my hair cut last night."

His sudden access of high spirits was built on illusion; the day his campaign died, five days before the election, he still thought he was winning. Fred Steeper had arrived at a meeting of the campaign core group in Bob Zoellick's office at the White House that morning with a fresh set of numbers suggesting that the president had at least a chance. Steeper had rounded up every reliable public and private poll he could lay his hands on, fed them into a computer, and blenderized them into a single trend line. It pointed to a 39-39 dead heat on Tuesday morning.

The electoral college still looked tough, maybe impossible. In the most generous count, Bush was behind in eleven of their twenty-nine target states, with only a long weekend in which to turn them around. But the flow of the popular vote at least seemed to favor the president. There were always miracles; maybe, as the saying had it, a rising tide would raise all ships, and Bush would somehow win.

The bubble burst just before three o'clock that afternoon when a communications staffer brought Charlie Black a copy of an Associated Press dispatch. Black scanned it. Lawrence Walsh, the independent counsel in charge of the long-running inquiry into the Iran-Contra affair, had just got an indictment against former Secretary of Defense Caspar Weinberger. The accompanying filings included some of Weinberger's in-the-room notes suggesting that Bush, as vice president, had not only known about but had favored the swap of arms for American hostages. The documents shredded the president's claim not to have been told what was up. The silver bullet had finally materialized, but *his* name was on it.

Clinton smiled broadly when an aide showed him the same dispatch.

Charlie Black folded his copy and slipped it into his breast pocket, a memento of the moment at which the Bush presidency effectively ended. "We're off track now," he told an aide. "This is really gonna make it damn tough."

In fact, Black was softening what he really felt. At dusk, Bob Teeter called in from Ann Arbor, Michigan, where he had taken an afternoon off to watch his son play in the state high-school football championships. Black told him the news.

"It's probably over now," he said.

Teeter agreed.

The timing of the indictment looked suspect to the more inflamed of Bush's generals; in their eyes, Walsh had been stalking the president for years like an avenging angel and had finally achieved his destruction. The stronger evidence suggested that the race was already over by then—that Clinton's stranglehold on the electoral college had made his narrowing lead in the national polls irrelevant to the outcome. But it was fair to argue, as one senior Bush-Quayle official did, that the disclosures in *United States* v. *Weinberger* were the last straw that broke the president's back. His character was in question now, and as the exit polls would reveal, his equivocations on Iran-Contra mattered more to voters than Clinton's on sex, dope, and the draft. The story dominated the news for forty-eight precious hours, blotting out anything else

Bush said or did. The movement in the polls stopped dead; the numbers froze where they were, with Clinton on top.

A note of desperation took over the campaign in the few remaining days, though the president bridled yet again when things threatened to get *too* personal. It was Dan Quayle instead who crossed the line his patron had drawn. The Friday before the election, Quayle had raised the Tower Test at an airport stop in Denver, insisting that Clinton ought to be subject to similar proofs of character; if skirt-chasing was a capital crime for a prospective secretary of defense, should it be tolerated in a president? Quayle had not cleared his plan beforehand, assuming that the nervous nellies on Fifteenth Street would reject it if he did. But once the deed had been done, he called his nonfriend Jim Baker to urge that the president take up the line of attack himself.

The entire senior command was on the road with Bush by then, on a whistle-stop tour of the Wisconsin heartland; their absence was itself the stuff of sardonic jokes on Fifteenth Street, to the effect that the campaign was doing better with the grown-ups out of town and the kids in charge. The top hands caucused in the observation car of the president's inaptly named "victory train." They had to do *something,* they all agreed, to counter the Iran-Contra story, and the Tower Test was the grenade nearest to hand. Bush seemed not uncomfortable with it, so long as he wasn't the one speaking the lines; he had read the story in the papers and had called the vice president that morning with a word of praise. Steve Provost, the speechwriter, phoned the Quayle road party to get the appropriate quotes from various Democratic senators waxing pious about Tower's alleged drinking and womanizing, and Jim Baker was sent forward to sell Bush the idea.

Baker was back in fifteen minutes, empty-handed. "He doesn't want to touch the Tower stuff," he told his colleagues; to the president, it was just a cute trick to raise the ghost of Gennifer Flowers, and he wasn't going to be party to it.

Quayle was in flight from Cedar Rapids, Iowa, to Chicago when Bob Teeter called to report the verdict and to suggest a possible way around it. Quayle would do his number one more time, on camera and with feeling. The press would surely ask the president about it, opening the subject without his having to raise it himself; who could fault him for answering a direct question?

Quayle was disgusted with the hesitancy at the top, guessing, incorrectly, that Baker and Teeter were behind it. "This is why we're gonna lose," he told his people. "They don't understand—you *have* to be on offense." He did his soldierly duty anyway, slapping Clinton with the Tower Test again when he hit Chicago, and waited for the president to respond to the cue. He didn't, not on Quayle's raw terms. His war council, this time with Marlin Fitzwater as their persuader, had got him to toughen up his counterattack on Iran-Contra; he dismissed the case against him as "these silly charges" and denounced Clinton for his "desperation" in trying to make a character issue of them. "I welcome this spotlight on character," he said at a raucous rally in Oshkosh, Wisconsin, "because, frankly, being attacked on character by Governor Clinton is like being called ugly by a frog." But the Tower Test was an infraction of Bush Rules, in the judgment of their author, and he never used it.

He was victim by then to the virus of futility that attacks losing campaigns; after what he would call "certainly probably the most unpleasant year of my life," the last believer was losing faith in his own reelection. He kept fighting till the end, slamming Clinton as a "tax-ophone artist" whose word was too slippery to be trusted. But he himself had become damaged goods on both of his own issues, taxes *and* trust, and whatever traction they had bought him was gone. He couldn't even afford to match his rival's closing TV special, having overspent on network time just to stay afloat; the money left in his media account went instead for more commercials in his target states.

Self-deception, the last refuge of candidates and handlers, was no longer easy to maintain. The boys and girls on the press plane were calling the president's last swing the Death with Dignity Tour and were predicting the imminent arrival of Dr. Jack Kevorkian, the famous broker in assisted suicides. Bush did not allow himself to show whatever pain he felt, but when Air Force One touched down in Detroit, a friend on the ground asked one of his Secret Service bodyguards how things were going. "He knows," the agent said. "He knows."

Clinton knew, too, though he didn't dare say so or slow down his 4,000-mile dawn-to-dawn sprint to the finish. He covered ten cities in nine states, and when his vocal cords failed him, he let his wife and his running mate do the talking for him, limiting himself to a few hoarse words and a smile. His crowds were big and adoring, the celebrants of a new beginning. Several thousand were waiting on the tarmac in Fort Worth when his charter, Express One, touched down at 1 A.M. When he reached Albuquerque three hours later, 3,000 people stood shivering in the early morning cold. Hillary by then was bundled up in a quilt, fast asleep, and he was feeling the mileage. "Even *my* iron body is falling apart," he said, teasing himself; then he stepped out into the chill of the air and the warmth of the crowd.

Day was breaking over Denver, the last stop, when the Clintons arrived, and the campaign's rock anthem, "Don't Stop Thinking about Tomorrow," filled the air. There 5,000 insomniac souls were waiting in a hangar. The great doors parted. The plane had nosed to a stop outside. The candidate and his wife started down the steps, and for the first time in more than a year, they no longer had to think about tomorrow. They were in it. It was theirs.

Its former proprietor, George Bush, had wakened early that morning in Houston and had gone out for a jog. Passersby waved at him as he went by, surrounded by his sweaty bodyguards; he answered with thumbs-up signs and smiles. When he had showered, changed, and voted, he joined some of his senior aides for breakfast in the atrium at his hotel, the Houstonian. It was a view widely held in the political community that they had failed him, but he resisted whatever temptation he might have felt to join the blame game.

"What do you guys hear?" he asked.

The good news was scanty. The bad was too painful to tell him, and too obvious.

Their evasions were transparent, and Bush saw through them. "Well," he said, "the polls don't look too good. But who knows?"

His people did, or soon would. Their final guess, faxed to Teeter and Malek in midafternoon, was that Clinton would win the popular vote by nine points, 47-38, with Perot sweeping up behind them at 15 percent. The electoral map looked even worse. One battleground state after another was turning blood red. Michigan was gone, and Ohio, Pennsylvania, New Jersey, and Georgia were going, all of them states Bush had to have to fill his impossible straight. It fell to Baker to deliver the numbers to Bush's condominium suite at the Houstonian. The two friends didn't leap to the obvious conclusion, or need to; they danced around its edges instead, agreeing that they had to get the wordsmiths going on a concession speech. "Keep it short," Bush said as they parted.

There had to be a victory speech, too, if for no other reason than to sustain morale for one more day, and Dick Darman's right-hand man Bob Grady was drafted to write it. "Move over, Harry Truman," he began, a tip of the hat to the last president to have won a new term after his political obituaries had been composed and published. But the day's real labor was assigned, tellingly, to Steve Provost in token of his rank as Bush's chief ghost. The speech of surrender he composed was short, at the president's wish, and gracious, as suited his person between elections.

He spoke in his valedictory of the regrettable smoke and fire of a campaign, as if he had not willingly been part of it. One of the sadder consequences of the politics of insult, which is to say practically all contemporary politics, is to diminish the winner and to reduce his authority in office. So it would be with Clinton, who had been damaged in ways that would haunt him long after his swearing-in as our forty-second president. The integrity of his word had been at issue all year, most violently at Bush's hands; the relentlessness of the attacks had driven up his negative ratings to a point nearly matching his positives and had dropped his grade on a 1-to-100 thermometer scale in Stan Greenberg's last survey to 50, a surprising level for a man on the edge of a rousing electoral victory.

But the outcome then taking form suggested that Bush had hurt himself with his stridency in the last weeks, and perhaps his party as well. "What do they stand for *now?*" Greenberg wondered; the president had governed without an ideology and had sought reelection without offering a clear reason for it, beyond the fact that he was there and was not Bill Clinton. His rival had joined in the slanging match, of course, but to the great relief of his team, he had finally got off it. His return to his positive themes in the final hours, on the road and in his television ads, rekindled that glow of energy, hope, and change he had captured at his convention. The contrast with Bush's negativism was striking and finally, so the numbers said, decisive. "I think," Greenberg said, scanning them, "that this happened in the last day."

What had come to pass was a seismic change in our politics, a shift of power from the ruling party of a quarter-century to its opposition; from the generation that had fought World War II to the generation sundered by Vietnam; from men who mistrusted government to men and women who believed in its affirmative uses. Its vessel was imperfect and its permanence uncertain, but its dimension made it plain indeed that, as Geoffrey Garin observed, something had happened. As night fell in Little Rock, the crowd in the War Room pondered the exit polls and told one another they had a fucking landslide on their hands. Clinton's lead would recede in the final count to 43-37, a victory of less than epic scale but solid still; no Democratic candidate in the postwar era had won by a bigger margin except Lyndon Johnson, in the freakish circumstances of 1964.

It was Ross Perot who made Clinton a minority president, with the smallest share of the vote since Woodrow Wilson; he had done just well enough to deny the winner a majority and, arguably, a landslide. Perot's success was extraordinary, given who he was and what he was attempting. Only two third-force candidates in our history, Millard Fillmore in 1856 and Teddy Roosevelt in 1912, had done better than his 19 percent of the vote, and both of them were former presidents. He was shut out where it finally mattered, in the electoral college, but his popular vote was itself a statement—a declaration that one American in five felt estranged enough to go outside the two-party universe of our politics and vote for an East Texas ET who somehow embodied their angst and their anger. "I'm like the grain of sand in the oyster that irritates the oyster, and out comes a pearl," he said in *his* concession speech. The words were gallant, but given how little the outcome resembled a pearl, by his lights, it was fair to guess that the Great Irritant wouldn't be going away.

His showing diverted attention from the real measure of Clinton's triumph: his 370-168 majority of the electoral vote against a sitting president. The Republican "lock" on the electoral college, if it had ever really existed, was broken; the challenger carried every region except, ironically, his own, and he was more competitive there than any nominee of his party since Jimmy Carter. He won all fifteen of the Top End states on his targeting list, and sixteen of the seventeen Play Hard and Play Very Hard states. Only North Carolina had got away; Clinton's sophisticated targeting, and Bush's inability to respond, had helped shape what Greenberg would call an authentic national victory.

Clinton made deep inroads as well into the coalition that had made the Republicans our presidential majority party for a generation. A plurality of the Reagan Democrats voted for a real Democrat again. So did the youngest voters, who had lived most of their lives under Republican presidents; their formative first or second votes were cast for a Democratic ticket, a bad omen for the losers and their dream of a durable realignment. The middle class, the suburbs, even veterans favored Clinton, in ad hoc alliance with the usual liberals and blacks; he had come closer than any Democrat in his own adult lifetime to rebuilding the old Robert Kennedy coalition.

Nothing, in politics, heals like the sense of imminent victory. In the last hours of his last tour of America, Clinton had sat aboard his jet with a traveling companion and reflected on his long, bruising quest for the presidency; it had been, he said improbably, a "good, noble, uplifting campaign," and it had finally ignited the "explosion of hope" he had always known would happen. The pain, the doubt, the self-pity had receded into a lost past; he had become the candidate of destiny, a condition common among the winners of offices from alderman to president, and had come to see his election as foreordained. He affected unsurprise during the afternoon and evening as aides brought him word of some of his more surprising state victories. "Oh, I expected that," he would say, forgetting how rattled he had been only a few days before. In fact, visitors to the governor's mansion described his mood and Hillary's as giddy.

But as his victory and his presidency became real to him, he seemed seized by a wave of emotion, even awe; it was Hillary who took charge of orchestrating their rite of passage while he fell to work redoing a staff draft of his speech. He was alone with his family when the networks declared him the winner; moments later, first Bush and then Quayle called to congratulate him.

"I've always admired how you hung in there," Clinton told Quayle, knowing something about the subject himself.

"Good luck, my friend," Quayle replied.

It was time then for Clinton to claim his prize. When his limousine finally arrived at the Old Statehouse, where he had declared for president an eternity ago, he lingered a while more over his speech. Then he stepped out to meet his future. He saw Dee Dee Myers and hugged her. Tears welled in his eyes.

The birth of a new presidency is a kind of rebirth, a moment of hope and renewal. Its air of promise was heightened in 1992 by the youth of the winners; the generation born before World War II had at last given way to the baby boomers—"the children," as Al Gore put it in his victory speech, "of modern America." But the Clinton presidency was coming into being under a cloud of civic anxiety and personal doubt. The voters, Fred Steeper said, had not so much rewarded Clinton as punished Bush for their discontents of the recent past. He had been borne to the presidency not so much by faith in him or what he could do as by a wave of anger at the way things were. He had four years in which to prove himself its master—or to join George Bush among its victims.

Stop time: The candidates take an ice-cream break on the trail. *(Ira Wyman)*

Go-go: The Gores and the Clintons enjoy a laugh on the bus. *(Ira Wyman)*

Partners: The Clintons shared a common goal. *(Ira Wyman)*

Teammates: The Gores joined up for the buscapade. *(Ira Wyman)*

Thunder on the right: Marilyn Quayle and Pat Buchanan helped set the angry tone at the Republican convention. *(Both, Wally McNamee/Newsweek)*

A place in the sun: The Bushes and Quayles celebrate their renomination in Houston. *(John Ficara/Newsweek)*

Beat the press: Clinton wasn't the only target of the president's attack campaign. *(Larry Downing/Newsweek)*

The undercard: Admiral Stockdale met Senator Gore and Vice President Quayle (not pictured) in the vice presidential debate. *(Both, John Ficara/ Newsweek)*

The main event: While Bush tuned out, the Great Empathizer stole the second presidential debate. *(Both, Wally McNamee/Newsweek)*

My turn: The debates put Perot and his plan on a level stage with the major-party candidates. *(Wally McNamee/Newsweek)*

Thumbs up: A whistle-stop ride in the heartland. *(Larry Downing/ Newsweek)*

Heads down: A somber walk with Jim Baker. *(John Ficara/Newsweek)*

Moments: On the road to the White House, the wail of a sax and the sweet sound of silence. *(Left, John Ficara/Newsweek; right, Ira Wyman)*

Reflections: Near the end of his quest, the president-to-be stares into his future. *(Ira Wyman)*

Healing: Barbara Bush welcomes a new First Lady. *(John Ficara/ Newsweek)*

Hail and farewell: The war over, the victor and the vanquished tour the White House together. *(John Ficara/Newsweek)*

Appendix
The Campaign Papers

A Note on the Documents

In the course of more than a year's reporting, we gathered a large number of confidential memoranda and other documents from the various campaigns. In the pages that follow, we have reproduced a number of them, those which struck us as most interesting to a general reader. They appear in chronological sequence, almost all in excerpted form; to publish our entire archive whole would require a second volume about as large as this one. In editing them, we have made every effort to preserve the integrity of the thoughts and arguments as the various authors intended them to be presented; we have limited our cuts to what we thought redundant or of marginal utility as part of the record of the 1992 campaign.

We published a comparable sampling in the 1984 book in this series and were sometimes surprised at the uses made of them by journalists and scholars. In the age of the handler, there is an unfortunate tendency to impute too much authority to strategy and polling memos, as if their arguments were commands punched into a computer rather than recommendations made to a living, breathing candidate with his own ideas and his own vanities and frailties. If a document exists, in this reading, it must have been obeyed.

A number of caveats should therefore be attached to this collection, first among them that the documents should not be read as a certain guide to what actually *happened* in the campaign or which advisers played the decisive roles. Instead, they reflect the thoughts, the brainstorms, and sometimes the frustrations of particular players at particular moments in the campaign. Politics runs more on the spoken than the written word, and some of its leading practitioners rarely if ever find it necessary to set their thoughts to paper. Polltakers, whose trade and habits of mind require it, are usually the most prolific authors; managers and strategists often are not. The reader who has got this far knows that James Baker, for one prominent example, and James Carville, for another, were central players in the events of 1992. But Carville appears only infrequently in this selection, usually co-signing memos by colleagues, and Baker is not represented at all.

Sometimes, memos strongly influence the conduct of a candidate and the strategy of a campaign. Sometimes they have no effect at all. (See, for instance, the united advice of Clinton's political team on the search for a runningmate: "The ideal nominee would not be a Southerner. . . .") Some represent the collective thinking of the strategists in a campaign. Some are lonely dissents, composed in anger or despair. Some are deadly serious in tone. Some resort to ironies and jokes to make a point or boost morale. Some could as easily have been written on water, for all their impact on events; all the Perot documents published here were produced by the hired professionals in his abortive first campaign, just before he fired them.

A campaign is a process, one whose development looks orderly and whose outcome seems inevitable only in retrospect. These papers should be read not as the story of the war of 1992 but as windows into the hearts and minds of some of its generals at some of its decisive moments.

BUSH: "A FEAR BORDERING ON PARANOIA"

In November, 1990, George Bush got a prophetic warning from Fred Malek, the corporate executive who would manage his reelection campaign:

November 26, 1990

MEMORANDUM FOR THE PRESIDENT
FROM: FRED MALEK

Congratulations on a magnificent trip. The appearances in Saudi Arabia were an emotional high, and there seemed to be a great deal of substantive progress with our allies and the Congressional leaders. These results should firm support for your policies here.

I'd like to take advantage of your invitation to offer follow-up thoughts to our luncheon two weeks ago. As stated then, I believe the American people have confidence in your handling of the Middle East but are less sure of your understanding and actions related to the country's economic problems. Yet, assuming the Iraqi problem is resolved in 1991, and we are otherwise at peace, our economic health will be, as usual, the principal measure by which voters will judge you in 1992.

Business and political leaders who are your friends were genuinely pleased to see your subsequent meetings with your economic team and then with a series of business and financial leaders. These sessions undoubtedly helped to accurately define the problem and its dimensions. Most likely these sessions have helped you and your team to conclude that:

- The country is indeed in a recession.
- It is selective, e.g., although the Northeast is a mess, the Northwest is healthy; while real estate is a true disaster, electronics/technological industries are doing fine.
- The recession has the clear potential of becoming deeper, larger, and more destructive than the 1981–2 recession.
- We do have an unprecedented credit crunch in the country, and bank regulators are unwittingly contributing to the problem. Their actions could drive a shallow recession into a major downturn, and will, at the least, mitigate against any rapid recovery.
- There is a sense of government apathy, unawareness, or insensitivity to the growing problems.

Now, let me be so bold as to suggest a few measures you can consider to deal with the problem, both perceptually and substantively:

Indicate your awareness and concern to the American people. Unfortunately, there is a serious fear, bordering on paranoia, developing among the American public. They see their economic future threatened as never before as homes—their single greatest asset—decline dramatically in value, jobs are threatened by recession and bankruptcies, financial services are in disarray, and former pillars (banks and insurance companies) appear vulnerable. They need you as a "father figure" to take them by the hand, acknowledge times are tough today, state that you are acting to improve the economy, and offer hope for the future. You should indicate that we have faced recessions before and will come through this one because:

- Your successful budget deficit efforts have already led to reduced interest rates, and have put us on a course designed to balance the budget over five years.
- Exports are increasing, and the balance of payments improving.
- Inflation is stabilizing and appears under control, and declining.
- You and your team are on top of this and taking further actions.

Continue to use your influence to press interest rates down. They are moving in the right direction, but need to fall further. [Federal Reserve chairman Alan] Greenspan seems to agree, but my fear is that the Fed is not moving fast enough. While there are risks involved, and subtlety is required, a visible meeting with Greenspan, prior to a likely move by the Fed, may help to demonstrate your leadership and your success in lowering interest rates.

Deal with the credit crunch. This problem is real, it is pervasive, and if unchecked it will cripple the economy. Regulators are holding banks to impossible standards and have established an atmosphere of fear and uncertainty that precludes lending even for worthwhile projects. Based on their fear of regulatory retaliation, banks are simply not lending to anyone, even the Fortune 500 companies are having trouble with credit; there is no longer such a thing as a real estate loan—for even the strongest developer with a fully leased building. Listen to your many friends from the business world on this one—yes, there have been excesses in the past, but the present atmosphere goes far beyond reason.

Work with business leaders to reduce the impact of massive layoffs. Business leaders do not want to engage in the massive layoffs now being announced at many financial and industrial companies, but they are concerned that the credit crunch and the softening economy mean inevitable revenue and profit reductions down the road. You can indicate that you are working on business leaders' concerns and want them to consider carefully their own contribution to the problem by trying to avoid precipitous, massive layoffs. The public would certainly approve of your expressed public concern about rising unemployment, which to date you have not really addressed.

Prepare economic measures for the State of the Union and new Congress. You can take advantage of the time available before the State of the Union address to develop measures to stimulate investment, savings and growth in the economy. By the time of the State of the Union address, we could be in a deeper recession than now, and there will be the inevitable Congressional call for Presidential leadership on the economy. A clear set of Presidential initiatives—some requiring Congressional approval and some not—will help convey the image that you are in command domestically as well as in foreign affairs.

If it would be helpful to you, I would be pleased to assemble a small and select group of highly thoughtful people from the business/financial community for an informal and private chat about all of the above issues.

*   *   *   *

Thanks for the opportunity to comment. Let me close with a personal and more upbeat note. My son, Fred, is now a Lieutenant on the

USS Juneau in San Diego and departs with his ship and 700 Marines for the Persian Gulf on December 1. He is proud to be serving and reports that morale is high, with solid across-the-board support for the Commander in Chief.

BUSH: "PREPARE FOR THE WORST"

On August 8, 1991, with Bush idling toward the starting line, Malek sounded the alarm again:

MEMORANDUM FOR THE PRESIDENT
From: Fred Malek
Subject: Campaign Planning

Thank you for including me in the Camp David meeting [on the reelection effort] last Saturday. I felt the discussions were productive and useful, and the key players had a good rapport and should work well together in the campaign.

You invited follow-up comments. This note is not intended to be definitive or inclusive but to underscore a few key points for your consideration.

Near Term Priorities

The need to be more visibly involved in domestic issues over the coming months was clearly articulated at Camp David. As we also discussed, the 1992 election will be far more influenced by the state of the economy than anything else. Unfortunately, the state of the economy is quite uncertain, a double dip back into recession is a distinct possibility, and you are perceived as somewhat detached from the problem.

I am not predicting there will be a double dip—in fact the vast majority of economists do not see this. However, the preponderance of anecdotal evidence from business people all over the country suggests the recovery is not yet on track and a double dip is enough of a probability to be dealt with. Thus, my argument is to prepare for the worst by taking steps now to substantively and perceptually invigorate the recovery. Here are a few suggested steps to start the process:

1. Commit a large part of your personal time in September and October to personally getting into the issue and developing your own firm convictions on the depth of the problem and possible solutions.

2. Start with some lengthy, substantive meetings with your eco-

nomic team (possibly including Alan Greenspan) to discuss and debate the issue and frame such concerns as the credit crunch, auto industry, housing sluggishness, etc.

3. Supplement the above with another round of give and take sessions with business and financial leaders from around the country. Include some smaller company and bank heads. Engage in a true dialogue and ask not only for a description of the problem but also their suggested solution.

4. Define the problem to your own satisfaction and develop a series of actions and public events to deal with the problem and the perception.

5. Ensure that you have a schedule the next six months that highlights for the American people your understanding of the economic realities, your empathy for those not doing too well, and your hands-on leadership to improve economic vitality.

BUSH: "THE PRESIDENT NEEDS A STRATEGY"

In November, 1991, soon after the defeat of Republican Richard Thornburgh in a Senate by-election in Pennsylvania, the president's poll-taker, Fred Steeper, saw portents of danger for his client:

MEMORANDUM

TO: Bob [Teeter]
FROM: Fred
DATE: November 15, 1991
SUBJECT: 1992 Presidential Campaign

What follows is only stating the obvious in the wake of the 1991 Pennsylvania U.S. Senate election. I outlined these thoughts a few days after the election and wish to share them with you for the record.

• The President needs a strategy that neutralizes the Democrats on domestic issues so his foreign policy successes can be the deciding factor in the 1992 election. His foreign policy successes, of course, are considerable:

✔ The significant reduction of the Soviet nuclear threat
✔ The end of communist expansionism
✔ The movement to democracy and free market economies
✔ A "new world order" that will not permit aggression by
   third world dictators

• In order to use these foreign policy successes, however, we also must have a domestic policy strategy that:

✔ Identifies with the voters' frustrations that most domestic problems are not getting better.

✔ Declares that the President and the Republicans have better solutions than do the Democrats.

✔ Focuses on one or two incremental solutions per problem that have significant public support and that can not be supported by the Democratic Party and the Democratic nominee.

✔ Blames the Congress for not enacting these incremental solutions.

BUSH: THE CHURCHILL PARALLEL

On December 18, 1991, Steeper reminded Teeter of what had befallen another leader who ran on his achievements abroad:

MEMORANDUM

TO: Bob

FROM: Fred

SUBJECT: 1992 Presidential Campaign: The Churchill Parallel

Several months ago I began to worry about a haunting episode in British history.

On May 8, 1945, the Allies declared V-E Day. Less than 60 days later, on July 5, Winston Churchill and his Conservative Party lost to Clement Attlee and the Labor Party, 48% to 40%. Historians concluded that the British voters felt Churchill was needed for war time, but he was not appropriate to rebuild Britain's economy during peace time.

During President Bush's first term, the Cold War ended, Germany reunited, the Warsaw Pact vanished, Eastern Europe turned to democracy and free markets, the Soviet Union disintegrated, Hussein's army was driven from Kuwait, the hostages returned, Noriega was arrested, nuclear arms began to be destroyed, apartheid faded, and the Israelis began negotiating with the Palestinians. The country also fell into a recession.

Leaders are not necessarily reelected for their foreign policy and wartime successes, even when monumental.

CLINTON: "THIS IS NOT A HOME GAME"

On December 26, 1991, Bill Clinton's polltaker, Stan Greenberg, used polling and focus groups to assess the Democratic primary race in New Hampshire and the message Clinton would use to take off there:

To: The Clinton Campaign
From: Stan Greenberg
Re: New Hampshire Update

There are signs of progress in New Hampshire and signs of a message that can make Clinton competitive in a difficult political environment. As of the third week in December, we were well positioned in third place where we get some cover against attack and, hopefully, the opportunity to overtake the field at the right moment. Tsongas is ahead at 26 percent, but his vote is very uncertain. He could easily drop further as public attention focuses on the top tier. Kerrey is at 17 (4 to 6 points ahead of us) and will be a serious contender.

The State of the New Hampshire Race

Let me summarize the main findings of the poll (with supplemental focus group material) in order to make strategic decisions for January:

Clinton can make headway in New Hampshire. We are at 11 percent and 13 percent within the likely electorate (up 4 points and within 4 points of Kerrey). After the presentation of messages, we move to 23 percent overall and 25 percent of the likely electorate—and into the lead. We can do well, but this is not a home game.

Clinton making progress. Clinton's favorability and recognition are up significantly. Unfortunately, Clinton's image lacks any serious definition. In focus groups, voters could recall almost nothing about him—except that he is a candidate.

Kerrey well-positioned. Kerrey is now second in the race and with the highest favorability of top-tier candidates. He was the immediate beneficiary of the Cuomo withdrawal. Voters are a little uncomfortable with Kerrey's current presentation of himself: seems a little bitter and angry and too focused on Vietnam. He wants to be a future-oriented candidate, yet the emphasis on biography sounds like old-stuff—as if he is having trouble escaping the past.

Harkin in trouble. Harkin is not catching on in New Hampshire. His support has dropped to 6 percent. We know from focus groups that New Hampshire voters are extremely uncomfortable with his style and message (too angry, too prairie populist, and too much Bush-bashing).

Message: New Hampshire

We conducted this poll primarily to refocus our message. As you probably recall, the new covenant message (still popular in Georgia) made little headway in New Hampshire. Voters were less interested in individual responsibility and welfare and more interested in middle class decline, economics, education, and radically changing government. That changed profile was largely responsible for the gains in the poll that moved us into a dead-heat with Kerrey.

The middle class messages should form the core of our media campaign in New Hampshire because they have the potential to take us into the lead:

Middle class values and economics. Under Reagan-Bush policies, the rich got richer and paid lower taxes, the politicians increased their pay, while the middle class declined. Most Americans worked harder for less and played by the rules. Clinton says we should respect individual responsibility again. He says end tax deductions for corporations using loopholes to export jobs or overpay their executives; create more work and less welfare; and Clinton says no more pay raises for politicians until the middle class gets tax relief and earns more. Clinton says he'll put Main Street before Wall Street and Washington.

Middle class tax relief. Under Reagan-Bush policies, the rich got richer and paid lower taxes, the politicians increased their pay, while the middle class declined. That's why he is the only candidate to offer his own proposal to cut middle class taxes by more than 10 percent, while asking the wealthy to start paying their fair share of taxes again. Clinton says we'll get this economy moving again when we restore the confidence and the incomes of the forgotten middle class.

The middle class values and economics message enable Clinton to make an 8 point gain and take the lead; the tax cut message alone produces a 6 point gain. Clinton makes gains, not just from the undecided but at the expense of both Tsongas and Kerrey—stealing about a quarter of their supporters. This broader middle class message is particularly effective in undercutting Tsongas.

Media presentation

The plan approach, developed by Greer, is extremely well-received. New Hampshire voters are hurting and cynical. It suggests that Clinton is serious about doing something on the economy; that he is not afraid to put his ideas out. In the end, they talk about Clinton as somebody with solutions, who is confident, smart and educated, somebody who makes sense and has a positive outlook.

Unfortunately, there is little sense of Clinton as somebody who cares and is concerned with people. The introductory spots have to become less intellectual and include more empathy for people in New Hampshire who are hurting.

CLINTON: THE POLITICS OF RACE

On December 27, Greenberg reported the results of a first scan of Georgia and how issues of color might come into play there:

To: The Clinton Campaign
From: Stan Greenberg
Re: Georgia: Baseline Survey

At last, we are playing with the home field advantage. In Georgia and probably most of the South, Clinton is well positioned to dominate the field. His message strikes a chord that moves voters and that allows Clinton to gather quickly a majority of the white vote. In Georgia—and in most Super Tuesday states—that will produce a decisive win. How decisive will depend on our ability to make inroads in the black community and hold down Wilder's vote and to limit the appeal of a New Hampshire winner, like Kerrey.

The poll suggests that the race could prove tight in states with large black [electorates]. Clinton makes only limited inroads in the black community (only 5 percent at this point) and a strong Wilder showing could prove troublesome. This poll suggests that Clinton could gather 25 to 30 percent of the black vote in a contest with Wilder which would ensure Clinton victories across the South.

The State of the Race

Clinton begins the Georgia primary in first place, with 15 percent of the vote, followed by Brown with 14 percent, Wilder with 12, Kerrey with 9, Harkins with 5 and Tsongas with 3. A near majority of 43 percent is undecided.

The undecided electorate is a Clinton majority in waiting. These undecided voters do not know Bill Clinton; those who know Clinton believe he is more conservative and Southern and pro-education, but they do not see him as pro-middle class. **The undecided voters, more** than any other segment of the electorate, score high on the middle class dimension. When they hear the Bill Clinton message, they shift to him in droves.

Making Inroads in the Black Community

We should understand at the outset that Wilder will run well in the black community—no matter how well he is doing elsewhere. We cannot measure whether his candidacy will generate turnout, but the voters are there for him. He begins with 31 percent of the black vote and quickly moves to 51 percent just by letting people know he is the black candidate. After the presentation of the Clinton message, Wilder still holds around 50 percent of the vote.

The black community favors a black southern governor to a white one by 48 to 9 percent. That is pretty close to our starting point. When the two candidates are put head-to-head, with their positions and attacks, Wilder wins out, 59 to 28 percent. **Clinton can clearly take 28 percent of the black vote in a head-to-head with Wilder; where Wilder does not contest the race, Clinton can run stronger (53 percent prefer a pro-civil rights, pro-education, pro work/not welfare, middle class white candidate).**

The Evolving Southern Message: Coming Home

The campaign will have to make a strategic judgment about the anti-liberal message. Clinton's support rises from 45 to 51 in the white community when he is anti-liberal, but that is balanced in part by slippage in the black community, from 25 down to 19 percent. In Georgia, the anti-liberal theme is a minor net plus, but [it] would hurt Clinton in states with larger black voting populations, like South Carolina, Alabama and Mississippi. **On balance, the anti-liberal theme only marginally enhances Clinton's candidacy; other additions will make more of a difference without costing Clinton in the black community.**

The **middle class message is still the center of the Clinton candidacy.**

CLINTON: "DUKAKIS WITH A DRAWL"

On January 7, 1992, one of Clinton's chief strategists, Paul Begala, addressed the problem of the passion gap in the early stages of the governor's campaign:

MEMORANDUM

TO: Frank Greer
      Anne Lewis
      Stan Greenberg
      David Wilhelm
      George Stephanopoulos
      Dee Dee Myers
From: Paul Begala
Re: Some Thoughts on the Message and How to Convey It

The [60-second] "Plan" spot lays a good foundation upon which to build a Clinton message in New Hampshire. The question is, where do we go from here?

Being the Man With The Plan, standing alone, is not good enough. On the stump, in the schedule and free press, and in the paid media we need a couple of things: more people, more energy, more passion. We need to be more emotional and less literal. We cannot simply be Dukakis with a drawl.

Now that we've laid the foundation for being Mr. Specific, I propose that we show folks how particular aspects of the Clinton plan can make a real difference in their daily lives. We could do this by selecting the three or four best ideas in the plan (that is, those things that Greenberg has determined people most want and that help to draw distinctions vis a vis the field) and showing how Bill Clinton's ideas can change the real lives of people.

This series of spots would be something like what United Way and John Hancock Insurance do. When United Way wants to get you to give, they don't appeal to your head; they appeal to your heart. You never see some coat-and-tie executive droning on about how "93 percent of United Way donations are applied to direct social services." Instead, you see a handsome, articulate jock bouncing a kid on his knee, talking about how your donation to United Way helped little Homer to overcome his tragic addiction to Twinkies. Then Homer looks in the camera, his chubby cheeks flush with a cherubic grin and says, "Thanks to you, it's working."

Dee Dee told me about a woman who wrote us a letter that would make a great spot. This woman had paid on her home mortgage for more than twenty years. She lost her job in the recession, and missed six payments in a row, for a total of something like $900. The bank foreclosed on her home. The following is very rough—and very much in need of the Greer Touch. But I think we should consider something like:

[JANE DOE]:   "I felt like my whole world was crashing down around me."

BILL CLINTON: "[Jane Doe] of Nashua made payments on this home every month for twenty-two years. But she lost her job in the recession and couldn't make the payments. The bank foreclosed. I'm Bill Clinton and my economic plan for America has an economic lifeline—so that people like Hazel won't lose their home and health care when they lose their job. If we can forgive two billion dollars of debt to the nation of Egypt, surely we can help our neighbors save their homes when they lose their jobs.

Join us. Together we can put government back on the side of the forgotten middle class."

I think we can do some variation of this on a host of issues, lifted straight out of the plan—the middle-class tax cut, the need for national health insurance, college opportunity, etc. In each one we can show an outrage that hurts working people—illustrated by the pain and suffering of one family, then show how Clinton's economic plan will stop this outrage.

I feel very strongly that our message and our media must be filled with emotion and energy, not bogged down in policy and process. Of course, I may be all wet in the way I've tried to achieve that goal here—and I welcome new, different and better ideas to convey the message. But I know this: If we grab them by the heart, their minds will follow.

CLINTON: GENNIFER AND ELVIS

On January 24, 1992, with the Gennifer Flowers scandal breaking over Clinton's head, Paul Begala wrote a "talking-points" memo to his colleagues intended as much to cheer them up as to tell them what to say:

TO: ALL STAFF, CONSULTANTS AND ELVIS IMPERSONATORS
FROM: PAUL BEGALA
RE: TALKING POINTS

Bill and Hillary Are Not "Victims"

- No other political couple has been more forthcoming about their relationship than Bill and Hillary Clinton.
- They understood this kind of thing would happen if they ran for President, but their commitment to each other is strong

enough, and their commitment to changing America is deep enough, that they jointly decided it was worth it.

- When they began this campaign, they took the unprecedented step of addressing a roomful of national reporters, and acknowledging that, like all relationships, theirs has had its ups and downs. If the standard is to be perfection, we won't measure up. But the important thing is that the commitment is real and lasting—they've been able to overcome adversity, and that's a tribute to their character and their commitment.
- We believe the American people are more concerned about the stresses and strains that are tearing middle-class families apart—job loss, declining wages, racial tensions, crime—than they are about what problems a political family has overcome in the past.

The *Star* Paid For The Story
- The woman in question felt so strongly that allegations of an affair were untrue that she had her lawyer threaten to sue someone who repeated them.
- Now that she's been paid-off by the *Star*, she's changed her story.
- The *Star* and the other tabloids are likely to litter the landscape of Little Rock with offers of cash—it's kind of like an Elvis sighting.

The Responsible Press Is Being Manipulated by the Tabloids:
- This is Lowest-Common-Denominator Journalism: If some scum-sucking rag like the *Star* prints something, the rest of the mainstream press allows it to dominate the agenda.

CLINTON: "RUNNING AGAINST OURSELVES"

On February 3, Stan Greenberg surveyed the changed lay of the land in New Hampshire after the Flowers story and the Clintons' reply:

TO: The Clinton Campaign
FROM: Stan Greenberg
RE: New Hampshire Update

We have been twice weekly (over four nights) conducting almost daily focus groups. The results have been used on an immediate basis to help govern media traffic decisions and a variety of other strategic judgments. As we enter the last two-week stretch, I wanted to highlight some patterns that are emerging:

• We are holding our lead in the race, with a couple of points slippage at the end of the week.

• Clinton's lead in the race is based on two attributes—leadership, that is, being presidential, and being for the middle class. He has only modest standing on the economy, and is weak on caring, standing up to special interests, on family values and honesty. In the next two weeks, we will have to reinforce the attributes that have gotten us here: advancing the economy (which is the most important consideration for many swing voters) and enhancing the personal traits.

• Tsongas is dangerous because his strengths and weaknesses closely complement ours and provide an easy alternative for those uncertain about Clinton. Tsongas is very high on family values and honesty and scores respectably on the economy and middle class. He is weakest on being presidential, which limits his electoral support somewhat.

• Kerrey's is a failed campaign. He has succeeded in establishing his identity with the health care and trade issues WITHOUT demonstrating that he cares or understands the economy. People do not see him as presidential.

• This race is still about Clinton. Most of the attention is focused on him AND CRITICALLY, Clinton is still the candidate that people want to know more about. Attention has not shifted to the other candidates. We are, in effect, running against ourselves on credibility. This is still an electorate positively predisposed to Clinton, despite their doubts.

CLINTON: "BACK KOPPEL OFF"

On February 12, Clinton was going on Nightline *to answer questions about his long-ago letter on the draft, and several aides offered him advice:*

To: Governor Clinton
From: Begala, Stephanopoulos, Boorstin
Re: Briefing on "Nightline"

Style and Format

The show is only 22 minutes long. You'll be live from New Hampshire, [Ted] Koppel will be in the studio in Washington, and you will only be able to hear him. Koppel always gives his guests a lot of leeway on the first couple of questions. Then he zeroes in and pins them down. So **feel free to run with the ball early in the show.** It is important—especially in the beginning of the show—that you turn questions and pivot into your message. **Literal, direct and limited answers do not serve your strategic interests.**

You can take control of the show from the beginning. Remember how Mandy [Grunwald] took control of the show from Koppel last month. She jumped on her message early; almost irrespective of what Koppel asked her, she kept hammering her indictment of the media, Nightline and even Koppel himself.

Pause a beat to collect yourself before you launch into an answer. If you launch into a too-perfect-to-be-true answer as soon as the question is out of Koppel's mouth, it feeds the Slick Willie problem.

Strategic Overview

We have an immediate problem in that ABC now says that you misunderstood—that Koppel never totally affirmed that their source was in the Pentagon. **I strongly think you should respond by saying:**

EVERYBODY IN AMERICA BELIEVES YOU, TED. SO DID I. I WAS TOLD BY YOU THAT THE SOURCE OF THIS LETTER WAS IN THE PENTAGON. NOW YOU SAY IT WASN'T. BUT THAT'S NOT WHAT'S IMPORTANT. WHAT'S IMPORTANT ARE THE JOBS AND THE FAMILIES AND THE CHILDREN AT RISK. WHAT'S IMPORTANT IS A PLAN TO GET THIS ECONOMY MOVING AGAIN.

While this is undeniably a problem, here's how we think you can try to make some chicken salad out of this chicken shit. Koppel is likely to be feeling sheepish that he misled you and you were burned. Not so sheepish that he'll admit that he screwed you, but probably sheepish enough to allow you more latitude in your responses. Take all that you can: get on your economic message and ride it as far as you can.

While it is unavoidable that the discussions will keep coming back to the letter and your draft record, we want as much as possible to re-focus the discussion on the Big Ideas that you've brought into the race. At every opportunity we want to return to the economy, and the reason why the Republicans want to talk about anything but their economic failings. Lines like the following should be wedged in whenever possible:

I DECIDED TO RUN FOR PRESIDENT BECAUSE I HAVE A SET OF IDEAS—A NATIONAL ECONOMIC STRATEGY THAT I BELIEVE CAN GET

THIS ECONOMY MOVING AGAIN. AND YET RATHER THAN DEBATING THE MERITS OF MY IDEAS WITH YOU, I FIND MYSELF ON "NIGHTLINE" OR "SIXTY MINUTES" NOT TO TALK ABOUT GETTING THE ECONOMY MOVING AGAIN, BUT INSTEAD DISCUSSING TABLOID STORIES AND 22-YEAR-OLD LETTERS.

AREN'T YOU TIRED OF TALKING ABOUT THESE DISTRACTIONS? I KNOW THE PEOPLE OF NEW HAMPSHIRE ARE.

SOMETHING IS GETTING LOST HERE. FAMILIES ARE LOSING THEIR HOMES. PEOPLE ARE LOSING THEIR JOBS AND THEIR HEALTH CARE AND THEIR PENSIONS. WE'RE LOSING OUR KIDS TO DRUGS AND DROP-OUTS. AND BECAUSE OF THESE DIVERSIONS, WE ARE LOSING OUR CHANCE TO HAVE A RATIONAL DEBATE ON THE FUTURE OF OUR NATION.

THIS HAPPENED IN 1988. GEORGE BUSH WAS ELECTED ON THE CHEAP. AND THE COUNTRY'S PAYING A TERRIBLE PRICE—THE PRICE OF A HOLLOW PRESIDENCY.

YOU KNOW, TED, WE COULD DO SIX SHOWS ABOUT THE VIETNAM WAR AND WHAT HAPPENED 22 YEARS AGO. AND THAT'S EXACTLY WHAT THE REPUBLICANS WANT. THEY CAN'T DEFEND THE ECONOMIC DISASTER OF THE LAST 11 YEARS. THEY WILL DO ANYTHING TO DIVERT, DIVIDE AND DISTRACT THE PEOPLE OF THIS COUNTRY.

Questions and Answers

Almost no matter what Koppel asks right out of the chute, you need to make the following point:

TED, THE LETTER YOU MENTIONED IS A LETTER I'M PROUD OF— A LETTER THAT FAIRLY REFLECTS MY ATTITUDES AND BELIEFS AT THAT TIME. I LOVED MY COUNTRY, BUT I HATED THAT WAR. THE LETTER CONFIRMS THE THREE MAIN POINTS I'VE BEEN SAYING ALL ALONG:

1. *I GAVE UP AN R.O.T.C. STUDENT DEFERMENT;*
2. *I VOLUNTARILY ENTERED THE DRAFT;*
3. *I HAD NO WAY OF KNOWING WHAT MY DRAFT LOTTERY NUMBER WOULD BE.*

Q: Didn't you release this because you're behind in the polls?

A: OH, THERE'S NO DOUBT I'VE FALLEN BEHIND IN THE POLLS, TED. THE PEOPLE OF NEW HAMPSHIRE HAVEN'T KNOWN ME VERY LONG. I'VE FALLEN IN THE POLLS BECAUSE OF TWO THINGS: CASH-FOR-TRASH TABLOID SLEAZE—COMPLETE WITH DOCTORED TAPES AND BOUGHT-OFF WITNESSES; AND SECOND BECAUSE OF OLD DISCREDITED STORIES FROM 22 YEARS AGO. THE QUESTION YOU AND YOUR COLLEAGUES AND THE AMERICAN PEOPLE HAVE TO ANSWER,

TED, IS: WILL WE ALLOW OUR PRESIDENTIAL ELECTIONS TO BE
CONTROLLED BY SLEAZY TABLOIDS AND 22-YEAR-OLD LETTERS?
THIS IS ABOUT MORE THAN ONE PERSON OR ONE CAMPAIGN. IT'S
ABOUT WHETHER WE'RE GOING TO BE ABLE TO CONTROL HOW WE
CHOOSE OUR PRESIDENTS.

To: Bill Clinton
From: Stan Greenberg
Re: Nightline

I will leave it to others to work through the specifics of the letter. No doubt we will have to deal with some of the language and
positions. But we have a larger problem—reflected in the overall
20 point drop over the past week and a half. We have to make a
much bigger statement tonight and in the next few days to regain
our base.

1. Back Koppel off. At some point, we have to back Koppel off by
putting the letter in context.

> Look, Ted. This letter was written 23 years ago, a quarter of a
> century ago, based in part on a paper written as a Georgetown
> undergraduate. I am proud that I wrote that letter in that era, but
> you are missing the real importance of the letter.

We should then move on to give the letter significance in a different
context, as below.

2. Reflects my generation. This letter reflects the experience of my
generation—and to some extent the country. We were conflicted over
the war and divided—and none of us would go back to relive that
experience.

For my part, I opposed the war, but chose in the end to put myself
in the draft. But my anguished letter reflected the experience of
a generation. Many of my friends accepted the obligation of service—
4 roommates; 4 of my high school classmates died in Vietnam, and I
still meet monthly with my friends from high school; some of my
roommates resisted the war and others committed suicide. So like
many others, I lived the pain that many of us felt. It's important that
those feelings and that experience be represented in our political life.
We need leaders who anguish about war and also understand their
responsibilities to their country.

That letter contains the account of a young man concerned with
right and wrong, who loved his country, who respected the military
(even when opposing the war) and who was ready to do his duty. I am

proud of those sentiments, and I suspect they reflect the sentiments of many Americans who lived that history. We need leaders who understand the American experience—and this is part of it.

2. Regret. Do I regret the excesses of that period—and even the letter? Of course, I do. There was not enough responsibility, not enough respect for our country and not enough respect for each other. We've all matured. The baby-boomers, the press, everybody. We have families and children, we pay taxes, we have the responsibility to assure the nation's security.

For my part, I have 2 decades of service to America. I've decried those who would burn the flag; I made sure the Arkansas National Guard was available to serve and train at the President's command; I supported the Persian Gulf War. I thought it was just. I've worked to build, not protest, to improve things for people. I have acted on values that matter to me in my life—rewarding hard work, educating kids, creating opportunity, understanding the burden of taxes on middle-class people.

I don't regret the idealism and passion, the desire to do right. We need more of that, not less.

3. Commander-in-chief. The Vietnam war weakened America. We all know that now wherever we stand. This country was divided; the war undermined confidence in the military; our leaders took the country to war without the support of the people.

Nobody running for President should weaken America. I understand the first responsibility of this office, etc., etc.

CLINTON: "TURN ON ALL YOUR CHARM"

On February 14, Mandy Grunwald and Paul Begala sent Clinton a critique of his performance at a town meeting in New Hampshire and some cues for an upcoming phone-in show on television:

MEMORANDUM

To: Governor Clinton
From: Grunwald, Begala
Re: Thoughts On Last Night's Show, And Tonight's
Last night's show was terrific. Outstanding. Wonderful.

Here's What Worked:

1. **You were personal about your own life and the lives of the people in the studio.** The first thing out of your mouth on the education question was a big smile—then a reminder that this is the issue to

which you've devoted more time than any other. Great. A direct personal connection will be more difficult to do with a disembodied voice on the phone. Turn on all your charm and empathy with your phone callers.

2. **You were engaged and you were thinking out loud.** None of the answers seemed canned or pre-programmed.

3. **You were animated.** You obviously love this stuff. You've been passionate about solving people's problems and making change all your life, and people can tell. Don't lose the gestures and the movement and the walking out from behind the podium just because your questioner is on the phone instead of in the studio.

4. **You were specific—without being a propeller-head.** It's a delicate balance, but you struck it well.

Here's What You Can Do Better than Last Night:

1. **Don't be a political analyst.** Don't talk about the polls.

2. **Look for something on which you can disagree with a questioner or some point where you've taken on a tough opponent.** It's important that you not be seen as all things to all people.

3. **Look for a couple moments of passion and outrage vs. Bush and the status quo.** Preferably on capital gains and middle-class tax cut. But race, division and diversion are excellent topics as well.

4. **Draw a starker populist contrast.** Your point of departure should be the 80s vs. the 90s: Reagan-Bush greed, corporate ethics versus the virtues of middle class people and their values. The middle-class people play by the rules. They should be rewarded for that.

CLINTON: "YOU'RE NOT THE FRONTRUNNER ANY MORE"

In the run-up to a scheduled debate on CNN on February 16, the Sunday before the New Hampshire primary, Clinton's strategists sent him two memos on what to expect and how to respond:

To: Governor Clinton
From: Your Debate Preppies
Re: Sunday's CNN Debate
Date: February 14, 1992

Style

In some ways, the strategy is the style. It's important to be engaged, energetic, personal and at times passionate. Use two recent performances as your guide: your performance on "Meet The Press" was great—when you leaned forward in your chair, eager to get the next question and engage in a dialogue. You looked like the eager young rookie on the bench during the big game saying "Put me in, Coach." Another moment to remember and pattern your performance on is your response to Steve Kroft when he asked you about your "arrangement" on "60 Minutes."

Inspire. Preach. Soar. Lift people. Do what you do at a rally, when you become the voice of a million frustrated, desperate, decent middle-class voters.

Strategy

Don't be careful. You're not the frontrunner any more. Go with your gut; always have the self-confidence to say the first thing that pops into your mind.

Go to the Big Idea, the Big Picture. From time to time, when the debate is descending into irrelevance or bickering, put it back on track. Comment on the debate as the leader of the pack. **Don't get sucked into some petty tit-for-tat with Harkin or Brown.** You're bigger than that. Or when Tsongas or Harkin is holding up a copy of their plan, remind them that a plan is just a piece of paper. **Remember, we're picking a president here.** This is Big Stuff. Big Consequences. Big Problems, Big Challenges.

Take on Bush. Pour it on.

Show that you're a fighter. Being a fighter does not mean bickering with your opponents, but rather being ready to defend yourself and your ideas vigorously. Show that you're the middle-class candidate. Show that you have an emotional commitment to people and your issues—especially on the economy. (Greenberg says that more than ⅔ of the voters agree with the statement that you have a plan for the nation's economic recovery. Press that advantage.) Don't be a propeller-head, buried in the arcana of some policy proposal. Be excited about your ideas.

Talk issues in terms of values, emotions and people. Don't ever forget that older woman who cried on your shoulder at the seniors center. Her story is about a tear in the social fabric of our nation; an example of the need to heal the wounds that cut to the very soul of our society.

Defend any attack against your record in Arkansas as an attack on the people of Arkansas. Don't attack the source, dispute the survey, or nit-pick about the methodology. Instead, defend the people of Arkansas, and compare what they've done with what's happened during the same time under Reagan and Bush in Washington. This is one of the times you want to show flashes of anger. Not about yourself or your record, but about your people.

Make the electability issue an excuse to draw distinctions vis-a-vis Bush. This is where you play to your strength: "Before you can argue that you're electable, you have to decide why you want to be President. . . ." Then rip Bush a new one on divide, divert, distract and destroy . . . Willie Horton . . . and the vision thing.

Think of the distinction with Tsongas in these terms: energy vs. lethargy; optimism vs. pessimism; challenge vs. punishment; middle class vs. corporate elite; Governor vs. Senator/lobbyist, and perhaps most importantly, Strength vs. Weakness, and Presidential vs. Weenie.

AND: CHALLENGE PEOPLE.

To: Governor Clinton
From: The Debate Preppies
Re: CNN Debate
Date: February 15, 1992

The three most important aspects of debate prep are, in this order: Mindset, Moments, and Lines.

Mindset

Your mindset has to be eager—almost to the point of aggressiveness. You should almost be on the edge of your chair—enthusiastic about your ideas and your message. You've taken more shit from more places that anyone in Presidential history, and you're still standing. There's nothing these bastards can do to you now. So come and get me—take your best shot, Bernie [Shaw]. I'm not gonna fold like Dukakis if you ask a goofy, unfair question about my personal life. I've heard worse things from better people.

This is a wonderful opportunity to speak to America about the things that are at stake in this country. For the last three weeks we've been bitching about how the media horde has blocked you from communicating directly with the American people. Now there's no excuses—you've got the microphone. This is a great chance to show folks what's really at stake, and to share the passions you've been fighting for for a decade.

Remember that you are the only person on that stage who has the ability to move this nation and lead us to a better place. You do it at every rally, you did it at the seniors center when that woman broke down. You can do it here. And those other poor bums can't hold a candle to you when you soar.

Never forget that it is George Bush and the Republicans who are the enemy here—not Harkin or Tsongas or anyone else. Keep your eyes on the prize.

Moments

In every debate there are Moments that capture and define what that debate was all about—and sometimes they capture what an election is all about. You know them: Reagan in '80 saying "I paid for this microphone, Mr. Breen"; and to Carter, "There you go again." Mondale in '84 saying, "Where's the beef?"; Dukakis in '88 unable to answer the Kitty question; Bentsen to Quayle: "You're no JFK." These were more than lines. They were Moments. We need to be prepared to create a few.

A Vietnam Moment—Any question about Vietnam is actually a question about your truthfulness or your patriotism, whether you understand and honor the emotions of military service. Whether you will understand how to be Commander in Chief. Make sure that any answer, no matter how they phrase the question, addresses those core emotions.

A useful guide is the 3 Facts/3 Emotions approach.

THREE FACTS:

A) I was reluctant to fight a war in which I didn't believe, so I asked for and received an ROTC student deferment;

B) But I felt that wasn't right, so I put myself back in the draft.

C) I received a high lottery number.

THREE EMOTIONS:

A) I grew up believing in America and the military. One of the few things I knew about my father. . . . veteran. . . . respect for service etc.

B) As a young man I took strong stands on the two great issues of the day—against racism and against the war in Vietnam. It was agonizing to me during Vietnam to be torn between loving my country and hating the war, hating what it was doing to the country.

C) As President, I will be the kind of Commander in Chief that I was in Arkansas, where I called on the National Guard to put down a riot at Fort Chaffee, and sent my Guard troops to train in Central America. I supported the Gulf War, and I will never ask this nation to fight a war that turns this country against itself, a war we don't believe in, and are not prepared to win. If I must ask the young people of this country to go to war, I can tell you we will know what we are fighting for and we will fight to win.

An Electability Moment: If asked about whether you're mortally wounded, whether Kerrey's more acceptable in the South, if you owe it to your party not to lead it off a cliff, or whatever horserace horseshit is out there, admit that it's true and withdraw from the race.

Let's really hope they don't ask it.

As a fallback: Take it to the Big Election, Big Deal answer. "To me, the test of electability is not found in a poll. The real test is whether you know why you want to be President and where you want to lead this country. I can win this election because I can offer not only a plan, but the energy, idealism, and the vision to lead the country to reject the hollow philosophy of Reagan and Bush and embrace the challenge of change."

On the Ethics of the Eighties. Look for an opportunity to pivot into a denunciation of the Decade of Greed. You know the riff—the worst legacy of the Reagan-Bush years is the greed, the get it while you can attitude; the to-hell-with-my-neighbor, quick buck mentality that created the S&L debacle, the looting of HUD, and the ransacking of our great companies. What that says to Michael Milken at the top, and a streetcorner crack dealer at the bottom, is that you don't have to play by the rules. What that says to all the hard-working middle class people who do the work, pay the taxes, and play by the rules is that the American system doesn't work for you. We're better than that.

BUSH: THEME MUSIC

On February 17, 1992, Fred Steeper outlined the best arguments for Bush's reelection, along with their potential drawbacks:

MEMORANDUM FOR ROBERT TEETER
FROM: FRED STEEPER
SUBJECT: Strategic themes

The following outlines my thoughts on the options for strategic themes for the President in 1992. These might be viewed as the President's options for positive themes. While I have largely described them in positive terms, they all have an implied comparative component. When the opponent does not possess the positive attribute described in the theme or is, otherwise, on the "wrong side" of our strategic theme, then it could be (and should be) part of our strategy to draw that contrast.

Economic Themes

1. *America as a Leader in the World Economy.*

The health of the U.S. economy depends on vigorous foreign trade, and a world at peace is beneficial to all international commerce. The end of the Cold War opens new trade opportunities and new resources to the West. The President has the proven experience to: keep the peace, maintain good relations with our current trading partners, improve upon these trade relationships, and open markets with the old communist bloc.

The country cannot solve its economic problems by returning to pre–WW II protectionism and isolationism. The country needs to make the reforms necessary to be a leader in the world economy.

Advantages: It deals with the voters' number one issue. It combines the domestic economy (a weakness) with foreign policy (a strength). It includes the traditional "peace" theme which is still relevant to voters.

The position is intellectually correct and will win much editorial support. An opponent who takes a protectionist position will be seen by editorial writers as demagoguing the issue. In short, we can "win the press" with this theme.

The theme lends itself to a second economic plan from the President. What reforms are needed for the country to become an economic world leader? This is different than the current plan to end the recession. The current plan is defensive and one that many think has come a bit late. The World Economic Leader Plan could be perceived as "pro-active." While maintaining a free trade policy, it could still have a strong note of nationalism in it, and, thereby, neutralize the America First attitude currently in the country. We do best against the Democrats when we can use nationalism.

Disadvantages: It may be playing on the opponent's field—the economy. The "America First" sentiment is running very high, and a pro-trade theme will drive some voters to each opponent.

2. *Economic Leadership.*

This theme features the President's experience, in general, rather than his foreign policy experience, and it makes no commitments on economic policy. The President has the most government experience of anyone to lead the country through these difficult times. He is prudent and responsible. He will not support quick fixes that will make things worse.

The experienced leadership theme could use the President's 1992 economic plan but would not feature it. It features his government experience.

Advantages: It deals with the voters' number one issue. "Experienced" is the number one positive perception of the President. Consequently, it pairs a strength (experienced) with the leading issue on the voters' agenda. By using government experience, in general, it does not feature foreign policy which has become a double edged sword for the President. This is the updated "resume strategy" that helped in 1988.

Disadvantages: It is entirely playing on the opponent's field—the economy. This is the old resume strategy which may not work again. The resume is mostly foreign policy experience.

3. *The President's Economic Plan*

This theme makes the primaries and possibly the general election a vote on whether people trust the President's approach or Congress's approach to the recovery. The President has a sound and workable plan for economic recovery. Congress refuses to pass it, and, instead, insists on passing a bill which emphasizes tax increases rather than spending cuts and incentives for investments in new jobs. The President's experience becomes a supporting argument rather than the featured argument to vote for him.

This theme could be used through November if the President vetoes all the plans passed by Congress. It can be used in the short term until the President does sign a bill.

Advantages: It deals with the voters' number one issue. The voters blame Congress more than the President for the length of the recession. The whole Party would be mobilized in a joint effort that might actually produce a Congress supportive of the President in 1993. It takes advantage of the unpopularity of Congress, which is greater than the President's.

Disadvantages: The Administration still has a ways to go in selling the plan to the American public. It may not be an issue by this fall.

Foreign Policy Themes

4. *A Safer World (for us and our children) #1.*

The President is one of the most experienced and most successful foreign policy Presidents in our history. His leadership helped secure the demise of communism and nurture the rise of democracy in its place, one of the most significant events of the century. The greatest danger to civilization, all out nuclear war, has been significantly reduced for the first time since it became a possibility. The situations in the former Soviet republics and Eastern Europe are still very delicate, and there is a real danger of counter revolutions against the young democracies. *This is no time to change presidents.* President Bush's experience is needed to ensure that this great gain for the world is not lost.

Advantages: These are profound events. They lend themselves to dramatic advertising more than any other possible theme for the President. The theme would work upon reflection of the voters, most of whom are concerned with domestic issues and the economy, i.e., "On second thought, we'd better stick with Bush." No opponent can match the President in this area, so the contrast potential is great.

Disadvantages: It is not the voters' number one issue. It may fall prey to the perception that the President spends too much time on foreign policy. The President's role in the changes in the old Soviet bloc is arguable. The theme would have to be used persistently, through an initial time when it did not seem to be working.

5. *A Safer World (for us and our children) #2.*
Desert Storm belongs here. We may end up merging this with the first version of the safer world, but, for now, I see the tone and meaning of this strategy to be different from the other version. This is more along the lines of the "New World Order's Top Enforcer." We know from polling data that the public now identifies international terrorism, international drug trafficking, and the development of weapons of mass destruction by third world dictators to be the most serious threats to our national security. This theme would spell out the President's vision of the New World Order where rogue dictators engaging in certain behavior would be met by joint U.S.-U.N. action, non-military at first; military, if necessary.

Advantages: This reintroduces the national security set of issues for the Republicans and the President. We have lost male support and Southern white support because of the recession. We had our male support and Southern white support partly because of the national security set of issues. It allows us to use Desert Storm in more than just a "patting ourselves on the back" way. Desert Storm becomes a message for other rogue dictators that is believable from this President.

Disadvantages: It is not the voters' number one issue.

Personal Quality Themes

6. *Experienced Leadership.*

The President is the most experienced candidate in the race on either side. His government resume is long and significant. No one in the race can be trusted to do all the things expected of a President as well as he can. His great experience is the most believable assertion about the President that we can make. It is the one the voters, themselves, volunteer the most often about the President.

Advantages: It elevates the essential question to the voters above immediate economic problems: who do you trust the most to do all the things expected of a president? No opponent can match the President on experience so the contrast potential is great.

Disadvantages: It is not the voters' number one issue. It can be a dull theme.

7. *Man of Basic Decency.*

For most voters, President Bush is a basically decent person in a profession they generally distrust.

Advantages: Many swing voters in the general election "vote for the man" not the party or ideology. This theme arguably is targeted to the only voters important to the actual campaign, the ones who still can be influenced after Labor Day.

Disadvantages: It is not the voters' number one issue concern in 1992. It needs an opponent who fits the mold of a "typical politician."

Ideological Themes

8. *Traditional American Values*

This theme has won many converts to the Republican Party and to Republican presidential candidates over the past three presidential elections, especially the so-called Reagan Democrats. Most voters, including traditional Republicans as well as Reagan Democrats, believe in standards of conduct; in right and wrong; and God. They do not believe all "alternative life styles" should be accepted with equal approval and full civil rights. Drug experimentation, homosexuality, and radical feminism are wrong. Racial quotas in hiring and promotion violate the principles of merit and equal opportunity. Our country has an important religious history, the expression of which should not be forbidden by the political system.

(The abortion issue remains divisive among our own voters. For some, "choice" is the traditional American value. For others, "life" is the traditional American value. It is not an issue to feature with this theme.)

Advantages: These are deeply felt beliefs and, consequently, they do move voters by the truck load. They can keep voters in the President's coalition [of] 1988 who are dissatisfied with him over the economy. This thematic area is very important to our Southern electoral base. With the possible exception of Governor Clinton, we should be facing another Democrat who is "liberal on the social issues," as Democrats put it.
Disadvantages: It is not the voters' number one issue. It can't be used against [Pat] Buchanan. It potentially could cause problems with our younger supporters and Northern moderate supporters although this has not been very evident in the last three presidential elections.

CLINTON: "MOSES VS. THE MECHANIC"

On February 18, primary day in New Hampshire, Clinton's strategists worked up a memo on how to respond to his expected second-place finish:

MEMORANDUM

To: Governor Clinton
From: Begala, Stephanopoulos, Grunwald, Boorstin
Re: Talking Points For Election Night

The Strategy

This is not the last speech in New Hampshire. That was last night. This is the first speech of the Southern Campaign. We want to set the agenda and change the news curve—to feed the feeling that now it's time for the media to focus on Tsongas, and make this a two-person race in case Kerrey is coming on.

Your most important strategic imperative is to draw a clear contrast with Tsongas. It's Moses vs. The Mechanic. The Visionary vs. The Technocrat. It's New Covenant vs. Atari Democrat. You challenge; he chastises. You promise hope and opportunity; he promises pain and limited horizons. You view the Presidency as the vital center of the nation, and this election as a struggle for the soul of the nation; he sees the President as Secretary of Commerce, and this election about his pure non-poll-driven truth triumphing over your intellectually and morally bankrupt pandering to the middle class.

Talking Points

THANK YOU, NEW HAMPSHIRE. YOU MADE ME FEEL LIKE THE
COMEBACK KID. I CAN'T WAIT TO TAKE THIS CAMPAIGN ACROSS THIS
COUNTRY, TO THE NOMINATION, AND ON TO VICTORY IN THE FALL,
AGAINST PATRICK J. BUCHANAN.

CLINTON: WHAT WOMEN WANT

*On March 10, a week before the Illinois primary, Clinton's pollsters
reported on the wary feelings of women voters toward him:*

To: Bill Clinton and company
From: Celinda Lake and Stan Greenberg
Date: March 10, 1992
Re: Illinois Focus Groups
           Phase III: Women Voters

Trusting the Man

College women and younger women voters are a difficult problem,
particularly as we move out of the south. Since Gennifer Flowers,
these women have been more negative about Bill Clinton. They have
ranked him significantly lower on being honest, trustworthy, having
family values, and being politically expedient. We took a toll with these
women voters who were introduced to us through the Gennifer Flowers
episode.

At the most fundamental and personal level, these women voters do
not "trust" Bill Clinton—a politician they have barely heard of. They
find it difficult to vote for a candidate that they do not trust at such an
elemental level. As one woman concluded, "it's an integrity issue that
is hard to overlook." Their introduction to Bill Clinton through Gennifer Flowers has produced a screen that tends to block out other
messages. It has also provided a powerful framework for interpreting
other messages. It is easy for these voters to see Clinton's commercials
as slick, politically expedient, and "saying all things to all people." Our
polls confirm that younger women and college educated women start
with and continue to hold higher doubts about Clinton's character,
and thus hold back from considering him as a candidate.

In our recent focus groups in Chicago, all but one woman volunteered the "affair" and "honesty" as something they knew about
Clinton. Even those who were less bothered wondered if "he can get
past the scandal." They "doubted" his personal morals, were "leery of

him," "untrusting of his morality." These feelings left them unsure of what he really believed in.

Voters in general are very cynical about politicians, convinced that they are untrustworthy and break promises. These voters believe they already know that Bill Clinton is "a liar," "untrustworthy," "not sure of his honesty," "lacks credibility." [He] broke a "personal promise" and these women voters wondered whether he would follow through on his promises to people as president. As one woman summed it up, "cheating on his wife, trying to cover that scandal up—his wife standing by his side." They want to make sure his ads are "not just one more of his promises with nothing concrete behind it." They wanted to believe that he is not just "telling people what they want to hear." They wanted to make sure "he will carry through."

Many of Clinton's advantages simultaneously compound these women voters' distrust. They think he is "good-looking," "articulate," "charismatic," but that has some down sides. Voters think Clinton is "like Kennedy," but with "all their affairs" that is hardly flattering. As one woman said, "get rid of the Kennedy look." Several said, "he's too sugary," "a sweet talker." Even when they liked him on the surface, they resisted those feelings. Women voters wanted to see the "real" Bill Clinton. In targeting younger women voters, we need to bend over backwards to avoid looking too slick, too political, and too polished.

Clinton's handling of the episode has convinced people that he is "strong," "articulate," "a fighter," "not a quitter," "powerful and able to overcome odds." However, it showed him being strong for himself, not necessarily for other people. Clinton seems political. One women asked, "if you covered up the affair with Ms. Flowers, what else will you try to cover up?"

The Issues: Education and Welfare

Education and welfare reform are the most powerful issues that Clinton can use to move women voters. Here his commitment seems real, for people, for America, against the current tide of politics. Women voters thought both issues showed "beliefs," that he "was a man for the people," that he "would get something done," and that he was talking about the basics—"the foundation for our country."

The Issues: Values

These voters rejected completely Clinton talking about his values and his mistakes. It seemed hypocritical and political to them, and only made them think "more about the affair" and "his family." These women voters agreed that "we all make mistakes and go on," but as one asked, "how many keep talking about it?" They do not want to be confronted with it and forced to use it as a standard—or implicitly forgive it.

Moreover, the bottom line is that if you do not trust someone, you want them to show their values and not talk about them. They did not even want to hear him use the word "values" but wanted him to illustrate his values. When Clinton talked to these voters about welfare and education, he showed his values far more powerfully than when he talked about them.

Hillary

Hillary does not solve this problem. These women voters' questions are about Bill Clinton, not Hillary Clinton; and at this point, only he can answer the questions for them. Ironically, using Hillary actually alienates women voters who say "stop trying to promote your wife in order to discredit the sex scandal," and "quit trying to convince us of your happy marriage." Even the college educated women who respond best to Hillary found the use of her as much too political.

Younger, non-college educated women also seemed threatened by her and want to hear from the candidate, not the spouse. As several said, "we don't need another Nancy Reagan," "keep your wife out of this, it brings up the question of who will be making the decisions," and one even harshly added, "put Hillary in the kitchen or the PTA and leave running the country to the President, whoever that may be."

CLINTON: SLICK WILLIE IN CAMELOT

In a March 11 memo on strategy for the Illinois primary, Greenberg looked at the emerging split vision of Clinton as a charismatic leader and a not wholly trustworthy man:

To: Bill Clinton and company
From: Stan Greenberg
Re: Illinois Strategic Memo

The Clinton Image

Clinton's favorability (pre–Super Tuesday) is very respectable in Illinois—about 2-to-1 positive to negative. His image, before this contest has begun, is dominated by being presidential (+18 over Tsongas), for the middle class (+9 points), and caring about people (+6 points).

Tsongas's candidacy, by contrast, is less-and-less compelling. His support is more tentative than Clinton's. Tsongas scores well on honesty but dominates no other dimension, including the economy. Clinton and Tsongas are now even on the economy, but over half of Tsongas's own voters do not choose him as the strongest on the economy or caring.

Voters have strong, competing visions of Clinton which offer the prospect of an even stronger candidacy. A stunning 40 percent agree that Bill Clinton reminds them of JFK. (That impression is even stronger in the black community, 53 to 37 percent.) A sizeable majority sees Clinton as a candidate of new and exciting ideas (57 percent) and almost two-thirds see him as someone on the side of average people. That is pretty extraordinary for an electorate that only gives him 40 percent of the vote. The seeds of a much more positive image have clearly been planted.

But voters are, at the same time, ambivalent about Bill Clinton. A sizeable 63 percent express some doubts—beginning with being too slick and smooth (19 percent), followed by he can't be trusted to tell the truth (16 percent), and other issues, may not be a moral person (8 percent), evaded the draft (8 percent), doesn't stand for anything (7 percent), and being a womanizer and adulterer (6 percent). When examining two responses, 30 percent speak of him as too slick; 30 percent as can't be trusted.

Slick and smooth is the downside of charisma. It is troubling, to be sure, but it can be turned positive. Those voters who think of Clinton as too slick have a somewhat positive view of him (51 to 37 percent). Clinton loses these voters (25 to 46 percent to Tsongas), but that compares favorably to the situation among those who can't trust him (35 percent favorable and 51 percent unfavorable and down by 19 to 61 percent in the vote). Obviously, "slick and smooth" is our first and easier task.

Tsongas voters seemed particularly focused on Clinton's "slickness." In the open-ended comments, they made the following observations: "he's a pretty face and that's all;" "extremely slick, facile;" "a little slick;" "too articulate, shifty, slick;" "he's a bullshitter;" "a little too polished;" "sounds really glossy, show biz;" "too glib."

BUSH: "OUR WORST POLITICAL NIGHTMARE"

On March 11, Fred Steeper sent a memo to headquarters arguing, yet again, that Bush was in deeper trouble than he and some of his handlers seemed to understand:

MEMORANDUM

TO: Robert Teeter
Charlie Black
FROM: Fred Steeper
RE: Taking Risks

I mentioned the other morning that I thought if we suddenly were in a 30 day campaign against Clinton, we would lose. Charlie disagreed. I thought I should expand on this thought because the correct assessment of the situation should influence your decisions on options involving various degrees of risk.

Step back a moment from the immediate choices and consider:

We face a 20 month recession, a 78% "wrong track" number, and a Southern Conservative Democrat.

In my mind, this is our worst political nightmare.

I expect this will materialize more clearly in the national trial heat results over the next month. We were ahead of Clinton and Tsongas a month ago by 10%. We now trail by a couple of points. We will read in a week or two that we are 10% behind, then 15% behind, moving to 20%. This is simply a function of a 40% Presidential approval rating and an electorate becoming familiar and more comfortable with the two alternatives.

The big difference in the Democrat lead this time compared to the similar time in 1988 is that we can not say, as we did in 1988, that the Democrat lead flies in the face of "peace and prosperity." Peace and prosperity provided the grease that helped us pull Dukakis back in 1988. We obviously, and very significantly, do not have prosperity working for us this election year.

I'm just pointing out that, to an impartial observer, who knows none of the details but just the broad picture, the outcome appears obvious.

Nothing is inevitable. But, I would consider this axiom: The lower the probability we think there is for an economic recovery this year, the greater the political risks we should be willing to take.

One sports analogy. Don't think of us as the team with the superior size, power, and speed. We are the underdogs (against the theories of presidential elections). To win, we need an imaginative, creative, take-them-by-surprise offense and defense.

We need to do some things we would not normally do.

CLINTON: "GO BIG"

On March 15, two days before the Illinois and Michigan primaries, Clinton's strategists primed him for a televised debate with his surviving rivals, Tsongas and Brown:

MEMORANDUM

To: Governor Clinton
From: Begala, Carville, Wilhelm, Stephanopoulos, Grunwald
Re: WLS-TV Debate

Strategic Overview

You had an excellent debate Friday night. The biggest improvement you can make is to take it to a higher plane—you're best when you soar, so don't get too bogged down in the minutiae.

Remember: Tsongas and Brown have to attack you. All you need to do is counter-punch and then soar. They'll come off nasty, you'll come off Presidential. Tsongas particularly is making this more personal and mean—he's out there directly questioning your character and saying he would not serve in your Administration. (That's a little like Carville piously declaring he won't sleep with Madonna; the thought is noble, but the offer isn't exactly on the table.)

Whenever you can, go big. Your moments should come on any opportunity to characterize the Ethic of the Eighties, the need for change, and the issue of race in America. Ronald Reagan carried Illinois twice. He never had a personal scandal; never bounced a check. And today's Chicago *Sun-Times* poll has Reagan's favorable rating down at 34, and his negative up to 50. People do not want more of the 80s. Tsongas's economic plan is more of the same, and Brown's flat tax would only make worse the excesses of the 80s.

The rebuttal to Tsongas is the simple, direct frontal assault you've used to bury him: If you think we need a kinder, gentler version of the 80s; if you think we need to focus only on capital for corporations, while ignoring education and training for people; if you think we need a 50-cent gas tax on working people and an across-the-board capital gains tax cut—then Paul Tsongas is your candidate. But if you want change; if you want to reject the ethic of the 80s; if you want to put people first, their jobs, their training, their education; if you want to win again; if you want to be one again, then I'm your candidate.

Charge and Response

CHARGE: *You're unelectable. You're carrying more baggage than Federal Express.*

ANSWER: I HAVE PICKED UP SOME BAGGAGE IN THIS CAMPAIGN. NEARLY ALL OF IT AROUND MY MIDSECTION.

BUT WE'VE HAD PRIMARIES OR CAUCUSES IN NEARLY HALF OF THE STATES BY NOW. PEOPLE FROM HAWAII TO MAINE HAVE HEARD THE WORST ABOUT ME. BUT THEY'VE ALSO SEEN THE BEST IN ME. AND THAT'S WHY I'M DOING WELL IN THIS CAMPAIGN. PEOPLE WANT CHANGE. THEY WANT TO CLOSE THE BOOK ON THE 80S AND MOVE INTO THE 90S BY PUTTING OUR PEOPLE FIRST. NO MORE SOMETHING FOR NOTHING FOR BIG CORPORATIONS AND THE RICH, BUT A NEW PEOPLE-BASED ECONOMICS—EDUCATION, TRAINING, HEALTH CARE. ULTIMATELY, PAUL, THE VOTERS WILL DECIDE WHO'S ELECTABLE. WE SHOULD STICK TO THE ISSUES.

BUSH: "THE VOTERS WANT CHANGE"

In mid-March, Fred Steeper found the outlines of a strategy in his raw polling and focus-group data:

3/16/92
Steeper
RESEARCH FINDINGS AND STRATEGY: CURRENT STATUS AND RECOMMENDATIONS

The Current Situation

Pat Buchanan is unimportant. His vote does not represent a right-wing revolt against the President on taxes or social issues. He is receiving a non-ideological protest vote on the economy and government inaction. We need to deal with the protest, not Buchanan.

The protest vote, the President's low approval rating, our whole political problem is the recession. Policies and perceptions to one side, a recession is a recession, and the President would be vulnerable because of it no matter what he did or did not do. However, we still need to meet this problem head-on.

The voters have two complaints against the president which we need to address through our paid media and all other communications with the voters. First, they think he has been late coming to the table on the recession. (They think, if he had been on top of things, he would have done something last summer.) Second, they are still not convinced that he considers the economy to be his number one priority. (Some think his first priority is now campaigning. Others think it is still foreign policy.)

Clinton and Tsongas are important. They both have "economic plans." The advantage of their plans is that they exist only on paper—voters can find hope in their plans. We are moving to a situation where it will be a choice of one of their "plans" against our track record. If there is no recovery, this choice is not a good one for us.

We face a 20 month recession, a 78% "wrong track" number, and (likely) a Southern Conservative Democrat. The situation is about as bad as it could be.

Research Findings Toward a Strategy

As bleak as all this sounds, here are some research results which we should be able to put together into a coherent strategy to, at least, neutralize the Democrats on the economic issue. (If we do not neutralize the economic issue and the general mood for change, the other two legs of our strategy, "peace" and "family," will not be enough.)

1. Reducing federal spending is the public's number one solution to the recession. (Reducing the deficit works almost as well.)

2. Restricting foreign imports is the public's second solution. (There is a way to turn this in our direction. Read this finding as the public's acknowledgment of the importance of the world economy [to] our own economy.)

3. The public blames Congress (not the Democratic Congress, but Congress) even more than the President for the lack of a recovery now.

4. The President's State of the Union proposals to help the economy give us something to work with, but they are far from having the solid public support that is needed.

5. The various uses of the tax code to stimulate the economy put us in a very dangerous issue area. The recession to one side, the voters want "tax fairness."

6. The voters want change. They want change on more than just the latest unemployment figures. They want reforms in education, welfare, crime, insurance rates, and health care.

7. The President is not perceived as a "foreign-policy one-note." Our focus groups said he is a strong leader once he decides to put his mind to it. They even went on to say that his foreign policy expertise could be put to our economic advantage by his opening new markets to American-made products.

8. The public is still with us on the general "tax and spend" issue.

For example, in our most recent national survey, it was no contest when the voters were asked to choose between the liberal view that government revenues need to increase so the government can meet the growing needs of the American people (18%) and the conservative view that government has grown too large and needs to shrink to fit its current revenues (75%).

9. The voters are in a strong "America First" frame of mine, but they are not isolationist, and they would oppose an isolationist candidate. A protectionist candidate would have a stronger appeal but [would] lose in the end.

10. The President, personally, is very credible. His number one personal asset is "experienced."

Recommendations

We face a huge problem on the economy requiring the greatest concentration of our resources. I recommend against paid media on any other subject but this one for the immediate future.

Rehabilitation

We need to counter the perception that the President has mostly ignored the economy for three years. We need a long list of past concrete actions and proposals for the surrogates and the media consultants to work with. However, this must be a list of actions taken before mid-1991.

Perhaps, we can use the 1990 budget agreement and tell the voters that the President risked his political standing with his party's right wing to get Congress to agree to restraints on spending to relieve the economy of the burden of an ever-growing deficit. This was the President's most publicized action at the beginning of the recession. We need a way to use it to counter the perception that he was ignoring the economy until recently.

The Need to Do Something, Not Just Talk about the Problem

One Seattle voter's recent comment: "Bush is sitting there and talking but not doing anything about it (the economy). I'm sick of hearing things and not seeing them done." Most of this memo is about "talking." But, there is nothing like action. Action by the President would go a long way in creating the perception that the economy is his first priority.

The unilateral use of the line item veto would be the ultimate action. [Media consultant] Alex Castellanos may have it right when he asks where is the bad news in a Supreme Court overturn? This dramatically sets up the President going to the voters and saying, "I did what needed to be done, but the Supreme Court says Congress must agree. Give me a Congress that will agree." The whole process would spotlight, day after day, the President as the outsider to the Washington government establishment, exactly where we need to be this year. And the issue it would be all about? "This government is too big and spends too much."

National Confidence

We know it is a communication mistake to tell voters "it is not as bad as you think." We will need to continually resist that temptation of incumbents especially this year. Having said that, I will completely reverse gears and suggest that there is a place in our strategy for "good news." Part of the current problem is that the voters think the country is in an economic decline. They hear [in the media] about the loss of jobs to foreign countries, and they see the foreign made products coming back to prove it. This bothers people a lot.

At the risk of committing the aforementioned communication mistake, I think it would help our political situation if the voters were to learn that America, not Japan, is the world's leading exporter.

I think people need to hear this good news for four reasons. First, the more decline the voters think we are in, the greater the shake-up they are going to make this fall, including putting a Democrat in the White House. Second, the Democrats will be stressing the negative, and at some point, they will commit the sin of "running down the country." Third, the good news component will give people a basis of optimism that the economic problems can be corrected. Fourth, we do well when we use nationalistic rhetoric and appeal to Americans' nationalism.

On the one hand, we do not want to disagree with the voters' perceptions of the economy. On the other hand, they may be in more of a funk than they need to be, and that pessimism means a Clinton or Tsongas vote, not a Bush vote.

Offense: Stage One

There will be some disagreements about this, but I think it is time to move from caring about the hurt caused by the recession to leadership to end the recession.

Rebutting the voters' retrospective evaluation of the President on the economy will be difficult. I recommend presenting the President's plan in two parts. The first part would include three areas most directly connected to the economy.

I recommend deficit reduction because it is important to the voters, we have some credibility on the issue, and there is the potential for a difference between the President and his fall opponent. I recommend foreign trade because this will allow us to use the President's greatest asset. I recommend education because it is important to the voters, the President has done some things to move the ball on this issue, and the voters support Republican-type reforms over Democrat-type reforms.

Offense: Stage Two

The first three areas would be the focus of our earned and paid media until such time as we thought we had sufficiently made our points. I would then move to three more items, which added to the first three, make a full agenda for change and support the theme line of "the man who changed the world will change America."

I recommend welfare reform because welfare continues to be a great annoyance to people and the Democrats are always vulnerable on the issue. I recommend tort reform because the public has picked up on this issue and understands its connection to insurance rates paid by themselves, by doctors, and by business. I recommend the crime bill because crime, too, remains a major complaint of the voters and we have the more credible approach to the problem. Most importantly, the public believes the situations in those three areas are acting as a major drag on our economy and our society.

Additional Thoughts

To give these messages some "edge" so they don't sound like so much political pablum, we need to identify the Enemies of the President's agenda for change. There certainly is sufficient data to support the strategy of making Congress Government Enemy Number One and run a Harry Truman type campaign. We should consider it. If we do the Truman strategy, then we definitely need to add term limits to the President's agenda for change. If we decide against the Truman strategy, then we should identify additional enemies of reform: trial lawyers, the education establishment, liberals, protectionists and isolationists, and maybe even the ACLU, again.

CLINTON: THE SIDEWALKS OF NEW YORK

On March 28, with Clinton's primary campaign limping out of Connecticut into New York and a fresh tabloid ambush, his strategy team sent him a fight-back memo:

To: Governor Clinton
From: All
Re: MESSAGE

1. We believe that New York must be treated with the same degree of urgency as the last days of New Hampshire. Taking on the tabloids. Taking on Brown. Taking the campaign to the people. Talking tough and passionate about the big issues. Demonstrating personal conviction. Getting New York to see the real you, not the tabloid's version.
2. Only confrontation and sharp edges get reported in this city. Only when you say the unexpected or the gutsy do people take notice. We want to define those sharp edges. Not by Brown. Not by the tabloids.
3. Here's the choice we want to set up: Jerry Brown and the tabloids want this campaign to be about bullshit attacks and side issues. They're more interested in division and distraction than talking about the real issues that are tearing this country apart. New Yorkers can believe the caricature of you they're painting or they can understand what you're really all about: changing people's lives and changing this country.
4. You KNOW what's wrong with this country. And it's a lot more than Jerry Brown is talking about or even understands. It's bigger than that. And you're going to challenge every audience from Wall Street to Harlem, every member of the press, and Jerry Brown to confront those issues and talk about real solutions. Because you have spent a decade trying to throw out the old book (Republican and Democratic) and find solutions that work.

[The same day, the team blocked out a strategy for a debate with Brown the next morning:]

To: Governor Clinton
From: Begala, Grunwald, Carville, Boorstin, Stephanopoulos
Re: WCBS Debate
      In reality, this is a knife fight, and there are no rules in a knife fight. **Don't point out when Jerry has broken the rules. Let the moderator do that. When you do you look whiny; when the moderator does Jerry looks silly.**

Strategy

Our biggest strategic goal is to slam-dunk Jerry on the flat tax. You know the points:
1. [Senator Daniel Patrick] Moynihan said it would put a silver bullet through the heart of Social Security;

2.   Triples taxes on the poor—even Reagan rejected this as too hard on the poor;
3.   Raises taxes on working people;
4.   Cuts taxes on the rich in half;
5.   Creates a "Double Thirteen" tax—including raising the sales tax to 21% in New York City;
6.   Ends deductibility for state and local taxes;

But here's the twist: **Challenge Brown to release his tax returns and show how he would personally profit from his tax plan.** This will require that you get your 1990 tax return out and compute how it would affect your taxes. At an opportune moment, pull out a sheet of paper that shows how the flat tax would affect you, Michael Milken, George Bush and a family with two incomes, both at minimum wage. (Our propeller-heads are preparing this for you.)

When you talk about the flat tax, **do not talk like a tax geek at Arthur Anderson! Talk like a guy who cares about clobbering the poor and the middle class.** Don't use words like "regressive" and "deductions" and "depreciation." Go back to words like "sucker-punch," "rip-off," "flatten," "declare war on New York," etc.

ON THE GOLF CLUB: If Jerry whacks you on the [all-white Little Rock] golf club, do two things:

1.   **Remind folks that you've admitted it was a mistake.** Nothing more. Don't elaborate, defend or explain. Say "Look, I've admitted that was a mistake." Then . . .
2.   Read this quote from Jerry (as reported in the *Village Voice*): JERRY, YOU ONCE SAID ABOUT SCHOOL INTEGRATION: "THE BLACK KIDS CAN TEACH THE WHITE KIDS HOW TO FIGHT AND THE WHITE KIDS CAN TEACH THE BLACK KIDS HOW TO READ." YOU KNOW, JERRY, A PERSON COULD READ THAT QUOTE AND ACCUSE YOU OF BEING A RACIST. BUT I KNOW YOU'RE NOT. AND I KNOW THIS ELECTION IS ABOUT A LOT MORE THAN ANY STUPID STATEMENT OR ANY GAME OF GOLF. IT'S ABOUT THE REAL PROBLEMS OF RACE AND DIVISION, AND I'M NOT GOING TO LET YOU OR THE TABLOIDS OR ANYONE ELSE KEEP ME FROM TALKING ABOUT THE FACT THAT THIS COUNTRY HAS BEEN DIVIDED BY RACE FOR TOO LONG.

IF ASKED ABOUT THE MEDIA AND ITS TREATMENT OF YOU: Try this: I'M A BIG BOY. I CAN TAKE CARE OF MYSELF. AND THE MEDIA ARE BIG FOLKS. THEY DON'T NEED ANYONE TO DEFEND THEM EITHER. WHAT BOTHERS ME ABOUT ALL THIS IS THERE ARE A LOT OF PEOPLE OUT THERE WHO WANT THIS ELECTION TO BE ABOUT THEM: THEIR PROBLEMS, AND STRUGGLES AND FIGHTS, NOT ABOUT SOME DIVER-

SION OR TABLOID TERRORISM. THE STAKES ARE TOO HIGH, AND I DON'T THINK THE PEOPLE OF NEW YORK WILL ALLOW ANYONE TO HIJACK THEIR ELECTION.

CLINTON: REMAKING THE CAMPAIGN

On April 27, three of Clinton's top strategists wrote an interim report on the Manhattan Project, the super-secret effort to reshape his candidacy for the fall election:

DRAFT/CONFIDENTIAL

TO: Bill Clinton
      Mickey Kantor and David Wilhelm
FROM: Stan Greenberg, James Carville and Frank Greer
RE: "THE GENERAL ELECTION PROJECT"
      Interim Report

This report of the "general election project" recommends a fundamental remaking of your campaign to reflect the new political realities and new phase of the campaign and, most important, to address the debilitating image that is dragging us down. We believe the campaign must move on an urgent basis before the Perot candidacy further defines us (by contrast) and the Bush-Quayle campaign defines us by malice. This is a critical window.

The recommendations here derive from wide-ranging discussions both within and without the campaign. They are not lightly arrived at, and everyone who has participated shares the sense of urgent opportunity and the need to move boldly.

Strategic Assessments

Bill Clinton is viewed unfavorably by a sizeable minority of Democratic primary voters (about 30 percent) and a plurality of general election voters (about 40 percent). We believe that these negatives (with their electoral consequences) can be greatly reduced, as they were for Reagan and Bush in previous elections. Voters are still open to a Clinton candidacy. A majority wants to vote against Bush and thinks they do not know the real Bill Clinton. (They are right!) After learning more about Bill Clinton in the focus groups, our support nearly doubled.

The core problem of the Clinton candidacy is Clinton's essential "political" nature. We have probed the whole issue of trust and honesty and, at the center, is the belief that Bill Clinton is a "typical politician." The two strongest negatives in [campaign and party polls] were the belief that Clinton is "a little too much of a politician" (53 perent) and that he will say anything to get elected (53 percent). The focus group participants spoke of Clinton as a typical politician, marketed well, but prepared to cater to any group.

For the most part, people were reluctant to write him off as corrupt, dishonest or immoral, but the highly publicized "shading of the truth" has reinforced an impression that he will do what is necessary to "look good." The questions about personal morality certainly matter, but their larger impact is contained in the general impression that he will say what is necessary and that he does not "talk straight."

The impression of being the ultimate politician is reinforced by Clinton's presentation (evasive, no clear yes or no, handy lists, fast talking, and all that political analysis). They think of him as "wishy-washy," not as "someone who will look you straight in the eye" and tell you the truth.

The impressions of Hillary reinforce the political image. In the focus groups, people think of her as being in the race "for herself" and as "going for the power." She is not seen as particularly "family-oriented." More than Nancy Reagan, she is seen as "running the show."

Obviously, we have created many of our own problems, but it is hard to underestimate the damage created by Tsongas and Brown, particularly the former. Each, in his own way, has tried to establish his identity by painting Clinton as political. There is every danger that the emergence of Perot will reinforce the same character traits and, thus, further undermine our candidacy, even if Perot eventually slips in the polls. Perot is seen as a straight, honest talker who worked for what he got, grew up "the American way," and who won't be intimidated by the money people and the special interests.

Clinton's political nature leads voters to a number of critical and debilitating conclusions:

1. **Clinton is not real.** He is "packaged," created by image makers. What he says, therefore, is discounted: rhetoric tailored to sound good, intended to reflect what people want. They do not believe they are hearing the "real Bill Clinton".

2. **Clinton is privileged, like the Kennedys.** Clinton's draft dealings and Ivy League/Oxford education leave voters with the impression that Clinton grew up with a "silver spoon." They think his path to high political office "was greased," requiring little effort and, therefore, little character. (Perot is, again, the looming contrast.)

3. **Clinton can't stand up to the special interests.** People think Washington and politics is a den of thieves. There are lots of "hands in the cookie jar" and "you've got to slap hands" if you are to lead, yet they doubt Clinton would slap anybody's hands. He wants to "appease everybody." That makes Clinton weak—controlled by the political establishment, "the powers" and the money people. (Voters already think that of Bush.)

4. **Clinton cannot be the candidate of change.** It is politics and politicians who are incapable of taking this country in a different direction. Clinton, therefore, as the ultimate politician, cannot be the voice of change. He is part of the "establishment," not a change agent. "With the current situation," one participant observed, "we can't afford another politician."

5. **Clinton's for himself, not people.** Voters are longing for a leader "who's going to look after us." Yet Clinton, as typical politician, is "self-centered," cares only about himself and getting elected. The unending array of character battles has left Clinton "self-absorbed," in voters' eyes. In the DNC survey, Clinton enjoys less than a 5 point advantage over Bush (the toady for the rich) on "cares about people," on being "on your side," and "representing me on the issues."

6. **Clinton's message/ideas are discounted.** When voters hear Bill Clinton's ideas, they are positive, but unexcited and reluctant to reassess their judgments about him. Sure he "understands" what we feel, but that is just it: "he knows what we want which is why he says it." His words are good but just political manipulation. It is hard for a politician to be heard these days, particularly one who wants to be the voice of change.

The campaign has to take radical steps to depoliticize Bill Clinton. The measures—tentatively supported by the research—fall in six strategic areas:

Biography. The "facts" of Clinton's life radically change the judgments about Bill Clinton: he is a human being who struggled, pulled his weight, showed strength of character, and fought for change.

Commitment. People need to learn about how Clinton struggled against special interests or difficult political forces to do what he believed in and to help people. People need to learn of a Bill Clinton who is willing to challenge convention and powerful interests on behalf of people.

Transition to people. Clinton needs to go from self-absorption to caring about people.

Non-political communication. The candidate needs to communicate in ways that sound less political, and the campaign needs to use media that are counter-political in style.

A plan. The campaign needs to communicate that it has a vision and ideas about how to change the country—not just a series of popular proposals that look political. Running against politics is also running against drift, and people are looking for a leader who knows where he is going.

Change. Clinton's candidacy will not catch fire unless voters come to understand what Bill Clinton wants to do to change America. Right now, they have no idea what he wants to do, except get elected. The change message cannot undo our current image problems, for voters now turn our ideas into self-serving rhetoric. But we must crystallize how Bill Clinton wants to change the country and begin advancing our ideas aggressively until we cross the threshold of believability.

Biography: The Real Bill Clinton

The presentation of biography, we know from the surveys and focus groups, has an extraordinary impact. After hearing "the facts" of Clinton's biography, voters who were previously preoccupied with Clinton the politician began speaking of him in radically new terms: "down to earth," "middle class boy," "self made," "earned it," "the opposite of Bush," "has some values," "honest, hard struggle," "no silver spoon." Indeed, after they heard "the facts," these voters felt cheated by the press, call it a "travesty," that "people are missing out." One person concluded, "it makes you want to find out more about his policies."

We should think of biography in two ways—first as personal character attributes and second as commitments. The personal character attributes include a widowed mother and standing up to alcoholic abusive stepfather, working his way through Georgetown and Yale, and returning home to one of America's poorest states. The commitments show a willingness to be tough and inventive trying to help people.

The campaign should produce a 60 second "character spot" that draws from these "facts" to present Bill Clinton, the person. The current bio spot, confined to the 30 second format and, therefore, too quick-moving, seems too political and packaged. We need to make a strong, non-political statement. (The model is Bush's 1988 "grandfather" spot which delivered a simple family, caring and values portrayal from June through October.)

The campaign should produce a 60 second or 2 minute spot introducing the real Bill Clinton, but on one issue, probably education showing Clinton's commitment, willingness to take on special interests, his belief in opportunity and responsibility, and how we can change America. The format must look non-political, giving full rein to spontaneity and sincerity.

The campaign should create a 30 minute Infomercial of the "Real Bill Clinton" to be aired in low-cost time slots from mid-May to Labor Day. The show should combine the biographical facts from above with testimonials in the appropriate areas, showing the Bill Clinton who came back to do good, fought powerful forces, and helped people.

Finally, we must begin immediately and aggressively scheduling the popular talk shows to introduce the real Bill Clinton. That includes the national popular culture shows and the regional radio interview and call-in shows. We should start with Johnny Carson, and move to Barbara Walters, Oprah and Donahue, Larry King and Rush Limbaugh. These shows must introduce these elements of biography, our principal change message and the human side of Bill Clinton (e.g., humor, sax and inhaling). Our goal is to break the political mold.

Transition to People

To break out of the political mold, we must take the campaign to the people: that is, Bill Clinton must move from self-absorption to caring about people, and the campaign itself must show Bill Clinton empowering people.

The popular culture/talk shows is one form of accessibility that should certainly distinguish Bill Clinton from George Bush—and perhaps Perot. We should barnstorm these shows over the next 2 months.

We need to make the "Ask Bill," Donahue format shows the signature of our campaign—Bill Clinton, completely comfortable with himself, answering questions in an entirely spontaneous format, where ordinary people can gain access to someone running for president. This is one president who will be accountable directly to the people. It is important that we create excitement about the concept before Perot's electronic democracy takes hold.

We need to make the transition from our self-absorption with being attacked by the press to running for president because we want to help people. We should seek to close the primary season on that theme— "the hits I've taken in this election are nothing compared to the hits the people of this state and this nation are taking every day."

Brave Enough to Challenge America

People believe change can only be brought about by a leader who lacks strings and who is strong enough to challenge powerful interests. That is the opposite of our current style which too often suggests compromises to organize political support.

Aggressive counter-scheduling and speeches are critical if we are to introduce this candidacy in a new light. Clinton should look unafraid and willing to brave the fire. However, our goal is not so much to antagonize as to challenge, hoping that the audience will applaud at the unexpected.

The "challenge" speeches should be organized from mid-May to mid-June—4 speeches, one a week under a common title. For the moment, we would suggest the following topics and audiences:

- Radically changing government, to a public employees audience. . . . The speech could also become radically reformist in cleaning out the mess in Washington—particularly the role of special interests.
- Lessons of Vietnam to a Veterans organization where we subtly talk about our own biography, the wrenching experience of a generation, the coming of age (discovering limits and patriotism), the Persian Gulf War, and the role of the modern military.
- Welfare, work, and middle class values to a black audience or audience of social workers. This is an opportunity to talk about our own biography, our values, and the willingness to fight hard for inventive programs.
- Education reform to a meeting of teachers—where we lay down our commitment but also our insistence on accountability, quality, curtailed bureaucracy, etc. This is also an opportunity to make education work as investment to reverse America's decline.

Obviously, there is room for further discussion on the topics, but we need to move now if these speeches are to happen. There is no room for the tentativeness of earlier speeches. These need to be billed as major addresses, and Bill Clinton needs the time to prepare for them.

The Hillary Clinton Campaign

The current presentation of Hillary Clinton and the Clinton marriage and family to the world is remarkably distorted. The absence of affection, children and family and the preoccupation with career and power only reinforces the political problem evident from the beginning. It also allows George Bush (and probably Perot) to build up extraordinary advantages on family values—32 points in the DNC survey.

We suggest the following steps to improve the situation, without endangering the family's privacy or trampling on reality:

- Hillary should have a lower profile in the immediate short-term, as we try to reintroduce Bill Clinton. It is important to do interviews with publications that have longer lead times, but, for the most part, Bill should appear alone on the popular culture shows. After the June primary, Bill and Hillary should do some joint appearances and Hillary should take up an aggressive schedule of interviews.
- Bill and Hillary need to talk much more of their own family, including Chelsea, and their affection for each other. If Chelsea cannot travel (which we understand) then we ought to figure out how protecting Chelsea from the press and protecting her childhood is an obsession of both parents. We need to make much more of Chelsea faxing her homework to Bill and/or something that Hillary does with Chelsea.
- The family needs to go on vacation together after the June primary, preferably in California (including Disneyland), though there is a minority for the Gulf Shores.
- After a short pull-back period, Hillary needs to come forward in a way that is much more reflective of herself—both her humor and her advocacy work for children. Linda Bloodworth-Thomason has suggested some joint appearances with her friends where Hillary can laugh, do her mimicry. We need to be thinking about events where Bill and Hillary can "go on dates with the American people." There is a suggestion that Bill and Chelsea surprise Hillary on Mother's Day.
- Bill and Hillary need to clarify Hillary's role as First Lady. Ambiguity looks like a power game. It is very important that voters feel comfortable with Hillary's role and not see her as an empowered Nancy Reagan.

The Hillary Clinton campaign needs to be organized and integrated into the overall campaign. What Hillary communicates is as important as what Bill communicates. Up until now, Hillary has had to devise the proper message or strategy. We think there ought to be a campaign manager for the Hillary Clinton effort, and that person ought to be a part of the message/strategy group of the campaign. It is time the campaign took this role seriously and recognized the central importance of Hillary's communication to what people believe about Bill Clinton as a prospective president.

Surrogates

Because Clinton is particularly exposed at this point, it is important that we develop a well-organized and aggressive surrogate program right now. This is not a substitute speaker program, as developed by most presidential campaigns, usually in the fall; this is an identifiable cabinet of substantial and outspoken leaders who would consistently praise or defend Clinton, attack Bush initiatives, and generally suggest a government in waiting. Clinton should not be hanging out there by himself, seeming vulnerable, isolated and weak.

Campaign of Ideas

Part of the public's aversion to politics is an aversion to slogans and promises. In the focus groups people yearned for a leader with a plan—concrete and well-formulated ideas on how to change the direction of the country. With Perot possibly emerging as quirky, it is critical that Clinton reemerge as substantive, with ideas on how to change America.

The plan needs to be reexamined, repackaged and prepared for a higher profile role. The plan should be reissued, with a broad array of university validation, including people who could emerge in important roles in a Clinton administration. We should use our popular culture appearances, our mall/Donahue type events, and speeches to communicate our ideas. At the same time, the schedule should allow Clinton more time to work on speeches, work through daily messages, communicate with campaign principals, read and work through ideas.

The Candidate of Change

The Clinton campaign will remain marginalized—no matter what we do to reduce Clinton's political image—if it does not present a compelling idea for change. That is our primary, immediate task.

CLINTON: BLITZING THE POP CULTURE

In April, Mandy Grunwald and Frank Greer pushed the stalled plan to have the Clintons blitz the pop-culture talk shows and magazines:

MEMORANDUM

To: Clinton Campaign
From: Mandy and Frank
Date: April 27, 1992
RE: FREE MEDIA SCHEDULING

We have spoken generally about the need to do pop-culture shows like Johnny Carson, but we have yet to lay out a plan to do this sort of thing, or to incorporate local radio talk shows into our schedule in any concerted way.

What are we waiting for?

We know from research that Bill Clinton's life story has a big impact on people. We know that learning about the fights he's taken on (education reform, welfare reform, dead-beat dads etc.) tells people a lot about his personal convictions. We know that moments of passions, personal reflection and humor do more for us than any six-second sound bite on the network news or for that matter any thirty-second television spot.

In tandem with our high road, serious speech effort, we ought to design a parallel track of pop culture national and local media efforts.

We must also coordinate this effort with a free media plan for Hillary. Which magazine should appear during the convention with Bill, Hillary and Chelsea on the cover? LIFE? Parade? We need to decide now.

This period leading up to the convention is CRITICAL for this kind of positive information. If we don't fill in the blanks now, we'll never get to it after the Republican Convention. That means time is pressing. Given the lead times for magazines and some TV programs, we have to move immediately.

I suggest a free media meeting (or call) as soon as possible to consider how to rethink scheduling to incorporate these opportunities and to consider some of the following kinds of ideas.

1. Which TV journalist should we invite to Arkansas for a tour with Bill of his childhood haunts etc.? Barbara Walters? Jane Pauley?

2. If Carson is booked, should Bill do Letterman? Arsenio? The new Jay Leno? All three?

3. What about Larry King, Oprah Winfrey, Sally Jesse Raphael?

Who would allow a focus on his childhood/accomplishments etc. without 1000 Gennifer Flowers questions?

4. What about national radio programs? Rush Limbaugh?

5. There's a Don Imus in every market in America, and a serious call-in political/talk radio show. Can we make a commitment that every day in every city we go to, we book Bill on those kinds of radio programs.

I understand that many people will say these kinds of things are "Un-Presidential." Bull. This is how people get information. These are forums for more personal and varied looks at Bill and Hillary and Chelsea.

Obviously, it would be better to be using these forums when the overall message of the campaign has been sharpened so that Bill's biography could be put in a more strategic context. But I'm not sure we have the luxury of waiting until that process is complete.

At least, let's get together and discuss these media options, so that decisions are not just made on an ad-hoc basis.

BUSH: "HE DOESN'T KNOW WHAT TO DO"

In late April, Steeper's firm, Market Strategies Inc., conducted a series of focus groups of 1988 Bush voters in suburban communities in California, North Carolina, and Michigan, in an effort to assess the mood of the nation and its implications for the president:

NATIONAL FOCUS GROUPS

REPORT

April 25–29, 1992

America's Future

By nature, Americans are an optimistic lot. Still, the overall mood of the groups was somber. *"We've always been positive. We're down on our knees right now, but we'll get up,"* is how one participant described the present state of affairs.

Among the host of problems weighing Americans down are crime and drugs, education, lack of affordable health insurance (i.e. care), interwoven with jobs and the economy. With a few regional variations, most participants are in agreement that jobs and the economy pose a serious threat to America's future.

People are cynically optimistic—*"it's as bad as I've seen it, it can only go up"*—they don't see things changing. For many, government, from the President to Congress is stymied. Participants are hard-pressed to name specific government policies that would stimulate the economy. By the same token, while the public realizes that they themselves don't have a plan, they are loud in voicing their concerns that the President doesn't either.

Almost all agree that it is very important for the United States to be a world leader economically. The caveat, however, echoed from group to group is *"but, we don't have to put our noses in everyone's business every time and bail everybody out."*

Foreseeing little help or support for a government solution to the problems that face America, the public is still hopeful about the economy and the opportunities that could develop. For many, the economy is on the upswing; they see it in their businesses. Opportunities for America to become economically competitive lie in the free trade and education arena.

The American Dream

The American Dream is easily described—a house, a good job, one's health, a good education, and a car—yet, more and more say it is unattainable.

The American Dream is divided along generational lines. While the dream is the same for many, older participants (especially in the California groups) feel that the dream is no longer attainable for today's young people. Everyone agrees that today's generation will be the first not to do better than their parents.

Of generational concerns, the greater anxiety is for the younger generations and its prospects for prosperity and safety.

Education is the engine that drives the American Dream. Most believe that given the chance through education, they would be able to achieve "their own" American Dream. Interesting comments emerge when you talk about the American Dream:

"Nowhere in the Constitution does it say that the government is responsible for the American Dream" (older, retired man)

"I work my butt off to get my American Dream. I can't understand why others don't want to work hard to get their dream" (young, father of two)

When discussing the American Dream, people harken back to the "old days." In order to achieve the American Dream we need to recapture the *"values that this nation has lost."* For many, America was a *"pretty good place back then."*

The End of the Cold War as an Opportunity

Saying that the end of the Cold War provides an economic opportunity for America is not a credible statement to most participants.

Psychologically, no one claimed to have been threatened by the Cold War. *"I'm more afraid of crime than a nuclear war,"* said one participant.

Financially, the universal view is that the end of the Cold War amounts to the creation of new and unwanted financial burdens for the United States in that now we must/should care for our former Cold War enemies. Few are able to recall the catch phrase of the 1990 political cycle—"the peace dividend," and even fewer believe that there really is a dollar savings which can be redirected to domestic programs.

Politically, the public does not believe that the Cold War ended under President Bush's watch, nor do they credit the President with being the primary motivator behind the Cold War's demise. For the California groups, unlike VE and VJ-day, the end of the Cold War was a process. For some, the Cold War has not been a threat since the days of the Cuban Missile Crisis.

Personal Situation

Almost all of the problems facing the country have become double-barreled in nature—important both for people's personal situation and for the nation.

Many of the personal problems mentioned by the groups stem from their own personal financial situation and the state of the U.S. economy:

✓ financially, Americans can't make ends meet
✓ fearful over never being able to retire
✓ lack of affordable health insurance
✓ lack of quality education
✓ crime and drugs

People are scared, not for fear of losing their own jobs, but seeing their neighbor lose his or her job. While most feel a sense of security about their own personal job situation, they are not immune to the host of pressures associated with keeping their jobs. *"I'm secure,"* said one young man, *"but they work us like a dog."*

Participants are unable to differentiate between personal and national problems. Like politics, all problems are local.

There is a consensus of mistrust about government. This negativism stems from an attitude that *"everything the federal government touches gets worse."* To these groups of Americans, there is little role left for the government to play in helping to solve the problems facing the country. Still, while most say the government should be doing little or nothing, they do cry out for the government to lend a helping hand. On the surface, people see the government as having just one solution to problems, "throw more money at it" and in these economic times that is not the solution the public is looking for. Said one young man in North Carolina, *"The government rewards people for messing up . . . like welfare programs."*

The undercurrent, though, of the mistrust of government is that people really do perceive the government as having a role in solving some of the nation's top problems, but they also feel that the government is unable to fulfill that role. Still, the public is short on solutions—federal, state or local:

"If you don't educate [people], you're going to have to feed them and house them and everything else."

"You solve problems through education. Education means better jobs; better jobs means higher wages; and higher wages equals a better quality of life."

Specific areas which the federal government can be working to solve some of the country's problems were probed for and revealed some interesting comments and discussion. For the most part, people see a role for the government in areas such as student loans, lower taxes, job training programs, and affordable health care. However, unaided, they are unable to come up with specific action steps the government can be taking in helping to solve some of these problems. Most interesting, though, and contrary to polling data, was the discussion on tax credits for first time home buyers. Young and old, most participants thought this was a poor idea and a *"political gimmick to prop up the economy."* Commonly heard was the theme, "nobody gave me a tax credit when I bought my first house."

President Bush

The emotions participants shared about President Bush were strong, hard-hitting and negative. The conversation on the President was begun by asking people to write the one or two words that best describe their feeling about him. Commonly shared perceptions and feelings include:

FEELINGS	PERCEPTIONS
disappointed	gotten away from home
luke-warm	out-of-it

satisfied	out-of-touch
bad	topsy-turvy
mistrust	traditional
guarded	silent
frustrated	uninformed
upset	captive
lazy	confused
uneasy	unfocused
sick & tired	wimpy
betrayed	incompetent
uneasy	scares me
secure	undecided
	phoney
	all mouth, no action

For the most part, the source of the public's anger was centered on the notion that the President has forgotten America.

"He has an air about him. . . . he just doesn't want to be bothered."

"He's gotten too carefree about the problems over here."

"If he can do any of the things he's saying he can do now, why hasn't he already done them?"

"George Bush has no idea how squeezed people are these days; he's a Texas millionaire."

"He kept saying the economy wasn't bad. We all knew it was bad, he wouldn't admit it. . . . Read my lips."

"He's living in the 'Leave it to Beaver' era. A mother and father in the home; two-point-one kids; a two-car garage. That's totally out of reality. He needs to get with the times, we're eight years away from the year 2000."

"He doesn't stand for anything . . . and that's where the problem lies."

"George Bush is an excellent Foreign Minister, but not a good President."

"Somehow when he's on TV he's a good man, but he frustrates me. Nothing is being done. Big words, big speeches; but nothing to show for it."

"He's got seven speech writers and a thousand points of light and 'read my lips.' That's not him, somebody wrote this for him and he says it. He needs to live up to his words. Look at all these things he promised. He wanted to be known as, and I quote, 'the education President.' What did he do for education? What . . . what . . . what?"

"I just don't think he's a doer. I think if the people get through this and they don't rebel, we're in for a long four years. . . . If we vote him back in without him giving us a plan for the next four years then we deserve what we get."

Few positive comments were heard about the President, but those that were aired honed in on the President's foreign policy leadership: *"[He] makes me feel safe. I don't think you have to worry about war. . . ."* For the President to convince these participants to hold less negative impressions of him, he would have to demonstrate a combination of:

genuine empathy . . .
"In his position he has concentrated in one area, international, and has not thought about the domestic . . . you get the feeling that at best he gives token concern."
as well as leadership,
"He's gotten himself hamstrung with politics—he couldn't make the changes we need."
and action,
"(Bush ought to) pick one issue and do something about it, just do something about it, do it without partisanship. We have to see him take action on the economy."
and finally, getting results in solving the country's problems,
"Results count; since results are worse, it's obvious Bush doesn't care."

The President may be slipping out of steady media contact with the public much as he did in 1988 after his nomination was assured: one group agreed that they had not heard much of the President lately, that he had been "pretty quiet" while the others were on the campaign trail.

The power and the longevity of the messages of the 1988 political campaign should not be underestimated. They are more enduring and come more readily to mind than any domestic policy accomplishment of the Administration. Without being offered an alternative issue agenda or a record of accomplishment, voters have chosen to hold the President accountable for the seemingly unfulfilled promises of the 1988 campaign.

In spite of the rough treatment the President receives, most participants say they could forgive him—but, forgive and vote for remain two separate avenues. While some in each group thought it was important for him to demonstrate greater concern than he has, the discussions seemed to lack the energy that usually is associated with hitting a topic that can motivate or is motivating people.

"I think he cares, but I think he doesn't know what to do about it."
"He's definitely a compassionate man. His demeanor . . . to listen to him speak, he's sincere."

There is a consensus that George Bush is at his core a kind and compassionate person, well-meaning and sincere, and his presidency is not dismissed outright as a failure. What is lacking is the perception of action and results in the issues important to people today: "He has to address health care, crime, and education, or I'm not voting for him." The groups are very critical of the campaign theme:

"This man who changed the world will change America."

They are critical of the premise (he didn't change the world) and the logic (he should have changed America first). To highlight some of their points:

"It makes him sound too much like God."
"If he can do it, why hasn't he done it."
"He's taking credit for changing the world? Is he taking credit for unemployment? Is he taking credit for the economy?"
"If he were going to change anything, he would have started four years ago, not now at the start of his second campaign."
"Now that the Cold War is over, we don't need a world leader."
"His priorities were all wrong, he should have changed America first."

Bill Clinton

Most of the participants in our groups have come to some harsh conclusions about Bill Clinton. Most importantly, the conversation about Clinton had the sound of voters dismissing him from serious consideration as President. Clinton is NOT presidential timber in the minds of these participants. Their comments come easily; there is no struggle to elicit their perceptions about a person they were probably unaware of a few a months ago.

"Maybe a great President, but if all this stuff is true about the guy, how much of a crook do we want in there."
"If he's the Democrats' best and brightest, the Democrats are in real trouble."
"There's too much slick things going on; they got him named right."
"He's scum. He's a liar. He got caught with his hand in the cookie jar and wouldn't admit it."
"At least we know what we got with Bush."

Throughout the groups, several participants confirmed that the real issue about Clinton is whether or not he is lying about the allegations surrounding him rather than the allegations themselves. Given the overall discussion about him and the fact that just two participants supported him in our three-way trial heat, they are concluding that there is too high a chance that he is lying, and, therefore, is a liar.

The voters, who were asked to assign an ideological label to Clinton, did so easily—Clinton is a liberal. (It took a long time to pin that label on Dukakis.)

Ross Perot

Perot strikes the participants in our focus groups as having the potential to be a good president. Participants are very intrigued by Perot. They believe he may be the answer. Some reservations are expressed about his ability to work in a political system that requires compromise, but as the trial balloting shows, these reservations are minimal at this moment.

In group after group, Perot's name comes up in the discussion unaided as a potential alternative candidate to either Bush or Clinton. Perot is not simply a vessel for voter discontent. Voters have a better command of his background and the defining events of his public life than they do of Clinton's. They connect many of these events to the solutions they seek in government. For example, it was concluded that since Perot built a $2 billion fortune from a $6,000 (sic) stake, he can handle the country's financial troubles.

"He's no nonsense, he's like Harry Truman."

"I respect someone who can make decisions."

"I like the way he comes across; he appeals to me. I don't know anything about him, but he says, 'If I'm doing a bad job, I'll quit,' I like that."

One of the many perceptions working in Perot's favor is the belief that he would finance his own campaign. Voters believe that he is above the motive of seeking personal gain in running for President, and he would not become beholden to special interests.

Even outside of Texas, Perot has an image of mythic dimensions.

"He worked his way up from nothing."

"He's the world's greatest salesman."

"He cares about America, education, and keeping money in the country."

"He's really into taking care of the people who work for him. The fact that he went and got the people out (of Iran) who were kidnapped from his company . . . if he takes care of the people who work for him, maybe he'll take care of the country."

"It's his job to be a good manager, and it is clear that his priority is America First, and that would be a good thing now."

The last comment shows how the public may not naturally see a strident dictator in Perot's business background as quickly as they see the beneficial manager or leader.

Still, all is not a perfect picture for a Perot candidacy. Among the few negative observations were:

"He hasn't come up with a single statement that makes sense on the issues."
"He may have started as one of us; but no more."
"He's arrogant, and that's negative.

After the discussions of the President, Clinton, and Perot, the participants were asked to write down their choice for President if the election were held today.

PRESIDENTIAL TRIAL HEATS

	Bush	Clinton	Perot
Van Nuys, CA	6	1	15
Charlotte, NC	4	—	14
Warren, MI	4	1	19
Totals	14	2	48

BUSH: "THE VOTERS ARE DISGUSTED"

On April 28, with the focus-group study still in progress, Steeper switched from a clinical to a political voice to convey his concern about what he was finding:

MEMORANDUM

FROM: Fred Steeper
DATE: April 28, 1992
RE: Implications of the April Focus Groups

Here is what I think I *also* heard in the focus groups in Van Nuys and Charlotte.

The voters are disgusted. They are disgusted with politicians, partisan politics, and government gridlock. They are more disgusted than angry. Surprise causes anger. They have been witnessing government failures for years. This year, however, they sound like their tolerance for politics-as-usual has worn out.

They see the country as facing enormous domestic problems—the deficit, crime, health care, education, and a weakened economy—and a political system incapable of offering any real solutions.

We are shut off from attacking Congress as a political strategy. To attack Congress would only reinforce the voters' perceptions of a political process gridlocked in partisan conflict. The voters want political leadership to pull together.

Because they see domestic problems in very bad shape, they are rationally concluding that America's problems should come first. They are sounding like America Firsters for good reasons.

The voters are looking for a domestic issue President.

They are less likely to recognize the national interest in world affairs than at any point since World War II. The voters think the President is very good at foreign policy, but not very interested in domestic problems. This also means, for them, that the President is not interested in their problems.

When it comes to domestic problems, they believe President Bush has been the "absent President." They do not recall his proposals on education, crime, deregulation, or any other domestic problem.

The swing voters have dismissed Bill Clinton as a serious alternative to President Bush. They have already reached their final conclusion about him—his character flaws are too great to put him in the White House. The voters that will count have made him a closed chapter in the 1992 election.

The voters' disenchantment with the President and their harsh appraisal of Clinton are so deep that they have set traps for both candidates. If Clinton does something that normally would be considered positive, voters will instead see it as an example of his slickness. If the President proposes something that normally would be considered positive, the voters will, instead, see it as yet another example of a problem he should have taken care of before he faced reelection.

The swing voters are very intrigued with Ross Perot. He is outside the political process that has failed them. Perot is a major threat to the President; Clinton is not.

CLINTON: THE MATCHMAKERS

On May 14, with Clinton's nomination all but certain, his strategists offered their ideas on the politics of the search for a vice-presidential candidate:

CONFIDENTIAL

MEMORANDUM
To: Vice Presidential Team
From: The Message Group
        Paul Begala, James Carville, Stan Greenberg,
        Frank Greer, Mandy Grunwald, George Stephanopoulos
Re: *Political Considerations*

We know that Bill's primary consideration in choosing his vice-presidential nominee is who would make the best president, not the best candidate.

However, those of us who are focused solely on winning, not governing, feel it's important to convey the factors we think would be helpful (and harmful) in a vice-presidential candidate.

We are not making any specific recommendations. That's not our job and we know it. Names are therefore used only as a point of reference, not to be taken as recommendations.

• *The ideal nominee would not be a Southerner:* We have already seen a lot of regional bias against Arkansas. Two southerners would obviously double that problem. We should note, however, that there are a few people who are from southern states who sound and seem like Northerners. Jay Rockefeller certainly falls in that category. (There is a minority of this group that believes that Al Gore, because of his environmental work, also transcends his region.)

• *The ideal nominee would appeal to college educated voters/suburbanites and independents:* In short, someone whose appeal is broader than the traditional Democratic base. We know this may be a difficult factor for you to determine about any individual you are considering. We would be happy to advise you on this, if it would be helpful.

• *The ideal nominee would not be a "typical" politician in the way he or she communicates:* Some candor (not gaffes, but *straight talk*) would be helpful in offsetting, not duplicating, the "Slick Willie" image we are battling. In short, someone unconventional either in style or background.

• *The ideal nominee would have a military record:* Another way to say this is that it would be detrimental if both members of the ticket had not served, particularly if the reasons were in any way unusual.

• *The ideal nominee does not have to have foreign policy credentials:* From a political point of view, we think this criteria is a trap we do not have to fall into.

• *The ideal nominee would have opposed the key elements of Reagan-Bush trickle-down economics:* A nominee's record should not undercut Bill's fundamental critique of the 1980s as a time when greed was encouraged, 60% of the growth went to the top 1% of the people and corporate irresponsibility was paid for with tax dollars, while the people who worked hard and played by the rules were abandoned.

• *To state the obvious, they ought to have good enough political instincts and communications skills* to duel with any member of the press, debate Dan Quayle or Jeane Kirkpatrick, and give a pretty good speech.

• *And to further emphasize the obvious, it should be someone who is seen as having the highest integrity.*

• *Finally, the ideal nominee, like Bill, should be a "different kind of Democrat."* This does not mean that the person must be a [Democratic Leadership Council] member or agree with all of Bill's ideas. It does mean, however, that they should have a more open mind about the direction of the Democratic Party than more traditional Democratic liberals and agree with Bill on core issues like choice.

Another issue to consider is the question of age. There are some who believe that an older, experienced vice-presidential nominee would offset Bill's youth. Others believe that a younger choice would create a ticket that provides a clearer contrast with both Bush and Perot. There is no "right" political decision; but Bill, in particular, should think about which of these directions he wants to go.

Finally, as you research each individual, you will, of course, find negative information in their past. When the choice is narrowed to a few people, we would appreciate the opportunity to "disaster check" each person; to make a political judgment about whether any aspects of their lives or records would be "lethal" from a press or political point of view.

As we saw from Bush's experience with Quayle, the press will immediately get to work on whoever is chosen, and we want to be sure the campaign knows all the answers before the press starts asking the questions.

We appreciate your request for this memo and would be happy to get involved in any way that would be helpful. And, by the way, if Colin Powell is interested, (pending the kind of financial check described above) you can pretty much throw this memo away.

CLINTON: "A CONTRACT WITH THE AMERICAN PEOPLE"

On May 21, on the eve of the key meeting with Clinton on the findings of the Manhattan Project, Stan Greenberg proposed a big-bang launch for the revised message when it was ready:

TO: George Stephanopoulos
FROM: Stan Greenberg
RE: JUNE SCHEDULE

The June schedule needs to be driven by the message and media campaign that we hope to kick off after Saturday's meeting. I am confident that the message will center in some way around investment. But whatever the rendering of the message, we need to make it mean something big—revitalizing America, the economy, and the country's spirit.

The [new Clinton economic] plan must come to embody our message and should be unveiled in some way. He may want to pass it out somewhere; hold a seminar at a university; sit in a bookstore; meet with a group of educators; go to a PTA meeting.

The plan and the message [have] to be elevated into something very serious—that can really change America. I suggest a series of validation events:

• 100 Economists with Clinton saying this is a breath of fresh air; somebody really ready to save America.

• Nation's governors: same theme; at last, a plan to save America; somebody taking responsibility nationwide.

• Nation's business leaders: surprised and in awe; somebody serious about changing America.

• Educators: Clinton's own education conference/summit— perhaps at site of Bush speech; somebody really serious about changing things; challenging the country, parents, kids and the schools.

You may want to then take the plan/message into the Platform Committee—and ask for a specific endorsement. Maybe you do something crazy. Challenge the platform committee to throw out the normal stuff for special interests and adopt the plan—a contract with the American people to invest in the country.

Finally, you need people's press conferences—or some other label— that shows you taking the plan to the people and elevating the level of national debate. This is an empowerment exercise that ought to center around Clinton's ideas.

cc: Message/strategy group
       Mickey [Kantor]

CLINTON: "A NEW KIND OF DEMOCRAT"

On June 5, Al From, the Democratic Leadership Council official representing Clinton before the committee drafting the party platform, urged his old DLC comrade to push a hard New Democratic line:

Memorandum to Bill Clinton
From: Al From
Subject: Platform Strategy

The platform game plan needs to be part of a bigger, short-term strategy to reestablish you (not Perot) as the candidate of fundamental change.

Fundamentally, you have two options on the platform: (a) you can use the platform as a means of unifying the party by accommodating every interest or constituency in the party that wants something in or out of the platform; or (b) you can use the platform to make a statement that you are a new kind of Democrat who is changing the party by presenting your version to the committee and pushing it through. There's not really a half way. Trying to reach a middle ground is likely to produce mush.

The first—the *accommodation* strategy—will keep the organized interests in the party happy, but is unlikely to give you a platform that reinforces your message. It is likely to produce a storyline that the candidate of change succumbed, without a fight, to the forces of the status quo. Not only is that a negative story, but it wastes one of the few premier opportunities you will have over the next two months to cast yourself as a new kind of Democrat in a sharp, dramatic, visible way. And, it will reinforce the rationale for a Perot candidacy.

The second—the *mastery* strategy—offers you an opportunity to demonstrate that you are now the leader of our party and are redefining it in your image. Essentially, it calls for the drafting committee to approve your platform that embodies your new message of change, not a compilation of demands from the usual suspects (as in 1984) or a bland directionless document (as in 1988). That's the strategy I recommend.

By demonstrating you have changed the party, you can take a giant step toward convincing the American people that you are a new kind of Democrat—not the kind they have been consistently voting against for the past 25 years. That is the essential first step to convince voters that you, not Perot, are the candidate of fundamental change.

What the Platform Should Say

The platform should be largely thematic—with specifics being limited to the signature ideas which you want to define your campaign. It is very important that you send out the word to committee members that you are willing to risk a fight to get a platform that sends a clear message and that you'd rather not have that message confused by adding a lot of other specific policy ideas—even ones you support.

I believe the platform should highlight the core themes that differentiate you from the old Democratic politics: revolutionizing government, championing the interests and *values* of the forgotten middle class, replacing the welfare state with an enabling or opportunity state, asking people to give something back to their country through national service, promoting strong families and going after deadbeat dads, expanding rather than restricting trade, and fighting crime.

If you pushed a platform through the committee that articulated those themes, you'd take a gigantic step toward reestablishing yourself as a candidate of fundamental change. Just as importantly, it would reaffirm your position as leader of the party and demonstrate to the political world that you are moving the party establishment to you, not vice versa. That, too, is a very important message to send.

First, you should insist that it be organized around the themes that have been the signatures of your campaign and your New Covenant speeches: Opportunity, Community, Responsibility, and Revolutionizing Government.

Second, you should insist that the platform retain and showcase the policy ideas that are the key illustrations of these themes. The danger is not that there will be moves to strike most of these ideas—though that may happen on some—but rather to water them down, to round them off so they become perfectly acceptable to the constituency groups and lose the edge that makes them "change." We can't let that happen if you want the platform to reinforce the idea that you are a candidate of change.

You should insist on language that specifically takes issue with the old Democratic philosophy. Examples include:

"Government doesn't raise children; families do."

"People don't want a top-down bureaucracy telling them what to do; they want a government that works at a price they can afford."

"Welfare should be a second chance, not a way of life."

"If supply side didn't create economic growth, neither will the old big government theory that says we can create a program for every problem and tax and spend our way to prosperity."

CLINTON: LOOKING FOR THE MAGIC WORDS

In early June, Stan Greenberg did a dial-group study in the Chicago suburbs, monitoring reactions to footage of all three candidates and testing some of Clinton's new thematics word by word:

Date: June 7, 1992
To: Bill Clinton and company
From: Stan Greenberg
RE: DIAL GROUPS AND SPEECH REACTIONS

First, Bush is in deep trouble. Simply seeing Bush drives the line downwards. Bush simply lacks credibility. When he says "the Republican party is building a stronger America," the line goes down; when his ad says Bush is a "strong leader" or "stands up to Congress and the Democratic leaders" the line goes down. Even when the Bush ad says something non-political, like having an "economic plan," or "Bush will change America," the line goes down. Bush is simply not credible as a leader, on economics or as a change agent. The Bush line heads up only when he shifts to welfare, insurance reform, family or Barbara Bush.

Second, the switchers to Clinton tend to be women (non-college), and they are particularly responsive on education issues. They also clearly begin with a more positive view of Clinton's character [and are] more neutral about Hillary: they begin to move up when Hillary talks about "a good marriage partnership."

Third, the Perot voters are distinguishable on a number of important dimensions that suggest our ability to compete for those votes:

• Perot voters are much more anti-Bush than other voters. The Perot line heads sharply colder at any mention of Bush, particularly on leadership, economics or change.

• Perot voters are willing to listen to Clinton: they begin neutral, do not move down when faced with the visual, and generally move sharply upward when Clinton delivers his message. They go down when Clinton talks about character and when Hillary appears on screen.

• The Perot voters are very responsive to populist, reward work and investment messages. They move upward when Clinton talks about "working harder, earning less, and paying higher taxes," "reward work" and "invest in our own country," "go after the excessive cost of government and insurance bureaucracy," "no tax breaks for corporations to move our jobs overseas," "we rewarded the quick buck" and "no more something for nothing," "middle class collapsing" and "invest."

Fourth, the stump speech is very powerful. It drives the mean [rating] almost immediately up to 70 (from 50) based on the critique of the 1980s ("working harder, earning less and paying higher taxes"). It moves up again (to 80) on the positive goals of "reward work," "invest in our country," and "education" as the key. Finally, it moves up to 90 when Clinton includes health care costs.

The **do right** language for those done wrong did not test well. It never produced a jump upward and in the post-group discussion, voters expressed some discomfort: sounding too rural and southern. Moreover, voters do not want to be victims. They want the country to reward work again to raise up the country and reward the right values, but the do right/wrong language does not capture the feeling.

Any reference to cutting the defense budget also brings the line down, particularly for Perot voters.

There are powerful ideas, not contained in the stump speech, that produce a strong response and must become integrated into our presentation:

• Welfare. The entire language of welfare, "second chance, not a way of life," etc., produces the sharpest increase in favorable responses.

• Anti-political. When Clinton talks about the "special interests that dominate Washington or the breakdown of confidence (from Watergate to S&Ls), he gets a strong response. People respond strongly to Clinton opposing "political gimmicks" or "quick fixes" in the balanced budget presentation. Conversely, when Clinton appears political—crowd scene with flags or when he analyzes Perot—the line moves sharply downward.

• Corporate responsibility. The stump speech that we test does not really hit this theme; however, the message drives the line up in other tests, particularly for Perot voters.

Fifth, the integrity response [in a television interview with David Frost] needs to be streamlined. The introductory comments were fairly neutral (except for the Perot voters) and became more negative when Clinton discussed being under attack ("withering set of personal attacks"). What moved the line up, above all, was the turn: why do people know more about inhaling than that we increased manufacturing jobs, children have a better chance, and moved people from welfare to work. Clearly the most powerful approach is being self-effacing and minimizing, and to turn to weighty issues: why aren't we discussing the things that matter to the people.

BUSH: "START A BELLICOSE VALUES WAR"

On June 13, Mike Murphy, a media consultant to the Bush campaign, warned the command team that the president would lose if he didn't go conservative—and confrontational—in what then looked like a three-way race:

CONFIDENTIAL MEMORANDUM

To: Mosbacher   Skinner
    Teeter   Kristol
    Malek   Kaufman
    Black
    Matalin
    Pinkerton
    Puris
    Lake
    Steeper
    Clarke

From: Mike Murphy
Re: Strategy

Some opinions, to provoke discussion:

Premise: The President is heading toward defeat in his re-election effort. The pervasive wrong track/anti-Bush feeling in the country is now exceeding 70% of the electorate. We must change our campaign strategy to win.

A Suggested Strategy: The President must embrace a right of center plurality coalition. The campaign and the White House must change tactics from accommodation to confrontation. Only by relentlessly *attacking* our policy enemies with a sharply defined ideological message can the campaign construct a winning conservative plurality. This right of center plurality can be won in enough states to win both a popular vote plurality and an electoral college majority.

Perot: Perot's candidacy is not yet mature. His support coalition is an ideological hodge-podge that cannot survive the cross-pressures of a five month campaign, especially an ideological campaign. Perot's campaign will be very self-indulgent. Contrary to popular wisdom, the more Perot spends, the *better* for his opponents, particularly the better for Clinton. (A manic egotist like Perot with a mammoth budget at his disposal is going to run an insufferable, lecturing, and ineffective campaign. His voters are very disaffected; they will be fickle and quick to find disappointment in their candidate, especially as the formal role of candidate forces Perot to act and appear more like the politician he says he is not.) [Ed] Rollins and [Hamilton] Jordan will be ineffectual and irrelevant; Perot cannot be managed.

Ross Perot is a man with an appealing twenty minute act now beginning a three hour performance. *The question is not how to defeat Perot, but how to keep Perot's disaffected voters from beating us with Bill Clinton.* The question is, will he take enough anti-Bush votes to help elect us. That depends on the success of Clinton, our true enemy, and what we do to stop him.

Clinton: I believe Bill Clinton is currently much better positioned than either the President or Perot to win the Fall election. Too many currently discount Clinton for reasons drawn out of the conventional wisdom of June rather than the reality of November. True, Clinton now has a negative rating of near 50%. So, however, does the President. If we believe a 50% negative must be fatal for Clinton, it must then also be fatal for the President. I believe Clinton still has an excellent chance to win if he uses Perot to redefine himself and if we continue thrashing about in the trap of trying to win while on defense.

The key is whether or not the Clinton people understand that they *must* successfully engage Perot to redefine Clinton into an electable candidate. My guess is that Clinton will soon adopt this strategy and begin a forward movement that may very well capture enough of the anti-Bush vote (about 70% of the electorate today) to defeat us.

Therefore, the essence of our strategy must be to: A.) shore up the President's natural right of center coalition and B.) prevent Clinton from emerging from a successful battle with Perot as the candidate of change.

President Bush: There is only one answer: take the strong offensive and define this election ideologically. Never has our right of center coalition become more important. We must begin a two fronted message war: conservative economics and family values. We can win with a conservative plurality if we adopt issues that have minority support, but also have *passion*. The politics of accommodation have hurt our effort tremendously. The president must *rule;* with an ideological agenda of change. It is vital that we attack our policy enemies forcefully. We will advance enormously by engaging the labor unions, Hollywood, the media, the soft on crime crowd, the welfare lobby and the miserable Congress. We will make news and we will erect our winning coalition, but only if we adopt the sharp edged campaign that we have chosen so far not to run.

Our Campaign: We are running a classically defensive and risk-averse incumbents' campaign despite having absolutely no lead or advantage to protect. First, we are too absorbed with day to day tactics at the expense of a strategy. We must stop our unproductive focus on process. We are continually working on irrelevant mechanical issues like increasing satellite feeds instead [of] supporting a 44% coalition strategy by developing a cutting and confrontational right of center message. Turning up the volume on static will not help us. If we get the message right, all the mechanical things will fall into place.

Message: We must be *confrontational:* defining ourselves through our enemies. Only attacks will bring the free media we need. We must be ideological, assembling minority viewpoints into a fierce 42% to 44% coalition. The 80% "wrong track" feeling we are measuring proves that there is a mighty voter market for leadership that pinpoints what is going wrong with America and offers a plan of action. This is an election for a Goldwater, not a Ford.

Our Strategy: We must build a right of center coalition and win with a plurality. Drive that coalition with a sharp ideological message, understanding that we can only survive on offense. We must recognize Clinton as our true threat and campaign aggressively against him.

Tactics:

1.) Start a bellicose values war with liberal America. (Crime, Workfare, Prayer, Pro-life.) Our winning coalition (and plenty of Perot's current voters) thinks the country is going to hell in a lawless, immoral hand basket. We need to start the national debate about right and wrong.

2.) Announce a first 100 days of the second term plan with plenty of conservative economic and social legislation (school choice, term limits, tax relief, balanced budget, spending cuts). Ask for public support to elect a new Congress to support this agenda.

3.) Relentlessly attack Clinton and his liberal base, especially the Congress. Force him left to his base. The "get along" data is wrong; this is a vicious, despondent political year that demands polarization and conflict.

4.) Refuse to debate process. Stop letting the process coverage in the *Washington Post* set the yardstick of success for our campaign.

5.) Stay on this message and do nothing else. No more changes. Discipline.

Tactics for the next three weeks:

1.) We should quickly attack Perot with a major speech calling him a fraud, plain and simple. We should do this not for our own benefit but instead to simply deny Clinton the long-term upside of being the first to engage Perot. Our focus should be Clinton.

2.) Immediately add a campaign-savvy and offense thinking ideological conservative to the very top level of the campaign or the White

House. (Vin Weber, Bill Bennett?) Our leadership does not look enough nor quack enough like our winning coalition.

3.) Develop a negative communications and advertising strategy to deny Clinton his major windows to redefine himself; particularly the Democratic National Convention. Clinton is our real threat; we must deny him all opportunities to come back to life. Writing him off would be a fatal mistake.

4.) Take charge of the debate on debates. We should go out, ask for and get fast agreement on several three candidate debates. We are going to have to debate anyway, and we want three-ways; we need the cover of Perot since one on one with Clinton would benefit Clinton. Since we know what we need, let's relish the combat and actually lead the debate on debates instead of being compelled to respond to it.

CLINTON: "PUTTING PEOPLE FIRST"

On June 18, Stan Greenberg set forth the final recommendation of the Manhattan Project that Clinton make "people-first" economics the theme of his fall campaign:

To: Bill Clinton and company
From: Stan Greenberg
RE: THE CLINTON MESSAGE

The general election research project has now settled, quite firmly, on a presentation of the Clinton message—that reflects your views and history, that contrasts sharply with the other candidates, and that moves voters to the Clinton candidacy. The message centers on *putting people first*. The words are deceptively simple, but they are packed with powerful ideas that give real force to this campaign.

The Clinton people-first profile changes this race—moving Clinton into a tie for first. The people-first profile (presented along with profiles of the other candidates) shifts 8 percent of the electorate to Clinton—double the impact of messages we tried at earlier points in this research. This is a message capable of changing the dynamics of the race.

In the *people-first* profile, Bill Clinton says—

America is in trouble because government is failing ordinary people and stacking the deck in favor of the rich. It is costing more but doing little about the economy or health care. Washington cuts taxes for the rich and honors the quick buck, while middle class people who play by the rules work harder, pay more taxes and get less from government. Bill Clinton says we need a national economic strategy that invests in our own people. That means getting value for their tax dollar while asking the rich to pay their share, a real investment in education and training, moving people from welfare to work, and taking on the insurance companies so that health care will be affordable and available to everyone. Clinton worked his way through school and fought for 10 years as governor to reform education and welfare and to create jobs. Bill Clinton says, the people deserve a president who will put our people first.

The people-first profile contrasts with George Bush who people believe has no understanding or commitment to ordinary people and who helped the rich get richer; and to Ross Perot who people are prepared to believe enriched himself by exploiting a corrupt system. Bill Clinton is the only candidate who will put people first.

It is extremely important that we understand the operative elements of this message. It is deceptively similar to ones employed earlier in the campaign, but this is an important new departure. *This message begins with the assertion that government has failed people.* That start point enables us to identify with the current mood, establish Clinton as an outsider, reach the Perot voters, and lay the foundation for an effective populist message. We deliver our powerful critique of the 1980s and the Reagan-Bush years through an attack on a failing government.

[The indictment of government, Greenberg wrote, was actually a blend of the ideas of two public-policy thinkers, David Osborne and Robert Reich.]

We tested a pure Reich critique of the current era and an Osborne one. Both tested well, but neither as strong as the synthesis presented below:

Americans are fed up with their government, and for good reason. It consumes more of our tax dollars yet delivers less value—producing worse schools, unsafe neighborhoods, more welfare, and less affordable health care. But for the wealthy and big corporations—the top 1 percent—it is producing massive tax cuts, deregulation and the S&L bailout. All the while, the middle class is shrinking. The trickle down experiment is failing. Government is failing. Our leaders have let things get out of control and demanded little in return for the country. America needs a new national economic strategy that invests in our own people, that puts people first.

(60 percent of target voters are more likely to support Clinton because of this critique.)

The critique begins with an identification with people's outrage about government. It complains that people are paying more and getting less. But the power of the critique lies in a two-pronged attack on government failing people—first, government is producing worse schools, more welfare and less affordable health care for ordinary people and second, government is producing massive tax cuts, deregulation and bailouts for the corporations and wealthy. It joins the failure of government and the failure of trickle down economics. That is the reason for a new national economic strategy and a government that will put people first.

Let us summarize the key elements of the people-first message because the campaign must center around them and incorporate their language:

• **Government failing ordinary people.** This is our entry point to the debate—why people alienated from politics will listen to us.

• **Government costing more but delivering less.**

• **Government is delivering for the top 1 percent.** There is irony in a government that cannot deliver for people in need but can stack the deck for the rich. The populist element in our critique potentially sets Clinton off from Perot, who is focused more on waste itself.

• **The middle class remembered.** The morality play is created by the hard working people at the center of this story—people who played by the rules, paid the taxes but got a government that gave little value and little service. Their plight contrasts with the rich who were able to make the quick buck but did little for the country.

• **The people first turn.** That is why we need a government and a president who put our people first again. The assertion sets Clinton against the tenor of our times where the government has been corrupted.

• **A national economic strategy.** The national economic strategy represents economic policies that put our people first and put the country on the right track. These are economic policies that invest in our own people.

PEROT: "SWINGING IN A DARKENED STADIUM"

On June 22, Peter Schechter, a member of Ed Rollins's team of campaign professionals, put together a to-do list of problems he and his colleagues thought were in need of urgent attention:

To: The Management Group
From: Peter Schechter
Re: *Decisions Memo*

As discussed, here is a stab at sketching out the principal decisions which will require attention and action over the next few weeks. They are in no particular order.

1. Running mate

Precious little time is left until we hit the first filing deadline on August 11th in South Dakota. After that the deadlines begin to cascade. Furthermore, we should take at least one month to do a minimal background review of the potential candidate; unless we want to "surprise" the nation as Bush did with Quayle. This means we need a name by the second week in July.

2. Announcement

We might want to consider announcing together with a Vice Presidential candidate. Need to consider carefully what type of an event accompanies an announcement.

3. Media and Advertising

Given the pummeling the campaign has taken in the past two weeks, it is more important than ever to have our media and advertising in place. The two lines of attack which seem to be taking hold are Perot's suspected "authoritarian" tendencies and his lack of specificity. Paid advertising will go a long way to deflect both attacks.

4. Basic Positioning Speeches

Whether the campaign addresses "specifics" or not is a strategic decision which will have to eventually be taken, preferably with the aid of good [public-opinion] research. Whatever we decide, there is no way to avoid making some "basic" positioning addresses to key groups. Some examples: NAACP Conference on race relations; AIPAC [the American Israel Public Affairs Committee] or the American Jewish Committee on U.S.-Israel relations; Council of La Raza on Hispanics; Mayors' Conference on urban renewal; Conference of Police Chiefs on crime; 4-H convention on future of America's youth.

5. Press Relations

We need a more aggressive press strategy to contest facts or change the spin on the story. As it stands, there has not been a Perot generated story for 10 days, with the exception of the California rallies. Recent media has been dominated by articles on Perot's "investigative tendencies" and his past. There needs to be more thought and management going into the campaign's relations with the press.

6. Research

We need to decide and stick to a tight schedule of focus groups and polls. The campaign is swinging at a fast pitch in a darkened stadium. We may be hitting, because we can hear the screams of the fans, but we have no idea where the ball is going. It is also critical to find out whether any of the negative press of the past few days is doing Mr. Perot any damage.

PEROT: SELLING CITIZEN ROSS

On June 30, two of Rollins's pros, Tony Marsh and Sal Russo, sent him a memo on advertising strategy:

PEROT PETITION COMMITTEE
Interoffice Memorandum
TO: Edward J. Rollins
FROM: Tony Marsh
       Sal Russo
REFERENCE: Media Ideas

Your plan to get Ross Perot's message directly to the voters free of the distortion from press filters is exactly correct.

Recent surveys and focus groups confirm the urgency of the need for an immediate media buy and a lot of it.

The elements of this first wave of television advertising are also clear: 1) Biography; 2) Ross Perot on the specific issues of the economy, education, and the budget deficit (or political reform); and 3) the testimonials of our supporters.

The message should be multi-dimensional, but easily understood. Ross Perot is someone who gets things done. He's not afraid to rock the boat, make waves and [take on] the powers that be. But he is also a smart, effective man who cares deeply about the future of America and our children.

It's our impression the [Hal] Riney spots can be re-edited to accomplish the 3rd element of this plan well. We haven't seen the current bio spot, but maybe that can be salvaged as well. In any event we should take the best 2 or 3 Riney spots and get them up ASAP. In the next couple of days, we can re-produce the bio spot as necessary. Then, we can move to create the issues spots in the following 2 or 3 days.

PEROT: "WE ARE ALMOST OUT OF TIME"

In late June, Tony Marsh supplied Rollins with a list of talking points for a meeting with Perot on what the pros considered the sorry state of the campaign:

1. NO STRATEGY

We need to develop a clear campaign strategy and plan—upon which decision making will be based. We can't make decisions on an ad hoc basis. The senior political staff can write a long term plan as well as daily action plans.

2. DECISION MAKING TOO CUMBERSOME

Decision making is too slow and cumbersome. I need to make quicker decisions. We need to increase the political staff involvement in developing our message and schedule.

3. OUR COMMUNICATIONS POLICY ISN'T WORKING

Our communications strategy is not appropriate for a campaign—it worked for petition gathering, we are done with petition gathering. We need a new Communications Director, 2 press spokespersons and a Media Relations Manager.

4. OUR FIELD OPERATION CAN'T GET UP TO SPEED FAST ENOUGH

There are terrific people in the field operation, but there is too much to learn before November. We need to put Mark [Blahnik] in a more limited role. I need to back up [senior staffer] Tim Kraft with 5 to 7 real smart political operatives for the states.

5. ANNOUNCEMENT DATE AND PLANS MUST BE FINALIZED

One of the most important decisions must be made and a good plan implemented. This is a very defining moment for the campaign.

6. VICE PRESIDENTIAL CANDIDATE MUST BE RECRUITED NOW

This is the most important decision of the campaign and we are almost out of time. A good decision could mean spectacular results, a poor decision could mean disaster. We have to bring our search to a rapid conclusion.

7. THERE WILL BE A BACKLASH IF WE DON'T RELEASE OUR ISSUE PAPERS

We are starting to see erosion in our support because voters do not believe you are addressing issues. We need a comprehensive plan to release our issues papers in a way to put this issue to rest.

8. OUR CONVENTION OPTIONS ARE RAPIDLY EVAPORATING

We have to make a final decision on the convention by next week or our options will be very limited. This could be another defining event in the campaign and must be carefully done. We have to start now.

9. STATE FUNDRAISING HAS POTENTIAL FOR DISASTER

As states complete the petition gathering process, they are eager to move forward with projects. Federal election law violations are rampant. We already have complaints from volunteers who believe you are going back on your word. If we are going to raise money, we need rules (e.g. no lobbyists) and modest limits (e.g. $100).

10. THE MEDIA BUYER MUST BE REPLACED BY A POLITICAL AGENCY
The television buy is the most expensive product in the campaign. It can't be in the hands of someone who does not understand major league politics.

PEROT: "DOUBT CAN KILL US"

At the end of June, Sal Russo made one more try at a detailed campaign plan that might somehow please Perot and his inner circle, starting with a get-real assessment of his situation:

Overview of Strategic Objectives
1. Maintain base of core voters.
We must maintain our base vote at all cost through the convention season. Whatever we do, the Perot phenomenon must continue to have the freshness of the American grassroots movement it has been so far. Alienate the voters that love (and made) Ross Perot and we begin to go under.

2. We got our core voter base through a message of radical change and taking the country back. But, recognize that it won't be enough. We must convince voters that Perot is not a jump into an unknown void.
Attacks on Perot will continue centering on converting the "driven," "can-do," "patriotic," "successful" businessman into a "quirky," "sick," "obsessive," "paranoid" billionaire. The best thing we can do is recognize that there can be a doubt sown in the mind of the electorate. That doubt can kill us because it will stop momentum and slowly erode our base vote.

3. Voters must be convinced that Perot knows where he wants to take the country. We do not have to succumb to the clamor for specificity. But they must believe he has a road map in his pocket.
This means weaving a greater clarity of direction into the message. He does not have to answer questions with enormous specificity, but he must raise voter comfort level with his answers. We cannot allow more questions such as [ABC anchorman Peter] Jennings', "you're defining the problem again, what's the solution?"

4. Research shows that people do not know the Ross Perot story. Attacks on him have begun to define him negatively. We need an immediate, direct, unfiltered link to the voters. Ross Perot must define Ross Perot.
Paid media should begin early and run continuously throughout

the summer. Paid media is the one way we can be sure of telling our story our way, both to our base voters and to potential swing voters.

5. Recognize Clinton for what he probably is: our main competitor in the race.

He will not attack as long as the White House and Perot are bullying each other. That will change when he feels we are getting more of Bush's disaffected vote than he [is]. But as a Democrat, our main contender's base is made up of coalition groups. Pick them off one by one. Core Democratic groups which can be picked off: Jews, Reagan Democrats, Labor. It must be done in bomber precision fashion; large names must be targeted and brought to our side.

6. Bush is more vulnerable in the election. His voters are the most disappointed and thus the most cynical. They must be made to believe change is possible. Target those voters.

Research shows that Bush's voters are particularly "tired" and apathetic. But this group is risky for Bush. Voters tired today can become "*sick* and tired" tomorrow. It is possible that as Bush becomes more panicky, he becomes more strident and seemingly unstable. What then happens is that Bush loses the one asset he has: i.e. the fact that he's already there. At the time Bush voters will accelerate their defections, we cannot afford to be seen as "unstable, stormy change."

7. Perot's image is of the radical change, can-do outsider. He is the incarnation of the non-politician. Keep it that way.

We must be creative about events that are non-political: a one term in office pledge; a surprising vice-presidential candidate; surprise visits to media outlets. We have to make sure that Perot's instincts as a fighter do not make him into a polemic, argumentative politician.

8. Identify core support by state, region and demographic groups, determine their priority issues and motivations for supporting Ross Perot and solidify their commitment to our candidate.

9. Position Ross Perot as a stable, strong, compassionate and experienced "can do" leader to counter charges of "weird, authoritarian and a dangerous unknown."

Focus groups have already demonstrated that his life story offers the first, best chance to convince voters that Ross Perot is a safe, even preferable, alternative to Bush and Clinton.

10. Convince voters that Ross Perot has the most appealing solutions to the "core" problems facing America.

This means we must quickly roll out substantive positions on job creation, tax reform, education reform and steps for improving our competitive position in the world.

It also means that we must discipline ourselves against debating trivial issues, or being persuaded to speak in detail to secondary issues.

In summary: we need specifics quickly on 4 or 5 issues, and stick to rhetoric—and downplay the importance—of most other issues.

11. Isolate the Bush campaign as a hollow, negative effort, void of ideas and desperately attempting to discredit both Perot and Clinton.

George Bush has no agenda and cannot make an appeal to "stay the course." His only strategy for success is to tear us down. We have to use this to our advantage and stay on the offensive against their negativism.

CLINTON: "WE NEED MORE RUNNING ROOM"

By July 1, the Clinton campaign was stirring to life, and Greenberg looked ahead to the Democratic convention, not quite two weeks off, as a launching platform:

TO: Bill Clinton and company
FROM: Stan Greenberg
         RE: PRECONVENTION: STRATEGIC CHOICES

Bill Clinton is currently in third place, holding steady with about 27 percent of the vote. We are in a position to move up—and perhaps move up dramatically—and change the dynamics of this race if we can advance our message clearly, introduce Bill Clinton as a man with conviction and ideas, and establish the right contrasts with our opponents. The convention period provides the only stage left in this election where we are alone—able to present Bill Clinton on his own terms. We were robbed of that stage in the late and post primary period by Ross Perot and thus dare not miss this opportunity. It will not come again.

It is critical that we make a strong statement now because we are at an important conjuncture: a high point of anti-Bush sentiment and voting before the GOP convention; rapidly growing doubts about Ross Perot; and growing openness to Bill Clinton. We have to give anti-Bush, change voters a reason and the confidence to vote for Bill Clinton.

We have two primary goals at this convention. All of our work ought to be judged by our ability to advance them.

First, we must show that Bill Clinton is a man with good values who believes in something. He is not merely a politician who will do and say anything to get elected. Bill Clinton grew up poor, worked hard to achieve great things, believed in people and their values, and struggled for a decade to make things better for them. In tough times, he is somebody you can put your faith in.

Second, we must put our marker down on why we are running for president, how we will change the country. Bill Clinton will put people first again. That simple idea contains our critique of government and the Reagan-Bush years, a reordering of priorities and values, and a new economic direction.

The simple message moves us ahead of George Bush and close to Perot: 34 percent, to 31 percent for Clinton and 26 percent for Bush. The message, combined with the newspaper critique of Perot, moves us into the lead, with 41 percent of the vote; Bush sits at 33 and Perot falls back to 20 percent. This is a broad message, reaching deep into the electorate—if we can get past the personal obstacles discussed below. A stunning 84 percent of the electorate agrees with the combined Osborne and Reich (anti-government and populist) critique, including 29 percent who strongly agree. Among our [heavily downscale] target voters, agreement reaches 90 percent, **with 40 percent strongly agreeing.**

Bill Clinton: Negative Images

We are weighed down in this effort by the negative image most people have of Bill Clinton. This is the reality, and it frustrates people's desire to vote for change and against George Bush. Barely a quarter of the voters believe Bush is doing a good job and more than 80 percent believe the country is headed in the wrong direction; 60 percent say they are angry or frustrated with politics in Washington. But a majority of the electorate (52 percent) does not now like Bill Clinton very much, and only 25 percent are positively predisposed. Just 50 percent say they are voting or considering voting for him. That limits our audience and ability to make gains. Many anti-Bush or Democratic voters are holding back or going with Perot.

The convention must change that. We need more running room.

The convention must convey new images—Bill Clinton, a real person (not a politician worried only about elections), with good values and a real commitment to people, somebody to trust. The Clinton image deteriorated between the New York primary and mid-June, with the mean rating dropping from 47 to 42 to 40 (with 0 the worst and 100 the best score); the percentage with negative feelings about Clinton rose from 39 percent to 47 percent to 51 percent in our latest survey. While the head-to-head race with Bush is close, the personal contrast is not very good: with 51 percent liking Bush more than Clinton, and only 34 percent liking Clinton more. The high Clinton negatives drive anti-Bush voters into the Perot camp.

Perot: Precarious Lead

Perot's position is very precarious. He is currently winning the support of the angriest and most anti-Bush voters in the electorate. But Perot's negatives are on the rise; in our national surveys, they have risen steadily, from 17, to 24 to 33 percent (nearly equaling his positives).

There are three lines of attack that move voters away from Perot.

1. Privacy and authoritarianism. Perot's willingness to dispense with warrants and such things raises very serious doubts for our target voters. The Republicans have figured out this weakness, particularly as it concerns more upscale and more Republican voters who are more likely to move to Bush.

2. Lobbyists and special tax breaks. These charges raise even higher doubts, and move more of the target Perot voters. There are good reasons why the GOP did not concentrate on this populist critique. These voters are more downscale and more likely to move to Clinton.

3. Nixon and [Oliver] North. Do not underestimate the power of these charges. Overall, they are not as strong as the other two, but financial adventurism and a Nixon-type presidency moves more of our target voters than the other two charges. These charges will be very important in bringing back Democratic and liberal voters.

Perot's current standing is rooted in politics and economics. He enjoys his strongest advantage over Bush and Clinton on cutting waste, not being a politician, breaking the logjam in Washington, and resisting special interests. Perot is seen as somebody who is unencumbered, who can take action and who will attack waste and the deficits. Perot also enjoys an advantage, not quite as pronounced, fortunately, on improving the economy.

Clinton enjoys a natural Democratic advantage on education, the environment and caring about people (over both Bush and Perot). He is also ahead on having good ideas. Clinton also has a natural Democratic advantage on health care and unemployment. The "people first" message turns those advantages into a much bigger statement about direction and priorities.

Bush establishes his advantage over Clinton and Perot on foreign policy, family values, moral standards, honesty, steadiness and trust to lead. These are powerful attributes that will always allow Bush to compete for the lead in this race.

Our task in this period is to make Bill Clinton less political, enliven his critique of government and ability to go to Washington and get things moving, and finally, show his single-minded devotion to changing this economy by focusing on people (our own people) again.

Economy and the Middle Class

Voters, more than anything else, want a president who will get this economy moving (36 percent) and who will put the middle class first (17 percent). This is our greatest area of opportunity. Not many of these voters are supporting us now—23 percent of the economy first and 29 percent of the middle class. But these voters are open to us. They like Clinton more and they are more open to voting for Clinton. Getting the economy moving is the strongest motivator both for those now voting and those considering voting for Clinton.

For those who want a president who will shake up government (15 percent), Perot is their man, taking over 60 percent of the vote. Over half these voters are still considering Clinton, suggesting that we could make gains here if Perot was to fade.

Clinton gets wiped out (scoring in the teens) among those looking for a president who will advance family values (13 percent) or show strong leadership (25 percent). Bush is currently winning among both these segments of the electorate.

It is clear that we want this race to be about the economy and the middle class. That is where the majority of the electorate is focused and that is where there is the greatest receptivity to Clinton.

There is broad support in the survey for Clinton's economic program, particularly for investment in education and training and for national health insurance. People want big economic ideas—a national health care program that gets costs under control and makes health care available to everyone, a CCC that creates jobs, a commitment to invest defense dollars in education and job training and in rebuilding America. Over half of all voters—and more than two-thirds of those considering Clinton—say they would be more likely to support a candidate advancing these ideas.

The entry to this discussion, however, is failed government—a government financed by the people that is failing to address their needs. People are much more upset with their political institutions than their economic ones. It is frustration with a government and leaders who are supposed to represent people that draws voters to Bill Clinton.

PEROT: "THE NEGATIVES ARE BUILDING"

On July 6, one of Perot's polltakers, Frank Luntz, reported on a sounding he had done in New York:

TO: Campaign Management Group
FROM: Frank Luntz
RE: Brief Summary of New York Ballot Test Results

New York's a three-way tie, with Bush at 30.5%, Perot at 29.7% and Clinton at 29.5%.

The better New Yorkers know Ross Perot, the more likely they are to support him. *Among those who feel they know "a lot" or "a good amount" about Perot, he gets 51% of the vote, easily beating Bush (24%) and Clinton (20%).* Among those who feel they know only "some" about Perot, his numbers still hold at 38%, with Bush at 29% and Clinton at 23%. However, among those who only know "a little" or "almost nothing," Perot receives only 13%.

We read 14 phrases to the respondents and asked them which candidate each phrase best described. Their responses, both favorable and unfavorable, help explain the narrow ballot gap between all three candidates:

Bush	has strong moral values; will win the election; is too much of a politician; is trustworthy; is a strong leader.
Clinton	would fight for the middle class; cares about people like yourself; would do or say anything to get elected.
Perot	will change the way things are run in this country; is too much of a risk; would best handle the economy; would get things done; has a vision for the future.

We have polled worse in New York than in most other states, so the three-way tie is a welcome relief. But the negatives are building and the hesitation is growing daily. Since voters still have trouble articulating anything specifically negative about Perot, we have not yet reached the abyss, but it's coming.

Our single most glaring weakness is in lack of voter familiarity with Ross Perot. The fact that almost 40% of the population now think "too much of a risk" best describes Ross Perot of the three candidates is alarming but not surprising.

Everyone agrees that we have to define Ross Perot now. However, how we accomplish that definition is still up for debate. *Different subgroups may have similar levels of support with Perot, but they back him for very different reasons. Only one finding is constant: the more you know Ross Perot, the more you like Ross Perot. New York provides still further evidence that the first ads must start now and must emphasize his personal background.*

CLINTON: THE CONFIDENCE GAP

On July 12, on the eve of the convention, Greenberg reported on his most recent national poll:

To: Bill Clinton and company
From: Stan Greenberg
RE: CONVENTION PREVIEW
The National Poll

The polling before the convention (and before Gore) is obviously very encouraging. In our own poll, we are in a statistical dead heat: 32 percent for Bush and Perot and 29 percent for Clinton. That represents a 4 point gain for Clinton since mid-June and a 5 point drop for Perot. But there is more going on, and we should understand that as we embark on the convention program.

Clinton: An Opening Electorate

The gains in votes are upstaged by the gains in favorability and declining negatives that suggest a more receptive electorate. Clinton's favorability is up 8 points to 32 percent and negatives are down 8 points to 43 percent. That is still fairly negative but a very different situation from mid-June. In the same period, Perot's negatives jumped 20 points to 34 percent. The percentage of the electorate voting *or considering voting* for Bill Clinton has risen to 56 percent (up 5 points), comparable to the level for Bush, while the percentage looking at Perot has contracted sharply (down 9 points) to 61 percent.

College-educated and older baby-boomers are already starting to move toward Clinton, particularly the younger women. (Seniors are moving as well, reflecting doubts about Perot that ought to be given a further push.) But the target audience that gets Clinton to a majority of the vote is down scale—over two-thirds without a college degree. Clinton has made no gains among non-college voters in the last month. He is not gaining with moderate/conservative Democrats or the swing Democrats (the group taking us from 40 to 55 percent). We will only make substantial gains if we can reach our down scale targets.

Changing Images: Feeling Confident

The overall gain in favorability reflects a growing feeling that Clinton cares about people (up 4 points to 52 percent), that he is competent (up 14 points to 63 percent), experienced (up 17 points to 65 percent), and determined (up 20 points to 80 percent). There is some progress on honesty and integrity (up 7 points to 42 percent).

But serious problems remain. There has been no progress on being a steady leader, a family man or in [the feeling that he] shares your values. Most disturbing, the number rejecting the statement, "makes you feel confident," has climbed 9 points to 60 percent; only 34 percent say Clinton makes them feel confident. Many more people think of Clinton as too political (up 12 points to 65 percent). Almost 60 percent of the electorate and 75 percent of the Perot voters describe Clinton as a typical politician.

It is important that we address the political problem at the convention. That is already underway. But we also have to show Clinton to be a steady leader, someone in whom you can put your confidence.

Worries and Doubts: Bush

For all of our problems, voters worry more about Bush (32 percent) serving as president for 4 more years than they worry about Clinton (26 percent); 27 percent worry about Perot. The worries about Bush in the White House for another 4 years are incredibly concentrated and simple: the economy and more-of-the-same gridlock.

Bush is associated with economic decline: "economy downfall," "he'll make the economy worse," "the economy will diminish into nothing," "economy not moving," "economy will continue to be bad," "downhill economy," "4 more bad years," "another 4 years of recession."

A Bush presidency would bring "another 4 years of the same," "continue screwing up things," "same old stuff," "no changes for the country," "things will stay the same," "more of the same," "no change," "not doing anything."

Worries and Doubts: Perot

The bad publicity of the last few months [is] taking a serious toll on Ross Perot, even and especially among his own supporters. This is a candidate in trouble. **First, people are increasingly concerned that he will turn out to be "dictator"**—venturing, perhaps, into a police state, producing turmoil, "by firing the Senate." **Second, voters are worried that he is an unknown with no specifics.** Perot voters are concerned that there is "no platform," "don't know enough about the man," "unpredictable," "don't know what to expect." There is also concern about his competence and his ability to get the economy moving. But also interesting is the **concern with gridlock and more of the same.** Voters are coming to see Perot "fighting everybody," "won't be able to do what he wants," "total chaos," "won't get along with Congress." A growing sense of disorder around his candidacy will undermine the perception of a can-do candidacy, central to this race and the contrast with Bush.

CLINTON: "WE CREATED AN OPENING"

On July 19, Greenberg reported on Clinton's triumph at the party convention and on the work remaining to be done:

To: Bill Clinton and company
From: Stan Greenberg
RE: CONVENTION ASSESSMENT

The convention and acceptance speeches were an extraordinary success, as is now apparent in the 20 to 23 point lead in post-convention national surveys. We began a process in mid-June that moved us up steadily in vote and favorability; the selection of Al Gore and the convention kick-off created the first surge, moving us into a clear lead with 40 percent of the vote nationally and, for the first time, a net positive image; and finally, the convention and speeches pushed Clinton into a 20 point lead over George Bush and a new race for president.

- Over 70 percent of the electorate is now considering voting for Bill Clinton.
- 35 percent of the electorate says they are absolutely certain Clinton voters.
- Almost half the voters like Bill Clinton and only 30 percent do not. That is a complete flip from mid-June.

The convention was successful on the things that mattered most—sincerity, standing up for beliefs, humble origins and working hard, vision and hope. We created an opening by filling out the picture of Bill Clinton—a man that might not be an ordinary politician, who might understand average people, who might believe in some things, and who might have ideas and the energy to change the country. Those who saw the [acceptance] speech became much more favorable to Clinton. Bill Clinton emerged from the convention as the candidate of change, even before Ross Perot dropped out of the race.

The convention left important things undone. The message of the speech was diffuse and off-target—leaving the economic plan and "people first" on the side and putting "new covenant" on center stage. The economic themes, when mentioned, scored very well, but new covenant themes fell completely flat.

Clinton emerged dominant on two main issues over his two rivals by Wednesday night. He was the candidate of change (47 percent, up 25 points in a week) and the candidate who understands the problems of average families (49 percent, up 18 points)—*change and people*, the essence of our message. We now have the credibility to deliver it.

Not surprisingly we did not succeed at everything. But who's greedy.

First, we did not succeed in presenting Bill Clinton's record in Arkansas. The perception of Clinton *with a record of accomplishment in Arkansas* rose only 5 points during the convention. That Clinton took on the *tough fights* rose only 7 points. Clinton's job rating in Arkansas is generally up, but that reflects an overall positive perception, not specific accomplishments.

Second and much more important, we only haltingly presented Clinton as strong on the economy and as a strong fighter for people. That Clinton *fights for the middle class*, though strong (64 percent), rose only 4 points during the convention. Clinton gained, in comparative terms, only 6 points on *improving the economy*.

A Note on Hillary Clinton

Hillary Clinton's favorability has risen steadily in this period, paralleling the gains for Bill Clinton. Her mean favorability stood at 41.7 degrees [on a 0–100 "thermometer scale"] before Gore, but rose steadily to 50 degrees and a net positive by Wednesday night. Moreover, there was an utterly new reaction to Hillary in the dial groups. In June, the mean line usually dropped down when Hillary appeared on the screen, but at the convention Thursday night that all changed: the line held steady or moved up.

BUSH: THE PRICE OF QUAYLE

On July 20, Fred Steeper delivered a clinician's report on his secret polling for the Bush campaign on the pros and cons of dumping Dan Quayle from the ticket.

MEMORANDUM FOR [Deleted]
FROM: Fred Steeper
RE: VICE PRESIDENT

There is a potential 4 to 6 percentage point net gain for the President by replacing Dan Quayle on the ticket with someone of neutral stature. This kind of survey extrapolation is made without figuring in the impact on public opinion of the reactions of the news media and party leaders to a change in the Vice-Presidential candidate.

Over one-half (55%) of the non-Bush voters report they would be "more likely" to vote for the President if he replaced Dan Quayle on the ticket. Only 17% say this would make them less likely to vote for him. The remainder (28%) say replacing Quayle would not make a difference. Even a 40% plurality of the Bush voters say replacing the Vice President would reinforce their intentions to vote for the President; 36% say it would make them less likely to vote for Bush. The results do not vary enough by region to imply a reversal in opinion in our key states.

These unfiltered results need to be viewed with a great deal of skepticism as they imply that the President would vault into a large lead from this action alone. Many of the Clinton and Perot voters are merely expressing their disapproval of the Vice President and don't really mean they would vote for the President despite the explicit wording of this question.

To place greater realism on this analysis we eliminated the 20% Democratic base voters and an additional 17% of the Democrats and Independents who are very negative toward the President. We then investigated the answers of the remaining 63% of the voters who more realistically might be moved in our direction by a change in running-mate.

From this filtered analysis, the President could conceivably gain or, at least, remove an obstacle for support among voters representing 17 percentage points (non-Bush voters more likely to vote for him). At the same time, he would be risking the support of 11 percentage points that he already has (Bush voters less likely to vote for him). The potential net gain is 6 percentage points.

Counting just those who react the most intensely to Quayle's removal ("much more likely" or "much less likely" to vote for Bush as a result), the President would potentially gain or begin to move 10 percentage points and lose or cause great dissatisfaction with 6 percentage points of the total vote. The potential net gain here is 4 percentage points.

These are fairly large numbers on both sides of the issue. Vice-President Quayle generates a lot of strong opinions, more against than for.

CLINTON: A WORD FROM "BOB TEETER"

On July 27, Stan Greenberg slipped into the role of "Bob Teeter," Bush's manager, and did a prescient make-believe strategy memo on how the Republicans might go about trying to destroy Clinton:

CONFIDENTIAL—LIMITED CIRCULATION

To: President George Bush
From: Bob Teeter
RE: DOING WHATEVER IT TAKES TO WIN RE-ELECTION

The polling results since the Democratic convention have not been encouraging. Bill Clinton maintains around a 20 point lead, taking around 56 percent of the vote to 38 percent for yourself. He begins this phase of the race with 38 percent who say they are absolutely certain Democratic voters, compared to just 24 percent who are firmly committed to us. Clearly, we have to regain our focus and determination to win. This memorandum suggests how we get there.

1. We have to abandon traditional assumptions about the Republican lock on the electoral college and look anew at the electoral map. We can win by abandoning the west and east coasts and a narrow stretch of southern border states to the Democrats. We easily carry the hard-core Republican states in the plains and the mountain west. The battle ground is the South where we make the Clinton-Gore ticket wholly unacceptable and in the industrial Midwest where the economy is in better shape and where Bush retains considerable popularity.

2. This election must be about leadership and values. If the election is about the economy, we lose. Right now, Clinton enjoys a 2-to-1 advantage on the economy. We must seek to change the subject and reduce Clinton's advantage, but very few voters think George Bush cares or has any idea how to get the economy moving. We must use the powers of incumbency to show Bush as steady and

comfortable in the presidential role, contrasted with Clinton who has failed as governor, fails to elicit confidence, and who lacks any world experience. We must create an agenda around family and social breakdown that gives our second term a sense of purpose. We must focus on education, crime and welfare—areas where there is a plausible agenda for average families. Bush can show himself to be firm and compassionate, guided by good values, prepared to shake up a political system that just spends money and closes out the people.

3. Bill Clinton must be made unacceptable. First, he must be seen as economically dangerous, that is, too willing to raise taxes and create big government programs and regulations. It is critical that we turn the tax debate—which could sink George Bush—into an attack that undercuts Clinton's advantage on the economy and ideas. Second, he must be seen as a weak leader, that is, a failed governor and untrustworthy person with little foreign policy experience. And third, he must be seen as culturally permissive, promising the world to gays, lesbians and extreme feminists and out-of-touch with southern voters in particular.

4. George Bush must emerge by the end as the best hope for a better future. Voters are desperate for change and desperate to feel better about America. The campaign must aim, in the end, to communicate your vision and hope for a more prosperous and united America. Clinton and Gore are soaring for the moment because voters, disillusioned with you and desperate for change, are putting their hopes on this young and energetic Democratic ticket. This campaign must rob them of that glow and offer them a Republican hope for the future.

Obviously, Clinton will try to keep this election focused on the economy and middle class America. We must wound Clinton on taxes, and then change the subject.

The biggest opportunity for us is leadership. A quarter of the electorate is looking to vote for a "strong leader." Right now, Clinton has a slight advantage among these voters, 54 to 41 percent. But that is the aspect of Clinton's current standing most subject to question. His leadership qualities—steady leader, makes you feel confident, honest and trustworthy, and record of accomplishment—fall 10 to 20 points short of his strongest attributes. In the head-to-head contest, Bush and Clinton are even on steady leader and honest and has integrity, and Clinton enjoys only a 12 point advantage on trust to lead.

The campaign will want the race to shift to leadership, particularly after we have had an opportunity to portray Clinton as unsteady and ineffectual and, in the end, unprepared to assume the office of president. This is ultimately a home game for us—and it is the only game that rivals the economy in importance.

*   *   *   *

The campaign needs to be patient and focused. Clinton will maintain a lead for some time, even as the race tightens. There is a strategy for defeating Bill Clinton. It requires determination in defining the race, clear attacks on taxes and record, and with good luck, some strategic caution on the part of the Clinton campaign. In the end, Bush must emerge as a steady hand—prepared to lead America and offering hope for a more moral and prosperous America.

To win, George Bush must offer hope that the country will not continue to decline and that things can be different. A new agenda of education, crime and welfare is probably not plausible now. But late in this race, after Clinton has become tarnished, voters will be looking for a way out of this malaise, and we must be ready to make George Bush the answer.

CLINTON: "THE CENTRALITY OF REASSURANCE"

On August 9, Stan Greenberg assessed the state of play between the two party conventions:

To: Bill Clinton and company
From: Stan Greenberg

RE: MID-CONVENTION MOOD

At mid-point between the conventions, Bill Clinton maintains a good 20 point lead over George Bush—58 to 36 percent in our latest poll. Despite our appropriate cautions about [the lead collapsing like a] "souffle," there is certain stability in our advantage that precludes any rapid slippage.

Underneath the strong vote for Clinton is some dulling of the convention glow. On nearly all image questions, Bill Clinton's positive profile has fallen off about 5 percentage points: steady leader (down 6 points), confidence (−6), shares values (−3), honesty (−5), trust to defend America (−4), too much of a politician (+4), say anything to get elected (+4), too liberal (+6), and too influenced by special interests (+2).

The faded glow has been produced mainly by waning enthusiasm among Republicans. George Bush has done little to enhance his own image on any characteristic and has, for the most part, failed to benefit from the slight Clinton image slippage. Clinton has lost no ground on family values, breaking the logjam, sharing values and moral standards.

Clinton has taken a real hit on two critical points:

- **Voters have growing doubts about Clinton's record as governor:** good record in Arkansas (down 10 points) and Arkansas job performance (down 10 points).
- **Voters have heard Bush charges on** *taxes:* too ready to raise taxes (up 8 points).

Obviously, the campaign has to address the question of Arkansas record and join and take control of the tax debate. The door is still open: on [the Arkansas] record, only a third say Clinton has done a bad job (28 percent do not know); on taxes, Clinton is still preferred to Bush, 47 to 32 percent.

The Thematic Battleground

Our first goal, of course, is to keep the campaign focused on the economy and to turn the tax attacks against the president. Economics, right now, trumps leadership.

But we also have an interest in guerrilla attacks that keep the president from turning this into an election about character, that is, trust to lead. The leadership issue, defined in the president's terms, is dangerous to us.

Right now, voters see Clinton as a stronger and steadier leader (47 to 40 percent). Voters believe that George Bush has failed to lead and take responsibility; he has failed to use the powers of the presidency; he has failed to honor a public trust by lying about taxes and other pledges. We should put that stamp on the leadership debate before Bush reduces it to one of personal honesty and risk.

The Anti-Bush Dynamic and the Centrality of Reassurance

We have surged into the lead and held our position because of two dynamics—the intense desire to vote against George Bush and the growing acceptance of Bill Clinton as a positive alternative. The two dynamics may be interrelated, with anti-Bush voters wanting to find and like the alternative.

Over 80 percent believe the country is headed in the wrong direction and almost three-quarters believe Bush is doing a bad job as president. A good 35 percent of the electorate dislikes Bush intensely [giving him a] thermometer rating between 0 and 25 degrees. There is probably a majority of the electorate that wants to vote against George Bush, given an acceptable alternative.

Bill Clinton's unfavorability began to drop as voters focused on the alternative: a 51 percent negative in mid-June, dropped to 43 percent by early July and 32 percent at the start of the Democratic convention. We were probably doing a lot of good things, but the scale of the shift suggests voters wanted to put aside their negative feelings—particularly as doubts grew about Perot.

The key to our victory, then, is reassuring voters that their positive feelings about Clinton, based on little information, are real. For the moment, Clinton runs ahead of Bush on every issue that Republicans consider their own: handling taxes (Clinton ahead by 15 points), cutting waste in government (Clinton ahead by 26 points), and advancing family values (Clinton ahead by 15 points). This is not a typical Democrat, and that is the key to keeping the current dynamic alive.

But the current advantages obscure the doubts that are already quite real—that Clinton is too liberal (40 percent), that he is too ready to raise taxes (44 percent), that he is too slick (47 percent), and that he is too risky to [be trusted as] president (42 percent). These doubts suggest a tendency for the race to close, unless Clinton reassures voters on these points.

BUSH: ACCENTUATE THE POSITIVE

On August 7, Martin Puris, the unhappy Madison Avenue huckster in charge of Bush's ad campaign, made a last, frustrated pitch to campaign headquarters to consider going positive with "A Battle Plan for the '90s":

AMMARATI & PURIS INC.

To: Bob Teeter
    cc: Fred Malek, Clayton Wilhite
From: Martin Puris

Dear Bob:

At the risk of seeming like a terrible bore, I feel I owe it to the President and the Campaign to enunciate once again the wisdom of considering "A Battle Plan for the 90's" as a theme for the President's program for America.

I certainly bow to the experience of the old Washington hands with regard to many aspects of this campaign. However, I must also say that I do bring an understanding of the consumer and an ability to communicate that is at least on a par with the assembled political experts.

At the very least, I'm certain that my point of view—however flawed—will be given serious consideration.

I believe that unless—and until—the President can convince people that he is in charge and that he has a forceful, clear plan for this country, no amount of Clinton bashing or character assassination will get him back in the White House.

I believe that anything less than a memorable, aggressive move at this time will fail to communicate what we need to communicate—fail to overcome the enormous credibility handicap we take with us into the fall—and cost us this election.

So, once again, I'm suggesting that the President announce at the convention: *President Bush's Program for America: A Battle Plan for the 90's* and a domestic assault team headed by James Baker with an all-star group that could conceivably consist of Colin Powell, Jack Kemp, Dick Cheney, Lynn Martin, etc.

I believe that the phrase, "A Battle Plan for the 90's"—combined with an impressive team—would accomplish exactly what we need to accomplish. It's memorable, clear and aggressive—it has plenty of energy and muscle and a positive rub off from the President's one shining moment, Desert Storm.

Further, it reduces Clinton and Gore to a couple of guys with a lot of words—a bunch of rhetoric that looks rather pathetic compared to a juggernaut of talent and commitment.

As everyone knows, the President put together an historic team to win a war in 100 hours—it's believed that he could put together an equally impressive team to shape up America—there's just no problem a team like that couldn't solve.

Ultimately, of course, we will charge down whatever path you choose. But I believe that nothing less will give people the security and peace of mind you say they crave. And if we can't dramatically change their minds now about the President—Bill Clinton will run off with a prize he doesn't deserve.

I urge you to consider this suggestion seriously—it could well be the life preserver we're all desperately seeking.

Sincerely,
Martin

CLINTON: "TAKE THE BATTLE TO BUSH"

In August, with the Republican convention less than a week away, Greenberg and Lake did a focus-group study testing some of the lines of attack Clinton could expect and some possible responses to them:

MEMORANDUM

TO: Bill Clinton and company
FROM: Stanley Greenberg and Celinda Lake
RE: Setting the Record Straight
DATE: August 13, 1992

The Arkansas Record—A Failed Governor

• The most salient attacks are those on the Arkansas record. Voters think they know very little about Bill Clinton's record in Arkansas. "He just appeared on the scene" . . . "I just found out about him a few months ago." As we noted in an earlier memo, voters did not come away from the [Democratic] convention with much sense of Clinton's record. We need to define that record before the Republicans do. Voters are worried that one "failed President" will be replaced by another "failed" governor.

• Voters worried significantly less about the charge of broken promises. The "read my lips President" was hardly one to make this charge—as one respondent added—"People who live in glass houses. . . ."

• Voters want desperately to believe. They crave information, particularly statistics and comparative rankings of the Arkansas record of Governor Bill Clinton. They want to believe that he succeeded and that what he did for Arkansas, he can do for the nation. They do not expect miracles. They just want to see that he made progress, since "he was governor for a long time," in the areas [in which] they believe a governor has responsibility. They respond strongly to statistics about education and children's welfare. They also respond to economic comparisons, particularly on jobs.

• Inoculation works. Repeatedly, when we had provided information about the Arkansas record before voters heard attacks, the attacks mattered less and voters wove together statistics to patch together a defense for Clinton themselves. The most powerful inoculation came from Clinton's welfare reform. His record and his proposal made him seem like a different kind of Democrat, made him seem more fiscally conservative, and held the promise that he would deliver on what he proposed.

• Voters also sought outside validation. They responded strongly to Clinton's being chosen best governor by his Democratic and Republican peers. These are the people who would be best able to judge his record and figure out what he had done.

Tax and Spend

• Voters worried about "taxes and spending." Voters respond to taxes and spending attacks most credibly when these are linked to Clinton's current economic plan. Voters are concerned that the economic plan includes $200 billion in spending and $150 billion in new taxes. They worry about "all those programs," "all the promises to groups." They do not believe that Bill Clinton wants to increase taxes on the middle class, but they worry "who will pay for all of this?" They need to hear more about Clinton's spending cuts, getting health care costs under control, welfare reform, and $144 billion in across the board administrative cuts.

• Balancing 12 budgets and having the second lowest per capita tax rate in the nation were powerful responses to this attack. They did not mind that Arkansas has a balanced budget requirement, because they believe the national government is supposed to have deficit reduction requirements and it never seems to work.

• Voters respond strongly to the comparisons of the Clinton/Bush records on jobs and on taxes. They are angry with Bush, who promised no new taxes and then responded with the 2nd highest tax increase in history, as reported by the Wall Street Journal. (The source is a critical part of our validation here.) With these statistics in mind, voters find charges on Bush's tax record effective—that Bush promised no new taxes and then worked for tax breaks for the wealthy, while Clinton wants to increase taxes on the wealthy. They resent that Bush promised 30 million new jobs and is 29 million short.

• Some statistics work strongly in advance. If we could get two statistics out before the attacks start, it would be that Clinton had balanced 12 budgets in a row and that he had created jobs at ten times the national average with wages that were fifth in the nation. Critically, these are the areas voters believe governors (and presidents) have charge of. They provide vivid and direct comparisons with the Bush record.

Other Attacks—Gays, Character, and Foreign Policy

• Other attacks also have some impact. Southerners are horrified by his support of gay rights, but find moving his answer that there is not one human to waste. Nevertheless, the campaign should take seriously attacks on support for gay teachers in the classroom. The attack on gays works most because it is about "special interests," "believable because he wants to be all things to all people," "about being too influenced by special interests." Southern voters are stunned by the attack because they find it unbelievable that "their" Clinton's values could be so out of the mainstream. They do, however, believe he could be that caught up in national special interest politics. His response works because it turns this issue from special interest groups to individuals. "It's true we are all human beings" . . . "he's mending the country."

• Finally, those voters, particularly women, who worry about "Slick Willie" find little in our response which is reassuring. They are troubled by the combination of answers on the draft, pot, and marital affairs which show the politician and poor judgment—much more than any attacks on switching issue positions. At the same time, if voters are reasssured about Clinton's public trust, they show little likelihood of voting their reservations [about] him personally. Voters want to be reassured that "he will do it [and] that he will be for us— for the people and not more broken promises." Talking about a concrete economic plan and inoculating positioning on the Arkansas record do much to reassure voters about public trust.

• In general voters also worried about Clinton's lack of experience in foreign policy and defense. They were worried about an "unknown," "untested" leader. At the same time they see Bush politicizing foreign affairs, somewhat unsuccessful even in his area of strength, and as the trade statistics would demonstrate—unable to turn his strength to national advantage. This attack [on Clinton] bothers men most and is really more about defense than foreign affairs. It is the one critique that George Bush has some credibility issuing, but works primarily because it builds on existing fears. Trying to demonstrate foreign policy and defense credentials [by picturing Clinton] as head of the Arkansas National Guard, a graduate in foreign affairs, or head of trade missions struck voters as ludicrous. The best defense is that voters ultimately want a domestic president, not a foreign policy one.

*   *   *   *

[In a follow-up memo to "Bill Clinton and company" three days later, Greenberg added a further bit of advice:]

Clinton wins if he joins the battle. At this point in the race, voters worry that Clinton is an unknown and risky leader and that he may raise taxes and hurt people financially (and the economy). They focus on his proposed $150 billion in new taxes. The attacks on Bill Clinton raise serious doubts for nearly 40 percent of the voters. But when we respond with record and contrast, the losses are cut in half; when we attack Bush, Clinton overtakes his original position. *The Clinton attacks on Bush are very strong, more than level the playing field and put Clinton in a 2-to-1 advantage among important swing groups.* Thus, do not just respond, take the battle to Bush.

CLINTON: "WE HAVE NO RIGHT LOSING GROUND"

On August 30, Greenberg scanned his latest national poll and did a worried memo on Bush's progress coming out of the Republican convention:

TO: Bill Clinton and company
FROM: Stan Greenberg
RE: PRE–LABOR DAY SURVEYS

We are still positioned to win this race and obviously sit atop a 10 to 13 point lead. But this race has changed dramatically over the past 3 weeks. The Bush campaign has repaired a great deal of the damage evident over the last year. It has nearly completed the job of bringing Republicans home; the South is nearly back in the GOP fold; the Bush campaign has narrowed the Clinton lead in key battleground states (like Michigan and Georgia) to low single digits; it has made major inroads among Catholics. And for the first time, there is some evidence of erosion among moderate Democrats. The tax issue has begun to bite.

But the basic contours of the race have not changed. People are still deeply unhappy about Bush and want to vote for change: over three-quarters of the voters believe the country is headed in the wrong direction; two-thirds still think George Bush is doing a bad job in office; and by a margin of 21 points, voters think Bill Clinton (not George Bush) can bring about the kind of change the country needs. Voters prefer Clinton's economic approach to Bush's by almost 2-to-1.

The Clinton campaign needs to assert its definition of the race, present its positive economic message to an electorate hungry for substance, put Bush on the defensive on taxes and economics, and show voters that Clinton is a moderate (not typical) Democrat. The campaign needs to go unabashedly after its own targets to create a new majority coalition.

The Bush Comeback

We should not fool ourselves. The Bush campaign has accomplished important things in the last 3 weeks. If the Bush people are shifting off of "family values," it is not because their efforts failed or backfired; it is because their efforts succeeded and they are ready to move on to other more moderate (and more economic) projects. Let us review what they have accomplished.

Tightening the race. Our lead has been cut in half—from 19 points preconvention to 10 now (probably 52 to 42 percent).

Consolidating the base. The Bush gains have come overwhelmingly in the Republican base. Bush is now getting 80 percent of Republicans, up from 70, leaving us with 16 percent.

Taking ownership of Republican issues. Republicans have taken complete charge of a number of key issues: family values (those who want a president who will advance family values are now voting for Bush, 73 to 19 percent) and control government spending (60 to 35 percent). Bush has established strong leads over Clinton on moral standards (by 21 points, up from 8 before the convention), honesty and integrity (by 12 points, up 10), on promoting family values (by 8 points, up 13 points).

Raising doubts about Clinton. Clinton's overall favorability has not deteriorated, but the character props underneath have: shares your values (dropped from 63, to 60, to 58, to 55 over the last 4 polls) and inspires confidence (58, to 53, to 52, to 49). From before the GOP convention, the percentage saying that [they] would not trust Clinton to defend America has risen 11 points and that [they] think Clinton is too liberal has risen 12 points.

Making taxes matter. The Bush campaign has hurt Bill Clinton on taxes. That Bill Clinton is too ready to raise taxes is now the biggest negative (56 percent, up 12 points). Clinton's pre-GOP convention lead on taxes of 18 points has evaporated to 2. (One could argue, of course, that any Democratic advantage on taxes is a plus.) Clinton's 29 point advantage on cutting wasteful government spending has fallen to 8. This is the one area where the Bush campaign is successfully defining the race: more voters say the tax-spend distinction is real and matters in their vote.

Reaching moderate Democrats. There is evidence that the Bush campaign may be reaching moderate Democrats—20 percent of whom are now voting for Bush. Clinton's lead—previously well over 70 percent—has dropped among Reagan Democrats (to 64 percent), union households (to 61 percent), and those looking for a middle class first president (to 60 percent).

Remember the Clinton/Democratic Advantages

The Republicans have certainly made gains, but we should not forget the clear advantages that have put us into the lead and provide us with the material to maintain and improve our position.

George Bush. Bush is slightly more popular this week: positive job performance up 6 points to 36 percent and now parity on favorability (40 percent favorable and 41 percent unfavorable). But those slight gains are just overwhelmed by the sense of Bush adrift: 62 percent say he has no realistic solutions to the country's problems; 54 percent say he does not care about them; 48 percent say he has no vision for the future; 60 percent say he is part of the Washington mess, and astonishingly, 68 percent say he has no idea how to get the economy moving. **We have no right losing ground to George Bush.** Voters want to turn him out of office, and we have to point the way to change.

Tough terrain for further Bush gains. The next 10 points for Bush must come from voters who think little of Bush. These "Bush targets" are the most Republican and pro-Bush voters who are not yet supporting him: however, 75 percent of these Bush targets think the country is headed off track, 53 percent say their income is falling, and 69 percent give Bush negative job marks; most of them still like Clinton (by 2 to 1); and perhaps most important, they strongly prefer Clinton's economic program to Bush's cut taxes/spending program (61 to 29 percent).

Clinton issue advantages. While Bush has narrowed Clinton's lead on most issues, Clinton maintains an overwhelming advantage on most issues that matter. In almost every case, Clinton has maintained his lead on these issues since the GOP convention:

Improving the economy	+19
Hope for the future	+17
Change needed for country	+21
Understands average family	+20
Break DC logjam	+24
Abortion	+17
Has a plan	+16
On your side	+16
Cares about you	+16
Stands up for American jobs	+14

These are the building blocks and language for the two distinctions that still put this race on our terms. *First, this race is about Clinton for change and Bush more of the same.* Voters think Bush has no idea how to get the economy moving or how to get Washington out of its current logjam. They are looking to Clinton for change, hope, economic improvement, and action.

Second, this race is about Clinton for people, and Bush for the wealthy. People scorn a Bush out of touch with ordinary Americans, and are reaching for a Clinton who will side with average Americans. The campaign needs to reassert a populist critique and positioning that emerged so powerfully at the convention out of the Clinton biography.

By keeping on the offensive, the Bush campaign has succeeded in keeping us off our issues. But our issues remain winning issues. The economy is the starting point.

The campaign must move to present its economic ideas in bold ways so they will be heard. Voters are hungry for positive information— what the candidates will do to get America moving.

BUSH: COURTING THE SWING VOTE

On September 3, Fred Steeper looked at the "expansion" voters Bush would need to target to get from his hard-core base of support to a majority:

Summary of Bush Expansion Voters and Conclusions: Attitudes, Perceptions, and Characteristics

SIZE

Fourteen percent of the voters are available to the President to add to his current 39%. They are either undecided or just soft Clinton supporters. In addition, they are absent strong Democratic characteristics that, in the end, probably would govern their choice.

ECONOMY

The President needs a major improvement in his credibility on the economy with the target voters.

Most, 55%, rate the economy higher or as high in importance to their voting decision as education, crime, health care, or family values.

Only 36% think the President has an economic plan (compared to 62% for Clinton).

Only 17% think the President has a plan and is committed to it (compared to 43% for Clinton).

Most prefer Clinton to handle the economy (59% Clinton to 16% Bush).

The Campaign needs to emphasize reducing the deficit and opening [foreign] markets as major parts of the President's economic plan.

Tax reductions and reducing government regulations have less punch.
Two thirds or more think reducing spending and the deficit and opening new markets would be extremely effective or very effective in helping the economy.
The target voters are not actively making this connection of who would open markets and who would best handle the economy. The campaign needs to form this missing link. Cutting spending and opening markets are considered much more credible than the centerpiece of Clinton's economic plan—"investments" in transportation, communications, and environmental technology.
Reducing taxes, by itself, is not seen as a major stimulant to the economy.
It will NOT help to draw comparisons to the Carter years.
Most (54%) believe economic problems today are worse than they were under Carter. Only 14% think our problems today are not as bad as the Carter years.
Most (57%) believe the country is, generally, worse off than it was during the Carter years.
Most (54%) believe the economy has gotten worse compared to a year ago.
Most (74%) believe the economy is not "fundamentally sound," but, instead, is "in deep trouble" and needs "far-reaching changes in government policies."

DOMESTIC PROPOSALS

Four items on the President's domestic agenda resonate extremely well with the target voters and should be fully incorporated into the campaign: (Each is considered a "very good idea" by two-thirds or more.)
A mutual cut in the administrative budgets of Congress and the White House. (81% very good idea)
Close "legal loopholes to keep criminals behind bars." (76% very good idea)
Legal reform: "reforming the legal system to stop trial lawyers from bringing frivolous and exaggerated lawsuits." (73% very good idea)
Term limits for Congress (66% very good idea)
Legal reform and term limits have the added advantage of placing Clinton on the defensive. Clinton's opposition or "doublespeak" on them should be part of the strategy in using them.
Clinton has been mostly silent on tougher measures against criminals which represent an open area for the President's campaign.

The balanced budget amendment has more resonance than the line item veto. Moreover, Clinton is vulnerable on the balanced budget amendment. It should be featured more in our communications on controlling spending than the line item veto.

PERCEPTIONS OF THE CANDIDATES

The President's appearances and advertising need to do a particularly good job [of] portraying him as optimistic and confident.

More assign "optimistic" to Clinton (59%) than to Bush (20%).

More assign "confident" to Clinton (45%) than to Bush (25%).

"Trust" is not a strong, persuasive theme for the Campaign to use until the President's overall standing has been significantly improved.

An unusually large 24% volunteer that "neither" candidate is "honest and trustworthy." Only 25% say that these traits belong to the President more than Clinton. Only 26% say they belong more to Clinton.

FOOTNOTE ON CURRENT BUSH VOTERS

The current Bush voters are significantly more conservative than the target voters. While the campaign needs to shift its emphasis to matters that are not necessarily germane to conservative values, it should not take its 39% coalition for granted. The President's supporters will need conservative reinforcement from time to time to hold them together.

They rate "family values" significantly higher in importance to their voting decision than do the target voters or the Clinton voters.

BUSH: THE RISK FACTOR

On September 4, Steeper studied his polling and saw danger in the argument that it would be too risky to elect Clinton president:

MEMORANDUM
FROM: Fred Steeper
RE: One Measure of the Risk Factor
The public may believe there is greater risk to NOT making a change.

If there are NO substantial changes in government policies on domestic problems under the next President, do you think things in the country will get better, stay about the same, or get worse?

Get better	18%
Stay about the same	26
Get worse	54
Don't know	2

CLINTON: "THE DOUBTS ARE REAL"

On September 22, with Clinton's lead narrowing and the draft issue back in play, Greenberg updated his analysis of the state of the race:

TO: Bill Clinton and company
FROM: Stan Greenberg
RE: RECLAIMING THE DIALOGUE
Post-Draft

Status Report

Bill Clinton is holding a pretty stable lead in the low teens— 11 points at the end of last week and 12 points this week (after a week of draft-bashing). That is impressive, given the steady pounding and Bush's ability to stay in the news. Clearly our disciplined focus on the economy and the hope for change is keeping the race on our terms.

Nonetheless, there are are concrete reasons for the nervous pit in all our stomachs.

First, we are not consolidating our vote. We achieved 39 percent strong Clinton support after the Democratic convention, and now we are at 38 percent. We have not been able to build confidence and firm up our support.

Second, slippage is being obscured by uneven gains. The Clinton margin was buttressed by our paid media which drove up, perhaps artificially, our vote in "play very hard" states and by a general swing away from Bush across New England. But those gains were balanced by losses elsewhere in the country.

Third, the doubts on the draft are real and strong enough to cut into our lead. By one model, our support could drop from 52 to 48 percent if the issue really heated up. Weak Clinton voters speak openly of "dodging the draft" and "dishonesty." While these swing voters have much to say that is positive, "too smooth," "personal morality," "slick Willy," "lying," "marijuana," and "untrustworthy" are top of mind impressions. Swing voters remain uneasy.

And fourth, Bush's paid media, highlighting leadership and strength, has highlighted the weakness of our current image. After Bush's 60 second spot, voters speak of him as very strong and power-ful, accentuating the contrast with a Bill Clinton who seems to waver and lack passion. Focus group respondents wonder out loud: Is he real? Can we believe him?

Readjusting the Campaign

Fortunately, we still have plenty of room to seize back the dialogue, provide reassurance and consolidate our support. This memorandum—based on two national surveys, focus groups in Michigan and Georgia and around 20 state surveys—suggests some helpful patterns:

1. Our paid media has proved immensely successful—moving up our vote in almost every target state.

2. Bush's image has deteriorated on an important dimension: he is seen, increasingly as much too political.

3. Bill Clinton is still winning the economy; voters have no idea that George Bush has an economic plan.

4. Bush's job performance rating is the best predictor of state vote (as opposed to attitudes toward Bill Clinton). Our main media task in the next six weeks is to drive down Bush's job performance.

5. Biography still needs to play an important part—to show Clinton is on the side of the average people and to show that Clinton's views are rooted in conviction.

6. After the economy and driving down Bush's job performance ratings, we need to provide voters with reassurance about Bill Clinton: that he's strong and steady, not a typical Democrat, and intends to do what he says.

7. Al Gore is important reassurance for voters who want to vote for Clinton (or against Bush) but who cannot resolve their doubts about Clinton. Gore needs to figure more prominently in our media and scheduling.

Bush: Too Much of a Politician

Bush's campaign over the past two weeks has opened up a new area of vulnerability, important to the way we run in the next 6 weeks. Obviously, we will run on Bush's failed record. We have always intended to use "read-my-lips" to underscore the inability to trust Bush. But Bush's new political phase—promising everything—creates a fundamental new problem for Bush. Bush has walked right into the anti-political mood of the country and, remarkably, has allowed us to gain an advantage where we have been vulnerable up until now. While in earlier periods, voters spoke of Clinton as a "politician," that discussion has now shifted decidedly to Bush.

The campaign should move quickly to make this an even more indelible impression of Bush, because his problems here are our best protection on "slick Willy." Of course, we have to avoid our own "political" statements (being all things to all people): note that the "both [are too political]" response has risen in most states.

Bush Job Performance: The electoral key

The regression analysis [of state-by-state polls] shows that **Clinton's vote is determined primarily by the way people evaluate George Bush's performance in office and by feelings about the Republican Party.** Attitudes toward Clinton and the Democrats are only a third or a fourth as important; feelings about Bush personally are similarly much less important. This finding has critical strategic implications. The best way to improve our margin is to drive down Bush's job ratings. *It is important to improve our image. It is important to raise questions about George Bush on trust. But it is much more important to raise questions about Bush and the Republicans' stewardship over the country.*

We must always keep coming back to Bush's failed record. The more we can highlight Bush's failure in office, the simpler our positive task becomes. Our message is primarily *change*—a new course after 4 years (perhaps 12 years) of failed governance. After hearing our media in the focus groups—positive about Clinton and negative about Bush—participants constantly associated their Clinton vote with "change."

We should not forget that "hope for the future" remains a powerful predictor of vote. It is hope that things can change (after Bush's failed performance) that moves voters to Clinton and that allows them to look beyond personal failings and inexperience. The lower Bush's job performance ratings, the greater the desire for change, the greater the hope that Clinton will make things better (and the greater the willingness to overlook the details about Clinton).

Al Gore: Profile and Reassurance

We need to rethink Al Gore's profile and purpose in this race. There is a tendency to equate his position with [Senator Lloyd] Bentsen's in 1988 which is wrong and leads us to incorrect strategic conclusions. In 1988, Bentsen was compared favorably to Quayle (stature versus bozo); his favorability ratings were consistently higher. But in the end, Bentsen did not help Dukakis very much, not even in Texas. The pundits concluded, perhaps correctly, that the [nominee for] VP does not make much of a difference. That analysis leads to a similar glorification of Gore and a comparable tendency to be dismissive of his ultimate effect.

But Gore's strength and importance, we suspect from the focus groups, is not about Quayle, but about Clinton. Gore's thermometer ratings are consistently higher than Clinton's. In focus groups, people regularly volunteer Gore as one of the good things about Bill Clinton.

Gore plays two important roles in this campaign. First, he is seen as young and dynamic. His association with the ticket reinforces the impression that we represent change. Second, Gore is an escape hatch for those who want to vote against Bush but have doubts about Clinton. He allows people to feel good about their change vote (while ignoring or minimizing their questions about Clinton).

Our media ought to use "Clinton-Gore" in all our change spots; in all our spots, except those meant to help Bill Clinton personally. We should consider producing media that shows Gore and Clinton together.

CLINTON: "VOTERS WANT TO MOVE ON"

On October 1, Celinda Lake took stock of the mixed impact of the draft issue on voters in the campaign's latest focus groups:

TO: Bill Clinton and Company
FROM: Celinda Lake
RE: Latest Focus Groups (September 27, 1992)

A portion of the women and almost all men still mention the draft as one of the negatives about Clinton, but only senior men and the [David] Duke voters in Louisiana seem likely to use this in their voting decision. *The Republicans have clearly overplayed this issue,* **making it political and drawing it out too long.** Voters volunteer "I'm tired of hearing about it," "there is nothing new," "heard it all before," "old hat," "dragging it around," "it's not an issue," "put it to rest."

This has become Bush's attack, making it less potent and more political. Voters find it "ridiculous," "belittling," "dirty campaigning." They also associate this attack with "the media again," making more of it than is real and engaging in muckraking, rather than the issues. Voters believe Bush is "belaboring the issue to avoid the real issues." It's "a smokescreen." **Voters agree with Clinton that it is far more important to talk about the future of America** than some issue of "a 22 year old . . . 20 years ago." As one voter said, "I don't want to hear any more about it. I want to hear about the issues. I don't care what he did 20 years ago. . . . I want to hear what he is going to do about the deficit and health care tomorrow."

As we have discussed in earlier memos, to the extent that this issue has any currency, it is not about Vietnam, but about honesty. As one voter said, "the problem is not the draft, but the different stories." Some voters appreciate a straight-forward answer, though they do not want a lot of details and "no side steps." "He said, 'I avoided the draft' . . . he dealt with it and he was honest." Another added, "he answered and moved on . . . me, too." "He said, 'I didn't believe in the war and I did not go because I did not want to' . . . I am not going to vote on this."

Voters have achieved as much closure as they are going to get and there is little that we can do to improve on the Republicans' mismanagement of this issue. **Answering this further seems to only create problems.** "I question if he is telling the truth now or will this change next week." Another added "nothing he says can make any difference. He has told so many stories how will I know the truth."

We ought to maintain that we have answered this issue and move on. At this point, it is unlikely that any additional explanation will work, or that we could say anything more that would reassure voters. Voters want to move on, and so should we. One voter put it eloquently, "I thought I would feel better if he explained, but I felt worse. I don't want to hear any more from him or from anyone else."

CLINTON: "ALL OF US ARE HUMAN"

On October 6, five days before the first debate, two of Clinton's coaches tried to anticipate some of the meaner questions he could expect from reporters on the panel—especially Bernard Shaw of CNN—and proposed some answers:

MEMORANDUM

TO: GOVERNOR CLINTON
FROM: PAUL BEGALA, MIKE DONILON
RE: TOUGH QUESTIONS, TOUGH ANSWERS

Ethics/Character

Q: GOVERNOR, AS A PUBLIC OFFICIAL HAVE YOU EVER TOLD A LIE? UNDER WHAT CIRCUMSTANCES IS IT PROPER FOR AN ELECTED OF-FICIAL TO WITHHOLD THE TRUTH FROM THE AMERICAN PEOPLE?

A: Every human being makes mistakes, but the last 25 years have seen an unprecedented breach of faith between the government and the people. From Vietnam to Watergate to Iran-Contra to the arming of Saddam Hussein, people are losing faith. Because of this loss of faith, I think the only time it is defensible for a President to withhold information from the American people is when our national security—American lives and American interests—are in immediate peril.

Q: WHAT MAKES YOU THINK YOU HAVE THE CHARACTER TO BE PRESIDENT?

A: I think character is developed and revealed by showing strength through adversity. In my years as an Attorney General and a Governor I've seen my share of tough times and had to make a lot of difficult decisions. The toughest test of character I've ever had to face came in the form of a phone call from the State Police to the Governor's Mansion late one night. It was my brother Roger. He was messed up in drugs. They wanted my authorization to arrest him in a sting. I approved it, and Roger went off to prison. At first he wouldn't speak to me. But now Roger's recovered. He's off drugs and out of prison and doing well with his career. And I couldn't be more proud of him.

Q: GOVERNOR CLINTON, IN YOUR 1990 CAMPAIGN FOR GOVERNOR, YOU MADE A PLEDGE TO THE PEOPLE OF YOUR STATE NOT TO RUN FOR PRESIDENT . . . AND YOU BROKE IT. YOU BROKE YOUR WORD TO THE R.O.T.C. YOU'VE ALL BUT ADMITTED THAT YOU'VE BROKEN FAITH WITH YOUR WIFE. HOW CAN THE AMERICAN PEOPLE KNOW THAT YOU'LL KEEP YOUR PROMISES AND THAT YOU HAVE THE CHARACTER TO BE PRESIDENT?

A: All of us are human, Bernie. All of us make mistakes. I believe character is strengthened and tested in times of adversity. I believe the American people have tested and examined my character—more than any other person who has ever sought this office—and found me not wanting. But this campaign is bigger than me. It's not about my life, Bernie. It's about the lives of millions of Americans who are working harder for less money; paying more in taxes and getting a failed government in return. This election is about our families' ability to earn a living, make the house payment, afford health care. The American Dream is at risk of fading, Bernie. We can either stay on the present course—and watch our economic strength continue to erode. Or we can change. We can reject the failed ways of the past—reject the brain-dead politics of both parties. We can revive our economy, renew the middle class and restore the American Dream.

The Draft and Vietnam

Q. AS A YOUNG MAN, YOU TOOK EXTRAORDINARY STEPS TO AVOID GOING TO VIETNAM. AS AN ADULT POLITICIAN, YOU'VE TOLD

SEVERAL DIFFERENT STORIES ABOUT THAT TIME IN YOUR LIFE. AS
PRESIDENT, WHAT WILL YOU SAY TO YOUNG MEN WHO WON'T
WANT TO GO WHEN *YOU* CALL THEM TO SERVE—AND WHAT DO
YOU SAY NOW TO THE FAMILIES WHO LOST LOVED ONES IN A WAR
YOU WOULDN'T SERVE IN?

A: I opposed the Vietnam War. I thought that war weakened and
divided America then, and I think that now. I would say that to
any family who lost a loved one: I mourn their loss and respect the
service of everyone who went to Vietnam. But as President I will
not commit America to any more Vietnams. I do not relish the
prospect of sending men into battle. Nor do I shrink from it. But
when I am President we will go into battle for clear and convincing reasons—with clear goals and objectives. We will send our
troops in well-armed and well-trained and well-equipped. It's
time we put the past behind us and focused on the future.

Q: GOVERNOR, YOU'VE HAD MANY SHIFTING STORIES ON YOUR AC-
TIONS TO AVOID MILITARY SERVICE IN VIETNAM. ONCE AND FOR
ALL, WITH ALL AMERICA WATCHING: WHAT DID YOU DO DURING
THE WAR?

A: I [arranged to enroll in] an ROTC unit, then thought better of it
and submitted myself for the draft. I got a high lottery number
and was never called. If some people want to vote against me for
that, that's their right. But it won't make their lives one bit better
the day after the election.

Conflicts of Interest

Q: YOU AND MRS. CLINTON WERE INVOLVED IN AN INVESTMENT
WITH A MAN NAMED JAMES MCDOUGAL, WHO OWNED A SAVINGS-
AND-LOAN. MRS. CLINTON REPRESENTED THE S&L BEFORE THE
STATE BANKING COMMISSION. IS SUCH AN INVESTMENT PROPER?
DOESN'T IT AT LEAST RAISE THE APPEARANCE OF IMPROPRIETY?

A: No. One of the things I am proudest of is that even after 12 years
as Governor, even my opponents have to admit we've had a
scandal-free Administration. I wish I could say the same about the
last 12 years of Presidential Administrations. But about that investment: we lost money on the deal, so it wasn't smart from that
standpoint. But you should understand that at the time we invested with Mr. McDougal he didn't own an S&L and I wasn't the
Governor. By the time he did own an S&L and I was the Governor
we were losing money hand over fist—and it would have been
impossible to find a buyer for a failed real estate deal.

Q: WHILE YOU'VE BEEN GOVERNOR, YOUR WIFE HAS MAINTAINED A
LUCRATIVE LAW PRACTICE WITH ONE OF THE BIGGEST AND MOST
POLITICALLY INFLUENTIAL FIRMS IN ARKANSAS. WHILE SHE DOES
NOT DO BUSINESS *FOR* THE STATE, HER FIRM CERTAINLY REPRE-
SENTS CLIENTS BEFORE THE STATE—A STATE GOVERNMENT THAT
YOU CONTROL. ISN'T THIS AS LEAST THE APPEARANCE OF A CON-
FLICT OF INTEREST? AND IF YOU WIN WILL MRS. CLINTON CON-
TINUE HER LAW PRACTICE IN WASHINGTON?

A: Hillary has gone above and beyond the highest ethical standards
in her law practice. She has refused to even collect her share of
partnership profits derived from state business—a practice that
has been praised by legal ethicists. I am proud that Hillary has
done such a wonderful job of balancing career and family. As First
Lady she has said she will not continue to practice law, but will
instead seek to be a "Voice for Children."

CLINTON: "THE DEBATES ARE A NAKED EVENT"

*On October 10, Celinda Lake reported on how focus groups had reacted
to some of the lines and arguments he might be using the next night in the
first debate:*

MEMORANDUM

TO: Debate Team
FROM: CELINDA LAKE
RE: Debate Preparation

Voters are looking for reassurance about the person and eagerly
await the opportunity to see "the real Bill Clinton." Voters repeatedly
said they "want to get to know him better" . . . "to see how [the
candidates] react and handle themselves." They want to get at the
person "beyond the 30 second spots," the consultants, and "his people." Voters are looking for one of their few opportunities to look at
the person, at the aspects of personal character that they believe are
behind political character. They want to see for themselves if they can
"trust Bill Clinton."

They say again and again "the way they look and the way they say
things is more important than what they say." This debate is much less
about issues in people's minds than about the people and their character.

This debate is about Bill Clinton in swing voters' minds. They have
given up on George Bush. They know more than they want to know

from the last four years and can only imagine that they want to hear an apology from him. Most are not seriously considering Ross Perot, a quitter, though they do think he brings issues to the debate. They "are not looking for any miracle" from Bill Clinton. But this is the place where voters hope to get "a lot of questions answered."

Reassurance

Voters are looking for a final reassurance that Clinton is honest. That he has the integrity to be President and that he will keep his political promises to them. In this deeply cynical period in American politics voters are trying to really assess if they "can believe either one of these guys." "I want to see Clinton with my own eyes . . . I want to look into his eyes . . . to see his personal intergrity." Women in particular are unnerved that they "always hear about one more thing," even though they believe these incidents are not important in themselves. They are looking for the debates "to put that to rest for myself."

Voters believe that the debates will allow them to judge the real men and to see if they measure to presidential standards. As one said, "I want to see if Clinton looks Presidential and where he stands on the big issues like the economy." The campaign has become mired in mudslinging, particularly by Bush. Voters are eager to compare these men on the issues.

Handling Pressure

Voters think the debates are a naked event, a pressure cooker. "It lets you see how the guy is going to handle himself" and "how they react to each other." [Voters] want to make sure "they don't panic, are straightforward," "and how they handle pressure." A debate is a real test that resembles the presidency for voters much more than the political campaigns. "You can't prepare for the debate with a set of questions." "Other candidates pick the questions and they are not the pleasant ones."

Voters like emotion and commitment, but they do not want their president to be hot-tempered. They have seen Clinton "blow up" and want to make sure that he does not do that. In earlier focus groups they often referred to Gore as someone who "brought stability" to the ticket. They want emotion and responded to passion and commitment, but do not want someone "who goes off."

Finally, voters like "comparisons," but they do not like gratuitous "digs at Bush." They are sensitive to negative campaigning and mudslinging. Clinton has the high road here and they dislike intensely when he gives it up in the debates. Their antennas are up. When Clinton says he will not attack Bush's character and uses that as a way to do just that, they notice and dislike it. This debate is about the presidency and they want it to be more than another campaign event.

Showing Commitment

In the groups, voters strongly responded to Clinton any time he said "I care," "I am committed," "I believe," "I firmly feel." Voters want to know what these candidates really care about and what they have done to back up that commitment.

Voters like to hear that Clinton has made tough choices and "taken on his party," "done unpopular things" because he believed in them—a belief they often share.

For the first time voters in the groups responded that they thought Clinton was sometimes "wishy washy," "taking a long time to make up his mind." They like that he is careful about big issues, but they want to see that he is decisive, knows where he wants to go, and seems confident about getting there. They want to see someone they trust as a leader.

They respond strongly to anytime Clinton mentions hope and change.

Taking Responsibility

The voters think both Bush and Clinton have trouble taking responsibility. On the one hand they believe that Bush "has not lived up to expectations" and "has not taken responsibility for it." "He has not taken control." On the other hand, from draft to pot to affairs, voters believe that Clinton frequently does not take responsibility. They do not want to hear that he did not inhale or forgot some of the details of the draft. They want closure on Clinton's personal life and they want to hear him take responsibility for policies and his own life. One voter summed it up: "I want to see how honest (Clinton is), whether he waffles, whether he backs off."

Being in Touch

Voters want the candidates "to talk to me," "to talk to the middle class." "Let me understand." One supporter counseled Clinton, "I want you to talk to me . . . don't use big words." Another added that she looked forward to a "one on one conversation . . . no sound bites . . . no speech."

The How's

Voters have a sense that Clinton has talked about a lot of changes and programs that they would like, but they want to "know how he will do it." They "want the details," "how he backs up his answers"— although we should note that they strongly rejected answers that were too long or detailed or complicated. What voters are really saying is that they are not sure how all this can be accomplished and paid for. They want to hear where the revenue will come from—"not just out of my pocket." They want to hear what Clinton will not do and what he will cut back, as well as what he will do.

Finally, voters responded positively in the groups every time Clinton said "I have a plan."

BUSH: "DEFINE YOUR SECOND TERM"

On October 13, Fred Steeper reported on how a dial group of thirty-two undecided and soft-for-Bush voters in Perrysburg, Ohio, responded to the president's performance in the first debate:

MEMORANDUM FOR THE PRESIDENT
FROM: Fred Steeper
RE: Voter Reactions to the First Debate

High Points

You had five high points in the debate: your explanation for not committing troops to Bosnia, your opposition to higher gas taxes, your opposition to legalizing drugs, your highlighting the impact of litigation on the costs of health care, and your point that one answer to the AIDS problem is for people to change their behavior.

Significantly, your high points all involve explanations of why you opposed something. You were more convincing in this context than when you were explaining what you are for. Keep counter-punching— you do it well. However, you need to improve your presentations of what you are proposing for your second term.

Fear of Nuclear War

It is important that you describe your own role in reducing the threat of nuclear war. People do not respond the way we want when you simply say "kids go to bed at night without the fear of nuclear war" as you did to the opening question. The lesson is that, if you do not give yourself direct credit, people assume that the reduction of the nuclear threat just happened on its own or because the Soviets unilaterally backed off.

"Country Coming Apart at the Seams"

You lost points when you said you took exception to Governor Clinton's position that "the country is coming apart at the seams." Voters agree with Clinton's assessment. In a way, they are deciding who can best stitch things back together. Your appeal to the basic confidence in the "United States" did not work; their confidence has been shaken.

I recommend not going against the grain on this one. Accept the negative perceptions of the country and focus on how you will make things better. Significantly, the one part of your answers that the group positively responded to was when you said, "Yes, there are problems. Yes, people are hurting."

"Misery Index"

People believe that the country is as bad off now as under Carter. Consequently, the use of the "misery index" [combining the unemployment and inflation rates] does not help you. Again, just accept this perception and explain how you will make things better. When you argue differently, you hurt your chances.

Protesting on Foreign Soil and Clinton's Rejoinder

The group did not immediately support your position that it is wrong to protest American policy while in a foreign country. Their first blush opinion is that Americans have a right to protest no matter where they are. (Nationally, a 52% majority agree with your position, and 39% disagree.) The group did come around to your side toward the end of your explanation when you related this issue to being Commander in Chief.

Even so, this is not the instant winner we thought it might be. I understand you feel strongly about this issue. I am just reporting that it, by itself, isn't deeply damaging for Clinton.

The issue *is* damaging for Clinton when it is combined with his draft dodging. In our national polling and focus groups, people indicate a problem with Clinton based on his *pattern* of behavior. For some, it is a pattern of his irresponsible behavior; for others, it is his pattern of deceptions and lies.

(Remember, that in 1988, it was not the weekend [prison] furlough issue alone that helped stop Dukakis. It was the accumulation or "pattern" of several liberal positions on crime and traditional values that caused the voter alienation from him.)

Because people have doubts about Clinton, his rejoinder to you was greeted with skepticism. Although he had obviously rehearsed this rejoinder with its reference to your father, it did not work for him. The results demonstrated that this is a very weak area for him if you keep in mind that it is the pattern the voters are concerned about and not just the one part on which you focused.

Other Observations

Clinton always scored positively when he used the word "change." You should view this word as the greatest single threat to your presidency and attack his use of it.

Some of your critical remarks about Clinton seemed to cause a negative reaction in the group. I would caution against using one-liner put downs. The one exception I would make is the suggested one liner, "Clinton should be for change, he changes all the time." However, be prepared to cite three examples of his changes so it is more than just a one-liner put down.

Recommendations for the Next Two Debates

Define your second term.
Define your second term.
Define your second term.

CLINTON: DIAL "B" FOR BILL

The day after the second debate in Richmond, two members of the Clinton polling team reported on how sixty-two swing voters in dial groups had reacted to the show:

MEMORANDUM
TO: Clinton Debate Team
FROM: Celinda Lake and Joe Goode
RE: Thursday Richmond Debate Dial Groups
DATE: October 16, 1992

Clinton clearly held his own and scored big jumps in being "honest and trustworthy" (up *30* points from 28 to 58 percent) and "trust to lead" (up 18 points from 54 to 72 percent). His favorable rating jumped from 52 to 76 percent. 77 percent thought his performance was "strong" or "very strong" (84 percent thought

Perot's peformance was strong while just 11 percent thought Bush turned in a strong performance).

Close to half, 43 percent, thought Clinton "won" the debate, 12 percent thought Perot won the debate, and just 2 percent picked Bush.

Post-Debate Discussion and Written Responses:

Clinton: Clinton's vote [among group members] went from 56 to 57 percent, but his favorable rating climbed from 52 percent favorable to 76 percent favorable. For the most part voters had a more favorable view of his performance this time than last time, and liked what they saw. Most of all voters liked his specific ideas and clear knowledge of policy. They found it reassuring that he seemed to know where he was going. Almost all commented: "impressive," "had specifics," "good ideas," "had facts," "a plan," "specific ideas and solutions," "strong points on his plan," "answers to all the questions," "clear cut ideas." Some still wondered how he would accomplish it all. Voters clearly thought about him as a leader. They spontaneously divided on his Arkansas record. Some found him "accomplished;" others thought it a long way from Arkansas to the nation and "Arkansas still needed help."

In general, voters thought he was less "programmed" and "rehearsed" and more comfortable than last time. Voters agreed that he was confident—some liked his "soft, caring" style; others found it "too soft." Some found him sincere; others still slick and polished. Several commented that he smiled too much during others' responses and did not like his "smirks." A few added that he was occasionally mudslinging. Finally, voters thought he was in touch with middle America or at least "seemed to be."

Perot: Perot went from 21 percent to 34 percent vote and gained in favorability from 45 percent to 72 percent favorable. Voters liked Perot for the most part and he picked up votes in this group. Voters found him "honest," "down to earth," "straight to the point," "roll up his sleeves," "positive," "up beat," "genuine," "gumption," "outspoken," "to the point." Most liked his combination of humor (and one liners) and strong, outspoken beliefs. They found him "a breath of fresh air" with his lack of "mudslinging" and his lack of campaign promises. As much as they liked him, however, many voters had serious reservations about him as President. They worry that "running a country is not like running a business." Voters repeatedly were still not sure of all his plans. They worried about how he would work with Congress and how he could get things done in a system with two parties.

Bush: Bush clearly lost this debate. He made few gains in vote or favorability (4 percent to 15 percent). Voters thought he often avoided the questions, "was evasive," "weak," "defensive." Voters thought him a nice guy personally and [felt he had] tried, but [had] no real answers. One dominant impression was broken promises. "He promised a lot four years ago and nothing happened." "He does his usual—promises things he can't deliver." "He has had four years." As one voter summed it up, "I just can't get into Bush's ideas any more." Another added, "he has to have a better explanation for himself." Voters also found him "out of touch," "completely missed the reality," "good ideas for the rich." Finally, some found his opening [statement] mudslinging. As one voter put it, "he had to get a lot of pressure from the audience to stop mudslinging."

THE PROFILE OF A CAMPAIGN

From the Sunday before Labor Day to the Sunday before the election, the authoritative Battleground '92 tracking poll charted the daily fluctuations in the race and in the ratings of the candidates. Major public events in the campaign, indicated by numbers in parentheses, are listed in the notes below; it should be borne in mind that it normally takes a day or two, and sometimes longer, for the full impact of such events to register in polls.

	The Race			Favorable/Unfavorable		
	Clinton	Bush	Perot	Clinton	Bush	Perot
WEEK ONE						
Sept. 6	47	43	3	54/35	43/49	—
7	48	42	4	53/34	43/49	—
8	50	40	4	53/33	42/50	—
9	52	38	2	54/33	42/50	—
10 (1)	50	39	2	52/34	42/50	—
WEEK TWO						
Sept. 13	51	39	3	54/35	43/51	—
14	51	39	3	54/36	42/51	—
15 (2)	49	40	4	53/36	43/50	—
16	49	40	5	53/36	42/51	—
17	48	41	5	52/35	43/48	—
WEEK THREE						
Sept. 20	47	41	5	49/37	43/49	—
21	48	39	6	51/36	42/49	—
22	48	39	5	52/36	42/49	—
23	49	40	5	51/37	41/52	—
24	49	41	5	51/36	42/51	—

		The Race			Favorable/Unfavorable		
		Clinton	Bush	Perot	Clinton	Bush	Perot
WEEK FOUR							
Sept. 27		49	40	4	51/36	40/51	—
28	(3)	48	41	5	49/37	40/51	—
29	(4)	48	39	5	48/38	40/51	—
30		49	38	6	49/38	38/50	—
Oct. 1	(5)	47	38	7	47/39	40/51	—
WEEK FIVE							
Oct. 4		46	35	10	49/39	40/52	—
5		48	35	9	50/39	40/53	—
6	(6)	48	36	8	51/40	41/53	—
7	(7)	49	35	8	52/39	40/54	—
8		49	34	9	53/38	40/55	21/63
WEEK SIX							
Oct. 11	(8)	47	34	10	53/38	41/54	25/59
12		45	34	13	53/38	41/52	32/51
13	(9)	43	34	13	52/39	42/51	36/46
14		41	35	14	50/42	44/50	41/44
15	(10)	43	33	15	51/41	42/52	41/44
WEEK SEVEN							
Oct. 18		45	32	14	52/42	41/55	41/46
19	(11)	45	33	16	52/42	42/55	45/43
20		46	32	17	53/41	41/55	49/38
21		46	31	18	54/41	42/55	56/33
22		45	42	17	53/42	43/54	56/34
THE HOMESTRETCH							
Oct. 25	(12)	45	32	18	53/43	43/54	56/34
26		44	32	18	52/43	43/54	53/38
27	(13)	42	34	18	50/44	44/52	49/41
28		40	35	19	50/45	45/51	48/43
29	(14)	41	36	17	50/45	46/50	44/46
30	(15)	40	36	17	51/45	48/49	44/46
31		41	35	17	51/45	47/51	45/45
Nov. 1		40	36	19	51/43	45/40	50/40
THE FINAL RETURNS							
Nov. 3		43	37	19			

NOTES: The events: (1) Bush outlines his "Agenda for American Renewal" to the Detroit Economic Club. (2) Clinton and Bush cross paths at the convention of the National Guard Association in Denver. (3) Delegations from the Clinton and Bush campaigns appear before a gathering of Perot's Volunteer leaders in Dallas. (4) Bush challenges Clinton to a series of weekly debates. (5) Perot enters the race. (6) Perot's first half-hour infomercial airs on CBS. (7) Bush, on *Larry King Live,* attacks Clinton's patriotism. (8) The first presidential debate, in Saint Louis.

(9) The vice-presidential debate in Atlanta. (10) The second presidential debate, in Richmond. (11) The third presidential debate, in East Lansing, Michigan. (12) Perot, on *60 Minutes*, accuses the Republicans of plotting to disgrace one of his daughters and disrupt her wedding. (13) A Gallup poll for *USA Today* and CNN shows Clinton leading Bush by one point. (14) Bush calls Clinton and Gore "bozos." (15) Papers filed in connection with the indictment of former Secretary of Defense Casper Weinberger undercut Bush's claim not to have known about the Iran-Contra affair.

The numbers in the Perot column from September 6 through October 1 combine the voters who preferred him with those who, while not stating an alternative, opposed both Clinton and Bush.

Index